How To Use This Book

This book is separated into three weeks, and each week builds on the previous one. The first week is a refresher for the background information you need for the second and third weeks. Week 2 is a complete guide to programming ADO, from start to finish, and Week 3 is a complete guide to ADC.

The three weeks of lessons have been divided into chapters that we believe can reasonably be covered in a day. However, we realize everyone is different, and you might be able to cover more than we had planned. If you feel you can do more, go for it! But don't become complacent. Try to work through the exercises even if you think you're ready to move on. At the same time, some chapters might challenge you, so don't lose heart. Just work at your own pace and try to get a thorough understanding of the subject material. Work through the exercises and use them to reinforce the material. The topics are presented in a progressive manner, designed to teach you things you don't know by building on those things you do know. We've used teaching methods that have proved successful in the past: first describing and explaining a concept, then demonstrating it in an easy-to-follow example, and finally discussing the results of applying that concept.

Who Should Read This Book?

If you're planning a Web site that includes database information, this book gives you a quick, easy, and inexpensive solution. An added bonus is that the technologies can easily be extended; you can add to the choices offered in this book to create the Web page *you* want.

D1407494

Teach Yourself

ACTIVE WEB
DATABASE
PROGRAMMING

in 21 Days

Teach Yourself
ACTIVE WEB
DATABASE
PROGRAMMING
in 21 Days

Dina Fleet
Matt Warren
Joyce Chia-Hsun Chen
Alexander Stojanovic

201 West 103rd Street
Indianapolis, Indiana 46290

To Wayne and Mom.   —Dina Fleet
This book is dedicated to Jean Warren and to both the red and green books.—Matt Warren
To my parents, who encouraged me.   —Joyce Chia-Hsun Chen
To my wife, Tatjana Jovanoska-Stojanovic, for her patience, and to my parents, Mirko and Lillian, for their constant encouragement and support over the years. Hvala.
(Hvala is Serbian for "Thank you.")   —Alexander Stojanovic

Copyright © 1997 by Sams.net Publishing

FIRST EDITION

International Standard Book Number: 1-57521-139-4

Library of Congress Catalog Card Number: 96-68598

2000   99   98   97   4   3   2   1

Interpretation of the printing code: the rightmost double-digit number is the year of the book's printing; the rightmost single-digit, the number of the book's printing. For example, a printing code of 97-1 shows that the first printing of the book occurred in 1997.

Composed in AGaramond and MCPdigital by Macmillan Computer Publishing

Printed in the United States of America

Trademarks

Publisher and President: Richard K. Swadley
Publishing Manager: Greg Wiegand
Director of Editorial Services Cindy Morrow
Director of Marketing Kelli S. Spencer
Assistant Marketing Managers Kristina Perry, Rachel Wolfe

Acquisitions Editor
Sharon Cox

Development Editor
Anthony Amico

Software Development Specialist
Brad Myers

Production Editor
Lisa M. Lord

Copy Editor
Howard A. Jones

Indexer
Bruce Clingaman

Technical Reviewers
Jeff Perkins
Jeff Shockley

Editorial Coordinator
Katie Wise

Technical Edit Coordinator
Lynette Quinn

Resource Coordinator
Deborah Frisby

Editorial Assistants
Carol Ackerman
Andi Richter
Rhonda Tinch-Mize

Cover Designer
Tim Amrhein

Book Designer
Gary Adair

Copy Writer
Peter Fuller

Production Team Supervisors
Brad Chinn
Charlotte Clapp

Production
Georgiana Briggs
Bruce Clingaman
Cyndi Davis
Sonya Hart
Mary Ellen Stephenson

Overview

Week 3 in Review **787**

Appendixes

Contents

Day 21   Interactive Web Application: The Virtual Library   739

Week 3 in Review   787

Appendixes

Acknowledgments

Dina Fleet: I would like to thank several Microsoft teams for making the information in this book available: IIS and the Active Server Pages, ADO, ADC, OLE DB, and VBScript. The information was made available before the ship dates of several of these products but it was necessary to get this book published.

Matt Warren: My thanks go to my wife, Betsy, who put up with me during the months it took to complete this book, who took on more than her share of the household chores, and who never complained when writing kept me up past midnight or when I devoted an entire weekend to finishing the latest chapter....okay, okay. She didn't complain excessively.

Joyce Chia-Hsun Chen: I would like to acknowlege Greg Hinkel, Jon Fowler, Robert Bradley, Qun Guo, and Charles Sterling for their assistance and encouragement. Thanks also to Rabih AbouJaoudé for providing some of the artwork used in the sample Web pages. Finally, I would like to thank Frank Hollander. Without his patience and support, I would not have been able to finish.

Alexander Stojanovic: I would like to thank the ActiveData Group (now Data Access Group) for their tireless efforts in shipping AdvancedDataConnector 1.0. Everyone (Program Management, Development, and Test) did a fantastic job in making sure we released the best possible product under very tight time constraints. I would also like to acknowledge Kamaljit Bath for his excellent white paper on ADC technology, which was a constant reference during my writing of the introductory ADC chapter.

A special thanks from all the authors to the Sams publishing team—Sharon Cox, Tony Amico, and Lisa Lord—for making this book possible.

About the Authors

Dina Fleet

Dina Fleet holds a bachelor's degree in computer science from Principia College in Elsah, Illinois. Her background includes hardware and network consulting, software development, networks, and Internet and database technology. She is originally from Midland, Texas, and now works for Microsoft in Redmond, Washington for the Normandy team. Dina can be contacted at dinaf@microsoft.com.

Matt Warren

Matt Warren is a software design engineer at Microsoft and is part of the Data Access Group, responsible for delivering ActiveX Data Objects, the Advanced Data Connector, and related technologies. Before Microsoft, he developed commercial applications for data analysis, graphics, network messaging, and office-style productivity software. He holds degrees in mathematics, computer science, and economics from the Universitiy of Washington. A native of Washington State, he currently lives in the Seattle area with his wife and three cats. Both he and his wife are avid scuba divers. The cats prefer to stay on land, but they do enjoy fish.

Joyce Chia-Hsun Chen

Joyce Chia-Hsun Chen has a Master of Science in computer science from the University of Houston. She has been working as a database specialist for over five years. She is currently working at Microsoft as a product support engineer.

Alexander Stojanovic

Alexander Stojanovic is a program manager with the Internet Application Server Group at Microsoft Corporation. He is currently project manager of the Advanced Data Connector technology. Before joining Microsoft, Alexander worked over five years as a systems analyst and software engineer, specializing in distributed application development, relational database design and programming, and object-oriented systems engineering. His current research interests include Java, object-relational database technology, and software metrics. Alexander lives with his wife, Tatjana Jovanoska-Stojanovic, in Bellevue, Washington. His avocational interests include linguistics, electronic music, and the fiction of Clark Ashton Smith.

Tell Us What You Think!

As a reader, you're the most important critic and commentator of our books. We value your opinion and want to know what we're doing right, what we could do better, what areas you'd like to see us publish in, and any other words of wisdom you're willing to pass our way. You can help us make strong books that meet your needs and give you the computer guidance you require.

Do you have access to CompuServe or the World Wide Web? Then check out our CompuServe forum by typing **GO SAMS** at any prompt. If you prefer the World Wide Web, check out our site at `http://www.mcp.com`.

NOTE

If you have a technical question about this book, call the technical support line at (317) 581-3833.

As the publishing manager of the group that created this book, I welcome your comments. You can fax, e-mail, or write me directly to let me know what you did or didn't like about this book—as well as what we can do to make our books stronger. Here's the information:

Fax: 317/581-4669

E-mail: `programming_mgr@sams.mcp.com`

Mail: Greg Wiegand
           Sams.net Publishing
           201 W. 103rd Street
           Indianapolis, IN 46290

Introduction

Using ActiveX Data Objects and Advanced Data Connector

Welcome to the fascinating world of database programming on the Web with the ActiveX Data Objects (ADO) and Advanced Data Connector (ADC).

The Web is currently the most interesting computer market and growth industry. Large and small corporations are developing business strategies to make use of their current technology and have an exciting presence on the Web. The most common store of information is a database, but in the past few years putting database information on the Web hasn't been easy. With the introduction of ADO and ADC, presenting database information is now easy and *fast*. The programming language used by these technologies is one of the easiest and most popular to date: Visual Basic Script (VBScript). If you have never programmed in VBScript, however, don't worry! This book explains everything you need to know to use VBScript, from beginning Web concepts all the way to real examples. This book also comes with sample code on the CD-ROM and an appendix of corresponding Web information.

Why Use ADO and ADC?

There are several reasons why you should use ADO and ADC:

☐ ADO and ADC rely on the event-driven programming model and the common programming language of VBScript. The event-driven programming model, which has been used by several Windows programming languages, states that the application is driven by events from the user. This is exactly how the Web works. Visual Basic is programmed by more than 3.5 million people and is an incredibly easy language to learn. Instead of having to learn the entire language, however, ADO and ADC depend on VBScript—a subset of Visual Basic—so you have to learn only the language constructs that apply to the Web.

☐ Accessing databases on the Web is as easy as accessing ODBC datasources. ODBC was designed to abstract the database specifics from the programmer, so the same code can access different kinds of databases. If you have an Oracle or Microsoft database, you can still get to the data. This flexibility means you don't have to know the nitty gritty about each database; you can focus on just one standard for accessing the data.

☐ ADO gives you easy server-side database access. Instead of having static Web pages that have to be kept updated on a regular basis, you can create dynamic pages with ADO. The only information that needs to change is the database. Once the ADO programming is written, you don't need to touch it again until you want to change the type of data presented. Suppose your Web pages contain time-sensitive information, such as a quarterly sales catalog. With ADO, you can easily modify and update the catalogs with a few quick changes in the database. Instead of writing time-consuming ISAPI or CGI scripts, you can write ADO scripts that are easy to write *and* read.

☐ ADC gives you easy client-side database access. By moving the data returned from a database query to the client, much of the processing load on the database is taken off the Web server's vital resources and placed in the hands of your user, who is the only one who really knows what information he or she was looking for. The kinds of data searches or changes a user can make aren't constrained by expensive trips across the Internet or a limited range of queries. ADC even handles the transaction processing to protect the database's integrity when the data is returned to the Web database through the Web server.

What Are Active Server Pages?

Active Server Pages (ASP) is a programming model that lets you create Web pages quickly, easily, and dynamically. By using ASP, a new feature of the Microsoft Internet Information Server (IIS) 3.0, you can tailor the Web pages returned to the client. They can be based on what browser type the client has, on what language the client's machine supports, and on what personal preferences the client has chosen on your Web site.

What Is ADO?

ActiveX Data Objects (ADO) is a programming extension of the Active Server Pages (ASP) supported by Microsoft Internet Information Server. ASP allows you to develop dynamic Web pages by offering a rich collection of client and server information. With ADO, you can make use of database information and display it to your users in an exciting, visually interesting manner.

What Is ADC?

ADC is an addition to the Web programming model. Instead of distributing data in HTML form, ADC ships an entire set of data (such as a result set) as well. The HTML pages and ActiveX controls can then coordinate with the dataset to give the user more control and a wealth of information.

What Are ActiveX Controls?

ActiveX controls are programming objects that sit on the client machine to give you more usability and a better display set than normal HTML allows. Instead of having a static HTML table of information, an ActiveX control can display the data so that you can manipulate both its display and its content. The user has more freedom to work with the data, and Web applications are more interactive.

Web Database Programming Is Fun

Remember the first time you saw a Web page? And how exciting and novel it was to see such a variety of information from all over the world? However, the way information is displayed seems to be 10 years behind Windows programs. Now with ADO, ADC, and ActiveX, those same Web pages can be just as exciting as any other computer application you have, and programming with these tools is both easy and fun.

NOTE

> Some of the examples in Week 3 have extensive, critical setup requirements. These setup requirements are listed in the "Week At a Glance" for Week 3.

Conventions Used in This Book

Over the years, we have found that a *Teach Yourself* book should be friendly and easy to read. Much of the text is formatted as you see here. We have also found that some important details should stand out and be separated from the normal text, so we have established some formatting conventions, as shown here:

- ☐ **Code/reserved words:** Terms, functions, variables, keywords, listings, and so on, that are taken from or are part of code are set in a monospaced type.
- ☐ **Placeholders:** Placeholders are words that stand for what you actually type. When they appear in regular text, they appear in *italic*. When they appear in code, they're formatted in `monospaced italic`.
- ☐ **New terms:** When new terms are introduced in the text, we use *italic* type to indicate them. Italics are occasionally used for emphasis, too.
- ☐ **Commands:** When we're identifying commands from menus, we separate the different levels by using a vertical bar. For example, File | Open means you pull down the File menu and choose the Open command.

☐ **Code Continuation:** When a line of code is longer than what we can show on a line in the book, we use a code continuation character: ➥. When you see this character, it means that the code continues on the next line. If you're typing, then you should just ignore the character and continue typing. Don't use the return key to separate the code.

Although we have many code snippets embedded in the pages to illustrate how to use important concepts, we also have longer, more involved examples. You should try to run these examples whenever possible. To help you keep track of your place as you review the code, the lines are numbered. If you're entering the code in an editor, make sure you don't type the line number.

These are some of the special visual elements we use in the book and what they mean:

WARNING

These boxes point out areas where care must be taken to prevent catastrophe, until you become more experienced.

NOTE

These boxes supply essential background material or different ways of viewing the information to help you understand the concepts behind the examples.

TIP

These boxes tell you about beneficial techniques that you might want to try for yourself.

ANALYSIS This icon tells you that we're describing an example in detail. You might think of it as a kind of detour to a scenic overlook on your journey to learning this new technology.

WEEK

1

1

2

3

4

5

6

7

At a Glance

During Week 1, you gain database skills and the fundamentals of Web scripting languages. By the end of the first week, you will be able to write a complete Web site as well as query the database.

Day 1: Database Connectivity and Visual Basic

Day 1 covers the development of some of the Web technologies up to their current state. In this chapter, you learn how the Web scripting of HTML started and where it is today. You also learn the difference between a static Web page and a dynamic Web page.

Day 2: The Client-Server Model

Day 2 introduces the client-server aspects of Web development. In this chapter, you learn the different network aspects of the Internet, including the protocols involved and the basics of Microsoft Internet Information Server (IIS).

Day 3: Database Fundamentals and ODBC

Day 3 introduces fundamental information for manipulating relational databases. In this chapter, you learn how to get information into and out of the database in many different ways. This chapter also explains the Open Database Connectivity (ODBC) standard.

Day 4: The HTML Scripting Language

Day 4 introduces some of the essential scripting tags that make up a Web page. In this chapter, you learn how to create a basic, as well as a more advanced, Web page by using the HTML scripting tags.

Day 5: The VBScript Language

Day 5 introduces the VBScript language constructs. You learn how to program the client-side page to act and react to your commands.

Day 6: Using an ActiveX Control

Day 6 shows you how to use and program an ActiveX control. This chapter focuses on how to manage the control through VBScript. It illustrates the concepts by using some free controls you can find on the Microsoft Web gallery site.

Day 7: Using Active Server Scripting

Day 7 explains how to write scripts that are executed on the server. In this chapter, you learn the basic objects and collections and how to use them.

Day 1

Database Connectivity and Visual Basic

by Dina Fleet

In this chapter, you will learn how far the Web has come in a few short years and how database information has been a critical step in driving some of the technology. You will also learn what the problems were at each step of the Web development of client and server pieces and what each new technology was meant to accomplish.

The Internet

The Internet started out as a project to connect scientists and researchers around the world and grew into a general communications tool. However, it had some problems. There were far too many access tools, and none of them were very user-friendly back in the days of text screens and command keys. The Internet didn't start out having a snappy graphical interface.

As access tools gained more functionality and new standards were put into place, HTTP (HyperText Transfer Protocol) and HTML (HyperText Markup Language) took over very quickly. HTTP allowed for an easy access protocol over a very popular protocol, TCP/IP (Transmission Control Protocol/Internet Protocol). Once HTML became the popular Internet language, people began working on making it more visually interesting.

The HTML Client and the Web Server

There's a relationship between the Internet technologies and how they developed. HTML is displayed in the browser on the client, and the Web server provides the HTML pages to the client. As HTML grew and developed, so did the technologies on the server. There are two different technologies on the server: first, the server scripting that controls what's returned to the browser, and second, the coordination of databases on the server with the server-side scripting.

The client and server technologies weren't being developed by a single "team." Their development was sporadic and meant to solve a specific problem. Getting the client and server technologies to interact in a meaningful way was difficult, and each of the technologies went through different stages of development. In Figure 1.1, you can see how each piece works together. The client-side browser can display only HTML text. As VBScript developed, other client-side processing was available. On the server side, everything must pass through the Web server. At that point, the Web server can determine whether any more work needs to take place. If no more work is needed, the Web server can return the page (a static page). If more processing takes place, the Web server passes the information to the server-side scripting, which is responsible for calling any other components, such as a database, it needs to fulfill the request.

Figure 1.1.
Client and server Web technologies.

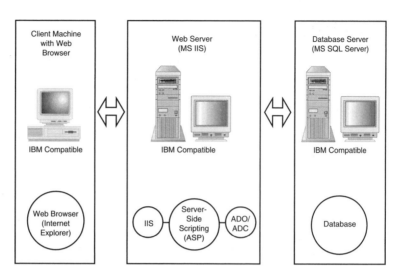

HTML Development on the Client

HTML is a growing language guided by the World Wide Web consortium (http://www.w3.org/). Anyone can submit a Request For Comment (RFC) that suggests changes to the language; both Netscape and Microsoft have submitted RFCs. When the language first came out, it supported the most rudimentary text layout, linking, and styles. The next versions added more functions to image support and more text styles. As people understood how interesting and easy-to-use the language was, they began defining ways to pass information to the server and more complex ways to display data.

The next step in developing HTML is the mathematical functions, which are still being considered. As the language grew, so did the browser's capability to display the language. The browser began to be produced faster than people on the Internet could upgrade. It became very important for the latest browser to be compatible with the oldest language requirements, which isn't as easy as it sounds.

The following figures show the progression of the Web in terms of visible differences. Figure 1.2 shows a Web page with just text formatting and links. This static page's only interactive component is the links. By *static*, I mean the information on the page is fixed at design time and doesn't vary based on the identity of the client. The page doesn't change unless someone rewrites the page. To all users, the page looks just as it does in Figure 1.2.

Figure 1.2.

A simple Web page.

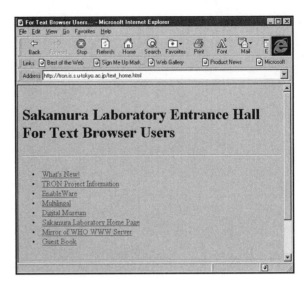

Adding Images to Web Pages

As the standards added more functionality, the need for presenting images became apparent. Not all image types were added—just a few common ones. As the Internet becomes more widely used, Netscape and Microsoft will define more image types to handle. Figure 1.3 illustrates a very simple Web page with images added. They can be handled in much the same way as text. You can align and size them to fit your needs; however, the page is still static and not very interesting.

Figure 1.3.

A simple Web page with images.

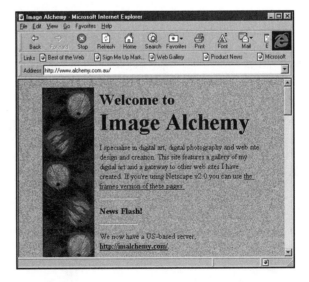

Using Web Pages to Get Information

As the Web became more popular, companies began to see the Internet as a new channel of revenue, but there wasn't a clear-cut way of getting to it. Three forms of commerce popped up: first, Internet Service Providers (ISPs) that host the Web sites; second, the revenue generated from advertising on a site; and third, direct marketing and selling goods on the Internet. This last form of commerce posed a problem because Web pages didn't have an attention-getting way to make products interesting (static Web pages are so boring), but it wasn't difficult to get and organize information from users. Many companies put a lot of money into expanding these forms of commerce.

Figure 1.4 shows a Web page asking for information from the user. For each piece of information, the user has to type something in. Before such tools as VBScript, validating data was difficult, so users could type in useless garbage that was still accepted.

Figure 1.4.

Querying the user for information.

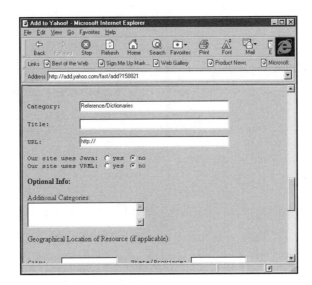

When information is used on a Web site, it must be filtered before it can be used. VBScript (on the client side) and CGI/ISAPIs (on the server side) were implemented to handle this kind of validation. CGI (Common Gateway Interface) scripts, generally written in Perl, were clunky and laborious, but then ISAPIs (Internet Server Application Programming Interfaces) came along. ISAPIs are DLLs (dynamic link libraries) that sit on the server. Because they are DLLs, they require more work to develop than the typical Web site administrator may be familiar with. Visual Basic Script from Microsoft solved the problem of client-side validation (as well as a lot of other problems) by using a language (Visual Basic) with a large programmer base (over 3.5 million programmers to date). This new scripting language made the esoteric work of Web sites easier for everyday programmers to handle.

Using More Advanced Images

The next features of Web pages to develop were more advanced images, such as image maps and animated images. *Image maps* are made up of a single image with specific regions that indicate a link. Animated images are basically screen "candy" and don't provide any true enhancement, but they are engaging and entertaining to the eye.

Figure 1.5 illustrates an animated image (of course, you can't see that it's animated here). This Web page is `http://www.emeraldcity.com/`. The text revolves around the globe that says "IWS" in the center of the page, which is definitely eye-catching.

Figure 1.5.

An animated image at `http://www.emeraldcity.com/`.

Figure 1.6 shows an image map on the left side of the Web page. Clicking on an oval and its corresponding text links you to a specific page, although the entire set of four ovals is just one image. This technique gives pages a uniform look, saves time by not downloading so many pictures, and easily moves users to a specific page when a region is clicked on. This Web page is `http://www.accessone.com/`.

The other major trend in Web pages is more organization of the text and images. Tables allow a Web page designer to organize text and images in rows and columns. With more advanced browsers, tables can be embedded within tables to allow subgrouping. The unique quality of tables that makes them very attractive as a design tool is that the rows and columns of a table don't have to be outlined, so the user doesn't even need to know that a table is on the page.

Figure 1.6.

An image map at
`http://`
`www.accessone.com/.`

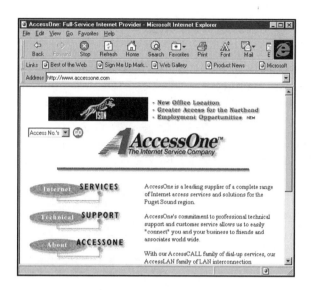

Figure 1.7 illustrates a page with embedded tables. The top grouping of images can be either an image map or a table embedded within another table. The left side of the page is used as an index bar, and the right-hand side can be used as the main content area. With tables, you can determine how large each row and column should be. On this page, for example, the left-hand column is only 30 percent of the screen, and the right-hand column takes up 70 percent of the screen.

Figure 1.7.

A page with an embedded table at
`http://`
`www.microsoft.com/.`

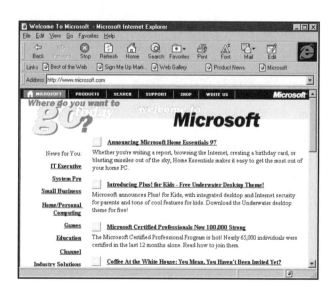

Using HTML Frames

The major HTML formatting addition is using frames. With tables, you could break up the page organization into rows and columns, but all the information had to come from one HTML page. With frames, however, the screen partitioning is a bit more sophisticated. Each screen division displays a different HTML page, and each division can be resized or scrolled (if you turn that feature on).

Figures 1.8 and 1.9 show Web pages with frames. They basically accomplish the same organization as Figure 1.7, but the content of each frame is captured in its own HTML page.

Figure 1.8.

A framed page at `http://` `digitalweb.com/.`

Using the <OBJECT> Tag

The next interesting addition to HTML is the <OBJECT> tag, which is what you use to add an ActiveX control to a Web page. ActiveX objects are downloaded to the client's machine and displayed (if there's a visual display) there. The display doesn't have to be in the browser screen area; the ActiveX control is independent of the browser in many ways.

The first type of ActiveX control you will look at is a visual one. Most Windows applications give you a menu list of choices. In HTML, you can offer this choice with a drop-down list box, but the list isn't very suitable to menu choices. Figure 1.10 illustrates a pop-up menu. The far-left button (Evaluating IIS) that invoked the pop-up menu is still pressed down, and the menu of choices is displayed to the right of that button. The pop-up menu overlaps the text on the page.

Figure 1.9.

Another framed page at `http://web.mso.nl/klaar/mosion/engels/frame.htm.`

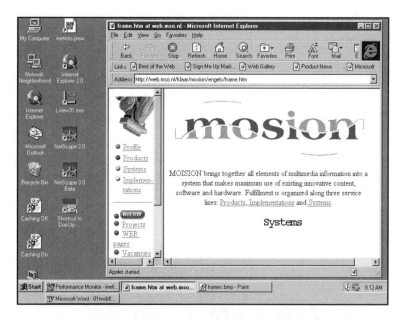

Figure 1.10.

A pop-up menu ActiveX control.

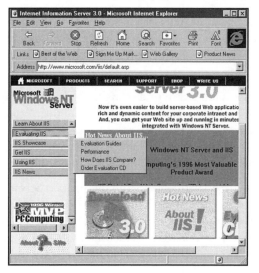

The second type of visual ActiveX control is illustrated in Figure 1.11. The XMailer window in the upper-right corner has information it would like to pass back to the Web server's database. This ActiveX control has two parts: the visible window, and the invisible work of passing information back to the server without interfering with the Web browser. This particular control passes the information back to the client through Windows Internet API calls.

Figure 1.11.

The XMailer ActiveX control.

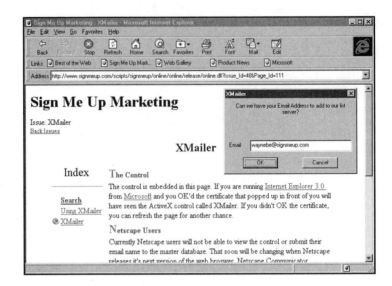

Web Development on the Server

The next kind of ActiveX control, or HTML function, is the Database component. To understand how these components work, however, you need a solid understanding of the Web server-side component history.

Web server technology has two components. The first component sends the Web page back to the user's browser to be displayed. The second component receives the browser's request for a page and figures out what to do with that request. On most Web servers, this second component can be handled with a CGI script that performs non-Web/HTML tasks to get the necessary information for the page. In this book, you're focusing on the requests for database information, but the CGI script is still used because it can cross over platforms.

However, the Microsoft Internet Information Server (IIS) added the ability to have a more standard DLL accept these requests for database information. This DLL, called ISAPI, gave Web developers some additional power beyond what a CGI script could offer. First, the ISAPI was incorporated into the Microsoft Visual C++ development environment, which made writing an ISAPI DLL very easy. Visual C++ added classes to handle many of the Web server issues, such as parameters passed to the ISAPI. The development environment also provided support for making requests from the database. However, writing an ISAPI DLL wasn't quite as easy as writing VBScript, and many Visual Basic programmers were expecting a tool they could easily use.

Active Server Pages

MS IIS made requesting information from databases easier by supplying a server-side scripting of VBScript called Active Server Pages (with a file extension of ASP, instead of HTML). This feature moved much of the work of C++ ISAPI coding capabilities into the hands of VB developers. By using VB in ASPs, ActiveX controls (previously called OLE controls) that had been available to VB programmers in non-Web applications are now available in Web applications, too. Visual Basic has an entire range of database controls that makes it a very rich tool for developers.

Before ASPs, VB programmers could get to databases through Data Access Objects (DAO). Now, with Active Server Pages, the same technology has been extended for the Web and is called ActiveX Data Objects (ADO). ADO script can be incorporated into ASP files to insert, retrieve, and update data. Just about anything you can do with the SQL database language, you can do with ADO.

ADO can be downloaded from `http://www.microsoft.com/iis` as part of the IIS 3.0 installation. The hardware and software requirements for ADO can also be found on those Web pages.

Database support for the Web still has two problems to solve. The first is displaying data, such as sales products or other information, that's already kept in a database. Formatting for that type of information generally tends to be static on a Web page. Figure 1.12 shows a Web page with tabled information from a database, done by using Active Server Pages. The information isn't very pretty, but you do get the sense that it came from a database.

Figure 1.12.

Database information in a Web page.

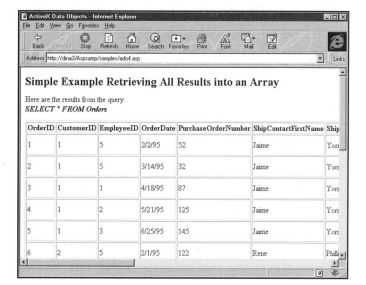

Figure 1.13 illustrates a much more interesting page composed of database information. This page, just one of many product pages, is part of the IIS 3.0 sample site called Adventure Works, a fictitious outdoor gear store. Notice that the pages look more like a product catalog, and the information is nicely displayed. This page was built by using ADO.

Figure 1.13.

The Adventure Works sample site.

Active Server pages return HTML text. Returning data in a Web page to a user's browser is simply returning static data, just as the surrounding text is static. Each time the user wants to change the data, view the data differently, or group the data in a different way, it requires a network trip from the client to the server and back. This requirement is inefficient because the range of information the client originally requested hasn't changed. If the client's machine could hold the entire range of data and manipulate it on the client, the server would be freed up to do other, more interesting, and more necessary processing—which is where the Advanced Data Connector comes into the picture.

Advanced Data Connector

The Advanced Data Connector (ADC) is a new tool from Microsoft that works with MS Internet Information Server and MS ADO to put the data on the client's machine. With some help from ADC components, the client's machine can now control the data without having to make a round trip to the server. All changes to the data can be made on the client. You can download ADC from http://www.microsoft.com/adc.

However, when it's time for those data changes to be incorporated into the database on the Web server, more ADC components are needed to make sure the final state of the database is correct. For example, suppose two clients have requested the same information to be updated. The ADC components on the server must incorporate each client's changes to the database.

ADC can give you a way to break up the processing of your Web application. What processing can be done on the client (far beyond displaying HTML pages) is moved to the client; this client-side processing includes data-aware ActiveX controls, invisible client-side cache of data, and one of Microsoft's newest database technologies, OLE DB. On the server side, ADC gives you all the transaction processing, server-side scripting, and Web product components you need. ADC is covered in depth starting in Chapter 15, "The Advanced Data Connector (ADC)."

Summary

ADO is an addition to Active Server Pages that allows server-side connections to databases. ADC is a joint client-server–based technology that moves the data to the client once, where the client can then manipulate and send it back in bulk.

By using ADO and ADC together, users' experiences with Web pages can be both fast (fewer trips across the Net) and exciting (because of a wide array of ActiveX objects to use). A Web page can be as simple or as complex as you need and can display and capture data from a wealth of stored information.

Q&A

Q If I want to display my Web site in an organized manner, what are my choices?

A You can use static pages that have a consistent menu for each page; framed pages, in which at least one frame is the consistent menu; Active Server Pages that have the menu statically stored in an ASP or include file; or a dynamic menu (Active Server Page) that can change based on information in the database.

Q How could I propose a change to the current Internet standards?

A You can submit an RFC (Request for Change) to the World Wide Web consortium (www.w3.org).

Quiz

1. What's the difference between HTML and Active Server Pages?
2. What's the difference between ADO and ADC?
3. What HTML component can load different Web pages into the same browser space?
4. Where can the rules for HTML be found?
5. Where can ADO be downloaded from?
6. Where can ADC be downloaded from?

Exercises

1. Download IIS 3.0 and Active Server Pages (ADO is included).
2. Download ADC.
3. Set up an ODBC database, preferably MS SQL Server or MS Access.

Day 2

The Client-Server Model

by Dina Fleet

In this chapter, you learn the architectural model that a browser and Web server emulate. Along the way, you will be subjected to some of the history of the client-server model; however, this knowledge makes it easier to understand why some technologies are the way they are today. You will also learn the terms and technology you need to set up your Microsoft Internet Information Server.

The Evolution of Client-Server

In the introduction, I used the term *architectural model* to describe client-server, but perhaps this term is a misnomer. When an architect designs a building, he has a vision of the finished product and produces a result based on that vision. Client-server, on the other hand, is more like a Darwinian model of the evolution of a living species. No one has a vision of the finished product; rather, it's affected by day-to-day events and gradual changes over time in reaction to those events. Just as you can't predict what humans will look like in 1,000 centuries, no one in 1957 could predict what client-server technology would be like in 1997. In fact, few people at that time could envision desktop computers or communications networks. But just as events that happen today affect a human's appearance in the distant future, so too did events from 1957 lay the foundation for client-server computing today. Table 2.1 shows a timeline of what I consider major events in the evolution of computing. The dates I show are subjective and approximate; they're used only to relate one event to another event. It wouldn't be a good idea to cite them in your doctoral thesis.

Table 2.1. Major events in the history of computing.

Approximate Date	Event
1804	Jacquard invents his loom.
1840	Babbage describes his "analytical engine."
1890	Hollerith develops his punched card machine.
1942	Eniac is built.
1945	von Neumann describes a "stored-program technique."
1947	First-generation computers use stored programs.
1948	deMestral invents Velcro.
early 1960s	CRT and disk are developed.
mid-1970s	Communications networks deployed.
1976	Terminals start to appear.
late 1970s	Xerox PARC develops Ethernet.
1979	Microcomputers.
1981	IBM PC appears.
early 1980s	Xerox PARC develops GUI-based computing.
mid-1980s	TCP/IP emerges.
late 1980s	Microsoft Windows appears.
1993	WWW and HTTP co-developed by CERN and NCSA.

OK, maybe Velcro isn't a major event in the history of computing, but it's an interesting fact. Other than Velcro, however, each of these events is vital to the concept of client-server computing. At the same time these hardware events were taking place, software was also evolving. It lagged behind hardware advancements but still emerged eventually to take advantage of the new capabilities. It's difficult to pinpoint an exact time that client-server computing appeared, but best guess would place it around 1990. However, even today, companies are yet to derive concrete benefits from these exciting new capabilities.

2

To set the stage for client-server computing software, you must go back to programming's roots. In the early days of business application programming (the mid-1960s), the operating system was very primitive. It was even more primitive than the MS-DOS of the early 1980s. This "operating system" was usually nothing more than a "loader" program for the application, running execution commands from a physical deck of cards, then later from stored commands. The application programs had to handle even low-level input/output functions. But over time, a commonality between functions in different applications and programs became apparent. To reduce the overall programming load, these common functions were gradually assimilated into the operating system, which simplified the applications at the expense of complicating the operating system—but that's another story. The operating system became much more robust, eventually handling thousands of interactive users and assuming more and more of the common tasks in applications.

While the operating system was evolving, a similar development was taking place in applications. In the beginning, applications were fairly simple, reading input transactions in a "batch," processing them against a data store, and then reporting the results. The input was usually punched cards, and the output was paper. Figure 2.1 shows a simplified functional representation of early applications. Although some applications became very elaborate, sorting data into different sequences, reporting different summaries, separating the input in many ways, they can all be broken down into those primary functions shown. You might note that I've separated the updating function into two parts, but this is done only for discussion's sake. Actually, record retrieval was usually a set of subroutines embedded in the updating program.

Figure 2.1.
Early software application structure.

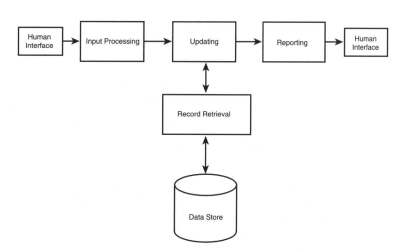

As I mentioned, common functions gradually migrated from the application to the operating system. Database processing was one of the first major functions to be removed from application control. This change in application structure is shown in Figure 2.2; however, the figure has been simplified. Much of the time database functions were added to existing functions instead of replacing them. The database functions in the application included retrieval, replacement, and insertion. Since it was impossible to handle these independent databases in a vacuum, a new function had to be introduced—database administration. This function was separate from the application code and involved defining the structure of the database, value ranges, backup, rollback, and so forth. From these simple beginnings, an entire multibillion dollar industry has blossomed.

Figure 2.2.
The database appli-
cation structure.

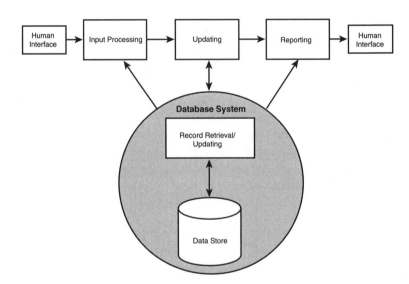

While these (r)evolutionary changes were going on in information storage and retrieval, a similar development was taking place on the communications side of applications. This change wasn't driven from inside the applications, but happened more as a defense against the applications. In some applications, a human interaction was required during operation; someone from the application would usurp the console—the controlling terminal for the computer—for his or her needs. Since it was often necessary to perform computer system functions at the same time, additional consoles were used to get the application people out of the way. These extra consoles eventually moved to functional areas (out of the glass house), adopted more roles, and evolved into dedicated terminals. The rest is history—unless you work in airline reservations, banks, and so on. Figure 2.3 illustrates this new structure. You must be aware that this new application structure didn't always replace the old structure. It

2

was used only when it was necessary for a person to interact with a single record in the database. In any case, it spawned a multibillion dollar communications industry, and programs became much more complex. Instead of several smaller programs communicating by using physical files, a mega-program assumed the entire job of input, updating, and reporting.

Figure 2.3.

The application structure using terminals.

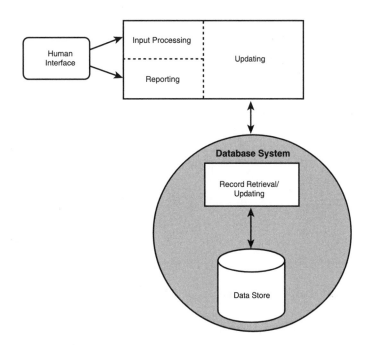

Although I'm trying to make this whole process seem orderly, there was a lot going on, and in many different directions. Terminals were becoming much smarter, taking over some editing functions and making the programs less clunky. The databases were becoming smarter, allowing applications to be built with predefined transactions kicked off by the smarter terminals. At the same time, minicomputers were being used as departmental computers and communication and print controllers, freeing the mainframe of many mundane tasks. Out in Palo Alto, Xerox was teaming up with DEC and others to develop Ethernet networks. Not to be outdone, the Army, in a remote area of Arizona not far from the Mexican border, was developing its own ideas for a worldwide communications network. Meanwhile, in the corner of a garage in California, three college guys were about to turn the whole industry upside down. 1980 was a very big year.

Now that I've set the stage, it's time to get back to client-server. To best illustrate this concept, I'll break down an application from a slightly different point of view: that of processing location rather than flow. This diagram is shown in Figure 2.4. In Figure 2.1, the processing flowed from input to output through many programs. However, in Figure 2.4, the application is shown in terms of functions to be performed, such as the dialogs with the program's users, the rules used for those dialogs and other processing, the high-level business rules applied before working with the data store, and, finally, the interaction with the data store. To illustrate a three-tier client-server structure, I've separated the processing rules and business rules. Most often, though, they exist in the same program.

Figure 2.4.

The client-server application function structure.

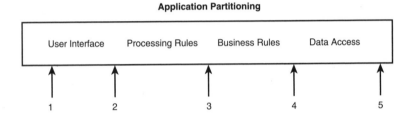

On the lower part of the diagram are a series of arrows numbered from 1 to 5. These arrows indicate places where an application (or a program) can be separated to implement client-server. When a separation (known as a *partition*) is done, communications routines and an external network replace the internal program function calls at that point in the program. Table 2.2 shows the different models based on implementing a partition at different points.

Table 2.2. Client-server partition models.

Arrow	Model
None	Traditional single-platform program, such as a standalone PC program.
1	Traditional dumb-terminal application, usually from a minicomputer or mainframe computer.
2	Smart terminal application; a Web browser application would fall into this model.
3	Heavy database application (usually happens when a database administrator designs an application!).
4	Light database application; that is, one in which the database is used more as a data store and doesn't implement the business rules.
5	Traditional back-end data store system.

2

This table also presents a very simplistic view. In actuality, client-server systems can be set up with wide variations and in multiple partitions. Proper client-server applications should balance the processing power available at different points and find its most suitable location in relation to cost. In some cases, a traditional mainframe application might be the best solution. Heaven knows, you wouldn't want the Social Security Administration's payroll run to be attempted on a Windows 95 system. At the same time, you wouldn't want Alice to write a letter to her mom on a $12,000,000 IBM ES9000.

2

The Advantages of a Client-Server Model

The major advantage of a client-server model is that the hardware and software can be placed where it will do the most good. In a mainframe model, the server has all the power and the dumb terminal has none. (The terminal is referred to as *dumb* because all the computing is done on the mainframe; the terminal is just a viewer into that information.) In the client-server model of PCs, the power can be spread across the client and server.

Say you have an Internet site (server) that looks up information in a database and displays the information (on the client) in an ActiveX object. The power to run this site can reside on one or two machines (there are other configurations as well). If the site was on a single machine, the Internet software and the database software would have to share hardware and software resources. If the machine is never running at full capacity, this configuration will work. However, if the machine begins to run at full capacity, the database software can be placed on a second machine. Now the server-side computer power is distributed to allow growth. On the client side, an ActiveX object is used to present the data. By having the client side do the work of presenting the data, that burden is removed from the server side so it can do more work. If the client machine reaches full capacity, it can't easily be distributed (although this is one of the emerging technologies). The common answer is to add more hardware.

A user of accounting software can make a request, such as calculating a range of inventory numbers. The client software supplies the interface (such as a windowed program) and the knowledge of how to pass the request to the server, and then formats the data for the user when it's returned from the server. The server's job is to manipulate the range of inventory numbers according to the user's request. This approach divides the processing across several computers, which has the advantage of not overloading any single processor. In this example, the user's computer is acting as a client by requesting another computer to do some work. The server is serving up the solution and passing it back to the client. Figure 2.5 illustrates which machine is doing what part of the work.

Figure 2.5.

The client is making the request, and the server is fulfilling the request and passing it back to the client.

1. User asks for report about employee salaries
2. Application sends request to operating system
3. Operating system passes request to the server

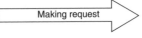
Making request

Returning answer

Personal Computer

Database Server

1. Server operating system finds resource, such as database
2. Server passes the request to the database
3. Database returns answer to operating system
4. Operating system passes answer back to personal computer's operating system
5. Personal computer's operating system returns answer to application
6. Application displays answer to user

Communications Protocol

The ability to request information from the server and have the server return that information depends on these two computers being able to communicate. The hardware involved in the communication process includes the network card and network wire on the personal computers and routers and hubs controlling the data flow. The software includes the protocols sitting on each of the computers. You can think of the *protocol* as the language between the two computers. If one computer knows only protocol A, and the other computer knows protocol B, the two computers can't exchange information. When an application on computer A needs a resource on computer B, the request goes through the application layers on both machines.

The Network Layers

The request from computer A to computer B takes a path on both machines from the highest layer (the application) to the lowest layer (the network wire). On computer A, the application must pass the request to a layer that decides whether the request can be answered on computer A or another machine is needed to fulfill this request. Since the request in this scenario is on computer B, assume that's the path. At the next layer, the information is then transformed

2

into a series of data packets. At the next layer, the packets are sent to the network card, which then sends the packets across the wire. Figure 2.6 illustrates the path a request takes from computer A to computer B.

Figure 2.6.

The network layers, including TCP/IP and HTTP.

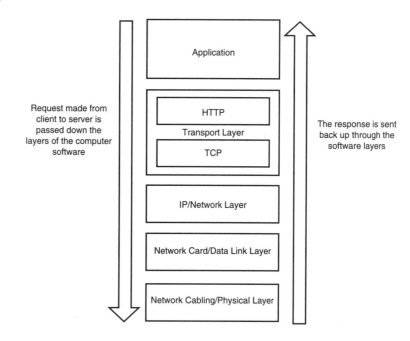

Notice that the path only resembles the request. If computer B needed to send information back to computer A, the opposite path would be taken. This layered system might seem like an overly complicated way to move data from computer A to computer B, but it has its advantages. The main advantage is that any layer in the system needs to know how to talk to only the layer above and below it. This restriction removes each layer from having to solve the entire problem of moving data; it's responsible for answering only one piece of the data request.

Suppose computer A is an MS Windows machine and computer B is a UNIX machine. Although the two operating systems are different, it's easy to move data between them as long as they understand how to talk to each other through the layers. Both machines must be using the same protocol (the set of standards about how to communicate), but each operating system uses a different version specifically designed for it. Figure 2.7 illustrates the differences in network communications when different operating systems are involved.

Figure 2.7.
*Different operating
systems implementing
the different network
layers.*

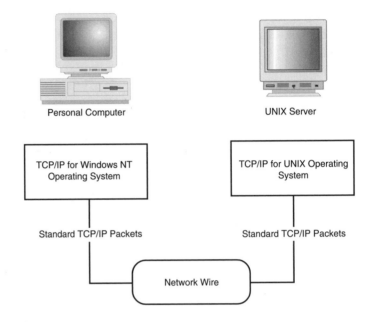

Personal Computer   UNIX Server

TCP/IP for Windows NT
Operating System

TCP/IP for UNIX Operating
System

Standard TCP/IP Packets   Standard TCP/IP Packets

Network Wire

Web Protocols

There are two main protocols for using the Web: TCP/IP and HTTP. HTTP sits on top of
TCP/IP and takes advantage of the market share that TCP/IP enjoys. HTTP could be
implemented on top of other protocols, but TCP/IP does rule the Internet because of its large
installed base and ease of use.

Transmission Control Protocol/Internet Protocol (TCP/IP)

TCP/IP (sometimes written as *TCPIP*) stands for *Transmission Control Protocol/Internet
Protocol.* It's a result of research funded by the U.S. government's project ARPA, the
Advanced Research Projects Agency. The original intent was to allow researchers from
around the world to communicate ideas and files so they could advance research projects
more easily. This network of research computers, which used TCP/IP as its protocol,
eventually became the Internet.

The Transmission Control Protocol determines how to divide the information into packets,
and the Internet Protocol transports these packets. The Internet Protocol doesn't guarantee
that the packets will be received in the order they were sent; it's up to the Transmission
Control Protocol to reassemble the packets in the correct order. Figure 2. 8 illustrates the
interaction between TCP and IP.

Figure 2.8.

The interaction between TCP and IP.

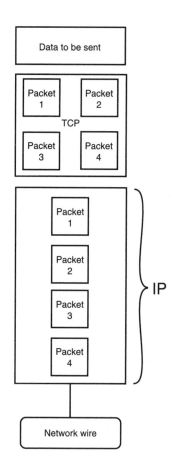

TCP/IP is a standard protocol of Windows NT and Windows 95 operating systems. Several applications are shipped with TCP/IP on the Windows platforms to configure and use TCP/IP. One of these TCP/IP applications is *FTP* (*File Transfer Protocol*). Although most browsers allow you to get to FTP sites, command-line utilities can also give you that access.

TCP/IP addresses are 16-digit numbers separated into four sections (known as *octets*), such as 255.14.130.12; the number in each section can't be higher than 255. Each section identifies, to some degree, the location of the recipient of the packets. The first two sections are generally considered the network address, the third section is considered the subnet mask, and the fourth section is the address of the physical machine.

There are three scenarios for using these numbers. In the first scenario, a company wants a direct connection to the Internet; for every direct connection, it needs a range of addresses.

This scenario isn't about the office worker who wants to surf the Net; it's a large company, with thousands of computers, that needs direct connections to the Internet so it can link geographically distant office locations. This is the server(s) that connects different office locations together. Scenario 1 is a company that leases a range of addresses and configures its servers as certain addresses. Figure 2.9 illustrates Scenario 1.

Figure 2.9.

Scenario 1: A company with Internet connections used to link different locations.

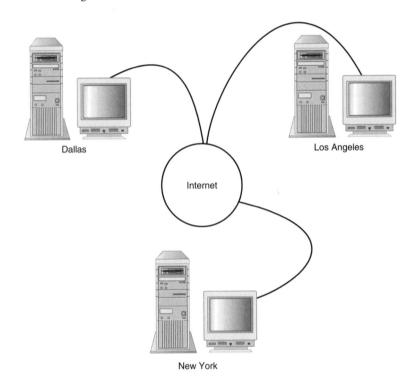

Scenario 2 is a company that doesn't have Internet connections but wants to configure the intranet with IP addresseses. This company doesn't have to lease the address but can choose the range of addresses. Generally, some schema, or a *Dynamic Host Configuration Protocol* (*DHCP*), is used to define these addresses. A DHCP server supplies a pool of addresses in some range, and a specific computer then borrows an address. When the computer is shut down, the address can go back in the pool and be used by another computer. Scenario 2, shown in Figure 2.10, is for small to medium companies. DHCP is different from Scenario 1 because computers that sit on the Internet must have a permanent connection with a permanent address. Address pooling would be a deterrent to Scenario 1, not a benefit.

Scenario 3, the most realistic scenario, combines portions of the first two scenarios. A large company needs both Internet and intranet connectivity. The company leases a range of Internet addresses and develops its own addressing system for intranet use. Figure 2.11 illustrates this scenario.

Figure 2.10.

Scenario 2: A company with no Internet connections, having DHCP-configured machines.

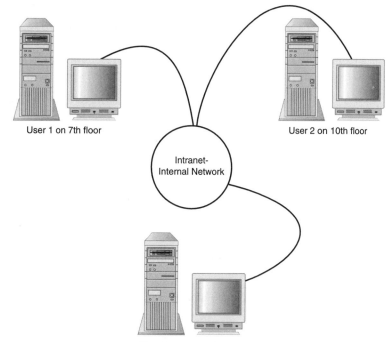

User 1 on 7th floor

User 2 on 10th floor

Intranet-Internal Network

User 3 on ground floor

2

Figure 2.11.

Scenario 3: A company with both Internet and intranet connections.

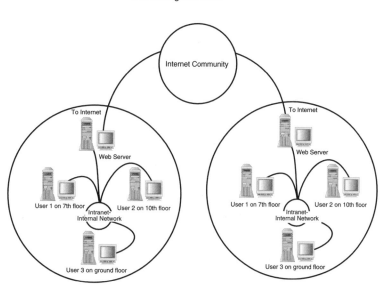

Internet Community

To Internet

Web Server

User 1 on 7th floor

User 2 on 10th floor

Intranet-Internal Network

User 3 on ground floor

To Internet

Web Server

User 1 on 7th floor

User 2 on 10th floor

Intranet-Internal Network

User 3 on ground floor

There are only a limited number of addresses and most are already leased, so there's great concern in the Internet community about what will happen when all the addresses run out. To handle this potential problem, an extended form of addressing is being proposed. It would handle 16 times the amount of currently available addresses.

A Web address is translated into the TCP/IP address with a domain server. To reach an Internet address, you can type the HTTP address, such as `http://www.sams.mcp.com`, or you can enter the actual TCP/IP address corresponding to that HTTP address. It doesn't really matter, because eventually the HTTP address is changed into a TCP/IP address, which is handled in a lookup table. Operating systems use lookup tables differently, but the idea is the same. When you type in the HTTP address at your client's browser, the browser passes this information to your domain server. If you're using a service such as MSN or AOL, these Internet services act as your domain server. If you're surfing the Net from within a corporation, it also has a domain server to figure out whether your request is inside the intranet or on the Internet. Once you have passed the HTTP address to the domain server, that server returns the TCP/IP address of the HTTP request. Then, the browser internally makes the request, using the TCP/IP address. Figure 2.12 illustrates how the request is made and returned.

Figure 2.12.

The HTTP request to the TCP/IP address.

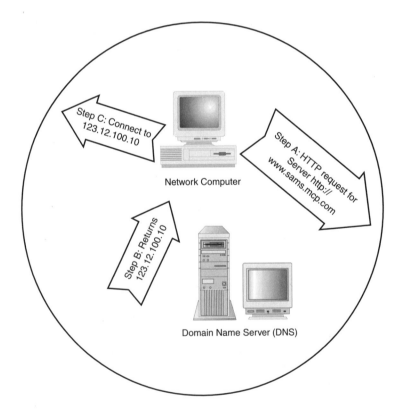

HyperText Transfer Protocol (HTTP)

HTTP is a protocol that sits on top of TCP/IP. The protocol translates requests from Web pages into requests over the network; it then takes browser requests in the format of a method. Although you will learn how to use these methods in Chapter 4, "The HTML Scripting Language," you should know what they mean, so I've offered a brief introduction of the four HTTP methods.

The HTTP methods are GET, PUT, POST, and DELETE. The GET method requests a file from the Web server. It's simply a method for linking from one page to another, not for handling any kind of form that you fill out. The POST method is used by forms to pass parameters to the Web server. The PUT method is rarely used because it allows a request to create a new file or append to the file if the file already exists. You can use the DELETE method to delete a file from the Web server. For security reasons, Web servers generally don't permit PUT and DELETE methods. Figure 2.13 illustrates the logic of each of the request types.

Figure 2.13.

How the HTTP methods work.

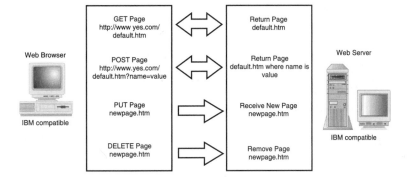

The HTTP model of Web browsing fits neatly into the client-server model. The Web browser, acting as the client, makes requests for pages to the Web server. The Web server fulfills these requests by responding with a Web page. Generally, each request is sent as a separate and unique connection.

All Web pages are sent as text files. Along with the request, the browser sends a header of information about itself, including what types of files it can handle. The server then uses this information to determine whether it should send the page. For the server to respond to the browser, the server sends a status code along with the page. If the page is sent, the status code is usually a success code; if the page isn't sent, the status code is some type of error code. The status codes are broken up into several categories identified by a numeric range from 100 to 599. The 100–199 range is information status; 200–299 indicates success status, but typically isn't displayed because the page was returned successfully; 300–399 means the page has been moved; 400–499 means there was an error on the browser's side; and 500–599 indicates there was a problem on the server's side.

Securing Web sites for commercial business needs is vital. Take using a credit card to pay for information across the Internet, for example. Without encryption of the request from the browser to the Web server, anyone who has a tool to read TCP/IP packets can see your credit-card information, as long as they are along the route of your packets. However, if the HTTP request is encrypted, the credit-card information could still be seen, but it would make no sense. This type of encryption in HTTP is known as *HTTPS*, also referred to as *secure server*.

The Web Server: MS Internet Information Server (IIS)

If you have surfed the Internet, you're probably very familiar with the browser side of Web pages. In this section, the focus is on the Web server. As an example of a server, I have used Microsoft Internet Information Server (IIS). If you have MS Windows NT 4.0, then you probably have IIS installed. However, if you don't have MS Windows NT 4.0, please visit the Microsoft site for information on installing IIS:

```
http://www.microsoft.com/iis
```

MS IIS comes with three Internet services: HTTP (Web), FTP, and Gopher, the most commonly used services on the Internet today. FTP is the file transfer protocol that allows you to place files on a server or get files from a Web server, and Gopher is a legacy service that incorporates some of the HTTP linking and includes a search server. Figure 2.14 shows the Microsoft Internet Service Manager. It's a very simple interface because the Web server doesn't have to do much; the actual Web pages do most of the work.

Figure 2.14.

The Microsoft Internet Service Manager.

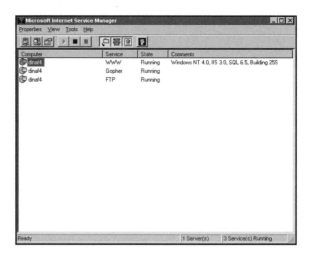

As with most server-management applications, the Internet Service Manager lets you manage any IIS as long as you have the appropriate permissions for, and can connect to, those machines. This feature is helpful for organizations that keep their Web servers in different locations. Instead of going to the server's physical location, you just connect to it through the Internet Service Manager.

Figure 2.15 shows the Service page of the Microsoft Internet Service Manager. In the TCP Port field, 80 is the default port for HTTP requests; however, you can configure it to your specific needs. The *connection time-out* means how long the server waits to respond to a request before it no longer answers. If your Web server is doing a lot of processing to answer the request, you should add more time to this field. In the Maximum Connections field, you see how many HTTP requests the Web server can handle at one time. If you allow anonymous connections to your Web server, don't change the Anonymous Logon fields. You can use the checkboxes in the Password Authentication area to indicate anonymous logons, HTML passwords (the Basic (Clear Text) checkbox), or Windows NT network logons. The common field is what shows up on Figure 2.14 as Comments. It's helpful for identifying locations and owners of Web servers for large intranet sites.

Figure 2.15.

Using the Service page of WWW Service Properties.

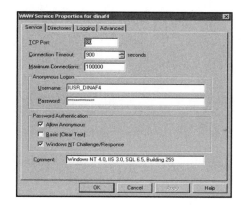

Figures 2.16 and 2.17 illustrate how to set up virtual roots on a Web server. Using a *virtual root* means that although the physical location for a file could be c:\web\files, the user would enter the Web location, not the physical location. Each Web server needs a default home location, which is used when the browser's HTTP address is generic, such as www.sams.mcp.com. However, if I wanted c:\web\files\account to appear as http://www.sams.mcp.com/account-ing, I need to add accounting as a virtual root. Figure 2.16 shows the physical location in the Directory column and the Alias column shows the virtual root name. The address would be specified if that virtual root was tied to a specific IP address.

The last two sections of the Directories page shown in Figure 2.16 give you more control of the entire Web server. The first checkbox is Enable Default Document. With the default installation of IIS, DEFAULT.HTM is the only default document, so if you want your MENU.HTM file to be displayed when a specific page isn't requested, add MENU.HTM in the Default Document text box. You can have more than one default document. In Chapter 7, "Using Active Server Scripting," you learn about Active Server Pages, which have an .ASP file extension. It's common to add the DEFAULT.ASP to the list of default documents; just make sure you use a comma as the separator between multiple items.

The last checkbox in Figure 2.16, Directory Browsing Allowed, is used to turn directory browsing on. Suppose you have a site that doesn't have a DEFAULT.HTM, but DEFAULT.HTM is the *only* default document. No page would be returned to the browser if directory browsing wasn't enabled. However, if it were, all the files in that directory would be listed. This feature saves the Web administrator from having to make sure a default page is available; however, it also gives full access to all the files in the directory.

Figure 2.16.

*Using the Directories
page.*

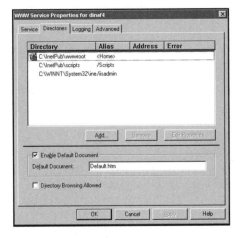

To add or edit a virtual directory, you can either click Add or select an existing directory and click Edit Properties; either action opens the dialog box shown in Figure 2.17. At the bottom of Figure 2.17, notice that access to the directory can be specified as Read or Execute. If the page is a straight HTML page, or other non-executable code, you need to set just the Read access. However, if the directory has CGI scripts, ISAPI DLLs, ASP files, or other executable files, enable the checkbox for Execute access. It's a good idea to separate out the files that can be read (HTM, HTML) and the files that can be executed (ISAPI, CGI, ASP). By making sure a directory has only one type of file and the corresponding permissions (Read or Execute), you're adding a layer of security to your site.

Figure 2.17.

*The Directory
Properties dialog box.*

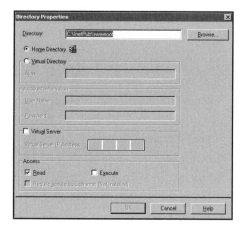

Figure 2.18 illustrates the Web server's logging capabilities. You can choose the log format (standard or NCSA), how often a new log file is created, and the directory where the log file will reside. The other choice is to log onto an MS SQL Server database through ODBC. Every Web page request (such as www.signmeup.com) made to the Web server is logged by time, and information about the request is stored.

Figure 2.18.

*Using the Logging
tab.*

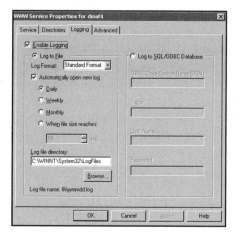

In Figure 2.19, you can see another Web server security choice. By setting options on the Advanced tab, you can grant or deny access to your Web server based on the requester's TCP/IP address or range of addresses. This method is a simple way to deny accessibility to your server. Please examine all your choices before deciding on a security method. To grant or deny a range of addresses, click the Add button, and to edit or delete a range of addresses, select the address from the list, then click Edit or Remove. Remember to select the Granted Access or Denied Access radio button; this dialog box defaults to Granted Access. The checkbox at the bottom is used to control how much information you allow your Web server (WWW, FTP, and Gopher) to deliver. This control is a benefit because you should know how fast your network or Internet connection is and deliver only up to that point. If you try to deliver more than your connection can handle, your network will probably crash.

Figure 2.19.

Setting options in the Advanced tab.

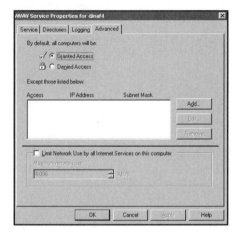

WARNING

When you install IIS, ODBC is installed, too. However, this version of ODBC may be older than the version you currently have on your computer. If any software adds ODBC to your computer, you should check both versions before accepting any installation because it could affect other programs on your computer.

Summary

In this chapter, you have learned about the client-server model and how a Web browser and Web server fit into that model. You have also learned the protocols used by the Web: TCP/IP and HTTP. The TCP/IP protocol is a standard, well-defined protocol (not specific to the Internet). HTTP is the method of moving Web pages across the Internet with certain commands such as GET or POST. Finally, you have seen how to manage your MS Internet Information Server. How you configure your IIS server is crucial to how secure and accessible your Web site is. After you have installed it, make sure to configure the Web server to fit your needs.

Q&A

Q **When I'm installing IIS, should I choose my own install options or take the default install options?**

A You should always choose your own install options. ODBC is installed by default, but this "added" component might conflict with other software you have. Never install an older version of ODBC, unless you know how it will affect your other installed programs.

Q **If I have both HTM pages and scripts to place on my Web server, how should I divide the information and what permissions should the directories have?**

A The HTM pages should be placed in their own directory (or directories) with read permission only. All scripts (ISAPI, CGI, ASP) should be placed in their own directory (or directories) with execute permission only. All links from an HTM page to a script should have an absolute reference, such as www.signmeup.com/scripts, instead of a relative reference, such as ../scripts. By making the reference absolute, you can move the HTM pages around and not have to re-edit the links.

Quiz

1. What are some of the protocols on the Web?
2. What's the difference between HTTP and TCP/IP?
3. How does the response/request model follow the client-server model?
4. What does HTTP's PUT command do? Why is it typically not used?
5. What does HTTP's DELETE command do? Why is it generally not implemented?
6. What is the difference between the functions of TCP and IP?
7. What is a virtual root?
8. What does the execute permission do on a virtual root?
9. How do you add default pages beyond DEFAULT.HTM?

Exercises

1. Design a Web architecture for your company.
2. Design a security architecture for allowing HTTP's PUT and DELETE.
3. Add a virtual root to your Web server.

Day **3**

Database Fundamentals and ODBC

by Dina Fleet

In this chapter, you gain some fundamental knowledge for using a database. First, you learn what a relational database is, and second, you learn how to design the database tables. As you learn about these topics, a new language called *Structured Query Language* (SQL) is introduced. Other skills introduced in this chapter include adding and manipulating data in the database, as well as how to choose data from the database. The last part of the chapter introduces the *Open Database Connectivity* (ODBC) standard. After you have read this chapter, you should be able to create a database and manipulate data by using SQL.

Databases are fundamental to businesses because they can store any kind of information that can then be retrieved and analyzed. Every time you make a request to your bank account, you're requesting information stored in a database. In the programming world, databases are separate from the program but vital to creating an application that manipulates information.

What Is a Relational Database?

A *relational database* is a collection of related data. A database usually represents some collection of real data, such as accounting information or a record of your music CDs. The data usually has some logical relationship; in other words, a random collection of data wouldn't be called a database. A database usually has a specific purpose, such as finding all the music CDs in a collection that fit the category of "Jazz" or an accounting database that finds all the entries for a particular client. A database has several areas of functionality, and each area is a component built to handle a specific task. These areas include the query processor that interprets your request, the transaction processor that ensures data integrity, the security model that allows only certain people to access certain data, the database language SQL, and concurrency issues (more than one person has access to the same data at the same time).

A relational database has some benefits; the main one being that duplicate data, such as many CDs from the same musical group, can be reduced. The information can be stored just once and then referenced by all the duplicates. This benefit is twofold. Each time a change has to be made to the information, it has to be made only once, instead of being changed for each reference to the information. The second benefit is that the amount of disk space needed is greatly reduced. This concept of reducing redundant data is known as *normalizing* a database. Issues of when and how to normalize a database are discussed later in this chapter.

Structured Query Language (SQL)

The first component of a relational database consists of methods for entering data into the database and getting data out of the database. Most databases support some sort of programming language for performing these tasks. In this book, you focus on the Structured Query Language (SQL) that most databases support. *SQL* is a programming language written specifically to deal with databases, so you wouldn't write an executable program such as Windows 95 with SQL. The language supports creating database structures, such as tables and indexes (called *Data Definition Language* or *DDL*), but also allows for data manipulation, such as entering and updating data (called *Data Manipulation Language* or *DML*).

The Query Processor

Another component of the relational database is the engine that interprets a SQL query's request. This component processes the SQL query and executes the request. To make sure the SQL query executes, the query engine must ensure that all the query's syntax is correct. If the syntax isn't correct, the query engine won't execute the request.

Security

A database should also have a component to handle security. Each person should have access only to the database he or she needs—but not anything else. For example, if someone goes to the library and looks through the database for a particular book, she shouldn't have the security privileges needed to add, change, or delete any information about that book; she should, however, be able to retrieve the information she needs. Similarly, a person who's responsible for making changes to a bank account should have enough security privileges to show the addition of funds in an account when a customer makes a deposit.

Transaction Processing

Transaction processing means making sure all changes to a database are correctly executed. If there's a problem executing the request, all the changes should be rolled back so that the database returns to its original state. Transaction processing is needed when you have, for example, a request to make changes to 10 accounts, each of which is related to the next; therefore, changes must affect *all* the accounts or none of them. If the database could fulfill five of the 10 account requests, but had a problem with the sixth request and stopped the changes there, the database wouldn't be correct. When the problem occurs with the sixth account, the database must return the previous five accounts to their original state, just as though the request hadn't been made.

If there's no problem with all 10 steps of the request, the data should be committed to the database. *Committing* data means that the data is now part of the database and can't be rolled back after the commit. There is no UNDO function in a database.

Concurrency Issues

A database also needs to control how data is affected when two or more people make a request to change that data. Each request must be scheduled in the database, which generally includes locking the data to just that request. This locking method keeps out the second request until the first is finished, making sure the final data is accurate and reflects both requests. Locking data eliminates the possibility of two people updating the same record simultaneously.

Taking a Closer Look at Relational Databases

This chapter focuses on a relational database. Although many types of databases exist (such as object-oriented databases), relational databases have a large share of the database industry for good reason. Relational databases consist of tables that have unique, definable relationships to each other.

A *relation* is a table that has columns and rows. Rows do not contain duplicate data, and each field in the table contains only one value. If you have worked with spreadsheet applications before, then you have a feel for how the row and column relationship works. A spreadsheet, however, can't be a true relational database because it can't enforce the rule that data in rows is unique.

Setting Up Sample Tables for a Relational Database

In a relational database, there are usually several tables that each contain information specific to that table. Going back to the database of musical CDs, what type of data could that database hold? Each CD has an artist or musical group, a record label, a producer, a style of music, specific songs with specific musicians on each song, the copyright date, cover art, and so forth. Some of these topics can be tables in a database; using those topics, I have set up the following table structures. I could have many more tables, but for demonstration purposes, these three tables are enough. Examine Tables 3.1, 3.2, and 3.3 and see how they relate to each other.

Table 3.1. The Music CD table contains information about each CD.

Column Name	Type of Data in Column
CD ID	Number
CD Title	Characters
Artist/Group	Characters
Record Label ID	Number
Date of Copyright	Date
Number of Songs	Number
Music Category	Characters

3

Table 3.2. The Song table contains information about each song.

Column Name	Type of Data in Column
Song Title	Characters
Author	Characters
CD ID	Number
Length of song	Time

Table 3.3. The Record Label table contains information about each record company.

Column Name	Type of Data in Column
Record Label ID	Number
Record Label	Characters
Address	Characters
City	Characters
State	Characters (2)
Zip Code	Number

Figure 3.1 illustrates the relationships between these tables. Each music CD can have multiple songs on it, but only one record label. Each row in the Music CD table corresponds to at least one row (and usually more than one) in the Song table, and each row in the Song table corresponds to one row in the Music CD table. This is called a *one-to-many relationship*, in which one row in a table (Music CD table) can correspond to many rows in another table (Song table). The relationship between the Music CD table and the Record Label table is also a one-to-many relationship because a record label can produce many CDs.

Determining Relationships Between Tables

There are two more types of relationships: one-to-one and many-to-many. In a *one-to-one relationship*, one row in Table X relates to only one row in Table Y. Figure 3.2 shows an example of this type of relationship. Assume that the companies in the Record Label table have only one location each. If the address information in the Record Label table had been placed in another table, each row of the Record Label table would have only one address and, therefore, only one corresponding row in a fictional Address table. To illustrate the many-to-many relationship, many versions of a single song can be performed by different artists, and that song could be on many different CDs.

Figure 3.1.

The relationship of the Music CD, Song, and Record Label tables (shown in Microsoft Access).

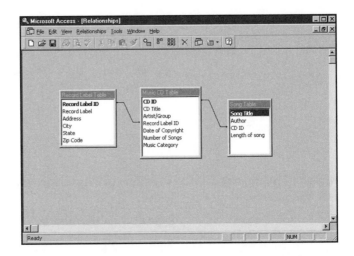

Figure 3.2.

An example of a one-to-one relationship.

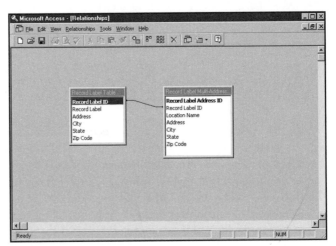

Identifying Columns

In Table 3.1, there are two columns that have "ID" in the label: CD ID and Record Label ID. They're used to do searches and compares quickly. Think about how many items have unique identification numbers: drivers' licenses, Social Security numbers, cars' VINs. Say, for example, that you wanted to find all the song titles on a CD called Samples. The database would have to compare the text (character by character) of the CD Title column in the Music CD table (refer to Table 3.1) with a corresponding column in the Song table (refer to Table 3.2). Comparing text generally takes longer than comparing numbers, so to speed up the search, the CD Title text column is kept in Table 3.1, and you add a column that's a unique identifier for the CD (usually a number). This way, a particular CD is known by its ID and the search is much faster. Table 3.4 illustrates how the ID number is unique to each CD.

Table 3.4. The Music CD table has a unique identifier for each CD title.

CD Title ID	CD Title
1	Title cb
2	Title ax
3	Title d
4	Title ba
5	Title a
6	Title ca
7	Title ab

Table 3.5 doesn't hold the CD title, but holds the unique identifier for each song so that searches are speedy.

Table 3.5. The Song table contains the song title and the relational identifier to the CD Title table.

Song Title	CD Title ID
Song Title A	3
Song Title a	5
Song Title ba	1
Song Title ac	2

NOTE

Notice that the information in the tables doesn't seem to be in any particular order. Don't worry—that's how a database works. Data sits in the tables in the order it was inserted. In Table 3.4, for example, Title cb was inserted first, then Title ax, and so on. The SQL language used to get information out of the database also handles sorting and shuffling data so that it's presented to you in the alphabetic or numeric order you're looking for.

Specifying Data Types

In programming languages, variables are of a specific type, which can be a number, characters, time, and so forth. Databases also use types. Although each database has specific types, there are a few that most databases have in common. In Tables 3.1, 3.2, and 3.3, the types characters, numbers, date, and time are used. In Table 3.3, the State column's type is two characters. States are usually represented as two characters, so the database needs to know that only two characters should be allowed in that field. If you don't specify a data type's length (there is a different way for each data type), the database creates the type with its default settings, which are usually the maximum for that type. If I wanted a field of characters that was a comment about the music in the CD, I would put a limit on the number of characters because a large comment (over 255 characters) might not be practical for my use of the information.

There's a special data type that the three tables depend on: the unique ID. The unique column identifier can be generated in two ways: You can keep track of how many rows are in the database and enter the unique ID as part of the data insertion, or (and this method is much better) the database can generate a unique ID for each row. This unique ID would have to be a data type that automatically increments as each row is inserted; the database would keep track of the next number.

WARNING

Before you create a database, be aware of the caveats of the data types you're choosing and what limitations they impose on executing queries. Suppose you have a data type that is, by default, 10,000 bytes. If you don't limit the size of the type, the database might reserve 10,000 bytes for each field, regardless of whether they're used. This is a waste of space, but there's another side-effect to the size of the types you choose. A database has to lock some portion of the data when you make a request. You might have a request to change one row on a database that locks 2K of data for each request. If the row is less than 2K, more than just that row will be locked until the request's execution is finished. If you try to create a row larger than 2K, the database might not let you do so. Consult the product reference information (the program's manual) for the specific database you're using.

Using Primary Keys

Primary keys are made up of a column or set of columns that uniquely identify each row. For example, the primary key for Table 3.1 is the CD ID, for Table 3.2, it's Song Title, and for Table 3.3, it's Record Label ID. Why should each row be different? Suppose I have two rows in the Song table called "My Love" on different CDs (by different artists and on different record labels). How would I distinguish one song from the other? I would have to compare each column in the Song Table until I found a column I knew also corresponded to the song I want. What if there are no other distinguishing columns? The correct record won't be found. To fix this, the database needs to know that each Song Title column must be unique. You can do this by using a primary key on the Song Title column to fix the problem of finding the right CD.

Say you're entering the first song title, along with the other information for that table—no problem so far. Next, try to enter the information for the second song title. The database doesn't let you do this, however, because there's already a song with that title. For argument's sake, try entering no song title but add the rest of the data, such as author and length of song. Because you placed a restriction of a primary key on the column, this entry isn't allowed by the database, either. If two rows of data were entered into the Song table without a Song Title, they wouldn't be unique. When a primary key is placed on a column (or columns), NULL data (an empty data field) can't be entered for that column.

WARNING

A common mistake is to think that textual data can be unique. To correct this problem of having more than one song title that's the same, create a Song ID column and place the primary key on that column.

There are other ways of making sure a row of data is unique, but setting primary keys is the most commonly used method.

Using Foreign Keys

A foreign key is a reference to a primary key, but the foreign key is not in the primary key's table. *Foreign keys* are similar to primary keys because they uniquely identify data, too, but they don't have to be unique in their table. For example, the Song table (refer to Table 3.2) has its own primary key (Song ID), but it also has a column (CD ID) that refers to the Music CD table's (refer to Table 3.1) primary key (CD ID). In this example, the Song table's CD ID column is the foreign key of the corresponding column in the Music CD table.

WARNING

In some databases, the primary key ID field is an auto-incrementing data type, but the foreign key ID field is just be a number. That's because the auto-incrementing type is specific only to that table. The Song table's foreign key (as an auto-incrementing column) would probably get out of synchronization with the primary key's auto-incrementing column. At this point, the database is responsible for the primary key's unique ID, and the programmer is responsible for making sure the foreign key's value for that corresponding row is exactly the same ID as the primary key's ID.

Using Indexes to Speed Up the Search

The previous section "Identifying Columns" mentioned using unique identifiers as a way to speed up searches when you're comparing textual data. Although there are several good reasons for using unique identifiers, it isn't always necessary to do so. Suppose the ID columns are removed from the three tables but an index—basically the same idea as a unique identifier—is placed on the table. The index consists of some unique identifier (it doesn't have to be a number; the database keeps this number internally) and the column of data indexed in a separate table. This table is only used internally by the database, and you should never try to access it. Table 3.6 is the Music CD table without the unique ID, and Table 3.7 is the index into the Music CD table.

Table 3.6. The Music CD table without any unique identifiers.

Column Name	Type of Data in Column
CD Title (column with unique index)	Characters
Artist/Group	Characters
Record Label ID	Number
Date of Copyright	Date
Number of Songs	Number
Music Category	Characters

Table 3.7. The Index table to the Music CD table.

Column Name	Type of Data
Index	Proprietary data type
CD Title	Characters

There are benefits to both systems of having a unique ID column on your table and having a unique index on that column. If the information in the table represents unique data, such as an account, billing, or product number, you should use a unique identifier. If you want to speed searches up, use an index, which generates a hidden table similar to Table 3.7.

In the database world, there are always trade-offs to be considered, and indexing is definitely one of them. Since the database keeps track of each row of data in two tables, each time you enter a new row of data, the database must work on two tables. Any operation that requires adding a new row of information or deleting a row requires more time. To determine whether updating a row costs time on an index, you need to know whether it's the indexed column that's being updated.

The second trade-off is a one-time problem. For example, a database might have a table with a million rows of data, and now the database administrator wants to add indexing to speed up searching. It will take quite a bit of time to create a row of indexing information for each row in the data table, but after that, searches will be very speedy.

TIP

Examine your database for tables generally used for finding information (searches) or for inserting information. Index the tables used for searching, but don't index tables used for inserting information.

Making Modifications to the Relational Database

Now that you know the terminology and understand some database design concepts, the original tables need to have this information added. Tables 3.8, 3.9, and 3.10 have been changed to include a unique index, a unique ID, and a primary key. These changes are meant to be a practical implementation of the issues discussed so far.

Table 3.8. The Music CD table, with a primary key, unique index, and unique auto-incrementing column identifier.

Column Name	Type of Data in Column
CD ID (primary key, unique index)	Auto-incrementing Number
CD Title	Characters
Artist/Group	Characters
Record Label ID (foreign key)	Number
Date of Copyright	Date
Number of Songs	Number
Music Category	Characters

Table 3.9. The Song table, with a primary key, unique index, and unique auto-incrementing column identifier.

Column Name	Type of Data
Song ID (primary key, unique index)	Auto-incrementing Number
Song Title	Characters
Author	Characters
CD ID (foreign key)	Number
Length of song	Time

Table 3.10. The Record Label table, with a primary key, unique index, and unique auto-incrementing column identifier.

Column Name	Type of Data
Record Label ID (primary key, unique index)	Auto-incrementing Number
Record Label	Characters
Address	Characters
City	Characters
State	Characters (2)
Zip Code	Number

Normalizing the Database

Beginners to designing a database might find one table much easier to deal with than three, so they often use the method of putting all the database information in one table. Table 3.11 shows you what this type of table might look like.

Table 3.11. The All Data table contains all the database information in one table.

Column Name	Type of Data
CD Title	Characters
Artist/Group	Characters
Date of Copyright	Date
Number of Songs	Number

Column Name	Type of Data
Music Category	Characters
Song Title	Characters
Author	Characters
Length of song	Time
Record Label	Characters
Address	Characters
City	Characters
State	Characters (2)
Zip Code	Number

Notice that because everything is in one table, a lot of information is duplicated. Every time a CD has a record label company that's not unique to another record label company, the five columns associated with the record label are duplicated. Users of a small table with little data (very few rows) might not notice a problem, but the more data that's entered into this kind of table, the slower the search is. Also, notice how much hard disk space is wasted with so much duplicated data. What if a record label company moved? That address information would have to be changed for every CD that used that record label company, which is a lot of work.

Normalization of a database is meant to break this kind of table down into smaller tables. This saves space in the database by eliminating duplicated information. Normalization also keeps the data's integrity because the update has to be done in only one place.

Data integrity generally means that the data is correct, such as updating all the instances of that data. Suppose the database tables are *denormalized* (so that the information you request can be found faster); then the same data might have to be kept in several tables, instead of just one table. Any changes to the data then must be made to each table's copy of that data. By normalizing the data, the need to make changes affects only one table instead of many. What could mess up the data's integrity? It isn't the database that would erroneously forget to make the change or make it incorrectly—it's the database programmer. By normalizing the database, the errors a programmer could make are minimized.

But with a table like Table 3.11, where do you start to break down the data? Look for a *unit* of information that's being duplicated; in Table 3.11, it's fairly easy to see that the record label company information is being duplicated. It's probably harder to see duplicated data in the Song table. If you have a fairly small CD collection, this extra break-out of a table might not be necessary. It's not that common that songs are covered by different groups, but it happens often enough that I wanted to handle that in my database.

Although normalization has its good points, it can have its bad points, too. Say you have a database of information with 15 large units of information and 10 small units of information that have been broken out into 25 tables. What happens if you have to use 10 tables to get the information you want? This task isn't impossible, but considering the search time (you have to look at all 10 tables) and insert time (you will probably insert data into all 10 tables), you might sacrifice query time to keep your database small. If database size isn't a problem, look for ways to denormalize the database. Doing so requires a thorough understanding of your database and what will be required of your tables for searching and inserting data. Denormalizing the database increases its size because the database will now have duplicate data over a range of tables.

A type of smaller table (referred to in the previous paragraph) is a *look-up table*, generally used only for searching and rarely for inserting. A table of state codes is a type of look-up table. If your company needed all state codes to have a numeric unique identifier (because numbers are easier to compare), the table might look like Table 3.12. This type of table can be used for fast searching because the table's data rarely changes.

Table 3.12. The Numeric State Code table used for fast searching.

Unique Identifier	Corresponding State
1	Alabama
2	Colorado
3	Minnesota
4	Texas
5	Wyoming

Tools for Looking at the Database

Databases generally store their data in files with a format so that you can't just open them up and read or change them. This format is *proprietary* because the specific database tools know how to access the information, and the data won't make sense unless you use the tools. The data is not in text files; you must use a query language (SQL) to make any searches or changes. But how and where do you write this query language?

Several query tools give you access to a database, but they generally come in two "flavors." The first is an application that usually comes from the same company and in the same software box as the database software. For example, Microsoft's Access database can be viewed from the Microsoft Access user interface. The second type of tool used for getting to a database is a generic one that gives you access to any database, as long as that application knows how to talk to that database. An example of this method is an ODBC (Open Database Connectivity) driver going to that driver's type of database, such as an Oracle driver going to an Oracle database. ODBC is discussed in detail later in the chapter; for now, the focus is on the first type of query tool.

Microsoft Access

Microsoft Access is a good small-business database system. In this section, you learn what the user interface shows; a discussion about when Access is the appropriate database choice is covered in a later section. Figure 3.3 is a view of Microsoft Access with a database open. Notice that you can access the tables discussed previously with a click of the mouse. You can also click Design to change the table definition or click New to create a new database. Microsoft Access doesn't require a great deal of database experience. It has wizards that walk you through each step of a process, from creating a database to selecting information from that database.

Figure 3.3.

Microsoft Access with the Day3 database open.

Figure 3.4 is the view of the table definition for the Music CD table. The data types are listed right after the column name (called the *field name* in this application). There's also room for a description of each column, as well as a Field Properties section for each column. Notice the little key to the left of the CD ID column. It indicates that the CD ID column is the primary key on the table. In the lower part of the window, you can see that the database window from Figure 3.3 is minimized but accessible at all times.

Figure 3.4.

The table definition of the Music CD table.

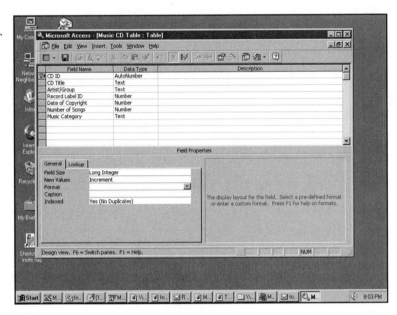

NOTE Microsoft Access generally "complains" if you don't have a column with the primary key in every table. If you don't know which column should have the primary key, it suggests one for you. Microsoft Access uses this primary key to help you build your database, tables, relationships, and so forth through wizards.

To see the information kept in a table, Microsoft Access gives you a few choices. You can look at the data as though it were a spreadsheet, or you can look at the data in a form. You might have noticed that one of the tabs in Figure 3.3's Database view is called Forms. Figure 3.5 shows you the Table view. Notice that not all the columns are visible, but you can see that there are four rows in the table and there's room after row 4 for the next entry. You can move around the table and change data in almost the same way you do with a spreadsheet application. However, you may not want everyone to have such unlimited access to your database. What if someone changed the Record Label ID and didn't notice? The data would then be corrupt and not very easy to track down.

Microsoft Access has another way for you to see data: Build a form, which can be done easily by using a wizard. The wizard gives you a way to restrict what your users see, and it's a very user-friendly default interface. Figure 3.6 shows a default form for the Music CD table with the two ID fields hidden from view. Notice that the table shows only one record at a time.

The user views the data by clicking on the left and right arrows underneath the data-entry section. This view is useful when you want to restrict what someone sees, but it's not very useful if you want a quick idea of what your data looks like.

Figure 3.5.

The Table view of the Music CD table in spreadsheet format.

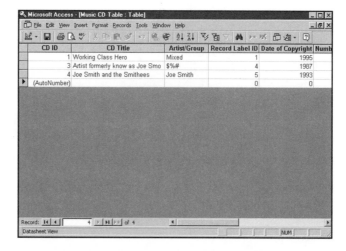

Figure 3.6.

The Form view of the Music CD table in a form created by the wizard.

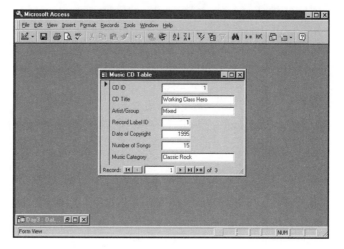

Microsoft Access can look at data beyond its own, which makes it a useful tool for looking into SQL Server. To access this data, you need an ODBC driver or ISAM (indexed sequential access method) of some kind. To get to this data, choose File | Get External Data | Link Tables from Access's menu. Your screen should look like Figure 3.7. At the bottom of the figure, notice that there are lists of file types you can choose from. Choose the file type you're interested in, and then you can see and access the data as though it were in Microsoft Access.

Figure 3.7.

Accessing other databases and files.

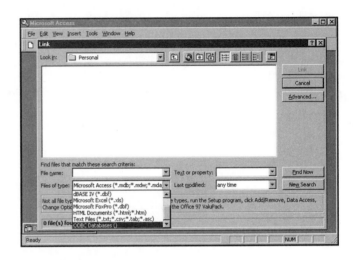

This section doesn't cover every feature Microsoft Access has to offer, but it does give you an idea of how to get to your data.

Microsoft SQL Server and ISQL_w

Microsoft SQL Server is built to be more robust than Microsoft Access, so you won't see many of the friendly user-interface features you saw in Microsoft Access. You can't view the tables in a spreadsheet or form, as you can in Microsoft Access, but you *can* view the data in SQL Server. It's not pretty, but it wasn't meant to be.

To reach the data in a Microsoft SQL Server database, you have a few choices. You can use ISQL_w or MS Query. ISQL_w is usually included only with Microsoft SQL Server, but MS Query comes with both the Microsoft Office suite and Microsoft SQL Server.

To use ISQL_w, you can either start the SQL Server Enterprise Manager or just open the ISQL_w tool. As a database administrator, you would probably want to use the Enterprise Manager; as a programmer, you would probably prefer using ISQL_w.

Figure 3.8 is a view of the Enterprise Manager. Notice that you have access to all objects on SQL Server (as long as you have the correct permissions). Also, notice the "tree" view of objects in the database.

To access data in the database, you must open ISQL_w. You can get to it from the Enterprise Manager by choosing Tools|SQL Query Tools from the menu. ISQL_w also has its own item in the SQL Server program group.

Figure 3.8.

The Microsoft SQL Server Enterprise Manager.

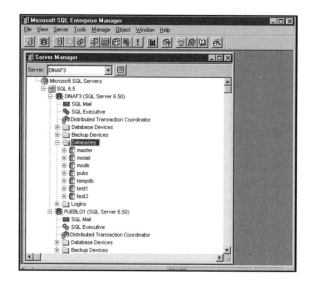

To get data out of a SQL Server database, you must know the SQL query language. SQL Server doesn't have a default view into a table, as Microsoft Access does in Figure 3.5. Figure 3.9 shows you what the data looks like when you have entered and executed a query. Notice that the data is formatted based on the width of data in a column. There's no numbering by each row to indicate which row you're looking at. When you scroll down through the data, the column headings scroll out of view, so you have to know what column you're in for the data to make sense. At the end of the data, a listing says how many rows were affected.

Figure 3.9.

A view of data from ISQL_w.

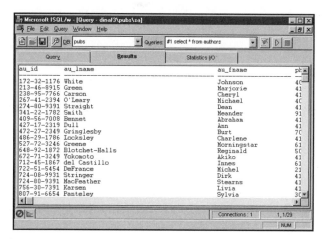

In Figure 3.9, I selected all rows in the Authors table from the Pubs database. The last line says 29 rows were affected, meaning that 29 rows were in the database. If an insert of one row is executed, the total rows affected should be just one. Some queries can affect zero rows, so be aware that "zero" could be a valid result.

ISQL_w saves your queries in a file with the extension of .SQL. Stored procedures also have a .SQL extension, so you can run stored procedures from the ISQL_w application.

MS Query

The MS Query tool is available from both MS SQL Server and MS Office. When you access ODBC data from an MS Office application, the MS Office application starts up MS Query and lets it do all the work. MS Query has the look and feel of MS Access, but it's not as robust. You can view data in a table, view the relationships between tables, and write SQL queries to get data out of tables.

Figure 3.10 shows MS Query with one table visible and four columns of data from the table. Notice that the column names aren't listed in the order they were created (the design order specified in Table 3.8). MS Query displays them in alphabetical order.

Figure 3.10.

Data viewed in MS Query.

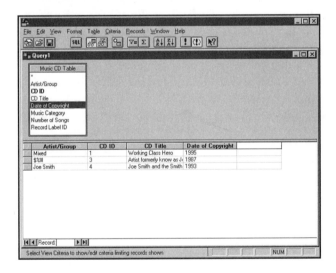

At the top of the figure, you can see several icons that match the MS Access toolbar. The exclamation point is the button used to run the query. Instead of writing the SQL query, MS Access and MS Query let you drag the columns on the grid you're interested in viewing. When you release the column, the data appears.

TIP
If you want to know which SQL query was executed for the dragged columns, click the SQL button on the toolbar. This is sort of a reverse way to learn SQL, but it's also a way to figure out why you didn't get the data you were expecting.

The Best Method of Viewing Data

It's easy to recommend a tool for viewing data, but you need to take into account what you're trying to accomplish. If you want to see all the data while you're working, MS Query and MS Access are better, and both go to ODBC data sources. If you want to execute stored procedures or other robust queries and go only to a SQL server, ISQL_w is your choice.

For the remainder of the SQL syntax and query sections, it shouldn't matter which query tool you use, but there could be differences. Since Access and ODBC have differences in the SQL language, my examples use SQL 92 (which is the standard) for all the exercises. Therefore, Tables 3.8, 3.9, and 3.10 from the section "Making Modifications to the Relational Database" are used as examples in the rest of this chapter.

Understanding the SQL Language

SQL is a language used to access relational data. It doesn't have a lot of bells and whistles. It does, however, have a lot of keywords you can't use for proper names of your tables, columns, or other objects. If you have programmed before, SQL might seem a little familiar, yet a little weird. You don't write "programs" in SQL; however, you can write several nested queries inside a single larger query. In that sense, SQL has a lot of functionality but not a big learning curve. It's a very straightforward language. Either your syntax is correct, or it's not. The objects you're referencing in your query either exist in that database, or they don't.

Before you start learning how to use SQL with the tables created in this chapter, make sure you have access to a database before starting the next sections.

NOTE
Some SQL databases are case sensitive, which means they might expect to see KEYWORD instead of keyword. It depends on whether the database has the option of being case sensitive, so you should check the documentation. For convenience (not out of necessity), the keywords in the rest of the chapters are capitalized, such as KEYWORD. This feature will help you find the keywords as you're learning the syntax.

NOTE Some SQL databases don't accept spaces in an object's name, such as Music CD Table. MS Access accepts spaces, but MS SQL Server doesn't. To handle this situation, the rest of the chapters don't use spaces in the names. Music CD Table will be written as Music_CD_Table.

NOTE Programming syntax standards are always an issue for businesses that want their code to be easily read by several different programmers. Although I agree these standards are necessary, I don't want you to be bogged down with figuring out how the object names are deciphered. The remaining sections, therefore, don't use coding notation standards.

Creating the Tables

The first thing that needs to be done is to create the tables in the database from Table 3.8, Table 3.9, and Table 3.10. Before you begin, you need to find the appropriate data types that match those listed. Since I'm using SQL Server, the tables have different types.

NOTE For readers using a Microsoft Access 97 database, you should find the DAY3.MDB file on the CD-ROM. It contains the three tables with the appropriate data types. Each table should have a few rows of data. For readers using a Microsoft SQL Server database, the *.SQL procedures you need to create the tables are on the CD-ROM. They're called Music_CD_Table, Song_Table, and Record_Label_Table, and have the appropriate data types. The end of each procedure enters a few rows of data into the table.

Refer to Tables 3.13, 3.14, and 3.15 to see the MS SQL Server types that are used. If you're using MS Access as your database, they have simpler types, which the Help files describe.

Table 3.13. The Music_CD_Table with data types added.

Column Name	Type of Data in Column
CD_ID (primary key, unique index)	Numeric Identity
CD_Title	VarChar
Artist_Group	VarChar
Record_Label_ID (foreign key)	Numeric
Date_of_Copyright	DateTime
Number_of_Songs	Numeric
Music_Category	VarChar

Table 3.14. The Song_Table with data types added.

Column Name	Type of Data
Song_ID (primary key, unique index)	Numeric Identity
Song_Title	VarChar
Author	VarChar
CD_ID (foreign key)	Numeric
Length_of_Song	Numeric

Table 3.15. The Record_Label_Table with data types added.

Column Name	Type of Data
Record_Label_ID (primary key, unique index)	Numeric Identity
Record_Label	VarChar
Address	VarChar
City	VarChar
State	Char (2)
Zip_Code	Numeric

3

> **NOTE** Other SQL Server data types of interest are Bit (also used for yes/no and true/false data), Image, Timestamp (for marking when data was initially entered into the database or last modified), and Money (to handle currency). There are other data types; if you aren't sure which type to use, consult your database application's documentation.

> **NOTE** The column names that correspond between tables don't have to be the same. However, some database applications, such as MS Access, take advantage of these names being the same. A true database application, such as MS SQL Server, has no way of making assumptions about table relationships. All relationships on MS SQL Server are preserved through SQL or other database mechanisms. MS Access is quite different. It has a tool called *Relationship* that makes relationship assumptions about table by default if the column names are the same. If the column names aren't the same, an Access user must explicitly indicate which columns are related.

This is the syntax needed to create a table:

```
CREATE table_name (column_name data type)
```

The command can fail for a number of reasons: The table already exists, the column data types aren't known to the database (you can have user-defined data types), or you have made a syntax error, such as leaving off the closing parenthesis. To make sure a column doesn't allow empty entries (known as NULL entries), you need to follow the column data type with the words NOT NULL, as shown here:

```
CREATE table_name (column_name data type NOT NULL)
```

Selecting Information from One Table

The first query you need to be familiar with is a *standard query*. It lets you view every column and every row, in the order it was inserted into the database. Although Listing 3.1 doesn't have very much information yet, it does have three keywords you should take note of: SELECT, *, and FROM. SELECT is a search keyword that fetches data. You can narrow your search to something like "only CDs that have 10 or more songs in the years 1980 to 1990," but that doesn't affect the use of the SELECT keyword. The * keyword is actually used as a wildcard character meaning "all." Therefore, if I wanted all the rows in a particular column or columns, the * would be replaced with those column names. The FROM keyword tells the database which object the query should act on. Basically, the query says you're going to SELECT column_name FROM table_name.

Listing 3.1. Get all rows and all columns from a specific table.

```
SELECT * FROM Music_CD_Table
```

Now that you can get data for an entire table, try narrowing the query down to select only one column from the table. Granted, that one column might not seem that interesting right now, but think of all the Windows or Web applications that have a drop-down box of just one type of item, such as what state you live in. This query is shown in Listing 3.2.

Listing 3.2. Get all rows of data but only one column from a specific table.

```
SELECT Music_Category FROM Music_CD_Table
```

This might be useful information, but there are times when more would be required, such as the music category *and* the CD title it corresponds to. One nice feature about SQL is that anytime you're requesting data of more than one item, all you have to do is add commas. Listing 3.3 illustrates how to get a CD title and the music category from the Music CD table.

Listing 3.3. Get all rows of data but only the Music_Category and CD_Title columns.

```
SELECT Music_Category, CD_Title FROM Music_CD_Table
```

Notice that it doesn't matter which order the columns are in, as long as both columns can be found in that table. The data is returned in the order specified, so the first column returned from Listing 3.3 would be the Music_Category column, and the second would be the CD_Title.

Selecting Specific Information from One Table

The previous section demonstrates how to get certain columns of data, but in this section, you learn how to get certain rows. You might, for example, want to find all the CD titles that have more than five songs. Figure 3.11 illustrates the difference between selecting certain columns and certain rows.

Figure 3.11.

CD titles that have more than five songs.

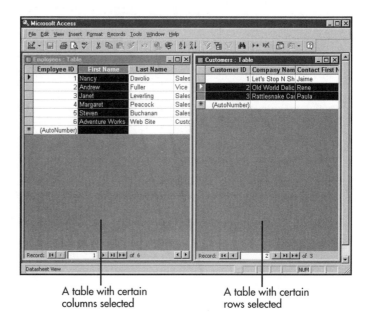

A table with certain columns selected

A table with certain rows selected

This type of restriction is done with a WHERE clause, which follows the initial SELECT statement with the specific criteria for each column you want to restrict. To find all CDs (and all corresponding information from that table) that have more than five songs, use this query:

```
SELECT * FROM Music_CD_Table
WHERE
Number_of_Songs > 5
```

TIP

The SQL text is on separate lines to make the code easier to read. SQL text doesn't have to be on the same line, and you don't need to use the line-continuation characters required in other languages. Another good way to make the code easier to read is to put each item of a comma-separated list (such as column names) on a separate line.

3

The WHERE clause can be as complicated or as simple as you need it to be. Say you have a query in which you need the CD Title and Artist or Group; the music group is equal to Jazz, and the number of songs on the CD is between 8 and 12. This query requests just two columns in the result and only certain rows from those two columns. Figure 3.12 illustrates how this more complex query differs from the two other methods of getting data.

Figure 3.12.

Results of a complex WHERE *clause.*

A table with certain columns selected

A table with certain rows selected

A table with certain columns and rows selected

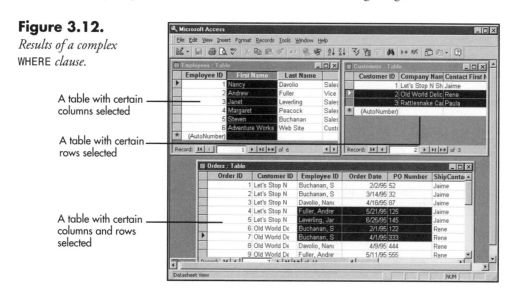

This is what the SQL syntax for the query of the Music_CD_Table looks like:

```
SELECT CD_Title, Artist_Group
FROM Music_CD_Table
WHERE
Music_Category = 'Jazz' AND
Number_of_Songs > 8 AND
Number_of_Songs < 12
```

In this example, the specific columns are listed in the SELECT clause and the specific rows are in the WHERE clause. The WHERE clause also has three criteria separated by AND. Notice that the text Jazz was enclosed in single quotes to let MS SQL Server know it should search for that text. You can also use the NOT and OR keywords between the WHERE clause conditions. Those keywords would help if you wanted all CDs in which the music category is Jazz *or* the number of songs is between 8 and 12.

```
SELECT CD_Title, Artist_Group
FROM Music_CD_Table
WHERE
Music_Catagory = 'Jazz' OR
(Number_of_Songs > 8 AND
Number_of_Songs < 12)
```

To have the query processor analyze the query with two conditions (jazz or song count), the second condition must be wrapped with parentheses. If the query didn't have the parentheses, it would be processed with three conditions. Placing parentheses around the first condition wouldn't interfere with the query processing and would help with readability, but that's a programming style issue. Here's what the query looks like when you're using two conditions:

```
SELECT CD_Title, Artist_Group
FROM Music_CD_Table
WHERE
(Music_Category = 'Jazz') OR
(Number_of_Songs > 8 AND
Number_of_Songs < 12)
```

NOTE   Other comparison operators SQL Server uses to compare two columns are >=, <=, <> or != (meaning "not equal to"), !>, and !<. The ! symbol is usually interpreted as "not." Other good comparison operators are BETWEEN and NOT BETWEEN, used when you want to say, for example, "Find me all CDs that have total songs between 8 and 12 or not between 1 and 8."

NOTE   If you're not using MS SQL Server, you need to look in your database application's documentation to see whether a character indicator is necessary.

NOTE   Text isn't the only kind of data that has a data type indicator. You need to check for all the data types you're using. For example, MS SQL Server prefixes the DateTime data type with a # symbol and the Binary data type with the characters 0x.

Getting Distinct Information

Most data has duplicates someplace for necessary reasons. For example, Music_CD_Table has duplicate Record_Label_IDs if all the rows are selected. Assume you want to know all the record label companies in your music collection. If you queried by using the statement SELECT Record_Label_ID from Music_CD_Table, you would get duplicate record IDs. To get rid of the duplicate data, you need to use the DISTINCT keyword. The query for all non-repeated record label companies would look like this:

```
SELECT DISTINCT Record_Label_ID from Music_CD_Table
```

Notice that the keyword DISTINCT is before the column name in which you want to reduce the duplicates.

Ordering the Data

In the previous section, all the record label IDs would be returned in the order they were entered into the database, which isn't as convenient as being ordered from largest number to smallest or smallest number to largest by using the ORDER BY clause. The ORDER BY clause can also work for text columns to put them in alphabetical order.

Assume you still want the distinct record labels, but want them in ascending order—that is, from lowest to highest. To do this kind of ordering, you must use the ORDER BY clause. Its syntax specifies which column you want ordered and whether the order is ascending or descending. If you don't specify ascending or descending, the database usually has a default of ascending. If you take the query from the last section and put an ascending order on it, the statement would look like this:

```
SELECT DISTINCT Record_Label_ID
FROM Music_CD_Table
ORDER BY Record_Label_ID ASC
```

Notice that the ORDER BY clause is after the FROM statement and that the ASC (for ascending) is after the column name. If the query had been descending, the keyword would be DESC.

Suppose you wanted to specify the criteria of the result set with a WHERE clause, as shown here:

```
SELECT CD_Title, Artist_Group
FROM Music_CD_Table
WHERE
Music_Category = 'Jazz' AND
Number_of_Songs > 8 AND
Number_of_Songs < 12
```

To specify an ordering for the query, you could order by CD_TITLE or by Artist_Group. The query would look like this:

```
SELECT CD_Title, Artist_Group
FROM Music_CD_Table
WHERE
Music_Category = 'Jazz' AND
Number_of_Songs > 8 AND
Number_of_Songs < 12
ORDER BY CD_Title ASC
```

The ORDER BY clause can be used with the WHERE clause to give you the exact data you're looking for in the order that suits you. Notice that the ORDER BY clause comes after the WHERE clause.

Adding Data Together

Suppose you have a calculation that needs to be performed for the data to make sense. You could have information in one column specifying the number of hours an employee worked and a second column that holds the employee's hourly wage. To find out how much the employee gets paid, the query could return both columns and you could do the math yourself, or you could have a column returned that held the total wages paid to the employee and have the database do the work.

Since this example doesn't fit the music CD collection tables, Table 3.16 is used as an example.

Table 3.16. Employee salary table used for multiplying the hours worked by the hourly wage.

Column Name	Type of Data
Employee_Name	Name
Hours_Worked	Number
Hourly_Wage	Number

The query selects the employee's name and the dollar value owed the employee. Since the second column required (dollar value owed the employee) isn't in the table, you have the database calculate it and return it in a default column (which means the database probably won't label the column). Here's what the SELECT statement is for this query:

```
SELECT Employee_Name, Hours_Worked * Hourly_Wage FROM Employee
```

The other operators are +, -, and /. You can use column data to perform numeric functions on or you can choose constant expressions. If each employee's hourly wage is $9, the query to find the same information would look like this:

```
SELECT Employee_Name, Hours_Worked * 9 FROM Employee
```

NOTE

In the previous two queries, the data for the calculated information was returned, but the column had no title. If you want to give this report to your boss, numbers in an unnamed column won't mean much to him or her. In MS SQL Server, use the = operator to title the calculated column, as shown here:

```
SELECT MyNewColumn = Hours_Worked * 9 FROM Employees
```

3

Numeric operators can also be used in the WHERE clause. Here's what the query would look like if you wanted to find all employees whose salary is over $30,000:

```
SELECT Employee_Name FROM Employee
WHERE (Hours_Worked * 9) > 30000
```

Managing Data in a Result

You should be confident now that you can select data from one table in a database with some options for what kind of data you want it to be. However, you might also want to have a summary or highlight of that data. Suppose you want the total number of music CDs in the collection. You could select all the rows and count them (some database applications tell you how many rows were returned from a query). In this example, the database would have to fulfill your query and rummage through the table. If you want to treat the data as a set, you can use some of the set functions: COUNT (total count), MAX (maximum), MIN (minimum), SUM (summation), and AVG (average).

Counting the Data

This is the query for a total count of CDs:

```
SELECT COUNT (*) FROM Music_CD_Table
```

Notice that this query doesn't request a specific column. The result set, then, isn't all rows and a count; it's just a count.

Suppose you need to know how many distinct songs are in the database. The query needs to specify the Song_Title column, as shown here:

```
SELECT COUNT(DISTINCT Song_Title) FROM Song_Table
```

The DISTINCT keyword is used to tell the database that the result should consider only unique songs.

Finding the Minimum and Maximum in Your Data

To find the largest and smallest instances of your data, you use the keywords MIN and MAX. Suppose you need to know the shortest and longest songs in your CD collection. You would then use a query that looks like this:

```
SELECT MAX(Length_of_Song) FROM Song_Table
```

You could also write the query this way:

```
SELECT MIN(Length_of_Song) FROM Song_Table
```

These queries are very similar; the only difference is the MIN or MAX keyword. If your song lengths were 2 minutes, 5 minutes, 6 minutes, and 10 minutes, the first query would return 10 and the second query would return 2.

Using SUM and AVG

Suppose you wanted the total amount of time it would take to play all the songs in your CD collection. The SUM keyword is perfect for this query, as shown here:

```
SELECT SUM(Length_of_Song) FROM Song_Table
```

Because all songs from all CDs are stored in the Song_Table, this query returns the total play time. If you wanted the average play time of all the CDs in the collection, the following query would return that information:

```
SELECT AVE(Length_of_Song) FROM Song_Table
```

Selecting Information from Two or More Tables

Now that you know how to get information from one table in several ways, you need to know how to get data from more than one table. To find out the CD titles and the record label name, you need information from the Music_CD_Table and the Record_Label_Table. This type of operation is considered a *join* because you're joining tables to get the information you want. By joining tables, the result of a query is still just one result. The join logic in the database program knows you're interested in having the information appear as though it were one single piece of information. To do this, the database program must check each row of the first table against each row of the second table to see whether it matches your criteria (the WHERE clause). Most joins are used to find where two columns match data, such as where the record label ID of the Music_CD_Table matches the record label ID in the Record_Label_Table. However, this type of equality isn't necessary; you might be looking for data where it *doesn't* match. Figure 3.13 illustrates the information a join would try to find.

The query for all CD titles and record label companies needs a few new pieces. The SELECT statement for one table includes the table name in the FROM clause. For a two-table (or more) query, the FROM clause must include each table. The order the tables are listed in isn't necessary, so the Music_CD_Table doesn't need to come before the Record_Label_Table. The WHERE clause contains the selection criteria that crosses the two tables. In this case, the Record_Label_ID of the Music_CD_Table is equal to the Record_Label_ID of the Record_Label_Table. The following query returns that information:

```
SELECT CD_Title, Record_Label
FROM Music_CD_Table, Record_Label_Table
WHERE Music_CD_Table.Record_Label_ID = Record_Label_Table.Record_Label_ID
```

Figure 3.13.
*The first table has the
ID field but needs the
address information
in the second table.*

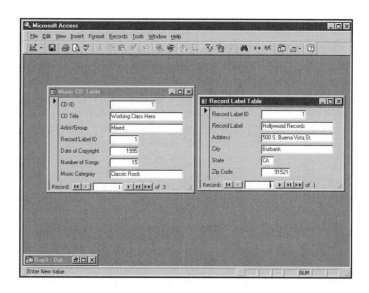

A period is used as the separator between the table and the table's column. The = operator was used in this query, but any of the comparison operators can be used in the join's WHERE clause.

NOTE

MS Access (and many other programming languages) uses the period separator between all its objects. In a form that accepts data into a text box, for example, you would use formx.textboxy to specify the textbox you wanted.

Inserting Data into a Database

Inserting the information into the database is similar to selecting data from the database. The biggest difference is how the database interprets column information. For example, there's a difference between how text and numeric data is interpreted. On MS SQL Server, to insert text data (data types of Text, Char, VarChar, DateTime, and SmallDataTime), a prefix and suffix of a single quote character must be added, as in 'My Name is John Doe'. Numeric data (data types of Numeric, Decimal, Bit, TinyInt, Int, SmallInt, Float, and Real) doesn't require a prefix or suffix character.

This is the syntax for inserting data:

```
INSERT INTO table_name
(column_name, column_name)
VALUES
(data_for_column, data_for_column)
```

This query specifies which columns are being inserted in the first list enclosed by parentheses and the corresponding data is in the second list within parentheses. Insert queries, in general, affect only one table. To insert a new row of data into the Music_CD_Table, write the query as shown:

```
INSERT INTO Music_CD_Table
(CD_Title,Artist_Group,Record_Label_ID,
Date_of_Copyright,Number_of_Songs,Music_Category)
VALUES
('The Best of','ACME',5,'1/1/1968',10,'Jazz')
```

The year has to be formatted and include single-quote prefixes and suffixes, just as strings do. Notice, too, that the first column of the table, CD_ID from Table 3.8, isn't mentioned in the INSERT statement . It was created as an auto-incrementing column, so you can't enter the data—only the database program can. This INSERT statement enters one row (every column except for the auto-incrementing column, CD_ID) into the table. Where the row is inserted into the table—at the beginning, the middle, or the end—is the database program's decision. You shouldn't depend on the location of the row; access it only through specific queries, such as a SELECT query with a WHERE clause that pinpoints that specific row.

NOTE   You have a few choices for formatting DateTime columns or similar data types. Please refer to your database application's documentation for a complete list.

Inserting every non–auto-incrementing column isn't necessary in an INSERT query. The only time a column must be part of the INSERT clause is when it's defined as NOT NULL. The rest of the columns in the Music_CD_Table are defined without the NOT NULL qualifier, so it isn't necessary to insert all the columnar data.

NOTE   The column CD_ID of the Music_CD_Table doesn't follow the NOT NULL rule mentioned in the preceding paragraph because it's inserted by the database program, which generates a new unique ID for each inserted row.

The INSERT statement also has an "insert all" type of query similar to the SELECT * FROM table_name query; it looks like this:

```
INSERT INTO Music_CD_Table VALUES
('The Best of', 'ACME', 5, '1/1/1968', 10, 'Jazz')
```

Because the column data to be inserted is in the same order as the columns in the table (refer to Table 3.8), the first clause within parentheses wasn't necessary. If the data clause hadn't been in the exact order of the corresponding columns, the database program would have tried to convert the data to the correct data type (such as Numeric to Text or Text to Numeric) and returned an error if that conversion wasn't possible.

Both of the preceding INSERT queries used all the columns so that each INSERT statement filled each column of data, but they don't have to insert data into all the columns of the table. However, this feature is handy when you don't know all the information, such as the Record_Label_ID. This might be information you enter at a later time or information entered by a different department (which requires the UPDATE query discussed in the section "Updating Data"). Listing 3.4 gives you an example of a query that doesn't insert all columns.

Listing 3.4. Inserting some (not all) columns of data into a table.

```
INSERT INTO Music_CD_Table
(Artist_Group, Music_Category)
VALUES
('ACME', 'Jazz')
```

In this simple query, not all the columns are inserted into the database. One benefit of listing the columns in the first clause enclosed by parentheses is that they don't have to be listed in the order they were created. What's important is that the first column in the list within parentheses corresponds to the data placed first in the second list within parentheses, and so on for each column and data pair. This requirement makes ordering the columns arbitrary, as shown in this example:

```
INSERT INTO Music_CD_Table
(Music_Category, Artist_Group)
VALUES
('Jazz', 'ACME')
```

Notice that the columns and the data have been re-ordered. This is a valid query that inserts a row of data of three columns: the CD_ID that the database creates, the Music_Category of Jazz, and the Artist_Group of ACME.

Updating Data

Updating data adds or alters a row's data. You update data for two reasons: to fill in any columns (as the information becomes available) not filled in by the INSERT query, or to change data currently in the database, such as changing the Record_Label_ID from 5 to 7. The previous code snippet gives you an example of filling in columns that weren't filled in by the INSERT query.

The UPDATE keyword is used to alter a column or columns of data. Unlike the INSERT statement, you have to know which row you want to update (or you can update all rows). To find the row(s) of data, the WHERE clause is used. This is the syntax for the UPDATE query:

```
UPDATE table_name
SET column_name = new_data
WHERE column_name = current_data
```

Using Listing 3.4, the UPDATE query to insert the remaining columns (CD_Title, Record_Label_ID, Date_of_Copyright, Number_of_Songs) looks like this:

```
UPDATE Music_CD_Table
SET
CD_Title = 'The Best of',
Record_Label_ID = 5,
Date_of_Copyright = '1/1/1968',
Number_of_Songs = 10
WHERE
Music_Category = 'Jazz' AND
Artist_Group = 'ACME'
```

WARNING

Don't take this example as a suggestion of how you should update your data. If there were two or more rows that fit the WHERE clause, all the rows would now have the column data from the preceding UPDATE query, which might not be what you want. This was only an example of the query, not a design or implementation suggestion.

Notice that the SET clause is used after the table name and that the column_name = new_data (column equals value pairs) are separated by commas.

There is an UPDATE query similar to the SELECT * FROM table_name that updates all the rows in the database:

```
UPDATE Music_CD_Table
SET
CD_Title = 'The Best of'
```

In this query, the WHERE clause is no longer necessary because *all* the rows are being updated.

At times, you might not know the data, but you know it's possible to calculate it. Suppose there are two columns added to the Music_CD_Table called Current_Value and Original_Value (both Numeric data types). The Original_Value column specifies the original purchase price, and Current_Value specifies the value of the CD with appreciation or depreciation taken into consideration. The appreciation or depreciation percentage should be multiplied by the Original_Value to get the Current_Value. The UPDATE query to appreciate a CD by 15 percent would look like this:

```
UPDATE Music_Cd_Table
SET Current_Value = Original_Value * 1.15
```

Notice that by not using the WHERE clause, all CDs in the Music_CD_Table are appreciated by 15 percent.

Deleting Data

Deleting data can be a dangerous operation if you aren't careful. Any deleted data *cannot* be recovered (unless the query is within a transaction). A DELETE query deletes an entire row or rows; it isn't fine-tuned enough to delete just a column of data (use UPDATE with a generic default value for affecting just one column). This is the syntax for deleting a row:

```
DELETE FROM table_name
WHERE column_name = value.
```

Notice that no column names are specified in the DELETE clause. You can't specify columns in a DELETE clause because *every* column (the entire row) is deleted. Of course, as with all queries, if you leave off the WHERE clause, all rows in the table are affected. Here's an example of deleting a single row:

```
DELETE FROM Music_CD_Table
WHERE CD_ID = 1
```

To delete all rows, the query would look like this:

```
DELETE FROM Music_CD_Table
```

Dropping a Table

Now that you know how to create a table and manipulate the data, you need to know how to delete the table. However, you should do this *only* when you know the data is no longer necessary.

TIP

> If you're new to database design or the SQL language, creating and playing with tables can be very informative. However, when you're done with your practice tables, delete them so they don't take up system resources.

To delete a table, you use a DROP TABLE query; the syntax for using it looks like this:

```
DROP TABLE table_name
```

The query doesn't have any other information besides the table name and the keywords. Don't confuse the DROP TABLE query with the DELETE query. The DELETE query removes rows from the table, and the DROP TABLE query removes the entire table from the database.

Parameterized Data

Assume that the CD tables used in this chapter are part of an application, and a user enters data such as Title of CD or Group of CD. The application can be written two ways. In the first method, the SQL statement is built on-the-fly every time the user enters data. The second way is to use a parameterized query.

A *parameterized query* has two parts. In the first part, you set the query and include placeholders for unknown data; in the second, you set the known data. The first part of the parameterized query looks like this:

```
INSERT INTO table
SET column_name = ?
```

Notice the use of the question mark to distinguish the unknown data. The question mark can be used in any of the previous queries to replace data, including data references in the WHERE clause. The second part of the query inserts the data into the database.

Microsoft SQL Server Versus Microsoft Access

There are fundamental differences between MS SQL Server and MS Access in three areas: design, transaction processing and error recovery, and security. MS SQL Server is meant to be used for large volumes of information for a traditional relational database. It handles all the major database issues but requires the administrator and users to be very knowledgeable about databases. MS Access is meant for small-business or personal home computer information. Access has a lot of wizards and prefabricated databases, such as address books and inventory. Much of the SQL code that would be used to manipulate data also has an easier interface that involves no code. The user drags and drops the columns she's interested in from the tables.

The benefits of MS SQL Server are that it has strength and speed in a true database fashion. Any application can interface with it and can be accessed from most programming languages, such as Visual Basic or Visual C++. The drawbacks are the price, the hardware required (Windows NT), and the level of knowledge to use SQL Server.

The benefits of MS Access are its ease of use for non-database people, its cost (it's bundled with MS Office, Professional Version), and its ability to be run on Windows NT or Windows 95. It has several great features and can still be programmed from languages such as Visual Basic or Visual C++. It works well for small databases, but once the database size grows beyond the recommendations given in the product manual, you will definitely see performance (in terms of speed) drop. You will also find the security model (it's just a file) might not be strong enough for your needs.

Design Issues

MS SQL Server is designed as a true client-server database application in which most data crunching happens on the server. The client makes requests and accepts results, which are simple operations compared to manipulating data. MS Access is designed as a file-sharing application, which means the data crunching is done on the client, regardless of where the database (*.MDB file) sits. The benefit that MS Access gains by using this file-sharing method is that it's easier to give someone access to the database.

Transaction Processing and Error Recovery

MS Access doesn't handle true transactions. Even when it says a transaction is committed, its caching schema might not allow other users to see the changes. Also, there's no way to roll back committed data, so if a delete erases important data, the only recovery you have is a backup of the *.MDB file. MS SQL Server, however, can handle these issues by including a transaction processor. When transaction processing is turned on (by using SQL commands), the data can be either committed or rolled back. When transaction processing isn't turned on, the data is automatically committed to the database (no caching involved).

Security

MS SQL Server uses a strong security model that can restrict a user's access rights on a very precise scale, such as allowing read-only access to Table A but full access to Table B. The MS Access database is just a file that can be erased if its location isn't secured by using the NT File System, for example.

What MS Access Is Built To Do

MS Access is a small, inexpensive database application with a strong emphasis on presenting data and making it easy to use. It has wizards built into the program that can do almost everything, including reports. Its programming language is easy to learn and the query tools use drag-and-drop technology. The learning curve for this program's database is small compared to MS SQL Server.

What MS SQL Server Is Built To Do

MS SQL Server is meant to be a full-blown true database application. Therefore, there's no windowed representation of the data and no built-in reports. All the functionality lies in its ability to handle and secure large amounts of data with many users, which is a huge amount of processing.

Open Database Connectivity (ODBC)

In decades past, companies would buy a database, including the hardware it ran on and the software to access it. There was no need for any other access to the information and no need to have another database (as these databases were very expensive). However, as companies grew, merged, and changed course, other databases filtered in. Moving an entire database of information from one system to another was time and labor intensive. People needed access to both databases and sometimes needed the data from both in a single report.

Systems and programmers had to accommodate two or more databases and find a way to make data from both seem as though it came from one. Applications were written in that language for that specific database. Each system (such as Oracle or IBM) had its own programming language, so programmers either had to know both languages or team up with other programmers to coordinate efforts. A program couldn't be adapted to handle both databases, so it was clear there needed to be one generic access method to databases.

This is where ODBC comes into the picture. ODBC allows a single uniform language to access different databases, instead of using the proprietary language of each database. It did this by designing a standard set of APIs (application program interfaces). Previously, a programming language talked directly to a database, but with ODBC, a programming language talks to the API. The API is developed for each database, so it knows what kind of database you're trying to talk to (because you told it), and it interprets your requests so that that database can return the information. Since every database driver has to follow the same standard for the APIs, the programming code doesn't have to change for each database.

This open connectivity to a database now allows an application to get data from any kind of database. The application becomes more flexible because you don't have to write code based on a particular database. The following figures illustrate the evolution of database access from proprietary systems to ODBC data connections. Figure 3.14 shows the traditional method of database access. The language and database are made by the same manufacturer (such as Oracle); no other languages can interact with that database, and the language can communicate only with databases made by that manufacturer. Figure 3.15 illustrates how data is accessed through an ODBC connection. The database can now be accessed (by using an ODBC driver that's proprietary to that database) with a variety of languages.

Figure 3.14.

How data was accessed on proprietary machines.

Figure 3.15.

How data is accessed on ODBC data.

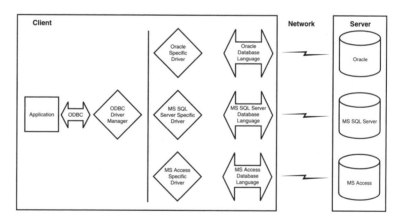

Since ODBC is a component used by other programs, such as MS Access or MS Excel, it has an install option with several programs. Microsoft provides free drivers to MS SQL Server and MS Access. To find drivers to other databases, please contact that database's manufacturer. ODBC can be installed from the following programs:

SQL Server
MS Office suite of products, including MS Access
MS Developer Studio suite of products
MS IIS
MS Active Server Framework (Denali) and ADO

Where Does ODBC Fit into the Client-Server Model?

The ODBC software sits on a client machine and is called from an application. The request from the client application is passed to the ODBC Driver Manager on the client. The ODBC Driver Manager decides whether the database driver is installed on the client and passes the request to the client database driver. The database driver does any validation required on the client, and then passes the request to the physical database, which can be on the client but is typically on the server. The database on the server fulfills or denies the request and passes the appropriate information back to the ODBC driver on the client. The ODBC driver interprets any errors and makes error information available on the client, if necessary. Finally, the ODBC driver returns the information to the client application.

Figure 3.16 illustrates how ODBC is called from the application and then fetches data when the application and database sit on one machine. In Figure 3.17, you can see how ODBC is called from the application on the client and the database on the server fulfills the request. Figure 3.18 shows how an ODBC database would be accessed through the Internet. The model is quite different because the Web server is also the ODBC client. All the ODBC/database software must sit on the Web server side of the picture, but the Web server and the database server can be physically different machines.

Figure 3.16.

Where ODBC fits into the client-server model on one machine.

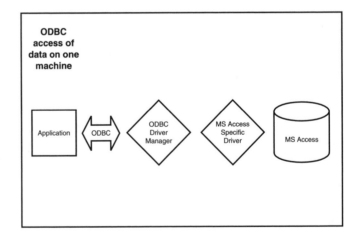

ODBC Drivers and the Administrator

A driver usually contains the callable API functions for a single database, such as MS SQL Server. The drivers and Driver Manager (also the ODBC DSN Administrator) need to be installed on every client machine. The drivers are dynamic link libraries (DLLs) and the Driver Manager is an executable program (in this case, odbcad32.exe). For each database you want the client to connect to, a *datasource name (DSN)* must be created. The DSN tells the driver where the database is located.

Figure 3.17.
Where ODBC fits into the client-server model on two machines.

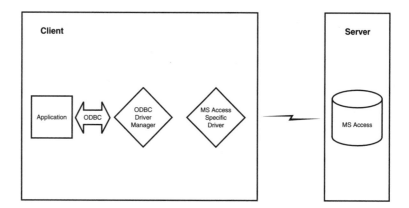

Figure 3.18.
Where ODBC fits into the client-server model across the Internet.

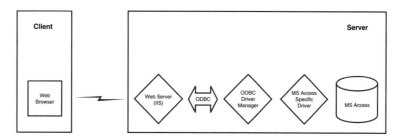

In the ODBC 3.0 version of the Administrator, you have three choices for what type of DSN you create: User, System, File. The *System DSN* allows every user of the computer and every system-level resource access to that database. The *File DSN* allows all users access to the same drivers, but the *User DSN* allows just a specific user to access this database. For example, if you're using a Microsoft Windows NT operating system machine (Server or Workstation), you can log on as an administrator and install a System DSN or File DSN or you can log on as that user and install a User DSN. The security to access the database is still necessary. If someone logged on with a System DSN tries to access the database, he must supply a user name and password that the database validates, or he won't be allowed into the database.

Cursor Models

When you're working with a text or spreadsheet application, the pointer (*cursor*) moves along to let you know where you are in the document. A cursor in a database also lets you know where you are—in which row, for example—in a table. In some databases, you can position the cursor by physical position, such as first or last row, or by finding a row based on a value in a column (by using the WHERE clause). Processing one row at a time is left to the database, but without a cursor, processing one row at a time is left up to you. You can also consider a cursor a "file" of information. Some files are read-only and can't be changed, but some files are writable and can be changed at will.

This section on cursors is meant to be just an introduction. Please refer to your program's documentation for a thorough understanding of its capabilities and possible limitations.

There are two kinds of cursors: scrollable and updatable. A *scrollable cursor* can move forward and backward through the rows of data. Imagine how difficult it would be to work with a list of data if you could go through it only from beginning to end; you couldn't go back and look at any of the previous rows without re-executing the statement and starting at the beginning again. A scrollable cursor saves you from having to re-execute that query. An *updatable cursor* allows you to modify data while you're sitting on that row.

You should also think about transaction management with cursors. If more than one user has access to data and is updating it, should other users of the data see the changes or not? Unfortunately, this issue requires a detailed discussion that's beyond the scope of this chapter, so check your program's documentation for more information on transaction management. The rest of this section focuses on ODBC cursors.

With cursors, you should also know what type of information you can see. When a cursor is opened with a statement such as SELECT * FROM Music_CD_Table, the cursor returns only that current data. But what happens if the data is updated? That row of data is already in the cursor. The database has the choice of not showing the change to the user or modifying the cursor to have that updated information. There's no need to expand the cursor (by adding more storage for another row) because the row already existed in the query's result set.

An insert is a little trickier. The space for the row didn't previously exist in the cursor, so adding this space and getting the right data into the cursor requires more work by the database. The database must allocate the storage (*buffer space*) for that row and then fill in the row's storage with the appropriate information. The database also has to make sure that constraints on the row are observed, such as ensuring that an ID is auto-incremented by the database or that a column can't be null. A delete, however, is simple. The database can either collapse that row as though it didn't exist, or it can hold the row but look empty, as though there were a "hole" in the data.

Static Cursors

With a *static*, or snapshot, *cursor*, the data is considered read-only. Any changes made to the data contained in this cursor aren't visible until this cursor is closed. The data is basically a copy of what's on the server at the time of the request. The static cursor gets data from the server only once, and then holds it until the cursor is closed. One benefit of the static cursor is that once all the rows are retrieved to the client, any scrolling happens on the client and doesn't cost a network trip back to the server. The downside of a static cursor is that another user can be making updates or inserts to the database, but the static cursor doesn't reflect those changes. Therefore, any changes made in the server aren't visible to other users until that cursor is closed. The static cursor is the default cursor returned by ODBC.

Dynamic Cursors

A *dynamic cursor* allows the user to see any changes and inserts made to the data in his result set after the cursor is opened, which allows up-to-the-minute changes based on real information. The dynamic cursor requires the database to reorder data in your cursor as it changes, which is an expensive operation in terms of the processing required. The database must figure out what you have in your cursor versus what's on the database, and then make a trip across the network to inform your cursor of those changes. Relative positioning is allowed, but absolute positioning on the rows is not. *Relative positioning* means that the current row's position is relative to the cursor's top or bottom row; *absolute positioning* means that the row can be uniquely identified, such as the nth row.

Keyset Cursors

The *keyset cursor* combines the best features of the static and dynamic cursors. The keyset cursor can see all inserts made into the database by other users and can fetch on absolute position (first, last, and so on). Updates are visible. The "key" is actually an index into the cursor. When the database has to update the value, it does so based on the row's key.

Cursor Summary

Each of the three cursor types covered have different levels in which they aren't true cursors, but allow more functionality before hitting the next level of cursor. This type of modification is database specific. If a programmer explicitly asks for a read-only cursor but is performing an insert or update into the cursor, the database has the choice of changing the cursor type or denying the request. These types of decisions give flexibility to the database, but also allow the database to stray from the traditional implementations of each of the cursor types. Please refer to your program's documentation for more information.

Summary

This chapter has given you a basic understanding of database design and SQL language syntax. A good database needs to start with a solid, normalized design and then create tables to carry out that design. The SQL query language gives you access to those tables so you can enter, change, or delete data.

Q&A

Q If I have a small company with potential for growth, should I buy a database such as MS SQL Server or MS Access?

A If you have the financial and technical ability to buy MS SQL Server now, do so. Financial considerations include the hardware, software, and training.

If you don't have the financial or technical resources to buy MS SQL Server, MS Access isn't a bad second choice. Many people can help you work with MS Access. The software has several cool tools and wizards to make working with databases as easy as possible. There are even tools to help you migrate from an MS Access database to a SQL Server database. However, don't assume that because you're a master at MS Access, you can automatically be a master at MS SQL. They are fundamentally different, so you still have to make the training and technical investment.

Q If I have a database that doesn't have its own ODBC driver, should I consider migrating to a different database, such as MS SQL Server?

A The rest of this book (regarding topics such as ActiveX Data Objects and Advanced Data Connector) won't be useful to you, unless you have ODBC connectivity to your database, a requirement of those two features. Any of the more accepted databases (including non-Microsoft databases) should have ODBC data connectivity. Look to migrate to one of those.

Quiz

1. What is data normalization used for?
2. What are indexes, unique identifiers, and primary keys used for?
3. What is ODBC?
4. What keyword is used to narrow a search criteria based on a column value?
5. What keyword is used to eliminate duplicate values from a search?
6. What is the difference between dropping a table and deleting a row?

Exercises

1. Design a database in which all the information is in one table. Include data types and type limits (such as two characters for a state).
2. Take the database from Exercise 1 and normalize the database (break it into smaller tables so each table has one focus).
3. Add an unique identifier to all tables.

4. Write INSERT statements for the tables.

5. Write SELECT statements for the tables.

6. Write DELETE statements for the tables.

7. Write join statements for the tables.

8. Improve the design of the database.

Week 1

Day 4

The HTML Scripting Language

by Dina Fleet

The HyperText Markup Language (HTML) was originally used to publish information (but not on the Web). Its ease of use made it a natural choice for people who wanted to distribute information on the Web. HTML has been standardized by the World Wide Web consortium. Understanding how these standards have changed and what the standards are will help you with programming languages. The best part of HTML is the page-layout programming, which lets you display the information to the Web browser in many different formats.

After you understand the format of an HTML page, you learn how to write the script for the page by using the HTML tags.

HTML Standards

HTML is governed by a standards committee called the World Wide Web consortium (www.w3.org). Any changes or proposed changes to the HTML language can be found on the consortium's Web page. This chapter focuses on those elements of the HTML language that are stable and generally supported by most current browsers. HTML has had many revisions, and not all browsers have been updated to support these changes. If you're concerned about a proprietary browser's behavior with any language elements discussed in this chapter, please refer to that browser's documentation.

HTML has different levels of support. If you want all or most browsers to see your pages, you should use HTML language structure of the lower levels. The lower level features don't give you as many choices for delivering your data as the higher level features do. You must decide between features and the quantity of browsers that can view your data.

If you're writing pages for your department, and you know that your company uses the latest browser, use the higher levels of functionality. Table 4.1 shows the different levels of support and the general features that were added with each level. Level 0 is necessary, regardless of the kind of browser you have, including text-only browsers.

Table 4.1. The levels of HTML support.

HTML Level	Features Supported
Level 0	Mandatory: Headings, lists, anchors, and so on
Level 1	Images, emphasis, text highlighting
Level 2	Forms, character definitions
Level 3	Tables, figures, and so on
Level 4	Mathematical formulas

WARNING

The information in this chapter tries to follow the stated standards as closely as possible. However, the browsers don't have to implement all the standards, or may implement the standards with their own interpretation.

The chapter discusses features that seem to be well supported and unaltered. Most tags discussed in this chapter have additional formatting choices or proposed extensions (which might not be implemented yet by your browser). Please refer to the HTML specifications on the www.w3.org site for more information.

Page Layout

An HTML Web page is filled with three kinds of information: The first is what you want the browser to finally display, such as company stock reports; the second is the HTML language with which you want to format your stock reports; and the third tells the browser any special information, such as the page name to display in the page window.

Figure 4.1 is a simple Web page as seen through the browser (display application), and Listing 4.1 is the text the browser interpreted to display this information. Notice that the words *head* and *body* can be seen on the page. The "HTML" text is also necessary; it's the text that tells the browser the file it's reading should be displayed by interpreting the HTML language tags.

Figure 4.1.

A simple Web page as displayed in the Microsoft Internet Explorer browser.

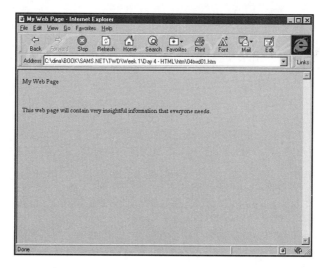

Listing 4.1. The HTML page text interpreted by a browser in Figure 4.1.

```
<HTML><HEAD><TITLE>My Web Page</TITLE></HEAD>
<BODY><FONT SIZE=2><P>My Web Page</P>
<P> </P>
<P>This Web page will contain very insightful
➥information that everyone needs.</P></FONT></BODY></HTML>
```

The Head

Within the head tags (`<HEAD></HEAD>`), you find general information about the HTML page—the title of your page (that the browser may choose to display), the base address of the page, and other information that the server or browser makes use of. In general, this information isn't displayed in the browser. In Listing 4.1, "My Web Page" could be displayed in the window's title bar (top left), as shown in Figure 4.1.

The Body

The body of the document should contain any text you want to display as well as the formatting tags to display that text. There are formatting styles to handle tables, lists, and programming code examples. With a bit of creativity, your page can be very interesting. Figure 4.1 shows only the body of the document in the browser window.

Adding Comments to the Page

Comments are a programmer's way of adding descriptions, references, or any other useful information. A comment doesn't interfere in the page's operations and is helpful if many people are changing a page or a page has a complex structure.

NOTE

HTML ignores any tabs or carriage returns you have embedded in the document.

Programming Language

The HTML programming language is easy to understand and use, as long as you know what the tag is and how to use it. Almost all language features for HTML have a keyword (or character). This keyword is enclosed in a tag. Some keywords must also have an ending tag.

4

A beginning tag looks like <KEYWORD> and the ending tag looks like </KEYWORD>. The forward slash indicates the ending tag.

Referring back to Listing 4.1, the HTML tag enclosed the entire document with <HTML> </HTML>. This is an example of tags (<HEAD>, <BODY>) being enclosed within other tags. You should remember that the language interprets the tags based on what the opening and closing tags are. An incorrect set of embedded tags would be <HEAD><TITLE></HEAD></TITLE>, for example. If a tag begins inside another tag, it must also end inside that tag. The correct example is <HEAD><TITLE></TITLE><HEAD>.

Some of the tags can be embedded in other tags—the bold tag <B>text</B>, for example. A table can be embedded into the cell of another table, too. The best way to see the different choices is to test the combinations of different tags and look at the text of the Web pages you like.

Required Tags on a Page

There are three sets of tags that make a page valid. All other tags are for formatting or browser interpretation. The other tags aren't necessary, but help to display the data you want in the manner you want. The required tags on a page are <HTML></HTML>,<HEAD></HEAD> and <BODY></BODY>. Notice that in Listing 4.1 there are other tags, as well as some text. The other tags and text aren't necessary, but remember that if you have no text, your document will be empty!

WARNING

The browser takes care of some of the work for you, such as what color the background should be and what color the text should be. Although you can change the color, you might want to leave it the way it is. If a user has changed his default text color to black, and you set the page's background color to black, the user won't be able to distinguish the text from the background, and will see only a black box.

Viewing Pages in a Browser

The two most popular browsers, Microsoft's Internet Explorer and Netscape's Navigator, can view HTML in two ways. The first is as a Web page, as shown in Figure 4.1, and the second is to actually view the text file of the Web page, generally referred to as the *source*. The HTML file is then opened with the application the extension is associated with. In Microsoft Internet Explorer, the default application is Notepad on all Windows 95 and Windows NT operating systems.

Making an HTML Page Easier to Read

The browser doesn't need the HTML page to be formatted in any special way, such as indenting code for easy readability. Listing 4.1 is a good HTML page, but it might not be easy to read. There are two things to consider here: first, the readability of the page. If you want to make changes, you must make sure you're entering code within the correct sub-tags to make that change. Adding tabs and spaces, such as those shown in Listing 4.2, is helpful. They're ignored by the browser, so they won't interfere with how the browser interprets the HTML page. However, they do take up space on a file, which is the second factor to consider. The larger a file is, the more time it takes to get from the Web server to your machine and to be interpreted by the browser, then displayed.

Listing 4.2. Adding white space to the page for easy reading.

```
<HTML>

<HEAD>
<TITLE>My Web Page</TITLE>
</HEAD>

<BODY>
<FONT SIZE=2><P>My Web Page</P>
<P> </P>
<P>This Web page will contain very insightful information that
➥everyone needs.</P>
</FONT>
</BODY>

</HTML>
```

Writing and Editing a Page

Several good applications can edit your HTML page. It's just a text file with an extension of .HTML or .HTM, so you can use any application you currently have that can edit text files. However, the more editing you have to do for Web pages, the less you might want to interpret tags and add or make changes to those tags with just a simple text editor. Take a look at Figure 4.2, which has a table of text. In a spreadsheet application, it might be easy to add columns or rows, but in an HTML text file that looks like Listing 4.3, it won't be as simple. You have to add the placeholder for the column or row and then add the data for each cell of the row. Many good programs (such as Microsoft FrontPage) let you add columns, rows, and data as though you were still working in a spreadsheet application.

A final consideration is the growth of the HTML language. Tables are just one feature that's difficult to edit in a text file. As extensions are added to the language, more HTML objects are cumbersome to edit in a text file.

Figure 4.2.

A table displayed in a browser.

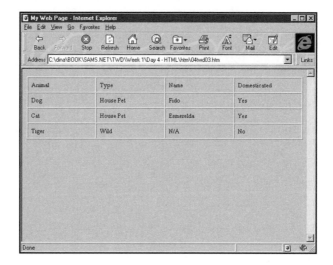

Listing 4.3. The HTML file displayed as Figure 4.2.

```
<HTML>

<HEAD>
<TITLE>My Web Page</TITLE>
</HEAD>

<BODY>

<TABLE BORDER CELLSPACING=1 CELLPADDING=7 WIDTH=590>
<TR><TD WIDTH="25%" VALIGN="TOP">
<FONT SIZE=2><P>Animal</FONT></TD>
<TD WIDTH="25%" VALIGN="TOP">
<FONT SIZE=2><P>Type</FONT></TD>
<TD WIDTH="25%" VALIGN="TOP">
<FONT SIZE=2><P>Name</FONT></TD>
<TD WIDTH="25%" VALIGN="TOP">
<FONT SIZE=2><P>Domesticated</FONT></TD>
</TR>
<TR><TD WIDTH="25%" VALIGN="TOP">
<FONT SIZE=2><P>Dog</FONT></TD>
<TD WIDTH="25%" VALIGN="TOP">
<FONT SIZE=2><P>House Pet</FONT></TD>
<TD WIDTH="25%" VALIGN="TOP">
<FONT SIZE=2><P>Fido</FONT></TD>
<TD WIDTH="25%" VALIGN="TOP">
<FONT SIZE=2><P>Yes</FONT></TD>
</TR>
<TR><TD WIDTH="25%" VALIGN="TOP">
<FONT SIZE=2><P>Cat</FONT></TD>
<TD WIDTH="25%" VALIGN="TOP">
<FONT SIZE=2><P>House Pet</FONT></TD>
```

continues

Listing 4.3. continued

```
<TD WIDTH="25%" VALIGN="TOP">
<FONT SIZE=2><P>Esmerelda</FONT></TD>
<TD WIDTH="25%" VALIGN="TOP">
<FONT SIZE=2><P>Yes</FONT></TD>
</TR>
<TR><TD WIDTH="25%" VALIGN="TOP">
<FONT SIZE=2><P>Tiger</FONT></TD>
<TD WIDTH="25%" VALIGN="TOP">
<FONT SIZE=2><P>Wild</FONT></TD>
<TD WIDTH="25%" VALIGN="TOP">
<FONT SIZE=2><P>N/A</FONT></TD>
<TD WIDTH="25%" VALIGN="TOP">
<FONT SIZE=2><P>No</FONT></TD>
</TR>
</TABLE>

</BODY>

</HTML>
```

Headings

Within the <BODY></BODY> tags, you can add headings similar to the "Headings" title for this section. There are six levels of headings, denoted from H1 to H6. H1 is the topmost heading and H6 is the most subordinate heading. H1 is the largest type size and H6 is the smallest possible heading type size.

Listing 4.4 illustrates how these headings should be used, and Figure 4.3 is the corresponding view of this HTML page from the browser. Even though the lines are spaced so the page is easy to read, the spacing is ignored when the page is displayed. Also notice that as the headers go from H1 to H6, the size of the text's font is reduced. The header tags don't distinguish the text. There are some useful tags that can be added to help the headers, such as horizontal lines and specific control of font size (discussed later in this chapter).

Listing 4.4. HTML text that uses all the header tags with recommended format uses.

```
<HTML>

<HEAD>
<TITLE>My Web Page</TITLE>
</HEAD>

<BODY>
<FONT SIZE=2><P>My Web Page</P>
```

```
<H1> A. Car Breakdown</H1>
    <H2> B. Automobile Maker Location</H2>
        <H3> C. Foreign </H3>
        <H3> C. Domestic </H3>
    <H2> B. Car Type </H2>
        <H3> C. 4 Wheel Drive </H3>
            <H4> D. Feature List </H4>
                <H5> E. Standard Features </H5>
                    <H6> F. Exterior Features </H6>
                    <H6> F. Interior Features </H6>
                <H5> E. Special Features </H5>
            <H4> D. Price Range </H4>
        <H3> C. Luxury </H3>
        <H3> C. Sports </H3>

<P> </P>
<P>This Web page will contain very insightful information
➡that everyone needs.</P>
</FONT>
</BODY>

</HTML>
```

Figure 4.3.

HTML text that uses all the header tags with recommended format uses.

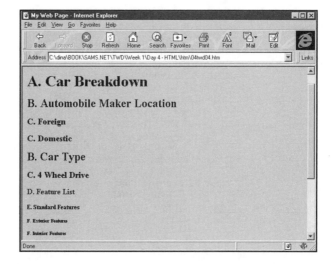

Paragraphs

Now that you grasp the concept of page layout and headings, adding information should make your page more interesting. Paragraphs are added with the `<P>text</P>` tag.

Taking the car example from Listing 4.4, add a paragraph about interior features. This example is shown in Listing 4.5 and displayed in Figure 4.4. In Listing 4.5, the paragraph is indented, but the text isn't affected when the pages are displayed.

Notice that the font size of Heading 6 is smaller than the paragraph's font size. You can control the size of the font only with the `<FONT=x></FONT>` tags discussed later in this chapter. The headings (and other kinds of text/tags) don't have an absolute font size to compensate for the screen resolution and preferences of the person using the browser.

The special quality of the `<P>text</P>` tag is that it indicates a paragraph separation from one set of text to the next. This separation is indicated by some space between the text above the paragraph and the text of the paragraph.

Listing 4.5. HTML text that uses the paragraph tag `<P>`.

```
<HTML>

<HEAD>
<TITLE>My Web Page</TITLE>
</HEAD>

<BODY>
<FONT SIZE=2><P>My Web Page</P>

<H1> A. Car Breakdown</H1>
    <H2> B. Automobile Maker Location</H2>
        <H3> C. Foreign </H3>
        <H3> C. Domestic </H3>
    <H2> B. Car Type </H2>
        <H3> C. 4 Wheel Drive </H3>
            <H4> D. Feature List </H4>
                <H5> E. Standard Features </H5>
                    <H6> F. Exterior Features </H6>
                    <H6> F. Interior Features </H6>
                        <P> The interior features of the 4 Wheel drive
                        include leather seats, automatic power steering,
                        automatic brakes, air conditioning, heated seats,
                        lighted vanity mirrors, and air bags.
                <H5> E. Special Features </H5>
            <H4> D. Price Range </H4>
        <H3> C. Luxury </H3>
        <H3> C. Sports </H3>

<P> </P>
<P>This Web page will contain very insightful information that
➥everyone needs.</P>
</FONT>
</BODY>

</HTML>
```

Figure 4.4.

HTML text that uses the paragraph tag <P>.

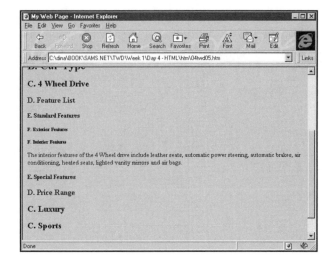

Lists

There are several styles of lists supported in HTML: numbered (ordered), bulleted (unordered), glossary list (term and definition), menu lists (one line per paragraph), and directory lists (short text items). A list (as well as tables and other HTML elements) has two sets of tags. The first tag indicates the type of list, and the second tag indicates an element in the list.

The ordered list is generally displayed as a numbered list. The tag to indicate list type is <OL></OL>, and the tag to indicate a list item is <LI>; there's no closing tag for <LI>. Listing 4.6 and Figure 4.5 illustrate using an ordered list. Notice that the tag doesn't have room for a tag name, such as "Ordered List," but is added with the paragraph <P> tag.

Listing 4.6. HTML text that uses an ordered list.

```
<HTML>

<HEAD>
<TITLE>Ordered List</TITLE>
</HEAD>

<BODY>

<P>Ordered List such as numbered</P>
<OL>
    <LI> First Item in List
    <LI> Second Item in List
    <LI> Third Item in List
</OL>
</BODY>
</HTML>
```

Figure 4.5.

HTML text that uses
an ordered list.

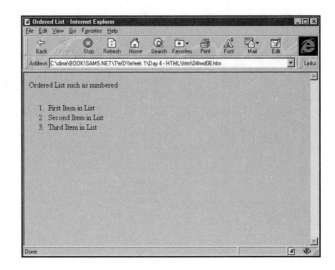

The unordered list is usually displayed as a bulleted list. The tag to indicate list type is <UL> </UL>, and the tag to indicate a list item is <LI>. There's no closing tag for <LI>. Listing 4.7 and Figure 4.6 illustrate using an unordered list. Your browser might display a different symbol to indicate each element in the list (instead of a bullet).

Listing 4.7. HTML text that uses an unordered list.

```
<HTML>

<HEAD>
<TITLE>Unordered List</TITLE>
</HEAD>

<BODY>

<P>Unordered List such as bullets</P>
<UL>
    <LI> First Item in List
    <LI> Second Item in List
    <LI> Third Item in List
</UL>
</BODY>
</HTML>
```

4

Figure 4.6.

HTML text that uses
an unordered list.

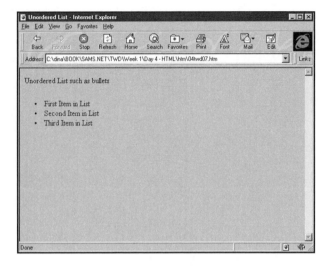

The glossary list is displayed as though a term were being defined. The tag to indicate the list
type is `<DL></DL>`. The tag to indicate an term being defined is `<DT>`, and the tag to indicate
the definition is `<DD>`. The term and definition tags don't have any closing tags. Listing 4.8
and Figure 4.7 illustrate using a glossary list.

Notice that the definition is on the next line and indented. Also notice that there's no specific
formatting of the term to indicate that it is one.

Listing 4.8. HTML text that uses a glossary list.

```
<HTML>

<HEAD>
<TITLE>Glossary List</TITLE>
</HEAD>

<BODY>

<P>Glossary List</P>
<DL>
    <DT> HTML
        <DD> HyperText Markup Language
    <DT> WWW
        <DD> World Wide Web
    <DT> TAG
        <DD> Indicates HTML formating
</DL>
</BODY>
</HTML>
```

Figure 4.7.

HTML text that uses a glossary list.

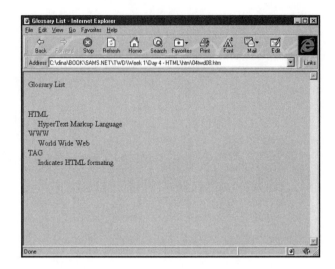

The use of menus and directory listings is left as an exercise for you to try.

Lists are powerful formats, especially because they can be nested. Suppose you want to create a TO DO list (numbered by priority), and in that list, you need a list of people to contact with their titles and phone numbers (glossary) and a list of equipment to finish the project (bulleted list). Listing 4.9 illustrates this kind of nested list, and Figure 4.8 demonstrates this HTML page in a browser.

Listing 4.9. A TO DO list using ordered, unordered, and glossary lists.

```
<HTML>

<HEAD>
<TITLE>TO DO</TITLE>
</HEAD>

<BODY>

<P>TO DO List</P>
<OL>
    <LI> Contact the following people
        <DL>
        <DT> John Doe - Marketing
            <DD> 555-1212, get his executive presentation
        <DT> Jane Smith - Finance
            <DD> 222-1212, get budget numbers
        <DT> Bill Jones - Manufacturing
            <DD> 123-3456, get design documents
        </DL>
    <LI> Get the following equipment/materials
        <UL>
```

```
                    <LI> Computers
                    <LI> Telephone Lines
                    <LI> Office Space
                    <LI> Lab Space
                    <LI> New Personnel
              </UL>
        </OL>
        </BODY>
        </HTML>
```

Figure 4.8.

A TO DO list using ordered, unordered, and glossary lists.

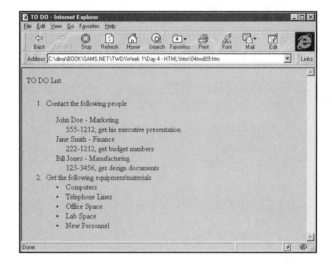

Tables

A table is a good formatting tool because you can put just about any other kind of tag in the cell of the table. The tag for a table works much like a glossary list because you must specify each element of the table. The tag to denote the entire table is the <TABLE></TABLE> tag, the tag to denote a row of a table is <TR></TR>, the tag to denote a cell of a table is <TD></TD>, and the tag to denote a column or row heading is <TH></TH>.

Listing 4.10 is an example of a table with column and row headings and data in the cells. Figure 4.9 shows what this table looks like in a browser. Notice that the <TABLE> cell also has the keyword BORDER, which allows the cells to be outlined so that it looks like a table, but this feature isn't necessary. The first few lines of HTML after the <TABLE> tag are header columns. The browser generally builds the page as it sees the text. If these <TH> lines had been at the end of the table (right before the </TABLE>), then the column headings would appear after the data rows. Also notice that each row's heading (to the left in bold) is incorporated into the <TR>, so each row begins with a heading cell, and then displays the data cells.

Listing 4.10. A simple table.

```
<HTML>
<HEAD>
<TITLE>Tables</TITLE>
</HEAD>
<BODY>

<TABLE BORDER=1 >
    <TH></TH>
    <TH> Animal </TH>
    <TH> Number </TH>
    <TH> Month </TH>
    <TR>
        <TH> Item 1 </TH>
        <TD>Dog</TD>
        <TD>1</TD>
        <TD>Jan</TD>
    </TR>
    <TR>
        <TH> Item 2 </TH>
        <TD>Cat</TD>
        <TD>2</TD>
        <TD>Feb</TD>
    </TR>
    <TR>
        <TH> Item 1 </TH>
        <TD>Cow</TD>
        <TD>3</TD>
        <TD>March</TD>
</TR>
</TABLE>

</BODY>
</HTML>
```

More Table Keywords

To control the table, more keywords need to be added in the table tags. For example, the table takes up only part of the screen (and will grow with more data). Suppose the table spans the entire screen and shrinks or grows as the browser is maximized or minimized. Figures 4.10 and 4.11 show the small HTML page with the browser at different sizes (nothing about the screen resolution changed, just the size the browser application took up onscreen). This is a nice way of controlling what the table looks like because you have no idea how the user will size the browser application.

4

Figure 4.9.

A simple table.

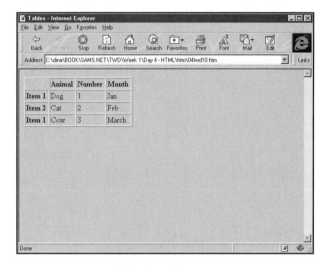

Figure 4.10.

Small HTML page with the browser not maximized.

Listing 4.11 and Figure 4.12 show the new keyword WIDTH inside the <TABLE> tag. Notice that the WIDTH has been set to 100 percent (the entire application window). The CELLSPACING keyword is the distance between two cells, and the CELLPADDING keyword is the distance between the cell's object (in this case, text) and the edge of the cell. Notice that by setting the WIDTH of the first header column in the first row to 80 percent, the first column is taking up most of the space onscreen.

Figure 4.11.
Small HTML page with browser maximized.

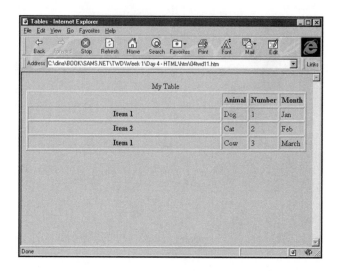

WARNING

The keywords, such as WIDTH, used in a table can be deceiving. You might want a great deal of control over your table and have a specific width for each item. If the browser doesn't support that level of detail on a table (or doesn't implement it correctly), you might not get the look you're after.

Listing 4.11. A simple table with more keywords.

```
<HTML>
<HEAD>
<TITLE>Tables</TITLE>
</HEAD>
<BODY>

<TABLE BORDER=1 CELLSPACING=3% CELLPADDING = 3% WIDTH=100%>
    <CAPTION> My Table </CAPTION>
    <TH WIDTH=80%></TH>
    <TH> Animal </TH>
    <TH> Number </TH>
    <TH> Month </TH>
    <TR>
        <TH> Item 1 </TH>
        <TD>Dog</TD>
        <TD>1</TD>
        <TD>Jan</TD>
    </TR>
```

```
    <TR>
        <TH> Item 2 </TH>
        <TD>Cat</TD>
        <TD>2</TD>
        <TD>Feb</TD>
    </TR>
    <TR>
        <TH> Item 1 </TH>
        <TD>Cow</TD>
        <TD>3</TD>
        <TD>March</TD>
    </TR>
    </TABLE>

    </BODY>
    </HTML>
```

Figure 4.12.

A simple table with more keywords.

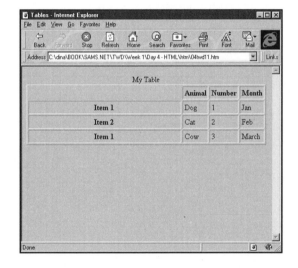

Nested Tables

Nested tables are a great tool for displaying and arranging information. To nest a table within another table, the cell of the outer table contains the entire inside table. The <TABLE> ... </TABLE> tag of the inside table is placed in the <TD> ... </TD> tags of the outside table. Listing 4.12 is an example of the code used to do this, and Figure 4.13 illustrates the result of this code when it's displayed in a browser.

Listing 4.12. A table nested inside another table.

```
<HTML>
<HEAD>
<TITLE>Tables</TITLE>
</HEAD>
<BODY>

<TABLE BORDER=1 CELLSPACING=10% CELLPADDING = 10% WIDTH=100%>
    <CAPTION> My Table </CAPTION>
    <TH></TH>
    <TH> Animal </TH>
    <TH> Number </TH>
    <TH> Month </TH>
    <TR>
        <TH> Item 1 </TH>
        <TD>
            <TABLE BORDER=2 WIDTH=100%>
                <CAPTION> Nested Table </CAPTION>
                <TH> Dogs</TH>
    <TH> Cats </TH>
                <TR>
                    <TD> Jenny </TD>
                    <TD> Joe </TD>
                <TR>
                <TR>
                    <TD> Wayne </TD>
                    <TD> Dina </TD>
                <TR>
            </TABLE>
        </TD>
        <TD>1</TD>
        <TD>Jan</TD>
    </TR>

</TABLE>

</BODY>
</HTML>
```

Adding Images to the Page

Most interesting Web pages contain images as well as text. GIF images are used in this chapter, but there are other image formats available. If you choose a type that isn't supported by all operating systems, however, the image isn't displayed in the browser.

Figure 4.13.

A table nested inside another table.

 TIP

It's easy to get distracted finding images to place on your Web site. Microsoft has a library of images and other useful Web design tools at www.microsoft.com/gallery. The images used in this chapter were pulled from this site.

Adding an image requires the <IMG> tag, such as <IMG SRC="image.gif">. Keep in mind that the image tag requires a specific location for the file. You have three choices: First, the image can be referenced from another Web site (or your own) with the http://www.dina.com/image.gif addressing. Second, the image can be in the directory of your Web server, such as ..\..\tree\image.gif or \image\image.gif. Third, the image can be in the current directory the Web page is stored in, referenced as image.gif. For simplicity's sake, this chapter assumes that the pictures are in the same directory and uses the image.gif file reference.

Listing 4.13 uses the image tag inside another tag (LI or line item) as well as outside the formatting tags. Notice in Figure 4.14 that the first figure (ORANGE_LINE.GIF) stretches across the width of the screen. The other images range in size and are in a bulleted list.

 WARNING

The larger the image (in screen pixels) and the sharper the image (more colors required), the longer the image download time and display time.

Listing 4.13. Using the image tag.

```
<HTML>
<HEAD>
<TITLE>Using the Image Tag</TITLE>
</HEAD>

<BODY>

<IMG SRC='orange_line.gif'>

<P>Using the Image Tag</P>
<UL>
    <LI> <IMG SRC='pen_pap.gif'>
    <LI> <IMG SRC='blue_arrow.gif'>
    <LI> <IMG SRC='gecko.gif'>
</UL>


</BODY>
</HTML>
```

Figure 4.14.

Using the image tag.

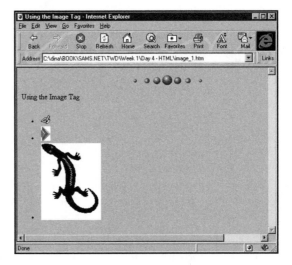

NOTE

A Web site reference has three sections: the protocol, the server name, and the page on the server. Using the example of http://www.microsoft.com/ default.htm, the protocol section is the http:, the server name is //www. microsoft.com/, and the page on the server is default.htm. Where is this page? It's at the root directory of the Web

pages. A Web site reference such as http://www.microsoft.com/
gallery/default.htm also has three sections. The protocol is http:, and
the server name is //www.microsoft.com. The Web page includes the
location—/gallery/—and the Web page is default.htm.

Cool Character Formatting Options

HTML does allow for some familiar formatting options, such as setting the text size or
specifying **bold** or *italic* text, and enables standard page formatting conventions such as line
breaks and horizontal lines.

Some of the formatting styles provide for font size and style, which you might want to control
yourself. Browsers can interpret general styles differently (such as how large a header should
be, and whether text should be bold or italic). By specifically stating the style and size, you
have more control (you still aren't guaranteed the exact look—remember that HTML is
meant to do the formatting work).

The text font is controlled with the <FONT> tag. To change the size, add the SIZE=x clause; to
change the color, add the COLOR=x clause. There are seven sizes (1–7) and several predefined
colors. Listing 4.14 is an example of a sentence in which every word is a different size and
color. Figure 4.15 shows what the page look like in a browser. Notice that use of the + and
- to increase and decrease the text size.

Listing 4.14. Using the `<FONT>` tag.

```
<HTML>
<HEAD>
<TITLE>Using the FONT keyword</TITLE>
</HEAD>

<BODY>

<P>
<FONT SIZE=7 COLOR=Black>Using </FONT>
<FONT SIZE=6 COLOR=Maroon>the </FONT>
<FONT SIZE=5 COLOR=Green>FONT </FONT>
<FONT SIZE=4 COLOR=Navy>keyword </FONT>
<FONT SIZE=3 COLOR=Red>is </FONT>
<FONT SIZE=2 COLOR=White>real </FONT>
<FONT SIZE=1 COLOR=Fuchsia>fun. </FONT>
```

continues

Listing 4.14. continued

```
<P>
<FONT SIZE=+7 COLOR=Black>Using </FONT>
<FONT SIZE=6 COLOR=Maroon>the </FONT>
<FONT SIZE=5 COLOR=Green>FONT </FONT>
<FONT SIZE=-4 COLOR=Navy>keyword </FONT>
<FONT SIZE=3 COLOR=Red>is </FONT>
<FONT SIZE=-2 COLOR=White>real </FONT>
<FONT SIZE=1 COLOR=Fuchsia>fun. </FONT>
</BODY>
</HTML>
```

Figure 4.15.

Using the <FONT>
tag.

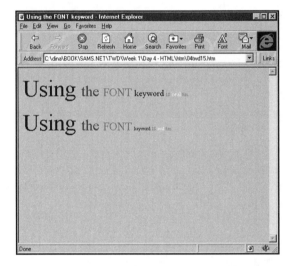

The other text attributes of bold, italic, and so on are also easy to use. The bold tag is <B>, and the italic tag is <I>. The horizontal line tag is <HR> for horizontal rules. The new line (also called carriage return) is <BR>. Listing 4.15 shows how these tags can be used, and Figure 4.16 illustrates what the final page looks like in a browser. Notice that the commenting tags are being used but aren't displayed in the page. The ordering of bold and italic doesn't matter.

Listing 4.15. Using bold, italic, horizontal rule, and new line tags.

```
<HTML>
<HEAD>
<TITLE>Using bold, italic, horizontal rule and new line tags</TITLE>
</HEAD>
```

```
<BODY>

<!-- Bold --!>
<FONT SIZE=7 COLOR=Black><B>Using </B></FONT>

<!-- Italic --!>
<FONT SIZE=7><I>the </I></FONT>

<!-- Horizontal Rule, notice no closing </HR> --!>
<HR>

<FONT SIZE=7>B,I, HR, BR </FONT>

<!-- New line, aka carriage return --!>
<BR>
<FONT SIZE=7>keywords </FONT>

<!-- Bold and Italic --!>
<FONT SIZE=7><B><I>is </I><B></FONT>

<!-- Italic and Bold --!>
<I><B><FONT SIZE=7>real </FONT></B></I>

<FONT SIZE=7>fun. </FONT>

</BODY>
</HTML>
```

Figure 4.16.

Using bold, italic, horizontal rule, and new line tags.

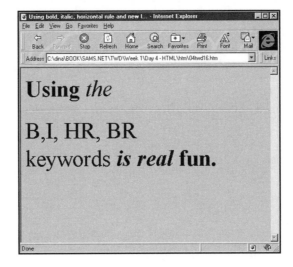

Move Around the Page with Anchors

Anchors give you the ability to jump from one part of a page to another. Don't confuse this with linking from page to page (to be discussed later). Anchors work well for pages that fill up more than one screen of information. Say you have a page of three related topics: sports cars, luxury cars, and four-wheel drive cars. The images and text of each section probably fill a few screens. Instead of scrolling through everything to find a particular topic, you can place anchors at the beginning of each section and then link those anchors to the top of the page (sort of a table of contents for the page). When a user clicks the anchor link at the top of the page, the browser automatically displays that section in the browser (very convenient for pages with a lot of content).

First, create the anchor in the section with the anchor tag `<A>`—`<A NAME="4Wheel">4 Wheel Automobiles</A>`, for example—so that the browser knows where to jump. Then, add the link the user clicks to jump to that section with `<A HREF=#4Wheel>Click Here to Go To 4 Wheel Cars</A>` (HREF stands for HyperText reference). The anchor must be given a name (`4Wheel`), and the link must refer to that name (`#4Wheel`).

Listing 4.16 shows an example of a Car page. The images on the car should be large enough so that you can't see all the cars (unless you have a large resolution or huge screen). The user should be able to link to the car section he's interested in and then click another link to get back to the top of the page. This kind of linking saves the user from having to scroll through a lot of information he isn't interested in. Notice that all the anchors have names and that all the links reference those names by placing the # character before the name. Figure 4.17 illustrates what this page looks like in the browser. Notice that the link is underlined in the figure; that's how the browser denotes a link.

Listing 4.16. Using anchors to maneuver around the page.

```
<HTML>
<HEAD>
<TITLE>Anchors</TITLE>
</HEAD>

<BODY>
<H1> Anchors </H1>
<A NAME="TOP"></A>
<BR><A HREF=#4Wheel>4 Wheel Automobiles</A>
<BR><A HREF=#Luxury>Luxury Sedans</A>
<BR><A HREF=#Sports>Sports Cars</A>

<HR>
<P>
<H2><A NAME="4Wheel">4 Wheel Automobiles</A></H2>
<IMG SRC='BIG_4WHEEL_CAR.jpg'>
<BR><A HREF=#TOP>Return to Top of Page</A>
```

```
<HR>
<P>
<H2><A NAME="Luxury">Luxury Sedans</A></H2>
<IMG SRC='BIG_LUXURY_CAR.gif'>
<BR><A HREF=#TOP>Return to Top of Page</A>

<HR>
<P>
<H2><A NAME="Sports">Sports Cars</A></H2>
<IMG SRC='BIG_SPORTS_CAR.gif'>
<BR><A HREF=#TOP>Return to Top of Page</A>
</BODY>
</HTML>
```

Figure 4.17.

Using anchors to maneuver around the page.

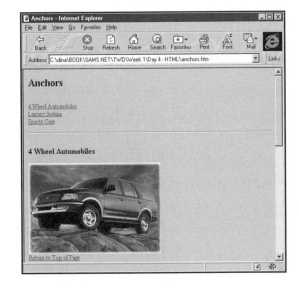

Move from Page to Page with Links

Now that you know how to create and move around the page, it's time to add links from page to page, which serves two purposes. It gives your users a way to maneuver through your site from page to page, and it gives your users links to other interesting information or other sites.

Because this kind of a link is similar to the anchors used in the previous section, the tag used is still <A>. Just as images can have three kinds of location references, links to other pages can have three kinds of location references. The first is a page in the directory: MYPAGE.HTM. The second is a page somewhere on my site: \more\pages\mypage.htm, and the third is a page on someone else's site: http://www.microsoft.com.

Listing 4.17 is the HTML page for these links, and Figure 4.18 shows the page displayed in a browser. Notice that the links are embedded in a bulleted list and that the first list uses text for the link; the second list uses pictures for the link. The spacing in the first list is uniform from one line to the next, but in the second list, the spacing isn't, to compensate for the pictures' vertical size.

Listing 4.17. Linking to other pages.

```
<HTML>
<HEAD>
<TITLE>Referencing Other Pages</TITLE>
</HEAD>

<BODY>

<H1>Referencing Other Pages</H1>

<H2> Links with Text</H2>
<UL>
<LI>Same site, dif directory:<A HREF="\sub\lists.htm">lists</A>
<LI>Same site, same direcotry:<A HREF="lists.htm">lists</A>
<LI>Different site:<A HREF="http://www.microsoft.com">Microsoft</A></UL>

<H2> Links with Images</H2>
<UL>
<LI>Same site, dif directory:<A HREF="\sub\lists.htm"><IMG SRC='pen_pap.gif'>
➥</A>
<LI>Same site, same directory:<A HREF="lists.htm"><IMG SRC='blue_arrow.gif'></A>
<LI>Different site:
➥<A HREF="http://www.microsoft.com"><IMG SRC='microsoft.gif'></A></UL>

</BODY>
</HTML>
```

Embedding Mailing Addresses

It's always convenient to include an e-mail address so that your customers can communicate with you. You could list your e-mail address as text, which your customers would then have to write down and enter in their e-mail system. An easier way is to incorporate your e-mail in its proper tag. When your customers click on it, your default e-mail application (if it exists and the browser knows about it) will open and the TO: line will have your address in it.

This e-mail feature uses the anchor tag <A> with the attribute of HREF=mailto:, as shown here:

```
<A HREF="webmaster@johndoe.com">Webmaster</A>
```

Figure 4.18.
Linking to other pages.

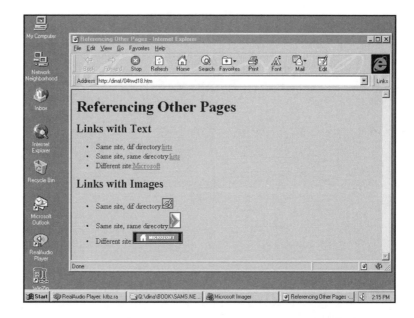

Listing 4.18 shows several examples, which are illustrated in Figure 4.19. Notice that the entire e-mail needs to be included. You can have the e-mail link display text or an image. There's no visual difference between this kind of link and a link to another page.

Listing 4.18. Adding e-mail to your page.

```
<HTML>
<HEAD>
<TITLE>Adding Email to your page</TITLE>
</HEAD>

<BODY>

<H1>Adding Email to your page</H1>

<UL>
<LI><A HREF="email:webmaster@johndoe.com"> Webmaster@johndoe.com </A>
<LI><A HREF="email:webmaster@johndoe.com"><IMG SRC='microsoft.gif'></A>
</UL>

</BODY>
</HTML>
```

Figure 4.19.

Adding e-mail to your page.

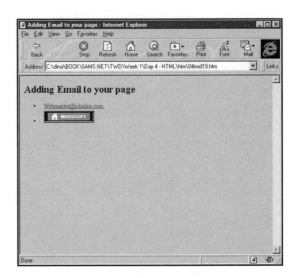

Page Backgrounds

The background of a Web page is generally a solid default color chosen by your Web browser (unless you change it). Most of the figures in this chapter use gray as the default for the background. In the <BODY> tag, you can change this color to a specific color, such as blue, or you can make the background a default image.

Background images are displayed as a backdrop for whatever content you have on a page. Backgrounds shouldn't interfere with a page's content or usefulness, but should add a sense of style to, or provide a context for, your page. A car company, for example, might use an image of its newest car as a background for its Web page. Figure 4.20 is an example of a Web page with a gray marble background. Because it's light gray, the background doesn't interfere with the page's black text. To add a background image, add the BACKGROUND attribute to the <BODY> tag, as shown in Listing 4.19. Notice that the image (if you pull it up in an image editor) is small compared to the size of your browser window. The browser tiles the image to fill up the entire browser screen.

Listing 4.19. A Web page with a gray marble background.

```
<HTML>

<HEAD>
<TITLE> Background Image </TITLE>
</HEAD>

<BODY BACKGROUND="background_grey.jpg">
```

```
<H1> Acme Music Company </H1>
<H2>

</BODY>
</HTML>
```

Figure 4.20.

This Web page uses a gray marble background.

You can also make the background a specific color by adding the BGCOLOR attribute to the <BODY> tag. The color choices are black, maroon, green, olive, navy, purple, teal, gray, silver, red, lime, yellow, blue, fuchsia, aqua, and white. The browser might not provide all colors, so test what your browser has. Figure 4.21 uses a blue background with white text. Listing 4.20 corresponds to this Web page.

Figure 4.21.

This Web page uses a navy background with white text.

Listing 4.20. A Web page with a navy background and white text.

```
<HTML>

<HEAD>
<TITLE>Background Color</TITLE>
</HEAD>

<BODY BGCOLOR="Navy">


<H1> <FONT COLOR="White">Acme Music Company </FONT></H1>
<H2>

</BODY>
</HTML>
```

Frame Support

Frames are one of the new "cool" extensions to the HTML language. Personally, I don't like frames on a Web site, but I can see their usefulness, so they're included here. One word of caution, though: Don't overdo it!

Figure 4.22 is an example of a framed page, which looks like physical boundaries on the page. These boundaries are not <HR> tags or other kinds of formatting divisions. They are frames dividing the screen so that more than one Web page can be viewed in the browser at a time.

Figure 4.22.

A framed page with physical boundaries on the page.

Frames break the Web page into specific units. Each unit is an HTML page, but because they're in a framed page, they can be viewed simultaneously. There might be some text or image material that you want at the top of every page, such as the company logo, date, and closing stock price. Instead of having to edit every page each time this information changes, you can separate out that information into its own page. This separate page could then be in the top frame of your window.

The frame's outer tag (similar to the <TABLE> outer tag of a table) is <FRAMESET></FRAMESET>. For a framed page, this tag replaces the <BODY></BODY> tag. Each frame has a <FRAME> tag, which doesn't have a closing </FRAME> tag, just as a table's data <TD> doesn't have a closing tag. Frames can be embedded within each other (just as tables can). The <FRAMESET> tag also has attributes. The most important attribute indicates the size of the FRAMESET, such as size across (COLS) or size down (ROWS). The FRAMESET must include one of these, but doesn't have to contain both. The * character is meant as *all*, as in "all the columns" or "all the rows."

Take an example of a <FRAMESET> page with two frames on the page. One frame is the table of contents. No matter what the user links to in the contents frame, that contents frame should always be in that frame. So, the second frame is where the linked page is displayed. To make sure the linked page is displayed in the second frame, the TARGET attribute must be added in the linked pages <A> tag.

To do this, there has to be a minimum of three HTML pages. The first is the <FRAMESET> page, FRAME_MAIN.HTM. This page contains the formatting for the <FRAMESET> and <FRAME> tags. The second page is the table of contents, CONTENTS.HTM. It contains the links to the pages of interest. The last page is a page from the table of contents, TODO_LIST.HTM. Figure 4.23 is a picture of the final Web page, FRAME_MAIN.HTM. The left frame of the page is the table of contents. When a user clicks a link in the contents, that page is displayed in the right frame. For this example, the first item in the table of contents is the TO DO list. When a user clicks on that link, the right frame is TODO_LIST.HTM.

The HTML code for FRAME_MAIN.HTM is in Listing 4.21. Notice that the browser page has been divided into a 30/70 split, in which the first <FRAME> tag has 30 percent of the browser screen, and the second <FRAME> tag has 70 percent of the browser screen. Each frame has a default HTML page to load and each frame is named. The left-hand frame name isn't used anywhere.

In each HTML page listed in the contents, the TARGET=contentFrame must be added so that the page is displayed in the right-hand frame. If this statement isn't added to each page listed in the table of contents, the left-hand frame changes to that page. Listing 4.22 is the HTML code for the CONTENTS.HTM page, and Listing 4.23 is the HTML code for the TODO_LIST.HTM (in a previous section of this chapter). Notice how both pages refer to the contentFrame. Before the user clicks any links in the contents frame, the right-hand frame appears empty. It isn't actually empty; it just refers to an HTML page that contains no text—so it seems empty. Listing 4.24 is the blank page, BLANK.HTM.

4

Figure 4.23.
The final framed Web page.

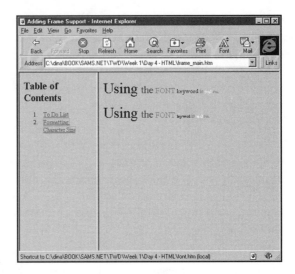

Listing 4.21. The main frame for the page: FRAME_MAIN.HTM.

```
<HTML>
<HEAD>
<TITLE>Adding Frame Support</TITLE>
</HEAD>

<FRAMESET COLS="30%,70%">
    <FRAME SRC="contents.htm" NAME="listFrame">
    <FRAME SRC="blank.htm" NAME="contentFrame">
</FRAMESET>
</HTML>
```

Listing 4.22. The menu in a separate frame: CONTENTS.HTM.

```
<HTML>
<HEAD>
<TITLE>Table of Contents</TITLE>
</HEAD>

<BODY>
<H1>Table of Contents</H1>
<OL>
<LI><A HREF="todo_list.htm" TARGET="contentFrame">To Do List</A>
<LI><A HREF="font.htm" TARGET="contentFrame">Formatting Character Size</A>
</OL>
</BODY>
</HTML>
```

Listing 4.23. A Web page that has a TO DO list, using ordered, unordered, and glossary lists.

```
<HTML>

<HEAD>
<TITLE>TO DO</TITLE>
</HEAD>

<BODY>

<P>TO DO List</P>
<OL>
    <LI> Contact the following people
        <DL>
        <DT> John Doe - Marketing
            <DD> 555-1212, get his executive presentation
        <DT> Jane Smith - Finance
            <DD> 222-1212, get budget numbers
        <DT> Bill Jones - Manufacturing
            <DD> 123-3456, get design documents
        </DL>
    <LI> Get the following equipment/materials
        <UL>
            <LI> Computers
            <LI> Telephone Lines
            <LI> Office Space
            <LI> Lab Space
            <LI> New Personnel
        </UL>
</OL>
</BODY>
</HTML>
```

Listing 4.24. A placeholder page loaded only when a specific page from the contents isn't chosen: BLANK.HTM.

```
<HTML>

<HEAD>
<TITLE></TITLE>
</HEAD>

<BODY>
</BODY>
</HTML>
```

WARNING

Frames are cool—there's no question about that. However, not every browser supports frames, so more work has to be done to compensate for that. Not every framed page is easy to understand. Having more frames doesn't mean a page is necessarily "cooler." Framed pages have their place only if they are easy to understand and use.

Example of a Simple Page of Static Data

Now that most of the elements of a Web page have been discussed, building a Web page that uses these elements correctly will be fun. The Web page is a home page (without frames, since I don't like them) for a bogus company. It will have a company logo, a table of contents (site map), a paragraph of text about the company, and a place to send e-mail to. Figure 4.24 shows what the page looks like in the browser.

The company logo is at the top of the page, and the table of contents and the paragraph about the company are in a table. The e-mail address comes after the table. The background is a gray marble.

Listing 4.25 is the code to build the page. Notice that there are a few new attributes in the tags, and that the tags are in lowercase letters (this shouldn't have any effect on how the page is displayed). The width attribute in the table tag tells the browser how much of the browser screen space to take.

Figure 4.24.

Sample page of static data.

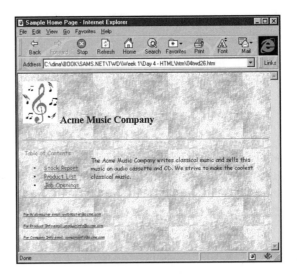

Listing 4.25. Sample page of static data.

```html
<html>

<head>
<title>Sample Home Page</title>
</head>

<body background="background_grey.jpg">

<h1>
<img src="music_note.gif" width="74" height="88">Acme Music Company
</h1>

<hr>

<table border="0" width="100%">
    <tr>
        <td width="15%"><font color="#008080"
        face="Comic Sans MS">Table of Contents </font><ul>
            <li><a href="home_sample_stock_report.htm"><font
                color="#008080" face="Comic Sans MS">Stock Report</font>
➥</a><font
                color="#008080" face="Comic Sans MS"> </font></li>
            <li><a href="home_sample_product_list.htm"><font
                color="#008080" face="Comic Sans MS">Product List</font>
➥</a><font
                color="#008080" face="Comic Sans MS"> </font></li>
            <li><a href="home_sample_job_openings.htm"><font
                color="#008080" face="Comic Sans MS">Job Openings
                </font></a></li>
        </ul>
        </td>
        <td width="40%"><font face="Comic Sans MS">The Acme Music
        Company writes classical music and sells this music on
        audio cassette and CD. We strive to make the coolest
        classical music. </font></td>
    </tr>
</table>

<hr>

<p><font size="1" face="Comic Sans MS">
<A HREF="email:webmaster@acme.com">For Webmaster email:
webmaster@acme.com</A></font></p>

<p><font size="1" face="Comic Sans MS">
<A HREF="email:productinfo@acme.com">For Product Info email:
productinfo@acme.com</A></font></p>

<p><font size="1" face="Comic Sans MS">
<A HREF="email:companyinfo@acme.com">For Company Info email:
companyinfo@acme.com</A></font></p>
</body>
</html>
```

4

The <FORM> Tag

Up to now, the HTML pages have been static (they are just files that never change unless *you* change them). They don't have any way to pass information from the browser back to the server. For example, a company might ask you a question when you visit its Web site. The answer you provide could be in the form of a text box you fill in, a series of checkboxes you select, or radio buttons you enable. To use these kinds of objects, they must be inside a <FORM> tag.

The <FORM> tag is the way to pass information from the browser back to the server. Information in the form designates what should be done and what information should be returned to the browser when the server is done.

Take, for example, a registration form used so the browser can download software. Many companies want to know who's downloading the software and keep track of how often. A user could jump to the software-downloading page. Before the server returns the downloaded software, the user must enter his name, address, and some information about his computer's capacity. When this information is passed back to the company's Web server, the Web server can pass this information on to the marketing department. Once this information is passed off, the Web server returns the software-downloading page to the user. The page returned to the browser didn't change based on the user input. To add more sophistication to the Web server, assume that the Web server recognizes the country the user is from and returns the Web page in that country's language. At this point, the page being returned depends on the information entered by the user.

The <FORM> tag contains the objects, such as text boxes, radio buttons, and so on, to insert the data, as well as the object to send the data to the server (the Submit button). Once the user has entered the information and clicked the Submit button, the browser configures the information for the objects to send back to the server.

The ACTION attribute of the <FORM> tag tells the server what server-side program to run. The METHOD attribute of the <FORM> tag tells the browser how to send the information back to the server. The two choices are the GET and POST methods.

GET sends a maximum of 1,000 characters back to the server and shows up in the browser's address box. If you have many objects, this probably won't work. The syntax of the address box looks like this:

```
program.exe?textbox1=helpme&radio1=item1
```

In this line, textbox1 and radio1 are objects in the <FORM> tag. The values of these objects follow the = sign. Each object/value pair is delimited with the & sign.

POST sends an unlimited number of characters back to the server, but the characters are sent in the body of the request.

The <INPUT> tag determines how objects such as the text box are used on the page. The objects should be names, which use the attribute NAME. If the object isn't a text box, you must use the VALUE attribute. For example, you might have two radio buttons: one for "new" and one for "old." To send new or old back to the server, they must be in the VALUE attribute of that object. The TYPE attribute of the <INPUT> tag tells the browser which object to display.

Figure 4.25 is an example of a Web page that uses the Form object as well as the text box, radio button, checkbox, and Submit button. Listing 4.26 is an example of the code needed to produce this page. Notice that the Form is sending the information to a Web server application called MYPROGRAM.DLL, which can be found in the Scripts directory on the server. The method is GET, so no more than 1,000 characters can be sent, including the program name, the object/value pairs, and all delimiters. The text box has been limited to 100 characters; the user can't enter any more. The checkbox and radio button names are the same for each choice. The value of the Submit button is the name that shows up on the button. The input tags don't have a closing </INPUT> tag, but the <FORM> tag does have a closing </FORM>.

Figure 4.25.

An example of a page with a <FORM> tag.

Listing 4.26. An example of a page with a <FORM> tag.

```
</HEAD>

<BODY>
<H1> Form Use </H1>
<HR>

<FORM ACTION="/scripts/myprogram.dll" METHOD="GET">
    <H2> The Text Box: Enter Your Name and Address </H2>
    <INPUT TYPE="TEXT" NAME="TextBox1" SIZE="100" MAXLENGTH="100">
    <HR>
    <H2> The Radio Button: Do you like the color RED? </H2>
    <INPUT TYPE="RADIO" NAME="RadioButton1" VALUE="Yes">
    <INPUT TYPE="RADIO" NAME="RadioButton1" VALUE="No">
    <HR>
    <H2> The Check Button: What colors do you like? </H2>
    <INPUT TYPE="CHECKBOX" NAME="CheckBox1" VALUE="RED">Red<BR>
    <INPUT TYPE="CHECKBOX" NAME="CheckBox1" VALUE="BLUD">Blue<BR>
    <INPUT TYPE="CHECKBOX" NAME="CheckBox1" VALUE="GREEN">Green<BR>
    <HR>
    <INPUT TYPE="SUBMIT" VALUE"SEND">Submit Now
</FORM>
</Body>
<HTML>
```

The HTTP Retrieval Methods

The HTTP methods of transferring pages are GET, PUT, POST, and DELETE. The GET method requests a file from the Web server. It's simply a way to link from one page to another, not to handle any kind of form you fill out. The POST method is used by forms to pass parameters to the Web server, as illustrated in the previous section. The PUT method is rarely used because it allows a request to create a new file or append to the file if the file already exists. This method could be dangerous and generally isn't allowed. You can use the DELETE method to delete a file from the Web server. For security reasons, Web servers usually don't permit PUT and DELETE methods.

Summary

This chapter is meant to give you an understanding of HTML so that you can begin writing Web pages. The format of the page includes the <HEAD> and <BODY> tags. Information is passed back to the Web server by using a form. Several tags allow you to format the page's look. In the next chapter, you look at how to manipulate the Web page with more scripting power from Visual Basic Script.

Q&A

Q If I want a uniform menu style for my Web page, what can I use?

A You have many choices, but the two most common are having the same HTML code on each page to represent the menu or having a framed page, in which one of the frames contains the menu.

Quiz

1. What is an HTML tag used for?
2. What does the <A> tag stand for, and what types are there?
3. What's the difference between the ordered list and the unordered list?
4. What tag is used to pass information from the browser to the Web server? What object tag must be inside the <FORM></FORM> tags?
5. How do you embed one table into another?
6. What is used to send mail as part of the Web page?
7. If you, as the Web administrator, wanted to retrieve information from the user, what would you use?
8. If you wanted to add a line between one paragraph and the next, what would you use?

Exercises

1. Design and write a Web page that uses a table with cells that contain images (not text).
2. Design and write a Web page that has a list embedded in a table.
3. Design and write a Web page in which objects of a form are embedded in a list or table.

Day 5

The VBScript Language

by Dina Fleet

The Visual Basic Script language (VBScript) is a slimmed-down version of the Visual Basic programming language. VBScript is built to program a Web page. The Microsoft Internet Explorer (browser) interprets the programming language and executes the script on the client (browser) side of the Internet (code that executes on the server side of the connections is discussed in Week 2, "Server-Side Rowsets with ActiveX Data Objects").

If you have programmed in Visual Basic before, this chapter should be a quick review of how VBScript can be used in the HTML page. First, you learn how to incorporate VBScript into your HTML page. Second, you learn some helpful VBScript functions that have already been written for you. Third, you learn about the HTML object model that's implemented in the Microsoft Internet Explorer program.

The code in this chapter is meant for the browser Microsoft Internet Explorer 3.01. The code listings have line numbers to help you view the code, but shouldn't be added to your own code.

The Event-Driven Programming Model

VBScript takes advantage of the event-driven programming model. The idea is that the application is driven by some event the user performs, such as clicking a button or entering text. When a user performs this kind of operation, the program executes that function and returns control to the user when it's done. It then sits in a wait state until the next event is fired off by the user. The user is driving the program through events.

The <SCRIPT> Tag

To use VBScript code, the <SCRIPT> tag must be used. The attributes of the tag tell the browser how to interpret the scripting code.

The LANGUAGE attribute can have two choices: VBScript or JScript. This book focuses on VBScript (although JScript could be used). The SRC attribute specifies a code file where the script can be found, if it's not in the current HTML file. Listing 5.1 shows a Web page that displays the text Hello World and has an empty <SCRIPT> tag. The <SCRIPT> tag is outside the <HEAD> and <BODY> tags. This listing is meant to be the shell of all the other listings in this chapter, although some listings might change to illustrate what changes are possible.

TIP

Plenty of browsers don't understand the <SCRIPT> tag, so it's important for you to add comments to the code after the <SCRIPT> tag. The code is still executed on browsers that understand the <SCRIPT> tag, and is properly ignored on browsers that don't understand the <SCRIPT> tag. Good form is as follows:

```
<SCRIPT>
    <!-- code here
    -->
</SCRIPT>.
```

Listing 5.1. The <SCRIPT> HTML file template.

```
<HTML>

<HEAD>
    <TITLE>The SCRIPT tag template</TITLE>
</HEAD>

    <BODY>
        <H1> Hello World </H1>
    </BODY>

    <SCRIPT LANGUAGE="VBScript">
```

```
    <!--
    -->
    </SCRIPT>

</HTML>
```

The `<FORM>` and `<INPUT>` Tags

Most Web pages use VBScript with the `<FORM>` and `<INPUT>` tags. The `<INPUT>` tag controls the user's input, and the `<FORM>` tag sends the information back to the Web server. If you aren't doing any Web server work on the data, the `<FORM>` tag isn't necessary.

The `<INPUT>` tag has several types: the text box, the text area, the password, the button, the checkbox, the radio button, the Submit button, and the Reset button. Listing 5.2 is a simple Web page with most of these `INPUT` tags; its output is shown in Figure 5.1. Since the information isn't being sent back to the Web server, the `FORM` tag isn't being used.

The first `INPUT` type is a text box (named `TextBox1`) with a maximum of 20 characters. The second `INPUT` type is a button (named `HelloButton`). When the button is clicked, it activates the `OnClick_Button` VBScript found in the `<SCRIPT>` section. The text box has the text `Hello World!` placed in it, which illustrates an `INPUT` type controlling another `INPUT` tag.

The third and fourth `INPUT` types are two radio buttons. Because they both have the `NAME` attribute as `Radio1`, they are treated as a group. When the first radio button is clicked, the `OnClick_Radio1_1` VBScript is executed. The script places the text `First Radio Button` in the bottommost `INPUT` type that's a text area. The second radio button's script places the text `Second Radio Button` in the text area.

The fifth and sixth `INPUT` types are two checkboxes. Unlike radio buttons, more than one checkbox can be checked at once. The script for the first checkbox is `OnClick_Check1_1`. The script places text similar to the radio button scripts in the text area.

The seventh `INPUT` type is a password text box. It can be limited in size like a normal text box can, but the entered text is shown as asterisks or some other character. The script for the button associated with the password box illustrates that a password is only as safe as you treat it. The real characters of the password are displayed in the text area. So if the password is "dog," the password text box displays three stars (one for each character) and the text area displays `dog`.

The last `INPUT` type is a Submit button; it usually sends the information from the `FORM` back to the server, but in this example, nothing is intended to be sent back to the server. A good reason for associating a script with the Submit button is for validation. Suppose that you ask the user to enter his state, such as `TX` for Texas. If the user enters character combinations that aren't associated with a state, you could warn the user of the incorrect state and give him another chance to enter the correct data before the trip back to the server.

5

NOTE

The VBScript procedures that these INPUT tags are calling look similar to the event that produced the call. For example, clicking a button produces an onClick event. The procedure associated with onClick was named OnClick_Button so that anyone reading the script has an easier time figuring out what's going on. The procedure name could have been this_thing_should_do_that. That's not a very descriptive name, but the procedure *would* be executed when the button is clicked.

Listing 5.2. The `<INPUT>` tag.

```
 1: <HTML>
 2:
 3: <HEAD>
 4:     <TITLE>The INPUT Tag</TITLE>
 5: </HEAD>
 6:
 7: <BODY>
 8:     <P> <INPUT TYPE=TEXTBOX NAME=TextBox1 SIZE=20> Textbox <br>
 9:     <P> <INPUT TYPE=BUTTON VALUE="Say Hello"
➡NAME="HelloButton" onClick="OnClick_Button"> Button <br>
10:     <P> <INPUT TYPE=RADIO
➡NAME=Radio1 onClick="OnClick_Radio1_1"> Radio Button 1 <br>
11:     <P> <INPUT TYPE=RADIO NAME=Radio1
➡onClick="OnClick_Radio1_2"> Radio Button 2 <br>
12:     <P> <INPUT TYPE=CHECKBOX NAME=Check1
➡onClick="OnClick_Check1_1"> Checkbox 1 <br>
13:     <P> <INPUT TYPE=CHECKBOX NAME=Check2
➡onClick="OnClick_Check1_2"> Checkbox 2 <br>
14:     <P> <INPUT TYPE=PASSWORD
➡NAME=Password1 > Password Box
15:         <INPUT TYPE=BUTTON VALUE="Enter Password"
➡onClick="OnClick_Password">
16:                 Button <br>
17:     <P> <INPUT TYPE=TEXTAREA NAME=TextArea1 SIZE="50,5"
18:             MAXLENGTH="200" onClick="OnClick_TextArea1"> Text area <br>
19:     <P> <INPUT TYPE=SUBMIT Value="Ok"
➡onClick="OnClick_TextArea1"> Submit Button <br>
20: </BODY>
21: <SCRIPT LANGUAGE="VBScript">
22:     <!--
23:     Sub OnClick_Button
24:         TextBox1.Value="Hello World!"
25:     End Sub
26:     Sub OnClick_Radio1_1
27:         TextArea1.Value="First Radio Button"
28:     End Sub
29:     Sub OnClick_Radio1_2
30:         TextArea1.Value="Second Radio Button"
31:     End Sub
32:     Sub OnClick_Check1_1
33:         TextArea1.Value="First Check Button"
```

```
34:        End Sub
35:        Sub OnClick_Check1_2
36:            TextArea1.Value="Second Check Button"
37:        End Sub
38:        Sub OnClick_Password
39:            TextArea1.Value=Password1.Value
40:        End Sub
41:        -->
42:    </SCRIPT>
43: </HTML>
```

The VBScript Procedure

In Listing 5.3, the procedure that was executed when the first button was clicked was started with Sub *namex* and ended with End Sub; *namex* is the procedure name. VBScript has two types of procedures: the subprocedure (Sub, End Sub) and the function (Function, End Function). Both types of procedures take parameters but only the function—such as adding two numbers, for example—returns a value.

Listing 5.3 and Figure 5.2 show a Web page with two text boxes (Value1 and Value2) where you enter a number, two buttons (BySub and ByFunction), and a final text box for the result (Total0). The first button adds the two numbers and places the text in the last text box by Sub; the second button does the same thing, but uses a Function procedure. The three text boxes don't need VBScript associations because the script associated with the buttons do the work.

VBScript treats the text box value (the number you entered) as a string (or text). Suppose that the first text box value is 1 and the second text box value is 2. The addition operator, +, for text adds the character 1 and 2 to make 12. Because this isn't the kind of addition the script is trying to perform, the cint function is used to convert Value1.value to a numeric number. The addition operator for numeric numbers makes the total 3.

The Function procedure isn't much good until it's called by another procedure (onClick_byFunc). Functions are useful when you want a single value returned. To have that value returned, the assignment of the Function name (AddThisTwoNumbers) has to equal the final value. The cint is wrapped around the parameters to AddThisTwoNumbers so that the correct addition is performed inside that function.

5

Figure 5.1.

*Using the <INPUT>
tag with VBScript
procedures.*

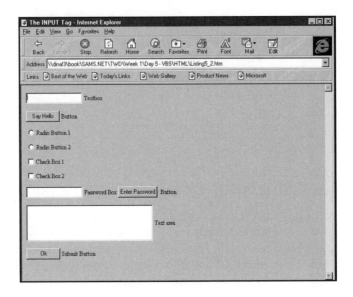

Listing 5.3. Adding two numbers by Sub and Function.

```
1: <HTML>
2:
3: <HEAD>
4:     <TITLE>Using Sub and Function procedures </TITLE>
5: <HEAD>
6:
7: <BODY>
8:     <INPUT TYPE=TEXTBOX NAME=Value1 SIZE=3>First Value <BR>
9:     + <BR>
10:    <INPUT TYPE=TEXTBOX NAME=Value2 SIZE=3>First Value <BR>
11:    = <BR>
12:    <INPUT TYPE=TEXTBOX NAME=Total SIZE=6>Total <BR>
13:    <INPUT TYPE=BUTTON NAME=BySub
➥Value="By Sub" onClick="onClick_bySub">
14:    <INPUT TYPE=BUTTON NAME=ByFunction
➥Value="By Function" onClick="onClick_byFunc">
15: </BODY>
16:
17: <SCRIPT Language="VBScript">
18: <!--
19:     Sub onClick_bySub
20:         Total.value = cint(Value1.value)
➥+ cint(Value2.value)
21:     End Sub
22:     Sub onClick_byFunc
23:         Total.value = AddThisTwoNumbers(cint(Value1.value),
➥cint(Value2.value))
24:     End Sub
25:     Function AddThisTwoNumbers(x,y)
26:         AddThisTwoNumbers = x + y
27:     End Function
```

```
28:              -->
29: </SCRIPT>
30: </HTML>
```

Figure 5.2.

Adding two num-bers by Sub *and* Function.

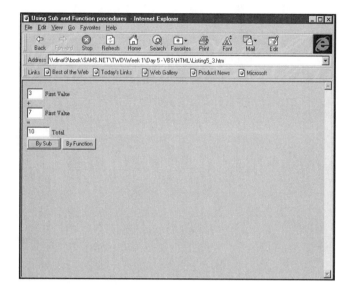

Passing Parameters from the INPUT Tag

Passing parameters to a function allows the function to be fairly generic and yet still accomplish its coding goal. An example is the AddthisTwoNumbers function from Listing 5.3, which takes any two numbers and adds them together. The first type of parameter passing is the kind used in Listing 5.3, where the INPUT type called a specific function with the appropriate values. This isn't true parameter passing, but you might want to use this kind of style. The second kind of parameter passing is the kind that VBScript supports internally.

An INPUT type can pass a parameter to the VBScript section of the page by following the sub-procedure name with a space and then the parameter. Listing 5.4 and Figure 5.3 illustrate passing parameters with the second method. This listing has a few new items. The first difference is that the <SCRIPT> section is after the <HEAD> section and before the <BODY> section (it shouldn't make any difference where the <SCRIPT> section goes).

The next difference is that the procedure onClick_Radio passes a parameter called radio_button_clicked. The parameter name could have been anything, but it's best to have it describe what's being passed. This procedure uses an If...then...else statement to control the flow of the procedure. Each radio button passes in a parameter (1 through 5) that determines what the procedure does. When the radio button is clicked, some text shows up in the text box at the bottom of the page.

5

The text written to the bottom of the page is going to be a date or type of date. In VBScript the Date function (which takes no parameters) returns the current system date and time. When you're executing this script on your client browser, the date is the client machine's date, not the server's date. The functions Month, Day, and Year take any date (Date) as a parameter and return the appropriate part of the date. The Time function returns the current system time.

Figure 5.3.

Passing parameters to the VBScript procedure.

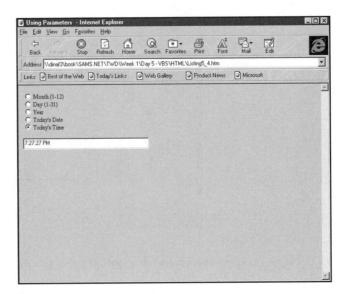

Listing 5.4. Passing parameters to the VBScript procedure.

```
 1: <HTML>
 2: <HEAD>
 3:     <TITLE>Passing Parameters </TITLE>
 4: <HEAD>
 5:
 6: <SCRIPT Language="VBScript">
 7: <!--
 8:     Sub onClick_Radio(radio_button_clicked)
 9:         If radio_button_clicked = 1 Then
10:             Total.value = Month(Date)
11:         Elseif radio_button_clicked = 2 Then
12:             Total.value = Day(Date)
13:         Elseif radio_button_clicked = 3 Then
14:             Total.value = Year(Date)
15:         Elseif radio_button_clicked = 4 Then
16:             Total.value = Date
17:         else
18:             Total.value = Time
19:         end if
20:     End Sub
21: -->
22: </SCRIPT>
23:
```

```
24: <BODY>
25:     <FORM NAME = "Now">
26:         <INPUT TYPE=RADIO NAME=Radio1
➥onClick="onClick_Radio 1">Month (1-12)<BR>
27:         <INPUT TYPE=RADIO NAME=Radio1
➥onClick="onClick_Radio 2">Day (1-31) <BR>
28:         <INPUT TYPE=RADIO NAME=Radio1
➥onClick="onClick_Radio 3">Year <BR>
29:         <INPUT TYPE=RADIO NAME=Radio1
➥onClick="onClick_Radio 4">Today's Date <BR>
30:         <INPUT TYPE=RADIO NAME=Radio1
➥onClick="onClick_Radio 5">Today's Time <BR>
31:     </FORM>
32:     <INPUT TYPE=TEXTBOX NAME=Total SIZE=50><BR>
33: </BODY>
34: </HTML>
```

TIP

> The VBScript interpreter seems to like having the script above the HTML when a parameter is being passed to the script from the HTML. If the script is below the HTML, and the HTML is passing a parameter, the interpreter may find an error on the parameter. In Listing 5.4 (if the script were after the HTML body), the error would look like Figure 5.4.

Figure 5.4.

A parameter error.

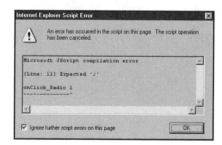

Declaring Variables

When declaring variables in VBScript, you don't need to specify the data type. VBScript supports the Variant type, which can support any numeric or text data. When declaring a variable such as my_variable, the variable name must be preceded by Dim, for *dimension*. The dimension keyword allocates enough space for the variable.

Listing 5.5 and Figure 5.5 illustrate declaring variables. This listing has some new elements. Using the Select statement allows a series of checks for different values. It's used when there are many choices. Using a `Select` statement doesn't have any added value over an `If...Then...Else` statement except that it's easier to read and executes faster. The value in the parentheses of `Select Case ()` determines which `Case` statement should be executed. The choices start with a numeric value 2, but could start with a string value, too.

> **TIP**
>
> The Boolean values of TRUE and FALSE usually disturb new programmers. Some programming languages assume that TRUE is any value other than zero or that it's any positive number. FALSE is almost universally considered to be zero. If you're programming in two languages and TRUE is different in each, you might program fewer bugs into your code if you always test against FALSE (zero).

The variable `data1` has the keyword `Dim` added at the beginning of the procedure. It's generally good coding style to declare any variables at the beginning of the procedure so that users can understand the variables and their purpose before they read the procedure.

The lines of code in the `Select` statement have a programmer's comments added. The comment in VBScript is denoted by the single quotation mark. Any text on the line after the single quote is ignored.

Figure 5.5.

Declaring variables.

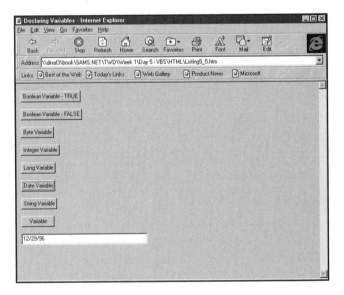

Listing 5.5. Declaring variables.

```
 1: <HTML>
 2:
 3: <HEAD>
 4:     <TITLE>Declaring Variables</TITLE>
 5: <HEAD>
 6:
 7: <SCRIPT Language="VBScript">
 8: <!--
 9:     Sub onClick_Button(datatype)
10:         Dim data1 'my first variable
11:
12:         Select Case (datatype)
13:             Case 2
14:                 data1 = TRUE
➥'True or False
15:             Case 3
16:                 data1 = FALSE
➥'True or False
17:             Case 4
18:                 data1 = 150
➥'0 to 255
19:             Case 5
20:                 data1 = -30000
➥'-32,768 to 32,767
21:             Case 6
22:                 data1 = 2000000
➥'-2,147,483,648 to 2,147,483,647
23:             Case 7
24:                 data1 = Date
25:             Case 8
26:                 data1 = "my name is Joe"
27:             Case Else
28:                 data1 = "no data type was chosen"
29:         End Select
30:
31:         VarValue.value = data1
32:     End Sub
33: -->
34: </SCRIPT>
35:
36: <BODY>
37:     <INPUT TYPE=BUTTON NAME=DimBool
➥Value="Boolean Variable - TRUE" onClick="onClick_Button 2"><P>
38:     <INPUT TYPE=BUTTON NAME=DimBool
➥Value="Boolean Variable - FALSE" onClick="onClick_Button 3"><P>
39:     <INPUT TYPE=BUTTON NAME=DimByte Value="Byte
➥Variable" onClick="onClick_Button 4"><P>
40:     <INPUT TYPE=BUTTON NAME=DimInt
➥Value="Integer Variable" onClick="onClick_Button 5"><P>
41:     <INPUT TYPE=BUTTON NAME=DimLong Value="Long
➥Variable" onClick="onClick_Button 6"><P>
```

continues

5

Listing 5.5. continued

```
42:        <INPUT TYPE=BUTTON NAME=DimDate Value="Date Variable"
➥onClick="onClick_Button 7"><P>
43:        <INPUT TYPE=BUTTON NAME=DimString
➥Value="String Variable" onClick="onClick_Button 8"><P>
44:        <INPUT TYPE=BUTTON NAME=Dim Value="Variable"
➥onClick="onClick_Button 20"><P>
45:        <INPUT TYPE=TEXTBOX NAME=VarValue size=50><BR>
46:    </BODY>
47: </HTML>
```

You can see a more realistic example of variables by examining how several variables are used in the script text and how the variable scope is used. *Scope* refers to where the variable is valid. If a variable is defined in the <SCRIPT> area but not in a procedure, it's considered *global* in the sense that any procedure has access to that variable. A variable defined inside a procedure is considered *local* because no other procedures can have access to that variable.

If the local and global variable have the same name, the local scope has precedence. Although you think you're changing the global variable (with the same name), you're actually changing the local variable.

Listing 5.6 and Figure 5.6 illustrate the concept of a variable's scope. There are two variables defined with the name myVar—one is global to any procedures, and the other is local to the procedure in which it's defined. There are three buttons and one text box. The first button chooses the first Select statement and prints out the global myVar value, which is set at the top of the procedure to be 1. It also prints out the text global so you know which variable you're accessing.

The second button chooses the second Select statement. Inside the statement, the second myVar is defined and the value of 5 is assigned. Then the text box is assigned the value of myVar. Because the scope of the local variable has precedence over the global variable, 5 is placed in the text box.

The third button goes to a different procedure that doesn't have any local variables. The procedure changes the global myVar to 10 and concatenates global.

The text should actually have the string 5 local. The + operator and the CStr function are used to do this. The CStr function converts the numeric value of 5 into a text value of 5, and the + operator concatenates the text value of local to the 5 string to get 5 local. This operation is called *string concatenation* and is fairly routine in the Visual Basic world.

Figure 5.6.

Variable scope.

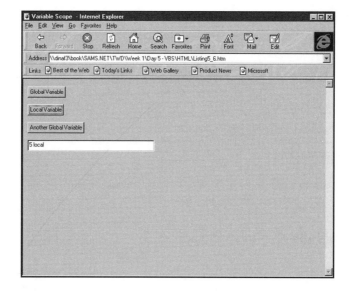

Listing 5.6. Variable scope.

```
 1: <HTML>
 2:
 3: <HEAD>
 4:     <TITLE> Variable Scope </Title>
 5: </HEAD>
 6:
 7: <SCRIPT Language="VBScript">
 8: <!--
 9:     Dim myVar    'global variable, any Sub or Function will have access to it
10:     myVar = 10
11:
12:     Sub onClick_Button(datatype)
13:
14:         myVar = 1  'set global variable equal to numeric 1
15:
16:         Select Case (datatype)
17:            Case 1
18:                Var.Value = CStr(myVar) + " global"
19:             Case 2
20:                Dim myVar
21:                myVar = 5
22:                Var.Value = CStr(myVar) + " local"
23:         End Select
24:     End Sub
25:     Sub onClick_AccessGlobal()
26:          Var.Value = CStr(myVar) +
➥" global" 'access the global variable, no local variable is defined
27:     End Sub
28: -->
29: </SCRIPT>
```

continues

5

Listing 5.6. continued

```
30:
31: <BODY>
32:        <INPUT TYPE=BUTTON NAME=DimGlobal
➥Value="Global Variable" onClick="onClick_Button 1"><P>
33:        <INPUT TYPE=BUTTON NAME=DimLocal
➥Value="Local Variable" onClick="onClick_Button 2"><P>
34:        <INPUT TYPE=BUTTON NAME=DimGlobal2 Value="Another Global Variable"
➥onClick="onClick_AccessGlobal"><P>
35: <INPUT TYPE=TEXTBOX NAME=Var size=50><BR>
36: </BODY>
37:
38: </HTML>
```

Helpful Functions

Visual Basic Script has many built-in functions to handle a variety of tasks, such as the Date function used in Listing 5.5 to automatically return the current date. There are several kinds of functions; some handle text and some handle numbers, and some are general functions, such as the Date function.

Text Functions

Text a user enters can be helpful, or can be completely wrong and harm any server-side applications. Listing 5.7 and Figure 5.7 show the Web page used to describe the text functions that VBScript supplies.

The page has two text boxes at the top, followed by 16 radio buttons, and then a text box at the bottom of the page. To demonstrate each of the functions, enter appropriate text into the first two text boxes and enable a radio button. The function executes and the result shows in the bottom text box.

Listing 5.7. Text functions.

```
1: <HTML>
2: <HEAD>
3:     <TITLE> String Functions </TITLE>
4: </HEAD>
5:
6: <BODY>
7: <INPUT TYPE=TEXTBOX NAME=Text1 size=50>First Text<P>
8: <INPUT TYPE=TEXTBOX NAME=Text2 size=50>Second Text<P>
9:
```

```
10: <OL>
11: <!-- 1  --> <LI> <INPUT TYPE=RADIO NAME=Window1
➥onClick="onClick_TextEqual">
12:              Does text 1 equal text 2
13: <!-- 2  --> <LI> <INPUT TYPE=RADIO NAME=Window1
➥onClick="onClick_TextNotEqual">
14:              Is text 1 Not Equal to text 2
15: <!-- 3  --> <LI> <INPUT TYPE=RADIO NAME=Window1
➥onClick="onClick_TextAdd">
16:              Text 1 + Text 2
17: <!-- 4  --> <LI> <INPUT TYPE=RADIO NAME=Window1
18:              onClick="onClick_TextFirstCharacter">
19:              Numeric value of first Character of Text 1
20: <!-- 5  --> <LI> <INPUT TYPE=RADIO NAME=Window1
21:              onClick="onClick_TextFirstCharacterAsASCII">
➥ASCII value of 100
22: <!-- 6  --> <LI> <INPUT TYPE=RADIO NAME=Window1
➥onClick="onClick_TextSearch">
23:              Find text 2 in text 1
24: <!-- 7  --> <LI> <INPUT TYPE=RADIO NAME=Window1
➥onClick="onClick_TextLength">
25:              Length of first text
26: <!-- 8  --> <LI> <INPUT TYPE=RADIO NAME=Window1
➥onClick="onClick_TextLeft">
27:              First two left characters of text 1
28: <!-- 9  --> <LI> <INPUT TYPE=RADIO NAME=Window1
➥onClick="onClick_TextRight">
29:              Last two right characters of text 1
30: <!-- 10 --> <LI> <INPUT TYPE=RADIO NAME=Window1
➥onClick="onClick_TextMid">
31:              Middle two characters of text 1
32: <!-- 11 --> <LI> <INPUT TYPE=RADIO NAME=Window1
➥onClick="onClick_TextStrCmp">
33:              Compare two strings
34: <!-- 12 --> <LI> <INPUT TYPE=RADIO NAME=Window1
➥onClick="onClick_TextLeftTrim">
35:              Trim text 1 of spaces from left
36: <!-- 13 --> <LI> <INPUT TYPE=RADIO NAME=Window1
➥onClick="onClick_TextRightTrim">
37:              Trim text 1 of spaces from right
38: <!-- 14 --> <LI> <INPUT TYPE=RADIO NAME=Window1
➥onClick="onClick_TextAllTrim">
39:              Trim text 1 of spaces from left and right
40: <!-- 15 --> <LI> <INPUT TYPE=RADIO NAME=Window1
➥onClick="onClick_TextLowercase">
41:              Convert text 1 to all lowercase
42: <!-- 16 --> <LI> <INPUT TYPE=RADIO NAME=Window1
➥onClick="onClick_TextUppercase">
43:              Convert text 1 to all uppercase
44: </OL>
45: <P>
46: <INPUT TYPE=TEXTBOX NAME=Answer size=100>Answer<P>
47: </BODY>
48:
```

5

continues

Listing 5.7. continued

```
49: <SCRIPT Language="VBScript">
50: <!--
51:     Sub onClick_TextEqual()
52:         if(Text1.Value = Text2.Value) Then
53:             Answer.Value = "TRUE"
54:         else
55:             Answer.Value = "FALSE"
56:         end if
57:     End Sub
58:     Sub onClick_TextNotEqual()
59:         if(Text1.Value <> Text2.Value) Then
60:             Answer.Value = "TRUE"
61:         else
62:             Answer.Value = "FALSE"
63:         end if
64:     End Sub
65:     Sub onClick_TextAdd()
66:         Answer.Value = Text1.Value + Text2.Value
67:     End Sub
68:     Sub onClick_TextFirstCharacter()
69:         Answer.Value = asc(Text1.Value)
70:     End Sub
71:     Sub onClick_TextFirstCharacterAsASCII()
72:         Answer.Value = chr(100)
73:     End Sub
74:     Sub onClick_TextSearch()
75:         Answer.Value = Instr(Text1.Value,Text2.Value)
76:     End Sub
77:     Sub onClick_TextLength()
78:         Answer.Value = len(Text1.Value)
79:     End Sub
80:     Sub onClick_TextLeft()
81:         Answer.Value = Left(Text1.Value, 2)
82:     End Sub
83:     Sub onClick_TextRight()
84:         Answer.Value = Right(Text1.Value, 2)
85:     End Sub
86:     Sub onClick_TextMid()
87:         Answer.Value = Mid(Text1.Value, 2, 2)
88:     End Sub
89:     Sub onClick_TextStrCmp()
90:         Answer.Value = StrComp(Text1.Value,Text2.Value)
91:     End Sub
92:     Sub onClick_TextLeftTrim()
93:         Answer.Value = Ltrim(Text1.Value)
94:     End Sub
95:     Sub onClick_TextRightTrim()
96:         Answer.Value = Rtrim(Text1.Value)
97:     End Sub
98:     Sub onClick_TextAllTrim()
99:         Answer.Value = trim(Text1.Value)
100:    End Sub
```

5

```
101:    Sub onClick_TextLowercase()
102:        Answer.Value = Lcase(Text1.Value)
103:    End Sub
104:    Sub onClick_TextUppercase()
105:        Answer.Value = Ucase(Text1.Value)
106:    End Sub
107:  -->
108:  </SCRIPT>
109:  </HTML>
```

Figure 5.7.

Text functions.

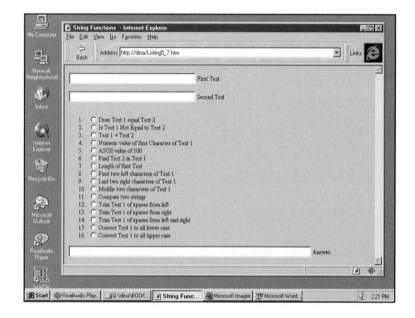

The first function (onClick_TextEqual) uses the comparison operator(=) to see whether the two strings are equal. If the two strings are dog and dog, then TRUE is printed in the Answer text box. If the two strings are dog and dog (there's a space after the *g*), the Answer text box prints FALSE. This function is a good way to verify an exact match of text.

The second function (onClick_TextNotEqual) is the opposite of the first function. The not equal operator is the left and right arrows (<>). The function returns TRUE (-1) if the two text strings aren't equal and FALSE (0) if the two text strings are equal. If the two text boxes have dog and dog , the Answer box is TRUE. If the two text boxes have dog and dog, the Answer box is FALSE.

The third function (onClick_TextAdd) uses the string concatenation operator +. When two strings are added together, they become one string. If dog and cat are concatenated, the Answer box is dogcat. Many strings can be concatenated, as shown in this example:

```
Answer.Value = "my dog's" + " name" + " is" + " spot"
```

The fourth function (onClick_TextFirstCharacter) uses the asc function, which returns the numeric equivalent of the character. All English characters have a numeric equivalent on the ASCII chart. The character *d* returns 100; *D* returns 68.

The fifth function (onClick_TextFirstCharacterAsASCII) is the opposite of the asc function. This function uses the chr function to convert the numeric value of a character into the character. For example, chr(100) returns d in the Answer text box.

The sixth function (onClick_TextSearch) uses the Instr function, which searches the first string to see whether the second string is in it. If the first string is mydog and the second string is og, the function returns 4, meaning that the second string can be found in the first string, starting at the fourth character of the first string. If the two strings are dog and cat, the function returns 0, meaning that the second string can't be found in the first string.

The seventh function (onClick_TextLength) uses the len function to determine how many characters are in the string. The string mydog returns 5, and the string my dog has fleas returns 18. The spaces are counted, too, as well as the characters.

The eighth function (onClick_TextLeft) uses the left function, which returns the number of characters specified, beginning from the left side of the string. If the code is left('mydog', 2), the function returns my. If the code is left('mydog'), the function returns the entire string mydog.

The ninth function (onClick_TextRight) uses the right function. This function returns the number of characters specified, beginning from the right side of the string. If the code is right('mydog',2), the function returns og.

The tenth function (onClick_TextMid) uses the mid function, which returns any number of characters from anywhere in the string. The function has to know what character to begin with and how many characters to read from that point. If the code was mid('mydog is ralph', 7, 2), the function returns is. I is the seventh character and beginning with the I, the function reads for two characters.

The eleventh function (onClick_TextStrCmp) uses the StrComp function to compare two strings. This function is a bit different from the equal operator =. The equal operator just returns TRUE or FALSE, but this function goes one step further to relate the two strings. If the two strings are exactly the same (dog and dog), the function returns 0. If the first string is closer to the front of the alphabet than the second, the function returns -1. If the first string is closer to the end of the alphabet than the second string, the function returns 1. If the first string is dog and the second string is cat (*c* is before *d*), the function returns 1. If the first string is 5 and the second string is b, the function returns –1 because numbers are before letters.

The twelfth function (onClick_TextLeftTrim) uses the ltrim function to trim any spaces from the left side of the string. If the string is dog, no spaces are in the string, so the original string is returned. If the string is dog , the function returns dog . The space after the *g* isn't trimmed.

The thirteenth function (onClick_TextRightTrim) uses the rtrim function to trim spaces from the right side of the string, so dog is trimmed to dog.

The fourteenth function (onClick_TextAllTrim) uses the trim function to trim any spaces from the string on the left and right sides. If the text is my dog is ralph , the function returns my dog is ralph.

The fifteenth function (onClick_TextLowercase) uses the lcase function to convert any uppercase characters into lowercase letters. The string mY Dog would be converted into my dog.

The sixteenth function (onClick_TextUppercase) uses the ucase function to convert any lowercase characters into uppercase letters. The string mY Dog would be converted into MY DOG.

Validation Functions

There are some functions that validate certain information. Assume that you expect a user to enter a number, but she enters text instead. You could validate that she hasn't entered a number and return to the page, letting the user know you expected a number.

Listing 5.8 and Figure 5.8 illustrate the validation routines. This Web page has two radio buttons at the top, five radio buttons in the middle, and a text box at the bottom. The first two radio buttons let the user choose the parameter to the validation function. If you choose to return TRUE, the parameter to the validation function is correct and the function returns TRUE.

The five middle radio buttons are the type of validation routines available. The text box at the bottom prints a -1 for TRUE and a 0 for FALSE. The global variables are as follows: True1 to indicate a valid or invalid parameter, myArray declared as an array of five elements, myDate with the current date set by the Date() function, myEmptyVariable with nothing in it, myNullVariable set to NULL (or nothing), and myNumeric set to the value of 5. Each valid parameter uses the correct variable, and each invalid parameter uses a different variable to get the FALSE returned.

The first function (onClick_IsArray) uses the IsArray function to determine whether the parameter passed to it is an *array*, which is a list of elements. Declaring a variable with parentheses, such as (5), would give your variable five elements. These elements could be numbers, such as days of the month (20, 1, 15, 5, 10), or the elements could be text (Monday, Tuesday, Wednesday, Thursday, Friday). If the variable passed to IsArray is just a single element declared without the parentheses, it returns FALSE, indicating that the variable isn't an array.

The second function (onClick_IsDate) uses the IsDate function to determine whether the parameter passed to it is a date.

The third function (onClick_IsEmpty) uses the IsEmpty function to determine whether the parameter passed to it has ever been initialized. A variable is initialized when it's set to a value. By setting the myDate variable to the Date function, it's initialized; by setting the myNullVariable to NULL, it's initialized to NULL.

The fourth function (onClick_IsNull) uses the IsNull function to determine whether the parameter is equal to NULL. If the variable is equal to a number or a string, it returns FALSE, indicating that data is currently in the variable.

The fifth function (onClick_IsNumeric) uses the IsNumeric function to determine whether a variable is a numeric value. This is a good way to distinguish between text and numeric data.

Figure 5.8.

Validation functions.

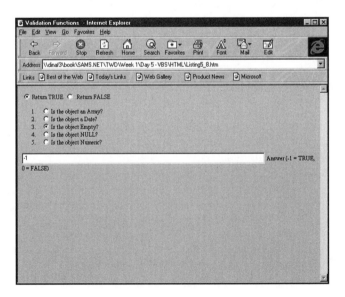

5

Listing 5.8. Validation functions.

```
 1: <HTML>
 2: <HEAD>
 3:     <TITLE> Validation Functions </TITLE>
 4: </HEAD>
 5:
 6: <SCRIPT Language="VBScript">
 7: <!--
 8:     Dim True1
 9:     Dim myArray(5)
10:     Dim myDate
11:     Dim myEmptyVariable
12:     Dim myNullVariable
13:     Dim myNumeric
14:
15:     myDate = Date
16:     myNullVariable = NULL
17:     myNumeric = 5
18:
19:     Sub onClick_IsTrue(istrue)
20:         if(istrue = 1) then
21:             True1 = TRUE
22:         else
23:             True1 = FALSE
24:         end if
25:     End Sub
26:     Sub onClick_IsArray()
27:         if(True1) then
28:             Answer.Value = IsArray(myArray)
29:         else
30:             Answer.Value = IsArray(myNumeric)
31:         end if
32:     End Sub
33:     Sub onClick_IsDate()
34:         if(True1) then
35:             Answer.Value = IsDate(myDate)
36:         else
37:             Answer.Value = IsArray(myEmptyVariable)
38:         end if
39:     End Sub
40:     Sub onClick_IsEmpty()
41:         if(True1) then
42:             Answer.Value = IsEmpty(myEmptyVariable)
43:         else
44:             Answer.Value = IsEmpty(myNumeric)
45:         end if
46:     End Sub
47:     Sub onClick_IsNull()
48:         if(True1) then
49:             Answer.Value = IsNull(myNullVariable)
50:         else
51:             Answer.Value = IsNull(myNumeric)
52:         end if
53:     End Sub
```

5

continues

Listing 5.8. continued

```
54:    Sub onClick_IsNumeric()
55:       if(True1) then
56:          Answer.Value = IsNumeric(myNumeric)
57:       else
58:          Answer.Value = IsNumeric(myDate)
59:       end if
60:    End Sub
61: -->
62: </SCRIPT>
63:
64: <BODY>
65: <INPUT TYPE=RADIO NAME=TRUE1 onClick="onClick_IsTrue 1">
66:             Return TRUE
67: <INPUT TYPE=RADIO NAME=TRUE1 onClick="onClick_IsTrue 0">
68:             Return FALSE
69:
70: <OL>
71: <!-- 1  --> <LI> <INPUT TYPE=RADIO
➥NAME=Window1 onClick="onClick_IsArray">
72:             Is the object an Array?
73: <!-- 2  --> <LI> <INPUT TYPE=RADIO
➥NAME=Window1 onClick="onClick_IsDate">
74:             Is the object a Date?
75: <!-- 3  --> <LI> <INPUT TYPE=RADIO
➥NAME=Window1 onClick="onClick_IsEmpty">
76:             Is the object Empty?
77: <!-- 4  --> <LI> <INPUT TYPE=RADIO
➥NAME=Window1 onClick="onClick_IsNull">
78:             Is the object NULL?
79: <!-- 5  --> <LI> <INPUT TYPE=RADIO
➥NAME=Window1 onClick="onClick_IsNumeric">
80:             Is the object Numeric?
81: </OL>
82: <P>
83: <INPUT TYPE=TEXTBOX NAME=Answer size=100>
➥Answer (-1 = TRUE, 0 = FALSE)<P>
84: </BODY>
85:
86:
87: </HTML>
```

The Object Hierarchy

The HTML object model shown in Figure 5.9 allows the VBScript to manipulate the objects in the browser window. By having access to all the contents of the browser and the HTML page, you can manipulate what the client sees and when. Most objects have three categories of functionality: properties, methods, and events. The HTML objects contain properties, such as name and current value. The objects also have methods, such as Open or Close, that act on the object. You must choose when a method is executed. The objects also have events, which are executed when some particular "event" occurs, such as OnLoad, which occurs when the page is first loaded. Some properties, methods, and events can apply to more than one object, such as the Name property. Every object has the Name property.

Figure 5.9.

The HTML object model.

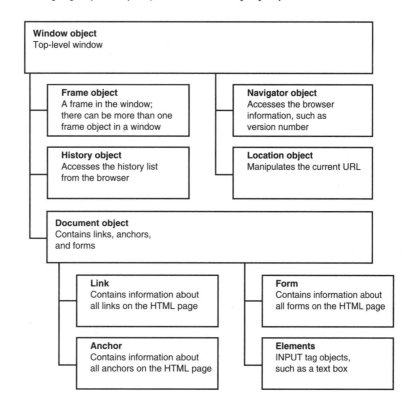

To maneuver through the object model, you must use the VB notation of object.property, such as window.name. In this example, the period between window and name is used to denote which element of the window object you're acting on. The hierarchy works so that the top element gives you access to the elements beneath, and so on. You can get to an element of a form with the following notation: window.document.form.element (this isn't the exact syntax but is meant to give you an idea of how the hierarchy works).

A property of an object is just denoted with the property name, such as Name, but methods and events can have parameters. An example of calling a method or event is object.method() or object.event(); any parameters are passed in the parentheses. If an object is in scope, such as the current window, the object name window doesn't have to be used. A property of the window can be accessed by just using the Name property. However, you need to use the entire object path when you want the name of a window other than the current one.

The Window **Object**

The Window object is the top-level object. Every window contains the Frame, History, Navigator, Location, and Document objects. However, if there are no frames in the window, the Frame object can be empty.

The Window object represents the browser window. The properties, methods, and events of the Window object can be executed from a VBScript.

Table 5.1 lists the properties of the Window object. If you have programmed in Visual Basic, these properties should be familiar. Some of these properties are read-only (you can't set the property), such as the Parent window. Other properties, such as Status, can be set.

Table 5.2 lists the methods of the Window object, and Table 5.3 lists its events.

Table 5.1. Window **properties.**

Property	Description
Name	Current window's name
Parent	Current window's parent
Opener	Window that opened current window
Self	Returns the current window object
Top	Topmost window
Location	Returns Location object
DefaultStatus	Sets the default status (in status bar)
Status	Sets the current status (in status bar)
Frames	Returns an array of Frame objects
History	Returns the History object of the current window
Navigator	Returns the Navigator object of the current window
Document	Returns the Document object of the current window

Table 5.2. Window **methods.**

Methods	Description
Alert	Displays a message box for an alert (OK)
Confirm	Displays a message box with OK or Cancel
Prompt	Prompts the user for input
Open	Opens a window

Methods	Description
Close	Closes a window
SetTimeout	Sets the timeout
ClearTimeout	Clears the timeout
Navigate	Moves the window to a new URL

Table 5.3. Window **events.**

Events	Description
OnLoad	Action to happen when window is loaded
OnUnload	Action to happen when window is unloaded

By controlling a window, you can change what page is visible in the browser. Listing 5.9 and Figure 5.10 illustrate two objectives. The first objective is determining how easy it is to control the browser window. The second objective is that the rest of the chapter uses frames to see the control more clearly. This listing has a button. When the button is clicked, it automatically loads the default Microsoft Corporation Web page.

The listing makes use of the Window object and its Location object by changing the HREF that the window loaded. This is a powerful feature. To show what each window is doing, the examples in the rest of the chapter use a framed page.

Figure 5.10.

A simple Window *object.*

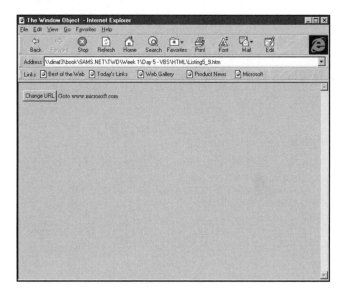

Listing 5.9. A simple `Window` object.

```
<HTML>
<HEAD>
    <TITLE> The Simple Window Object </TITLE>
</HEAD>

<SCRIPT Language="VBScript">
<!--
    Sub onClick_Button
        window.location.href="http://www.microsoft.com"
    End Sub
-->
</SCRIPT>

<BODY>
<INPUT TYPE=BUTTON VALUE="Change URL"
➥onClick="onClick_Button">Goto www.microsoft.com
</BODY>
</HTML>
```

Listing 5.10 and Figure 5.11 are the framed page, with the page broken up into two columns. The first column takes up 30 percent of the window, and the second column takes up 70 percent of the window. The first column shows the table of contents (TOC.HTM), and the second column displays whatever is chosen from the table of contents.

In Listing 5.10, notice that there is no `<BODY>` tag—it has been replaced with the frame tag `<Frame>`. `RIGHT.HTM` is just a placeholder and can be an empty Web page.

Listing 5.11 is the TOC.HTM. When the button is clicked, the top window's second frame (an array starts at `0`, so `1` would be the second element) now has a new HREF. The page then changes to the referenced Web page.

Listing 5.10. The framed page.

```
<HTML>
<HEAD>
    <TITLE> The Framed Window </TITLE>
</HEAD>

<FRAMESET COLS="30%,70%" FRAMEBORDER=1>
    <FRAME NAME="TOC" SRC="TOC.HTM">
    <FRAME NAME="DISPLAY" SRC="RIGHT.HTM">
</FRAMESET>
</HTML>
```

Figure 5.11.

The framed page.

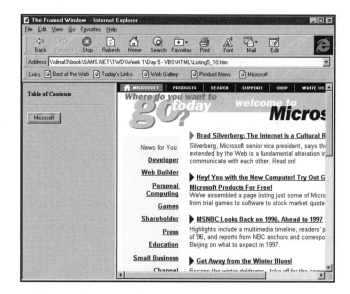

Listing 5.11. The table of contents.

```
<HTML>
<HEAD>
    <TITLE> Table of Contents </TITLE>
</HEAD>

<SCRIPT Language="VBScript">
<!--
    Sub onClick_MS()
    top.Frames(1).Location.HREF=
➥"http://www.microsoft.com"
    End Sub
-->
</SCRIPT>

<BODY>
    <B> Table of Contents
    <HR>
    <INPUT TYPE=BUTTON VALUE="Microsoft"
➥onClick="onClick_MS">
</BODY>
</HTML>
```

5

The Frames Object

The Frames object is just an array of frames. The first frame (the first frame listed in FRAMESET) is Frames(0), and the second frame in the frames array is Frames(1). Because Frame is a subclass of Window, it has the same properties, methods, and events as Window.

The History Object

The History object gives you access to the Web pages in the history list. You can access this list through VBScript. Microsoft Internet Explorer keeps a list of Web pages you have viewed; you can travel through that list with the arrow keys on the toolbar. This feature can also be used in your VBScript by using the properties in Table 5.4 and the methods in Table 5.5.

Table 5.4. History properties.

Property	Description
Length	Number of Web pages in history list

Table 5.5. History methods.

Methods	Description
Back	Loads the previous Web page in history list
Forward	Loads the next Web page in history list
Go	Loads a specific Web page in the history list

To use this object, surf through some Web pages. The main page for this is Listing 5.10, the frame page. The TOC.HTM is changed to Listing 5.12. This page navigates through the history list. The script has three buttons for Forward, Back, and Go that put the referenced history page into the right-hand frame.

Listing 5.12. The table of contents with the History object.

```
<HTML>
<HEAD>
    <TITLE> Table of Contents with the History Object</TITLE>
</HEAD>
```

```
<SCRIPT Language="VBScript">
<!--
    Sub onClick_Forward()
        top.Frames(1).location.href=top.Frames(1).history.forward
    End Sub
    Sub onClick_Back()
        top.Frames(1).location.href=top.Frames(1).history.back
    End Sub
    Sub onClick_Go()
        top.Frames(1).location.href=top.Frames(1).history.go(1)
    End Sub
-->
</SCRIPT>

<BODY>
    <B> Table of Contents
    <HR>
    <INPUT TYPE=BUTTON VALUE="Forward" onClick="onClick_Forward">
    <INPUT TYPE=BUTTON VALUE="Back" onClick="onClick_Back">
    <INPUT TYPE=BUTTON VALUE="Go" onClick="onClick_Go">
</BODY>
</HTML>
```

The Navigator Object

The Navigator object has information about the browser being used, including the version number and application name. Table 5.6 lists the properties for the Navigator object, which doesn't have any methods or events.

Table 5.6. Navigator **properties.**

Property	Description
AppCodename	Browser's code name
AppName	Browser's released name
AppVersion	Browser's version
UserAgent	Browser's user agent

Copy Listing 5.13 into the TOC.HTM page. The table of contents contains one button and four text boxes. Each text box is a piece of the Navigator information.

Figure 5.12 illustrates what the page looks like after the button is clicked; it's generally information passed to the server in the header block.

Figure 5.12.

*Table of contents with
the* Navigator
object.

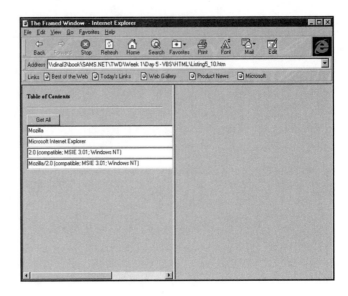

Listing 5.13. Table of contents with the Navigator object.

```
<HTML>
<HEAD>
    <TITLE> Table of Contents with the Navigator Object</TITLE>
</HEAD>

<SCRIPT Language="VBScript">
<!--
    Sub onLoad_Fill()
        NavText1.Value=window.navigator.appCodeName
        NavText2.Value=window.navigator.appName
        NavText3.Value=window.navigator.appVersion
        NavText4.Value=window.navigator.userAgent
    End Sub
-->
</SCRIPT>

<BODY>
    <B> Table of Contents
    <HR>
    <INPUT TYPE=Button Value="Get All" onClick="onLoad_Fill">
    <INPUT TYPE=TEXTBOX NAME="NavText1" SIZE=100>
    <INPUT TYPE=TEXTBOX NAME="NavText2" SIZE=100>
    <INPUT TYPE=TEXTBOX NAME="NavText3" SIZE=100>
    <INPUT TYPE=TEXTBOX NAME="NavText4" SIZE=100>
</BODY>
</HTML>
```

The Location **Object**

The Location object controls the current URL. Each part of the object can be controlled separately. Table 5.7 lists all the properties of the URL. You can get or set these properties.

Table 5.7. Location **properties.**

Property	Description
Href	Complete URL
Protocol	Protocol portion of the URL (such as HTTP or FTP)
Host	Controls the host and port portions of the URL
Hostname	Either name or IP address of host
Port	Port of the URL
Pathname	Path from root of Web site
Search	Any parameters
Hash	Hash portion of URL

Listing 5.14 and Figure 5.13 illustrate what the Location information looks like for http://www.microsoft.com/msoffice. Listing 5.14 should be copied over the old TOC.HTM. The button loads the Web page into the right-hand frame, and then loads the location information into the text boxes in the left side of the frames.

Figure 5.13.

Table of contents with the Location *object.*

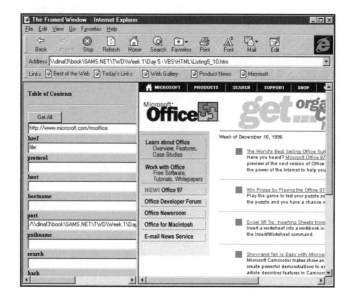

Listing 5.14. Table of contents with the Location object.

```
 1: <HTML>
 2: <HEAD>
 3:     <TITLE> Table of Contents with the History Object</TITLE>
 4: </HEAD>
 5:
 6: <SCRIPT Language="VBScript">
 7: <!--
 8:     Sub onLoad_Fill()
 9:         top.Frames(1).location.href=
➥"http://www.microsoft.com/msoffice"
10:         NavText1.Value= top.Frames(1).location.href
11:         NavText2.Value= top.Frames(1).location.protocol
12:         NavText3.Value= top.Frames(1).location.host
13:         NavText4.Value= top.Frames(1).location.hostname
14:         NavText5.Value= top.Frames(1).location.port
15:         NavText6.Value= top.Frames(1).location.pathname
16:         NavText7.Value= top.Frames(1).location.search
17:         NavText8.Value= top.Frames(1).location.hash
18:     End Sub
19: -->
20: </SCRIPT>
21:
22: <BODY>
23:     <B> Table of Contents
24:     <HR>
25:     <INPUT TYPE=Button Value="Get All" onClick="onLoad_Fill">
26:     <INPUT TYPE=TEXTBOX NAME="NavText1" SIZE=100>href
27:     <INPUT TYPE=TEXTBOX NAME="NavText2" SIZE=100>protocol
28:     <INPUT TYPE=TEXTBOX NAME="NavText3" SIZE=100>host
29:     <INPUT TYPE=TEXTBOX NAME="NavText4" SIZE=100>hostname
30:     <INPUT TYPE=TEXTBOX NAME="NavText5" SIZE=100>port
31:     <INPUT TYPE=TEXTBOX NAME="NavText6" SIZE=100>pathname
32:     <INPUT TYPE=TEXTBOX NAME="NavText7" SIZE=100>search
33:     <INPUT TYPE=TEXTBOX NAME="NavText8" SIZE=100>hash
34: </BODY>
35:
36: </HTML>
```

The Document Object

The Document object is the most complex object in the hierarchy. The HTML Web page content is contained in this object. With the Document object, script can control the colors, links, anchors, and forms in the document. Table 5.8 lists the Document properties, and Table 5.9 lists the Document methods.

Table 5.8. Document **properties.**

Property	Description
LinkColor	Color of links in a document
ALinkColor	Color of active link (clicked but not released)
VLinkColor	Color of visited links
BgColor	Background color
FgColor	Foreground color
Anchors	Array of anchors in document
Links	Array of links in document
Forms	Array of forms in document
Location	Location object (read-only)
LastModified	Date the page was last modified
Title	Title of page (<TITLE> tag)
Cookie	Cookie of document
Referrer	URL of referring document

Table 5.9. Document **methods.**

Method	Description
Write	Appends text to document
WriteLn	Appends new line character to document
Open	Opens document for output
Close	Updates window with all text written to document after it was last open
Clear	Closes document and updates display of the page

5

The Anchor, Link, and Form objects are discussed later in this chapter; the Location object was discussed earlier.

At the document level, there are two cool things you can do—control the color of the document, and control the content of the document. Currently, controlling the document's colors is already provided for in HTML, but controlling the content of the document through script gives a Web page programmer much more flexibility than a static page does.

A browser generally has default values for the objects that can have color, such as a link, but this can be changed in your code. Listing 5.15 and Figure 5.14 illustrate the control you can have over the colors of a Web page. Listing 5.15 should be copied into the TOC.HTM.

Figure 5.14.

Table of contents with the Document *object.*

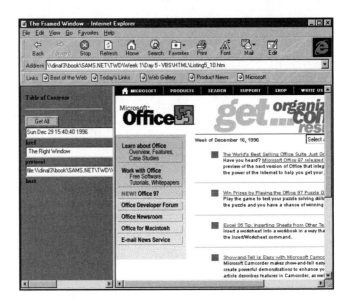

Listing 5.15. Table of contents with the Document object.

```
<HTML>
<HEAD>
    <TITLE> Table of Contents with the Document Object</TITLE>
</HEAD>

<SCRIPT Language="VBScript">
<!--
    Sub onLoad_Fill()
        top.Frames(1).location.href=
        ➥"http://www.microsoft.com/msoffice"
        top.Frames(0).document.linkColor = "navy"
        top.Frames(0).document.aLinkColor = "black"
        top.Frames(0).document.vLinkColor = "white"
        top.Frames(0).document.bgColor = "red"

        NavText1.Value= top.Frames(1).document.lastModified
        NavText2.Value= top.Frames(1).document.title
        NavText3.Value= top.Frames(1).document.referrer
    End Sub
-->
</SCRIPT>

<BODY>
```

```
     <B> Table of Contents
     <HR>
     <INPUT TYPE=Button Value="Get All" onClick="onLoad_Fill">
     <INPUT TYPE=TEXTBOX NAME="NavText1" SIZE=100>href
     <INPUT TYPE=TEXTBOX NAME="NavText2" SIZE=100>protocol
     <INPUT TYPE=TEXTBOX NAME="NavText3" SIZE=100>host
</BODY>

</HTML>
```

The Link Object

The Link object is an array of links, similar to the Frames object, containing an array of frames. Each <A> tag that contains an HREF attribute is considered a *link*. The first link of the document is document.links(0). Table 5.10 lists the Link array properties, and Table 5.11 lists the Link array events.

Table 5.10. Link properties.

Property	Description
Href	Complete URL
Protocol	Protocol portion of the URL (such as HTTP or FTP)
Host	Controls the host and port portions of the URL
Hostname	Either name or IP address of host
Port	Port of the URL
Pathname	Path from root of Web site
Search	Any parameters
Target	Target of the link (such as the FRAME name)
Hash	Hash portion of URL

Table 5.11. Link events.

Method	Description
OnMouseMove	Event is fired when cursor moves over the link
OnMouseOver	Event is fired when cursor is over the link
OnClick	Event is fired when link is clicked

5

Listing 5.16 and Figure 5.15 illustrate the information you can get from the Link object. Listing 5.16 should be copied into the TOC.HTM file. Notice that because the listing has only one link, the reference in the script is links(0). Also notice that the target is the second frame named from Listing 5.10, DISPLAY.

Figure 5.15.

Table of contents with the Link object.

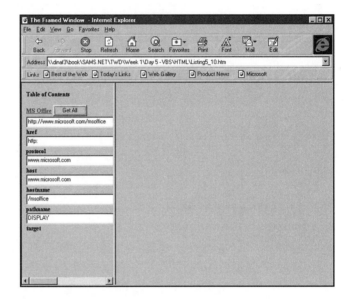

Listing 5.16. Table of contents with the Link object.

```
 1: <HTML>
 2: <HEAD>
 3:     <TITLE> Table of Contents with the Link Object</TITLE>
 4: </HEAD>
 5:
 6: <SCRIPT Language="VBScript">
 7: <!--
 8:     Sub onLoad_Fill()
 9:         NavText1.Value= document.links(0).href
10:         NavText2.Value= document.links(0).protocol
11:         NavText3.Value= document.links(0).host
12:         NavText4.Value= document.links(0).hostname
13:         NavText6.Value= document.links(0).pathname
14:         NavText8.Value= document.links(0).target
15:     End Sub
16: -->
17: </SCRIPT>
18:
19: <BODY>
20:     <B> Table of Contents
```

```
21:     <P>
22:     <A HREF="http://www.microsoft.com/msoffice"
➥TARGET="DISPLAY">MS Office</A>
23:     <INPUT TYPE=Button Value="Get All" onClick="onLoad_Fill">
24:     <INPUT TYPE=TEXTBOX NAME="NavText1" SIZE=100>href
25:     <INPUT TYPE=TEXTBOX NAME="NavText2" SIZE=100>protocol
26:     <INPUT TYPE=TEXTBOX NAME="NavText3" SIZE=100>host
27:     <INPUT TYPE=TEXTBOX NAME="NavText4" SIZE=100>hostname
28:     <INPUT TYPE=TEXTBOX NAME="NavText6" SIZE=100>pathname
29:     <INPUT TYPE=TEXTBOX NAME="NavText8" SIZE=100>target
30: </BODY>
31:
32: </HTML>
```

The Anchor **Object**

The only property of the Anchor object is Name. The Anchor object is also an array, so the name of the first anchor is document.anchors(0).name.

The Form **Object**

The Form object is an array of all forms held in a document, but the forms can also be referred to by name. The elements of a form are the <INPUT> tags. Table 5.12 lists the properties of the form, Table 5.13 lists the only event for the form, and Table 5.14 lists the only method for the form. By making a Submit method, the script can fire off the submit without the page having a Submit button (<INPUT TYPE=SUBMIT>).

Table 5.12. Form **properties.**

Property	Description
Action	Address of the URL
Encoding	Valid MIME type
Method	GET or POST
Target	Target of the returned page
Elements	Array of form elements

Table 5.13. Form **events.**

Event	Description
OnSubmit	Event is fired when Submit button is clicked

5

Table 5.14. Form **methods.**

Method	Description
Submit	Submits the form to the Web server

The Element **Object**

Elements of a form are considered to be any <INPUT> tags or any <OBJECT> tags. <OBJECT> tags are used for ActiveX controls discussed in the next chapter. Because a form can have many <INPUT> tags, the <INPUT> tag can be accessed through an array or by name. Some of the properties depend on what type of element you're referring to. A text box has a length of characters that's acceptable, but a checkbox doesn't. Table 5.15 shows the Element properties, Table 5.16 shows the Element events, and Table 5.17 shows the Element methods.

Table 5.15. Element **properties.**

Property	Description
Form	Name of form
Name	Name of element
Value	Value of element
DefaultValue	Default value
Checked	Checked value
DefaultChecked	Element checked by default
Length	Length of element
Options	Options of element
SelectedIndex	Selected index of element

Table 5.16. Element **events.**

Events	Description
OnClick	Event is fired when element is clicked
OnFocus	Event is fired when element is in focus
OnBlur	Event is fired when element is blurred
OnChange	Event is fired when element is changed
OnSelect	Event is fired when element is selected

5

Table 5.17. `Element` **methods.**

Method	Description
Click	Forces element to be clicked
Focus	Forces element to have focus
Blur	Forces element to be blurred
Select	Forces element to be selected

Differences Between Visual Basic and VBScript

VBScript is a very "slim" version of Visual Basic. It's not meant to recreate an entire programming language, but to give you enough flexibility to control the browser.

VBScript supports only one type (`Variant`), but Visual Basic supports most of the common programming language types. There's no control to the Clipboard in VBScript. Collections can't be numbered or referred to with the ! symbol, and there's no conditional compilation in VBScript. There are no intrinsic contents and no line numbers or line labels. There's no intrinsic debugging, but new development environments are being released (such as Microsoft's Internet Development Studio). There's no file I/O and there are no financial functions. All graphics functions have been removed, and most functions that end with the dollar sign have been removed.

Summary

This chapter has given you a basic understanding of VBScript. This language is just the beginning of controlling the browser on the client side. You can control how the page is manipulated by where and how you write your script. You can also control the page with VBScript functions that do the most common work for you. You can also access the object collections to manipulate the page. In the next chapter, ActiveX controls are added to the VBScript you just learned.

Q&A

Q How can I make sure a user fills in a form before submitting it?

A You can use a validation routine.

Q What's a good name for a subprocedure created for the `OnClick` event of a button named Yes?

A `OnClick_Yes`

Quiz

1. What's the syntax for passing parameters to a subprocedure?
2. What Link property gives you the name of the frame a page was opened into?
3. Why do some of the objects contain arrays?
4. What is VBScript?
5. What is the tag that enables scripting, and how can you make sure any non–script-supporting browser can still read your page?
6. What is the topmost object of the object model?

Exercises

Design a Web page that sets and accesses some of the objects from the object hierarchy.

Day 6

Using an ActiveX Control

by Dina Fleet

ActiveX controls give a Web page the look and behavior of a more typical Windows application and extend the ability of what the browser can do. This chapter covers what you need to know to use ActiveX controls on your Web pages. It doesn't, however, cover how to create ActiveX controls; that's beyond the scope of this chapter.

At the end of this chapter, you will know how to do the following things:

- ☐ Incorporate ActiveX controls into your Web page
- ☐ How to write code to handle these ActiveX controls
- ☐ Where to get ActiveX controls

Why ActiveX Controls Are Needed

A general Web page can function only inside the browser through the controls defined by HTML or the browser. The list of available HTML controls is small, and the controls aren't very graceful compared to a Windows program such as Microsoft Word. People who are familiar with Windows applications expect much more functionality and can be disappointed when they reach a site that has only HTML controls. ActiveX controls can bridge the gap between HTML's limited controls and a typical Windows application. They reach far beyond Web pages; as a matter of fact, they existed *before* the Web page.

What Is an ActiveX Control?

An ActiveX control is a binary file with an .OCX filename extension. That's the simple explanation. Beyond that simple explanation, however, an *ActiveX control* is an object that has methods, properties, and events (which should be familiar now from Chapter 5, "The VBScript Language"), which allow you to control the object's look and behavior and instruct it to perform certain functions. You can find ActiveX controls in Windows applications, operating systems, and Web pages. An application can require many listboxes and buttons, but a control is meant to fulfill a specific need, such as creating a listbox or a button. Each listbox or button in the application can be based on a single ActiveX control.

An ActiveX control can make use of all the OLE technologies from Microsoft, as well as extend itself to something specific to fit your needs. An ActiveX control doesn't have to be a visible control, such as a listbox or checkbox. It can be a database tool, audio tool, video tool, or just about anything else you want to make it. And yet, even though ActiveX controls can do all that, you don't have to write your own controls. If you're running Windows 95 or Windows NT 3.51 or higher, you have controls on your machine already; they're being used by the operating system.

Any file that ends with the extension .OCX is a control, and you can find more than one control in an OCX file. Microsoft places all its common controls in the file COMCTL32.OCX. Most controls are kept in the system directory. On a Windows NT machine, for example, that directory might be C:\WINNT40\SYSTEM32.

Declaring ActiveX Controls in HTML

The <OBJECT> tag is used to place a control (or a Java applet) on a page; it should be placed in the body of the HTML page, after the <BODY> tag. The <OBJECT> tag has several attributes, but as with the other HTML tags, not all attributes are necessary.

To get an ActiveX control working on your page, however, the <OBJECT> tag needs the CLASSID attribute. This attribute specifies the *CLASSID* (the unique identifier of an ActiveX control). The CLASSID of each object is stored in the Registry of your Microsoft operating system. There are several easy ways to find the CLASSID and several advanced ways to find the CLASSID. I explain only one method because it's free software and gives you the CLASSID (and much more). That method is discussed in the section "The ActiveX Control Pad" later in this chapter.

Also, you need a way to refer to the control in VBScript, so it needs a name in the ID attribute. The name isn't the control's "official" name; it's only a variable name you use in your VBScript code to refer to the control. As with all variables, it's a good idea to use a name that reflects the object. If you're using a Tree control, for example, ID="TreeCtl1" would be fine. The NAME attribute is used in a similar way to submit information through a <FORM> tag.

Most controls don't have a specific size, so you should state their size in the WIDTH and HEIGHT attributes. You can also use the ALIGN attribute to determine where to place the control. The BORDER attribute is handy to help set off controls visually on a page. HSPACE and VSPACE are used to add space between the object and any text or other controls surrounding it.

The following code snippet illustrates an <OBJECT> tag with all these attributes:

```
<OBJECT ID="Inetctl1"
WIDTH=200
HEIGHT=300
HSPACE=10
VSPACE=10
ALIGN=CENTER
NAME="listbox1"
CLASSID="CLSID:7B784E43-3C11-11D0-B91A-00AA00688898"
CODEBASE="http://jaypil4/activebp/controls/ActiveBP.cab">
</OBJECT>
```

Remember, though, you don't have to use all of them. If you wanted to set a property for this control in VBScript, the code could simply be Inetctl1.SetColor(Green). The width and height are determined in pixel units. On my screen with my resolution, the image might be about 2 × 3 inches with a very small border around it (set by the HSPACE and VSPACE attributes). The control would be centered within this 200 × 300 area. If the control were used in a form, the name passed to the server from the page would be listbox1. The CLASSID attribute is the GUID (Global Unique IDentifier) number that should be registered on the client's machine, and the CODEBASE attribute indicates where the control is downloaded from.

Downloading an ActiveX Control to the Client

Downloading the control to the client machine is done with the CODEBASE attribute, as shown here:

```
CODEBASE="http://mysite/mycontrol.cab"
```

NOTE

The CODEBASE attribute of the <OBJECT> tag indicates where the file should be downloaded from. The parameter to the attribute is a URL. The preceding example is a full URL, but it could have used a virtual address, such as /download/myctrl.cab. By using a full URL, however, I can move the page containing this CODEBASE attribute and not worry about the download, because the code knows exactly where to get the file. If I used a virtual address, the code might not find the location when the page containing this CODEBASE attribute is moved.

This example specifies the location for the file to be downloaded. It's done from a CAB file. When the client's machine reads this part of the <OBJECT> tag, it does several things. First, it checks whether the control is already on the machine; if it is, the control isn't downloaded. Second, it makes sure that the correct version (if one is specified) is on the machine. If it is, it doesn't download the file. If the correct version isn't on the machine, then it's installed. Third (assuming Steps 1 and 2 didn't find the control), it downloads the CAB file and makes the necessary arrangements for the system to use the ActiveX control. In most cases, this means registering the control with the operating system (with the command-line program REGSVR32.EXE). If you develop your own control, you may have other files that need to go in specific places. To control how the ActiveX control and any other files are installed, you must build the CAB file correctly.

The CAB File

CAB files are a simple way to compress data and deliver it in some sort of installable fashion. It's more than just a way to download ActiveX controls; it can be used to install software from floppy disks, CD-ROMs, or over the network (which is basically what you need to do). The CAB file is compressed, so it can save you up to 70 percent download time. It contains the control and a file to register the control on the client system (.OCX files and .INF files). The .OCX file *is* the control, and the .INF file is built for you to tell Internet Explorer how to handle the installation. The .INF file can contain, among many other things, information about what files you want installed and where you want them installed and information about any Registry entries (beyond your control) you might need. In short, the .INF file specifies everything you need to install a large Windows application, which is much more power than you need to install an ActiveX control. The CAB file, compressed with the DIAMOND compression algorithm, is built by using the DIANTZ.EXE command-line program.

You have two choices for building your CAB file. First, write a DIAMOND directive file (DDF) that specifies where everything goes and what should be done with it. Once you have written it, you can have this .DDF file turned into an .INF file, which saves you from having to learn the intricacies of the INF format. However, you still have to learn the DIAMOND directive format—which is simpler but still has a learning curve. The second choice is to write the .INF file yourself. What are the trade-offs? .INF files are complex, looking much like .INI files, and there are a lot of choices. Understanding the trade-offs is a serious undertaking. However, if you're in the business of manufacturing hardware, you have to learn INF file formats anyway.

Listing 6.1 is an example of an .INF file for a fictitious ActiveX control. .INF files are divided into sections, each of which contains a piece of information. The [DefaultInstall] section should be included in your .INF file. The subsection RegisterOCXs=RegisterFiles tells the installation process to jump down a few sections to the [RegisterFiles] section for information on what control to register. Notice that the control name ends in .OCX; if the control ended in anything else, it wouldn't be an ActiveX control. All these sections, and many more, are described in complete detail in the Cabinet Development Kit.

NOTE

> The Cabinet Development Kit is available to help you provide your controls to the browser. This includes tools and documentation to get you on your way. You can find the Cabinet Development Kit at http://www.microsoft.com/intdev/sdk. The kit has its own downloadable file, and it's also shipped with the ActiveX SDK, which can be downloaded, too. Regardless of where you get the Cabinet Development Kit, its complete documentation covers a multitude of development choices.

Listing 6.1. Fictitious .INF file for an ActiveX control.

```
 1: ; INF file for comdlg32.ocx
 2: [DefaultInstall]
 3: CopyFiles=install.files
 4: RegisterOCXs=RegisterFiles
 5: [DestinationDirs]
 6: install.files=11
 7: [install.files]
 8: comdlg32.OCX=comdlg32.OCX
 9: [RegisterFiles]
10: %11%\comdlg32.OCX
11: [comdlg32.OCX]
12: file-win32-x86=thiscab
13: RegisterServer=Yes
14: FileVersion=5,0,34,22
15: [version]
16: signature="$CHICAGO$"
17: AdvancedINF=2.0
18: [SourceDisksNames]
19: 1="default",,1
```

6

WARNING

You have several choices when it comes to registering ActiveX controls on a client's machine. The control can be self-registering, meaning that when the REGSVR32 program is called to register the control, all the work is actually done inside the control. The control adds the appropriate entries into the Registry so that the control is usable. Self-registering is the more difficult of the two methods, so you probably won't use it with "home grown" ActiveX controls.

Your other choices for making entries in the Registry are too numerous to list here. These other methods are also more prone to error, so I don't recommend them. For all professional-quality controls, you should expect them to be self-registering.

NOTE

The REGSVR32.EXE program is part of the Windows operating systems. It's a command-line program, so it doesn't have a windowed interface. As a general user of your computer, you should never have to use this program. However, as an ActiveX developer, or developer of Web pages that use ActiveX controls, you need to become familiar with it.

Once you have the .INF file written, you need to create a CAB file. At the command prompt, follow the program name (DIANTZ.EXE) with the file you're "pushing" into the CAB file, then the CAB file itself. Here's an example of what you might enter at the command prompt:

```
DIANTZ.EXE mycontrl.ocx mycontrl.cab
```

You must also push an .INF file into the CAB file to register the control on the client's system. If the control isn't registered in the client system, it can't be used on the Web page. The client's browser won't know where to find the control until it's registered. The STANDBY attribute shows a message while the object is loading. For example, most Windows applications show a progress bar or hourglass when the application is busy. This signal tells the user that the application won't accept user input or control. The Web browser can also indicate the same busy state with the STANDBY attribute. The parameter for STANDBY is the message you want the user to see, such as STANDBY="Downloading file...".

6

The <OBJECT> tag also has another tag it works with: the <PARAM> tag. Because each control can have properties (such as background color), you need a way to pass them to the control when it's loaded. You can use the <PARAM> tag (or the DATA attribute of the <OBJECT> tag). The <PARAM> tag can set any property the control supports with the NAME attribute and the VALUE attribute.

Listing 6.2 and Figure 6.1 show an example of a Web page with a Marquee control, which scrolls a Web page (any HTM) inside a specific area, for a specific amount of time and at a specific speed. The PageInit function is used to load the information into the control when the page is loaded; it's called within the <BODY> tags, but the code has been left out because it's discussed in more detail later in the chapter, a section specifically for the Marquee control. The Marquee control loads the file listed in the szURL parameter.

Listing 6.2. Using the Marquee control on a page.

```
 1: <HEAD>
 2: <TITLE>Marquee Control</TITLE>
 3: </HEAD>
 4: <SCRIPT LANGUAGE=VBScript>
 5: <!--
 6: Sub PageInit
 7: 'Code will be discussed later
 8: End Sub
 9: -->
10: </SCRIPT>
11: <BODY ONLOAD=PageInit>
12: <H1> The OBJECT Tag </H1>
13: <P>
14: <OBJECT ID="Marquee1" WIDTH=500 HEIGHT=400 ALIGN=TOP BORDER=1
15: CLASSID="CLSID:1A4DA620-6217-11CF-BE62-0080C72EDD2D">
16: <PARAM NAME="szURL" VALUE="text.htm">
17: <PARAM NAME="ScrollStyleX" VALUE="Circular">
18: <PARAM NAME="ScrollStyleY" VALUE="Circular">
19: <PARAM NAME="ScrollPixelsY" VALUE=90>
20: <PARAM NAME="ScrollPixelsX" VALUE=0>
21: <PARAM NAME="DrawImmediately" VALUE=1>
22: <PARAM NAME="WidthOfPage" VALUE=500>
23: <PARAM NAME="ScrollDelay" VALUE=500>
24: </OBJECT>
25: </BODY>
26: </HTML>
```

6

Figure 6.1.

*Using the Marquee
control on a page.*

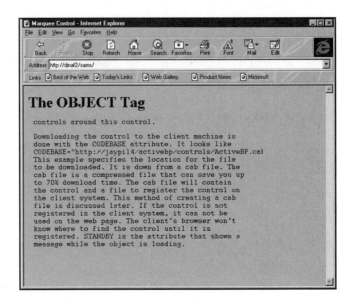

The Controls Used in This Chapter

The controls used in this chapter can be found at `http://www.microsoft.com/activex/gallery/` under the Microsoft section of ActiveX controls (unless stated otherwise). This site has the control, a demonstration of the control, and sample code and documentation. The following controls, described in Table 6.1, are discussed: Label, Marquee, Menu, Popup Menu, and Popup Window. Please download these controls now. Read the documentation carefully to see what browsers they are compatible with.

Table 6.1. Free Microsoft ActiveX controls.

Control	Description
Label	Controls text layout
Marquee	Presents a Web page in a scrollable marquee
Menu	Normal menu control on the top bar of most applications
Popup Menu	Pops up a list of menu choices
Popup Window	Pops up a window loaded with an HTML page

NOTE

> Using these controls isn't necessarily a promotion of them. You can find better controls for a cost, but they're worth the investment.

Using Controls with VBScript

Placing the <OBJECT> tag on the page places the control on the page. To make the control do something, however, you must have a SCRIPT section on the page with procedures that access this control. It could be a control that doesn't need any more code once the <PARAM> tags are set, but this is a rare case.

A control has properties such as color, size, and data. You can set them in your VBScript code by naming the object myobj, then following the name with a period and the property name, as shown in this example of changing the Caption property:

```
myobj.Caption = "New Caption"
```

You can also set properties in the <PARAM> tag. Use the NAME attribute to specify the property's name—NAME="Caption", for example— and the VALUE attribute indicates the new value, such as VALUE="New Caption".

Methods are how you make the control do things, such as change color or load another HTML page. The syntax is similar to that for setting properties:

```
control.Method(param21, param2)
```

If the method doesn't take any parameters, you don't need the parentheses. Also, you can't set methods in <PARAM> tags.

An event is an occurrence that's captured by the Windows operating system. Events are occurrences such as moving the mouse over the control or clicking on the control. You can't control when an event happens, but you can program what your control does when that event is fired. Most controls "listen" for only a few events, such as the Click event.

The ActiveX Control Pad

Setting the <OBJECT> tag attributes might seem difficult at first, but Microsoft has developed a free tool—called the ActiveX Control Pad—to help you place ActiveX controls on a page. The best feature of this tool is that it writes the <OBJECT> and <PARAM> tags for any object, which means you don't have to hunt for the CLASSID, and you can set the parameters in an easy-to-use windowed interface. You can download the ActiveX Control Pad from this site:

```
http://www.microsoft.com/workshop/author/cpad/
```

NOTE

Although there are other good tools for handling ActiveX controls on an HTML page, I mention the ActiveX Control Pad because it fills in the `<OBJECT>` and `<PARAM>` tags for you, and it has the advantage of being free and easily accessible. If you plan on doing a great deal of work with ActiveX controls, you should spend some time researching your available options for products in this area.

Figure 6.2 shows the dialog box used to choose the control you want from the ActiveX Control Pad; in this figure, the Marquee control is highlighted.

Figure 6.2.

Step 1: Choosing a control in the Insert ActiveX Control dialog box.

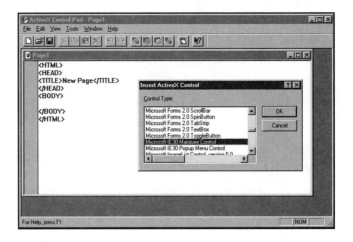

Figure 6.3 illustrates setting properties for the Marquee control in the ActiveX Control Pad. In this figure, you can see the actual HTML page in the background. The ActiveX Control Pad has already added the page's basic structure, and in the lower-left area of the figure, you can see a visual representation of the control. Use that Edit window to size the control visually, instead of supplying a count of width and height. On the right side of the figure, you can see the Marquee control's property page; all the properties listed are default ones. Use the `<PARAM>` tag or VBScript to set these properties.

Figure 6.3.

Step 2: Setting properties for an ActiveX control.

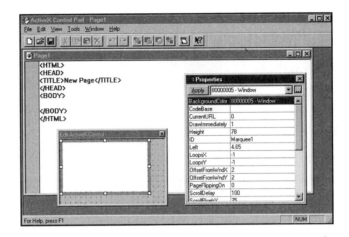

Figure 6.4 shows what the HTML page looks like when the ActiveX Control Pad has inserted the control.

Figure 6.4.

Step 3: The HTML page with the ActiveX control added.

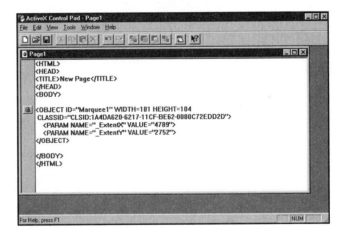

The Label Control

The Label control gives you a great deal of control over a specific region of text. Most text can be controlled through normal HTML tags, but what makes this control special is that it allows you to control the angle and style of the text and change the color of the text's background. Depending on your flare, this control could fit your needs. The sample HTML page for this control uses some of the Label control's properties, methods, and events and gives you an opportunity to control them through VBScript.

Figure 6.5 shows the Label control; its code is given in Listing 6.3. The page has four buttons to manipulate the control:

Figure 6.5.

The Label control.

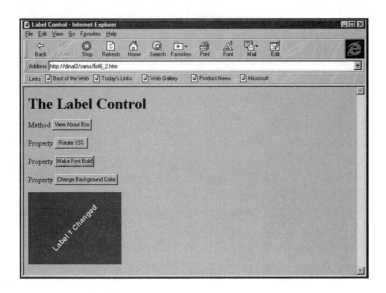

☐ Clicking the View About Box button lets you do just that by calling the AboutBox method.

☐ The Rotate 15% button rotates the caption 15 percent counterclockwise each time you click it.

☐ The Make Font Bold button toggles the caption between bold type and regular type and makes the caption alternate between Label 1 and Label 1 Changed.

☐ The Change Background Color button randomly changes the Label control's background color.

The most common way to fire an event is to click on the control. The sub-procedure Label1_Click, for example, pops up a message box with the text single click. Another event is used in this example. In the Label1_Change() sub-procedure, the caption is rotated 30 degrees clockwise each time the caption changes (which happens only when the Make Font Bold button is clicked).

Listing 6.3. The Label control.

```
 1: <HTML>
 2: <HEAD>
 3: <TITLE>Label Control</TITLE>
 4: </HEAD>
 5: <BODY>
 6: <SCRIPT LANGUAGE=VBScript>
 7: <!--
 8: Sub Label1_Change()
 9: Label1.Angle = (Label1.Angle + 30) mod 360
10: end sub
11: Sub onClick_Rotate()
12: Label1.Angle = (Label1.Angle - 15) mod 360
13: end sub
14: Sub onClick_Bold()
15: if Label1.Caption = "Label 1" then
16: Label1.Caption = "Label 1 Changed"
17: else
18: Label1.Caption = "Label 1"
19: end if
20: if Label1.FontBold = -1 Then
21: Label1.FontBold = 0
22: else
23: Label1.FontBold = -1
24: end if
25: end sub
26: Sub onClick_About()
27: Label1.AboutBox
28: end sub
29: Sub Label1_Click()
30: MsgBox "Single Click"
31: end sub
32: Sub onClick_Back()
33: Label1.BackColor = rnd() * 16777216
34: end sub
35: -->
36: </SCRIPT>
37: <H1> The Label Control </H1>
38: <FORM>
39: Method
40: <INPUT TYPE=BUTTON NAME="ABOUT" VALUE="View About Box"
➥onClick="onClick_About"><P>
41: Property
42: <INPUT TYPE=BUTTON NAME="ROTATE" VALUE="Rotate 15%"
➥ onClick="onClick_Rotate"><P>
43: Property
44: <INPUT TYPE=BUTTON NAME="BOLD" VALUE="Make Font Bold"
➥ onClick="onClick_Bold"><P>
45: Property
46: <INPUT TYPE=BUTTON NAME="BACK" VALUE="Change Background Color"
➥ onClick="onClick_Back"><P>
```

6

continues

Listing 6.3. continued

```
47: </FORM>
48: <OBJECT
49: ID="label1"
50: CLASSID="clsid:99B42120-6EC7-11CF-A6C7-00AA00A47DD2"
51: WIDTH=200
52: HEIGHT=150
53: ALIGN=left
54: >
55: <PARAM NAME="Angle" VALUE="0">
56: <PARAM NAME="Alignment" VALUE="4" >
57: <PARAM NAME="BackStyle" VALUE="1" >
58: <PARAM NAME="BackColor" VALUE="#0000ff" >
59: <PARAM NAME="Caption" VALUE="Label 1">
60: <PARAM NAME="FontName" VALUE="Courier">
61: <PARAM NAME="FontSize" VALUE="12">
62: <PARAM NAME="ForeColor" VALUE="#F0f000" >
63: <PARAM NAME="FontBold" VALUE="1" >
64: </OBJECT>
65: </BODY>
66: </HTML>
```

NOTE Remember, you *can* have more than one control on a page, but for simplicity's sake, these examples use one control each.

The Marquee Control

The Marquee control allows you to add scrolling text to your page. The text can scroll once or in a continuous loop. The Marquee actually scrolls another Web page (an *.HTM file). You can set how fast the page scrolls and specify which page should scroll. You can also pause and resume the scrolling.

Figure 6.6 illustrates the Marquee control; the code is given in Listing 6.4. The page has the Marquee control at the top and four buttons at the bottom. The first button displays the About box, the second button pauses the scrolling, the third button restarts the scrolling, and the fourth button zooms the display.

Figure 6.6.

The Marquee control.

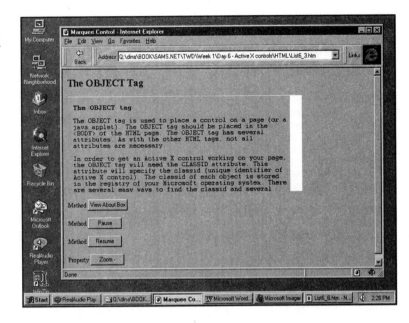

Listing 6.4. The Marquee control.

```
 1: <HTML>
 2: <HEAD>
 3: <TITLE>Marquee Control</TITLE>
 4: </HEAD>
 5: <SCRIPT LANGUAGE=VBScript>
 6: <!--
 7: Sub onClick_About()
 8: Marquee1.AboutBox
 9: end sub
10: Sub onClick_Pause()
11: Marquee1.Pause
12: end sub
13: Sub onClick_Resume()
14: Marquee1.Resume
15: end sub
16: Sub onClick_ZoomSmaller()
17: if Marquee1.Zoom > 10 Then
18: Marquee1.Zoom = (Marquee1.Zoom - 10)
19: end if
20: end sub
21: Sub Marquee1_OnLMouseClick
22: MsgBox "single click"
23: End sub
24: -->
25: </SCRIPT>
```

continues

Listing 6.4. continued

```
26: <BODY>
27: <H1> The OBJECT Tag </H1>
28: <P>
29: <OBJECT ID="Marquee1" WIDTH=500 HEIGHT=200 ALIGN=TOP BORDER=1
30: CLASSID="CLSID:1A4DA620-6217-11CF-BE62-0080C72EDD2D">
31: <PARAM NAME="szURL" VALUE="text.htm">
32: <PARAM NAME="ScrollStyleX" VALUE="Bounce">
33: <PARAM NAME="ScrollStyleY" VALUE="Bounce">
34: <PARAM NAME="LoopsX" VALUE=3>
35: <PARAM NAME="LoopsY" VALUE=3>
36: <PARAM NAME="ScrollPixelsY" VALUE=90>
37: <PARAM NAME="ScrollPixelsX" VALUE=0>
38: <PARAM NAME="DrawImmediately" VALUE=0>
39: <PARAM NAME="WidthOfPage" VALUE=500>
40: <PARAM NAME="ScrollDelay" VALUE=300>
41: <PARAM NAME="Zoom" VALUE=100>
42: </OBJECT>
43: <FORM>
44: Method
45: <INPUT TYPE=BUTTON NAME="ABOUT" VALUE="View About Box"
➥ onClick="onClick_About"><P>
46: Method
47: <INPUT TYPE=BUTTON NAME="PAUSE" VALUE="Pause"
➥ onClick="onClick_Pause"><P>
48: Method
49: <INPUT TYPE=BUTTON NAME="Resume" VALUE="Resume"
➥ onClick="onClick_Resume"><P>
50: Property
51: <INPUT TYPE=BUTTON NAME="ZOOMS" VALUE="Zoom -"
➥ onClick="onClick_ZoomSmaller"><P>
52: </FORM>
53: </BODY>
54: </HTML>
```

The Menu and Popup Menu Controls

The Menu control places a menu on the page; the Popup Menu does this, too, except that the menu items appear only when the PopUp method is invoked. When the page is first loaded, only the top-level menu item (item 0) is visible. To make the rest of the menu visible, you must click on the first item. Most of the applications you're familiar with have several menus, such as File, Edit, Window, and Help. This Menu control handles only one menu, however. To have several menus, you must place several Menu controls, each with a different name, on the page.

The cool thing about this control is that the items in the menu list and the caption (what you see as the top-level item) can be set by using VBScript code. As your Web site changes, this menu can be altered dynamically to reflect those changes in the site.

You can see both the Menu and Popup Menu controls in Figure 6.7; Listing 6.5 provides the code for these controls. The menu on the left is the actual control, and its menu items are visible without having to do anything. The button on the right is used to invoke the Popup Menu control, but the button is not the Popup Menu control itself.

Figure 6.7.

The Menu and Popup Menu controls.

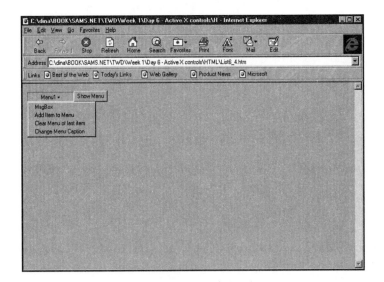

The sub-procedure pmenu1_Click is executed only when there are no items in the list. The first Popup Menu control pops up a message box saying it was the first item selected. The second Menu control adds a new item to the bottom of the list. You could add a second parameter to the AddItem() function to specify where to insert the new item. Notice that this second menu item names the item based on the current count of the menu list, which you determine by using the ItemCount method. The third Menu control removes the last item from the list. You must specify which item to delete. The fourth Menu control changes the menu's caption. Try clicking the "Add Item to Menu" control several times, and then click the "Clear Menu of last item" control. Notice that only the last item is deleted. (See Figure 6.8.)

Figure 6.8.

The Menu control with several items added.

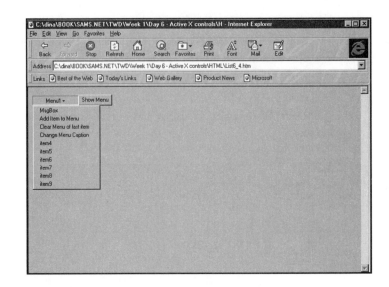

The Popup Menu control is invisible until you call the PopUp method to invoke the control from the button. In this example, I use a button to activate the pop-up menu. Also notice that there's no caption. Other than these differences, the Popup Menu control behaves just like the other Menu control. Figure 6.9 shows the pop-up menu activated.

Figure 6.9.

Invoking the Popup Menu control.

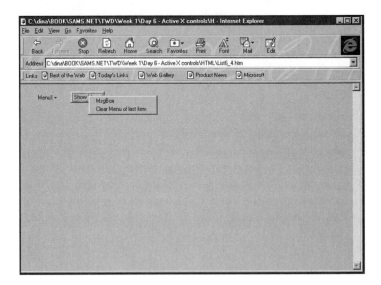

Listing 6.5. The Menu and Popup Menu controls.

```
 1: <HTML>
 2: <HEAD>
 3: <TITLE>New Page</TITLE>
 4: </HEAD>
 5: <BODY>
 6: <SCRIPT LANGUAGE="VBScript">
 7: <!--
 8: Sub pmenu1_Click()
 9: MsgBox  "Single Click"
10: end sub
11: Sub pmenu1_Select(item)
12: if item = 1 then
13: MsgBox  ("First Item Selected")
14: end if
15: if item = 2 then
16: pmenu1.AddItem ("item" + CStr(pmenu1.ItemCount))
17: end if
18: if item = 3 then
19: pmenu1.RemoveItem (pmenu1.ItemCount)
20: end if
21: if item = 4 then
22: if pmenu1.Caption = "Menu1" then
23: pmenu1.Caption = "Menu1 Changed"
24: else
25: pmenu1.Caption = "Menu1"
26: end if
27: end if
28: end sub
29: sub Iepop1_Click(ByVal x)
30: if x = 1 then
31: MsgBox  ("First Item Selected")
32: end if
33: if x = 2 then
34: Iepop1.RemoveItem (Iepop1.ItemCount)
35: end if
36: end sub
37: Sub ShowMenu_onClick
38: call Iepop1.PopUp()
39: End Sub
40: -->
41: </SCRIPT>
42: <OBJECT ID="pmenu1" WIDTH=100 HEIGHT=20
43: CLASSID="CLSID:52DFAE60-CEBF-11CF-A3A9-00A0C9034920">
44: <PARAM NAME="_ExtentX" VALUE="1244">
45: <PARAM NAME="_ExtentY" VALUE="529">
46: <PARAM NAME="Caption" VALUE="Menu1">
47: <param NAME="Menuitem[0]" value="MsgBox">
48: <param NAME="Menuitem[1]" value="Add Item to Menu">
49: <param NAME="Menuitem[2]" value="Clear Menu of last item">
50: <param NAME="Menuitem[3]" value="Change Menu Caption">
51: </OBJECT>
52: <INPUT TYPE="button" NAME="ShowMenu" VALUE="Show Menu" ALIGN=RIGHT>
```

continues

Listing 6.5. continued

```
53: <OBJECT ID="IEPOP1" WIDTH=1 HEIGHT=1
54: CLASSID="CLSID:7823A620-9DD9-11CF-A662-00AA00C066D2">
55: <PARAM NAME="_ExtentX" VALUE="4207">
56: <PARAM NAME="_ExtentY" VALUE="1296">
57: <PARAM NAME="Caption" VALUE="Menu2">
58: <param NAME="Menuitem[0]" value="MsgBox">
59: <param NAME="Menuitem[1]" value="Clear Menu of last item">
60: </OBJECT>
61: </BODY>
62: </HTML>
```

WARNING

The menu items must be in numeric order: 0, 1, 2, 3. If an item number is skipped—by using 0, 1, 3, for example—the item marked 3 isn't displayed.

The Popup Window Control

The Popup Window control pops up a window displaying an HTML page when it's invoked. You can shrink the HTML page to be sized for this pop-up window, or you can leave the HTML page unsized, which crops it (on my machine, the window popped up as large as the page). This is a good control to use for a page preview, but be careful: All images, controls, and so forth from that page are loaded in the pop-up window.

Listing 6.6 shows the code for the Popup Window control. As with the Popup Menu control, you need some way to invoke the control. This example uses two buttons: one with the shrink parameter set to TRUE (the Show Window, To Scale button) and one with the shrink parameter set to FALSE (the Show Window, Clip Display button).

Figure 6.10 shows the Popup Window control invoked with the shrink parameter set to TRUE (very tiny print). In Figure 6.11, the shrink parameter has been set to FALSE.

6

Figure 6.10.

The Popup Window control with its shrink parameter set to TRUE.

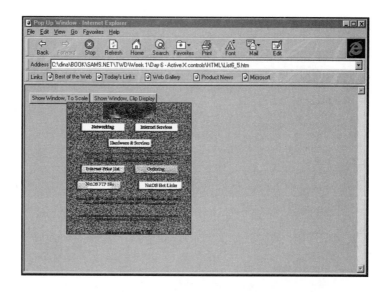

Figure 6.11.

The Popup Window control with its shrink parameter set to FALSE.

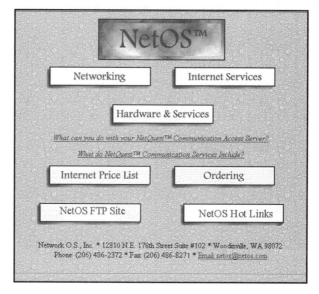

Listing 6.6. The Popup Window control.

```
 1: <HTML>
 2: <HEAD><TITLE>Pop Up Window</TITLE></HEAD>
 3: <BODY>
 4: <INPUT TYPE="button" NAME="ShowWindow" VALUE="Show Window, To Scale"
➥ALIGN=RIGHT>
 5: <INPUT TYPE="button" NAME="ShowWindow1" VALUE="Show Window, Clip Display"
➥ALIGN=RIGHT>
 6: <SCRIPT Language="VBSCRIPT">
 7: Sub ShowMenu_onClick
 8: PopObj.Popup "http://www.netos.com", TRUE
 9: End Sub
10: Sub ShowMenu1_onClick
11: PopObj.Popup "http://www/netos.com", FALSE
12: End Sub
13: </SCRIPT>
14: <OBJECT
15: ID="PopObj"
16: CLASSID="clsid:A23D7C20-CABA-11CF-A5D4-00AA00A47DD2"
17: WIDTH=400
18: HEIGHT=20
19: >
20: </OBJECT>
21: </FONT>
22: </BODY>
23: </HTML>
```

Getting Information from the Web Server into the Control

All the preceding examples have the data for the control on the HTML page itself. However, you might want the data to come from the Web server, perhaps from a database. You have a couple of choices for doing this. First, you can have another control (not visible to the user) on your page that communicates with the server. You would then call this control's methods to get your information. This technique is fairly common, but you would probably have to write that control yourself.

The second choice is to build the HTML page from Microsoft Internet Information Server (IIS) and, possibly, ADO script. You wouldn't be calling functions from the HTML page to IIS. You would have an Active Server Page (.ASP is the file extension) build the entire HTML page, including procedures and objects. This method is also fairly common. What you need to determine is whether using IIS and ADO will get you the information you're looking for. If it won't, then you need to write your own control. You don't have to resort to long C++ programs, however. You can write ActiveX controls by using Visual Basic 5.0, and because VBScript is very much like Visual Basic (the language), it's simpler to learn than C++ code is.

Summary

ActiveX controls are easy to use on Web pages. You can use a tool such as the ActiveX Control Pad to fill in the <OBJECT> and <PARAM> tags, and by adding VBScript to the page, you can easily access and manipulate the control. An ActiveX control can be used on a Web page to give it more of a Windows "look and feel."

In this chapter, you have learned that an ActiveX control is basically an object used in any type of application (including an operating system) that you can control through code. You have also learned how to find and program ActiveX controls. To use these controls, you need to know what methods, properties, and events they support and how to use them. Most professional controls come with documentation. Armed with the knowledge of how to use the control in a Web page, you should now be able to incorporate controls into your Web site to give it an interactive look and behavior.

Q&A

Q If I wanted to program an ActiveX control, what tools could I use?

A The ActiveX Control Pad is an easy tool to learn and is free to everyone. It adds the necessary information and provides all the properties and methods the control has.

Q If I want to make sure the control is on the client's machine, what should I do?

A Download the Cabinet Development Kit and learn about making cabinets. Then, include information in the <OBJECT> tag to make sure the appropriate version is downloaded to the client.

Quiz

1. What's the file extension for an ActiveX control?
2. Where can you set the properties of a control?
3. What's the difference between a method and an event?
4. What's the syntax for passing parameters to a method?
5. Where are ActiveX controls listed?
6. What does the CODEBASE attribute of the <OBJECT> tag allow you to do?

Exercises

1. Use two controls from this chapter on the same page.
2. Design a Web page as though it were an application (with controls), and then find those controls and build the page.

Day 7

Using Active Server Scripting

by Dina Fleet

Active Server Scripting Versus Visual Basic Script

In this chapter, you learn how to use Active Server scripting to create dynamic Web pages and access information at the client's request or from the server. Visual Basic Script is executed on the client machine, so any objects on the page or any procedures are executed on the client machine, too. Active Server scripting, however, is executed on the server and then returns the page to the client. At that point, any VBScript or objects are executed from the client's machine.

Where To Get Active Server Scripting

Visual Basic Script is supported on Microsoft's Internet Explorer (a Web browser). Microsoft's Web server (Internet Information Server; IIS) is supported on the Windows NT operating system. Active Server scripting is one of the new features of IIS 3.0. You can download the product and information from `http://www.microsoft.com/iis`. Make sure to choose Active Server scripting. To use it, you might need to upgrade your NT operating system or your IIS.

TIP

You installed the Active Server Pages but you don't know where to look for documentation on your computer! Where did it go? The ASP documentation is installed in your IIS program group. The first place to look for information is the Active Server Pages Roadmap.

To use the examples in this chapter, open the IIS Manager and add a virtual root. Figure 7.1 illustrates adding a virtual root called /day7. This virtual root's real location on the computer is in c:\tmp. The directory must have Execute privileges because you will be executing ASP files in the directory. Suppose the server name was `www.joe.com`; a browser would access those ASP files by using the following address:

```
http://www.joe.com/day7/xyz.asp
```

NOTE

For Internet Information Server 3.0, there are two relevant Web directory permissions for this chapter: Read and Execute. *Read privileges* is a permission used for HTML Web pages because the page doesn't perform any "action" on the server, but it does need to be read. *Execute privileges* is a permission used for server-side scripts, such as CGI (Common Gateway Interface), ISAPI (Internet Server Application Programming Interface), and ASP (Active Server Pages). The scripts are "executed" on the server by requiring the server to do some type of work. If you store scripts and HTML pages in the same directory, that directory must have both Read and Execute permissions.

Figure 7.1.

Adding the virtual root /day7 at c:\tmp with Execute privileges.

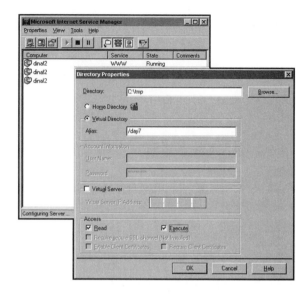

The Magic of Active Server Scripting

The magic of Active Server scripting is in the code's syntax. The Active Server Page either *is* an HTML page or generates one. The points where the code should be executed on the server begin with <% and end with %>. These symbols are the *delimiters* in Active Server scripting.

 TIP

> If you get an error that your page doesn't load on the client, the first thing to check is whether your Active Server scripting delimiters *do* enclose all your server-side code. Microsoft Visual C++ color-codes the ASP file so you can easily see whether you're missing a delimiter.

The Active Server scripting file has an extension of .ASP (which stands for Active Server Page). There are two other extensions that Active Server scripting supports—.INC and .ASA—but they're secondary to the .ASP extension and are discussed later in the sections "The Include File" and "The ASA File." Your Active Server Page is meant to generate an HTML-like page, which means all the normal tags an HTML page uses are included in the ASP file. Listing 7.1 is a very short Active Server Page: LIST7_1.ASP. It must have an extension of .ASP. Figure 7.2 illustrates this page in a browser. The code on the ASP page looks exactly like an HTML page, except for the Active Server scripting. It's good form to have the delimiters on their own lines, but it's not necessary. Don't worry about what the Active Server code means right now; it's covered later in the section "The Response Object."

Figure 7.2.

The first ASP file.

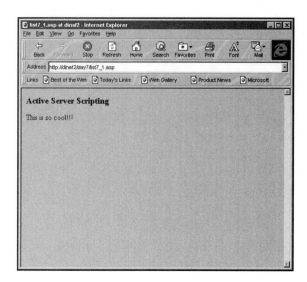

Listing 7.1. Generating your first Active Server Page.

```
1: <HTML>
2: <HEAD> <TITLE>Active Server Scripting<TITLE></HEAD>
3: <BODY>
4: <H3> Active Server Scripting </H3>
5: <%
6: Response.Write "This is so cool!!!"
7: %>
8: </BODY>
9: </HTML>
```

The Active Server Object Model

You learned about the VBScript object model in Chapter 5, "VBScript Language," but Active Server scripting has an object model, too. Although the VBScript model is meant to manipulate the browser and its contents, the Active Server scripting model is meant to access information about the request a browser makes and the response the server gives.

The Active Server object model includes five objects: Application, Server, Session, Request, and Response. Most of the functions and features of the object model are supplied by the Server, Request, and Response objects. The syntax for using these objects is the same as it is in VBScript, and the following "rules" still hold true for the Active Server object model:

☐ The object can have properties, methods, and events.

☐ Properties can be read-only or can be set by assigning variables.

☐ Methods and events are procedures you can call.

☐ To refer to a property, you must add the object name and a period (used as the object delimiter) before the name of the property, as shown here:

```
Response.Status
```

☐ Methods and events are called by adding the object name and a period (used as the object delimiter) before the name of the method or event, as shown in this example:

```
Response.Write()
```

☐ Any parameters to the method or event are placed within parentheses and separated by commas.

TIP

Adding comments to your ASP code is very helpful, so you should use them liberally. Remember that a comment in VBScript is marked by a single quote at the beginning of the line and must be inside the `<SCRIPT></SCRIPT>` tags and within the ASP delimiters `<% %>`. Any single quote that isn't inside either the VBScript tag or the Active Server delimiters might cause your page to be displayed incorrectly or not at all. A comment placed outside the VBScript tags or Active Server delimiters should use the HTML comment style of `<!-- -->` .

NOTE

This chapter may not cover all the objects in the Active Server object model, but it covers the most commonly used objects.

HTTP Refresher and the Active Server Objects

Remember that the HTTP protocol is a request/response protocol: The client makes a request from the server, and the server returns a response. This definition makes it easier to distinguish between the Request and Response Active Server objects. When a client makes a request, the Request object includes a header of information, such as what type of browser the client is. This information allows the server to distinguish between information the browser does and doesn't understand. The server can then return a page with the functions

7

and features the browser can support; an old browser, for example, might not be able to handle embedded tables or framed pages. The server can discover these limitations by querying the appropriate headers. It then returns a page that doesn't have objects that aren't supported; instead, it finds another way to display the required information.

The Request Object

The Request object holds information about what kind of request the client's browser is making, including the header information, any parameters from a form, cookies (explained in the section "Cookies: Request and Response Objects"), and so forth. The Request object is actually made up of a collection of objects. To get information from the collection, you refer first to the collection and then to a specific member of the collection. To refer to information in the request's second form (<FORM>), for example, you would use this syntax:

```
Request.Form[index].property
```

In this code line, index refers to the form you want to access. You don't always have to use the collection's index, however; if there's only one form, the statement Request.Form.property would do the job. To better understand the Request object, you need to look at the collections included in it. These collections—Form and QueryString—are explained in the following sections, along with the Request object's ServerVariables method.

The Form Collection

The Form collection gives you access to <FORM> tag information that's passed from the client to the server. The <FORM> tag can have objects such as text boxes, buttons, option buttons, checkboxes, select boxes, and so on. The Submit button that the user clicks passes the <FORM> tag information from the client to the server.

Figure 7.3 and Listing 7.2 illustrate a form that has most of the objects mentioned in the preceding paragraph. Notice that the form is named, the objects are named, and values are associated with each object. This is an HTML file because you don't need any Active Server scripting to have a Form object.

The page that's generated sits on the server. Notice that in the <FORM> tag, the file LIST7_3.ASP is mentioned, which means the page in Listing 7.2 requests the LIST7_3.ASP file from the server.

Figure 7.3.
*The HTML page
generated from the
Form file.*

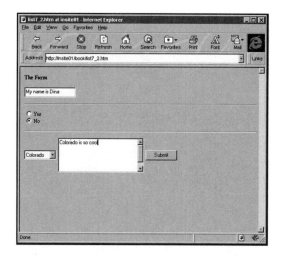

Listing 7.2. Using objects in the Form collection.

```
 1: <HTML>
 2: <HEAD> <TITLE>The Form<TITLE></HEAD>
 3: <BODY>
 4: <H3> The Form </H3>
 5: <FORM NAME="Form1" METHOD=POST ACTION="List7_3.asp">
 6: <INPUT TYPE=TEXT NAME="Text1" VALUE="Enter Text here" SIZE=20>
 7: <HR><INPUT TYPE=RADIO NAME="Radio1" VALUE="Yes">Yes
 8: <BR><INPUT TYPE=RADIO NAME="Radio1" VALUE="No">No
 9: <BR>
10: <HR><SELECT NAME="Select1">
11: <OPTION> Texas
12: <OPTION> Colorado
13: <OPTION> Washington
14: </SELECT>
15: <TEXTAREA NAME="TextArea1" SIZE="10,10" VALUE="Enter Text Here"> Text Area
16: <INPUT TYPE=SUBMIT NAME="Submit1" VALUE="Submit">
17: </FORM>
18: </BODY>
19: </HTML>
```

The ASP file that Listing 7.2 requests is in Listing 7.3. Notice that the information written
in the form is returned as text. (See Figure 7.4.) Each object of the form is referred to by its
name (as the form named it) and the statement Request.Form("Text1") returns the value of
the data entered in the Text1 Form object.

Figure 7.4.

Returning requested information as text.

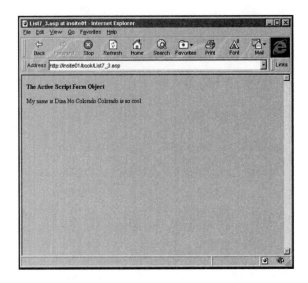

Listing 7.3. The ASP response file.

```
 1: <HTML>
 2: <HEAD> <TITLE>The Active Script Form Object<TITLE></HEAD>
 3: <BODY>
 4: <H3> The Active Script Form Object</H3>
 5: <%
 6: Response.Write Request.Form("Text1")
 7: Response.Write chr(13) & chr(10)
 8: Response.Write Request.Form("Radio1")
 9: Response.Write chr(13) & chr(10)
10: Response.Write Request.Form("Select1")
11: Response.Write chr(13) & chr(10)
12: Response.Write Request.Form("TextArea1")
13: Response.Write chr(13) & chr(10)
14: %>
15: </BODY>
16: </HTML>
```

TIP

When using the Request.Form collection, make sure that the page making the request, such as the one in Listing 7.2, has the METHOD attribute of the <FORM> tag set to POST. Otherwise, you might not see any response text. When making a request through the anchor tag <A>, the method is GET.

7

The `QueryString` **Collection**

The anchor tag <A> can return information to the Web server, much as the `Form` collection does. When requesting a page, the Web server receives the Web page name, such as `http://dinaf1/default.asp`. When using a form, the browser formats the variables passed to the Web server. These variables are passed in *name=value pairs*; in these pairs, *name* is the name of the object, such as `company name`, and *value* is the name of the company entered in a text box. Each `name=value` pair is separated by an ampersand. When using an anchor tag, you must write this formatted string of `name=value` pairs like this:

`http://dinaf1/default.asp?name=sams&chapter=7`

The question mark denotes the beginning of the `name=value` pairs. Figure 7.5 and Listing 7.4 illustrate this anchor tag used in a Web page. Figure 7.6 and Listing 7.5 illustrate how to read this tag and return it in another page. The `Request.QueryString` collection is the way to access these `name=value` pairs.

Figure 7.5.

Passing name=value *pairs.*

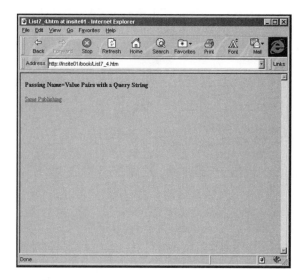

Listing 7.4. Using the `QueryString` collection.

```
1: <HTML>
2: <HEAD><TITLE></TITLE></HEAD>
3: <BODY>
4: <H3>Passing Name=Value Pairs with a Query String</H3>
5: <A NAME="product" HREF="querstr2.asp?name=dina&pub=sams">Sams Publishing</A>
6: </BODY>
7: </HTML>
```

Figure 7.6.

*Reading the anchor
tag's query string.*

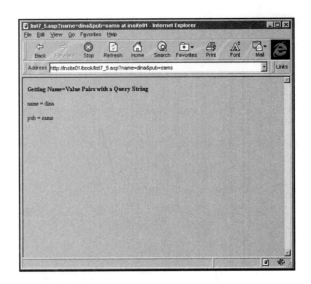

Listing 7.5. The anchor tag's query string.

```
1: <HTML>
2: <HEAD><TITLE></TITLE></HEAD>
3: <BODY>
4: <H3>Getting Name=Value Pairs with a Query String</H3>
5: <P>
6: name = <%= Request.QueryString("name") %><P>
7: pub = <% = Request.QueryString("pub") %>
8: </BODY>
9: </HTML>
```

The ServerVariables Method

At times, you need to know and use information about the Web server, such as the length of the content being returned or the software the Web server is running. The Request object has a method to return just this type of information: ServerVariables. This method takes one parameter as text; this parameter corresponds to the specific information to return, and there are several predefined parameters. The client's browser can send proprietary header information that this method can then retrieve, as long as you can supply the name of the header.

Listing 7.6 and Figure 7.7 illustrate how to retrieve server variables. Assume that this ASP file is on an IIS 3.0 server. Table 7.1 explains what the parameters do.

Listing 7.6. Getting the server variables from the client.

```
 1: <HTML>
 2: <HEAD><TITLE></TITLE></HEAD>
 3: <BODY>
 4: <H3>Getting the client's Server Variables</H3>
 5: <BR>
 6: AUTH_TYPE = <%= Request.ServerVariables("AUTH_TYPE") %><BR>
 7: CONTENT_LENGTH = <% = Request.ServerVariables("CONTENT_LENGTH") %><BR>
 8: CONTENT_TYPE = <% = Request.ServerVariables("CONTENT_TYPE") %><BR>
 9: GATEWAY_INTERFACE = <% = Request.ServerVariables("GATEWAY_INTERFACE") %><BR>
10: LOGON_USER = <% = Request.ServerVariables("LOGON_USER") %><BR>
11: PATH_INFO = <% = Request.ServerVariables("PATH_INFO") %><BR>
12: PATH_TRANSLATED = <% = Request.ServerVariables("PATH_TRANSLATED") %><BR>
13: QUERY_STRING = <% = Request.ServerVariables("QUERY_STRING") %><BR>
14: REMOTE_ADDR = <% = Request.ServerVariables("REMOTE_ADDR") %><BR>
15: REMOTE_HOST = <% = Request.ServerVariables("REMOTE_HOST") %><BR>
16: REMOTE_METHOD = <% = Request.ServerVariables("REMOTE_METHOD") %><BR>
17: SCRIPT_MAP = <% = Request.ServerVariables("SCRIPT_MAP") %><BR>
18: SCRIPT_NAME = <% = Request.ServerVariables("SCRIPT_NAME") %><BR>
19: SERVER_NAME = <% = Request.ServerVariables("SERVER_NAME") %><BR>
20: SERVER_PORT = <% = Request.ServerVariables("SERVER_PORT") %><BR>
21: SERVER_PORT_SECURE = <% = Request.ServerVariables("SERVER_PORT_SECURE")
➡%><BR>
22: SERVER_PROTOCOL = <% = Request.ServerVariables("SERVER_PROTOCOL") %><BR>
23: SERVER_SOFTWARE = <% = Request.ServerVariables("SERVER_SOFTWARE") %><BR>
24: URL  = <% = Request.ServerVariables("URL") %><BR>
25: </BODY>
26: </HTML>
```

Figure 7.7.

Retrieving the server variables.

Table 7.1. The ServerVariables **parameters.**

Parameter	Purpose
AUTH_TYPE	Authentication method of the server, such as the user's name
CONTENT_LENGTH	Length of the request, such as the <FORM>
CONTENT_TYPE	Type of Request object indicated after the ? delimiter, such as POST or GET
GATEWAY_INTERFACE	The CGI specification used
HTTP_*HeaderName*	Proprietary header that you create
LOGON_USER	Windows NT account used
PATH_INFO	Virtual path on the server of the file requested
PATH_TRANSLATED	Physical path on the server of the file requested
QUERY_STRING	Query string from an anchor tag placed after the ? delimiter
REMOTE_ADDR	Address of the client machine
REMOTE_HOST	Name of the client machine
REQUEST_METHOD	Can be POST, GET, or PUT
SCRIPT_MAP	Domain name of the URL
SCRIPT_NAME	File requested with the virtual root
SERVER_NAME	Port that the client sends the request to
SERVER_PORT	Name of the Web server answering the request
SERVER_PORT_SECURE	1 = a secure port (such as Secured Socket Layer); 0 = not a secure port
SERVER_PROTOCOL	Protocol that the Web server uses to return the file
SERVER_SOFTWARE	Web software running on the server
URL	File requested, including the virtual path

The Response **Object**

The Response object controls how you send output to the client's browser. You are building either an HTML or ASP file to return to the browser. There are several properties and methods for the Response object, explained in the following sections.

The Buffer **Property**

You can use either of these statements for setting the Buffer property:

```
Response.Buffer = TRUE

Response.Buffer = FALSE
```

The first property of the Response object is the Buffer property. The server has a buffer where the ASP page is processed. The page is either processed entirely in this buffer and then sent to the client or not processed in the buffer, meaning it's sent directly to the client. You can set the Buffer to TRUE or FALSE. If it's set to TRUE, the server waits until the whole page is processed (or the FLUSH or END methods are called) before sending the page to the client. If the Buffer is set to FALSE, the server sends the page as it's being processed.

If the Buffer property is set to TRUE and the page doesn't call FLUSH, then the next request by the client is processed faster because the server treats it as a keep-alive request. If you have a large page, the page isn't sent to the client immediately, so it's kept waiting. This wait makes it seem as though you have a slow server. With the Buffer property set to FALSE, however, the client's browser gets parts of the page (from top to bottom) as it's being processed, which reduces the wait for the client.

NOTE   A *keep-alive request* is the ability to keep the TCP/IP connection to the server open instead of closing it after the page is sent. The request and response are faster because the connection doesn't have to be re-established.

The ContentType **Property**

This is the syntax for setting the ContentType property:

```
Response.ContentType = "text/plain"
```

The ContentType property specifies what the content of the page returned to the browser looks like. The default is text/HTML, meaning that the stream of data should be interpreted as text and HTML tags should be used for formatting. Another common content type is text/plain, which means the data stream is displayed as text with no HTML formatting.

7

The Expires **Property**

Use this statement to set the Expires property:

```
Response.Expires = 0
```

The Expires property tells the browser how long to cache a page before retrieving it again. If you know your data is being updated every five minutes, you can set the Expires property to 5. When the page expires, the next fetch brings the new page in five minutes. By setting the Expires property to 0, you're setting the cache time to zero minutes. If you want each client to request the new page from the server every time, and not from the client's browser page cache, you would set this property to zero.

Setting the Expires property to zero can be very useful if you have a Web page with information changing continuously (minute to minute), such as those used for a late-breaking news story, the stock market, or the weather.

The ExpiresAbsolute **Property**

You can use either of these statements for setting the ExpiresAbsolute property:

```
Response.ExpiresAbsolute = #January 1, 1998#
```

```
Response.ExpiresAbsolute = #January 1, 1998, 1:00:00#
```

The Expires property sets a time length, but the ExpiresAbsolute property specifies a particular date and time of day. If no time is specified, the page expires at midnight, and if no date is specified, then the page expires at that time on the current day.

The Status **Property**

This is the syntax for setting the Status property:

```
Response.Status = "401 Unauthorized"
```

Every page that's requested must return a status from the server. If the page isn't found, that's one kind of status; if the page *is* found, that's another. Here's a list of the more common return status codes:

Status	Code
OK	200
Created	201
Accepted	202
No content	204
Moved permanently	301
Moved temporarily	302

Status	Code
Not modified	304
Bad request	400
Unauthorized	401
Forbidden	403
Page not found	404
Internal server error	500
Not implemented	501
Bad gateway	502
Service unavailable	503

The AppendToLog Method

This is the syntax for using the AppendToLog method:

```
Response.AppendToLog "Kilroy was here"
```

The AppendToLog method is a way to add information to the IIS log file. The maximum length of the text you can add is 80 characters. There are several applications that analyze log files for particular pieces of information, so be careful what you add. However, you could write your own application that also analyzes the log file, looking for something you specifically entered. Because each line of the log file is comma-separated, you can't have any commas in your text.

Figure 7.8 shows what the log file entry look likes after you enter the sample syntax at the beginning of this section.

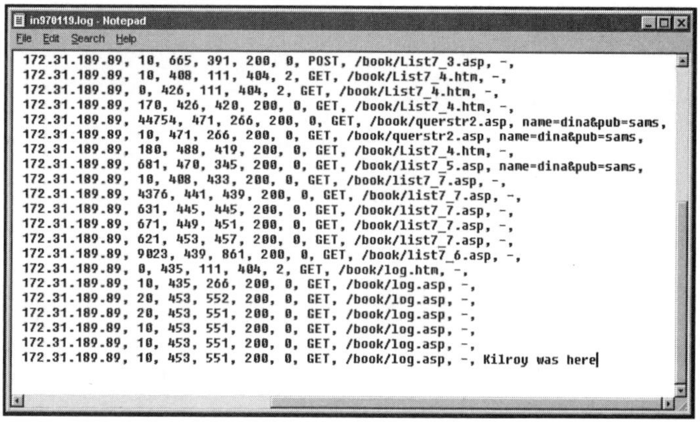

Figure 7.8.

Adding text to the IIS log file.

The WriteBinary Method

This is the syntax for using the WriteBinary method:

```
Response.WriteBinary picture
```

In this sample syntax, *picture* is a stream of binary data. The WriteBinary method is a way to add a stream of data to the browser as binary data. It's a good way to handle non-text data, such as image files, sound files, or video files. You can open the object, assign a variable to it, and then pass that variable as the parameter to WriteBinary.

The Clear Method

This is the syntax for using the Clear method:

```
Response.Clear 'no params
```

The Clear method works when the Response object's Buffer property is set to TRUE. It allows you to erase all the buffered data. This method is a good alternative in case the code runs into an error condition on the server. However, if Buffer is set to FALSE, using the Clear method produces a runtime error.

The End Method

Here's the syntax for using the End method:

```
Response.End 'no params
```

The End method allows the server to stop processing the Active Server script and return the page. This method should be used when a page has buffering set to TRUE and has finished processing because of specifications you set in the code, such as the end of a loop.

The Redirect Method

This is the syntax for using the Redirect method:

```
Response.Redirect URL 'where URL is the new page
```

The Redirect method allows you to redirect a request to another page. You use this method when you have moved a page but don't want to make the user search for it. When a user makes a request for the page that's been moved, the server doesn't respond with the requested page; instead, it "redirects" the client by returning the page the client was looking for. The Redirect method moves directly to the correct location the user specifies. It's done automatically, so the client side shouldn't be aware it's happening.

The Write Method

Here's the syntax for using the Write method:

```
Response.Write "<INPUT TYPE=BUTTON>"
```

The Write method allows you to write out the page's text or HTML. You can "write" VBScript to the page, controls, and objects or write HTML text or regular text to the page.

If you want to add a newline feed through code, you can use the following:

```
Response.Write Chr(13) & Chr(10).
```

If you want to add double quotes through code, you can use the following:

```
Response.Write """"
```

Cookies: Request and Response Objects

Cookies are a unique identifier you place on the client's machine; they're a good way to tell whether a user has visited your site before and to get information about the user. Much as a Web page passes a name=value pair to a Web server, the cookie is passed as a name=value pair with each request to the Web server. To place the cookie on the client machine, use the Response.Cookies collection; to retrieve a cookie from a client's machine, use the Request.Cookies collection.

The purpose of the information in the cookie is completely up to you, but here are a few examples. Suppose a user hits your Web page and you want some personal information about him or her. Users might fill out this information once, but they will probably stop visiting your site if they have to fill out the form on each visit. You can capture the information once (in a database on your Web server, for example) and then assign a unique identifier for each user, which is then placed in the cookie. The next time the user visits your site, you look for the cookie first. Once you have retrieved the cookie, you can access the information about the user from the database. However, if you don't want something as elaborate as a database, you can keep multiple name=value pairs in the cookie.

A cookie isn't some magical entry on your client's machine. It's simply a text file (you can read any cookie file with a text editor) in which the name of the file corresponds to your Web site. Every site that gives out cookies places a file on the client's machine.

Listing 7.7 creates a cookie on the client, reads the cookie from the request, and displays it on the Web page, shown in Figure 7.9. Each time you refresh the page, more text is added to the cookie.

Imagine the first time a user hits your site; the first file returned to the client's browser contains the response code in Listing 7.7 (not very pretty, but functional). Every request after that first one also passes the cookie information to the server. You can keep track of people

7

ng your site through the cookie. You're responsible for setting the value of the
value pair to a unique identifier, but then only you know the meaning of the pair (the information in the cookie is meaningful only to you).

If you don't set the Response object's Buffer property to TRUE (by using Response.Buffer = TRUE), you must have the Response.Cookies assignment on the first line with the <%. If you do have buffering turned on, you can place the Response.Cookies assignment on the next line of the ASP file.

Figure 7.9.

Creating and reading a cookie.

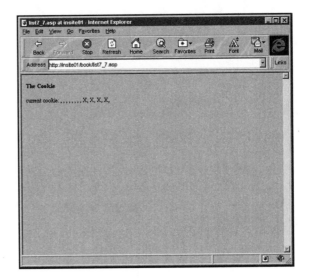

Listing 7.7. Creating and reading a cookie.

```
 1: <% Response.Buffer = TRUE
 2: it = Request.Cookies("mycookie")
 3: it = it + "X, "
 4: Response.Cookies("mycookie") = it
 5: Response.Cookies("mycookie").Expires =  "July 4, 1997"
 6: %>
 7: <HTML>
 8: <HEAD> <TITLE>The Cookie<TITLE></HEAD>
 9: <BODY>
10: <H3>The Cookie</H3>
11: current cookie: <%= it %>
12: </BODY>
13: </HTML>
```

7

The Session **Object**

The Session object is used as a way of remembering, between visits, information about a visitor to your site. This object is supported only by browsers that support cookies (if your browser gives you a choice of rejected cookies, please make sure that option is turned off for these examples, meaning you will accept cookies). Basically, the Session object stores and retrieves a cookie for you, but this cookie is marked as the Session object. Therefore, the Session methods return information about this Session's cookie only. A Session is automatically created for each user who doesn't already have one.

Properties and Methods of the Session **Object**

The properties for the Session object are SessionID and Timeout. SessionID is a unique number that the Web server generates when the session is created (when the user first visits your site). If the Web server is stopped and restarted, a session ID may be duplicated.

The Session object's Timeout property sets in minutes how long the client browser has to make a request before the session is ended. The default is 20 minutes.

The method for the Session object is Abandon, which releases the Session object. If the Abandon method is not called, the server destroys the Session object when the length of the session reaches the Timeout value. Listing 7.8 shows you how to set up the Session and read the session value.

Listing 7.8. Setting up the Session object.

```
 1: <HTML>
 2: <HEAD><TITLE></TITLE></HEAD>
 3: <BODY>
 4: <H3>Setting and Getting the Session Object</H3>
 5: <BR>
 6: <%
 7: Session.Abandon 'Kill any current sessions this visitor has
 8: Session("visitor_name") = "Dina" 'reset session value
 9: %>
10: </BODY>
11: </HTML>
```

The Server **Object**

The Server object gives you access to functions on the server. Some of these functions provide information that's useful but not specifically tied to either the response or the request. This object has one property and two methods, covered in the following sections.

7

The `ScriptTimeout` **Property**

This is the syntax for setting the `ScriptTimeout` property:

```
Server.ScriptTimeout =120
```

The `ScriptTimeout` property lets you set how long a server can take to respond with a page. If the `Response.Buffer` is set to TRUE and the timeout occurs, the page might not be returned to the client browser. The minimum amount of time in seconds is configured in the Registry and defaults to 90 seconds. You can set the maximum timeout to be longer than 90 seconds, but if you set the timeout to be shorter than 90 seconds, the timeout in the Registry setting will supersede your timeout in the Active Server script. However, you can change the Registry setting for the timeout length.

The `MapPath` **Method**

You can use either statement for the `MapPath` method:

```
Server.MapPath("/myvroot/file.asp")

Server.MapPath("file.asp").
```

There will be times you want to manipulate files from ASP scripts but can't count on the file's physical path. For example, you might have a Web site where several servers are fulfilling requests. Each server might have the physical paths configured differently, but the virtual roots remain the same across all the machines. The only path you should count on is the virtual root path. To find the file's physical path, you can use the `MapPath` method. Its only parameter is the file's virtual, or relative, path. If the path you pass as a parameter starts with either a forward slash or a backslash, `MapPath` assumes you want the full physical path that maps to the full virtual path. If the path parameter doesn't start with any slash, then `MapPath` assumes you want the physical path in relation to the location of the calling ASP file.

The `CreateObject` **Method**

The `CreateObject` method allows you to invoke objects on the server. In this respect, you can think of an object as an ActiveX object, but instead of being executed on the client, it's executed on the server. This method is covered in more detail in Week 2, "Server-Side Rowsets with ActiveX Data Objects," but there's one feature of `CreateObject` you might want to use now. You can make the Active Server script write to a text file. You could use this feature in a variety of ways, from generating a site log for your Web site to creating a chat server (although it will probably be slow and bulky) by adding to a file at a certain place to creating new HTML files and adding links to them in other files. This file capability is provided by using the `FileSystemObject ActiveX object`. You can open a file, create a file, move the file around, and add text and line returns to the file.

Listing 7.9 illustrates how to open a file and append a line of text to it, as well as return a link to that newly created file.

Listing 7.9. Creating a text file from an ASP page.

```
 1: <HTML>
 2: <HEAD>
 3: <TITLE>Writing to a Text File</TITLE>
 4: </HEAD>
 5: <BODY>
 6: <H3>Writing to a Text File</H3>
 7: <%
 8: textfile = Server.MapPath ("/dina") & "\test1.htm"   9: Set FileObject =
➡Server.CreateObject("Scripting.FileSystemObject")
10: Set OutStream= FileObject.CreateTextFile (textfile, True, False)
11: mystring = "<HTML><HEAD><TITLE>Writing to a File</TITLE></HEAD>"
12: OutStream.WriteLine mystring
13: mystring = "The time is now " & now
14: OutStream.WriteLine mystring
15: mystring = "</BODY></HTML>"
16: OutStream.WriteLine mystring
17: Set OutStream = Nothing
18: Response.Write "<A HREF=" & """" & "test1.htm" & """" & ">
➡My New Text File </A>"
19: %>
20: <BR>
21: <BR>
22: </BODY>
23: </HTML>
```

On line 8, the Server.MapPath is used to find the physical address of the virtual root dina and then append the new filename \test1.htm, so the new file is placed in the virtual root dina and referred to as test1.htm. On line 9, notice that the Server.CreateObject method is used to get the FileSystemObject. You have to use the Set keyword to assign the new file object.

On line 10, the file is created. The first parameter, textfile, is the path and name of the file. The second parameter, TRUE, indicates whether there's already a file in that location with the same name that it could overwrite. The third parameter indicates that the file should be written in ASCII text instead of UNICODE. Line 12 writes the variable mystring to the file stream, and Lines 13 and 15 change the variable. Lines 14 and 16 write another string to the file stream, and Line 17 resets the outstream by setting it to nothing (setting something to nothing is common). Line 18 sends back a reference to the new text file.

Figure 7.10 illustrates the response, and Figure 7.11 is the new file, TEST1.HTM.

7

Figure 7.10.

Creating a new file.

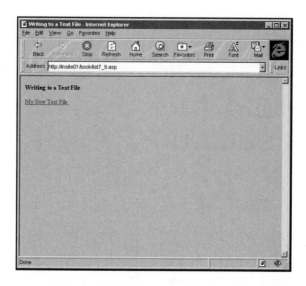

Figure 7.11.

Looking at the new file.

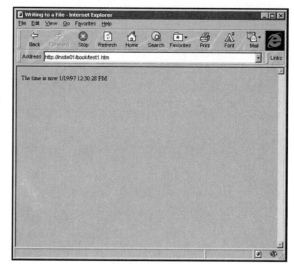

The Application **Object**

The Application object allows you to treat a virtual root and all its subdirectories as though they were a single application. Most applications need a common set of data and functions across the entire application. In Web page terminology, this means that a variable set in page A should be accessible from page B. Suppose that when a visitor enters your site, you collect information about her, such as name, age, location, and so on. You might want to use her name on every page to make the Web site more personal, but you might want to use the location information only when displaying regional news. You could use her age for demographic information. Although you gather this information on the first page of your site, you want the information visible to all the pages that make up your site.

Active Server Pages allow you to do this, with a couple of restrictions. An application in Active Server Pages is defined as the virtual root and all its subdirectories. If you set up a virtual root in the beginning of this chapter, then that's your application level. A variable set in the DEFAULT.ASP, for example, at the top level of your virtual directory is accessible from WEATHER.ASP in the /region/weather/ directory. The other restriction is that information from a single page's Active Server objects, such as Request, Response, Server, Application, and Session, can't be set into application-level variables.

The Application object can be compared to a global variable in most other programming languages. Because many people can access Web pages at the same time, you need to surround the Application objects (anywhere they're set) with the application-level method Lock. This method ensures that the variable will be changed by only one visitor at a time. The Lock method is how Active Server Pages handle the multithreading issue that all other Web applications have to deal with.

Listing 7.10 is the entry page (ASP file) where a visitor enters his name and age and selects his city. (See Figure 7.12.)

Listing 7.10. The entry page for entering information about the user.

```
 1: <HTML>
 2: <HEAD><TITLE>Please Add Your Name, Age, and City</TITLE></HEAD>
 3: <BODY>
 4: <H3>Please Add Your Name, Age, and City</H3>
 5: <p>
 6: <FORM METHOD=POST NAME="Personal" ACTION="list7_11.asp">
 7: Please enter your name:
 8: <INPUT TYPE=TEXTBOX SIZE=50 MAX=47 NAME="name" VALUE=""><P>
 9: Please enter your age:
10: <INPUT TYPE=TEXTBOX SIZE=5 MAX=3 NAME="age" VALUE=""><P>
11: Please select which city your are living in:
12: <SELECT NAME="city" ><P>
13:     <OPTION VALUE="Seattle">Seattle
14:     <OPTION VALUE="Denver">Denver
15:     <OPTION VALUE="Miami">Miami
16: </SELECT>
17: <INPUT TYPE=SUBMIT>
18: </FORM>
19: </BODY>
20: </HTML>
```

7

Figure 7.12.

Entering information about the user on the entry page.

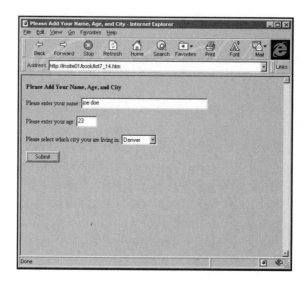

The information entered by the user is then passed to Listing 7.11, another ASP file that sets the application-level variables name, age, city. These variable names are of my choosing; Active Server lets you name variables whatever you want, except for keywords and other known variable exceptions.

Listing 7.11. The ASP file used to set the application-level variables (in the same directory).

```
 1: <HTML>
 2: <HEAD><TITLE></TITLE></HEAD>
 3: <%
 4: Application.Lock
 5: Application("name") = Request.Form("name")
 6: Application("age") = Request.Form("age")
 7: Application("city") = Request.Form("city")
 8: Application.Unlock
 9: %>
10: <BODY>
11: <H3>Hello <%= Application("name") %>, thank you for filling out the form</
➥H3>
12: <% if Application("city") = "Seattle" then %>
13: The weather in <%= Application("city") %> is grey skies and plenty o'rain.
14: <% elseif Application("city") = "Denver" then %>
15: The weather in <%= Application("city") %> is cold and snowy.
16: <% else %>
17: The weather in <%= Application("city") %> is warm and sunny.
18: <% end if %>
19: <FORM NAME="age" METHOD=POST ACTION="/html/list7_12.asp">
20: <INPUT TYPE=SUBMIT VALUE="OK">
```

```
21: </FORM>
22: </BODY>
23: </HTML>
```

Notice that Listing 7.11 finds the name information from the `Application` object, not the `Request` object. This is one example of a global application-level variable. Also notice that the methods `Application.Lock` and `Application.Unlock` surround where you set the variable. Locking and unlocking the variables are necessary only when you're setting or changing the variable, *not* when you're reading the variable.

To run correctly, Listing 7.12 should be placed in the /html subdirectory of the virtual root that Listing 7.10 and Listing 7.11 are in. When run in the browser, Listing 7.12 displays the application-level variables set from Listing 7.11. This illustrates how a parameter set from one page can be reused in another page where the two pages don't pass the parameter. Figure 7.13 shows the ASP file that reads the application name in a subdirectory that uses the application-level variables.

Listing 7.12. The ASP file in the subdirectory that uses the application-level variables.

```
1: <HTML>
2: <HEAD><TITLE></TITLE></HEAD>
3: <BODY>
4: <H3><%= Application("name") %> is accessing an Application variable from
➥ a subdirectory.</H3>
5: </BODY>
6: </HTML>
```

Figure 7.13.

The ASP file that displays the application-level variables.

Most of the work done in an Active Server Page is creating the page to return to the client, which might require string manipulation or math manipulation. You can use VBScript functions within your ASP files, as long as these functions are also in the Active Server Page delimiters.

The Include File

Most programming languages have a mechanism to include more than one function that can be used by a file. Active Server Pages supply a similar mechanism: the include file. The include file can have HTML or Active Server scripting, but it must have the extension .INC.

There are two important ways to use an include file. First, you can give a consistent look to your pages by adding, say, a menu. If you have a menu on every page, then normally you would have to edit every page when the menu needs to change. However, the menu text can be placed in a MENU.INC file, such as the one shown in Listing 7.13. Notice that there are no beginning or ending HTML tags, such as <HTML> or <BODY>. That's because when the #include statement in the calling file is processed, the include file is entered at that point. Generally, that point is already in the middle of a file being processed. By using an include file, the editing of the menu (or whatever common HTML code you need) takes place in only a single file. You don't have to touch multiple files—only the necessary include files.

Listing 7.13. The MENU.INC include file.

```
1: <!-- menu.inc -->
2: <A HREF="top.htm">Top</A><BR>
3: <A HREF="next.htm">Next</A><BR>
4: <A HREF="previous.htm">Previous</A><BR>
5: <P>
```

Listing 7.14 uses the include file to add a menu to the response. Notice how the include file is named and the FILE keyword is used. The other keyword is VIRTUAL, which points to a virtual directory path to get the include file. Also notice that the statement is included in an HTML comment instead of an Active Server delimited statement. Figure 7.14 illustrates what this file looks like when it's called.

Listing 7.14. The calling file for the `#include` statement.

```
 1:  <HTML>
 2:  <HEAD>
 3:  <TITLE> Form Use </TITLE>
 4:  </HEAD>
 5:  <H3> Form Use </H3>
 6:  <!--#INCLUDE FILE="menu.inc"-->
 7:  <%
 8:  Response.Write Request.Form("text1")
 9:  %>
10:  </HTML>
```

Figure 7.14.

Creating a menu through an include file.

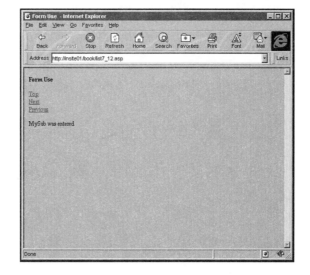

The second use for an include file involves a set of functions used by most of your ASP files. These would be good functions to place in an include file. As an example, suppose that each page you have must make sure that the text input from a user doesn't have any characters the database won't accept. This would be a function. Every page with a form needs this function, but with include files, you need to write it only once, then include it. Listing 7.15 is a revised FORM.ASP file, with the first `#include` statement calling an ASP file. By listing FUNCT.ASP as an include file, all of its text is included. The line `Call MySub` is the reference to the function in the FUNCT.ASP.

7

Listing 7.15. Including functions.

```
 1: <!--#INCLUDE FILE="funct.asp"-->
 2: <HTML>
 3: <HEAD>
 4: <TITLE> Form Use </TITLE>
 5: </HEAD>
 6: <H3> Form Use </H3>
 7: <!--#INCLUDE FILE="menu.inc"-->
 8: <%
 9: Call MySub
10: %>
11: <%
12: Response.Write Request.Form("text1")
13: %>
14: </HTML>
```

Listing 7.16 is the FUNCT.ASP file. Notice that the Active Server script still must be placed within the Active Server delimiters.

Listing 7.16. The included file.

```
1: <!-- funct.asp -->
2: <%
3: Sub MySub()
4:     Response.Write "<P>MySub was entered <P>"
5: End Sub
6: %>
```

The ASA File

The ASA file is used as the application-level "glue." Because a Web site isn't a single "application," the ASA file handles things that should happen at an application level. The ASA file should contain any startup or shutdown events for the Application or Session object as well as any objects that the application's ASP pages will use.

The ASA file is read by the Web server the first time a user makes a request or when a user doesn't have a session. The ASA file should be placed in the Web server's root directory for the files that are considered the application. If you have two different groups of Web pages, such as Human Resources and Finance, you would probably have each in its own directory of the main root. The /hr alias and the /finance alias, for example, each need an ASA file in those directories (these need to be explicit aliases created through Internet Information Server). ASP files in any subdirectories will know to find the ASA file.

If your Web "application" doesn't need to keep track of users-per-session information or global application-level startup or shutdown events, don't worry about ASA files. Your site can do just fine without them.

Summary

In this chapter, you have learned about Active Server scripting, which has five objects: `Server`, `Request`, `Response`, `Session`, and `Application`. The `Request` object is sent from the client's browser to request a Web page from the server, and the `Response` object accesses information that's sent in the response to the client's browser. The `Application` and `Session` objects allow a programmer to treat the Active Server Pages as an `Application` object with a connection from the client's browser. The `Server` object gives you access to information about the Web server. With Active Server Pages, you can control the Web page through programming as it's processed on the server.

Q&A

Q If I wanted to include a file, does the extension have to be .INC?

A No, the normal .ASP extension will work.

Q If I wanted to pass parameters to an ASP file, what's the difference between the `Request.QueryString` and the `Request.Forms` collections?

A The only difference is that the information in the `Forms` collection comes from a `<FORM>` and the `QueryString` collection comes from an `<A>` anchor tag with a link that includes parameters, such as `<A HREF=mypage.asp?param1=yes&param2=no">My Page</A>`.

Q What's the difference between using VBScript in an ASP file and using VBScript in a HTML page?

A Nothing will be different about what the VBScript does. The only difference is that HTML code uses the `<SCRIPT>` tag as a delimiter, but ASP pages need all script, including VBScript, delimited with the `<% %>` markers.

Quiz

1. What's the file extension for an Active Server Page?
2. What permissions do you have to set on a virtual root to have the Active Server Page process correctly?
3. If you have a single file of global functions that all Active Server pages may need to get to, how can you access that file?

4. How do you create a virtual root?

5. What is considered an *application* in Active Server Page terminology?

6. What is the syntax for passing parameters to a method?

7. What is buffering?

8. What does `Response.Write` do?

Exercises

1. Create Web pages with buffering on and with buffering off, and note differences when you use different Active Server objects.

2. Create a Web page that creates an instance of an OLE control and has code to manipulate that control when the page is loaded.

3. Create a Web site that uses the application-level variables and session-level scope as well as cookies to store clients' interests.

4. Create a Web page where the form is built and written to the client's browser by using scripting.

WEEK

1

In Review

During Week 1, you learned database skills and the fundamentals of Web scripting languages. You should now be able to write a complete Web site as well as query the database.

Day 1: Database Connectivity and Visual Basic

Day 1 covered the development of some of the Web technologies up to their current state. In this chapter, you learned how the Web scripting of HTML started and where it is today. You also learned the difference between a static Web page and a dynamic Web page.

Day 2: The Client-Server Model

Day 2 introduced the client-server aspects of Web development. In this chapter, you learned the different network aspects of the Internet, including the protocols involved and the basics of Microsoft Internet Information Server (IIS).

Day 3: Database Fundamentals and ODBC

Day 3 introduced fundamental information for manipulating relational databases. In this chapter, you learned different ways to get information into and out of a database. This chapter also explained the Open Database Connectivity (ODBC) standard.

Day 4: The HTML Scripting Language

Day 4 introduced some of the essential scripting tags that make up a Web page. In this chapter, you learned how to create a basic, as well as a more advanced, Web page by using the HTML scripting tags.

Day 5: The VBScript Language

Day 5 introduced the VBScript language constructs, and you learned how to program the client-side page to act and react to your commands.

Day 6: Using an ActiveX Control

Day 6 covered how to use and program an ActiveX control by using some free sample controls from the Microsoft Web gallery. This chapter focused on how to manage the control through VBScript.

Day 7: Using Active Server Scripting

Day 7 explained how to write scripts that are executed on the server. In this chapter, you learned the basic objects and collections and how to use them.

At a Glance

The first week acted as an introduction to the applications and tools you will be using to perform data access over the World Wide Web. Week 2, "Server-Side Rowsets with ActiveX Data Objects," leaves the introductions behind and jump-starts you into building your own dynamic Web pages.

Data access over the Web can be done in two different, yet complementary, ways. It can be restricted to a server-only operation in which Web pages and tabular results are generated and sent back to the client as HTML documents, or it can be done interactively with queries originating from the client, resulting in data made directly available to client scripts.

This second week focuses on server-only data access, which is tied directly to a server-based Web-programming model. In this model, the burden of your online application is placed on the server. Using Microsoft Active Server Pages, you add your own extensions to the Web server that automatically generates the pages composing your application in response to user interactions from the client. A major benefit of a server-based programming model is that the client browser needs to understand only HTML. Your Web application will be accessible by everyone, everywhere.

Data access is the key component in determining both the content of your pages and the methods by which you take meaningful action based on user input. You learn how to use Microsoft's ActiveX Data Objects with Active Server Pages and Visual Basic Script on the server to accomplish these goals and build compelling Web applications.

Day 8

ActiveX Data Objects (ADO) Overview

by Matt Warren

After reading this chapter, you will be able to do the following:

- ☐ List the advantages of using ActiveX Data Objects (ADO) for database access
- ☐ Describe what it means for an object to be *programmable*
- ☐ List the three main objects in the ADO model
- ☐ Associate each main ActiveX Data Object with its particular use
- ☐ Show how to create ActiveX Data Objects by using Visual Basic, Visual Basic Script, and Visual Basic Script for Active Server Pages
- ☐ List the advantages of using Active Server Pages for delivering HTML content
- ☐ Describe the primary differences between ADO, DAO (Data Access Objects), and RDO (Remote Data Objects)

Why ADO Is So Cool

ADO (ActiveX Data Objects) is a technology that can be used by Web page developers to add database access to their online content. Database access opens up a world of information that can be used to customize Web site offerings based on user preferences, past usage history, or up-to-the-minute news. Database applications, with ADO, can now be written as online applications, accessed anywhere over the global Internet; orders can be filled, purchases can be tracked, and inventory can be kept up to date based on real information from the same sources that drive current business operations.

ADO is a technology meant for application and Web-site developers with modest programming skills. It's capable of condensing otherwise complex and lengthy programming tasks into simple-to-use statements and strong enough to grow as the demand for more advanced features grow with any project. ADO couples ease-of-use with a full range of advanced features. ADO makes both common and advanced operations simpler to use than ever before.

ADO is consistent, no matter what database program is actually used to store the information. ActiveX Data Objects gives programmers the same interface and offers the same sets of features, whether the data is stored locally in products such as Microsoft Access or Microsoft FoxPro or resides in servers from companies like Microsoft, Oracle, Informix, or Sybase.

ADO is *cross language*, which means that besides being consistent across database vendors, ADO is consistent across different programming environment, from Visual Basic to C++ to Java. Skills from programmers knowledgeable in one environment can be easily transferred to another. Programmers developing commercial products with C++ can just as easily take advantage of ADO as programmers developing corporate business applications in Visual Basic or online content in Visual Basic Script, JavaScript, or Java. The product they use is the same in each case. A company can leverage a single database access technology without sacrificing access to multiple database back-ends or limiting application development to a single programming environment.

ADO is available today on the platforms you use. ActiveX Data Objects are accessible on any operating system that supports both the Component Object Model (COM) and OLE Automation. This includes Windows 95, Windows NT Workstation, and Windows NT Server running on Intel, DEC Alpha, and PowerPC, in addition to any platform governed by Microsoft's Active Platform product line. Online applications can be built by using ADO on the server to deliver customized content through the World Wide Web. In this way, any platform supporting a modern Web browser can automatically take advantage of data access. Users of Windows PCs, Macs, UNIX workstations, or other types of consumer Web devices can easily tap into your online application to make inquiries and order products.

8

The Benefits of Basing ActiveX Data Objects on Microsoft's COM

COM is advantageous because it enforces an agreement between software producers and software consumers, guaranteeing a consistent calling mechanism between them. The layout of a COM interface doesn't vary across platforms or programming environments. Many separate objects can share the same definition of a single interface, allowing them to be easily interchanged. No longer do applications need to be written to talk to proprietary tools. Breaking tools down into components with well-defined interfaces gives you a simple, consistent way to customize software. Functions and parameters behave the same in Basic, C, C++, or Java, whether the tool is written by me or by you.

COM objects are multifaceted. They aren't restricted to a single set of functions, so they can take on the appearance of many well-defined interfaces. You might want to build a tool that appears as a database to one application but as a file system to another. Similarly, you're free to choose among the interfaces supported by a commercial tool to get the level of functionality you want for your application.

COM objects are easily distributed. They automatically gain the ability to be used across multiple processes and multiple machines. Often difficult to program, interprocess communication and remote procedure calls are automatic to developers using COM objects. They can be passed back and forth through function calls as easily as normal parameters. Neither function needs to know that the other doesn't exist in the same process space on the same machine, and no code needs to be changed. Whether local or remote, your code is exactly the same.

The ADO Model

The ADO model defines a hierarchy of programmable objects that can be used by the Web page developer to access information stored in a database. A *hierarchy* is a group of related objects that work together for some useful purpose. Figure 8.1 shows a hierarchy; each box represents an object, and each line represents a direct association between objects.

The term *object* has many different meanings, depending on who you ask. In the world of information systems and database development, it can often mean the data stored in the database. There's a lot of talk today about object databases, persistent object stores, and other merging ideas between programming and databases that might make your eyes either glaze over in frustration or gleam with anticipation. ADO uses the term in a more pragmatic sense, in the same manner used when discussing object-oriented programming languages, such as C++, Smalltalk, and, yes, even Visual Basic.

Figure 8.1.
A hierarchy chart.

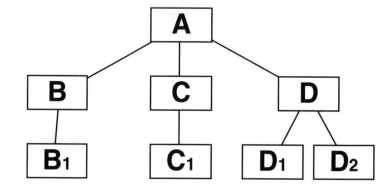

An object is best understood as a logical association between program variables and program functions. (See Figure 8.2.) For example, a variable declared in the Visual Basic statement `Dim x as integer` is intended to hold information—in this case, a number. A function declared in the same language is expected to take an action, to do something: change the value of a variable, paint a picture on the screen, or send out for pizza.

Figure 8.2.
A "generic" object with its associated variables and functions.

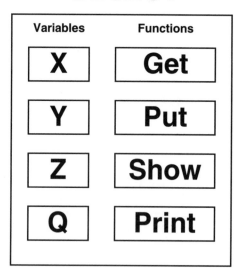

An object is more than just a variable, or many variables, and it's more than just a function, or many functions. An object is an organization of variables and functions that the programmer has decided belong together because together they do something useful.

For example, variables and functions organized together into an object might represent an airline flight reservation. The prospective passenger's name and phone number may be part of the object's variables, and the act of assigning a seat or even canceling the reservation might be considered some of the object's functions. To a programmer who's concerned with manipulating flight reservations, it's much more convenient to work with objects than with a smattering of variables and functions. If the programmer wants to work with 10 reservations at once, for instance, it's easier to have 10 objects than hundreds of independent variables. If the programmer wants to know at a glance what common and useful things can be done with a reservation, he need look no further than the object's description. Instead of needing to understand the details of a flight reservation, the programmer can remain fixed on the problem at hand, such as booking 10 people on an itinerary of six flights and eight hotels over four weeks and three continents. Good organization is the key to making difficult problems seem simpler.

Similarly, it's often more convenient for programmers to offer useful functions and features to other programmers by organizing them into objects. If you remember back to Chapter 6, "Using an ActiveX Control," ActiveX controls are a way to add canned functionality to a Web page. Those controls can be manipulated by using Visual Basic Script or JavaScript to change properties (variables) and call methods (functions). ActiveX controls are objects, in the same way that the flight reservation was an object in the previous example.

Because these objects can be manipulated in programming or scripting languages, they are called *programmable*. Some controls might have only a visual user interface with canned responses to mouse clicks and key presses. These types of controls or objects are considered *non-programmable*. ActiveX Data Objects are programmable objects. They are also technically ActiveX controls, but since they have no visual interface, they draw no graphical representation of themselves on the screen; it's less confusing to simply talk about them as programmable objects.

ActiveX Data Objects are collections of variables and functions that are organized together because together they do unique and useful things. They connect to databases, issue queries, and gather responses. They let you step through the records you have queried for, make changes, and send those changes back to the database. They do this without you, the programmer, needing to know the intricate details of communicating directly to any number of databases that you might otherwise need to know to perform the task set before you.

The ActiveX Data Objects

The ADO model defines three general-purpose objects—Connection, Command, and Recordset—that can be created by the programmer and used to access data. There are other objects in the model as well, such as Field, Property, and Parameter, that are accessible as sub-objects of the main three; they're described in the following list:

Object Name	Description
Connection	The direct link to the database server
Command	The query to be issued against the server
Recordset	The result of the query; all the data
Fields	A collection of multiple Field objects
Field	An individual Field object
Properties	A collection of multiple Property objects
Property	An individual extended Property object
Parameters	A collection of multiple Parameter objects
Parameter	An individual Command Parameter object
Errors	A collection of multiple Error objects
Error	An individual Error object

The Connection object can be used to establish a dedicated line of communication between a software application and a database. The Command and Recordset objects use the Connection object to perform their individual tasks. Imagine that the Connection object is a telephone call. The act of creating a Connection object is just like picking up the receiver of the phone, and the act of opening the Connection object is similar to dialing. Both the Command and Recordset objects, in turn, speak over the open line to the database, requesting and updating information.

The Command object can be used to specify a database query. Often this query is expressed in terms of a SQL statement. If you recall from Chapter 3, "Database Fundamentals and ODBC," *SQL* stands for "Standard Query Language." Most database servers accept requests written with this language. ADO allows the programmer to use whatever query language is native to the database server. A programmer, using an ADO Command object, can take a SQL query and assign it to the Command object's CommandString property. Later, when the command is executed, the query is sent to the database server, and the results are retrieved and stored in a Recordset object.

8

8

The Recordset object is by far the most useful of all the ActiveX Data Objects. A *recordset* represents the records resulting from a query against a database; aptly named, a recordset is simply a set of records. If a database is a gold mine, the records are the gold nuggets, the actual bits and pieces of information the database query was sent to retrieve. You can use the Recordset object to examine each record one at a time, independently accessing the values held for each of the record's fields. With the help of a server-side scripting environment, you can step through each record and construct a corresponding visual representation of the data.

A typical, albeit minimal, example is a program that generates a Web page containing a table of information—an up-to-date pricing list for an online store. The Web site could display customized inventory lists, customer purchases, virtual shopping baskets, and more. If your application requires it, you can even use the Recordset object to update the field values for one or more records and then submit them back to the database. More than simply displaying data, your Web site can function as a true interactive application, one that's comparable to a fully functional order-entry, billing, or any other production system used in a large corporation, and that can be accessed as easily across the World Wide Web as it can within centrally controlled corporate computer networks.

A Recordset cannot do its work, however, without a Command object to issue a query, and neither object would be of any use without a Connection object. If there's no Connection, there might as well be no database; nothing to query, no gold to mine. These three main objects of the ADO hierarchy work together to deliver data access to your application or Web page. Each is necessary, and none can be used alone. It's best to understand them as a hierarchy of dependence, illustrated in Figure 8.3. A Recordset depends on both a Command and a Connection, the Command depends only on the Connection, and the Connection depends merely on the information you give it to find the correct database.

Figure 8.3.

A simple ADO hierarchy chart.

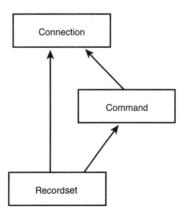

Letting Recordsets Do the Work

These three objects—Connection, Command, and Recordset—are always working together, even if you, the programmer, don't explicitly create them. You can accomplish everything you need to do, such as connecting to a database, executing a query, and manipulating the results, by programming with the Recordset object alone. It's powerful enough to do the work for you of creating a Connection and a Command object without you having to write code to create them and link them into the hierarchy.

Still, the ADO model does allow the programmer to piece together the object hierarchy at runtime. You can create both the Connection and Command objects separately and associate them later. The Command object has a property that can be used to associate an active Connection object to it directly. An *active connection* is one that has already been created and opened to establish a link to the database. Likewise, the Recordset object has properties that can be used to associate it to both a Connection object and a Command object.

What's not so readily apparent, however, is that just about anything can be used as a Connection or a Command. You don't have to specifically assign a Connection object to the Recordset's ActiveConnection property . You can simply assign a character string describing the connection, the same string you would have used to inform the Connection object about the database you wanted to establish a link to. The Recordset object is capable of taking that string and converting it into a Connection object or taking a string containing a SQL query and converting it into a Command object.

You can save yourself a lot of typing and confusion by simply using the Recordset object alone. You have the choice of assigning character strings to properties that automatically turn themselves into objects, instead of writing code that explicitly creates them. To make it even easier, the Recordset object has the Open method that takes a SQL query and a connection string as two of its parameters. You can essentially go from nothing to a fully functional Recordset, ready to manipulate, in one line of code.

Doing It Yourself

There are, however, very good reasons to do the work yourself. Both Connection and Command objects can be customized, altering their behaviors to fit the particular tastes of the programmer or the specific needs of the application. These changes can affect how the query is performed, how the server produces results, and how updates, if any, are managed between the client and the server. It's important to be able to customize a connection before the link is established. This level of customization isn't possible, however, if you leave the work of creating the connection to the Recordset object. There's a trade-off between advanced features and ease-of-use to consider when you're choosing which method you'll use to construct your object hierarchy.

Taking Advantage of Shared Command Objects

Other advanced features, discussed later in this book, give equally compelling reasons to choose creating Connection and Command objects separately. Both Connection and Command objects can be created once and shared across multiple Recordsets. Chapter 11, "Transactions and the Connection Object," will show you how. This ability gives you a huge performance benefit, one that every Web page developer will want to take advantage of. Not only can you share connections across multiple queries, you can also share connections across multiple Web page hits, for the same client or for many clients. More often than not, Web sites are designed to repeatedly access the same database, using the same or similar queries. Shared connections mean less workload placed on the database server, quicker response time, and more successful page hits per minute.

Shared Command objects take this concept one step further. Chapter 12, "Commands and Stored Procedures," will show you how a *shared Command object* can be prepared for execution once, saving a lot of time that would otherwise be needed to execute the query. Most database servers allow queries to be optimized. An optimized query can execute faster than a non-optimized one because analysis of the query and the database has already determined the most efficient way to retrieve the data. This analysis might be as simple as determining which of many indexes to use against a database table, or it could be as complicated as determining in which sequence sub-queries must be processed to produce the results of a complex multilevel join in the shortest time or with the fewest resources. Regardless of whether the query is optimized before execution, the work must still be done. A shared Command object allows the programmer to re-use the optimization work from a previous query.

ADO in VBScript

Visual Basic Script, or *VBScript*, is one of many programming environments that can readily accept ADO as a native extension to its built-in services. Java, JavaScript, Visual Basic, and Visual C++ all use ADO in exactly the same way to get the same data access. You can leverage your knowledge of ADO in one environment when moving to the others. The same objects, methods, and properties exist in each environment. You can even program with ADO in the macro language found in Microsoft Office applications. It is, after all, Visual Basic, too.

A scripting language, however, is the best choice when developing Web-based applications because the client-side browser and the Web server both understand how to insert scripting code into HTML pages. The scripting code is what brings your Web pages to life; it's the glue that binds together all those ActiveX controls and Java applets. When the user opens a form created by HTML tags and clicks a button, the scripting code takes over. The code you added is executed interactively on demand. You can do a lot with scripting code, including writing your entire Web-based application in it.

If you're already familiar with Visual Basic, then Visual Basic Script is by all means the best choice to get started with. You won't find yourself digging through stacks of documentation just to write your first line of code. The code you write will look practically identical to the code you would have written using Visual Basic. The concepts are the same, and so is the syntax. The main difference between Visual Basic and its scripting counterpart is that the scripting code knows how to work inside an HTML document. Embedded between a pair of HTML tags, actual code lies in wait for the moment it's urged into action.

The only real difference between using ADO in Visual Basic Script and using it in Visual Basic is how you go about creating those three main ADO objects. Books focused on Visual Basic will undoubtedly teach you to declare every object before you use it, which requires you to use a `Dim` statement, of course.

Visual Basic and the `Dim` Statement

The `Dim` statement was introduced in Basic long ago, during the dinosaur years when the Basic language was the new kid on the block. It was originally used to declare arrays of values. `Dim` stood for *dimension*, as in `Dim x(10)`, which meant "declare the variable x to contain 11 elements, 0 through 10." Later, Microsoft developed Basic further and extended the command to allow explicit naming of data types. The statement `Dim x(10)` turned into `Dim x(10) as Single`; `Single` meant a single-precision floating-point number. Likewise, `Dim x(10) as Integer` would declare an array of 11 integers. Then, someone got the brilliant idea to extend the `Dim` statement to include variables that weren't arrays. Soon statements like `Dim Q as String` started popping up. In the dinosaur years, if you wanted to use a string, you had to add a suffix of a dollar sign ($), so you had to type `Q$`. This latest extension of the `Dim` statement gave you the keen ability to type `Q` instead of `Q$`.

Alas, Visual Basic came along and extended Basic once again. No longer are you limited to simple primitive data types, such as `Single`, `Double`, `Integer` or `String`. You can now extend Basic by adding in new data types. Your own objects, implemented as OLE Automation/ ActiveX servers, can appear simply as normal, built-in primitives. All you have to do is tell Basic about your wonderful new custom object/data type by pulling down the Tools | References menu and picking the library you want to use. You can immediately begin using your new data type or object. To declare a variable of type `MyType`, all you have to do is use the statement `Dim x as new MyType`.

In Visual Basic, declaring ActiveX Data Objects is just as simple. The following three lines of code each declare a unique and different ADO object:

```
Dim rs as new Recordset

Dim cn as New Connection

Dim cm as New Command
```

This syntax for declaring objects is extremely useful when you start doing advanced operations, such as building custom business objects, in Chapter 19, "Client-Server Business Objects." Until then, however, it's nice to be able to forget about the intricacies of the Dim statement. Visual Basic Script, in an attempt to simplify the language and provide a more streamlined virtual machine (the engine that actually executes your basic code), has dropped all the added syntax extensions. The Dim statement still exists, but it's reserved, as it originally was, for declaring dimensions of arrays. VBScript has forsaken the descriptive power of the declaration for the eloquence of simplicity. It has taken to heart the motto "Everything is an object."

Everything Is a Variant

In Visual Basic Script, all variables are objects, or rather they are all *Variants*. A Variant is a data type that not only varies in value, but also in type. Each variable has the type of whatever data was last assigned to it. Instead of being allowed to use only integers with variables declared as Integer, a variable can change its apparent type from one part of the program to the next. A variable can start out being an Integer at the beginning of the program, but by the middle, it can be a String, or a Single, or even a Recordset. This change is not, however, a wide divergence from Visual Basic proper. Visual Basic Script's more strongly typed "big brother" can do all that VBScript can and more. It's possible to declare individual variables as Variant and gain all the same advantages of VBScript. In Visual Basic, you can even declare a variable as type Object, much more restrictive than Variant, but still allow the variable to take on the identity of any custom data type.

Using an Alternative to the Dim Statement

All this preceding discussion means you won't be using a Dim statement to declare a Recordset object in VBScript. You will, however, be using an alternative method of getting a custom data type or object, a method equally available in all forms of Visual Basic.

The CreateObject() function was originally supplied in Visual Basic as a means of creating custom typed objects at runtime, without knowing at design time what the actual type was going to be. This was done by passing a String value to the function as its sole parameter. A programmer could, if he wanted, change the custom type he planned to create by storing the type's name in a String variable and using that variable as the parameter to the CreateObject() function. The developers of VBScript kept this function as the sole object-creation mechanism because it was both powerful and data-type–agnostic. No matter what custom data type is actually created by the function, it returns a value typed as Object to the programmer. The catch-all type Variant can quite easily take on the appearance of an Object, so VBScript was free to use the CreateObject() function without alteration.

Creating an ActiveX Data Object in VBScript is as simple as calling the `CreateObject()` function. As with the Visual Basic example before, the following three lines of code each create a unique and different ActiveX Data Object:

```
Set rs = CreateObject("ADODB.Recordset")

Set cn = CreateObject("ADODB.Connection")

Set cm = CreateObject("ADODB.Command")
```

Make sure you notice the prefix ADODB used in each of the `CreateObject()` function calls. The string that's passed as a parameter to `CreateObject()` is the name of the object type you want to create. This string is sometimes referred to as the *PROGID* of the object. Pronounced "PROG-I-D," meaning "Program ID," this name is used by the operating system as a key for finding the library of code associated with the object. The prefix ADODB is actually the name given to the library. Microsoft's first release of ActiveX Data Objects, affectionately named *ADODB*, is designed to be an easy-to-use front-end to Microsoft's premier database technology OLE DB. When you specify ADODB in your code, you're asking for the OLE DB version of ADO. Fortunately, ADODB is a component that's included with Internet Information Server 3.0 or higher, and is available for use on all servers with IIS installed. Programmers familiar with Visual Basic and the various uses of the `Dim` statement might know that the library name is optional when declaring a variable typed as an object. The library name, however, is *not* optional when using the `CreateObject()` function. Visual Basic needs the full name, including the library prefix, to find all the information about the object from the operating system's registry.

ADO and Active Server Pages

Active Server Pages is a technology introduced by Microsoft in Internet Information Server 3.0. It adds the capability of customizing Web pages on the server before they're transmitted over the network to the browser requesting them. Although there are other means to customize Web pages, none is more elegant and powerful than Active Server Pages. Programmability is its key feature, but more important is the ease of adding that programmability. With Active Server Pages, program scripts can be added directly to the Web page and inserted precisely between the HTML instructions that need to be customized. Instead of writing lengthy, hard-to-read C programs or Perl scripts that disguise the HTML instructions and leave you wondering just what obfuscated output the programs generate, with Active Server Pages, you can put the code you want right were you want it. You can start with a complete, viewable HTML document and incrementally customize it with small fragments of script code that automatically direct the changes to the document when the code is executed on the server.

With Active Server Pages, the code you add to the HTML documents is not unlike the code you might normally add to the same document to have interactive behavior that runs on the client side. Most browsers, for some time, have been able to host scripting code that's executed after the Web page is downloaded from the Web server to the client. Internet Explorer can add programmability with either Visual Basic Script or JavaScript, depending on the tastes and skills of the Web page developer, and Active Server Pages has added this same capability to Internet Information Server. A Web page developer can use both Visual Basic Script and JavaScript to add scripting code that's executed by the server, instead of the browser, before the document is transferred across the network. The ability to use the exact same scripting language when developing Web pages that exhibit interactive behavior and customization allows a developer with modest skills to control the entire operation of an online application.

Customizing with Scripting Code

It's also possible to use client-side scripting to customize a Web page after it has been downloaded. For example, VBScript statements added to an HTML document, but not placed inside explicit functions or sub-routines, execute immediately after the page has finished transferring from the server. This code could actually alter the page's appearance by modifying the HTML instructions before the browser has examined it. This technique does have a place in Web developers' tool belts, but it shouldn't be the primary technique because it has many drawbacks. With tools such as Active Server Pages, however, you can overcome these drawbacks by server-side customization.

Web pages with extensive customization code are much larger than pages that are designed once and always have the same appearance. Smaller Web pages are more popular than larger ones because they transfer faster and are more likely to be revisited. Customization on the server allows the workload to be placed on the server, not the client. More important, the code executed by the server isn't transferred to the client. Only the resulting Web page is transferred, and it's often as small and streamlined as a non-customized page.

The most important use of server-side scripting is, perhaps, the one that's equally as important to the developers reading this book. Customization is worthwhile only if it results in Web pages that are compelling to either the company developing the Web site or the user accessing it. There may be reasons to add tricks such as randomizing ads so that different images are displayed each time a Web page is hit, but these reasons are rather trivial compared to Web sites that can automatically customize themselves based on user preferences, history of previous visits or purchases, current events, or news. Information is the missing piece, and more often than not, information is tucked away inside overwhelmingly arcane databases.

One great advantage to customizing with Active Server Pages is that the Web server has access to databases that are hidden from client computers. Web servers on the Internet are often placed behind corporate *firewalls*, which act as barriers that protect computers in a company from the wild, unguarded chaos of the global Internet. Requests, such as those for Web pages, are often allowed to travel through the firewall. These requests are considered harmless and are usually the main reason a corporate network is connected to the Internet in the first place.

Reducing the Risk to Database Servers

Database servers, however, are often considered too critical to a company's existence to risk opening them up for direct contact with the outside world. Web servers are privileged because they exist logically on the same side of the firewall as the database server, so they can access the databases directly. This restriction is compounded by most databases being accessible only to machines on a local area network. Local area networks have the advantage of being faster and more reliable than distributed networks, such as the Internet, and databases are often designed with this advantage as a requirement for operation. The more reliable a network, the less likely data will be lost during transmission or a transaction will be broken in mid-step. Proprietary protocols are often devised to reduce these risks even further. Unfortunately, these protocols are often bound to the same local area networks the databases were designed for, so even if the database servers could be connected directly to the global Internet, it's unlikely they could be communicated with.

Many companies, like Microsoft, are trying to come up with ways to ensure reliable, safe access to databases across the Internet. The Advanced Data Connector, discussed in Chapter 15, "The Advanced Data Connector (ADC)," is Microsoft's first attempt at bridging the gap between local area networks and distributed networks. For online applications that demand a more robust, interactive experience with data, the Advanced Data Connector is a useful tool.

There are trade-offs, however, when choosing client-side tools such as the Advanced Data Connector. HTML documents become increasingly larger, and the pages aren't accessible to all browsers on all platforms. If your audience is limited, and you can guarantee their hardware is of a certain type and above a certain par, and their network connections operate at an acceptable speed, then the Advanced Data Connector is a good choice. If not—if you need to make your online application available to a general audience with a widely diverging set of computer hardware and software—it's better to control all customization and all data access by scripting code run on the server. Although they can be completely customized by using scripting code with direct access to secure databases, Active Server Pages transmit as pure HTML documents to the client's browser. No matter what browser is used, the customized Web page is fully functional.

8

Using Active Server Pages

This discussion on database access, of course, brings you back to ActiveX Data Objects, the fundamental means of accessing data from scripts written within HTML documents. These scripts can, based on the data, customize the appearance of the Web page by altering the HTML instructions within it. ADOs can be integrated into Active Server Pages as simply as they can with Visual Basic. In fact, Active Server Pages, being a mix between HTML instructions and scripting code, give the programmer as simple a mechanism of introducing ADO as VBScript alone.

The `CreateObject()` function is available in the scripting code embedded in the Web page. It's supplied as a method of the built-in `Server` object. The Active Server environment offers five built-in objects: `Server`, `Session`, `Request`, `Response`, and `Form`. These objects aren't available to scripting code running on the client; they're special objects that encapsulate a lot of functionality the programmer would otherwise have to invent to write server-side code. The examples in this book take advantage of these built-in objects extensively.

The following statement written in VBScript for Active Server Pages demonstrates the straightforward nature of getting an ADO `Recordset` object:

```
<% Set rs = Server.CreateObject("ADODB.Recordset") %>
```

Active Server considers everything that appears between the bracketing symbols, `<%` and `%>`, to be scripting code. All VBScript statements executed by the server before the page is transmitted must appear between these two brackets. Almost any valid script can be used, as complex as many statement lines and complete functions or sub-routines, or as simple as partial fragments of statements or expressions. As far as Active Server is concerned, all scripting code placed between these brackets is seen as one long sequential script. When processing the Web page, Active Server ignores the HTML instructions, executes the combined program, and replaces the bracketed sections with new HTML instructions generated by the code in the corresponding locations. None of the code that appears between brackets, or even the brackets themselves, end up in the HTML document that's eventually sent to the client. In the preceding VBScript statement, the recordset is created during the execution on the server. Other VBScript code later in the document can make use of the recordset, but none of the statement as shown appears in the document sent to the client. In fact, since the statement itself doesn't generate any HTML output, the entire statement is removed.

ADO, DAO, and RDO

ActiveX Data Objects are, indeed, the best way for programmers to get access to databases. They offer a simple programming model that can also provide advanced functionality for those seeking it. They aren't, however, the first of their breed. They aren't even a new idea—just a practical one.

Microsoft, in its never-ending attempt at refining ease of use and expanding functionality, had previously released two other products that achieved much the same goal. Packaged with both Microsoft Access and Microsoft Visual C++, *DAO (Data Access Objects)* was the first of the object models to see the light of day. DAO, like ADO, introduced an object model complete with a hierarchy of programmable objects. DAO included recordsets, fields, properties, and more—objects that a die-hard database programmer could easily sink her teeth into. In fact, DAO is still in use today; Microsoft Office 97 includes DAO version 3.5.

The difference between DAO and ADO, other than rearranging the letters of their respective acronyms, is that DAO was designed specifically to reveal direct access to Microsoft Access's underlying database technology, known familiarly as the JET database engine. ADO, on the other hand, wasn't designed with any particular database in mind. It has a general design, so it meshes more cleanly with programming models designed around proprietary databases and with those designed around open standards. ODBC, Open Database Connectivity, is one such open standard.

Originating from Microsoft, ODBC has become the recognized standard for providing database technology to consumers. For database development companies such as Microsoft, IBM, Oracle, Sybase, Informix, and others, ODBC has given programmers a way to directly access their database technology through a single consistent, common interface. Products like Microsoft Access, Microsoft FoxPro, and PowerSoft's PowerBuilder all use ODBC to access databases from other manufacturers and their own native technology. ODBC is an *API (application programming interface)*, a set of standards defining a library of function calls that can be used in programming languages like C to access databases on remote servers. Unfortunately, although ODBC was considered a good interface for supplying data, it left a lot to be desired when used as a programming interface. Many attempts were made to disguise this difficult-to-use interface with *wrappers*, language-specific packaging layered on top.

To solve the ease-of-use problem with ODBC once and for all, Microsoft invented another technology parallel to the already existing DAO object model. *RDO (Remote Data Objects)* took the stage and found its way into consumers' hands in a heavy, cube-shaped box known as Microsoft Visual Basic Enterprise Edition. RDO had its own equivalents to DAO objects. Rooted in ODBC terminology, RDO used `Resultsets`, not `Recordsets`, and `Statements`, not `QueryDefs`. RDO was necessary because the DAO model wasn't a clean match to ODBC.

Altering the DAO model would ruin its attractiveness to Microsoft Access programmers. To compromise ODBC functionality by introducing it through DAO would be devastating to the Visual Basic crew because access to ODBC was what the Enterprise Edition was all about. Change was in the wind, and the common use of databases was shifting away from the Access database model based on file-sharing to the new contender: remote servers. Microsoft FoxPro had undergone a redesign that left it strongly positioned as a database server. For the Fox database engine, ODBC meant life or death. And, of course, there was Microsoft SQL Server, on its way to becoming Microsoft's flagship database server product. It, too, depended on ODBC as a primary mechanism to deliver its goods to the consumers.

There had never been a more confusing time for Microsoft databases or for programmers using Microsoft products. Which model was for the future? Which would be supported? Should programmers dump DAO in favor of RDO? What about DAO's complete coverage of the JET database engine? Not all that functionality was available through ODBC. Should DAO be expanded to encompass all that was RDO? Should RDO go beyond ODBC generality and add extensions for Microsoft Access and JET? Microsoft chose the wisest path. It let each product continue on its own way, expanding in directions more favorable to the body of programmers who entrenched themselves as dedicated users of each.

Microsoft knew that something larger loomed on the horizon, something that would not only find answers to these questions, but also leave them behind in the dust. The real debate didn't lie in the difference between DAO and RDO. It sat quite comfortably in the underlying technology, the difference between file-sharing databases and remote servers. That world was about to be bridged by a newer technology promising to lift the database programming community into the world of distributed object programming. OLE was becoming distributed, databases would soon become synonymous with OLE, and OLE DB was the technical specification that was going to take them there. It was destined to surpass ODBC as the recognized standard for providing database technology to consumers. OLE DB was component-object based, meaning the same technology could take on different appearances, depending on the consumer. A single database could seem to have the functionality of a local file store, yet appear to be a fully functioning remote server to another application.

Unfortunately, OLE DB had an even more difficult-to-use interface than ODBC: more difficult to learn, more parameters, more options, more structures, more properties, more settings, more of everything that made it easier for database development companies to add system-specific features. This, of course, left the database programmer with more possibilities and less chance of guessing which set of features would be supported by which set of database engines. OLE DB certainly needed a fresh dose of simplification for the average programmer.

The DAO team and the RDO team joined forces, determined to settle differences and merge the two programming models so that the richness of OLE DB would be simpler and easier to use. ActiveX Data Objects were designed to sit side-by-side with OLE DB and act as a kinder, gentler way of programming. The database development companies could supply expansive features through OLE DB, with no need for private, system-specific APIs. Commercial products obsessed with power and efficiency could program to OLE DB directly, but end-user programmers—those building corporate database applications, the dedicated workers under the gun of short deadlines and high expectations—could take the quicker route and use ADO. ActiveX Data Objects would cut out months of programming time. Getting up and running with ADO would be as simple as creating your first Recordset.

Summary

This chapter has given you an overview of ADO, ActiveX Data Objects, and discussed how Active Server Pages and ADO are used together to build database-centered Web applications. You have been introduced to the ADO object model and seen the primary mechanism for creating each ADO object using Visual Basic and Visual Basic Script. You have also learned the role played by each top-level ADO object and how they depend on each other to perform their individual tasks. Finally, this chapter has offered a complete synopsis of the advantages gained by using ActiveX Data Objects, Visual Basic Script, and Active Server Pages independently, along with a detailed history of the evolution of Microsoft's data access models, which culminated in the easy-to-use, full-featured, cross-language, database-agnostic programming model known as ADO.

Q&A

Q Can I use ADO in the VBScript that runs under the browser?

A Yes, it's possible, but unless you use technology similar to that covered in Chapter 15, you will be restricted to accessing databases that are visible to the client machine. That may be desirable in an intranet scenario, where all clients are actually within the same organization on the same local network.

Also, take into consideration that ADO is not currently marked as safe for scripting. This means ADO objects can be created by the Web page only if the user of the browser accepts each object directly. Under Internet Explorer 3.0, the user is required to click the Accept button of a security warning dialog box. This feature can be overridden, however, by having the user reduce the browser's security level, but it's not recommended.

Q Can I create ActiveX Data Objects using HTML object tags?

A Yes, you can, but doing so falls under the same restrictions described in the first question. Using the <object> HTML tags, you must specify the entire Class ID

(CLSID), not the PROGID you're familiar with when using the CreateObject()
function. Class IDs are globally unique identifiers. No other class in existence,
whether invented by you or a software company, can have exactly the same CLSID
because a unique sequence of numbers is used instead of a name. Although names
are easy to remember, they're also easy for independent developers to accidentally
use for completely different sets of objects.

Use this statement to create a Recordset using HTML <object> tags:

```
<OBJECT NAME=rs CLSID="CLSID:00000281-0000-0010-8000-00AA006D2EA4">
</OBJECT>
```

To create a Connection using HTML <object> tags, use this statement:

```
<OBJECT NAME=cn CLSID="CLSID:00000293-0000-0010-8000-00AA006D2EA4">
</OBJECT>
```

Here's how you create a Command using HTML <object> tags:

```
<OBJECT NAME=cm CLSID="CLSID:0000022D-0000-0010-8000-00AA006D2EA4">
</OBJECT>
```

Q What editor should I use to build my Web pages?

A Use whatever editor is available that lets you insert HTML instructions directly
into the document. ActiveX Control Pad is a good choice, and so is a bare-bones
text editor, such as Notepad. You can also use a layout package, such as FrontPage,
to design the initial pages, and then edit them separately under another editor to
add scripting.

Microsoft Visual InterDev lets you do both, but documenting Visual InterDev is
beyond the scope of this book. All the examples in this book can be easily repro-
duced using a simple text editor.

Q Where do I get ADO? How do I know if I already have it?

A If you have a complete installation of Internet Information Server 3.0 or higher,
ADO is automatically installed on your computer and can be used anytime.

Another way to get ADO by itself is to install the OLE DB Software Development
Kit (SDK).

Q Do I have to buy Visual Basic to use Visual Basic Script in my Web pages?

A No. Visual Basic Script is a subset of Visual Basic and is provided with both
Microsoft Internet Explorer 3.0 and Microsoft Internet Information Server 3.0 or
higher.

**Q Can I use JavaScript instead of Visual Basic Script when I add customization
code to my Web pages?**

A Yes. Microsoft Internet Explorer 3.0 and Microsoft Internet Information Server 3.0
support both scripting languages. However, this book and all the examples in it

have been built using Visual Basic Script. For those knowledgeable in JavaScript, a simple exercise would be to convert the examples from VBScript into JavaScript.

Q Can scripting code running on the client call functions in scripting code running on the server?

A The server-side scripting code is executed only once and is the means by which Web pages are customized before they are transmitted to the client. Once the client gets the custom HTML document, the server script that previously existed in the Web page is removed and generated HTML instructions are inserted in its place (if anything at all is inserted). The server-side scripting code is then no longer running, so it's inaccessible to the client-side scripting code.

To call code running on the server from code running on the client, investigate by using server-side business objects, discussed in Chapter 19.

Q Can I access more than one database at a time?

A Yes. Multiple Recordsets, Commands, and Connections can all be open and functioning at the same time in the same scripting code. You can't, however, include tables from databases associated through separate connections in the same query. For example, if you have one connection made to an Oracle database server, and another, separate connection made to a Microsoft SQL server, you can't form a query that uses tables from both databases. You might get an acceptable result by using a single connection to a single server and by using product-specific features of that server to do the cross-table/cross-database join.

Q Can I have more than one Recordset open per connection?

A Yes, many Recordsets may be open per connection. Likewise, many commands may be pre-optimized (prepared) over the same connection.

Q Can I use either DAO or RDO with Active Server Pages instead of ADO?

A Yes, but some restrictions may apply. Neither DAO nor RDO are optimized for use in a multi-threaded environment such as Active Server Pages. Applications that have been written to use these earlier object models normally access only a handful of objects and are intended for use by only a single client-application process at a time. Active Server Pages are accessible to hundreds, if not thousands, of clients at a time. Furthermore, ActiveX Data Objects have been tested for reliability over lengthy runtimes and hundreds of thousands of repeated uses. This level of reliability and performance were never expected from either DAO or RDO.

8

Quiz

1. List all three main ADO objects.
2. What does the acronym ADO stand for?
3. What's the name of Visual Basic Script's built-in function that's used to create individual ADO objects?
4. To do its work, the ADO Recordset depends on what two other objects?
5. Although the ADO Recordset object depends on other objects to do its work, the programmer doesn't need to manipulate them directly. True or False?
6. The prefix ADODB, used when creating ADO objects, refers to what?
7. ADO can be used in which programming languages or environments?
8. ADO objects are, in fact, ActiveX objects. True or False?

Exercises

1. Show the Visual Basic statement needed to create an ADO Recordset object.
2. Show the VBScript statement needed to create an ADO Recordset object under the server-side scripting environment Active Server Pages.

Day **9**

Dynamic Pages and the ADO Recordset

by Matt Warren

After reading this chapter, you will be able to do the following:

☐ List the methods, properties, and common uses of the ADO `Recordset`
object.

☐ List the methods, properties, and common uses of the ADO `Field`
object.

☐ Write a simple dynamic Web page using ADO technology that
generates HTML-formatted representations of database queries.

Recordset **Fundamentals**

The ADO Recordset object was designed precisely for manipulating the data retrieved as the result of a database query. The Recordset, in a single object, represents a way to find all the database's records that match the query's constraints. The Recordset interface supplies functions that allow you, the programmer, to access individual data elements, either one at a time or in multiple record blocks, depending on which is more natural to the application you're building.

The most common means of getting information is done by accessing records one at a time. For this, the Recordset maintains a sense of *currency*—that is, it uses the concept of a current record position, like a finger pointing at a particular row of a table. When the Recordset is first retrieved, or opened, the position is always on the first record (if there are any records that match the query constraints). If no records match, then the Recordset is considered empty, and the record position is said to be "past the end" of the data. As long as the Recordset is positioned on a good row of data, it isn't past the end or before the beginning; then the application is free to access the individual field elements. Figure 9.1 illustrates all three cases: before the beginning, on a good row, and after the end.

Figure 9.1.

The current record position.

— BOF —

	First Name	Last Name
1	John	Bird
2	Lucy	Lion
3	Art	Walrus
4	Pam	Giraffe
5	Donald	Mallard
6	Yvonne	Ostrich
7	Doris	Tortoise
8	Nancy	Zebra

— EOF —

Opening the Recordset

The easiest way to start manipulating data is to use the Recordset by itself. The Recordset interface has all the functions you need to make commonplace connections to database servers and to perform a wide range of queries. Both of these tasks can be performed by simply choosing appropriate parameters to the Open method.

The Open method is often the first method you use after creating the Recordset. In a single statement, you can both establish a connection to the database server and issue a request for data. A typical use of the Open method is shown as it would appear in a scripting section of an Active Server Page:

```
<%
SET rs = Server.CreateObject("ADODB.Recordset")
rs.Open "Select * from employee", "DSN=pubs;"
%>
```

The first parameter is generically referred to as the Source parameter. In the previous example, the query "Select * from employee" is the Source. Although the database itself is obviously the true source of the data, the query specifies exactly which fields from which tables should be retrieved. In a sense, it represents how the data is transferred from the server and cached (stored) for later use. The Source parameter can be specified as either a Command object or a query string. If a query string is specified, the Recordset automatically converts it to a Command object internally.

The second parameter specified is commonly referred to as the ActiveConnection, which is the connection that's already been established as a link to the database server. It may be specified as either a Connection object or a connection string. In the previous example, the string "DSN=pubs;" is the connection string being used as the ActiveConnection parameter. As you might have already noticed, a connection string doesn't truly represent an established link. However, the Recordset automatically establishes the connection for you, just as it did with the Source parameter when specified as a query string.

A connection string is composed of a series of associations. Terms understood by the database are matched with values supplied by the programmer. An individual association looks like the name of an item—DSN in this example—followed by an equals sign (=), followed by the value pubs, and terminated by a semicolon (;). A well-formed connection string may be composed of many associations, each immediately following the other and always separated by a semicolon.

If you're familiar with ODBC, DAO 3.5 (ODBCDirect), or RDO, you might recognize the term *DSN*; it means *Data Source Name*. The value pubs is the name of a sample database installed by Microsoft SQL Server. Some of the examples in this chapter use pubs as a datasource.

Confirming the Data

Once the Recordset is open, it's easy to determine whether the query has retrieved any data. The Recordset has two properties that can be used just as easily to determine the state of the Recordset: RecordCount and EOF.

The RecordCount property gives the exact number of records retrieved in the query. A query that results in no matched records has a RecordCount of zero. Unfortunately, not all types of Recordsets can easily determine the true count. A forward-only Recordset, the default type, has no way of determining the count of records because the query remains incomplete on the server until all records have been individually read by the client application. Other types of

Recordsets are capable of determining the count, but at a cost of waiting for the full query to finish.

Using the EOF (end of file) property makes it just as easy to check whether the query has retrieved any records; this method has the advantage of always being the most efficient. If you don't really need to know the number of records in the set, simply test the EOF property. It determines whether the current record position is placed after the end of the data. Although "file" terminology isn't entirely applicable to a Recordset, it has historic significance, is familiar to most programmers, and so remains in the lexicon of ActiveX Data Objects. The following Active Server Page script shows the proper use of the EOF property:

```
<%
SET rs = Server.CreateObject("ADODB.Recordset")
rs.Open "Select fname, lname from employee", "DSN=pubs;"
IF NOT rs.EOF THEN
    ' do something with the data here
END IF
%>
```

The EOF property returns a Boolean value that can be either true or false. The IF statement in the preceding script specifically negates the value of the EOF property by using the NOT function. In this fashion, whatever statements that might be added to sit between the THEN and the END IF are executed only when Recordset isn't empty.

Accessing the Data

Now that you know at least one record is available for use, the next thing you should do is actually take a look at it. Just as the database tables themselves are broken down into records and fields, and the corresponding field names are used in the database query, you use these same field names to look at the individual data items. The simplest syntax to use to get the field values is shown in the following statement:

```
<% Firstname = rs("fname") %>
```

In this statement, the variable Firstname is assigned the value from the field "fname" of the first record in the set. Since the variable Firstname is a Variant type, the value from the Recordset field can be of any known type. For example, although "fname" is actually stored as text in the database and appears as a string in VBScript, it could just as easily have been an integer, a floating point number, a date, a currency value, a Boolean true or false, or even an object.

This method of accessing data is a shortcut. The Recordset object is actually a bit more complex in its natural layout. Each field of the Recordset is represented by its own object. The Field objects are grouped together in a collection of objects known as the *Fields collection*. In reality, the Recordset object has as part of its membership the entire Fields collection. For example, you could use the following statement to determine the number of fields in the Recordset:

```
<% n = rs.Fields.Count %>
```

Instead of the original statement used to access the "fname" field from the Recordset, you could have written the following statement:

```
<% Firstname = rs.Fields("fname") %>
```

Normally, the indexing operator is reserved for arrays and collections. The *indexing operator* makes the object look like either a function or an array with many elements. With it, you can specify either the item number or the name of the item you want to find in the collection.

This shortcut method exists because the Recordset isn't a collection in the truest sense. It does represent an entire set of records, but the access methods available allow you to get at only a single record at a time. Unless a query results in a very small set of records, only a narrow span of the data is available to the Recordset. Most database servers can efficiently feed records to the client by streaming sequences of records backward or forward through the results. It would be unnecessarily time-consuming to jump around the set of records haphazardly. There are ways to do this, but they aren't offered as the default means.

Because there's no default record-lookup facility, the Recordset isn't a true collection. When you use the indexing operator to retrieve a field value from the Recordset directly, you're really using the indexing operator of the Fields collection.

Navigating the Records

Now that you know how to get at the data, how about accessing more than just the first record? There are many records, and you can get at them all, but you just have to do it one at a time, by changing the Recordset's current position. Fortunately, you have many ways to do this. The easiest method is to instruct the Recordset to move to the very next record in the set. This method is called, aptly enough, MoveNext. This statement shows how to use it:

```
<% rs.MoveNext %>
```

It's just that simple. You can also modify this example so that instead of working with just the first record, MoveNext uses all of them, one at a time, in a loop:

```
<%
SET rs = Server.CreateObject("ADODB.Recordset")
rs.Open "Select fname, lname from employee", "DSN=pubs;"
WHILE NOT rs.EOF
    ' do something with the data here
    rs.MoveNext
WEND
%>
```

There are three items you should notice in this enhanced example. First, instead of the IF statement used before, this example uses the WHILE statement, which allows the code to operate repeatedly over different records, using the same Recordset and the same sequence of statements. Second, the rs.MoveNext statement advances the Recordset to the next record. Third, notice how the EOF property is still used. When moving forward through the records, it tells you when you have gone past the end of the records. By using the same property that told you when there were no records in the set, you can also determine when you have moved past the end. Without adding extra code, you can handle both looping over the data and confirming that its contents exist.

Moving backward through the data and moving to a particular position within the set are just as easy. However, these methods are considered advanced because not all database servers support all the required modes of operation. Be careful when matching what features are needed by your application to those supported by the different types of Recordsets and databases. Fortunately, the Recordset object is explained in detail in the next section. You'll find descriptions of all the methods, properties, and modes of operation that are useful when developing online applications and dynamic Web pages.

The Recordset Interface

Every object has at least one interface, and each method is a member of the interface. *Interfaces* are merely the set of functions or methods that the object makes available to the programmer. For example, a television could be an object and its remote control the interface you use to control the television—unless, of course, you like to get up and turn the knob. In that case, the knob, too, is an interface; it's just a different one.

The Recordset object has an interface you have already been introduced to. It includes the methods Open and MoveNext and the property EOF. Don't let the existence of properties confuse you. They are actually methods, too; they just behave by Visual Basic syntax rules that allow them to appear as data members. In fact, all members of an interface are methods, but to reduce confusion, they're discussed separately in the following sections.

Recordset Properties

Table 9.1 lists, in alphabetical order, all the properties available on the ADO Recordset object. Following the table, each property is discussed in detail.

Table 9.1. Properties of the Recordset object.

Property	Description
AbsolutePage	Page of current position
AbsolutePosition	Current position
ActiveConnection	Active Connection object
BOF	Beginning of file
Bookmark	Bookmark of current position
CacheSize	Number of records cached
CursorLocation	Server or client
CursorType	Forward, static, dynamic, keyset
EOF	End of file
EditMode	Whether an edit is in progress
Filter	Hide types of records
LockType	Record locking for edits or updates
MaxRecords	Maximum records retrieved
PageCount	Number of pages total
PageSize	Number of records per page
RecordCount	Number of total records
Source	Source Command object
Status	Status of the last action

NOTE   The following descriptions have a phrase on the right-hand side of the page, just after the section title. The words to the left of the separating slash (/) pertain to the Recordset before it's been opened, and those to the right apply while it's open.

AbsolutePage

Contains a PositionEnum (Integer) value   NA / Read-Write

The AbsolutePage property may contain an integer between 1 and the total page count or one of the constant values: adPositionUnknown (-1), adPosBOF (-2), or adPosEOF (-3). You can use this property to determine the exact page number the current position resides on. Pages are broken into separate (*discrete*) blocks of a fixed size that you determine by setting the `PageSize` property. The following calculation shows how the absolute page is determined manually:

```
AbsolutePage = ( AbsolutePosition / PageSize ) + 1
```

In the equation, fractions are ignored. If the current position is the 27th record and the page size is set to 10, then the `AbsolutePage` property reports a value of 3.

You can both get and set the value of the `AbsolutePage` property. When it's assigned, the `Recordset` tries to move the current position to the first record on the designated page. If the `AbsolutePage` property is set to 7 and the `PageSize` is currently 10, then the current position is moved to the 61st record.

If the current position is presently before the first record, the constant value `adPosBOF` is reported. Likewise, if the current position is past the last record, the constant value `adPosEOF` is returned.

AbsolutePosition

Contains a `PositionEnum` (Integer) value   NA / Read-Write

The `AbsolutePosition` property may contain an integer between 1 and the total record count or one of the constant values: `adPositionUnknown` (-1), `adPosBOF` (-2), or `adPosEOF` (-3). It's used to determine the exact ordinal value of the current record position in relation to the entire set. The first record in the set has the `AbsolutePosition` of (1), and the last record in the set has the `AbsolutePosition` of `RecordCount`.

You can both get and set the `AbsolutePosition` property. When it's assigned, the `Recordset` tries to move the current position to the exact position specified.

If the current position is presently before the first record, the constant value `adPosBOF` is reported; if the current position is past the last record, the constant value `adPosEOF` is returned.

ActiveConnection

Contains a `Variant` value   Read-Write / Read-Only

The `ActiveConnection` property can be used to discover the actual `Connection` object being used by the `Recordset` to communicate to the database server.

You can assign either an open `Connection` object or a string containing connection information to this property.

NOTE The `ActiveConnection` parameter of the `Open` method, overrides the `ActiveConnection` property of the `Recordset` object. If you omit this parameter from the call to `Open`, the property's value is used.

9

BOF

Contains a `Boolean` value   NA / Read-Only

The `BOF` property may contain the value of `TRUE` or `FALSE`. It's used to determine whether the current record position is actually before the first record of the set. This can happen when you're trying to move the position backward by using `MovePrevious` or specifying a negative offset to the `Move` method.

CacheSize

Contains an `Integer` value   Read-Write / Read-Write

The `CacheSize` property can be used to tell the `Recordset` how many records to keep in its internal cache. This value also determines how many records are fetched each time data is retrieved from the database server. Changes to the cache size take affect the next time the `Recordset` fetches data.

Cache size is important only when the underlying data provider is functioning as a *server-side cursor*, which is the default mode of operation. *Client-side cursors* store the entire query result on the client machine, so the cache size is identical to the total number of records in the set. When ADO is used with the Advanced Data Control, starting in Chapter 17, "The `AdvancedDataControl` and the ADO `Recordset`," it's operating with a client-side cursor.

CursorLocation

Contains one of the following values: Read-Write / Read-Only

Cursor Location	Value
adUseClient	1
adUseServer	2
adUseClientBatch	3

The `CursorLocation` property can be used to control where the underlying data provider maintains the query results. A client-side cursor maintains the results primarily on the client, and a server-side cursor keeps them on the server. A *client-batch cursor*, however, is special because it can be disassociated from its server side, transmitted to the client, modified, sent back to the server, and reconnected to the database for updating.

This property is especially important to developers of online applications intended for the Internet. It allows interactive access to data without requiring a constant connection to the back-end database server. You will learn more about the CursorLocation property's use during Chapter 20, "Business Objects and ADO."

CursorType

Contains one of the following values: Read-Write / Read-Only

Cursor Type	Value
adOpenForwardOnly	1
adOpenKeyset	2
adOpenDynamic	3
adOpenStatic	4

The default value is adOpenForwardOnly.

The CursorType property can be used to control how the underlying data provider retrieves records from the database server. Each type has unique benefits and drawbacks.

adOpenForwardOnly	Bookmarks are unavailable and the Recordset can be navigated only by using the MoveNext or GetRows methods. This cursor type has the fastest response time.
adOpenKeyset	Changes to the database made by other users, except for additions, are visible whenever the Recordset fetches data. Bookmarks are always available, and the Recordset is fully navigable, forward and backward.
adOpenDynamic	Changes to the database made by other users (including additions) are visible whenever the Recordset fetches data. Bookmarks might be available (but not always), and the Recordset is fully navigable, forward and backward.
adOpenStatic	Query results are kept in isolation from the rest of the database. Changes to the database made by other users are invisible. Bookmarks might be available, and the Recordset is fully navigable, forward and backward.

EditMode

Contains one of the following values: NA / Read-Only

EditMode Constant	Value
adEditNone	0
adEditInProgress	1
adEditAdd	2

You can use the EditMode property to determine the current record's edit status. This property exists primarily for backward compatibility with DAO and RDO object models. For more complete status information, use the Status property.

adEditNone   No edit is in progress. The current record has not been modified.

adEditInProgress   An edit is currently in progress. Some of the current record's fields have been modified.

adEditAdd   The current record was previously created by a call to AddNew and hasn't been added to the database yet.

EOF

Contains a Boolean value   NA / Read-Only

The EOF property may contain the value of TRUE or FALSE. It's used to determine whether the current record position is actually after the last record of the set. This can happen when you're trying to move the position forward by using MoveNext or specifying a positive offset to the Move method.

Filter

Contains a Variant value   Read-Write / Read-Write

Filter Constants	Value
adFilterNone	0
adFilterPendingRecords	1
adFilterAffectedRecords	2
adFilterFetchedRecords	3

The Filter property can be used to temporarily examine just a subset of the full set of records. The Recordset behaves as though only the filtered records exist.

adFilterNone   All records are visible.

9

endingRecords	Only records pending update, insertion, or deletion are visible.
AffectedRecords	Only records affected by the last call to `UpdateBatch`, `CancelBatch`, `Delete`, or `Resync` are visible.
terFetchedRecords	Only records in the current cache are visible.

u can also specify either a constraint expressed as a text string or an array of bookmarks that define a subset of the records within the set.

A constraint expression might look like the WHERE clause of a SQL expression. The following string, for example, describes a valid constraint:

```
"Age > 25 AND Sales < $1000.00 AND FirstName <> 'Bob' "
```

Valid operators include <, >, <=, >=, <>, =, and LIKE. You can string several constraints together by separating them with the term AND. You must surround dates with pound signs (#) and enclose strings within single quotes ('). With the LIKE operator, you can use either the asterisk or the percent sign as wildcards, as long as the wildcard is the last character in the string. Both wildcards are equivalent and can be used to match any sequence that starts with the character sequence preceding the wildcard symbol.

LockType

Contains one of the following values: Read-Write / Read-Only

LockType *Constants*	*Value*
adLockReadOnly	1
adLockPessimistic	2
adLockOptimistic	3
adLockBatchOptimistic	4

You can use the LockType property to control how the underlying data provider handles record locking for updates.

adLockReadOnly	The Recordset is opened in the read-only mode. No updates, inserts, or deletions are allowed.
adLockPessimistic	Records are locked during editing. This is the safest mechanism.
AdLockOptimistic	Records aren't locked during editing, but updates, inserts, and deletions are still allowed.
adLockBatchOptimistic	Records aren't locked during editing. Updates, inserts, and deletions happen in Batch mode.

NOTE

> Although optimistic locking isn't as safe as pessimistic locking, because no locks are used at all, you can still manage safe interactions with the database by using transactions.

MaxRecords

Contains an Integer value   Read-Write / Read-Only

The MaxRecords property can be used to preset the total number of records to retrieve in the query when the Recordset is opened. The default value of zero indicates that all records will be retrieved.

PageCount

Contains an Integer value   NA / Read-Only

You can use the PageCount property to determine the total number of pages available in the Recordset. The following calculation is used to determine the page count manually:

```
PageCount = (RecordCount + PageSize - 1) / PageSize
```

PageSize

Contains an Integer value   Read-Write / Read-Write

You can use the PageSize property to assign a value to the Recordset so that it can conveniently keep track of the AbsolutePage property for you. The page size is simply the number of records you have determined will fit on an actual page of output, such as a printed page or a Web page.

RecordCount

Contains an Integer value   NA / Read-Only

You can use the RecordCount property to determine the total number of records retrieved by the query issued when the Recordset was opened.

WARNING

> Some Recordsets, in particular a forward-only server-side cursor, are incapable of determining the RecordCount. Forward-only cursors retrieve data while the database is still processing your query. The act of moving forward through the Recordset instructs the database server to

continue finding matches. You won't know how many records match your query until the database server has found them all, and by that time you have already retrieved them.

Source

Contains a Variant value   Read-Write / Read-Only

You can use the Source property to preset the query used when the Recordset is opened. You can assign either a Command object or a string containing a query appropriate to the type of database being communicated with. Once the Recordset is opened, the Command object being used can be discovered by reading this property.

NOTE

The Source parameter of the Open method overrides the Source property of the Recordset object. If you omit this parameter from the call to Open, the property's value is used.

WARNING

If a Command object is assigned to the Source property or used in the Open command, and that Command object is already associated with a Connection object, the Command object's Connection overrides any connection that's been preset by using the ActiveConnection property or passed as the second parameter to Open.

Status

Contains one of the following values: NA / Read-Only

Status Constant	Value
adRecOK	0
adRecNew	1
adRecModified	2
adRecDeleted	4
adRecUnmodified	8
adRecInvalid	16

9

Status *Constant*	*Value*
adRecMultipleChanges	64
adRecPendingChanges	128
adRecCanceled	256
adRecCantRelease	1024
adRecConcurrencyViolation	2048
adRecIntegrityViolation	4096
adRecMaxChangesExceeded	8192
adRecObjectOpen	16384
adRecOutOfMemory	32768
adRecPermissionDenied	65536
adRecSchemaViolation	131072
adRecDBDeleted	262144

You can use the Status property to determine the status flags for the current record. These flags are usually affected by methods that either update, insert, delete, or change the current record position.

Status Flag	*Meaning*
adRecOk	The last operation succeeded.
adRecNew	The current record is new and hasn't been added to the database yet.
adRecModified	The record has been modified and hasn't been updated yet.
adRecDeleted	The record has been deleted.
adRecUnmodified	The record hasn't been modified yet.
adRecInvalid	The update failed because the bookmark was invalid.
adRecMultipleChanges	The update failed because it would have required changes across multiple records.
adRecPendingChanges	The update failed because it depends on other pending changes.
adRecCanceled	The update failed because the operation was aborted.
adRecCantRelease	The update failed because required locks couldn't be obtained.
adRecConcurrencyViolation	The update failed because optimistic locking was in use and the database was changed before this update was attempted.
adRecIntegrityViolation	The update failed because the record violated constraints imposed by rules within the database.
adRecMaxChangesExceeded	The update failed because there were too many pending changes.

continues

Status Flag	*Meaning*
adRecObjectOpen	The update failed because a required storage object was already open.
adRecOutOfMemory	The update failed because the computer ran out of memory for some reason. This situation is very rare, so it's best to notify the user when it happens.
adRecPermissionDenied	The update failed because of insufficient user access privileges.
adRecSchemaViolation	The update failed because the record violates the integrity of the database structure.
adRecDBDeleted	The update failed because the record has already been removed from the database.

The status of the current record can actually contain one or more of the listed flags. To determine whether any particular flag is true, simply use the AND operator to extract the particular status flag from the value returned by this property. The following statement illustrates how this is done:

```
<%
IF rs.Status AND adRecNew THEN
  ' do something here when the record is new
END IF
%>
```

Recordset **Methods**

Table 9.2 lists all the methods available on the Recordset object. Following the table, each method is discussed in detail.

Table 9.2. Methods of the Recordset object.

Method	Action
AddNew	Add a new record to set
CancelBatch	Cancel pending batch updates
CancelUpdate	Cancel pending update
Clone	Create identical Recordset
Close	Close the Recordset
Delete	Delete the current record
GetRows	Get multiple records
Move	Move to the specified record
MoveNext	Move forward one record

9

Method	Action
MovePrevious	Move backward one record
MoveFirst	Move to the first record
MoveLast	Move to the last record
NextRecordset	Move to the next set in multi-set query
Open	Execute the query
Requery	Re-execute the same query
Resync	Synchronize data with server
Supports	Determine supported features
Update	Update the current record
UpdateBatch	Update pending records

AddNew

This is the syntax for using the AddNew method:

```
Recordset.AddNew [Fields, Values]
```

Parameter	Type	Description
Fields	Variant	Either a single field name or an array of field names
Values	Variant	Either a single value or an array of values

You can use the AddNew method to add new records to the database associated with an open Recordset. The AddNew method can be used in one of two ways.

Specifying AddNew with no parameters adds a blank record to the Recordset. The blank record can then be modified by assigning values to individual fields. Finally, the Update method must be called to truly add the new record to the database.

Specifying AddNew with parameters allows you to add a completely defined new record in one statement. The following code fragment illustrates how to add a new record this way:

```
<%
  Dim fields(2)
  Dim values(2)

  fields(0) = "Name"
  fields(1) = "Age"
  values(0) = "Fred"
  values(1) = 35

  rs.AddNew fields, values
%>
```

NOTE

The Recordset is positioned on the new record. The new record position isn't necessarily near its position before the call to the AddNew method. The new position depends on how the underlying data provider is used.

CancelBatch

Here's the syntax for using the CancelBatch method:

Recordset.CancelBatch

You can use the CancelBatch method to cancel a pending batch update. You're in Batch Update mode when you have selected adLockBatchOptimistic for the LockType and have successfully opened the Recordset. A batch update is pending any time after a record has been modified, added, or deleted and before the UpdateBatch method has been called.

CancelUpdate

Recordset.CancelUpdate

You can use the CancelUpdate method to undo any changes you have made to the current record before calling the Update method. This includes undoing AddNew calls that require a call to Update before taking effect.

WARNING

Calling a method that changes the current record position is the equivalent of a call to Update.

Clone

Set clonedRecordset = *Recordset*.Clone

You can use the Clone method to generate a Recordset identical to the current one. Both Recordsets maintain their own separate current record position, but share the same internal cache of records. Changes made to records in one of the Recordsets are immediately visible to the other.

It is important to note that you can clone only Recordsets that support bookmarks.

Close

Recordset.Close

You can use the Close method to indicate you're done using the Recordset as a means of accessing the records from the query. Any resources used by the Recordset are then released.

Clones aren't affected by closing a Recordset. Each clone must be closed independently.

Closing the Recordset happens by default as soon as there are no references to the Recordset remaining. This may happen because the variables used as references to the Recordset were constrained to the scope of a function or script and the execution has left that area, or you have reassigned that variable to a new value or object. If you don't explicitly close the Recordset object, it's automatically closed for you.

Delete

Recordset.Delete *affect*

Affect *Constants*	*Value*
adAffectCurrent	1
adAffectGroup	2

You can use the Delete method to delete records from the database. The method takes one optional parameter.

adAffectCurrent   Delete the current record only. This is the default value.

adAffectGroup   Delete all records matching the current Filter property.

Once the records have been deleted, you can't access them except to determine their individual status. When adLockBatchOptimistic has been specified for LockType, the records aren't really deleted until the UpdateBatch method has been called.

When deleting the current record, the default behavior is that the current record position remains on the deleted record. However, this may not always be the case. In environments that share the same Recordset among many objects, those objects may indeed alter the behavior of the Recordset without your knowledge. Another object might find it necessary to automatically position the Recordset on the next record in the set. For instance, a data grid doesn't usually display deleted records. It might forcibly move the current position to a non-deleted record when it's notified that the record at the current position has been removed.

GetRows

`Set rows = Recordset.GetRows( count, start, fields )`

rows   An array of rows returned by the `GetRows` method. Each row itself is an array of values.

count   The number of rows to read from the `Recordset`. This parameter is optional and defaults to the value of (`-1`), which will read the entire `Recordset`.

start   The bookmark of the first record to read. This parameter is optional and defaults to the current record.

fields   The exact fields arranged in the order you want them to appear in the resulting array. This parameter can be a single field name or index or an entire array of field names or indexes. This parameter is optional and defaults to all the fields in the `Recordset`.

You can use the `GetRows` method to get a static copy of the records in the `Recordset` as a two-dimensional array of values.

After calling the `GetRows` method, the `Recordset` has a current position of the next record after those read by the call. If no more records exist in the set beyond those read, the current record position is after the end of the records. In that case, the `EOF` property will be `true`.

Move

`Recordset.Move count, start`

count   The number of records to move in relation to the start position. A value of 1 means move to one record after the start position, and a value of -1 means to move to one record before the start position.

start   A bookmark declaring the start position of the `Move` method. This parameter is optional because it defaults to the current record position.

You can use the `Move` method to change the current record position, which is by far the most powerful of all the move methods. It allows you to use a single statement to move many records forward or backward at the same time.

Not all `Recordsets` can move the current position backward. `Recordsets` opened with adOpenForwardOnly for `CursorType` can move in the forward direction only. Because of this, once you have moved beyond a record, you can't move back to it.

NOTE

A move that would cause the position to be placed anywhere after the end of the set instead places the current position exactly after the end of the records. The edges of the Recordset act like barriers. There's only one imaginary spot beyond each edge.

WARNING

A move made in relation to the current position (which is either after the end or before the beginning of the set) that would cause the position to be moved even further beyond the edge is considered an error.

MoveNext

Recordset.MoveNext

You can use the MoveNext method to move the current record position to the very next record in the set. If the current position is the last record in the set, the EOF property gets the value True after the call to MoveNext.

If MoveNext is repeatedly called while the current position is after the end of the Recordset, an error is generated.

MovePrevious

Recordset.MovePrevious

You can use the MovePrevious method to move the current record position to the previous record in the set. If the current position is the first record in the set, the BOF property gets the value True after the call to MovePrevious.

If MovePrevious is repeatedly called while the current position is after the end of the Recordset, an error is generated.

Not all Recordsets can move the current position backward. Recordsets opened with adOpenForwardOnly for CursorType can move in the forward direction only. Because of this, records can't be revisited.

MoveFirst

Recorset.MoveFirst

You can use the MoveFirst method to move the current record position to the first record in the set. The Recordset is automatically positioned on the first record when it's opened.

Recordsets opened with adOpenForwardOnly for CursorType or those without bookmark support can't move back to the first record once the current position has moved beyond it.

MoveLast

Recordset.MoveLast

You can use the MoveLast method to move the current record position to the last record in the set. However, Recordsets opened without bookmark support can't move directly to the last record.

NextRecordset

Set *nextRecordset* = *Recordset*.NextRecordset(*affected*)

nextRecordset   An entirely separate Recordset object returned as the result of this function, or the value Nothing if no more Recordsets are available.

affected   A variable used as an output parameter to report the number of records affected by the operation associated with the next Recordset.

You can use the NextRecordset method to retrieve the next Recordset associated with a multi-Recordset query. Both SQL queries with compound statements and stored procedures can return multiple Recordsets.

Many SQL statements may affect the data without returning records in a Recordset. In this case, the affected parameter reports the number of records affected by the statement, and the Recordset itself is empty. This situation differs from having no more Recordsets at all. An empty Recordset has the EOF property set to True. The following code fragment shows both of these mechanisms used together:

```
<%
  WHILE rs <> Nothing
    IF NOT rs.EOF THEN
      ' do something with the recordset
    END IF
    SET rs = rs.NextRecordset( recordsAffected )
  WEND
%>
```

Open

Recordset.Open *source, connection, cursor, lock, type*

source	Either a command object or a string containing a query acceptable to the database server. This parameter is optional. If it's not specified, the value of the Source property is used.
connection	Either a Connection object or a string containing connection information descriptive enough to establish a connection to a database server. This parameter is optional. If it's not specified, the value of the ActiveConnection property is used.
cursor	Any constant value normally used to assign the CursorType property. This parameter is optional. If it's not specified, the value of the CursorType property is used. The default value of the CursorType property is often adOpenForwardOnly, but it may depend on the CursorLocation property as well. For languages incapable of expressing optional parameters, the value of adOpenUnspecified (-1) can be used to get the same result.
lock	Any constant value normally used to assign the LockType property. This parameter is optional. If it's not specified, the value of the LockType property is used. The default value of the LockType property is adLockReadOnly. For languages incapable of expressing optional parameters, the value of adLockUnspecified (-1) can be used to get the same result.
type	Any constant value normally used to assign the CommandType property of a Command object. This parameter is optional. If it's not specified, the value of the adCmdUnknown (8) is used. For languages incapable of expressing optional parameters, the value of adCmdUnspecified (-1) can be used to get the same result. This parameter can be used to help the Recordset optimize the query execution by hinting at the type of the query being used. This parameter is only of use when a query string is being specified as the source.

You can use the Open method to establish a connection to a database server and to execute a query. If a Connection object is supplied instead of a connection string, the Open method uses that connection to the database server without establishing a new one. If a Command object is supplied instead of a query string, a Connection object may already be associated with the Command. The Command object's connection overrides any Connection object or connection string supplied as either a property or a parameter to Open.

9

Requery

Recordset.Requery

You can use the Requery method to completely re-execute the query you used when opening the Recordset. All caches on the client and the server are refreshed to reflect the new query results. The Recordset remains open with the same properties and parameters used when it was initially opened.

Resync

Recordset.Resync *affect*

Affect *Constants*	Value
adAffectCurrent	1
adAffectGroup	2
adAffectAll	3

You can use the Resync method to refresh the records held within the Recordset to reflect the database's current state without re-executing the query. Some or all of the records may be refreshed during this operation. Additions and deletions made by other users won't suddenly appear in the refreshed set of records.

adAffectCurrent   Only the record at the current position is refreshed.

adAffectGroup   All records matching the constraints imposed by the Filter property are refreshed.

adAffectAll   All records in the set are refreshed.

Supports

doesSupport = *Recordset*.Supports(*option*)

doesSupport   A Boolean value set to True only if the feature is supported by the Recordset.

option   One of many constants of the type CursorOptionEnum.

CursorOption *Constants*	Value
adAddNew	16778240
adApproxPosition	16384
adBookmark	8192
adDelete	16779264
adHoldRecords	256

CursorOption *Constants*	*Value*
adMovePrevious	512
adResync	131072
adUpdate	16809984
adUpdateBatch	65536

You can use the Supports() method to determine whether a particular feature is available in the open Recordset.

adAddNew	The data provider supports adding records to this Recordset.
adApproxPosition	The data provider supports positioning based on ratios. This feature is used by the Recordset to provide absolute positioning. Both AbsolutePage and AbsolutePosition properties depend on it.
adBookmark	The data provider supports the use of bookmarks for navigation of this Recordset.
adDelete	The data provider supports deleting records from this Recordset.
adHoldRecords	The data provider supports the Recordset holding multiple discrete blocks of records. This feature allows you to read more records without committing pending changes.
adMovePrevious	The data provider supports returning to records that have already been read once, without requiring the support of bookmarks.
adResync	The data provider supports synchronization of the records held outside the database as results of the query with their corresponding values held within the database.
adUpdate	The data provider supports updating changes to the records in this Recordset.
adUpdateBatch	The data provider supports updating batch changes to the records in this Recordset.

You can combine multiple constants, either by adding their values or by using the OR operator, and determine whether multiple features are available in one function call. The following code fragment shows how the Supports() method is used:

```
<%
  IF rs.Supports( adAddNew + adDelete ) THEN
    ' do something special here
  END IF
%>
```

Update

`Recordset.Update` *fields, values*

fields	Either the name or ordinal position of a single field, or an array of names or ordinal positions of many fields. This parameter is optional. If it's not specified, the *values* parameter can't be specified either.
values	Either a single value or an array of values corresponding to the fields specified in the *fields* parameter. This parameter is optional and isn't specified when the *fields* parameter is not specified.

You can use the Update method to alter the field values of the record at the current position and to submit them to the database. If the optional parameters are omitted, then only the changes made before calling the Update method are submitted to the database.

Note, however, that if the Recordset is currently in batch update mode, if it was opened with a LockType of adLockBatchOptimistic, then the changes made aren't really submitted to the database until the UpdateBatch method is called. You may omit calling Update for changes made to the current record if they're the last set of changes made before calling UpdateBatch.

Most operations that change the current record position cause the equivalent of a call to Update. Trying to move to the next record when there are pending changes to the current record first updates the current record and then moves to the next one.

UpdateBatch

`Recordset.UpdateBatch` *affect*

Affect *Constants*	*Value*
adAffectCurrent	1
adAffectGroup	2
adAffectAll	3

You can use the UpdateBatch method to update all pending changes, additions, and deletions from the Recordset. UpdateBatch can be used only if the Recordset is currently in batch update mode, which happens when it's opened with a LockType of adLockBatchOptimistic.

You can limit the records that are updated by choosing one of the following Affect constants:

adAffectCurrent	Only pending changes of the record at the current position are updated.
adAffectGroup	Pending changes for all records matching the constraints imposed by the Filter property are updated.
adAffectAll	Pending changes for all records in the Recordset are updated.

Some or all of the records submitted in the batch update may fail the update because of conflicts arising in the database. If all records submitted fail the update, then the method call returns an error. If only some of the records submitted fail, then the Connection object's Error object collection contains a warning.

You can use the Filter property to isolate the records that failed the update by setting it to adFilterAffectedRecords. You can then determine the cause of each failure by stepping over the records and examining the Status property for each current record.

Recordset **Fields**

Recordset fields are objects that give independent access to each data field of the record at the Recordset's current record position. The Recordset has a property called Fields that provides direct access to a collection of Field objects. Each Field object has a name and an ordinal index position. The Field name corresponds to the name used to identify a particular column of the database table or the name given to the column within the query string used to open the Recordset. The Field's index position corresponds to the order in which the column was listed in the query.

You can access the collection of Field objects by using this statement:

```
<% Set fields = rs.Fields %>
```

You can specify a Field object from the collection by following the examples shown in these code fragments:

```
<% Set field = rs.Fields( "name" ) %>

<% Set field = rs( "name" ) %>

<%
  Set fields = rs.Fields
  Set field = fields( "name" )
%>
```

Fields **Collection Properties**

There is actually only one property available in the Fields collection itself: the Count property.

Count

Contains an Integer value   NA / Read-Only

You can use the Count property to determine the total number of fields in the Fields collection.

Fields **Collection Methods**

The Fields collection also contains a couple of methods that can be called from scripting code.

Refresh

```
Fields.Refresh
```

You can use the Refresh method to force the Fields collection to re-read the information about the columns used in the query.

Item

```
Set field = Fields.Item( index )
```

index   The name or ordinal position of the requested Field.

The Item method is the default method called when you use the parentheses as indexing operators on the Recordset or the Fields collection. This method is normally hidden from view in program editors that understand the type-library format of OLE Automation objects.

Field **Properties**

Each Field object has its own set of properties. These are not the same as the properties available in the Fields collection. The table below lists the properties available for each individual Field object:

Property	*Description*
ActualSize	The length of the data value
Attributes	Attributes describing the value
DefinedSize	Length as defined in the database
Name	Name of the field
Type	Data type of the field
Value	Actual data value
Precision	Precision of the numeric value
NumericScale	Scale of the numeric value

9

ActualSize

Contains an Integer value NA / Read-Only

You can use the ActualSize property to determine the full length of the field's actual data value before you copy the value into a program variable. This value won't necessarily match the length used when declaring the corresponding column of the database table. The field's actual size can be unknown; in this case, the ActualSize property returns the constant value adUnknown (-1).

Attributes

Contains one or more of the following values: NA / Read-Only

Attributes *Constants*	*Value*
adFldMayDefer	2
adFldUpdatable	4
adFldUnknownUpdatable	8
adFldFixed	16
adFldIsNullable	32
adFldMayBeNull	64
adFldLong	128
adFldRowID	256
adFldRowVersion	512
adFldCacheDeferred	4096

You can use the Attributes property to determine special information about the Field and its value before you try to access it. Each Field can be described by one or more of these attribute flags:

Attribute Flags	*Meaning*
adFldMayDefer	The value isn't retrieved from the database server until it's explicitly referenced, which happens often with fields containing large data values.
adFldUpdatable	The value can be changed.
adFldUnknownUpdatable	It's not known whether the value can be updated.
adFldFixed	The value is fixed in length. Use the DefinedSize property to determine the exact length.
adFldIsNullable	The field may be assigned the value of NULL in addition to the normal values for the field's data type.
adFldMayBeNull	The field may or may not contain data. A special value of NULL is returned when the actual data doesn't exist.

continues

Attribute Flags	Meaning
adFldLong	The value of a type that can be considerably large, such as Long Binary.
adFldRowId	The value contains information that can uniquely identify the current record.
adFldRowVersion	The value contains information that can be used to verify the last time the data was changed.
adFldCacheDeferred	The value is read from a cache each time it's accessed, instead of being re-fetched from the database server.

The following example illustrates a common use of the Attributes property:

```
<%
  IF rs("name").Attributes AND adFldUpdatable THEN
    ' do something here
  END IF
%>
```

DefinedSize

Contains an Integer value   NA / Read-Only

You can use the DefinedSize property to determine the maximum length of the field as specified when the corresponding column of the database table was declared.

Name

Contains a String value   NA / Read-Only

You can use the Name property to determine the name of the field as specified in the query. This same name can be used as a key when retrieving the Field object from the Fields collection.

Type

Contains one of the following values: NA / Read-Only

Type Constant	Value	Description
adBigInt	20	8-byte signed integer
adBinary	128	Binary encoded bytes
adBoolean	11	Boolean true or false
adBSTR	8	Unicode character string
adChar	129	ASCII character string
adCurrency	6	Numeric currency
adDate	7	System style date

Type Constant	Value	Description
adDBDate	133	Date encoded as YYYYMMDD
adDBTime	134	Time encoded as HHMMSS
adDBTimeStamp	135	Time stamp
adDecimal	14	Numeric value with fixed precision
adDouble	5	Double-precision floating point
adError	10	System error code
adGUID	72	Globally unique identifier
adIDispatch	9	COM/OLE Automation object
adInteger	3	4-byte signed integer
adIUnknown	13	COM/OLE object
adNumeric	131	Numeric value with fixed precision
adSingle	4	Single-precision floating point
adSmallInt	2	2-byte signed integer
adTinyInt	16	1-byte signed integer
adUnsignedBigInt	21	8-byte unsigned integer
adUnsignedInt	19	4-byte unsigned integer
adUnsignedSmallInt	18	2-byte unsigned integer
adUnsignedTinyInt	17	1-byte unsigned integer
adUserDefined	132	A value defined by the user
adVariant	12	An OLE Automation Variant
adWChar	130	Unicode character string

You can use the Type property to determine the exact data type used to declare the corresponding column in the database table.

Note, however, that there are more types listed than are available in the Variant data type. All data is coerced into an appropriate Variant data type before it's returned by using the Value property. For example, Variants have only one Date type. Variant Dates contain both data and time information. Fields typed as adDate, adDBDate, adDBTime, and adDBTimestamp all appear as the Variant Date type before the values reach your program.

Value

Contains a Variant value   NA / Read-Write

You can use the Value property to both get and set the data value for the current record's corresponding field. Assigning a data value to the Value property is one way of making changes to the current record. If the Field object supports updating, the Attributes property has the adFldUpdatable flag turned on, and the Recordset is not read-only, then the Value property can be used to change the Field's value.

Precision

Contains a Byte value   NA / Read-Write

You can use the Precision property to both get and set the maximum number of digits allowed in the representation of the numeric data value. The maximum includes those digits used to represent the scale or the fractional portion of the data value.

NumericScale

Contains a Byte value   NA / Read-Write

You can use the NumericScale property to both get and set the number of digits used in the representation of the fractional portion of the numeric data value. The NumericScale property can never have a value greater than the Precision property.

Field **Methods**

The following table lists the methods available on each Field object. Afterward, each method is discussed in detail.

Method	Description
AppendChunk	Append data to a field in pieces.
GetChunk	Get data from a field in pieces.
OriginalValue	The value before modification.
UnderlyingValue	The value as stored in the database.

AppendChunk

Field.AppendChunk *bytes*

bytes   A Variant containing the data to append to the end of the current value.

You can use the AppendChunk method to add data bytes onto the end of the current value. The first time you call AppendChunk on a Field object, the data value is assigned the bytes passed as a parameter to the method. Repeated calls to AppendChunk append the bytes passed onto the end of the current value.

You may use AppendChunk with only one field at a time. If you use AppendChunk with another field and then try to use it again with the original Field, the append semantics start over as though it were the first time you called AppendChunk on the original field. The field's previous value is then overwritten with the new information.

9

GetChunk

Set *variable* = *Field*.GetChunk(*count*)

variable   A variable that's assigned a portion of the field's data value.

count   Typed as Long, a parameter specifying the exact number of bytes to be gotten as a chunk of the field's data value.

You can use the GetChunk method to retrieve sequential portions of the field's data value. The first call to GetChunk retrieves the first count bytes of the data value, the second call retrieves the next count bytes, and so on.

You may use GetChunk with only one field at a time. If you use GetChunk with another field and then try to use it again with the original field, the retrieval semantics start over again as though it were the first time you called GetChunk on the original field. The first count bytes are retrieved instead.

If you ask for more bytes than what remains in the data value, the bytes returned are less than you requested.

WARNING

> Both the AppendChunk and GetChunk semantics revert to their initial conditions whenever another field value is read from or written to. You can't use GetChunk and AppendChunk in tandem to copy data from one field to another in the same Recordset. You can, however, do this with fields from entirely separate Recordsets. Clones don't count as separate Recordsets in this circumstance.

OriginalValue

Set *variable* = *Field*.OriginalValue

You can use the OriginalValue method to retrieve the Field's last known official value. This can either be the value that existed when the Recordset was first opened or the value that existed immediately after that last call to the Update method. If the Recordset is using batch updating, the original value is considered the value that existed immediately after the last call to the UpdateBatch method.

UnderlyingValue

```
Set variable = Field.UnderlyingValue
```

You can use the UnderlyingValue method to retrieve the Field's value as it's currently stored in the database server. This value may be different from the OriginalValue because other sources might have changed the value stored in the database since the current record was fetched from the server.

Dynamic Pages

Dynamic Web pages are a fundamental means of distributing your application across the Internet. Dynamic pages can be customized each time a user requests them from the server and interact with databases using ADO technology to deliver up-to-the-minute information. You can automatically generate product listings, brochures, order forms, or anything else that can be represented as an HTML document.

A Simple Dynamic Page

It's best to start your exploration into the world of dynamic Web pages with an example that demonstrates the basics: the integration of HTML instructions and Visual Basic scripting. Listing 9.1 shows a complete Web page that randomly generates a magic number each time a user requests the page.

Listing 9.1. The Magic Number page.

```
<HTML>

<TITLE>Example 9.1: The Magic Number</TITLE>

<HEAD>
<H1>Hello World Wide Web</H1>
</HEAD>

<BODY>

<% randomize timer %>

Your new magic number is <%= int(100*rnd) %>

</BODY>

</HTML>
```

9

The code can be entered by using Notepad or retrieved from the samples on the book's CD-ROM under the filename 09TWD01.ASP.

 TIP *ASP* is the standard extension for all Active Server Pages. Use ASP instead of HTML or HTM when you're creating dynamic Web pages.

The Magic Number sample is a mix of both HTML tags and Visual Basic Script. It contains the standard set of tags defining the common regions of an HTML document: <HTML>, <TITLE>, <HEAD>, and <BODY>. The VBScript sections are the ones enclosed between the <% and the %> symbols.

There are two separate sections of VBScript in the example. The first section attempts to start the randomization processes by using the Timer object's current value.

 NOTE Functions that generate random numbers in most computers don't actually generate *random* numbers. For practical purposes, random numbers are impossible to calculate. The functions really generate a sequence of numbers that doesn't repeat for a very long, seemingly infinite, period. However, the calculations involved need a starting point, some number to start crunching with. This starting point is known as the *seed*. Pseudo–random-number generators produce the same sequence of results if given the same seed.

Each time VBScript is started on a new page request, the starting point for the rnd() function is the same, so you need to do something to change it. The magic number isn't truly random at all, but is based on the exact moment that the Web page was executed. Luckily, it looks random to everyone else.

The second section of VBScript actually calculates a pseudo-random integer to a number between 0 and 99. If you study the code carefully, you'll notice a peculiarity. At first glance, the statement looks normal enough. It takes the randomly generated floating-point value between 0 and 1, shifts the decimal point over two digits by multiplying by 100, and then rounds off the fractional part, using the Int() function. But even though the calculation looks innocent, there's something sinister going on.

The equals operator (=) placed just after the opening <% symbol is something special to Visual Basic Script for Active Server Pages. You will find this nowhere else in any other computer language. It's special because it tells Active Server Pages to take the output generated by the expression and insert it into the HTML document. Everything outside the <% and %> symbols automatically becomes part of the generated Web page, and everything inside the <% and %> symbols is executed as scripting code. Special regions designated with an initial equals sign are executed, and the output inserted into the HTML document in the exact place taken by the scripting code.

To get a better understanding of what actually happens when the Web page is requested, executed, and transferred back to the client's browser, take a look at this generated document:

```
<HTML>

<TITLE>Example 9.1: The Magic Number</TITLE>

<HEAD>
<H1>Hello World Wide Web</H1>
</HEAD>

<BODY>

Your new magic number is 73

</BODY>

</HTML>
```

The text generated from the second script section is in bold. Since the number generated is pseudo-random, it will most likely be different from the number generated when you view the Web page yourself. Everything else is the same HTML document from the example, except that the scripting sections have been removed. Using Active Server Pages to create dynamic pages is just that simple.

The generated document is what's finally transferred over the network to your browser. The browser interprets the HTML instructions and displays them as a viewable Web page.

Dynamic Information Lists

The next step in learning how to build dynamic Web pages is to actually take a look at one that uses ADO to gather information for generating part of the page. The simplest thing to do with ADO is to convert the information from the Recordset directly into HTML text. The example in Listing 9.2 takes the field values from the ADO Recordset and forms a list of all the information.

Listing 9.2. Generating dynamic lists.

```
<HTML>
<TITLE>Example 9.2: Dynamic Lists</TITLE>
```

```
<HEAD><H1>Dynamic Lists</H1></HEAD>

<BODY>

<%
set rs = Server.CreateObject("ADODB.Recordset")
rs.Open "Select lname, fname FROM employee", "DSN=pubs;UID=sa;PWD=;

while not rs.EOF
    %><%=rs("lname")+", "+rs("fname")%><BR><%
    rs.MoveNext
wend

rs.Close
%>

</BODY>
</HTML>
```

9

This example is not much more complicated than the previous Magic Number example. It does, however, have a few more lines of VBScript code.

The first line of the code creates the ADO Recordset. Chapter 8, "ActiveX Data Objects (ADO) Overview," introduced you to the CreateObject() function and how it's used with the Active Server Pages Server object. This line is the same one used as an example in Chapter 8.

The second line establishes a connection to the Pubs database and executes a simple SQL query by using the Open method of the Recordset object. The beginning of this chapter described this procedure, as well as the next few statements.

The WHILE-WEND looping structure is standard in Visual Basic. It's commonly used with the ADO Recordset instead of other looping mechanisms because of the Recordset's convenient EOF property. The loop, including the MoveNext statement near the bottom, continues to execute the statements within it for every record in the Recordset. The WHILE loop uses the EOF property to tell it when to stop looping, or rather, whether it's still all right to continue looping. When the execution reaches the WEND instruction, it branches back up to the matching WHILE instruction and tests the expression. If the expression evaluates to TRUE, it continues on with the next instruction just inside the loop; otherwise, it skips back down the WEND instruction and the execution continues on to the next instruction.

The interesting parts of this example are the instructions placed just inside the WHILE loop. Mixed together with a few <% and %> symbols are a few discernible expressions that use the Recordset object rs:

```
%><%=rs("lname")+", "+rs("fname")%><BR><%
```

You know from earlier discussions that `<%` and `%>` symbols are used to surround VBScript statements embedded in the HTML document. In fact, the code in this sample is completely surrounded by these very same symbols. Why, then, are there extra `<%` and `%>` symbols placed inside the code? Do Active Server Pages have even stranger symbols with even more bizarre meanings?

The simple truth is that they are *not* extra. They aren't placed inside the code. The first symbol is an end-script symbol (`%>`). It corresponds to the first begin-script symbol (`<%`) a few lines above it. Together, they form a complete VBScript section.

Immediately following is another VBScript section:

```
<%=rs("lname")+", "+rs("fname")%>
```

This section begins with an equals sign signifying that the result of this expression, when executed on the server, will be placed in the document at this exact position.

Following this section, a third one begins. The HTML tag `<BR>` is placed between the second and third scripting sections. This last section extends to the end of the scripting code.

Even though the example looks strange because the VBScript `WHILE-WEND` loop is broken across three separate code sections, the three sections are actually viewed as one by the VBScript executor.

You can also write a single script section that does the work of all three. Instead of breaking the script section into discrete parts so that the second section can take advantage of the special equals operator, you could have used a method of the built-in `Response` object to accomplish the same thing. The `Response` object has a method named `Write` that can be used to insert text into the HTML document being generated.

For example, the following statement

```
<% Response.Write "Hello " + userName %>
```

is equivalent to the statement

```
<%= "Hello" + userName %>
```

and is also equivalent to this statement:

```
Hello <%= userName %>
```

It's possible to write any of these statements using the `Response.Write()` method instead of using the `<%=` and `%>` symbols. Listing 9.3 shows the previous listing, Listing 9.2, rewritten to use calls to `Response.Write()`.

Listing 9.3. Dynamic lists using `Response.Write`.

```
<HTML>`
<TITLE>Example 9.2: Dynamic Lists</TITLE>

<HEAD><H1>Dynamic Lists</H1></HEAD>

<BODY>

<%
set rs = Server.CreateObject("ADODB.Recordset")
rs.Open "Select lname, fname FROM employee", "DSN=pubs;UID=sa;PWD=;"

while not rs.EOF
    Response.Write rs("lname") + ", " + rs("fname")
    Response.Write "<BR>"
    rs.MoveNext
wend

rs.Close
%>

</BODY>
</HTML>
```

This dynamic Web page produces the same output as Listing 9.2; however, instead of using multiple script sections, it has only one.

The use of the `Response.Write` method has been broken into two separate calls to illustrate the difference between the two expressions. In the original example, the first expression accessing the `Recordset` fields was inside its own pair of begin-script `<%` and end-script `%>` symbols, and the `<BR>` tag was just on its own outside the scripting sections. The drawback of the single-section technique is that HTML tags that would otherwise have been represented as a natural part of the document now must be handled as pieces of data to the script code, which makes the VBScript code look a bit more confusing. The file starts to look more like a VB program and less like a HTML document.

TIP

Which method is most straightforward? Active Server Pages allow you to decide for yourself by putting the power in your hands. If you think the begin-script `<%` and end-script `%>` symbols look too intrusive, go for the single-section technique. If you think you're losing too much HTML into the hands of VB code and you can no longer understand the overall structure of the document, break out of the code more often and back into raw HTML. It's a delicate balance that only you can decide.

Summary

This chapter has explained the fundamentals of using the ADO Recordset object. You have seen examples of the common methods used to create, open, and read data elements, how to determine whether data existed in the results of your query, and how to navigate through all the records from beginning to end. You have also been given a detailed list of all properties and methods of the Recordset object and its subordinate Field objects, along with descriptions on the uses and capabilities of each. Finally, you have seen a series of examples showing not only how to write a dynamic Web page, but also how to use ADO to add data directly to that Web page.

Q&A

Q The chapter talks about five parameters to the Open method, but your example uses only two. Why don't you need any of the others?

A Each parameter to the Open method is optional. You may specify some or all of them. The ones you don't specify take on default values. Opening a Recordset without specifying cursor type, lock type, and options results in a forward-only non-updatable Recordset, which is precisely the best type for the examples.

Examples in later chapters make full use of these other parameters.

Q If I have two separate VBScript code sections, can I use a Recordset I create inside another one?

A Yes. When the page is executed, all script sections are appended together and run as though they were one continuous program.

Q If the scripting code is really VBScript, can I write my own sub-routines and functions?

A Yes. You may write your own sub-routines and functions, and you can also add to the scripting sections whatever you think is necessary to generate the HTML you want. If your code is more understandable to you when broken down into sub-routines, then by all means write them.

Q I have some Visual Basic code modules that I built for another project. Can I use them in VBScript?

A No. Visual Basic modules aren't compatible with VBScript. What you can do is output the VB modules to a text file, modify the code to conform to VBScript syntax (which is a subset of VB syntax), and then use the server-side include feature of Internet Information Server to automatically add the code to each Web page.

You can implement server-side includes with the following syntax:

```
<!-- #include virtual="mycode.txt" -->
```

Place a line similar to this near the top of your .ASP file. It merges your subroutines and functions into this document whenever it's run.

Q Can I have pictures stored in the database and put them on my Web page?

A Yes and no. What you're asking is actually many separate problems.

To an HTML document, embedded pictures are really references to picture files stored on the server. They don't actually exist in the Web page; they exist as URLs or filenames only.

URL names to specific pictures could be stored in the database instead of actual picture data, and `<Image>` tags could be generated to point to the pictures accessible through a Web server, such as IIS.

Another method might be to put the pictures themselves into the database stored as `Long Binary` data or objects, if supported by the particular server. The only problem that remains is transferring them to the client.

You can solve this problem, however, by using technology such as the Advanced Data Connector (ADC), covered in Week 3, and then hooking the data connector to an ActiveX data-bound control that just happens to support that particular picture format.

An even more bizarre scenario might include using ADO to retrieve portions of the picture binary, converting the binary into some form of encoded ASCII, and generating HTML statements. These statements, when run on the client, would pass the ASCII sequences to either an ActiveX control or a Java applet that would in turn convert the sequences back into a picture and display it.

Q How do I know if the query succeeded when I open a `Recordset`?

A Without doing anything special to the scripting code, a query that doesn't succeed reports an error message. Most ADO objects have conditions in which they may raise errors. When an error is raised, a message is placed inside the HTML at the current insertion point and the execution stops. The client browser receives the HTML with the error message inside, and that message is displayed on the user's machine.

Of course, no one wants an end-user to see a nasty error message. You can avoid error messages in the generated HTML but still recover from error conditions. To do this, use this Visual Basic statement:

```
On Error Resume Next
```

This statement basically makes the code ignore all errors. The code proceeds from the statement that fails to the next one without hesitation. You can, however, determine whether an error occurred by examining the value of the `Err` variable that's built into Visual Basic and VBScript. If the value of this variable is anything but zero, the previous statement has generated an error.

You can check this variable after calling the Open method. If it has a value of zero, the Recordset has been opened successfully.

Chapter 13, "Errors and Provider Properties," goes into this subject in much more detail.

Q Can I split a single statement across multiple code sections?

A Yes, with these exceptions—you can't split a symbol name or a data value. Sections beginning with the special equals operator must contain a complete expression.

For example, this statement is OK:

```
<% Response.Write %>  <% "Hello" %>
```

However, this statement is not OK:

```
<% Respon %>  <% se.Write "Hello" %>
```

This statement is allowed:

```
<%= height * width %>
```

This statement, however, isn't allowed:

```
<%= height * %> <%= width %>
```

Q Your example builds a list out of data in a Recordset, using all the records in the table. Is there a way to show only some of the records?

A Yes. You could limit the records by specifying more constraints in the SQL query with a WHERE clause.

You could also distribute the results across multiple Web pages; you'll see an example of this in Chapter 10, "More Dynamic Pages."

Q Can I use the Recordset to get the values from another query?

A Yes. When you're done using the Recordset for the first query, simply call Close and then call Open again, specifying the new query.

Q What happens if I use a query that uses two tables and two different fields, one from each table, that have the same name?

A Both fields will appear in the Fields collection of the Recordset. However, you can access only the first one by name. If you know the order of the fields in the query, you can reference them by number instead.

The following VBScript statements show the short-hand methods of accessing field values both by name and by number:

```
<% desc1 = rs("description") %>
```

```
<% desc2 = rs(8) %>
```

The best way to resolve the problem is to assign a new name to one of the columns inside the query itself.

Quiz

1. The Open method can be used to perform two distinct operations. What are they?

2. Name two properties of the Recordset object you can use to determine whether the query just issued resulted in any records.

3. List all methods of the Recordset that can be used to explicitly change the current record position.

4. Name two states that the current record position can be in other than pointing at a valid record.

5. Show at least two different ways to reference the data value held in the first field of the Recordset.

6. List the methods that can be used to change the current record position of a default style Recordset.

7. It isn't necessary to call the Close method before the end of the scripting code in an HTML document. True or False?

8. You can access the fields of the Recordset object before the Recordset is opened. True or False?

9. List the standard parts of the WHILE loop used to step forward through each record of the Recordset.

10. Name a property that can be used to determine the total number of fields in each record of the Recordset.

Exercises

1. Write a dynamic Web page that lists the authors from the Authors table in the Pubs database.

2. Write a dynamic Web page that displays all the fields from the first record of the Authors table in the Pubs database, with each field on a separate line.

3. Write a dynamic Web page that lists all the employees from the Employees table in the Pubs database whose last names start with *A*.

Setting Up the Pubs Database

The Pubs database is the sample database that comes with Microsoft SQL Server. However, it doesn't come configured for use through the ODBC Data Source Administrator. The default data provider that ADO uses is actually ODBC. You need to configure the Pubs database in the ODBC Data Source Administrator before the examples in this chapter will work.

1. Go to the Control Panel on the computer where you have installed Internet Information Server. To do this, first click the Start button at the bottom of the screen, select the Settings sub-menu, and then choose Control Panel. The Control Panel is a window containing a bunch of icons, much like a normal file window. The ODBC Data Source Administrator is named ODBC in this window. If you don't find the ODBC icon, then SQL Server probably isn't installed correctly.

   Clicking the ODBC icon brings up the dialog box shown in Figure 9.2.

Figure 9.2.

The ODBC Data Source Administrator.

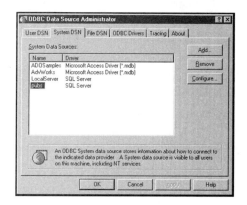

Make sure the System DSN panel is showing by clicking on its tab.

If the Pubs datasource is listed, double-click on it and go immediately to Step 5.

2. To add the Pubs datasource to the list, click the Add button to open the dialog box shown in Figure 9.3.

Figure 9.3.

Adding the Pubs datasource.

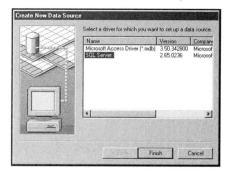

3. Select SQL Server as the driver, and click the Finish button to open the dialog box shown in Figure 9.4.

Figure 9.4.

The ODBC SQL Server Setup dialog box.

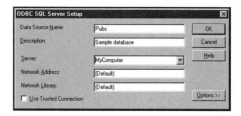

4. For the Data Source Name field, enter Pubs, and for the Description field, enter Sample database. In the Server field, enter the name of your computer that has SQL Server installed.

5. Click the Options button to enter more information. The dialog box should expand to look like Figure 9.5.

Figure 9.5.

The advanced setup dialog box.

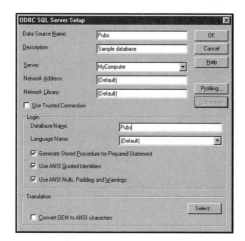

6. For the Database Name field, enter Pubs again. Leave everything else as default, and click the OK button to save the information and add it to the list.

Day 10

More Dynamic Pages

by Matt Warren

Chapter 9, "Dynamic Pages and the ADO `Recordset`," introduced not only the `Recordset` object and how it's used, but it also gave two examples of dynamic Web pages. The second example used the `Recordset` object inside Visual Basic Script to generate a custom Web page based on information from the database. This chapter continues along those same lines; it's made up entirely of examples that show you new ways to use both the `Recordset` object and dynamic Web pages. Together, they can be used to perform many kinds of data-entry and data-retrieval operations.

After reading this chapter, you will be able to do the following:

☐ Display data as an HTML table

☐ Generate dynamic input forms

☐ Manipulate data you get from input forms

☐ Keep ADO objects alive across multiple pages

☐ Build a simple data-entry system

Displaying Data as Tables

Although the example from the previous chapter was useful for showing how database information can be fed directly into an HTML document so that it seems like part of the text, there's actually a better way to represent raw information to the viewer. Information displayed in a table is easier to read and makes for a more visually attractive presentation.

To convert your data into a table, you could do one of two things. You could write a bunch of Visual Basic code that formats each field of each record by padding the text and numbers with enough blanks and tab characters so that, when shown by a browser, all the data appears to line up in individual columns. You would have to invest a lot of time and effort, and the end product would be error prone. Also, depending on the display mode and the character fonts used by the browser, determining spacing between text is unpredictable. The best you could do is hope for a monospace font.

Fortunately, HTML has a built-in feature that makes displaying tables easy. The <TABLE> tag and its siblings are meant to be used for tabular data layout. Using these tags, you can name each column and then declare the data for each field of each row independently.

Here is a table showing the HTML tags used to create tables, listed in the order you would use them:

HTML Tag	Description
<TABLE>	Start the table
<TD>	Start data item
</TD>	End data item
<TR>	Start table row
</TR>	End table row
</TABLE>	End the table

The <TD> and </TD> tags can be used to declare both column names and individual field values. When used inside the <TR> and </TR> pair, the <TD> tags define field values by surrounding the text of the value. When used inside the table, but not inside any particular row, the <TD> tags define column names.

For example, this HTML fragment could conceivably contain text that appears as either data in a single cell of the table or a column name:

```
<TD>This is data</TD>
```

This fragment definitely defines data that appears in a cell; each <TR> </TR> pair denotes its own row of data:

```
<TR> <TD>This is data</TD> </TR>
```

Likewise, the following fragment defines all the data for three individual columns of a single row:

```
<TR>
<TD>This is the first data</TD>
<TD>This is the second data</TD>
<TD>This is the last data</TD>
</TR>
```

If you were to place three separate `<TD>` definitions before the `<TR>` row definitions, you could just as easily have described the column names. The following fragment shows column names and row data defined in one concise block of HTML; each row of the tables displays a unique pairing between a person's name and phone number:

```
<TABLE>
<TD>Name</TD>
<TD>Phone #</TD>
<TR> <TD>John Smith</TD>  <TD>555-2121</TD> </TR>
<TR> <TD>Alice Copperfield</TD>  <TD>555-3927</TD> </TR>
<TR> <TD>Vincent Van Gogh</TD> <TD>555-3210</TD> </TR>
<TR> <TD>Danielle Boone</TD>  <TD>555-8955</TD> </TR>
</TABLE>
```

The most compelling reason to use the `<TABLE>` tags is not that it saves you coding time. It's that by using these tags, you can represent your data in a way that's viewer neutral. Each user's browser interprets the table, tags, and data and chooses the best way to display the information. The browser may simply display the data in nicely spaced columns, in the same way you might have been restricted to had you not had this feature:

Name	Phone #
John Smith	555-2121
Alice Copperfield	555-2927
Vincent Van Gogh	555-3210
Danielle Boone	555-8955

Or it might look as fancy as the graphically adorned tables in Microsoft's Internet Explorer. For example, if the HTML shown in Listing 10.1 were viewed using Internet Explorer, the data would be displayed in a series of outlined boxes, with each cell having a 3-D appearance. Figure 10.1 shows Internet Explorer 3.0 displaying this HTML document from Listing 10.1.

Listing 10.1. A static data table (10TWD01.HTML).

```
1: <HTML>
2: <TITLE> Example 10.1: Static Data Table </TITLE>
3: <HEAD><H1>Static Data Table</H1></HEAD>
4: <BODY>
```

continues

Listing 10.1. continued

```
 5: <TABLE BORDER=1>
 6: <TD>Name</TD>
 7: <TD>Phone #</TD>
 8: <TR> <TD>John Smith</TD> <TD>555-2121</TD> </TR>
 9: <TR> <TD>Alice Copperfield</TD> <TD>555-3927</TD> </TR>
10: <TR> <TD>Vincent Van Gogh</TD> <TD>555-3210</TD> </TR>
11: <TR> <TD>Danielle Boone</TD> <TD>555-8955</TD> </TR>
12: </TABLE>
13: </BODY>
14: </HTML>
```

Figure 10.1.

Tables in Internet Explorer 3.0.

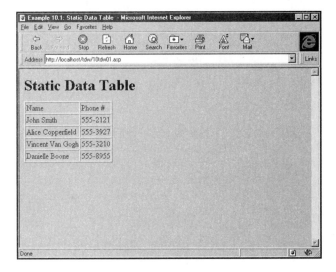

 NOTE Notice the BORDER=1 statement in the <TABLE> tag. This special property tells the browser to draw borders around the table elements. Tables are often used to simulate setting tab stops in a word processor. Borderless tables can be used to arrange any group of HTML, text, and pictures into neatly aligned regions.

The Dynamic Tables Web Page

Of course, displaying static data in an HTML table isn't the goal of this chapter, nor this section. Displaying dynamic data, however, is. In the same way you read data from the database in Chapter 9's listing example, you can easily create a table showing the same information. The code in Listing 10.2 shows how to use the <TABLE> tag syntax in place of generating a comma-separated list.

Listing 10.2. Dynamic tables (10TWD02.ASP).

```
 1: <HTML>
 2: <TITLE>Example 10.2: Dynamic Tables</TITLE>
 3: <HEAD><H1>Dynamic Tables</H1></HEAD>
 4: <BODY>
 5: <%
 6: set rs = Server.CreateObject("ADODB.Recordset")
 7: rs.Open "Select lname, fname FROM employee", "DSN=pubs;UID=sa;PWD=;"
 8: %>
 9: <TABLE BORDER=1>
10: <TD>First Name</TD>
11: <TD>Last Name</TD>
12: <%
13: while not rs.EOF
14:    %>
15:    <TR>
16:    <TD VALIGN=TOP><%= rs("fname") %></TD>
17:    <TD VALIGN=TOP><%= rs("lname") %></TD>
18:    </TR>
19:    <%
20:    rs.MoveNext
21: wend
22: rs.Close
23: %>
24: </TABLE>
25: </BODY>
26: </HTML>
```

10

Taking the Program Apart

This example is so close to the Dynamic List example from Chapter 9, it may be important to note only the distinct differences between the two. However, for completeness, and to act as a refresher of what you learned yesterday, each step is explained in this section.

Just as in the previous example, this Dynamic Table example has one unique scripting section used to make the initial link with the database. A Recordset is created by using the CreateObject() method of the built-in Server object. That Recordset is then opened with the Open method, passing in the explicit SQL query and connection information as parameters:

```
<%
set rs = Server.CreateObject("ADODB.Recordset")
rs.Open "Select lname, fname FROM employee", "DSN=pubs;UID=sa;PWD=;"
%>
```

Next, using the HTML <TABLE> tags, the table is started outside the initial scripting section. Directly following it are two sets of <TD> tags used to name the table's columns:

```
<TABLE BORDER=1>
<TD>First Name</TD>
<TD>Last Name</TD>
```

Then, the fun begins with the Recordset. Inside another scripting section, a WHILE loop begins, terminating only when the Recordset has run out of records:

```
<%
while not rs.EOF
  %>
```

Outside the second scripting section, a sequence of four lines describes an individual row of the table. Because the code overall is running inside a WHILE loop, each pass through the loop generates a table row declaration for each record in the Recordset. Between each <TD> and </TD> pair, a scripting expression section is re-entered, and the current value for each particular field is evaluated and inserted into the generated HTML. An *expression section* is one that begins with the special equals (=) operator. The expression immediately following it is evaluated, and the visual representation of the calculated value is inserted into the HTML in place of the scripting section itself:

```
<TR>
<TD VALIGN=TOP><%= rs("fname") %></TD>
<TD VALIGN=TOP><%= rs("lname") %></TD>
</TR>
```

Finally, the last scripting section ends the WHILE loop by first advancing the Recordset's current record position with the MoveNext method, and then using the Visual Basic WEND statement to signify the end of the loop. After that, the Close method is called on the Recordset to guarantee that the resources are freed:

```
<%
  rs.MoveNext
wend

rs.Close
%>
```

TIP

Calling Close when you're through using a Recordset isn't absolutely necessary. The Recordset is closed automatically when the script ends. It does, however, allow you to minimize the time lag between when a script ends and when the resources are returned to the system. Use it as a way to guarantee exactly when the resources are freed.

10

In addition, after the last scripting section has ended, a single </TABLE> tag indicates the end of the table definition. The rest of the tags are among the usual suspects found at the bottom of a Web page: the closing tags to the body and the HTML document itself.

The Generated HTML

If the names in the Pubs sample database were Sam Woody, Thomas Tank, Wendy Darling, and Maureen Moccasin, the generated HTML document would look like the following code lines. Notice that each name is associated with its own <TR> to </TR> sequence.

```
<HTML>
<TITLE>Example 10.2: Dynamic Tables</TITLE>
<HEAD><H1>Dynamic Tables</H1></HEAD>
<BODY>
<TABLE BORDER=1>
<TD>First Name</TD>
<TD>Last Name</TD>
  <TR>
  <TD VALIGN=TOP>Sam</TD>
  <TD VALIGN=TOP>Woody</TD>
  </TR>
  <TR>
  <TD VALIGN=TOP>Thomas</TD>
  <TD VALIGN=TOP>Tank</TD>
  </TR>
  <TR>
  <TD VALIGN=TOP>Wendy</TD>
  <TD VALIGN=TOP>Darling</TD>
  </TR>
  <TR>
  <TD VALIGN=TOP>Maureen</TD>
  <TD VALIGN=TOP>Moccasin</TD>
  </TR>
</TABLE>
</BODY>
</HTML>
```

The actual names, and the actual output as viewed by Internet Explorer 3.0, are shown in Figure 10.2.

Figure 10.2.

Dynamic tables shown in Internet Explorer 3.0.

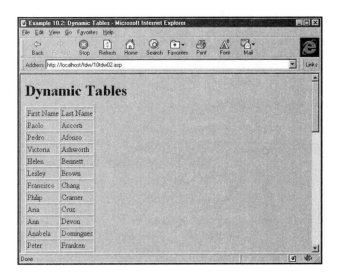

The Whole Enchilada

Now that you can quite easily write dynamic Web pages to generate tables of data with two columns, you might be thinking about generating tables of data with more than two columns. What if you want to generate a table with six or eight or more columns?

The immediate solution might be to simply add more columns to the query and more to the HTML table definition. If, in addition to first name and last name, you want to display job title and work phone number, you could simply add these to the SQL statement and add column names inside the <TABLE> tags and extra value calculations inside the <TR> table row tags.

But what if you don't know how many columns there are going to be? This could happen quite easily. A common way to specify "all columns in the table" in SQL is to use the asterisk (*) in the SELECT statement. You might know at the time you write the query what the table's true layout should be, but over time it could change. Columns could have been added or removed. Any change to the table's structure could easily cause your dynamic Web pages to fail during their execution and generation. If you have many Web pages dependent on the same data table, fixing them every time the structure changes can be a real chore.

You might choose not to use the asterisk at all, and instead specifically list each and every field. However, this method has the drawback of failing if and when columns are removed, and being incomplete when columns are added.

You might not even have control over the form of the query at all. A co-worker may have built predefined database procedures that can be called through queries, and these procedures could be the means of getting your Recordset. The use of database-stored procedures is common practice for the information systems departments of many organizations. Businesses often hide functions in the database as being simply "business rules," so instead of interacting with the database directly by using SELECT statements, interactions are controlled through procedure calls. That method leaves the definition of the Recordset you end up working with completely out of your control.

One way of handling any and all of these cases is to write your script code generically so that it can handle any Recordset given to it. Instead of individually requesting the first name and then the last name, do the calculations for each and every field of the Recordset in one fell swoop. If you recall from Chapter 9, the fields of the Recordset can be accessed by either name or number. The Fields collection of the Recordset object has the Count property to tell you the exact number of fields in the Recordset. So instead of writing separate script expression sections for each field, just add a FOR loop to the code and step through each field repeatedly.

The code in Listing 10.3 shows this method in action. You actually end up writing less code than you would have by writing separate expressions for each column.

Listing 10.3. A general dynamic table (10TWD03.ASP).

```
1: <HTML>
2: <TITLE>Example 10.3: General Dynamic Table</TITLE>
3: <HEAD><H1>General Table</H1></HEAD>
4: <BODY>

5: <%
6: set rs = Server.CreateObject("ADODB.Recordset")
7: rs.Open "Select * FROM Employee", "DSN=pubs;UID=sa;PWD=;"
8: %>
9: <TABLE BORDER=1>
10: <%
11: for i = 0 to rs.fields.count - 1
12:    %> <TD><%= rs(i).Name %></TD> <%
13: next
14: while not rs.EOF
15:    %> <TR> <%
16:    for i = 0 to rs.fields.count - 1
17:      %> <TD><%= rs(i) %></TD> <%
18:    next
19:    %> </TR> <%
20:    rs.MoveNext
21: wend
22: rs.Close
23: %>

24: </TABLE>
25: </BODY>
26: </HTML>
```

10

Dissecting this code reveals the difference between it and its fixed-column predecessor. It starts with the same code section—creating and opening the `Recordset`—and is followed immediately by the same `<TABLE BORDER=1>` tag. Just after that point, however, is where the two programs begin to diverge.

Instead of a series of `<TD>` to `</TD>` tags defining the column names, another code section takes its place. The Visual Basic `FOR` loop is used to repeatedly count though the numbers zero to one less than the total numbers of fields in the `Recordset rs.fields.count`:

The `FOR` loop specifies the variable `i` and the lower and upper boundaries: `0` and `rs.fields. count - 1`, respectively:

```
<%
for i = 0 to rs.fields.count - 1
```

At each pass through the loop, the value of the looping variable `i` is incremented by one. The loop stops executing whenever the looping variable exceeds the upper boundary. The `NEXT` statement marks the end of the loop. When the code reaches the `NEXT` statement, the looping variable is incremented, and the execution is resumed just inside the loop, the statement immediately after the `FOR` statement, unless the upper boundary has been exceeded. In that case, the execution drops to the code immediately after the `NEXT` statement.

Inside the `FOR` loop, the column names are generated automatically by calculating them directly, based on the `Field` in the `Recordset` object at the particular index. `Recordset Field` objects are numbered starting at zero. The first column in the query can be accessed using Field number zero, the second column in the query at Field number one, and so on.

First, the scripting code is exited using an end-script symbol (`%>`), and then a column is declared by the `<TD>` tag, the column name is evaluated using a script expression section (`<%= %>`), the column name is finished using the reciprocal `</TD>` tag, and finally the scripting code is re-entered with the begin-script symbol (`<%`):

```
%> <TD><%= rs(i).Name %></TD> <%
```

After all that, the `NEXT` statement ends the loop.

The `WHILE` loop has very similar improvements. Instead of a series of item definitions enclosed inside `<TD>` tags, another `FOR` loop is embedded between the row declaration `<TR>` tags:

```
  (%>) <TR> <%
for i = 0 to rs.fields.count - 1
    %> <TD><%= rs(i) %></TD> <%
  next
  %> </TR> <%
```

The scripting code containing the `WHILE` statement is exited by using the end-script symbol (`<%`), the `<TR>` tag declares the beginning of a row of data, the scripting code is re-entered using the begin-script symbol `%>`, and then the `FOR` loop takes over.

The FOR loop looks almost identical to the loop used when generating the column names. In fact, the only difference between the two is that inside the expression section, the Field's value is being inserted instead of the name.

> **TIP**
>
> The value of a Field object is considered its default property, so it doesn't actually have to be identified directly. Instead of typing rs.Fields(0).Value, you can simply write rs.Fields(0). In the same way, since the Fields collection is considered to be the default property of the Recordset, instead of typing rs.Fields(0), simply type rs(0).

The statements following the FOR loop are almost identical to the ones preceding it: an end-script symbol %>, followed by the end-table-row tag </TR>, followed by the begin-script symbol <%.

Everything else in the example is exactly the same. The WEND statement ends the WHILE loop, and the Recordset is closed with a call to the Close method. The last bit of the script section exits, and the terminating </TABLE> tag declares the end of the table.

The entire table of data is generated without knowing beforehand the exact structure of the Recordset object. You could easily go back to the query at the top of the page and change the SELECT statement. You could even query different fields from a different table, and the code following the query would still generate a valid table. Unless there are other extenuating circumstances, code written to handle general cases is much more durable because you don't have to change it every time the query changes.

Working with Sub-routines

Of course, even general code starts to look confusing when there are many context changes in and out of scripting code. The general code has only a few transitions and the specific "brute-force" code has many more, but what happens when you find yourself writing general table-generating scripts over and over for different pages, or for pages that display multiple tables? Soon, the simple logic of the table generation becomes lost in the transition in and out of hundreds of percentage symbols and angle brackets (<%)(%>).

What you want to be able to do is isolate that general table-generating script and reuse it. Then you have to look at only one set of code and the intricacies of its context changes, not two or three or ten. Even better yet, you have to get it right only once. Instead of eye-balling the coordination of modifications throughout several code blocks when you find that you have indeed made an error, you have to do it to only one code block.

Visual Basic allows you to define sub-routines, each with its own name and its own block of code. You can use the sub-routine's name as though it were a built-in function of Basic, and call it by passing parameters that can then be accessed by the code associated with the sub-routine. In this way, you can use sub-routines to factor reusable code out of the mainstream logic. These sub-routines can then be called one or more times to do the work of the code that would otherwise have to be repeated inline.

The following code fragment shows the declaration of a sub-routine in Visual Basic Script for Active Server Pages:

```
<%
Sub Credits()
  %> This page was designed by me <%
End Sub
%>
```

The Credits() sub-routine, each time it's called by mainstream code, inserts the message This page was designed by me into the HTML. Instead of explicitly inserting this message everywhere you might want it displayed in the generated Web page, you simply call the Credits() sub-routine that you defined. The following statement calls the sub-routine:

```
<% Credits %>
```

A sub-routine can be written that generates a table based on a Recordset object. If you need multiple tables generated, instead of writing separate code blocks that do practically the same work, call the sub-routine each time.

The following code fragment defines a sub-routine that generates a table of data based on a Recordset:

```
<%
Sub GenerateTable( rs )
  Response.Write( "<TABLE BORDER=1>" )
  ' set up column names
  for i = 0 to rs.fields.count - 1
    Response.Write("<TD>" + rs(i).Name + "</TD>")
  next
  ' write each row
  while not rs.EOF
    Response.Write( "<TR>" )
    for i = 0 to rs.fields.count - 1
      v = rs(i)
      if isnull(v) then v = ""
      Response.Write( "<TD VALIGN=TOP>" + CStr( v ) + "</TD>" )
    next
    rs.MoveNext
  wend
  Response.Write( "</TABLE>" )
End Sub
%>
```

10

At first glance, the `GenerateTable()` sub-routine is recognizably different from the `Credits()` sub-routine because it has a parameter. The variable `rs` is listed inside the parentheses following the sub-routine name. Each variable listed within the parentheses is considered a parameter. Different values can be passed to this sub-routine each time it's called, meaning different `Recordsets` can be used to generate HTML tables.

Notice also that instead of having end-script `%>` and begin-script `<%` symbols placed throughout the code, calls to `Response.Write` are being used. In Chapter 9, you saw that `Response.Write` can be used as another means of inserting text or HTML tags into the generated document. It's left to the programmer to decide which method can be used more comfortably. Often, this decision hinges on whether the document is primarily HTML or scripting code. It's easy to begin writing dynamic Web pages by adding indiscrete code sections directly into the predominantly static HTML; this method makes the code look less intrusive. However, once the balance swings to a document that's primarily scripting code with very little, if any, static HTML, it's easier and less confusing to work with everything as code.

The first call to `Response.Write` inserts the `<TABLE BORDER=1>` tag directly into the generated HTML. This is the same tag used in all the previous examples. In fact, you can make direct comparisons to each `Response.Write` statement and corresponding lines of code from Listing 10.3.

The call to `Response.Write` inside the first `FOR` loop simply combines the tag `<TD>` with the field name and the reciprocal tag `</TD>` into a single text string, before it writes that string into the HTML output.

The call to `Response.Write` inside the second `FOR` loop does primarily the same things. Instead of the field name, however, it combines the field value with the `<TD>` tags and writes them into the output.

The only part of this sub-routine's code that's at all different in function from the code in Listing 10.3 is the few lines of code inside the second `FOR` loop before the call to `Response.Write`. In these two lines of code, the value of the `Field` in question is copied into the variable `v`; that variable is then tested for null data with the following statement:

```
if isnull(v) then v = ""
```

The `isnull()` function evaluates to `TRUE` if the variable `v` contains null data. Sometimes columns in database tables are allowed to contain *null values*, which are values that don't truly exist. They're used in place of real data when the true data isn't known. Unfortunately, HTML has no concept of null data. Null has no textual representation, so you can't write null data into a generated HTML document. The `THEN` clause of the `IF` statement overwrites the null value with an empty string, which is as close to the concept of a null value as HTML can come.

The only other minor difference is the use of the CStr() function in the very next line of code. The CStr() function converts data of any type into its equivalent string representation. Using this function allows you to use the string concatenation plus operators (+), for the sake of brevity, instead of having multiple calls to Response.Write. The string concatenation plus operator works only with string data, but the Response.Write method works with any applicable data type.

Listing 10.4 shows the entire dynamic Web page, including the declaration of the GenerateTable() sub-routine.

Listing 10.4. The dynamic table sub-routine (10TWD04.ASP).

```
 1: <HTML>
 2: <TITLE>Example 10.4: Dynamic Table Sub-routine</TITLE>
 3: <HEAD><H1>Dynamic Table Sub-routine</H1></HEAD>
 4: <BODY>

 5: <%
 6: Sub GenerateTable( rs )
 7:   Response.Write( "<TABLE BORDER=1>" )
 8:   ' set up column names
 9:   for i = 0 to rs.fields.count - 1
10:     Response.Write("<TD>" + rs(i).Name + "</TD>")
11:   next
12:   ' write each row
13:   while not rs.EOF
14:     Response.Write( "<TR>" )
15:     for i = 0 to rs.fields.count - 1
16:       v = rs(i)
17:       if isnull(v) then v = ""
18:       Response.Write( "<TD VALIGN=TOP>" + CStr( v ) + "</TD>" )
19:     next
20:     rs.MoveNext
21:   wend
22:   Response.Write( "</TABLE>" )
23: End Sub
24: %>

25: <%
26: set rs = Server.CreateObject("ADODB.Recordset")
27: rs.Open "Select * from Employee", "DSN=pubs;UID=sa;PWD=;"
28: GenerateTable rs
29: rs.Close
30: %>

31: </BODY>
32: </HTML>
```

10

The code has been separated into two separate scripting sections. The first one simply defines the sub-routine, but the second one is the mainstream logic of the program. When the scripting code is combined and executed, the sub-routine declarations are skipped over. The first line of code that's executed is the CreateObject() function, down near the bottom of the ASP file. None of the code inside the GenerateTable() sub-routine is executed until the explicit call to the sub-routine, the third statement in this second scripting section.

This example opens a Recordset by using the exact same query and exact same database as the previous two full examples. It then passes that Recordset into the GenerateTable() sub-routine that actually does the work of generating the table. The fact that the variable rs used inside the GenerateTable() sub-routine and the variable rs in the mainstream code have the same name is purely a coincidence. They are actually two separate variables, and either one could have been named something completely different.

It's easy to see that if another Recordset object were created and opened in a similar fashion as the first one, it too could be passed to the GenerateTable() sub-routine.

10

Dynamic Input Forms

Input forms are a common feature of many Web pages. When you visit a site and are asked to fill out information on yourself, you're using input forms. Some sites might require you to type in a name and password to identify yourself before you go deeper into their network of pages. Others may simply want to collect addresses to use for a mailing list or to send you products or literature by mail. Whatever the reason, input forms are used so commonly that they're a built-in feature of HTML. Just like tables, forms have their own HTML tags that describe what you want done, but not explicitly how to do it.

The <FORM> family of HTML tags can be used to specify a series of input fields that the browser can use to interact with the user. You can specify text fields, checkboxes, radio buttons, pushbuttons, and drop-down lists. The browser takes this information and turns it into actual controls or widgets, interactive user-interface elements that can be typed into or clicked on. Because the browser chooses how the interaction is controlled, the same form can be used by any client.

Static Input

The most common type of form used on the Web today is a *static form*, one that doesn't change based on user interaction with the Web site. Static forms are part of static Web pages. No matter when the page is retrieved, or by whom, the form is always the same. A static form might, for example, ask you to enter your name and mailing address. If the form always starts out blank and is always the same, it's probably static.

Dynamic input forms do change, however. They can look different, depending on previous interactions with the online application. Based on who you are or how you have navigated to the dynamic page, the page can look different. Different fields can be prompted for input, different validation rules can be applied to the response, and different values can be filled in initially, based on all those same factors.

Static input forms can be of some use, however, since they're always associated with another application or dynamic page that does something interesting with the data they collect. The form always appears constant to the user, but the server application may react in different ways, depending on the data supplied.

The Form

The code in Listing 10.5 shows a static Web page that uses HTML forms to gather user input. Although your goal is to eventually build dynamic input forms, examining a static one helps you review basic HTML form concepts.

Listing 10.5. A static input form (10TWD05.ASP).

```
 1: <HTML>
 2: <TITLE>Example 10.5: Static Input</TITLE>
 3: <HEAD><H1>My Email List</H1></HEAD>
 4: <BODY>

 5: <FORM METHOD=POST ACTION="10tdw06.asp">
 6: Please add yourself to my email list
 7: by entering your name and email address.
 8: <BR>
 9: <BR>
10: First Name:
11: <INPUT TYPE=TEXT NAME=fname> <BR>
12: Last Name:
13: <INPUT TYPE=TEXT NAME=lname> <BR>
14: E-mail:
15: <INPUT TYPE=TEXT NAME=email> <BR>
16: <BR>
17: <INPUT TYPE=CHECKBOX NAME=sendnow CHECKED>
18: Please send me information today! <BR>
19: <BR>
20: How did you hear about me?
21: <SELECT NAME=how>
22: <OPTION SELECTED>Web Link
23: <OPTION>Television
24: <OPTION>Magazine
25: <OPTION>Radio
26: <OPTION>Friend
27: </SELECT>
28: <BR>
29: <BR>
```

10

```
30: <INPUT TYPE=SUBMIT VALUE="Add Me Now"> <BR>
31: </FORM>

32: </BODY>
33: </HTML>
```

The first line of interest is line 5, the one containing the original <FORM> tag. Inside the tag itself, two properties are assigned: METHOD and ACTION. The value POST is assigned to the METHOD property. A form can use one of two methods—GET or POST—to transmit user input back to the server. Forms that use the GET method transmit all user input back as part of the URL that declares the Web page or server application that deals with the response. Forms that use the POST method transmit data separately from the URL submission, so they aren't constrained by the limits the server may place on URL size or encoding.

The ACTION property is assigned the URL of the Web page or server application that's invoked when the form is submitted. In this example, the Active Server Page 10TWD06.ASP is the Web page that's invoked. Active Server Pages are both Web pages and server applications. After the user has keyed in the appropriated information and has clicked the Submit button, the ASP file 10TWD06.ASP is executed on the server, and data that was typed in is then accessible by the executing code.

A message is displayed within the form, and immediately following it are three plain text input fields: fname, lname, and email. If you're familiar with HTML, you might recall that input fields can be any one of the following types:

Input Types	Description
TEXT	Plain text entry
TEXTAREA	Multiline text entry
PASSWORD	Used for entering passwords
CHECKBOX	Check any that apply
RADIO	Check only one from many
SUBMIT	A button that submits the data
RESET	A button that cancels the edit
BUTTON	A pushbutton that can invoke scripting code
SELECT	Choose one or many from a list
HIDDEN	A field that can't be directly edited

All input types use the <INPUT> tag to declare them, except for TEXTAREA and SELECT, which have their own tags. Text fields are created by using a HTML statement, as in the example above.

This tag tells the browser to insert a user-editable field at this exact location in the Web page:

```
<INPUT TYPE=TEXT NAME=fname>
```

The fourth input field is a checkbox. Normally, a checkbox appears as a small square that can be marked with a check:

```
<INPUT TYPE=CHECKBOX NAME=sendnow CHECKED>
```

The fifth input field shows up as a drop-down combo box. A combo box initially appears as a text field with a button next to it. Clicking the button drops down a scrollable list of options. This special kind of input field can be specified by using the <SELECT> tag. Each option that can appear in the list is specified using its own <OPTION> tag. Option tags precede each separate section of text. A special SELECTED property can be identified inside the <OPTION> tag that's meant to represent the default value. In the following example, the value Web Link is specified as the SELECTED option. When the form is first presented to the user inside a Web browser, the value Web Link appears in the text field portion of the drop-down combo box.

```
<SELECT NAME=how>
<OPTION SELECTED>Web Link
<OPTION>Television
<OPTION>Magazine
<OPTION>Radio
<OPTION>Friend
</SELECT>
```

The last input field is the Submit button; it's drawn onscreen as a normal pushbutton with the title Add Me Now:

```
<INPUT TYPE=SUBMIT VALUE="Add Me Now">
```

When the user clicks the button by using the mouse or keyboard, the form and all its data are submitted to the server with the ACTION property specified in the original <FORM> tag.

The Submission

Of course, the form would be of no use if there wasn't an application running on the server that could do something with the data. In the past, the CGI (Common Gateway Interface) application has filled this need. When CGI applications are referenced in the URL of the ACTION property, they're executed on the server after the data is submitted. These applications take the data, perform some task, and respond by sending a stream of HTML instructions back to the client.

With Active Server Pages, you don't need to develop a separate application to deal with the results. You simply write a dynamic Web page that makes use of the Request object. When an Active Server Page is used as the ACTION property of a <FORM>, all the data collected on the form is accessible through the built-in Request object.

The document in Listing 10.6 shows a dynamic Web page that uses the Request object to identify the data entered in the previous form (from Listing 10.5).

Listing 10.6. A dynamic reaction page (10TWD06.ASP).

```
 1: <HTML>
 2: <TITLE>Example 10.6: Dynamic Reaction</TITLE>
 3: <HEAD><H1>Thank You</H1></HEAD>
 4: <BODY>

 5: <BR>
 6: <BR>
 7: Name:
 8: <%= Request.Form("fname") + " " + Request.Form("lname") %>
 9: <BR>
10: email:
11: <%= Request.Form("email") %>
12: <BR>
13: <% if Request.Form("sendnow") = "on" then %>
14: You wanted information sent today!
15: <% else %>
16: You do not require information to be sent today.
17: <% end if %>
18: <BR>
19: You heard about me via:
20: <%= Request.Form("how") %>
21: <BR>

22: </BODY>
23: </HTML>
```

The page is primarily a simple HTML document, and the text in it is the actual text that's going to be sent back to the user who submitted the data. However, in a few places, the HTML switches over to scripting code, and in those places the Request object is used. The Request object has a sub-object called Form associated with it, as though it were simply a property of the Request object. In this way, it is just like the Fields collection of the Recordset object. The Form sub-object is a collection of all the data elements sent from the client browser to the server. The elements are named in exactly the same way they were expressed in the original form.

To get the data from a form sent to the server, just use the Visual Basic indexing operator:

```
<%= Request.Form("fname") %>
```

This statement accesses the first name field of the data sent from the form to the server. It uses the name fname because that's the name given to the input field on the form in Listing 10.5.

It's easier to understand what transpires between these two Web pages by taking a look at a physical example. Figure 10.3 shows Internet Explorer being used to access the Web page from Listing 10.5.

Figure 10.3.

Submitting the data.

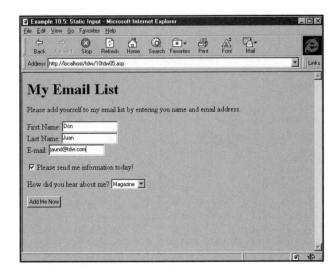

The next picture, Figure 10.4, shows the generated response from the Web server after the Add Me Now button has submitted the data.

Figure 10.4.

The reply.

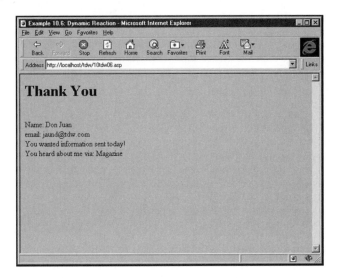

Note that this page doesn't actually do anything with the data sent back to the user, except to send it right back to the user in the form on another HTML page.

Because Listing 10.6 uses scripting, both pages seem to be dynamic in nature when you compare them. However, the first Web page was completely static, and the second page was dynamic because its generation depended on input from the user interacting with the first page. Together, they are partially dynamic and partially static. The next example shows you a fully dynamic data input form.

Dynamic Input

You can generate the input form on demand, just as the Dynamic Table example generated the table based on the query and the fields from the database. This method might be useful for database administrators who want remote access to the database for maintenance reasons. In this case, the same arguments presented with the Dynamic Table example apply. The administrator would want to see all fields from each table without needing modifications to the Web page each time the database's structure was changed. The administrator might even be accessing the database with the express purpose of adding a column to a table.

Luckily, Recordsets and Visual Basic Script give you an easy way of building input forms on-the-fly. The following code in Listing 10.7 shows a sub-routine defined in Visual Basic Script that generates an input form based on the fields obtained from a Recordset.

Listing 10.7. Building an input form on-the-fly.

```
Sub GenerateForm( rs, action, maxsize, usedata )

  ' start form
  %> <FORM METHOD=POST ACTION="<%= action %>"> <%

  ' build input field for each recordset field
  for i = 0 to rs.fields.count - 1

    ' determine size of input field
    size = rs(i).DefinedSize
    if size > maxsize or size < 1 then
      size = maxsize
    end if

    ' determine initial value of field
    if useData then
      value = rs(i)
      if isNull(value) then value=""
    else
      value=""
    end if
```

continues

Listing 10.7. continued

```
   ' determine name of field
   name = "fld"+cstr(i)

   ' create input field as html
%> <P><%= rs(i).Name %>   <%
%> <INPUT TYPE=TEXT SIZE=<%= size %> VALUE=<%= value %> NAME=<%= name
➥%>><BR> <%

next
%>  <BR>
<INPUT TYPE=HIDDEN NAME="x" VALUE="y">
<INPUT TYPE=SUBMIT VALUE="SUBMIT">
</FORM>
<%

End Sub
```

The routine takes four parameters: rs is a Recordset that has already been opened, action is the name of an Active Server Page that acts as the recipient of data from this form, maxsize is the maximum size of a text input field, and usedata is a Boolean flag that tells the sub-routine whether to populate the form with data from the Recordset fields or to leave it blank.

The routine starts by generating the original <FORM> tag into the HTML output stream. The ACTION argument of the <FORM> tag is generated to refer to the same value contained in the action variable passed to the sub-routine. The METHOD argument is always set to POST.

Immediately after, the familiar FOR loop begins to repeat over each field of the Recordset in succession.

The size of the input field is calculated based on the size of the Recordset field as defined in the database; however, it can't exceed the maximum size specified by the code calling this sub-routine.

The default value of the input field is determined to be the same value held by the current record of the Recordset if the usedata option is turned on. Otherwise, the default value is initialized as an empty string, which is the equivalent of being blank for text fields.

Finally, a name for the input field is generated based on the prefix fld and the ordinal value of the Field object in the Recordset. Input field names can be anything, but since <FORM> fields have stricter naming conventions than Recordset Fields do, they have been assigned generated names—fld0, fld1, fld2, and so on—instead of using names known to the Recordset.

10

After all the information describing the input field is calculated, the prompt for the field is inserted into the generated HTML. This prompt is given the name of the Recordset field because it's more descriptive than a generated name.

The declaration of the input field itself follows on the heels of the prompt, complete with scripting calculations for each of its properties.

This sequence of calculations and input field generation is repeated for each field of the Recordset. Once all the fields have been generated, two final fields are added at the bottom. One is a hidden field populated with a simple value. This field can be used in the Web page that gets the data as a verification that it's genuine and that it did indeed originate from this generated form.

TIP

Use hidden fields with automatic values as a trick to determine whether the Active Server Page has been accessed by an initial request or by posting data from a HTML form. With Active Server Pages, you can use the same Web page to act as both the input form and the code that handles the reply.

The second final input field is actually a button, the Submit button that the user clicks on. The data isn't submitted to the server until the button has been clicked.

You can see the entire Web page in its full glory in Listing 10.8. The same dynamic Web page is used both for generating the input form and for acting on posting the data back to the server.

Listing 10.8. A dynamic input page (10TWD07.ASP).

```
 1: <HTML>
 2: <TITLE>Dynamic Input</TITLE>
 3: <HEAD><H1>Dynamic Input</H1></HEAD>
 4: <BODY>

 5: <%
 6: Sub GenerateForm( rs, action, maxsize, usedata )
 7:    ' start form
 8:    %> <FORM METHOD=POST ACTION="<%= action %>"> <%
 9:    ' build input field for each recordset field
10:    for i = 0 to rs.fields.count - 1
11:       ' determine size of input field
12:       size = rs(i).DefinedSize
```

continues

Listing 10.8. continued

```
13:     if size > maxsize or size < 1 then
14:        size = maxsize
15:     end if
16:     ' determine initial value of field
17:     if useData then
18:        value = rs(i)
19:        if isNull(value) then value=""
20:     else
21:        value=""
22:     end if
23:     ' determine name of field
24:     name = "fld"+cstr(i)
25:     ' create input field as html
26:     %> <P><%= rs(i).Name %>   <%
27:     %> <INPUT TYPE=TEXT SIZE=<%= size %>
➥VALUE=<%= value %> NAME=<%= name %>><BR> <%
28:   next
29:   %>
30:   <BR>
31:   <INPUT TYPE=HIDDEN NAME="x" VALUE="y">
32:   <INPUT TYPE=SUBMIT VALUE="SUBMIT">
33:   </FORM>
34:   <%
35: End Sub

36: if Request.Form("x") = "" then
37:    ' first time page-hit, no request yet!
38:    set rs = Server.CreateObject("ADODB.Recordset")
39:    rs.Open "select * from orders", "DSN=ADOSamples"
40:    set Session("rs") = rs
41:    GenerateForm rs, "10twd07.asp", 60, true
42: else
43:    Set rs = Session("rs")
44:    if not rs.EOF then
45:       rs.MoveNext
46:    end if
47:    if rs.EOF then
48:       Set Session("rs") = nothing
49:       rs.Close
50:       %> This is the end of the road. <%
51:    else
52:
53:       GenerateForm rs, "10twd07.asp", 60, true
54:    end if
55: end if
56: %>
57: </BODY>
58: </HTML>
```

10

The form-generating function you saw earlier is contained in the first part of the scripting section. Because it's a sub-routine, it isn't immediately executed when the page is first run. It's skipped over, and the first execution begins on the IF statement:

```
if Request.Form("x") = "" then
```

The IF statement checks the Request object for the hidden field x that's part of the generated form. If this page is being accessed directly from a Web link, then no form is being submitted and the x field contains no data. It's blank, so it's equivalent to the empty string it's being compared against in this statement.

If this is the case—that submitting FORM data hasn't been the cause of this page's activation—the following code accesses the database, queries for information, and then generates the input form based on that information:

```
' first time page-hit, no request yet!
  set rs = Server.CreateObject("ADODB.Recordset")
  rs.Open "select * from orders", "DSN=ADOSamples"
  set Session("rs") = rs
  GenerateForm rs, "10tdw07.asp", 60, true
```

Notice that another trick is being used in this same code. Not only is the same Web page being invoked twice, once to generate the form and a second time to receive the submitted data, but it's also remembering information across the two invocations. The Recordset itself is being opened only once.

NOTE

> Active Server Pages have a special built-in object called Session that can be used by the scripting code to store information across separate accesses made by the same user. Session is a storage bin for anything you might want to associate with the user accessing your application.

You can store a Recordset in the Session object by assigning the Recordset to a named element of the Session collection. In Listing 10.8, it's done by using this statement:

```
set Session("rs") = rs
```

This statement uses the name rs to store the Recordset named rs. It is purely by coincidence that the two have the same name. The name used to store an object or a value in the Session collection can be any name you want. You just have to use the same name you used before to get the object or value back out. For example, the following statement could have been used just as well:

```
set Session("timbuktu") = myRecordset
```

NOTE

Using the Session object isn't restricted to functioning across repeated calls to the same page. Any page can use the Session object and find objects and values in it that were stored by other pages accessed by the same user.

Finally, the last instruction in the top portion of the IF statement is a call to the sub-routine GenerateForm():

```
GenerateForm rs, "10tdw07.asp", 60, true
```

This call to the sub-routine passes information to generate an input form based on the Recordset rs, using this same ASP file as the receiver of the submitted response, to keep input fields from being larger than 60 text characters wide and to default the form fields to values in the current record of the Recordset.

The other half of the IF statement is executed only after the data from the input form has been submitted back to the server. In this case, one of two things can happen. If there's more data in the Recordset, the input form is sent back to the user with data from the most recent record. If no more data exists, the message This is the end of the road is sent back instead.

Each time the user submits the input form, a new input form is sent back containing the next record of data, until it reaches the end of the Recordset.

Although this advanced input form isn't all that useful, it's a good example of a dynamic input form. Each time the page is accessed, a new form is generated with a new set of default data. The data can then be altered and sent back to the server by clicking the Submit button. The server can do something with the data—record it or update it—and send back a Web page representing a response to the submission. It just so happens that, in this example, the response is a form similar to the original one submitting the data, containing the next record. Nothing is actually done with the data; it's not written back into the database.

Dynamic Input Fields

Most often, a complete dynamically generated form isn't what you think would be useful for getting user input to your online application. That doesn't mean, however, that the input form should remain static.

Just as you can generate every input field automatically, you can also write scripting code that picks and chooses the fields to display for editing. A Web page that generates a form in this manner is free to choose the exact representation of each input field. Instead of automatically generating them all as simple text input fields, you can choose to use different types of input: checkboxes, radio buttons, selection lists, and so forth.

This next example illustrates how dynamic Web pages can not only control which fields appear in the generated input form, but also *how* they appear. Listing 10.9 is an ASP file that contains VBScript code full of sub-routines for defining different kinds of input fields. The most important one for this example is the SELECT field. Instead of having static tables of choices to build a selection list from, Recordsets can offer an up-to-date list of choices.

Listing 10.9. Using dynamic input fields (10TWD08.ASP).

```
 1: <HTML>
 2: <TITLE>Dynamic Input Fields</TITLE>
 3: <HEAD><H1>Dynamic Input Fields</H1></HEAD>
 4: <BODY>

 5: <%
 6: '********************************************************
 7: '* FORM UTILITY SUBROUTINES

 8: Sub FormBegin( action )
 9:    %> <FORM METHOD=POST ACTION=<%= action %>> <%
10: End sub

11: Sub FormEnd( mode )
12:    %>
13:    <INPUT TYPE=HIDDEN NAME="mode" VALUE="<%=mode%>">
14:    </FORM>
15:    <%
16: End Sub

17: Sub FormInput( name, prompt, size, value )
18:    %>
19:    <P>
20:    <%= prompt %>
21:    <INPUT TYPE=TEXT SIZE=<%=size%> VALUE="<%=value%>" NAME="<%=name%>" >
22:    <BR>
23:    <%
24: End Sub

25: Sub FormSelect( name, prompt, size, value, items )
26:    %>
27:    <P>
28:    <%= prompt %>
29:    <SELECT NAME=<%=name%>>
30:    <%
31:    for i = 0 to UBound(items,2)
32:      if value = items(0,i) then
33:        Response.Write "<OPTION SELECTED>" + cstr(items(0,i))
34:      else
35:        Response.Write "<OPTION>" + cstr(items(0,i))
36:      end if
```

continues

10

Listing 10.9. continued

```
37:    next
38:    %>
39:    </SELECT>
40:    <BR>
41:    <%
42: End Sub

43: Sub FormSubmit( name, value )
44:    %>
45:    <INPUT TYPE=SUBMIT NAME=<%= name %> VALUE=<%= value %> >
46:    <%
47: End Sub

48: Function GetItemList( fld, table, cn )
49:    set rs = Server.CreateObject("ADODB.Recordset")
50:    rs.Open "select "+fld+" from "+table, cn
51:    GetItemList = rs.GetRows(-1)
52: End Function

53: '*****************************************************
54: '* MY FORMS

55: Sub ProductForm( action, mode )
56:    products = GetItemList( "ProductName", "Products", "DSN=ADOSamples" )
57:    FormBegin action
58:    FormSelect "prod", "Choose a Product", 40, "", products
59:    Response.Write "<BR>Please fill out the following information<BR><BR>"
60:
61:    FormInput  "fname", "First Name: ", 40, ""
62:    FormInput  "lname", "Last Name : ", 40, ""
63:    FormInput  "email", "Email Address: ", 40, ""
64:
65:    Response.Write "<BR>"
66:    FormSubmit "submit", "SUBMIT"
67:    FormEnd mode
68: End Sub

69: Sub YesNoForm( action, mode )
70:    FormBegin action
71:    FormSubmit "yes", "YES"
72:    FormSubmit "No", "NO"
73:    FormEnd mode
74: End Sub

75: '*****************************************************
76: '* THE MAIN CODE

77: mode = Request.Form( "mode" )
78: if mode = "" then
79:    ProductForm "10twd09.asp", "1"
80: elseif mode = "1" then
81:    %>
82:    You chose:
83:    <%= Request.Form("prod") %>
```

```
 84:   <BR>
 85:   Your name is:
 86:   <%= Request.Form("fname") + " " +_
 87:       Request.Form("lname") %>
 88:   <BR>
 89:   Your email address is:
 90:   <%= Request.Form("email") %>
 91:   <BR>
 92:   <BR>
 93:   <BR>
 94:   Is the information correct?
 95:   <%
 96:   YesNoForm "10twd08.asp", "2"
 97: elseif mode = "2" then
 98:   if Request.Form("yes") = "YES" then
 99:     %> <HR><H3> Thank you, very much </H3> <%
100:   else
101:     ProductForm "10twd08.asp", "1"
102:   end if
103: end if
104: %>
105: </BODY>
106: </HTML>
```

The Utility Sub-routines

The first sub-routine, FormBegin(), is called to generate the HTML sequence for starting a <FORM>. It takes one parameter, action, which correlates to the ACTION property of the <FORM> tag:

```
Sub FormBegin( action )
  %> <FORM METHOD=POST ACTION=<%= action %>> <%
End sub
```

Its counterpart is the sub-routine FormEnd():

```
Sub FormEnd( mode )
  %>
  <INPUT TYPE=HIDDEN NAME="mode" VALUE="<%=mode%>">
  <INPUT TYPE=SUBMIT VALUE="SUBMIT">
  </FORM>
  <%
End Sub
```

This sub-routine must be called to finish defining an HTML input form. It adds the hidden field named *mode*, initialized with the value mode supplied as a parameter to this sub-routine. In the last example, a hidden field named *x* was added to the form that always contains the value y. In this example, the hidden field "mode" does the same job, but its value isn't fixed to any particular string. Each form may set the mode field to any value. This method can be used to distinguish the input from many different forms, all flooding to the same dynamic Web page.

The sub-routine `FormInput()` is equally straightforward:

```
Sub FormInput( name, prompt, size, value )
  %>
  <P>
  <%= prompt %>
  <INPUT TYPE=TEXT SIZE=<%=size%> VALUE="<%=value%>" NAME="<%=name%>" >
  <BR>
  <%
End Sub
```

It takes four parameters defining the makeup of a normal text input field and then generates the appropriate HTML to add the input field to the form.

The most interesting sub-routine is `FormSelect()`; it's used to generate a `<SELECT>` instruction that builds a selection list into the form:

```
Sub FormSelect( name, prompt, size, value, items )
  %>
  <P>
  <%= prompt %>
  <SELECT NAME=<%=name%>>
  <%
  for i = 0 to UBound(items,2)
    if value = items(0,i) then
      Response.Write "<OPTION SELECTED>" + cstr(items(0,i))
    else
      Response.Write "<OPTION>" + cstr(items(0,i))
    end if
  next
  %>
  </SELECT>
  <BR>
  <%
End Sub
```

The selection list is populated with values contained between the `<SELECT>` and `</SELECT>` tags. Each value, or option, must be represented in the HTML as it's sent to the client browser; otherwise, it wouldn't be available for the user to select. A dynamic Web page using Active Server Pages can generate the full `<SELECT>` instruction with a complete set of options represented by a database table.

The `FormSelect()` sub-routine takes, in addition to same parameters used to define an input field for the `FormInput()` sub-routine, an additional parameter containing an array of items. These items are then converted into `<OPTIONS>` that make up the `<SELECT>` instruction.

The item array being accessed in the `FormSelect()` sub-routine is actually a two-dimensional array. Think of the item array as a table of data. The first index of the array specifies the column of data within the table, and the second index specifies the row.

TIP

The Recordset object has a method called GetRows() tha range of records into a two-dimensional array of data. Thi contains a copy of the data found in the records.

Calling the GetRows() method with the first parameter set to (-1) copies the entire R into a local variable as a two-dimensional array. The FormSelect() sub-routine has been written assuming that only the first column of the array is meaningful.

The GetItemList() function, shown here, gets the array of values for you:

```
Function GetItemList( fld, table, cn )
  set rs = Server.CreateObject("ADODB.Recordset")
  rs.Open "select "+fld+" from "+table, cn
  GetItemList = rs.GetRows(-1)
End Function
```

10

This function takes the name of a field, the name of a table, and a connection string and returns an array containing all the unique values of that field as contained in the specified table.

 NOTE

A *function* in Visual Basic Script is just like a sub-routine, except that it can return a value. A function is defined by using the Function and End Function keywords instead of the Sub and End Sub keywords.

For example, the GetItemList() function may be used in the following way:

```
mylist = GetItemList( "x", "y", "z" )
```

A variable with the same name as the function acts as a storage bin for the return value. The last line of the GetItemList() function shows the result of the GetRows() function being assigned to a variable named GetItemList. It is through this variable that the array of data is passed back to the caller.

 TIP

Storing the results of a query in an array as a cache allows you to reuse the same set of information for multiple selection lists without re-reading the data from the database. For small tables, this method is useful. The query can be executed with the fastest access method—a forward-only read—yet the data can be reused for multiple selection lists without having to reexecute the query.

The last utility function, `FormSubmit()`, adds a Submit button to the form:

```
Sub FormSubmit( name, value )
  %>
  <INPUT TYPE=SUBMIT NAME=<%= name %> VALUE=<%= value %> >
  <%
End Sub
```

`FormSubmit()` is defined as its own sub-routine instead of being incorporated into either `FormBegin()` or `FormEnd()` for two reasons: First, you might want to choose not only what the button is called, but where it's located in relation to the other fields on the form; second, you might have more than one Submit button.

TIP   Each Submit button can have its own name and its own value. Both the name and the value are transmitted to the server as part of the form's data, but only the value of the Submit button that's clicked by the user gets sent. This trick can be used to determine an additional choice made by the user.

The Form Sub-routines

There are two sub-routines that generate forms. The first, `ProductForm()`, builds an input form requesting the user to make a product choice and then fill in some personal information:

```
Sub ProductForm( action, mode )
  products = GetItemList( "ProductName", "Products", "DSN=ADOSamples" )
  FormBegin action
  FormSelect "prod", "Choose a Product", 40, "", products
  Response.Write "<BR>Please fill out the following information<BR><BR>"
FormInput  "fname", "First Name: ", 40, ""
  FormInput  "lname", "Last Name : ", 40, ""
  FormInput  "email", "Email Address: ", 40, ""
  Response.Write "<BR>"
  FormSubmit "submit", "SUBMIT"
  FormEnd mode
End Sub
```

The sub-routine has two parameters: `action` and `mode`. These parameters are identical to the parameters used for the `FormBegin()` and `FormEnd()` sub-routines. They are intended to be passed down to their respective utility sub-routines and are a way to potentially reuse `ProductForm()` for different purposes. The `action` parameter eventually tells the browser which Active Server Page will process the results, and the `mode` parameter tells the browser where the information came from.

10

In the code, the `ProductForm()` sub-routine makes use of the `GetItemList()` function to generate an array of product names. It then uses this array of products as a parameter to the `FormSelect()` sub-routine that generates a selection list of all the products.

The other fields are laid out with their respective sub-routine calls. The call to `FormSubmit()` generates a standard Submit button, named `submit`, that displays the message SUBMIT when drawn by the browser.

Aptly named, the last form generates a simple YES or NO selection. The `YesNoForm()` sub-routine makes use of the multiple Submit button trick, naming one `yes` and the other `no`:

```
Sub YesNoForm( action, mode )
  FormBegin action
  FormSubmit "yes", "YES"
  FormSubmit "no", "NO"
  FormEnd mode
End Sub
```

When the user sees this form, he or she must choose which button to click. Either button will submit the data. Only one of the button's values is sent to the server page that processes the submission, so that page can determine the user's exact choice.

The Main Code

After everything else has been broken out into separate sub-routines or functions, the main code ends up looking fairly simple, which is good. The main control logic of your dynamic Web page should always seem easy to understand.

The primary structure of the main code is a single IF-THEN-ELSEIF structure that checks the "mode" field of the `Request` object to determine which step the user is making—which form was last entered—so it can take the appropriate action:

```
mode = Request.Form( "mode" )
if mode = "" then
  ProductForm "10tdw08.asp", "1"
elseif mode = "1" then
  %>
  You chose:
  <%= Request.Form("prod") %>
  <BR>
  Your name is:
  <%= Request.Form("fname") + " "
      + Request.Form("lname") %>
  <BR>
  Your email address is:
  <%= Request.Form("email") %>
  <BR>
  <BR>
```

```
<BR>
Is the information correct?
<%
YesNoForm "10tdw08.asp", "2"
elseif mode = "2" then
  if Request.Form("yes") = "YES" then
    %> <HR><H3> Thank you, very much </H3> <%
  else
    ProductForm "10tdw08.asp", "1"
  end if
end if
```

The first time the user accesses the page, no forms have been entered, so the mode field is empty. The first comparison of the IF-THEN-ELSEIF structure checks to see whether the field is empty. If so, the product form is generated for the user by calling the ProductForm() sub-routine.

If the mode field contains the value 1, you know immediately that the product form has been filled out by the user and the Submit button has been clicked. In this case, the information entered by the user is displayed back to the browser, and a small YES-or-NO form is appended, giving the user a chance to revoke the submission. This form is generated by calling the YesNoForm() sub-routine.

If the mode field contains the value 2, you know that the user has clicked on the YES-or-NO form. The only way the mode can be set to 2 is if the user has already submitted the product form and then seen the YES-or-NO form. The Request object has the information needed to determine which Submit button was clicked. If the Yes button was clicked, then the Yes field will exist in the form's data, and it will have the same text displayed on the button's face.

If the Yes button was indeed clicked, a sincere "thank you" message is sent back, acknowledging that the multistep data entry has been successful. Otherwise, the original product form is regenerated with another call to ProductForm() so the user can have another try at entering the correct information.

Dynamic Updating

It takes only a minor leap in logic to imagine creating input forms that update information directly into a database. You might want to keep a mailing list of everyone who has visited your site or let customers post orders for products.

In the previous examples, the only thing missing was code that actually did something constructive with the submitted data. The examples seemed to lack a real purpose because nothing ever happened to the information that was entered. The lack of purpose wasn't an oversight, however; it was a simplification made so you could focus on entering and submitting information, without worrying about what was going to eventually happen to it.

Now it's time to take a look at the ways you can take the submitted informati███ it back to the database.

Updating Data Using Recordsets

The first thing you need to know is how to go about writing information into the database. Chapter 9 touched on all the methods and properties of the Recordset object. Some of the methods could be used to add new records, and others to update single or multiple records at a time. Before you can use any of these methods, however, you need a Recordset object that has been opened for writing.

Any Recordset that isn't read-only has been opened for writing. The LockType property is used to control the type of updating the Recordset uses. If you recall, Chapter 9 listed four possible values for the LockType property:

LockType *Constants*	*Value*
adLockReadOnly	1
adLockPessimistic	2
adLockOptimistic	3
adLockBatchOptimistic	4

The first one, adLockReadOnly, is obviously the one LockType constant meant for creating a read-only Recordset and is of no use when opening a Recordset meant for updating.

Of the remaining three, adLockBatchOptimistic is meant for batch processing. It's best to use batch processing when changes to many records need to be made and the cost of updating each one independently is too great, which can happen when updates are sent across a slow network connection, for example. You would want to batch-up as many changes as possible before taking the time to send them across the wire.

Fortunately, with dynamic Web pages, the Recordset object isn't responsible for communicating over a slow link. That bridge is made between the input form and the submission of data to the server application. The server application in turn uses the Recordset to communicate to the database over a fast communication link, so batch processing is unnecessary for most applications.

The only real choice is between adLockPessimistic and adLockOptimistic. Of the two, a *pessimistic lock* is better at guaranteeing the database's integrity. It locks out everyone else from the record you're editing, safeguarding your changes from those made by others. It keeps the record locked from the time you make your first change until you call the Update method.

Optimistic locking, on the other hand, locks the record only during the call to Update. Someone else could have made a change to the record between the time you made your first

date. With optimistic locking, you could accidentally undo
⌐e time you update yours. It does, however, take up fewer
⌐ing because your changes happen all at once instead of over
⌐resources needed, you might find optimistic locking superior
⌐g online applications. You aren't required to design around the
⌐cess to a record or the update failing.

(in left margin, rotated: ...on and apply / 329)

...ordset

⌐nat can be used for updating, simply assign the `LockType` property
⌐cordset:

```
<%
rs.LockType = adLockOptimistic
rs.Open "query", "connection", adOpenDynamic
%>
```

You can also pass the appropriate `LockType` property as the fourth parameter to the `Open` command:

```
<% rs.Open "query", "connection", adOpenDynamic, adLockOptimistic %>
```

Notice how, in either case, the third parameter to `Open` has been specified as `adOpenDynamic`. This constant is one of the constants available to describe cursor types. The default `CursorType` property has always been `adOpenForwardOnly`. Forward-only cursors can be navigated only by using the `MoveNext` method; that is, you can visit each record only once. However, you often want to revisit records when writing applications that update data.

Updating Fields

Updating the data in a `Recordset` is as natural as assigning new values to individual fields. The first time you make a change to any field's value, you have begun to edit the current record. You're finished editing when you either change the record position or explicitly call the `Recordset`'s `Update` method.

For example, the following lines of code make changes to separate fields of the current record:

```
<%
rs("fname") = "Harry"
rs("lname") = "Yoddleman"
rs("hobby") = "Model Trains"
rs.Update
%>
```

If you opened the `Recordset` using `adLockPessimistic` for `LockType`, then the record is immediately locked as soon as the first change is made on the first line of code. If you opened the `Recordset` using `adLockOptimistic`, then the record is locked, updated, and unlocked all during the single call to `Update`.

10

Adding New Records

Adding new records is just as easy as updating them. In fact, the code can look surprisingly similar:

```
<%
rs.AddNew
rs("fname") = "Harry"
rs("lname") = "Yoddleman"
rs("hobby") = "Model Trains"
rs.Update
%>
```

In this example, when the AddNew method is called, an empty record is added to the Recordset. The fields are modified one by one, and the entire changed record is sent to the database server at once.

Special Cases

There are other ways to add new records and update them that require using arrays of field names and arrays of values. Both the AddNew and Update methods can operate in this manner.

You may have to preset a handful of fields before the record is added to the Recordset because of constraints placed on the table within the database. For example, a database table containing mailing list information could be considered invalid if it has an incomplete mailing address at the time the record is added.

You can guarantee that all the fields are defined when you add the record by passing them all at once to the AddNew method:

```
<%
  Dim names(2)
  Dim values(2)
  names(0) = "fname"
  names(1) = "lname"
  names(2) = "hobby"
  values(0) = "Harry"
  values(1) = "Yoddleman"
  values(2) = "Model Trains"
  rs.AddNew names, values
%>
```

If you add new records using this sequence of steps, there's no need to call the Update method. However, if there are more fields to be changed after the initial AddNew is called, then Update is still necessary:

```
<%
  Dim names(1)
  Dim values(1)
  names(0) = "fname"
  names(1) = "lname"
```

10

```
      0) = "Harry"
      (1) = "Yoddleman"
    .dNew names, values
   hobby") = "Model Trains"
   .Update
```

331

.n the preceding code, you can assume that the database requires both the first name and last name fields to exist in all records. This requirement is often the case when particular fields are included in either a primary or secondary key. The hobby field wasn't a required portion of any key, so it can be modified after the initial call to AddNew.

The Data Entry Application

The dynamic Web page in this section is the most comprehensive example so far. It not only handles displaying and entering data, but also adding new records and updating existing ones.

The VBScript portion of the ASP file can be broken down into three logical pieces. The first is a bunch of form-generating utility sub-routines similar to those in the previous examples. The second is a pair of sub-routines for manipulating the customer form and its data. The final piece is the main logic of the program. It handles coordinating the display presented to the user and directs the processing of input forms.

Listing 10.10 is rather long, so examine it carefully before you continue to the discussion following it.

Listing 10.10. A dynamic data-entry form (10TWD09.ASP).

```
 1: <HTML>
 2: <TITLE>Dynamic Data Entry</TITLE>
 3: <BODY>

 4: <!--#include file="adovbs.inc" -->

 5: <%
 6: '****************************************************
 7: '* FORM UTILITIES

 8: Sub FormBegin( action )
 9:    %> <FORM METHOD=POST ACTION="<%= action %>"> <%
10: End sub

11: Sub FormEnd( mode )
12:    %>
13:    <INPUT TYPE=HIDDEN NAME="mode" VALUE="<%=mode%>">
14:    </FORM>
15:    <%
16: End Sub
```

10

```
17: Sub FormInput( name, prompt, size, value )
18:    if isNull(value) then value = ""
19:    %>
20:    <B><%= prompt %></B>
21:    <INPUT TYPE=TEXT SIZE=<%=size%> VALUE="<%=value%>" NAME="<%=name%>" >
22:    <%
23: End Sub

24: Sub FormText( name, prompt, rows, cols, value )
25:    if isNull(value) then value = ""
26:    %>
27:    <B><%= prompt %></B>
28:    <TEXTAREA NAME="<%=name%>" ROWS=<%=rows%> COLS=<%=cols%>
29:    ><%= value %></TEXTAREA>
30:    <%
31: End Sub

32: Sub FormSubmit( name, value )
33:    %>
34:    <INPUT TYPE=SUBMIT NAME="<%= name %>" VALUE="<%= value %>" >
35:    <%
36: End Sub

37: '********************************************************
38: '* CUSTOMER FORM

39: Sub CustomerForm( rs, action, mode )
40:    FormBegin action

41:    if mode = "browse" then
42:    %><H3>Contact</H3><%
43:    %><%= rs("ContactFirstName") + " " + rs("ContactLastName") %><BR><%
44:    %><%= rs("ContactTitle") %><BR><%
45:    %><%= rs("CompanyName") %><BR><BR><%
46:    %>Phone#: <%= rs("PhoneNumber") %><BR><%
47:    %>Fax#: <%= rs("FaxNumber") %><BR><%
48:    %>Email: <%= rs("EmailAddress") %><BR><BR><%
49:    %><H3>Billing Address</H3><%
50:    %><%= rs("BillingAddress" ) %><BR><%
51:    %><%= rs("City") + ", " + rs("StateOrProvince") +_
➥" " + rs("PostalCode") %><BR><%
52:    %><%= rs("Country") %><%
53:    else
54:    %><H3>Contact</H3> <%
55:    FormInput "cofname", "Name", 20, rs("ContactFirstName")
56:    FormInput "colname", "", 20, rs("ContactLastName")
57:    %> <BR> <%
58:    FormInput "cotitle", "Title", 60, rs("ContactTitle")
59:    %> <BR> <%
60:    FormInput "coname", "Company", 60, rs("CompanyName")
61:    %> <BR><BR> <%
62:    FormInput "phone", "Phone#", 16, rs("PhoneNumber")
63:    FormInput "fax", "Fax#", 16, rs("FaxNumber")
64:    %> <BR> <%
65:    FormInput "email", "Email", 40, rs("EmailAddress")
66:
```

10

continues

Listing 10.10. continued

```
67:    %> <H3>Billing Address</H3> <%
68:    FormText "address", "", 1, 60, rs("BillingAddress")
69:    %> <BR><BR> <%
70:    FormInput "city", "City", 20, rs("City")
71:    FormInput "state", "State", 2, rs("StateOrProvince")
72:    FormInput "zip", "Zip", 12, rs("PostalCode")
73:    FormInput "country", "Country", 10, rs("Country")
74:  end if

75:  %> <BR><HR> <%
76:  '** add appropriate submit buttons **
77:  if mode = "browse" then
78:    rs.MovePrevious
79:    if not rs.BOF then
80:      FormSubmit "prev", "<<"
81:    end if
82:    rs.MoveNext
83:    rs.MoveNext
84:    if not rs.EOF then
85:      FormSubmit "next", ">>"
86:    end if
87:    rs.MovePrevious
88:    FormSubmit "edit", "Edit"
89:    FormSubmit "add", "New"
90:    FormSubmit "exit", "Exit"
91:  elseif mode = "edit" then
92:    FormSubmit "submit", "Update"
93:    FormSubmit "cancel", "Cancel"
94:  elseif mode = "add" then
95:    FormSubmit "submit", "Add"
96:    FormSubmit "cancel", "Cancel"
97:  end if
98:  FormEnd mode
99: End Sub

100: Sub UpdateCustomer( rs )
101:   rs("ContactFirstName") = Request.Form("cofname")
102:   rs("ContactLastName") = Request.Form("colname")
103:   rs("ContactTitle") = Request.Form("cotitle")
104:   rs("CompanyName") = Request.Form("coname")
105:   rs("PhoneNumber") = Request.Form("phone")
106:   rs("FaxNumber") = Request.Form("fax")
107:   rs("EmailAddress") = Request.Form("email")
108:   rs("BillingAddress") = Request.Form("address")
109:   rs("City") = Request.Form("city")
110:   rs("StateOrProvince") = Request.Form("state")
111:   rs("PostalCode") = Request.Form("zip")
112:   rs("Country") = Request.Form("country")
113:   rs.Update
114: End Sub
```

10

```
115:  '*****************************************************
116:  '* THE MAIN CODE

117:  thisForm = "10twd09.asp"
118:  mode = Request.form("mode")

119:  if mode = "" then

120:     %><H1>Customer Info</H1><%
121:     set rs = Server.CreateObject("ADODB.Recordset")
122:     rs.Open "select * from Customers", "DSN=ADOSamples", _
➥adOpenKeyset, adLockOptimistic
123:     set Session("rs") = rs
124:     CustomerForm rs, thisForm, "browse"

125:  elseif mode = "browse" then

126:     set rs = Session("rs")
127:     if Request.Form("next") > "" then
128:       rs.MoveNext
129:       %><H1>Customer Info</H1><%
130:       CustomerForm rs, thisForm, "browse"
131:     elseif Request.Form("prev") > "" then
132:
133:       rs.MovePrevious
134:       %><H1>Customer Info</H1><%
135:       CustomerForm rs, thisForm, "browse"
136:     elseif Request.Form("edit") > "" then
137:       %><H1>Edit Customer</H1><%
138:       CustomerForm rs, thisForm, "edit"
139:     elseif Request.Form("add") > "" then
140:
141:       rs.AddNew
142:       %><H1>New Customer</H1><%
143:       CustomerForm rs, thisForm, "add"
144:     elseif Request.Form("exit") > "" then
145:
146:       set rs = Session("rs")
147:       set Session("rs") = Nothing
148:       rs.Close
149:       %> <H3>Have a nice day!</H3> <%
150:     end if

151:  elseif mode = "edit" then

152:     set rs = Session("rs")
153:     if Request.Form("submit") > "" then
154:       UpdateCustomer rs
155:       %><H1>Customer Info</H1><%
156:       CustomerForm rs, thisForm, "browse"
157:     elseif Request.Form("cancel") > "" then
158:       %><H1>Customer Info</H1><%
159:       CustomerForm rs, thisForm, "browse"
```

continues

Listing 10.10. continued

```
160:   end if

161: elseif mode = "add" then
162:
163:    set rs = Session("rs")
164:    if Request.Form("submit") > "" then
165:      UpdateCustomer rs
166:      %><H1>Customer Info</H1><%
167:      CustomerForm rs, thisForm, "browse"
168:    elseif Request.Form("cancel") > "" then
169:      rs.CancelUpdate
170:      %><H1>Customer Info</H1><%
171:      CustomerForm rs, thisForm, "browse"
172:    end if

173: else
174:    %> Error: Unknown mode <%
175: end if

176: %>
177: </BODY>
178: </HTML>
```

Server-Side Includes

The first thing you should notice in Listing 10.10 is the special HTML comment placed near the top of the listing:

```
<!--#include file="adovbs.inc" -->
```

It's known as a *server-side include*. Many Web servers, such as Internet Information Server, recognize this special HTML comment as a directive to include another file before processing.

The file ADOVBS.INC has definitions of all those ADO constants identified in Chapter 9. Including this file in your own ASP file lets you use the ADO named constants in your script code instead of using the numeric values.

The Utility Sub-routines

For the most part, the utility sub-routines are similar to those found in Listing 10.9. A new addition is the FormText() sub-routine that generates <TEXTAREA> tags for specifying multi-line text input.

The Customer Form

The sub-routine CustomerForm() generates HTML instructions for displaying an input form for the customer table. It takes three parameters: rs, a Recordset; action, a URL to an Active

Server Page that handles processing the submitted data; and mode, a value denoting the application's current state. Compare these parameters to the ProductForm() sub-routine from Listing 10.9. The action and mode parameters do exactly the same job they did in that example. The action parameter is used in the call to FormBegin(), and the mode parameter is used in the call to FormEnd().

The first thing that happens in this sub-routine, just after the call to FormBegin(), is an IF statement checks the value of the mode parameter. The CustomerForm() routine is slightly more advanced than the ProductForm() routine from Listing 10.9; it uses the mode parameter to determine exactly what the display should look like.

If the mode parameter is set to browse, the sub-routine generates a modest display of the information, but it doesn't actually generate input fields for the data fields. In browse mode, editing the data is not allowed.

If the mode parameter is not browse, it must be either add or edit. In either case, a complete set of input fields is generated so the user can manipulate the data.

After the display is generated, CustomerForm() once again uses the mode parameter to determine the type of Submit buttons to display at the bottom. Browse mode displays get forward and backward VCR-style navigation buttons, as well as buttons for editing and adding new records. Edit mode displays get an Update and a Cancel button, and Add mode displays get Add and Cancel buttons.

Updating the Customer

The UpdateCustomer() sub-routine copies the submitted data from the Request object and into the Recordset object at the current record's position. It's encapsulated into its own sub-routine to isolate it from the application's main logic and to associate it more directly with the Customer form.

The sub-routine operates by copying each field one by one. The names used in the input form aren't the same names used in the Recordset. You could possibly shorten this code to a looping algorithm, with the field names stored in a fixed array. The code has been written in a straightforward series of assignments to make it seem similar to the Recordset updating example discussed earlier; it consists of several assignments into the Recordset and a call to the Update method.

The Main Code

The main code acts primarily as a dispatcher to the other code. It retrieves the mode field from the input form and uses it to process and generate new HTML pages accordingly.

TIP

It's good coding practice to isolate the majority of your application's details away from the main code logic. The main logic should be legible as an outline of the broad paths of execution your code may take. If your dynamic Web page consists of more than a modest amount of scripting code, separate the top-level decision-making code from the detailed HTML-generating code and encapsulate details in reusable sub-routines.

The main code consists of one overall IF-THEN-ELSEIF statement that breaks the application down into separate sequences of code, depending on how the page was activated. Each form the user sees is associated with a unique mode and special value identifying which Submit button he or she clicked. With these two bits of information, the main code determines the precise action to take.

In browse mode, one of four buttons could have been clicked to submit data and reactivate the Active Server Page. If the Next button is accessible as part of the Request object's data, then the user clicked the Next button. In this case, the current record position is advanced to the next record, and the form is regenerated showing the new record. If the Prev button was clicked, the current record position is moved back to the previous record. If the Edit button was clicked, then the form is regenerated in the edit mode. Similarly, if the Add button was clicked, the form is regenerated in the add mode.

In edit mode, either the Update or Cancel button has been clicked. If the Update button was clicked, the current record is updated by calling the UpdateCustomer() sub-routine, and the form is regenerated back in browse mode. If the Cancel button was clicked, the submitted data is ignored, and the form is again regenerated back in browse mode.

In add mode, either the Add or Cancel button has been clicked. Both of these cases are similar to the edit mode cases, except that canceling an AddNew requires a call to CancelUpdate(). The edit mode cancel didn't require such a call because no data was actually updated before the button was clicked.

Lights, Camera, Action

To take a look at the code in action, bring up a Web browser and point it at the file 10TDW09.ASP. Figure 10.5 shows the Customer form displaying the first record in the Customers table. It hardly looks like a form because there are no input fields, but the Submit buttons at the bottom are a tell-tale sign.

10

Note You might want to make a backup copy of the ADVWORKS.MDB database stored in the ASPSamples\AdvWorks subdirectory of your Web browser's Internet publications directory. The default publications directory is InetPub for Internet Information Server.

Figure 10.5.
The first customer.

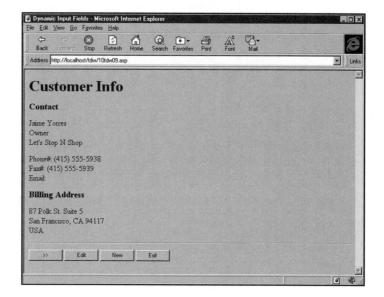

Clicking the Edit button changes the display to a full-fledged input form. Figure 10.6 shows the input form initialized with data from the first record.

Go ahead and change the e-mail address for this person. The sample database is missing e-mail addresses, so add an imaginary one. Clicking Update adds the information to the database and returns the display to browse mode.

From browse mode, use the navigation button (>>) to advance to the next record. The second record shows two navigation buttons, one for forward and another for reverse. Eventually, if you keep advancing, on the third record you can see that the original forward button is gone, and only the reverse button remains. The application is "smart" enough to figure out the Recordset's end-points. If you're curious, go back and inspect the CustomerForm() subroutine to see how it's done.

Clicking the New button brings up the New Customer form, which surprisingly resembles the Update Customer form. The only difference is the two buttons on the bottom: one marked Add and one marked Cancel, as you can see in Figure 10.7.

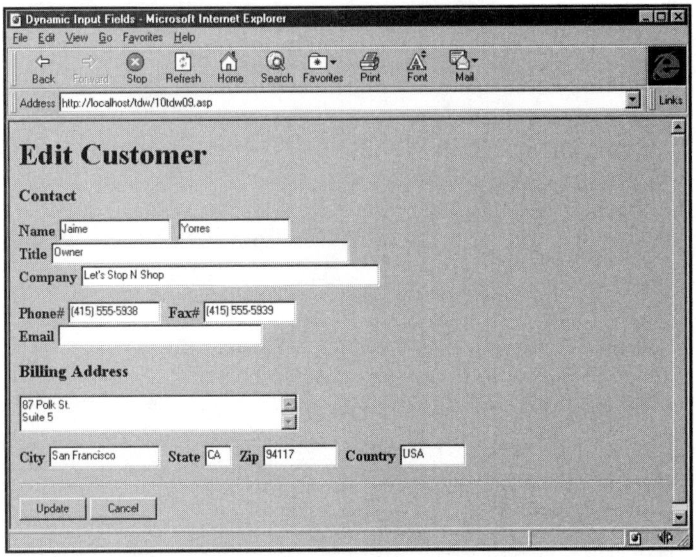

Figure 10.6.

Editing the customer.

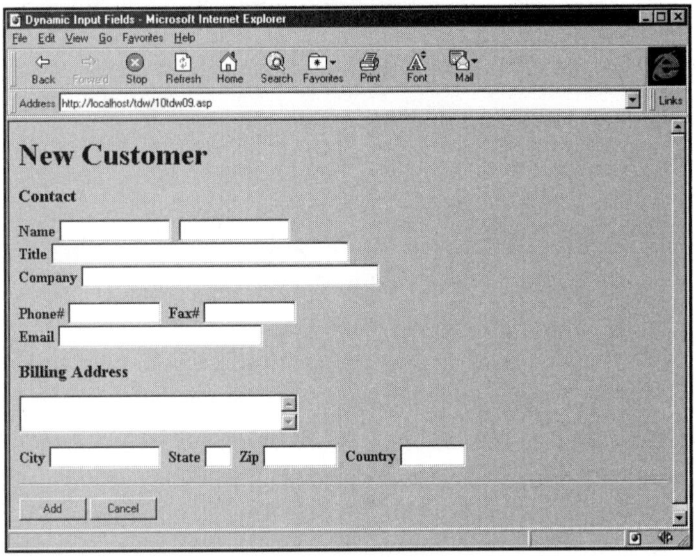

> **Dynamic Input Fields - Microsoft Internet Explorer**
>
> File   Edit   View   Go   Favorites   Help
>
> Back   Forward   Stop   Refresh   Home   Search   Favorites   Print   Font   Mail
>
> Address http://localhost/tdw/10tdw09.asp
>
> ## Edit Customer
>
> **Contact**
>
> Name Jaime   Yorres
> Title Owner
> Company Let's Stop N Shop
>
> Phone# (415) 555-5938   Fax# (415) 555-5939
> Email
>
> **Billing Address**
>
> 87 Polk St.
> Suite 5
>
> City San Francisco   State CA   Zip 94117   Country USA
>
> Update   Cancel

Figure 10.7.

Adding a new customer.

> **Dynamic Input Fields - Microsoft Internet Explorer**
>
> File   Edit   View   Go   Favorites   Help
>
> Back   Forward   Stop   Refresh   Home   Search   Favorites   Print   Font   Mail
>
> Address http://localhost/tdw/10tdw09.asp
>
> ## New Customer
>
> **Contact**
>
> Name
> Title
> Company
>
> Phone#   Fax#
> Email
>
> **Billing Address**
>
> City   State   Zip   Country
>
> Add   Cancel

Go ahead and add a new customer, filling out any information you find appropriate. Click the Add button when you're done to add the new customer to the database.

Again, you're returned to the browse mode form. To exit the application and release the resources associated with your session, click the Exit button at the bottom.

Summary

This chapter has explained dynamic Web pages and given many examples of using them with the ADO Recordset object to produce three of the most important pieces of a data-centered Web application: information display, input forms, and database updating. With tools like these, you can easily get information to people formatted as plain HTML, retrieve information from them using HTML forms, and manipulate the data once it's submitted by using the ADO Recordset.

Information display, whether it's HTML tables or the layout of an input form, can be based algorithmically on a query's structure and the information it returns. You can generate both tables and forms that include all the columns from a query, and you can populate input fields with live data from Recordset objects, even building up-to-date selection lists.

Active Server Pages can store information for you across multiple Web pages or over multiple hits on the same Web page. You can store live Recordsets in a Session object to keep a memory of what happened before that will help you plan what's going to happen next. You can overcome the Web's static nature once you begin to keep track of individual users' actions, allowing each a personal view of your site and your online application.

Q&A

Q How can I reuse code like your form utilities without copying and pasting them into every Web page I build?

A Simply copy the code in question into its own standalone file. Using the same server-side include trick used in Listing 10.10, include this new utility file at the top of your application:

```
<!--#include file="myfile.asp" -->
```

When building your own Web applications, think ahead about portions of code that could be reused by many pages. Put these pieces of code into sub-routines, and then put the sub-routines in a file all by themselves. It's good practice to have many separate code files.

Q Your input form examples always submit the data back to the same ASP file that generated the form. Is this a good idea?

A It depends on how complicated your pages get. It might make more sense to you to distribute the work across many ASP files. This distribution keeps the parsing overhead down because the server doesn't have to re-digest the entire program and all its facets for each submission the user makes.

However, unless you have good skills at source-control, it might be less confusing to put all the application code associated with the same task in a single ASP file.

Q **If I keep a** `Recordset` **open across multiple page hits, and I have several concurrent users accessing the same Web page, won't the resources on the server be overloaded?**

A At some point, that may be true. Keeping `Recordset`s alive between page hits is expensive; you're limited by your server's capacity.

Fortunately, you have other, less resource-intensive ways to build online applications. Only if you need to keep the current record position around do you definitely need to keep the entire `Recordset` alive. If not, you can close the `Recordset` after each use, and then use SQL statements to send updates to the database. This technique is covered in Chapters 11, "Transactions and the `Connection` Object," and 12, "Commands and Stored Procedures."

Q **Can you have more than one form in a Web page running under the browser?**

A Yes, you can have many separate forms, but only one can be submitted back to the Web server.

Q **Can an HTML table be generated without column names on top?**

A Yes. Just don't put the extra `<TD>` tags outside the `<TR>` tags.

Q **How can I know when the data I've put into a table will reach the edge of the screen? I want to show only as many columns as will fit.**

A It's impossible to know. The `<TABLE>` tag syntax is generic and simply states what *should* be displayed, not necessarily *how* it should be displayed. You don't know how much space is available on the client browser.

You might need to look into other methods of presenting tables on Web pages, such as ActiveX controls or Java applets.

Q **If I write client-side scripting code and put it in the Web page, can the script access the form variables?**

A Yes. You can access the form variables through the `Document` object when running under the client Web browser. A field with the name "fname" can be accessed by typing `Document.Form.fname`, or, if the form has its own name, `Document.Formname.fname`.

Quiz

1. List the HTML tags used for generating tables and explain the role played by each.

2. Given a `Recordset` named `rs`, write the HTML instructions that generate a text input field for the field named "title." This input field has a display size of 40 characters and defaults to the current value of the `Recordset`.

3. A `Session` object can be used to keep information across multiple page accesses. True or False?

4. A single `Session` object is shared by all users accessing the same Web page. True or False?

5. List all types of input fields that can be used with input forms.

6. List all types of input fields that can be defined by using the `<INPUT>` tag.

7. List three primary ways to turn static HTML Web pages into dynamic Web pages.

8. Describe two different ways you can use the `Recordset` object to update a record.

9. Describe two different ways you can use the `Recordset` object to add a new record.

10. List the four types of locking that can be performed with a `Recordset`.

Exercises

1. Write a dynamic Web page that generates a table listing of data from your own database (assuming you have some of your own data).

2. Make your own version of the General Dynamic Table example, Listing 10.3, that presents the columns in reverse order.

3. Write a dynamic Web page that builds an HTML input form and responds to the submitted data.

4. Complete the form utilities by writing sub-routines that help generate radio buttons, password fields, and multi-select listboxes.

5. Write a dynamic Web page that 1) builds a form for user input of multiple fields, 2) on submission, stores the results in the `Session` object and then generates a Yes/No validation form, and 3) on submission of a YES, uses the data stored in the `Session` object to generate another display.

6. Extend Exercise 5 by adding `Recordset` updating. Open a `Recordset` to a table in your own database or in one of the sample databases. Default the original input form with data from the first record. After submission of a YES on the second input form, update the `Recordset`, close the `Recordset`, and remove the `Recordset` from the `Session` object.

7. Write a dynamic Web page that displays HTML tables spanning several pages. Limit each page to 10 records.

    You will need skills you learned for both table and input form generation. Make a modified version of the `GenerateTable()` sub-routine to produce only a specified number of rows. Next, build an input form that offers the user a More Records button that retrieves the next 10 records when clicked.

    Hint: Use the `Session` object to hold a live `Recordset` across multiple page hits.

8. Write a dynamic Web page that generates an input form not actually used for input, but to display combo boxes for each column of the table. Each box contains a list of all the unique values found in the table for the respective column.

9. Make your own version of the data-entry example shown in Listing 10.10 that includes a Delete button in addition to Edit and New.

Day 11

Transactions and the Connection Object

by Matt Warren

The Connection object represents the physical link between your application and the remote database server. All communication between your Recordsets or Commands and the back-end database is negotiated through the Connection.

Transactions make your interactions with the database "bulletproof." A series of changes can be grouped together to look like a single, all-or-nothing change. Other users don't see partial updates, and the database's integrity can't be undermined by dangerous—albeit unlikely—failures occurring on the Web server. In other words, by using transactions, your information isn't lost.

After reading this chapter, you will be able to do the following:

- ☐ List the methods and properties of the Connection object.
- ☐ Use the Connection object for simple SQL execution.
- ☐ Reduce the resource load placed on both the database and Web server by sharing Connections.
- ☐ Show how the Connection object and Recordset object work together.
- ☐ Explain why transactions are important for online applications.
- ☐ Show how transactions are used to consolidate multiple updates into one.

Connections

The ADO Connection object was designed as a tangible representation of the link between your application and the database server. With the Connection object, you control how the link is established and when it's shut down.

Because it's a separate object, you can decide at any time what objects are associated with your connection. Recordsets and Commands are both tools used to manipulate data. They can be used and reused for different jobs, plugged into one connection initially, closed, and plugged into another to do something completely different. They both need to be plugged into a physical link to the database, however, before they can be used to do any work. The Connection object is that link.

In addition to acting as the plumbing for the data to travel along, the Connection object is the control point for all the general settings that affect the Recordsets and Commands hooked to the connection.

As far as the database is concerned, users don't interact with the database; Connections do. To the database, Connections are the points of contact with the outside world. You might have many open Recordsets at one time, but if they're all using the same Connection, the database sees them as one multifaceted interaction. You and a group of friends may hop in a car and stop a local restaurant with a drive-up window, but the driver usually does the talking for the rest of the car. The driver is the point of contact for all the passengers.

Many things have an overriding effect over the entire Connection and its associated objects. Transactions in particular can be manipulated only at the level of the connection, just as the driver is the one who pays the bill—handles the transaction—at the drive-up window.

Transactions allow you to make multiple changes to the database, but make them behave as though only one occurred. Either they all succeed, or they all fail. The cashier at the drive-up window doesn't care who in the car is short on money; either the entire bill is paid, or no one gets a burger.

Overview of the Connection C

Before you delve too deeply into this chapter, I've given
Connection object to help you absorb the details in the fol

Imagine the following scenario: You're a top-secret agent
headquarters. First, you find an available telephone—mayb

```
<% Set cn = Server.CreateObject("ADODB.Connection") %
```

Next, you dial. A person answers, but instead of letting you blurt out whatever it is you have
to say, she asks you for your identification. You tell her, but she's still not sure. She wants you
to tell her the secret password, the one only you would know. You look around to see if anyone
is listening, and then you whisper it:

```
<% cn.Open "Headquarters", "Max", "WYB?" %>
```

She buys it. You ask to speak to your partner, Charlie, who will know what to do with your
startling information:

```
<% cn.DefaultDatabase = "FactsForCharlie" %>
```

He listens while you pass on what you know:

```
<% cn.Execute "update location='library' in hideouts where thug = 'The Kidd'" %>
```

Opening the Connection

As with the Recordset object, the first thing you need to know how to do is to create the object
and then open it. Creating the Connection is like picking up the receiver of a telephone, and
opening it is like dialing. Getting to a phone is simple, but for dialing you need to know who
you're calling and what the number is. Connections don't come with phone directories.

You create a Connection the same way you created a Recordset, with the CreateObject()
command. Using Visual Basic Script under Active Server Pages, this is a method of the built-
in Server object:

```
<% Set cn = Server.CreateObject("ADODB.Connection") %>
```

You open it by calling its Open method, specifying the datasource name, the user ID, and the
password, respectively:

```
<% cn.Open "bigdb", "me", "ungalungaloo" %>
```

This is much easier than specifying a connection string, but if you would prefer to do that,
you have two ways to do so. You could assign the connection string to the ConnectionString
property, and then call Open with no parameters at all:

```
constr = "data source=bigdb;user=me;password=ungalungaloo"
cn.ConnectionString = constr
cn.Open
%>
```

Or you could pass the connection string as the first parameter to the Open method:

```
<%
constr = "data source=bigdb;user=me;password=ungalungaloo"
cn.Open constr
%>
```

Either way, opening a Connection requires a datasource, user ID, and password. Unless the database is configured to use something like NTLM, Windows NT's user authentication system, to provide automatic authentication, or has guests accounts or accounts with no password, you need all three pieces of information.

Issuing Queries

You can issue queries by using the Connection object without involving a Recordset at all. Many queries sent to the database don't actually retrieve any information; often, they just perform updates, deletions, or insertions. Simple forms of these queries can be expressed easily in a native query syntax, such as SQL.

Instead of opening a Recordset, transferring copies of records from the server, and then sending changes back, you can specify the explicit changes in the form of a query. The benefit of using the Recordset is that you can algorithmically inspect the data and, after inspection, decide what changes should be made. If you know beforehand exactly what changes to make, it's faster to send them directly, as shown here:

```
<% cn.Execute "INSERT INTO workout (weight,reps,day)
               VALUES (80,30,CURRENT_DATE)" %>
```

In addition, commands that instruct the database to restructure itself—by creating tables and adding fields, for example—can be done easily without involving a Recordset, as shown in this example:

```
<% cn.Execute "CREATE TABLE coffee(id int, name varchar (30))"
```

Connecting a Recordset

If you insist on issuing queries that return results, there are two ways to go about using a Connection object to do that. You could use the Connection object's Execute method to issue the query, as in the previous examples. The Execute method is willing to hand you back a Recordset, if there is one to be had:

```
<% Set rs = cn.Execute "select * from coffee" %>
```

This method works, but has the drawback of handing you back a forward-only, read-only Recordset. Without being able to call the Open method on the Recordset itself, it's impossible to ask for anything but the default style of Recordset.

The other method is to use the Recordset to issue the query:

```
<% rs.Open "select * from coffee", cn, adOpenKeyset %>
```

Using the Recordset, you get to decide the cursor type and the lock type. Passing the Connection object in as the second parameter to the Recordset's Open command tells the Recordset to use your Connection object as its link to the database.

After the Recordset is opened, the ActiveConnection property points back to your Connection object. This is true for the Recordset that was created by using the Connection object's Execute method, as well.

Using Properties of the Connection Object

Property	Description
Attributes	Retains the transaction behavior.
CommandTimeout	Time lapse before Execute method aborts.
ConnectionString	Series of inline property assignments.
ConnectionTimeout	Time lapse before Open method aborts.
CursorLocation	Default cursor location.
DefaultDatabase	Name of database implicit in the query syntax.
IsolationLevel	Level of transaction isolation.
Mode	Control over shared access.
Provider	Default provider that manages communication.
Version	Current version of ADO.

NOTE   As in Chapter 9, "Dynamic Pages and the ADO Recordset," the following descriptions have a phrase on the right-hand side of the page, just after the section title. The words to the left of the separating slash (/) pertain to the Connection before it's been opened, and those to the right apply while it's open.

Attributes

Contains one or more of the following values: Read-Write / Read-Write

Attributes Constant	Value
adXactCommitRetaining	131072
adXactAbortRetaining	262144

You can use the Attributes property to control how transactions are re-engaged once they have been committed or aborted. A connection that renews itself after it has been committed or aborted is said to be *retained*. That transaction ceases to exist, but a new one is put in its place.

adXactCommitRetaining   After a call to CommitTrans, a new transaction is begun automatically, without requiring you to call the BeginTrans method.

adXactAbortRetaining   After a call to RollbackTrans, a new transaction is begun automatically, without requiring you to call the BeginTrans method.

You can change the Connection's retaining behavior at any time, regardless of whether the Connection is open or closed or whether a transaction is in progress. However, many providers might not be able to support either feature.

NOTE

> It's common practice to explicitly add scopes to transacted updates between calls to BeginTrans and CommitTrans because you rarely want all your database interactions to be governed by transactions. Only paired statements that transfer information across separate tables should be governed directly. The resource cost of a transaction is too steep for anything other than groups of updates that need to appear atomic.

If the entire goal of your application or sub-routine is to perform many updates, and each successive update is composed of many subordinate updates that together move data between tables, then retained transactions could be beneficial. They require less communication with the database server, so subsequent transactions take less time to initiate.

CommandTimeout

Contains an Integer value   Read-Write / Read-Write

You can use the CommandTimeout property to set a limit on the number of seconds an execution is allowed to take. If the execution takes longer than the time-out period, the query is aborted and the call to the Execute method fails.

In cases of slow network response or backlogged servers, commands might take longer than you'd like to execute. The Execute method can be preset to fail in either of these cases, instead of waiting indefinitely for a query to succeed.

The CommandTimeout property can be used to control the default behavior of Command objects. Any Command object with an ActiveConnection property pointing back to this Connection object automatically uses the Connection object's CommandTimeout property as a default, unless the particular Command object overrides the CommandTimeout value. Both the Connection and Command objects have CommandTimeout properties.

The default value of the Connection object's CommandTimeout property is 30 seconds. Changing this to a value of zero allows the Connection or Command object to wait indefinitely for the Execute method to finish.

ConnectionString

Contains a String value   Read-Write / Read-Only

You can use the ConnectionString property to supply provider-specific information before a connection is opened to the database. This is the same information you give to the ActiveConnection property of the Recordset object when you expect the Recordset to implicitly create the Connection object for you.

A *connection string* is composed of a series of associations. Terms understood by the database are matched with values provided by the programmer. Each association is formed by four pieces: the name of a provider-specific property, an equals sign (=), the value to associate with the named property, and a semicolon (;) at the end.

The following string is an example of a syntactically valid connection string:

```
"size=10;height=20;weight=15;"
```

Connection string properties aren't the same as built-in object properties, such as ConnectionString; however, sometimes they do coincide.

ADO connection strings recognize the following special property names:

Provider	Identifies the type of datasource provider and the code library that interacts with it. An ADO provider is similar to an ODBC driver. The default provider for ADO 1.0 is MSDASQL.
Data Source	Identifies the name of the datasource that can be accessed with the chosen provider. Often, it's the same name as the default database.
User	Identifies the name of the user trying to gain access to the database.
Password	Identifies the user's password that must be verified before access is permitted.
File Name	Identifies a file that may contain saved connection information.

Each of these connection string properties is intercepted by the ADO Connection object and dealt with internally. All other properties are sent on as they are to the provider for processing. Only properties recognized by either ADO or the provider are used.

The Provider connection string property is equivalent to the Connection object property Provider. It can either be assigned to the object directly or included in the connection string.

The examples from Chapters 9 and 10, "More Dynamic Pages," used the connection string properties DSN, UID, and PWD. These are special ODBC connection properties and are equivalent to Data Source, User, and Password, respectively. When using the special ADO property names, make sure you include a space in double-word names, such as Data Source. Leave no extra spaces before or after the equals sign or between the data value and the semicolon.

Although it was necessary to specify Data Source, User, and Password properties inside a connection string when working with a Recordset alone, it's not required when working with a Connection object. The Open method of the Connection object accepts three parameters that just happen to be Data Source, User, and Password. Most often, these are the only properties specified. It's easier to pass them as parameters to the Open method instead of remembering their particular names and forming a well-punctuated connection string.

ConnectionTimeout

Contains an Integer value   Read-Write / Read-Only

You can use the ConnectionTimeout property to limit the number of seconds the Open method is allowed to take before it's considered a failure.

In cases of slow network response or backlogged servers, connection requests might take longer than you'd like to succeed. The Open method can be preset to fail in either of these cases, instead of waiting indefinitely.

The default value for the ConnectionTimeout property is 15 seconds. Changing this value to zero allows the Connection object to wait indefinitely for the Open method to succeed.

CursorLocation

Contains one of the following values: Read-Write / Read-Only

Cursor Location	Value
adUseClient	1
adUseServer	2
adUseClientBatch	3

You can use the CursorLocation property to assign a default value for Commands and Recordsets associated with a particular Connection object. The Connection doesn't actually use this information—the Recordset does. Recordsets created by calling the Execute method of either a Connection or a Command have a cursor location determined by this property.

The CursorLocation property can be used to control where the underlying data provider maintains the query results. A client-side cursor maintains the results primarily on the client, and a server-side cursor on the server. A client-batch cursor, however, is special because it can be disassociated from its server-side, transmitted to the client, modified, sent back to the server, and reconnected to the database for updating. This feature is of primary importance to developers of online applications intended for the Internet. It allows interactive access to data without requiring a constant connection to the back-end database server. You'll learn more about the CursorLocation property's use in association with the Active Data Connector during Week 3, "Client-Side Rowsets with the Advanced Data Connector."

DefaultDatabase

Contains a String value   Read-Write / Read-Write

You can use the DefaultDatabase property to declare the name of the database used as the default when issuing queries. Normally, query languages such as SQL let you qualify a table's name by specifying what database it belongs to. This choice is important because datasources may contain several databases, and only one per connection is considered the default.

Changing the default database affects only queries that take place after the change of database. Recordsets that are currently open won't suddenly change their behavior.

IsolationLevel

Contains one of the following values: Read-Write / Read-Write

Isolation Constant	Value
adXactUnspecified	-1
adXactChaos	16
adXactBrowse	256
adXactReadUncommitted	256
adXactCursorStability	4096
adXactReadCommitted	4096
adXactRepeatableRead	65536
adXactIsolated	1048576
adXactSerializable	1048576

You can use the IsolationLevel property to set the degree of isolation before a transaction begins. The level of *isolation* determines whether each change is postponed until the transaction is committed and to what degree changes made by other transactions are visible during your transaction's time span. A fully isolated transaction has no overlap with other transactions occurring in the same database at the same time.

adXactUnspecified	Use this value when calling BeginTrans in languages that don't support missing parameters.
adXactChaos	All transactions occurring at the level of "chaos" can overwrite each other's changes before the transactions are committed, which is like having no transactions at all, except for the guarantee that the changes did indeed take place.
adXactBrowse	All changes are atomic at the time they're committed. However, changes made by other transactions are visible to you before they're committed.
adXactCursorStability	All changes are atomic at the time they're committed. Changes made by other transactions are visible to you only after they have been committed, which is the default behavior.
adXactRepeatableRead	All changes are atomic at the time they're committed. Changes made by other transactions aren't visible, unless the changes have been committed and you have called the Requery method on your individual Recordsets.

adXactIsolated   All changes are atomic at the time they're committed. The transaction is held in complete isolation, so changes made by other transactions aren't visible during the scope of this transaction.

Mode

Contains one of the following values: Read-Write / Read-Only

Mode *Constants*	*Value*
adModeUnknown	0
adModeRead	1
adModeWrite	2
adModeReadWrite	3
adModeShareDenyRead	4
adModeShareDenyWrite	8
adModeShareExclusive	12
adModeShareDenyNone	16

You can use the Mode property to set the acceptable level of sharing between your connection and other connections made to the same datasource. Using this property, you can restrict the type of connections that can be made to the same datasource in addition to your connections.

adModeUnknown   May be returned by the Mode property when the provider can't determine the actual sharing level.

adModeRead   Your connection may have read access.

adModeWrite   Your connection may have write access.

adModeReadWrite   Your connection may have both read and write access. Note that the value of this constant is merely the sum of adModeRead and adModeWrite.

adModeShareDenyRead   No other connections may exist that require read access.

adModeShareDenyWrite   No other connections may exist that require write access.

adModeShareExclusive   No other connections may exist that require either read or write access. Note that the value of this constant is merely the sum of adModeShareDenyRead and adModeShareDenyWrite.

adModeShareDenyNone   No other connections may exist at all.

11

Provider

Contains a `String` value   Read-Write / Read-Only

You can use the `Provider` property to identify the name of the datasource provider, which corresponds to the registered PROGID (program ID) of a dynamically loaded library of code that manages communication between ADO and the remote database server. (Remember, ADODB is the registered PROGID of ADO v1.0.) You can also set the provider name as an argument in the connection string.

The default value of the `Provider` property for ADO v1.0 is `MSDASQL`, which controls access to all current ODBC datasources.

Version

Contains a `String` value   Read-Only / Read-Only

You can use the `Version` property to determine the current version of ADO you're using. The `Version` property returns a string identifying the version of ADO in a readable form.

Using Methods of the `Connection` Object

Method	Description
BeginTrans	Starts a transaction
Close	Closes a connection
CommitTrans	Commits a transaction
Execute	Executes a query
RollbackTrans	Aborts a transaction
Open	Opens a new `Connection`

BeginTrans

`n = Connection.BeginTrans`

n   The nesting level of the newly begun transaction.

You can use the `BeginTrans` method to start a new top-level transaction or to start a new inner, nested transaction within the scope of an outer transaction.

A transaction defines the boundary within which many database interactions can be made, yet still appear as a single atomic interaction. For example, once a transaction is begun, an application can make updates to multiple records, add new records, and delete old ones. The effect of these changes is held in isolation from the rest of the database and the rest of the active connections until the transaction is committed. At that time, all the changes are made simultaneously against the actual database, without changes made by other connections mixing with them.

Some databases allow transactions to be *nested*. Many smaller, inner transactions can exist within an outer transaction. The BeginTrans method returns the nesting level of the newly started transaction. A value of 1 identifies the topmost transaction, 2 identifies the second level, and so on.

Close

`Connection.Close`

You can use the Close method to explicitly break the link between the Connection object and the remote database server. Once a Connection has been closed, it can be reopened again with a call to the Open method. If a live transaction exists on the Connection, the call to Close fails.

All Recordsets and Commands directly associated with the closed Connection become immediately disassociated from it, so their ActiveConnection properties report a value of Nothing. In addition, Recordsets are automatically closed, and all changes that haven't been updated yet are lost. Fields, Properties, and Parameters collections are either inaccessible until the parent object is reopened or empty because of the lost ink.

CommitTrans

`Connection.CommitTrans`

You can use the CommitTrans method to end a transaction, forcing all changes made since the transaction began to be saved into the database.

If the current transaction is a nested transaction, only the innermost transaction is committed, and the transaction level reverts to the next outer one. Changes committed by a nested transaction are added to the next level's pending changes and are fully committed to the database only when the outermost transaction is committed.

Execute

`Set rs = Connection.Execute Query, Count, Options`

rs	A Recordset object created as the result of the query's execution. SQL SELECT statements and stored procedure calls can both return Recordsets.
Query	A string containing the text of a query.

`Count`	A variable that gets the count of the total number of records affected by the query's execution. It's the total number of records updated, inserted, or deleted. If the query results in a `Recordset` object, a value of `-1` is returned in the variable. The `Count` parameter is optional.
`Options`	A constant entered as `CommandTypeEnum`. It takes on the same values and serves the same purpose as the `Options` parameter of the `Recordset` `Open` method. It can be used as a hint to specify the type of query being issued in the `Query` parameter. You can specify the constant values `adCmdText (1)`, `adCmdTable (2)`, and `adCmdStoredProc (3)`. The `Options` parameter is optional. The value `adCmdUnspecified (-1)` can be used for languages that don't support missing parameters.

You can use the `Execute` method to issue a query directly against the database linked by an open connection. If the query is a SQL `SELECT` statement or its equivalent, the name of a table, or a stored procedure that returns records, an open `Recordset` is returned by the call to `Execute`. Otherwise, a closed `Recordset` is returned and can simply be ignored.

NOTE

> `Recordsets` created as a result of calling the `Execute` method have a forward-only cursor and are read-only. To get another type of cursor or write access, create a `Recordset` on your own and use its `Open` method instead.

Use the `Execute` method as a shortcut for executing simple queries, such as SQL `UPDATE`, `INSERT`, or `DELETE` commands. Any command recognized by the database provider—such as table-definition statements or even granting and revoking user permissions—can be sent in this manner.

For executing more complex commands, those with parameters not easily expressed in a query string, you have to use a `Command` object, which is explained in Chapter 12, "Commands and Stored Procedures."

`Recordsets` created by the `Execute` method are directly associated with the `Connection` object, which can be confirmed by inspecting the `Recordset`'s `ActiveConnection` property.

RollbackTrans

`Connection`.RollbackTrans

You can use the `RollbackTrans` method to end a transaction and undo all changes made since the transaction began. The state of the database reverts to what it was before the first change was made. Deleted records reappear, and added records vanish.

Calling RollbackTrans on a nested transaction undoes only those changes made in the deepest level of nesting. Outer transactions remain intact, with all other changes still waiting for a future call to Commit. It's possible to roll back changes on an inner transaction and still commit changes on the outer levels.

Open

```
Connection.Open Data Source, User, Password
```

Data Source	A string containing either the name of an explicit datasource or a connection string containing a series of associations. See the ConnectionString property in this chapter for further details. This parameter is optional.
User	The name or ID of the user whose access permissions will be used for this connection. This parameter is optional. The information could also be supplied as part of a connection string.
Password	The password associated with the user ID; this parameter is optional. The information could also be supplied as part of a connection string.

You can use the Open method to establish a link between the Connection object and a remote database server identified by the name of the Data Source.

Once the connection is opened, it becomes active and can be used as the ActiveConnection property of a Recordset or Command object.

Using the Errors Collection

Each Connection object contains a collection called Errors, which has a set of errors or warnings generated by the last method call made on the Connection object or any associated Recordset or Command objects. See Chapter 13, "Errors and Provider Properties," for an in-depth discussion of the Errors collection and how it can be used to your advantage when programming dynamic Web pages.

Using the Properties Collection

As with all top-level ADO objects, the Connection object has a collection called Properties containing special properties defined by the datasource provider that can affect and enhance the interaction between ADO and the database. These properties can change from datasource to datasource and from provider to provider, so to make use of them, you must be certain of the type of datasource you're connecting to. Chapter 13 offers an in-depth discussion of the Properties collection and how it can be used to your advantage when programming dynamic Web pages.

Sharing Connections

One of the best features of a Connection object is that it can be reused to do many jobs. The same link to the same database can host many activities, queries, and updates that can even be happening simultaneously.

Using Multiple Recordsets

The first example shows how to use a single Connection object with multiple Recordset objects at the same time. The Connection is communicating to the back-end database for both Recordsets.

Listing 11.1 shows a dynamic Web page that displays two independent tables on the same page. You can get each table from the sample database ADOSamples by using a separate Recordset object, yet use only a single connection to the database.

Listing 11.1. Multiple Recordsets (11TWD01.ASP).

```
 1: <HTML>
 2: <TITLE>Example 11.1: Multiple Recordsets</TITLE>
 3: <HEAD><H1>Multiple Recordsets</H1></HEAD>
 4: <BODY>

 5: <%
 6: Sub GenerateTable( rs )
 7:   Response.Write( "<TABLE BORDER=1>" )
 8:   ' set up column names
 9:   for i = 0 to rs.fields.count - 1
10:     Response.Write("<TD>" + rs(i).Name + "</TD>")
11:   next
12:   ' write each row
13:   while not rs.EOF
14:     Response.Write( "<TR>" )
15:     for i = 0 to rs.fields.count - 1
16:       v = rs(i)
17:       if isnull(v) then v = ""
18:       Response.Write( "<TD VALIGN=TOP>" + CStr( v ) + "</TD>" )
19:     next
20:     rs.MoveNext
21:   wend
22:   Response.Write( "</TABLE>" )
23: End Sub
24: %>

25: <%
26: set cn = Server.CreateObject("ADODB.Connection")
```

```
27: cn.Open "ADOSamples"
28: %>
29: <h3>Employees</h3>
30: <%
31: set rs1 = Server.CreateObject("ADODB.Recordset")
32: rs1.Open "select FirstName, LastName from employees", cn
33: GenerateTable rs1
34: %>
35: <h3>Customers</h3>
36: <%
37: set rs2 = Server.CreateObject("ADODB.Recordset")
38: rs2.Open "select ContactFirstName, ContactLastName from customers", cn
39: GenerateTable rs2
40: %>
41: <%
42: cn.Close
43: %>

44: </TABLE>
45: </BODY>
46: </HTML>
```

Listing 11.1 borrows the GenerateTable() sub-routine used in Listing 10.4. It's used here to generate HTML tables for two separate Recordsets.

The code immediately following the sub-routine creates a Connection object by using the CreateObject() method of the built-in Server object. It then calls the Open method to establish a link to the datasource.

The next section of code does almost exactly the same thing, except it creates and opens a Recordset object instead. Notice how the Connection object cn is used as the second parameter to the Recordset's Open method. The Recordset actually uses the open, live Connection to communicate to the datasource and issue the query. The data retrieved by the query is sent back to the Recordset along this same channel.

Following the call to Open, the Recordset is passed to the GenerateTable() sub-routine, where the data is used to generate an HTML table.

A third scripting section uses code that's equivalent to the previous section. A second Recordset object is created and opened using a different query but the same Connection object. It's then passed to the GenerateTable() sub-routine, just as the first Recordset was.

Both Recordsets are live and functioning, using the same Connection object at the same time. If you wanted to continue using the first Recordset, it would be available to do so. You could, in fact, interleave calls to the separate Recordsets. The single Connection object and the database server would honor all requests.

Working with Multiple Pages

Just as you can with the Recordset object, you can keep a Connection object alive across accesses to several Web pages or multiple hits on the same Web page. After creating a Connection, you can store it in the Session collection, and it will be there waiting for you the next time you come looking for it.

Listing 11.2 shows a dynamic Web page with a multi-stage input form. The first form prompts the user for name and password. This information is then used to get the connection to the database on behalf of the user. The second form is simply a request to choose between two different tables available for display. Clicking a button associated with a table generates that table on the next page displayed.

Listing 11.2. Multiple pages (11TWD02.ASP).

```
 1: <HTML>
 2: <TITLE>Example 11.2: Multiple Pages</TITLE>
 3: <HEAD></HEAD>
 4: <BODY>

 5: <%
 6: Sub GenerateTable( rs )
 7:   Response.Write( "<TABLE BORDER=1>" )
 8:   ' set up column names
 9:   for i = 0 to rs.fields.count - 1
10:     Response.Write("<TD>" + rs(i).Name + "</TD>")
11:   next
12:   ' write each row
13:   while not rs.EOF
14:     Response.Write( "<TR>" )
15:     for i = 0 to rs.fields.count - 1
16:       v = rs(i)
17:       if isnull(v) then v = ""
18:       Response.Write( "<TD VALIGN=TOP>" + CStr( v ) + "</TD>" )
19:     next
20:     rs.MoveNext
21:   wend
22:   Response.Write( "</TABLE>" )
23: End Sub
24: %>

25: <% Sub LoginForm() %>
26: <H3> Login </H3>
27: <FORM METHOD=POST ACTION="11tdw02.asp">
28: <B>User Name:</B>
29: <INPUT NAME="USER" WIDTH=20>
30: <BR>
31: <BR>
32: <B>Password :</B>
33: <INPUT TYPE=PASSWORD NAME="PASS" WIDTH=20>
34: <BR>
```

11

```
35: <BR>
36: <INPUT TYPE=HIDDEN NAME="Mode" VALUE="Login">
37: <INPUT TYPE=SUBMIT VALUE="Enter"
38: </FORM>
39: <% End Sub %>

40: <% Sub PickTableForm() %>
41: <H3> Choose a Table </H#>
42: <FORM METHOD=POST ACTION="11tdw02.asp">
43: <INPUT TYPE=SUBMIT NAME="Employee" VALUE="Employee">
44: <INPUT TYPE=SUBMIT NAME="Customer" VALUE="Customer">
45: <INPUT TYPE=SUBMIT NAME="Exit" VALUE="Exit">
46: <INPUT TYPE=HIDDEN NAME="Mode" VALUE="Pick">
47: </FORM>
48: <% End Sub %>

49: <!-- THE MAIN CODE -->
50: <%
51: mode = Request.Form("mode")
52: if mode = "" then
53: LoginForm()
54: elseif mode = "Login" then
55: set cn = Server.CreateObject("ADODB.Connection")
56:    cn.Open "ADOSamples", Request.Form("USER"), Request.Form("PASS")
57:    set Session("cn") = cn
58:    PickTableForm
59: elseif mode = "Pick" then
60:    set cn = Session("cn")
61:    set rs = Server.CreateObject("ADODB.Recordset")
62:    if Request.Form("Employee") > "" then
63:
64:      rs.Open "select FirstName, LastName from employees", cn
65:      %><h3>Employees</h3><%
66:      GenerateTable rs
67:      PickTableForm
68:    elseif Request.Form("Customer") > "" then
69:      rs.Open "select ContactFirstName, ContactLastName from customers", cn
70:      %><h3>Customers</h3><%
71:      GenerateTable rs
72:      PickTableForm
73:    elseif Request.Form("Exit") > "" then
74:      cn.Close
75:      Set Session("cn") = Nothing
76:      Session("cn") = ""
77:      %> Have a good day! <%
78:    end if
79: end if
80: %>

81: </TABLE>
82: </BODY>
83: </HTML>
```

The first scripting section, just like Listing 11.1, restates the GenerateForm() sub-routine that first appeared in Listing 10.4. It's used later to generate the displays of the two separate tables.

Following the definition of the GenerateForm() sub-routine are two more sub-routine definitions that individually create the two input forms used in this example. For brevity's sake, the form utility sub-routines used in the last chapter have been ignored; instead, the forms are specified in pure HTML inside the sub-routines.

The first form is the login form, generated in the LoginForm() sub-routines. It's a form with two simple input fields: a user name and a password. The password field uses the special "password" field type so that the keystrokes are disguised as asterisks. The field really contains the characters that were typed; only their appearance is changed so that curious eyes don't accidentally see what you type.

The form has an Enter submit button and a hidden "mode" field that contains the value Login. This hidden mode field is used by the main code to recognize which form is being processed each time the page is invoked. When the Enter button is clicked or the user presses the Enter key, the fields are submitted to the same ASP that generated them.

The second form is even simpler than the first. It has no input fields at all. It merely displays three different Submit buttons. The first button is labeled Employee, the second, Customer, and the third, Exit. Clicking Employee or Customer asks the ASP file to generate HTML tables of the respective database tables; clicking Exit is a request to exit the session and explicitly close the Connection.

After the sub-routines, the main code provides the details for the logic of the dynamic Web page. Based on the value found in the Request object's mode field, different actions take place. This decision is controlled by the trusty Visual Basic IF-THEN-ELSEIF statement.

The first time the page is accessed, or whenever it's accessed from a link other than the input forms themselves, there's no mode field in the Request object because the Request object itself is empty of any information, since no request has been made. In this case, the first input form is generated and sent back to the user.

Any user name and password will do. The ADOSamples database works without one specified. Your own database, however, will have the individual user accounts you set up for it.

When the first input form with user and password fields is submitted, the value of Login is automatically assigned to the mode field of the Request object. This value assignment is made by your input form. The input form's hidden field "mode" defaults to the value Login when it's generated. This is the same field that appears in the Request object's Form collection, and it has the same value as you gave it originally.

Whenever the mode field has the value of Login, the dynamic Web page takes the second branch in the IF statement and generates the second form by calling the sub-routine PickTableForm(). This sub-routine generates the form with three different Submit buttons.

11

Also hidden within the form is the same hidden field named "Mode," except this time it has defaulted to the value Pick. When this form is submitted back to the same ASP file for processing, the mode field declares that the user has picked a table.

The third branch of the IF statement handles the case of the returned form. The code then breaks down the paths even further by checking which button the user clicked. This checking is done by examining the Request object's Form collection for the fields with the same name as the buttons. Only the button that was clicked is passed along as part of the submission, so only that field name will contain data.

A test is made for each button, looking for values greater than an empty string.

NOTE

When fields don't exist in the Request object's Form collection, they appear to contain a value equivalent to an empty string.

The first two conditions check for the buttons that are requests for tables to be generated. In each circumstance, the particular table is opened by using a Recordset.

Notice that before the inner IF-THEN-ELSEIF statement begins, the current Connection object is retrieved from the built-in Session object. It was put there when the Login form was being processed. At that time, the user's information on name and password were available, so the Connection was opened and stored for safekeeping.

Now, when there's a query to be made or a Recordset to be opened, the live Connection is retrieved from the Session object and used as the second parameter to the Recordset's Open method.

For each button, Employee or Customer, the appropriate table is generated by passing the opened Recordset to the GenerateTable() sub-routine.

The last button is the Exit condition. Clicking the Exit button is a request to shut down the connection. In this case, the Connection object is explicitly closed by calling the Close method. All the resources used on the Web server and the database server to maintain this connection are released.

Using Connection Pooling

Sometimes Web servers host many online applications, and each application is formed by a network of many Web pages, both dynamic and static. The dynamic Web pages that use ADO to access database servers put a high demand on that server each time a Connection object is opened and a link is established.

Keeping Connection objects alive is expensive. They take up resources on the server even when no communication is occurring. The database server might have a limit on the number of Connections that can be active at any one time, and so may the Web server. This limitation might make you think you shouldn't keep Connections alive, that instead, you should reopen a new Connection each time a dynamic page is activated and the database is interacted with.

Microsoft's ODBC 3.0 Driver Manager has one solution. It has a special feature called *connection pooling* that can make regaining a connection fast. Without any significant changes to how you use Active Server Pages, connections opened to the same datasource using the same properties and options might not require a new link to be established. Connection pooling keeps old, closed connections alive for a short time, allowing subsequent requests to immediately make use of them, instead of handling all the negotiations for opening a new one.

Figure 11.1 shows a connection pool. Each time the Connection object is opened, it can get one of the pooled physical links already established to the database.

Figure 11.1.

The connection pool.

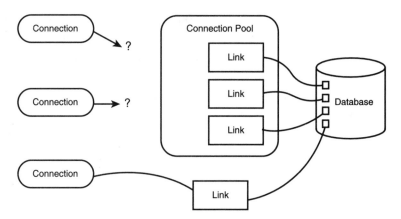

Starting the Connection Pool

To start connection pooling, you must modify a Registry setting; to do that, you have to use the system application REGEDIT:

1. From the Start button, choose Run. Enter the name REGEDIT and press the Enter key.

2. Once REGEDIT is started, you need to find the section devoted to Active Server Pages. This might seem daunting, but REGEDIT displays information in much the same way that Explorer shows files and folders. The ASP section is inside many levels of Registry folders. The following pathname shows you which folders to open:

HKEY_LOCAL_MACHINE\SYSTEM\CurrentControlSet\Services\W3SVC\ASP\Parameters

Figure 11.2 shows the REGEDIT program viewing the Active Server Pages Parameters window.

Figure 11.2.

Finding the parameter.

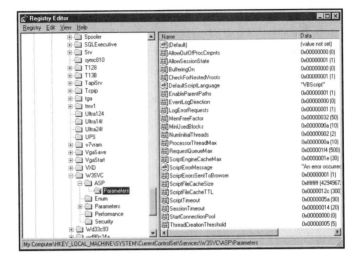

3. Double-click on the StartConnectionPool item in the list of parameters, and change its value from 0 to 1, as shown in Figure 11.3.

Figure 11.3.

Starting the connection pool.

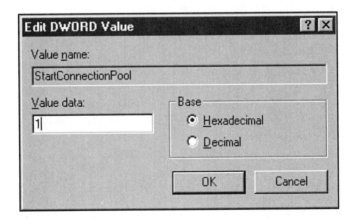

4. Press the Enter key or click OK. To save the changes to the Registry, choose Registry | Exit from the menu.

Transactions

Transactions and `Connection` objects are practically synonymous; they both govern the entirety of the interaction that occurs over the wire. Everything that's done to a database happens through the keyhole of a `Connection`. Each open `Recordset` and executed `Command` must issue its instructions through a single portal, and the `Connection` object is the point of contact between the database and each independent query or update. (See Figure 11.4.)

Figure 11.4.

The `Connection` *object as the point of contact.*

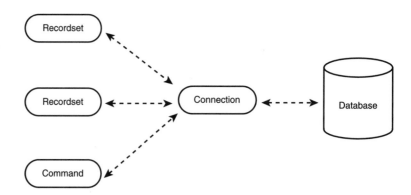

You can perform transactions on multiple changes made to the database from a single `Connection`. Once they're started, all interactions made over the same `Connection` take part in the single transaction.

A transaction acts as a veil of invulnerability that blankets a sequence of changes and keeps them isolated from the chaos of updates hitting the database server from all other sides. During this period, changes made by others can be screened out, so the transacted sequence may believe that it's alone.

A transaction defines a boundary enclosing many database interactions that still appear as a single atomic interaction. For example, once a transaction is begun, an application can make updates to multiple records, add new records, and delete old ones. The effect of these changes is held in isolation from the rest of the database and the rest of the active connections until the transaction is committed. At that time, all the changes are made simultaneously against the actual database, without changes made by other connections mixing with them.

Together, the changes that make up a single transaction take on an all-or-nothing behavior; either they all succeed or they all fail. The database might contain integrity rules that changes being made would breach. An update made to a record could fail, or the application could simply determine that three changes down the road, the database's current state no longer matches what's required for the entire set of changes to make sense.

Transactions can be rolled back. If an event occurs that spoils the intent of the sequence of changes, all the previous changes can be undone to restore the database to its original form. For example, imagine an application that moves money from one account to another. If the accounts were separate records in the same table, or worse yet, in separate tables, two individual updates must be made to deduct money from one account and add it to another. Transactions make certain that the two separate updates appear as one to all outside observers. If transactions didn't exist, then after the first change is made, it's possible that many other queries could accidentally see this change before the second one is made, and calculation errors could result. Other applications could mistakenly assume there was too much or too little money in either account.

Figure 11.5 shows the different stages of a transfer between two accounts. If other users could see the intermediary steps, their calculations would be incorrect.

Figure 11.5.

Accidental inequity.

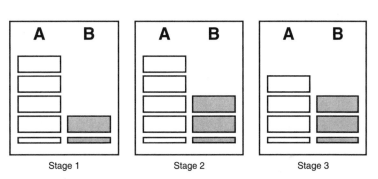

Worse yet, what if the second update actually failed? What if the application requesting the changes accidentally crashed? What if the machine was accidentally turned off? Transactions guarantee that either all changes are made successfully, or none are. A transaction that's stopped short in the middle never actually makes it into the database.

An application determines when a transaction is over. It commits the transaction explicitly, and it knows that if the commit operation succeeds, then all the changes have been accepted by the database.

You can use transactions in your dynamic Web pages as easily as you turn on a light switch. To begin a transaction, tell the `Connection` object to start the transaction by calling the `BeginTrans` method:

```
<% cn.BeginTrans %>
```

After the transaction has begun, go about using the `Connection` object as you normally would. Any open `Recordsets` are automatically brought under the wing of the transaction. Any updates, additions, or deletions are all assumed to be part of the transaction. They seem to operate as they usually do and updates seem to update, but none of the changes become official until the transaction has been committed.

To commit a transaction, call the `CommitTrans` method of the `Connection` object:

```
<% cn.CommitTrans %>
```

If a problem arises and you want to back out of all the changes made since the last call to `BeginTrans`, simply roll them all back by calling the `RollbackTrans` method:

```
<% cn.Rollback %>
```

Everything you did is then automatically undone.

Transacting with Cash

Transferring money is an obvious, straightforward example that takes advantage of transactions. Other good places to use transactions are when stock is bought or sold, when inventory is moved, or when reservations are placed.

Listing 11.3 shows a small dynamic Web page that allows the user to transfer money from one account to another. It generates an input form to ask for details, and then processes the request by issuing SQL UPDATE commands against the database.

Listing 11.3. Moving money (11TWD03.ASP).

```
 1: <HTML>
 2: <TITLE>Example 11.3: Moving Money</TITLE>
 3: <HEAD><H1>Moving Money</H1></HEAD>
 4: <BODY>

 5: <!--#include file="adovbs.inc" -->

 6: <%
 7: '*******************************************************
 8: '* TABLE UTILITIES

 9: Sub GenerateTable( rs )
10:    Response.Write( "<TABLE BORDER=1>" )
11:    ' set up column names
12:    for i = 0 to rs.fields.count - 1
13:      Response.Write("<TD>" + rs(i).Name + "</TD>")
14:    next
15:    ' write each row
16:    while not rs.EOF
17:      Response.Write( "<TR>" )
18:      for i = 0 to rs.fields.count - 1
19:        v = rs(i)
20:        if isnull(v) then v = ""
21:        Response.Write( "<TD VALIGN=TOP>" + CStr( v ) + "</TD>" )
```

```
22:    next
23:    rs.MoveNext
24:   wend
25:   Response.Write( "</TABLE>" )
26: End Sub

27: '********************************************************
28: '* FORM UTILITIES

29: Sub FormBegin( action )
30:   %> <FORM METHOD=POST ACTION="<%= action %>"> <%
31: End sub

32: Sub FormEnd( mode )
33:   %>
34:   <INPUT TYPE=HIDDEN NAME="mode" VALUE="<%=mode%>">
35:   </FORM>
36:   <%
37: End Sub

38: Sub FormInput( name, prompt, size, value )
39:   if isNull(value) then value = ""
40:   %>
41:   <B><%= prompt %></B>
42:   <INPUT TYPE=TEXT SIZE=<%=size%> VALUE="<%=value%>" NAME="<%=name%>" >
43:   <%
44: End Sub

45: Sub FormText( name, prompt, rows, cols, value )
46:   if isNull(value) then value = ""
47:   %>
48:   <B><%= prompt %></B>
49:   <TEXTAREA NAME="<%=name%>" ROWS=<%=rows%> COLS=<%=cols%>
50:   ><%= value %></TEXTAREA>
51:   <%
52: End Sub

53: Sub FormSelect( name, prompt, size, value, items )
54:   %>
55:   <B><%= prompt %></B>
56:   <SELECT NAME=<%=name%>>
57:   <%
58:   for i = 0 to UBound(items,2)
59:     if value = items(0,i) then
60:       Response.Write "<OPTION SELECTED>" + cstr(items(0,i))
61:     else
62:       Response.Write "<OPTION>" + cstr(items(0,i))
63:     end if
64:   next
65:   %>
66:   </SELECT>
67:   <%
68: End Sub

69: Sub FormSubmit( name, value )
70:   %>
```

continues

Listing 11.3. continued

```
71:    <INPUT TYPE=SUBMIT NAME="<%= name %>" VALUE="<%= value %>" >
72:    <%
73: End Sub
74: Function GetItemList( fld, table, cn )
75:    set rs = Server.CreateObject("ADODB.Recordset")
76:    rs.Open "select "+fld+" from "+table, cn
77:    GetItemList = rs.GetRows(-1)
78: End Function

79: '*****************************************************
80: '* SAMPLE DATA UTILITIES

81: sub CreateAccounts()
82:    set cn = CreateObject("ADODB.Connection")
83:    cn.Open "pubs", "sa", ""
84:    on error resume next
85:    ' create accounts table
86:    cn.Execute "drop table accounts"
87:    cmd = "CREATE TABLE Accounts( "
88:    cmd = cmd + "AcctNo int NOT NULL"
89:    cmd = cmd + ", Dollars money NULL"
90:    cmd = cmd + ", CONSTRAINT pk PRIMARY KEY ( AcctNo ) )"
91:    cn.Execute cmd
92: cn.Execute "INSERT INTO Accounts (AcctNo, Dollars) VALUES (1234, 8092)"
93:    cn.Execute "INSERT INTO Accounts (AcctNo, Dollars) VALUES (1367, 1024)"
94:    cn.Execute "INSERT INTO Accounts (AcctNo, Dollars) VALUES (1450, 4096)"
95: end sub
96: %>

97: <%
98: '*****************************************************
99: '* TRANSFER FORM

100: Sub TransferForm( cn )
101:    accounts = GetItemList( "AcctNo", "Accounts", cn )
102:    FormBegin "11tdw03.asp"
103: FormSelect "From", "From", 10, "", accounts
104:    FormSelect "To", "To", 10, "", accounts
105:    FormInput "Amount", "Amount: ", "", 10
106:    %><BR><BR><%
107:    FormSubmit "submit", "Enter"
108:    FormEnd "Transfer"
109: End Sub
110: %>

111: '*****************************************************
112: '* ACCOUNT SUBROUTINES

113: Sub Withdraw( a, d, cn )
114:    cn.Execute "UPDATE Accounts SET Dollars = Dollars - " + _
➡                  d + " WHERE AcctNo = " + a
115: End Sub
```

```
116: Sub Deposit( a, d, cn )
117:    cn.Execute "UPDATE Accounts SET Dollars = Dollars + " + _
                    d + " WHERE AcctNo = " + a
118: End Sub

119: Sub Transfer( a1, a2, d, cn )
120:    cn.BeginTrans
121:    Withdraw a1, d, cn
122:    Deposit a2, d, cn
123:    cn.CommitTrans
124: End Sub
125: %>

126: <%
127: '********************************************************
128: '* THE MAIN CODE

129:    set cn = CreateObject("ADODB.Connection")
130:    set rs = CreateObject("ADODB.Recordset")
131:    cn.Open "pubs", "sa", ""
132:    mode = Request.Form("mode")
133:
134:    if mode = "" then
135:      CreateAccounts
136:
137:    elseif mode = "Transfer" then
138:      vfrom = Request.Form("From")
139:      vto = Request.Form("To")
140:      amount = Request.Form("Amount")
141:      Transfer vfrom, vto, amount, cn
142:    end if
143:    rs.Open "select * from Accounts", cn
144:    %><H3>Current Balances</H3><%
145:    GenerateTable rs
146:    %><H3>Transfer</H3><%
147:    TransferForm cn
148:
149: %>

150: </BODY>
151: </HTML>
```

The Utilities

The first scripting section contains sub-routines defined under two separate topic headings: Tables and Forms. By now, you should be familiar with both of these sets of sub-routines, as they have been used in many previous examples.

Listing 11.3 makes use of both generated HTML table output and dynamic input forms.

The Accounts Table

The sub-routine CreateAccounts() is unique. It actually creates the Accounts table inside the sample database. The code inside it is a good example of how ADO can be used to manipulate database structure. Future versions of ADO may have more built-in methods for defining table structures and stored procedures, but it's still possible to manipulate databases that respond to a full range of the SQL syntax.

A call to the Execute method of the Connection object removes any previous version of the table using the SQL drop table statement:

```
cn.Execute "drop table accounts"
```

An error is generated the first time this statement is executed because the table doesn't exist yet. Normally, the page generation would be terminated, if it weren't for the statement a few lines above it:

```
on error resume next
```

This entire line is a single command in Visual Basic that tells the runtime virtual machine to basically ignore all errors. It says, in case of any error, continue execution on the next line. This is exactly what would happen if no at all error occurred. Discover more about errors and how to use them to your advantage in Chapter 13, "Errors and Provider Properties."

Following the first Execute statement, a few lines are dedicated to building up a query string. They are separated over multiple lines to make them easier to read in this book, but you could easily change them so that the query string appears on just one line.

After the query string is assembled, it's executed with another call to Execute. This query is actually a CREATE TABLE command in SQL. It asks the database to make up a new table called Accounts from the sample database Pubs. The table has two columns: AcctNo, the account number, and Dollars, the current balance. A third column specification is actually a constraint that's been named pk; it defines the table's primary key.

All tables have primary keys; they're used to declare the uniqueness of each record. Normally, no two keys in the same table can ever be alike. The Accounts table uses the AcctNo field as its primary key.

Finally, three separate calls to Execute send SQL INSERT commands to the database. Each one adds a new record to the table. It's possible, and often desirable, to use SQL INSERT commands to add new records to a database, instead of using the Recordset method AddNew. Before AddNew can be used, a Recordset must be opened, meaning a query must be executed that returns records from the database. This is time consuming and wasteful, if all you need to do is add a new record.

The Form

The TransferForm() sub-routine generates an input form that asks the user to specify an account to transfer money from, a second account to transfer money to, and the total amount of money to transfer. In addition, it has an Enter button used to submit the data back to the Active Server Page.

It has three parameters, two of which are familiar: action and mode. Both of these are used as expected, to pass on directly to calls to FormBegin() and FormEnd(). The third parameter, however, is special. It's an ADO Connection object that's going to be reused in the code to follow.

The first thing that happens in the function is a call to the GetItemList() sub-routine introduced in Chapter 9. This sub-routine opens a Recordset, queries for an individual column from a table, and funnels all the records into a two-dimensional array.

The array is reused in the next two lines, with calls to the FormSelect() sub-routine. Each call generates a combo-box selection list that gives the user a convenient means of selecting both the From and To accounts for the transfer.

A simple text input field is generated to ask for the amount of the transfer; following it, the Submit button is added.

Accounting

The next script section has three sub-routines used to manipulate the balances of an individual account.

The Withdraw() sub-routine takes three parameters: a, the account number; d, the amount to withdraw; and cn, an active connection to the database. It contains a single call to the Execute method, using a SQL UPDATE statement that decrements the current dollar amount by the withdrawal amount.

The Deposit() sub-routine does just the opposite. It takes the same three parameters, as the Withdraw() sub-routine did, and it too contains a single call to the Execute method, but the statement it sends to the database is a SQL UPDATE statement that *increments* the account balance.

Finally, the third sub-routine, Transfer(), takes four parameters: two account numbers, the amount to transfer, and an active Connection. It reuses the previous two sub-routines by calling them in succession. First, the transfer amount is withdrawn from the first account, and then it's deposited in the second account. Notice, however, that these statements are not alone. The Transfer() function uses a transaction.

A call to the BeginTrans() method is made before the first sub-routine call, and a call to the CommitTrans() method is made just after the second sub-routine call. In effect, a transaction is started, two successive SQL UPDATEs are processed, and then the transaction is committed. This sequence of events has the effect of making both updates look like a single exchange.

The Main Code

The main code for this example has only two possibilities; it's a modest example of a dynamic form. The first time the page is activated, it generates an input form; on subsequent activations, it processes submitted data and does the appropriate money transfer.

First, the main code creates both a Connection and a Recordset object. It does this beforehand because it knows that all execution paths eventually require each of them.

The Connection object is opened, establishing a link to the Pubs sample database. Then the mode field of the submitted form is examined to determine under which state the page has been activated.

If the activation wasn't caused by submitting data, the code calls the CreateAccounts() sub-routine to regenerate the Accounts table. Most real applications wouldn't destroy and then re-create a database table after each access to its site, but because of this action, the example appears the same each time it's run, no matter how much the accounts are altered in the previous run.

If a form was submitted, the code picks out the appropriate information from the built-in Request object and calls the Transfer() sub-routine to do the work.

In both cases, the resulting HTML page is the same. It's a table showing the current balances of all accounts and an input form asking for transfer information.

A Recordset is opened with a query that selects all the columns from the Accounts table. A call to GenerateTable() generates the HTML instructions that display the table of information on the browser. Next, a call to TransferForm() generates the input form.

Summary

This chapter has explained the ADO Connection object and covered the topics of execution, reuse, sharing, and transacting. It has shown you how to use the Connection object to execute query strings immediately, without involving a Recordset. It has also discussed and explained, by example, how to use a single Connection object with multiple open Recordsets. You have been introduced to the concept of transactions and seen how to use them in your own dynamic Web page. In addition, you have been given a complete description of all the properties and methods of the ADO Connection object.

Q&A

Q **Can I include updates made on separate Connections in the same transaction?**

A No, not without tools outside the ADO object set. The transactions used by the Connection object are explicitly those services supplied by the database provider. Most providers organize transactions' scope based on the individual user connections. Some don't even support transactions.

Still, other types of transactions are possible. Future Microsoft products will give you greater control of distributed transactions.

Q **Is there a way I can store a single Connection object for everyone to use?**

A Yes, but it's not recommended.

You can put objects into a built-in Application object. It's a collection just like the Session object, but contains a single set of objects and values accessible by all users.

Connection objects, if marked as "free threaded," can be used simultaneously by several people. The problem is that even though ADO supports multi-user interactions, not all providers do, especially not all ODBC drivers that may be accessed by using ADO's default provider.

Q **Can I turn connection pooling on and off within my VBScript code?**

A No. Connection pooling must be enabled or disabled at the start-up of the application, before the ODBC Driver Manager's first use. In this case, the application is the Web server itself.

See the section "Starting the Connection Pool" earlier in this chapter to find out how to turn connection pooling on.

Q **Can I reuse the Recordsets that I get back from the Execute method?**

A Yes. If the Recordset was opened when you received it, close it and then call the Open method.

All top-level ADO objects—Recordsets, Connections, and Commands—can be reused.

Q **How can I tell if the Recordset I get back as a returned value from the Execute method is truly open or not?**

A There are two ways to do this. The ADO Help file tells you that to do this, you must try to access a property, like EOF, and check to see whether the access fails. To do this, you need to turn off error trapping in Visual Basic by using the On Error Resume Next statement. This statement causes the execution to continue, even in the face of an error that would normally halt it. You can then check the value of the built-in Err variable. If it's anything other than zero, then an error has occurred on the statement before the check.

Another way to tell whether the Recordset is really open is to retrieve the count of the affected records. The second parameter to the Execute method accepts a variable that's filled in with the number of records affected by the query:

```
<% set rs = cn.Execute querystring, count %>
```

This is normally done to determine how many records were actually updated by a SQL UPDATE statement. ODBC drivers return the value of -1 if the query actually produced records instead of modifying them.

Q What happens if I have a ConnectionString property containing things like DSN=, UID=, and PWD=, and then I open the Connection passing in different values for datasource, user id, and password as parameters?

A The result is unpredictable. The DSN=-like arguments in the connection string get sent to the provider separately from the information supplied in the Open method. The provider either resolves this conflict in some proprietary way or fails.

Q What happens if I make a Web page that keeps Connections alive in the Session object, and the user, after starting my application, never follows through to the point where I clean up my Connections?

A The Session object will, at some point, become out of date and be purged from the system. It might be quite some time after it has been created, but eventually it will go away on its own, and the Connection will be closed.

If you anticipate that the users of your application may have huge breaks between page hits, then you either need to design your application to be stateless and store nothing in the Session object or anticipate that the information kept alive could vanish from time to time.

Q After I commit an inner nested transaction, can I start another one?

A Yes. You can do as many sequential transactions, one after another, as you want, whether they're nested or top-level.

Q How deep can I nest transactions?

A The specific data provider places realistic limits on how deep you can nest transactions. Remember, some providers might not support nested transactions at all, just top-level ones.

You will have to investigate the data providers you intend to use. The default ADO provider communicates by using ODBC, which passes the burden off onto ODBC and the individual driver.

Q Why would someone do Recordset updating if it's just as easy to call Execute and pass separate SQL commands?

A It depends on the type of application you're writing.

You might be supplying a navigable interface to a user because his or her knowledge is what's needed to determine which records get updated, and how and when.

Or you may have an update logic that's so complex you can't efficiently specify updates to individual or grouped records with a SQL statement. You might just have to step through the records one at a time or even bounce back and forth within the set.

In addition, some providers might not be sophisticated enough to understand a full ANSI SQL syntax. You may be talking to a primitive datasource that means you're actually thumbing through physical records as you navigate the `Recordset`. For example, the provider could be talking to a text file or a linear data stream, and the updates you make happen directly to those sources.

ADO gives you the best of both worlds. It allows you to manipulate server-based, SQL-centered databases with broad, sweeping `SELECT`, `INSERT`, `UPDATE`, and `DELETE` commands, and it also gives you a way to talk to less sophisticated sources of data, like a data range in Excel or an array of numbers you have stored in Basic.

The `Recordset` is just another means of manipulating data. It goes beyond simply examining records one by one. It treats the results of queries as separate cached tables that have a minimal flat-file database behavior.

Quiz

1. List the three kinds of information needed to open a connection.
2. A `Connection` object establishes a link to a single datasource. True or False?
3. A `Connection` object can be used by only one `Recordset` at a time. True or False?
4. What is a connection string?
5. Transactions make a series of database interactions look like a single one. True or False?
6. What is the method you can call to stop a transaction and undo all previous changes?
7. After a transaction is committed, all associated `Recordsets` are immediately closed. True or False?
8. Retained transactions automatically restart after they have been committed. True or False?
9. What property can be used to control the "retained" behavior of a transaction?
10. Connection pooling allows `Connections` with three or more `Recordsets` to travel along the "fast lane" of communication bandwidths, bypassing most network bandwidths. True or False?

Exercises

1. Write a dynamic Web page that uses multiple transactions, one after the other, and also takes advantage of retained transactions.

2. Write a dynamic Web page that inserts a new record into a table. The form accepts input from all of a record's applicable fields and, when the data is submitted back to the page, adds a new record to the database with that information. The page should use the Execute method of the Connection object by sending a SQL INSERT statement to add the record.

3. Write a dynamic Web page that updates a single record at a time. The form has two input forms. The first asks for enough information to identify an individual record that already exists in a table. The second form allows the user to edit the record's fields. When the data is submitted from the second form, use the Execute method to send a SQL UPDATE statement to modify the record in the database with the user's changes.

4. Write a dynamic Web page that moves a record from one table to another. The page generates one input form that asks for enough information to identify an individual record that already exists in a table. When the data is submitted, use a call to Execute to retrieve the single record identified by the user's input. Insert a new record into a separate table that has most or all of the original record's information by using a second call to Execute. A final call to Execute should delete the record from the original table. Surround the operation in a transaction.

5. ADVANCED: Write a dynamic Web page that displays a record of data and offers forward and backward buttons for navigating to the next and previous records in a table. Don't keep a Recordset or a Connection live across invocations.

   Hint: This problem has more than one solution.

Day 12

Commands and Stored Procedures

by Matt Warren

The ADO Command object is the best tool to use when issuing queries against a database. Its power goes beyond executing the simple text queries understood by the Connection and Recordset objects. The Command object can be tuned for reuse to save you time and processing power. Common statements can be precompiled and then, by using parameters, altered each time they're executed. In the same way, procedures stored in the database can be called with parameters to modify their behavior.

Stored procedures are fragments of SQL code, sub-routines bound into the database itself that give you another means of manipulating data. Instead of expecting end-users to issue direct SQL statements against the database, you can design stored procedures to hide such complexities, leaving a more concise interface available for application development.

After reading this chapter, you will be able to do the following:

- ☐ List the methods and properties of the ADO Command object.
- ☐ List the methods and properties of the ADO Parameter object.
- ☐ Show how the Command and Recordset objects work together to get better results.
- ☐ Use the Command object to precompile queries so they execute faster.
- ☐ Use the Command object to reuse a query with different arguments.
- ☐ Use the Command object to called stored procedures.

Command **Objects**

Command objects are the common language of the database world. If Recordsets are the means of digesting the database's contents, Commands are the means of paring the information feast down to a respectable plateful. Without a Command, you couldn't even find your place at the table.

Commands are the SQL statements used to issue queries and make broad alterations in the database's contents. They are the SELECT, UPDATE, INSERT, and DELETE phrases combined with their WHERE, SORT, GROUP, and FROM clauses that allow you to pinpoint the groups of records you want to review and potentially make changes to.

Command objects are literally the commands you make to the database server, with a twist. They are the explicit orders you invoke when you want something specific done, but they're also something more. The Command object is an abstraction, a placeholder for a query that wraps around it like a suit of armor. A *query* is a text string that expresses the words or the intent, and a Command object is the vessel in which the query comes alive. It's both the actor and the script.

The Command object is more than just the text of a query; it's the tool with which you manipulate how a query is fully expressed. The Command object has the power to change the query each time it's used, customizing it for particular purposes. For example, SQL statements can be left partially vague, with question marks substituted for values that can change regularly. You might want to issue a series of commands that vary only slightly, such as the value of a column tested in a WHERE clause or the assignment of a field in an UPDATE statement. With a Command object, you can specify the final bits of information on-the-fly. As easily as field values are changed in a Recordset, portions of a query can be altered moments before execution.

Some queries even return values that aren't part of a Recordset. Stored procedures can have both input and output parameters, just as sub-routines in Basic or functions in C++ do. With a Command object, you can pass parameter values into these procedures each time they're called and retrieve values that are sent back. The Command object has a collection called Parameters, the same way that the Recordset object has a collection called Fields. Each parameter has a name and can be interacted with by scripting code.

Creating a Command

You create a Command object in Visual Basic Script the same way you create all other top-level ADO objects—by using the CreateObject method:

```
<% Set cm = Server.CreateObject("ADODB.Command") %>
```

A Command object is created and assigned to the variable cm. You can now use cm in places that take a Command object or query strings, such as the Recordset's Open method.

Connecting the Command

Once a Command is created, it needs to be associated with an active Connection before it can be used to execute queries. The Command object must be plugged into a database or it can't send instructions to do your bidding.

Just as with the Recordset, you can assign only the value of a Connection object that has already been opened to the ActiveConnection property of the Command object. In addition, you can save yourself the work of creating the Connection object by assigning a connection string to the ActiveConnection property.

You could use statements like these two examples:

```
<% Set cm.ActiveConnection = cn %>
```

```
<% Set cm.ActiveConnection = "DSN=Pubs;UID=sa;PWD=;" %>
```

However, by using the latter, you lose control over the type of connection that's made.

Specifying the Query

Specifying the query is as simple as assigning a string to a property. The CommandText property, in fact, is what you need to set before you can execute the command, as shown here:

```
<% set cm.CommandText = "Select * from employee" %>
```

The string can contain any query accepted by the data provider and can be any one of three types of statements: a normal query string, the name of a database table, or a stored procedure. You can help the data provider discover the exact type of statement by filling out the CommandType parameter.

12

For example, if you want to select all columns and all rows of a known database table, there's no need to spell out a lengthy SQL SELECT statement. Supplying the name of the table is enough, as shown in this example:

```
<%
  set cm.CommandText = "employee"
  set cm.CommandType = adCmdTable
%>
```

In the same way, if you want to call a procedure defined in the database, all you need to specify is the name of the procedure, and then set the CommandType property to adCmdStoredProc:

```
<%
  set cm.CommandText = "NewHires"
  set cm.CommandType = adCmdStoredProc
%>
```

If your query requires you to fill in parameters, you can call them out by name, as follows:

```
<%
  cm("@rate") = .10
  cm("@period") = 24
  cm("@balance") = 20000
%>
```

Or, you can call them out by number:

```
<%
  cm(0) = .10
  cm(1) = 24
  cm(2) = 20000
%>
```

Executing a Command

There are two ways to execute a Command, and you have already seen both of them in action. The first is the Execute method. It's the same name and practically the same method that was defined for the Connection object. It differs in only a single parameter. The Execute method of the Connection object took an optional query string as the first parameter. The Command object's Execute method forgoes the query string parameter. You have to assign the query string separately as the CommandText property. What the Command object's Execute method has that the Connection object doesn't is an optional parameters parameter.

The second parameter of the Execute method accepts an array of values that are substituted for the current parameter values held in the Parameters collection before the Command is executed. If you find it convenient to keep a series of values at the ready, in a predimensioned array, you can save yourself many keystrokes and a lot of execution time by passing the array directly into the call to Execute.

But before you get too deep in the more advanced features, keep in mind that in its simplest form, the Execute method can be used without any parameters at all, as it is here:

```
<% Set rs = cm.Execute %>
```

Just as with the Connection object, the Execute method returns a Recordset object. Queries that implicitly produce records of data return those records in the form of a Recordset. Those that don't most likely operate on one or more records in some other fashion. For this purpose, the first parameter of the Command object's Execute method is an output parameter that returns the total number of records affected by the execution:

```
<%
Set cm.CommandText = "UPDATE employee SET Salary = Salary*1.10 WHERE rating >=
4.0
Set rs = cm.Execute count
%> I raised the salary of <%= count %> employees
%>
```

The second parameter is the parameters parameter. It can be used to pass an optional array of values, overriding the current values held by the Parameters collection, as shown in this example:

```
<%
Dim p(2)
p(0) = .10
p(1) = 24
p(2) = 20000
set cm.CommandText = "amort"
set cm.CommandType = adCmdStoredProc
set rs = cm.Execute count, p
%>
```

This method is actually faster than assigning each Parameter object individually. The assignment work is done inside the Command object. Instead of having to call into ADO many times, you need to do it only once.

Remember, the statement

```
<% cm(0) = .10 %>
```

is equivalent to this statement:

```
<% cm.Parameters(0).Value = .10 %>
```

The former appears to be as simple as the assignment to the array element, but it isn't.

The last parameter is a last-chance option. Use it to specify the CommandType if you intended to but simply never got around to doing it earlier:

```
<% cm.Execute count, ,adCmdStoredProc %>
```

NOTE You don't have to specify optional parameters in an ADO method call. You can skip over optional parameters by specifying nothing at all in place of where the parameters would normally be.

The second method of execution is to not call the `Execute` method at all. You can use the `Recordset`'s `Open` method to do the same thing if you already have a `Recordset` you can use, or one that has been closed and is ready for reuse, as shown here:

```
<% rs.Open cm, cn %>
```

You can pass both the initialized `Command` object and the active `Connection` object to the `Open` method as parameters. Use this method, as shown in the following example, to execute queries when you expect to get records back:

```
<% rs.Open cm, cn, adOpenKeyset, adLockOptimistic %>
```

If you do this, make certain that the `Command` object has not yet been associated with an active `Connection` object. If it has, then you should specify the call to `Open`, like this:

```
<% rs.Open cm, , adOpenKeyset, adLockOptimistic %>
```

The `Recordset` you end up using is one that you set up. You determine the cursor type, and you decide if you want to do updating.

Properties of the Command **Object**

Unlike the `Connection` and `Recordset` objects, all properties of the `Command` object can be both read from and written to at any time. `Commands` are never opened or closed.

The following table lists the properties available for the `Command` object. After the table, each property is discussed in detail.

Property	Description
ActiveConnection	The associated Connection object
CommandText	The query string
CommandTimeout	The amount of time before the execution is aborted
CommandType	A hint at the type of query string
Prepared	Indication whether the command should be precompiled

12

ActiveConnection

Contains a `Connection` or `String` value

The `ActiveConnection` property can be used to assign or discover the actual `Connection` object being used by the `Command` to communicate to the database server.

The property can be assigned either an open `Connection` object or a string containing connection information.

CommandText

Contains a `String` value

You can use the `CommandText` property to assign the text of the query you want to execute. The text could include a query statement in the syntax that's understood by the provider, the explicit name of a table, or a stored procedure, if it's supported by the provider.

CommandTimeout

Contains an `Integer` value

You can use the `CommandTimeout` property to set a limit on the number of seconds an execution is allowed to take. If the execution takes longer than the time-out period, the query is aborted and the call to the `Execute` method fails.

In cases of slow network response or backlogged servers, `Commands` might take longer than you'd like to execute. The `Execute` method can be preset to fail in either of these cases, instead of waiting indefinitely for a query to succeed.

The default value of the `CommandTimeout` property is 30 seconds. Changing this to a value of 0 allows the `Command` object to wait indefinitely for the `Execute` method to finish. The default value of the `CommandTimeout` property can be overriden by the `CommandTimeout` property held by the associated active `Connection` object.

CommandType

Contains one of the following values:

Type Constants	Value
adCmdText	1
adCmdTable	2
adCmdStoredProc	4
adCmdUnknown	8

12

You can use the CommandType property to give the Command object a hint about the type of query assigned to the CommandText property. Setting this property isn't required for proper execution of the Command object, but it does speed it up. If the CommandType is adCmdUnknown, the default, ADO asks the provider to determine the appropriate type; otherwise, the CommandType property must match the type of query specified in the CommandText property.

Prepared

Contains a Boolean value

You can use the Prepared property to request that the query be compiled the first time it's executed. On subsequent executions of the same query, the provider is saved the trouble of compilation, and the Command executes faster. If the provider doesn't support compiling queries, this property is reset to false; however, the Command is still executed.

Methods of the Command Object

Both of the Command object methods are listed in the following table and discussed in the following sections.

Method	Description
CreateParameter	Creates a new Parameter object
Execute	Executes the current CommandText query

CreateParameter

Set p = Command.CreateParameter(n, t, d, s, v)

- n The name of the parameter.
- t The type of the parameter. This argument is optional and is equivalent to the Parameter object's Type property.
- d The direction of the parameter. This argument is optional and is equivalent to the Parameter object's Direction property.
- s The maximum size of the parameter. This argument is optional and is equivalent to the Parameter object's Size property.
- v The value of the parameter. This argument is optional.

You can use the CreateParameter method to create a new Parameter object. The Parameter object must be appended to the Parameters collection of a Command object before it can be used. At the time that the Parameter is appended, the Type and Size properties are validated.

Execute

```
Set rs = Command.Execute( count, parameters, options )
```

count	A variable that's assigned the number of records affected by the query's execution. This argument is optional.
parameters	A variable containing an array of parameter values. This argument is optional.
options	A CommandType constant. This argument is optional and defaults to the value supplied to the CommandType property.

You can use the Execute method to execute the query specified by the CommandText property. The Command object must have an active Connection object for it to operate successfully.

If the query is a SQL SELECT statement or its equivalent, the name of a table, or a stored procedure that returns records, an open Recordset is returned by the call to Execute. Otherwise, a closed Recordset is returned and can simply be ignored.

NOTE

> Recordsets created from a call to Execute have a forward-only cursor and are read-only. To get another type of cursor or write access, create a Recordset on your own and use its Open method instead.

Use the Execute method as a means of executing complex, non–record-producing queries, such as SQL UPDATE, INSERT, or DELETE commands. Any command that's recognized by the database provider—such as table definition statements or granting and revoking user permissions—can be sent in this manner.

Queries executed through a Command object work just the same as those executed through the Connection object's Execute method, except that the queries used by a Command object can be precompiled and re-executed with different sets of parameters.

For executing record-producing queries, it's better to create your own Recordset object and use its Open method, passing in the Command object as the first parameter. This technique lets you specify the exact style of Recordset you end up with.

Recordsets created by the Execute method are directly associated with the Command object and its active Connection, as are Recordsets opened with a Command object as a Source parameter.

12

Command **Parameters**

The Command object contains an entire collection of Parameter objects because each query can take one or more parameters. This collection is known by the name Parameters and is accessible from the Command object as though it were a property, in the same way that the Fields collection is accessible from the Recordset object.

Parameters **Collection Properties**

The Parameters collection has only one property.

Count

Contains an Integer value

You can use the Count property to determine the total number of parameters in the Parameters collection.

Parameters **Collection Methods**

Unlike other collection objects, like the Recordset's Fields collection, the Parameters collection can be altered by the programmer. Because of this, the Parameters collection has a few more methods than are normally found in other collections.

The Parameters collection's methods are listed in the following table and discussed in the following sections.

Property	Description
Append	Add a Parameter object to the collection
Delete	Remove a Parameter object from the collection
Item	Retrieve a particular Parameter object
Refresh	Reconstruct the collection

Append

Parameters.Append *parameter*

parameter   A newly created Parameter object to be appended to the Parameters collection.

You can use the Append method to add a new Parameter object at the end of the Parameters collection when defining a Command yourself.

If you know the makeup of a stored procedure or a parameter-based query, you can save yourself a lot of time by building up the `Parameters` collection by hand. This method saves you from having to call the `Refresh` method and performing an additional communication with the remote server.

Delete

Parameters.Delete index

    index   The name or ordinal index of the `Parameter` you want to remove from the `Parameters` collection.

You can use the `Delete` method of the `Parameters` collection to remove a `Parameter` object from the collection. After a `Parameter` has been removed, it can be used again as a `Parameter` for another `Command` object.

Item

`Set` *parameter* `= Parameters.Item(` *index* `)`

    index   The name or ordinal position of the requested `Parameter`.

The `Item` method is the default method called when you use the parentheses as an indexing operator on the `Command` or the `Parameters` collection. This method is normally hidden from view within program editors that understand the type-library format of OLE Automation objects.

The statement

`Set p = cm( 0 )`

is equivalent to

`Set p = cm.Parameters( 0 )`

and is also equivalent to

`Set p = cm.Parameters.Item( 0 )`

Refresh

Parameters.Refresh

You can use the `Refresh` method to force the `Parameters` collection to read the schema information from the data provider. After a call to the `Refresh` method, a `Command` object with a live link to the data source and a valid `CommandText` property will have a populated `Parameters` collection that matches the query statement specified by the `CommandText` property.

12

Parameter **Properties**

Since each `Parameter` object is somewhat similar to a `Field` object, they share many of the same properties. The following table lists the properties available for each `Parameter` object. Each property is discussed separately in the following sections.

Property	Description
Attributes	Combination of attribute flags
Direction	`Parameter` is used for input, output, or both
Name	The name of the `Parameter`
NumericScale	Decimal places after the "dot"
Precision	Total number of decimal places
Size	Size of variable data in bytes
Type	Type of data being sent
Value	Current value of the `Parameter`

 NOTE

As in Chapter 9, "Dynamic Pages and the ADO `Recordset`," the following descriptions have a phrase on the right-hand side of the page, just after the section title. The words to the left of the separating slash (/) pertain to the `Parameter` before it's added to the `Parameters` collection, and those to the right apply after it has been added.

Attributes

Contains one of the following values: Read-Only / Read-Only

Attributes *Constants*	Value
adParamLong	128
adParamNullable	64
adParamSigned	16

You can use the `Attributes` property to determine special information about the `Parameter` and its value before you try to access it. Each `Parameter` can be described by one or more of these attribute flags:

adParamLong	The value of a type that can be considerably large, such as `Long Binary`.

12

adParamNullable	The Parameter may be assigned the value of NULL in the normal values representative of the Parameters (
adParamSigned	The Parameter may contain signed values.

Direction

Contains one of the following values: Read-Write / Read-Write

Direction *Constant*	*Value*
adParamInput	1
adParamOutput	2
adParamInputOutput	3
adParamReturnValue	4

You can use the Direction property to assign the flow direction of each individual property.
Most parameters are used to pass information into a query or to a stored procedure; however,
sometimes parameters are used to get information back.

adParamInput	The Parameter passes information to the database server.
adParamOutput	The Parameter is used to get values back from the data server after the Command is executed.
adParamInputOutput	The Parameter is used to pass information to and receive information from the database server.
adParamReturnValue	The Parameter is the explicit returned value from a stored procedure.

Name

Contains a String value   Read-Write / Read-Only

You can use the Name property to determine or assign a name to the parameter for your own
convenience. This same name can be used as a key when retrieving the Parameter object from
the Parameters collection. Once appended to the Parameters collection, the name of a
Parameter becomes read-only.

If the Command object is being used to access a stored procedure, the Name property reflects, by
default, the name specified by the procedure stored in the database server, after a call to the
Refresh method of the Parameters collection.

12

NumericScale

Contains a `Byte` value　　　　　　　　　　　　　Read-Write / Read-Write

You can use the `NumericScale` property to both get and set the number of digits used in representing the fractional portion of the numeric data value. The scale can never have a value greater than the precision.

Precision

Contains a `Byte` value　　　　　　　　　　　　　Read-Write / Read-Write

You can use the `Precision` property to both get and set the maximum number of digits used to represent the numeric data value. The maximum includes those digits used to represent the scale or the fractional portion of the data value.

Size

Contains an `Integer` value　　　　　　　　　　　　Read-Write / Read-Write

You can use the `Size` property to determine the exact size of a fixed-size parameter or the maximum size of a variable-length parameter (which *must* have a maximum size specified). For `Parameters` typed as variable length, this property must be set before the `Parameter` is appended to the `Parameters` collection. If the parameter was appended earlier and has since changed to a variable-length data type, you must still set the `Size` property before the `Command` is executed.

Type

Contains one of the following values:　　　　　　　Read-Write / Read-Write

Type *Constant*	*Value*	*Description*
adBigInt	20	8-byte signed integer
adBinary	128	Binary encoded bytes
adBoolean	11	Boolean `True` or `False`
adBSTR	8	Unicode character string
adChar	129	ASCII character string
adCurrency	6	Numeric currency
adDate	7	System style date
adDBDate	133	Date encoded as `YYYYMMDD`
adDBTime	134	Time encoded as `HHMMSS`

Type *Constant*	*Value*	*Description*
adDBTimeStamp	135	Time stamp
adDecimal	14	Numeric value with fixed pr
adDouble	5	Double-precision floating poi
adError	10	System error code
adGUID	72	Globally unique identifier
adIDispatch	9	COM/OLE Automation object
adInteger	3	4-byte signed integer
adIUnknown	13	COM/OLE object
adLongVarBinary	205	Large variable-length binary value
adLongVarChar	201	Large variable-length character string
adLongVarWChar	203	Large variable-length Unicode string
adNumeric	131	Numeric value with fixed precision
adSingle	4	Single-precision floating point
adSmallInt	2	2-byte signed integer
adTinyInt	16	1-byte signed integer
adUnsignedBigInt	21	8-byte unsigned integer
adUnsignedInt	19	4-byte unsigned integer
adUnsignedSmallInt	18	2-byte unsigned integer
adUnsignedTinyInt	17	1-byte unsigned integer
adUserDefined	132	User-defined data type
adVariant	12	An OLE Automation Variant type
adVarBinary	204	Variable-length binary value
adVarChar	200	Variable-length character value
adVarWChar	202	Variable-length Unicode string
adWChar	130	Unicode character string

You can use the Type property to determine the exact data type used when input parameters are sent to the database server and output parameters are sent back.

For parameters to stored procedures, this type must match the type defined for the parameter inside the database. For parameters to queries, this type must match the type of the associated column.

12

Value

Contains a `Variant` value   Read-Write / Read-Write

You can use the `Value` property to both get and set the data value for the corresponding `Parameter` of the `Command` object. Assigning a data value to the `Value` property allows that value to be sent to the database server when the `Command` is executed.

Parameter **Methods**

The two methods of the `Parameter` object operate much like their counterparts on the `Field` object. The following table lists the methods, and they are discussed in the following sections.

Method	Description
AppendChunk	Add data to the `Parameter` value
GetChunk	Get a portion of the `Parameter` value

AppendChunk

`Parameter.AppendChunk bytes`

bytes   A `Variant` containing the data to append to the end of the current value.

You can use the `AppendChunk` method to add data bytes onto the end of the current value. The first time you call `AppendChunk` on a `Parameter` object, the data value is assigned the bytes passed as a parameter to the method. Repeated calls to `AppendChunk` append the bytes passed onto the end of the current value.

You may use `AppendChunk` with only one `Parameter` at a time. If you use `AppendChunk` with another `Parameter` and then try to use it again with the original `Parameter`, the append semantics start over as though it were the first time you called `AppendChunk` on the original `Parameter`. The field's previous value is overwritten with the new information.

GetChunk

`Set variable = Parameter.GetChunk( count )`

variable   A variable that's assigned a portion of the field's data value.

count   Contains a `Long` value. A parameter specifying the exact number of bytes to be gotten as a chunk of the parameter's data value.

You can use the `GetChunk` method to retrieve sequential portions of the `Parameter`'s data value. The first call to `GetChunk` retrieves the first `count` bytes of the data value, the second call retrieves the next `count` bytes, and so on.

You may use `GetChunk` with only one parameter at a time. If you use `GetChunk` with another parameter and then try to use it again with the original parameter, the retrieval semantics start over again as though it were the first time you called `GetChunk` on the original parameter. The first `count` bytes are retrieved instead.

If you ask for more bytes than what remain in the data value, the bytes returned are fewer than you requested.

Commands with Parameters

The biggest benefit of using a `Command` object instead of specifying query strings is that you can manipulate the query, adjusting its minor nuances without resorting to massive string concatenations. Not all data types have values that can even be expressed in simple textual form. Some values like `Binary`, especially `Long Binary`, need to be fed to the database precisely. There's no telling what an incorrect bit could mean to the application that uses the data.

The `Command` object has another object that's one of its direct members. In the same way that the `Recordset` object has its `Fields` collection, the `Command` object has a `Parameters` collection, an ordered group of `Parameter` objects. Each `Parameter` object contains a name, a value, a data type, and other schematic information that describes how the `Parameter` behaves.

The `Parameter` object can be easily understood as the counterpart to the `Recordset`'s `Field` object. Both manipulate a single data element at a time and represent an item from the query string. The `Field` object manipulates values returned from queries as parts of records. The `Parameter` object manipulates values sent to the database server by means of the query and sometimes even individual values that are sent back. If you can't retrieve the data with a `Field` object, you can usually get it with a `Parameter`.

Accessing the Parameters

You can access each `Parameter` by using either its name or ordinal position in the collection. The ordinal position matches the order that the parameter appears in the query string.

For example, this statement

```
<% cm("name") = "Humphry" %>
```

can be equivalent to

```
<% cm(2) = "Humphry" %>
```

You use question mark placeholders in a query string to specify where parameters replace values:

```
<% cm.CommandText = "SELECT * FROM Hats WHERE style = ? AND color = ?" %>
```

12

Parameters represented by question marks have default names of Param1, Param2, and so forth, unless you override them:

```
<%
cm("Param1") = "Frumpy"
cm("Param2") = "Black"
%>
```

Refreshing the Parameters

Parameters don't appear in the Parameters collection by magic. In fact, they don't exist at all immediately after the query string is assigned to the CommandText property.

The query string must first be examined before you can determine the number of parameters and their individual data types. To force ADO and the back-end data provider to examine the query string before execution, call the Refresh method of the Parameters collection:

```
<% cm.Parameters.Refresh %>
```

Calling the Refresh method automatically sends the query string to the data provider, which reports back the appropriate parameter information.

Once Refresh has been called, the Parameters collection comes alive, populated with enough parameters to match the number of question mark placeholders specified in the query string.

ADO automatically names these parameters for you with the names Param1, Param2, and so forth:

```
<%
cm.Parameters.Refresh
cm("Param1") = 100
cm("Param2") = "Heidi"
cm.Execute
rv = cm(0)
%>
```

If the query is actually a stored procedure, the first Parameter, index zero, contains a parameter named RETURN-VALUE. After execution, this parameter contains any explicitly returned value from the stored procedure.

If you reuse the Command object by changing the CommandText property, make sure you call the Refresh method again; otherwise, the parameters might not match.

Declaring the Parameters

You can save yourself considerable time by declaring the Parameter objects manually instead of calling the Refresh method. The Refresh method works by sending a message to the database server and receiving a separate message back. This extra network round trip can be a significant portion of the total time it takes to initialize a Command object and execute a query.

The Parameters collection is different from the Fields collection because you can add your own Parameter objects to it, and a Parameter object is different from a Field object because you can create one by hand. Field objects are created automatically when the Recordset is opened or the Command is executed, but Parameter objects can be created individually.

Top-level ADO objects use the CreateObject() method or any other standard means of creating new object instances. Parameter objects are different, however. They're not top-level ADO objects and they can't be freely created. The Command object itself controls how Parameter objects are built, so the CreateParameter() method of the Command object must be called to generate a new Parameter.

The CreateParameter() methods takes five parameters of its own: the name of the Parameter, the data type, whether it's input or output (the *direction*), the maximum size, and the current value. All but the first parameter are optional. For a detailed description of this method, see the CreateParameter method described in the section "Methods of the Command Object," earlier in this chapter.

You most likely need to pass in the first three parameters—the name, type, and direction—to get a Parameter object that can be used:

```
<% set param = cm.CreateParameter( "x", adInteger, adParamInput ) %>
```

Input parameters, called adParamInput, are sent to the database server when the Command is executed. Output parameters, called adParamOutput, are sent back when the execution is finished. Other directions that parameters can take are adParamInputOutput, when the same parameter is used to send and receive information, and adParamReturnValue, when the parameter is a stand-in for the explicitly returned value from a stored procedure.

Parameters that aren't fully specified can't be used when a Command is executed. The data type of the Parameter must match the data type of the associated column in the query or the type of the stored procedure argument, depending on the type of command being sent. The maximum size must be specified if the data type is a variable-length type, and the direction must match the query. If a SQL SELECT, UPDATE, INSERT, or DELETE statement is augmented by parameters, the Parameter's direction must be adParamInput. If the query is actually a stored procedure call, the direction must match the direction defined by the procedure.

Parameters are added to the Parameters collection one at a time. The Append method of the Parameters collection accepts a Parameter object as input and adds the object to the end of the set, as shown in the following example. Only Parameter objects that aren't currently appended to a collection can be used in the Append method.

12

```
<%
set p = cm.CreateParameter("x", adInteger, adParamInput)
cm.Parameters.Append p
%>
```

If you're clever, you can combine the two statements into one that creates the `Parameter` object and appends it to the `Parameters` collection all at one time:

```
<% cm.Parameters.Append cm.CreateParameter("x", adInteger, adParamInput) %>
```

Replacing Values

Use the `Parameters` collection to update the values used in a query. Instead of laboring over a series of concatenations each time you want to change the values used to constrain a query, change each `Parameter` value individually with a simple function call.

Without `Parameters`, you would have to reconstruct your query each time you wanted to execute it, as shown here:

```
<%
set cmd = "SELECT * FROM employee WHERE"
set cmd = cmd + "lname = " + lname
set cmd = cmd + "AND fname = " + fname
set cm.CommandText = cmd
%>
```

With `Parameters`, however, you can simply state the query once and modify the parameters later, as shown in this example:

```
<%
set cm.CommandText = "SELECT * FROM employee WHERE lname = ? and fname = ?"
cm.parameters.refresh
cm(0) = lname
cm(1) = fname
cm.Execute
cm(0) = lname2
cm.Execute
%>
```

Using Dynamic Commands

The easiest feature to take advantage of is the ability to turn conventional queries into `Parameter`-based queries. `Parameter`-based queries have question mark placeholders where values would normally be. Instead of using a lot of confusing string concatenation to finalize a query before execution, you can make use of the `Command` object's ability to send parameters to the back-end database server along with the query text.

The following example, Listing 12.1, shows a dynamic Web page that uses a `Command` object to specify a `Parameter`-based query. The query is made `Parameter`-based by substituting a question mark for a constraint value. In this way, large values, or even values that couldn't normally have been inserted into the query text, can be used just as easily as others.

Listing 12.1. Command Parameters (12TWD01.ASP).

```
 1: <HTML>
 2: <TITLE>Example 12.1: Command Parameters</TITLE>
 3: <HEAD><H1>Command Parameters</H1></HEAD>
 4: <BODY>

 5: <%
 6: '*****************************************
 7: '* NameForm

 8: Sub NameForm( action, mode )
 9: %>
10: <FORM ACTION="<%= action %>" METHOD=POST>
11: Last Name:
12: <INPUT NAME="lname" WIDTH=40>
13: <INPUT TYPE=SUBMIT VALUE="Find">
14: <INPUT TYPE=HIDDEN NAME="mode" VALUE="<%= mode %>">
15: </FORM>
16: <%
17: End Sub
18: %>

19: <%
20: '*****************************************
21: '* DisplayEmployee

22: Sub DisplayEmployee( rs )
23: %>
24: <code>
25: <br><pr>First Name: </pr><b><%= rs("fname") %></b>
26: <br><pr>Last Name:  </pr><b><%= rs("lname") %></b>
27: </code>
28: <%
29: End Sub
30: %>

31: <%
32: '*****************************************
33: '* THE MAIN CODE

34: mode = Request.Form("mode")
35: if mode = "" then
36:    %>
37:    Enter the last name of the employee
38:    <BR><BR>
39:    <%
40:    NameForm "12twd01.asp", "find"
41: elseif mode = "find" then
42:    Set cn = Server.CreateObject("ADODB.Connection")
43:    Set cm = Server.CreateObject("ADODB.Command")
```

continues

Listing 12.1. continued

```
44:    cn.Open "pubs", "sa", ""
45:    cm.ActiveConnection = cn
46:    cm.CommandText = "select * from employee where lname = ?"
47:    cm.Properties.Refresh
48:    cm("Param1") = Request.Form("lname")
49:    Set rs = cm.Execute
50:    if rs.EOF Then
51:      %><BR>There were no matches<%
52:    else
53:
54:      %>I found the following matches<BR><%
55:      while not rs.EOF
56:        DisplayEmployee rs
57:        %><br><%
58:        rs.MoveNext
59:      wend
60:    end if
61: end if
62: %>

63: </BODY>
64: </HTML>
```

Dissecting the Page

The first point of interest is the first section of scripting code. It contains the sub-routine `NameForm()` that generates a simple input form requesting the last name of an employee. It uses the familiar trappings of a Submit button and a hidden "mode" field. The main code makes use of the mode field later on.

The sub-routine takes two parameters, `action` and `mode`, that are subsequently inserted as values in the `<FORM>` tag and the hidden mode field.

Following `NameForm()` is another small sub-routine. This one, `DisplayEmployee()`, takes a `Recordset` as an input parameter and generates HTML that displays the current record's first and last name. The `<code>` and `<pr>` tags have been used together to line up the output, making it more readable.

The main code is really where all the action occurs. It consists of an `IF-THEN-ELSEIF` Visual Basic statement that breaks the code down into separate chunks, which are executed based on the value of the mode field handed back from the form submission.

If the form wasn't submitted, the mode field has a value equivalent to an empty string. In this case, a prompt is inserted into the HTML and an input form is generated by a call to the sub-routine `NameForm()`.

The action really begins when the form is submitted. Both a `Connection` and a `Command` object are created through calls to `Server.CreateObject()`. The `Connection` is opened to the Pubs sample database, and the `Command` object is linked to the `Connection` object through `Command`'s `ActiveConnection` property.

The next line states the query:

```
cm.CommandText = "select * from employee where lname = ?"
```

The query contains a question mark to the right of the equals operator in the SQL `SELECT` statement's `WHERE` clause. Normally, a value of some sort, a `string` in this case, would have been placed there; instead, the question mark acts as a placeholder. Later, a `Parameter` from the `Command` object is used to replace the question mark.

Following that line is a call to the `Refresh` method of the `Properties` collection:

```
cm.Properties.Refresh
```

This call requests information from the data provider about the query. The `Command` object sends a message to the provider, which then communicates with the database server. The query is analyzed, the appropriate parameters are determined, and the schematic information is returned back to the provider and, ultimately, the `Command` object.

With the schema in hand, the `Parameters` collection is filled out. The next statement in the script code assigns a value to the parameter named `Param1`:

```
cm("Param1") = Request.Form("lname")
```

The value just so happens to come from the submitted information of the input form.

NOTE

> `Parameters` that are automatically generated in response to a call to `Refresh` are named based on their equivalent stored-procedure name or from the sequence `Param1`, `Param2`, and so forth, if the server doesn't know specific names.

Finally, the `Command` object is executed with a call to the `Execute` method:

```
Set rs = cm.Execute
```

The `Recordset` containing all the matches is assigned to the local variable `rs`.

The rest of the dynamic Web page tries to generate a display of the matching information. If the `EOF` property of the `Recordset` is `false`, the `Recordset` has no records; therefore, instead of information, the message `There were no matches` is reported. Otherwise, a `WHILE` loop is used to step through each record, one at a time. A call to the sub-routine `DisplayEmployee()` takes the current record and generates output showing the first and last names.

12

Viewing the Example

Figure 12.1 shows the page as it's first seen. No forms have been processed yet, and no commands have been issued.

Figure 12.1.

Entering the
`Parameter.`

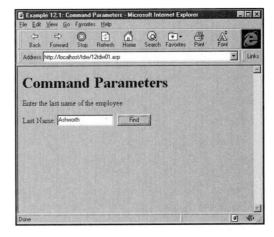

Entering the last name `Ashworth` produces one record in response. Figure 12.2 shows the page as it looks after a valid record has been found by the search parameter.

Figure 12.2.

A record found.

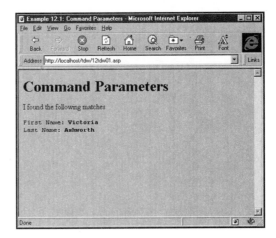

Of course, there's always the possibility that invalid information could be entered. The last name Yoyo produces a different effect. The same command is used, but the match condition is different. Since no records are found that match, the message `There were no matches` is displayed. (See Figure 12.3.)

Figure 12.3.
No matches found.

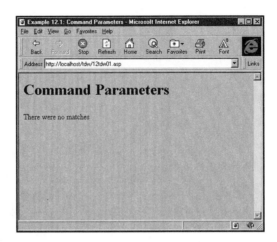

Using Prepared Commands

You can save yourself a lot of execution time by using prepared Commands. Commands that are executed often, especially those that might be executed more than once in the processing code of the same dynamic Web page, can benefit from precompilation.

Before queries are actually executed by the data provider on the database server, they are examined, optimized, and compiled into a pseudo-code that's later used to drive the data-retrieval system. You can take advantage of this knowledge by holding onto the compiled portion of the execution process and reusing it the next time you need to execute the same command.

Command objects can be *prepared*, meaning they instruct the data provider to give back a token representing the compiled pseudo-code that it uses internally. The Command object then remembers this token for you. The next time you use the same Command object, and as long as the CommandText hasn't changed, the same token is fed back to the data provider, allowing the execution code to skip ahead to the data-retrieval section. The query has already been parsed, and the optimal scheme for data retrieval has already been determined and programmed into the pseudo-code.

To prepare a Command object, simply set the Prepared property to true. The Command object does the rest of the work. If the data provider can support precompilation, the query is compiled the first time the Execute method is called. Subsequent calls to Execute on the same Command object take advantage of the precompilation and actually return results faster.

12

The following example updates the counter field of the Ticker table for a unique ticker four separate times:

```
<%
Set cm.CommandText = "UPDATE ticker SET counter = counter + 1 WHERE tickid =
100"
cm.CommandType = adCmdText
cm.Prepared = true
cm.Execute
cm.Execute
cm.Execute
cm.Execute
%>
```

A prepared Command object allows the server to identify the quickest means of finding the correct record and updating it. Even the knowledge that the query is precompiled might indicate to the server that the query will be re-executed soon, so the best access strategy could be to cache the record.

A more realistic example actually combines using prepared Commands with Parameters. It isn't often that you re-execute the exact same query with the exact same text. It's more likely that a Command you execute often is one that changes slightly between each execution. Commands with Parameters make doing this possible:

```
<%
Set cm.CommandText = "UPDATE ticket SET counter = counter + ? WHERE tickid = ?"
cm.CommandType = adCmdText
cm.Prepared = true
cm.parameters.append cm.CreateParameter( "val", adInteger, adParamInput )
cm.parameters.append cm.CreateParameter( "id", adInteger, adParamInput )
cm("val") = 1
cm("id") = 200
cm.Execute
cm("val") = 5
cm("id") = 300
cm.Execute
cm("val") = 10
cm("id") = 400
cm.Execute
cm("val") = 25
cm("id") = 500
cm.Execute
%>
```

The combination of Parameter-based Commands with prepared Commands is unbeatable. You get the benefit of not having to reconstruct your command each time it's used, which means the Command can be pre-compiled. You save both the concatenation work and the recompiling that would be required if you didn't use Parameters at all.

Dynamic Preparation

The following example, Listing 12.2, makes use of both Parameter-based Commands and precompilation. The dynamic Web page is an interface to an application that grants bonuses to employees. It makes use of a novel interface, allowing a supervisor or manager to pick and choose exactly which employees get bonuses. The publishers of this book don't necessarily condone this method of distributing employee compensation; it's just used as part of this example because it makes use of a table from the sample Pubs database and highlights the use of prepared Commands that are called repeatedly.

Listing 12.2. Prepared Commands (12TWD02.ASP).

```
 1: <HTML>
 2: <TITLE>Example 12.2: Prepared Commands</TITLE>
 3: <HEAD></HEAD>
 4: <BODY>

 5: <%
 6: '****************************************************************
 7: '* CheckListForm

 8: Sub CheckListForm( action, mode, submit, array, columns, fields )
 9: %><FORM ACTION="<%= action %>" METHOD=POST><%
10: %><TABLE BORDER=1><%
11: records = UBound( array, 2 )
12: rows = Int( (records + columns - 1) / columns )
13: for col = 0 to columns - 1
14:   %><TD><TABLE BORDER=0><%
15:   for row = 0 to rows - 1
16:     %><TR><%
17:     rec = col * rows + row
18:     if rec < records then
19:       for fld = 0 to fields - 1
20:         %><TD><%= array(fld,rec) %></TD><%
21:       next
22:       name = "cb"+cstr(rec)
23:       %><TD><INPUT TYPE=CHECKBOX NAME="<%= name %>"></TD><%
24:     end if
25:     %></TR><%
26:   next
27:   %></TABLE></TD><%
28: next
29: %>
30: </TABLE>
31: <HR>
32: <INPUT TYPE=SUBMIT VALUE="<%= submit %>">
33: <INPUT TYPE=HIDDEN NAME="mode" VALUE="<%= mode %>">
34: </FORM>
35: <%
36: End Sub
```

continues

Listing 12.2. continued

```
37: '******************************************************************
38: '* CreateBonusTable

39: sub CreateBonusTable( cn )
40: on error resume next
41:    ' create accounts table
42:    cn.Execute "drop table Bonus"
43:    cmd = "CREATE TABLE Bonus( "
44:    cmd = cmd + "emp_id char(9) NOT NULL"
45:    cmd = cmd + ", bonus money"
46:    cmd = cmd + ", CONSTRAINT pk PRIMARY KEY ( emp_id ) )"
47:    cn.Execute cmd
48: end sub

49: '******************************************************************
50: '* GiveBonuses

51: Sub GiveBonuses( cn, array, idFld, amount )
52:    Set cm = Server.CreateObject("ADODB.Command")
53:    cm.ActiveConnection = cn
54:    cm.CommandText = "INSERT INTO Bonus (emp_id, bonus) VALUES (?,?)"
55:    cm.Prepared = true
56:    cm.Parameters.Refresh
57:    ' for each emp_id in the array
58:    for rec = 0 to UBound(array,2)
59:      name = "cb"+cstr(rec)
60:      if Request.Form(name) = "on" then
61:        cm("Param1") = array(idFld,rec)
62:        cm("Param2") = amount
63:        cm.Execute
64:      end if
65:    next
66: End Sub

67: '******************************************************************
68: '* DisplayBonuses

69: Sub DisplayBonuses( cn )
70: set rs = Server.CreateObject("ADODB.Recordset")
71:    ' display the employees
72:    rs.Open "Select fname, lname, bonus from employee, " & _
➥"Bonus WHERE employee.emp_id = Bonus.emp_id", cn
73:    %><TABLE BORDER=0><%
74:    while not rs.EOF
75:      %><TR>
76:      <TD><%= rs("fname") + " " + rs("lname") %></TD>
77:      <TD><%= rs("bonus") %></TD>
78:      </TR><%
79:      rs.MoveNext
80:    wend
81:    %></TABLE><%
82: End Sub

83: '******************************************************************
84: '* THE MAIN CODE
```

```
 85: set cn = Server.CreateObject("ADODB.Connection")
 86: cn.Open "Pubs", "sa", ""
 87: mode = Request.Form("mode")
 88: if mode = "" then
 89:    set rs = Server.CreateObject("ADODB.Recordset")
 90:    rs.Open "SELECT fname, lname, emp_id FROM employee ORDER BY lname", cn
 91:    ' get the entire table of data
 92:    employees = rs.GetRows
 93:    ' save the list for later
 94:    Session("employees") = employees
 95:    ' display the page title
 96:    %><H1>Employee Bonuses</H1><%
 97:    %><B>Check the employees to give a bonus to</B><%
 98:    ' build the checklist table
 99:    CheckListForm "12twd02.asp", "check", "Move", employees, 4, 2
100: elseif mode = "check" then
101:    ' get the array of employees for before
102:    employees = Session("employees")
103:    ' create the table for demo
104:    CreateBonusTable cn
105:
106:    ' add bonus records for employees
107:    GiveBonuses cn, employees, 2, 1000
108:    ' display the page title
109:    %><H3>Employees with bonuses</H3><%
110:    DisplayBonuses cn
111: end if
112: %>

113: </BODY>
114: </HTML>
```

The Check List Form

As in most of the previous examples from this chapter and others, the bulk of the dynamic Web page is actually scripting code broken down into logical sub-routines.

The first sub-routine, CheckListForm(), builds an input form based on an array of information. This array is exactly the same kind of two-dimensional array returned from a call to the GetRows() method of the Recordset object. CheckListForm() makes use of an HTML trick not yet seen in the other examples. Take a look at the logic, and you'll find not only an input form, but also two HTML tables. The tables and the input <FORM> tags are mixed together. The tables are actually being used to lay out the display of the form, aligning all the fields and prompts:

```
%><FORM ACTION="<%= action %>" METHOD=POST><%
%><TABLE BORDER=1><%
. . .
    for fld = 0 to fields - 1
      %><TD><%= array(fld,rec) %></TD><%
    next
```

```
. . .
</TABLE>
<HR>
<INPUT TYPE=SUBMIT VALUE="<%= submit %>">
<INPUT TYPE=HIDDEN NAME="mode" VALUE="<%= mode %>">
</FORM>
```

TIP

Use HTML tables and forms together to generate a cleaner display. <TABLE> tags can be used inside <FORM> tags to surround input fields and prompts. The form elements appear within individual cells and are automatically aligned with one another when displayed on the user's browser.

The CheckListForm() sub-routine takes the normal action and mode parameters, but also takes submit, the submit key name; array, the two-dimensional array of data; columns, the number of columns to display the data in; and fields, the number of fields to use from the array.

The sub-routine actually produces an input form listing each data record from the array, with each field side by side, in a column of records running from top to bottom, with multiple columns per page. In addition, each record has a checkbox input field next to it, used to get the actual input. Each checkbox input field is named, starting with cb and followed by the ordinal value of the record. For example, the first three checkboxes have the names cb0, cb1, and cb2.

Creating the Bonuses

The next sub-routine in the bunch is CreateBonusTable(). Given an active Connection object as an input parameter, the CreateBonusTable() sub-routine does just what its name implies—it creates a table called Bonus in the database. Bonus is a temporary table that exists merely for this example. Creating tables on-the-fly isn't a common occurrence for dynamic Web applications.

Handing the Bonuses Out

Following CreateBonusTable() is yet another sub-routine. GiveBonuses() does the actual work of recording the bonuses allocated to each employee. It does this by taking as parameters an active Connection, an array of data, the field number of the elements of the array used to match records, and the amount of money to allocate to each employee in the table.

What the sub-routine does is match up the records in the array with the fields of checkbox information held in the built-in Request object. When the CheckList form is submitted, one input field per record is returned to this Web page, and each field contains a value distinguishing the checked records from the non-checked ones.

The employees getting bonuses are the ones the user checked. Each checked field from the Request object corresponds to a record in the array of employee information. The field at index idFld within the array is the information corresponding to the emp_id field from the database's Employee table.

The sub-routine creates a Command object with a CommandText that uses a SQL INSERT statement to add records to the Bonus table:

```
cm.CommandText = "INSERT INTO Bonus (emp_id, bonus) VALUES (?,?)"
```

The Command is prepared in the next statement by assigning the value true to the Prepared property, but nothing happens at this time. The query is actually compiled the first time it's executed. The Parameters collection is populated with a call to Refresh. Because of this, the names Param1 and Param2 are used to access the individual Parameters.

A FOR-NEXT loop is used to step through each record of employee information. If the input field corresponding to the individual record is checked, the Parameters of the Command object are assigned values based on the emp_id field from the array and a constant bonus amount. For the sake of this example, just assume everyone gets the same bonus.

For each employee that was checked, the Command object is re-executed, with different parameters each time. The Command is compiled only during the first execution. Each successive call takes advantage of the work that's already done.

The Display

Finally, the last sub-routine, DisplayBonuses(), lists each employee who is part of the Bonus table. It opens a Recordset with a query that joins the Employee table with the Bonus table, extracting the names of each employee along with the bonus amount.

The Main Code

The main code consists of the standard dynamic Web page IF-THEN-ELSEIF statement, using the mode field of the Request object to direct the flow of execution.

When the page is first accessed, it reads the Employee table using a Recordset object, transfers the data into an array by calling GetRows(), and then generates the input form by calling CheckListForm(). The actual array of information is stored in the Session object because each field in the input form corresponds to an exact index in the array. The array is used later to help process the submission.

When the form is submitted with its set of checkboxes—some checked, others not—the main code performs four tasks. It retrieves the stashed array of employee information from the

Session object. Next, it calls the sub-routine CreateBonusTable() to actually create the Bonus table in the database. Then it calls the GiveBonuses() sub-routine to do the actual work of adding records to the new table, and finally, it generates the list of employees with bonuses as a response to the submission by calling the DisplayBonuses() sub-routine.

NOTE

This example creates a table on-the-fly, but you probably won't ever need to do this. It was done here so that the table remains fresh each time the example is run; that way, you see the same thing everyone else sees each time.

Running the Code

It's best to examine the code while it's actually running to see what the input form looks like. Remember the form is interleaved with <TABLE>, <TR>, and <TD> instructions that help lay out each prompt and field. The following image, Figure 12.4, shows the Web page as it looks the first time the page is accessed.

Figure 12.4.

An input form for selecting which employees get bonuses.

Go ahead and check any name you want. The employees who correspond to the checked boxes are then inserted into the new Bonuses table when the form is submitted back to the server. The next image, Figure 12.5, shows the response from the ASP file after the form, complete with checked boxes, is submitted.

Figure 12.5.
A list of the employees who received bonuses.

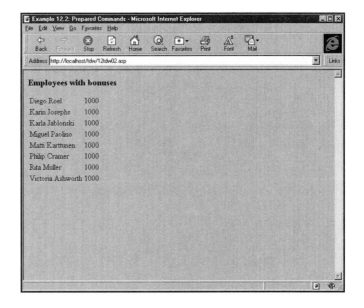

Stored Procedures

Sophisticated back-end database servers, such as Microsoft SQL Server, allow you to store named sequences of SQL statements in the database, just as though they were any other database object, such as a table or view.

The Benefits of Stored Procedures

Stored procedures are beneficial because they can be used to hide the complexity of a SQL query from the application programmer. A single person or a group of people in an organization can design the intricacies of a data-storage system and lay out all its rules and dependencies. Instead of expecting each and every programmer to learn and follow the rules, they can offer programmers an alternative interface.

An interface composed of named procedures can direct application programmers to a narrow range of interactions guarded against integrity violations. Each time a procedure is called, you have control over what happens. You guarantee exactly which queries are made and which fields are accessed. You even have the opportunity to execute multiple queries in the same stored procedure.

For example, a stored procedure can be written that handles updating records in a database. The following example gives bonuses to employees based on a percentage rate and length of employment:

```
CREATE PROCEDURE GiveBonuses @BasePercent int
AS
  UPDATE employees
    SET bonus = salary * @BasePercent / 100.0 * 0.5
    WHERE months < 24;
  UPDATE employees
    SET bonus = salary * @BasePercent / 100.0 * 0.75
    WHERE months >= 24 and months < 48;
  UPDATE employees
    SET bonus = salary * @BasePercent
    WHERE months >= 48
GO
```

Three separate updates are used to hit employees in different ranges, but the programmer doesn't need to know this. The application programmer who's building an application that presents a menu of options to the boss doesn't have to remember how bonuses are passed out. The programmer simply calls the GiveBonuses procedure.

Another example is a procedure that does the work of adding a new subscriber to a magazine subscription database:

```
CREATE PROCEDURE AddNewSubscriber
    @Id        int,
    @Name      char(20),
    @Address   char(80),
    @City      char(20),
    @State     char(2),
    @Zip       char(11),
    @Title     char(80),
    @Months    int
AS
  INSERT INTO subscribers
    (Id, Name, Address, City, State, Zip)
    VALUES
    (@Id, @Name, @Address, @City, @State, @zip);
  INSERT INTO subscriptions
    (Id, Title, Months)
    VALUES
    (@Id, @Title, @Months)
GO
```

The subscriber being added to a table different from the subscription information is hidden from the programmer. An additional procedure might add subscriptions for current subscribers. Here's a complementary stored procedure that contains a SELECT query combining the information from these two tables:

```
CREATE PROCEDURE AllSubscriptions
AS
  SELECT * FROM subscribers, subscriptions
    WHERE subscribers.Id = subscriptions.Id
    ORDER BY subscribers.Zip, subscribers.Address
GO
```

You might need just such a table to generate mailing labels for each outgoing magazine.

Calling Stored Procedures

Like functions you might build in a programming language such as Visual Basic, VBScript, C++, or Java, stored SQL procedures accept parameters and return values. They behave very much like normal queries and can be manipulated with Command objects in the same way. However, unlike Visual Basic Script, procedures stored in the database have explicitly defined parameters, each with a specified data type and size.

To call a stored procedure, the Parameters collection must be set up to precisely match the number and type of parameters defined on the server. You can do this by using the same two methods explained earlier. You can either take the time and pay for a network round trip by calling the Refresh method of the Parameters collection or you can build the Parameters collection by hand.

Building the Parameters collection by hand is the preferred method because it results in faster execution. The code, however, ends up looking a bit more complex, as shown here:

```
<%
cm.CommandText = "AddNewSubscriber"
cm.CommandType = adCmdStoredProc
set p = cm.Parameters
p.Append cm.CreateParameter("@Id", adInteger, adParamInput)
p.Append cm.CreateParameter("@Name", adChar, adParamInput, 20)
p.Append cm.CreateParameter("@Address", adChar, adParamInput, 80)
p.Append cm.CreateParameter("@City", adChar, adParamInput, 20)
p.Append cm.CreateParameter("@State", adChar, adParamInput, 2)
p.Append cm.CreateParameter("@Zip", adChar, adParamInput, 11)
p.Append cm.CreateParameter("@Title", adChar, adParamInput, 80)
p.Append cm.CreateParameter("@Months", adInteger, adParamInput)
cm("@Id") = 40239
cm("@Name") = "Bob Boogie"
cm("@Address") = "1122 BW Ave"
cm("@City") = "Redmond"
cm("@State") = "WA"
cm("@Zip") = 99999
cm("@Title") = "Monster Mag"
cm("@Months") = 12
cm.Execute
%>
```

Looking at the Results

Stored procedure that return explicit return values send the data for the return value back to the Command object's Execute method. After the Command is executed and the examination of the Recordset is finished the first Parameter of the Parameters collection contains the return value:

```
<% v = cm(0)%>
```

Parameter collections that are generated by calling the Refresh method have an initial parameter named RETURN-VALUE at index 0. If you're building the Parameters collection yourself, you must specify the return value as well by appending it to the collection:

```
<%
set p = cm.CreateParameter( "retval", adInteger, adParamReturnValue )
cm.Parameters.Append p
cm.Execute
v = cm("retval")
%>
```

The Stored Procedure Query

The query you use to specify a call to a stored procedure can look as simple as the name of the procedure itself. However, this simple form is available only when you have explicitly told the Command object that the CommandType is adCmdStoredProc. If the command type is left unknown, you're going to have to do a bit more work.

Fortunately, the expanded form of the stored procedure call looks much like the Parameter-based query shown earlier:

```
<% cm.CommandText = "{ ? = myproc( ? ) }" %>
```

In addition to the name of the procedure, all parameters are labeled with their own question mark placeholders.

The preceding statement assigns a query string to the CommandText property. The query is a call to a stored procedure in its expanded form; the call is placed inside braces: { and }. The placeholder for the return value appears as a question mark to the left of an equals (=) operator. On the right-hand side is the procedure name itself, followed by its parameter list. Each parameter in the list is represented by a question mark of its own.

A procedure call with multiple parameters would look like the following statement:

```
<% cm.CommandText = "{ ? = myproc2( ?, ? ) }" %>
```

And a call to the same procedure with a constant parameter would look like this:

```
<% cm.CommandText = "{ ? = myproc2( ?, 10 ) }" %>
```

You can save yourself the trouble of having to specify the procedure call in the expanded form by assigning the value adCmdStoredProc to the CommandType property.

Even if you do specify the appropriate command type, you can take a look at the query's expanded form by reading the CommandText property back out again. ADO automatically converts the short form into the expanded form for you.

12

Dynamic Procedure Calls

The following example, Listing 12.3, shows a dynamic Web page that uses the Command object to call a procedure stored in the database. A sub-routine from this Web page actually stores the procedure in the database by using the SQL CREATE PROCEDURE statement. The example is far simpler than Listing 12.2 and does very much the same thing that Listing 12.1 did. It asks for user input to help narrow a search. When the input is submitted, the search is performed and the matching records are displayed.

Listing 12.3. Stored procedures (12TWD03.ASP).

```
1: <HTML>
2: <TITLE>Example 12.3: Stored Procedures</TITLE>
3: <HEAD></HEAD>
4: <BODY>

5: <!--#include file="adovbs.inc" -->

6: <%
7: '*****************************************
8: '* CreateQuery

9: Sub CreateQuery( cn, name, params, query )
10:    on error resume next
11:    cn.Execute "drop procedure " & name
12:    cn.Execute "CREATE PROCEDURE " & name & " " & params & " AS " & query
13: End Sub

14: '*****************************************
15: '* NameRangeForm

16: Sub NameRangeForm( action, mode )
17: %>
18: <FORM ACTION="<%= action %>" METHOD=POST>
19: From (inclusive):
20: <INPUT NAME="lo" WIDTH=40>
21: To
22: <INPUT NAME="hi" WIDTH=40>
23: <INPUT TYPE=SUBMIT VALUE="Find">
24: <INPUT TYPE=HIDDEN NAME="mode" VALUE="<%= mode %>">
25: </FORM>
26: <%
27: End Sub

28: '*****************************************
29: '* DisplayEmployees

30: Sub DisplayEmployees( rs )
31:    %><TABLE BORDER=1><%
32:    while not rs.EOF
33:      %><TR>
34:      <TD><%= rs("fname") + " " + rs("lname") %></TD>
```

continues

Listing 12.3. continued

```
35:     </TR><%
36:     rs.MoveNext
37:    wend
38:    %></TABLE><%
39: End Sub

40: '********************************************
41: '* THE MAIN CODE

42: set cn = Server.CreateObject("ADODB.Connection")
43: cn.Open "pubs", "sa", ""
44: mode = Request.Form("mode")
45: if mode = "" then
46:    '*** DISPLAY INPUT FORM ***
47:    %><H1>Find Employees</H1><%
48:    %>Enter range for last names<BR><BR><%
49:    NameRangeForm "12twd03.asp", "find"
50: elseif mode ="find" then
51:    '*** CREATE stored proc for this demo ***
52:    proc = "FindEmployee"
53:    params = "@lo char(40), @hi char(40)"
54:    query = "SELECT * FROM employee WHERE lname >= @lo AND lname < @hi"
55:    CreateQuery cn, proc, params, query
56:    '*** Call stored procedure ***
57:    set cm = Server.CreateObject("ADODB.Command")
58:    'set up command
59:    cm.ActiveConnection = cn
60:    cm.CommandText = "FindEmployee"
61:    cm.CommandType = adCmdStoredProc
62:    cm.Parameters.Refresh
63:    ' set up parameter values
64:    cm("@lo") = Request.Form("lo")
65:    cm("@hi") = Request.Form("hi")
66:    ' execute command to call procedure
67:    set rs = cm.Execute
68:    '*** display the results ***
69:    %><H3>Employees between
70:    <%=Request.Form("lo")%> and
71:    <%=Request.Form("hi")%>
72:    </H3><%
73:
74:    DisplayEmployees rs
75: end if
76: %>

77: </BODY>
78: </HTML>
```

Creating the Query

The `CreateQuery()` sub-routine is a helper function that adds any procedure specified in a character string to the database. The sub-routine takes four parameters: an active `Connection`

to the database, the name of the procedure to store, a list of any parameters, and a SQL expression that constitutes the body of the procedure.

The Name Range Form

The second sub-routine of this example generates a form that asks the user for two pieces of information—the boundaries of a range of values for the last name field in the Employee table. The two input fields are named `lo` and `hi`. In addition, a Submit button with the value of `Enter` and a hidden field named "mode" are added to the form. You should be familiar with both of these features by now.

The Display

The third and last sub-routine of this example, `DisplayEmployees()`, simply takes a `Recordset` of employee names and generates a table with each employee in its own cell.

The Main Code

The first time the page is accessed, an empty string is stored in the mode field of the `Request` object so that the NameRange input form is generated and sent back to the user.

When the form is submitted, the main code creates a `Command` object used to make the call into the stored procedure. The `ActiveConnection` property is hooked to the opened `Connection` object. The name of the procedure is assigned to the `CommandText` property, and the `CommandType` property is set to the value `adCmdStoredProc`.

A call to `Refresh` fills the `Parameters` collection with the parameters of the procedure defined in the database. Each parameter is then set, copying the appropriate data from the `Request` object's `Form` and into the individual `Parameters`.

Next, a call to `Execute` sends the query, which consists of the procedure name and the parameters to the database to be processed. The procedure actually contains a SQL `SELECT` statement augmented by the parameters passed to it. The `SELECT` statement generates a `Recordset` as output, which is fed back to the application and stored in the local variable `rs`.

A prompt is generated, and a call to `DisplayEmployees()` finishes the application by building a table of all the employees names contained in the resulting `Recordset`.

Executing the Procedure

You can see this code in action by testing out the dynamic page. Figure 12.6 shows what the page looks like the first time it's accessed.

12

Figure 12.6.

*Enter the letters
defining the range of
valid values for the
employees' last names.*

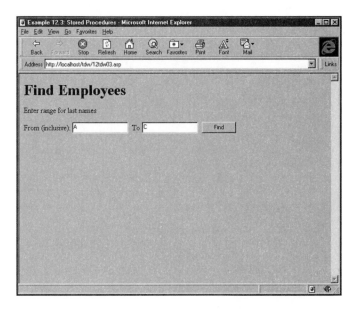

Enter A for the From field and C for the To field, and press the Enter key or click the Find button to submit the data. The stored procedure takes the submitted information and uses it as part of its internal query. The results are shown in Figure 12.7.

Figure 12.7.

*The matching
employees.*

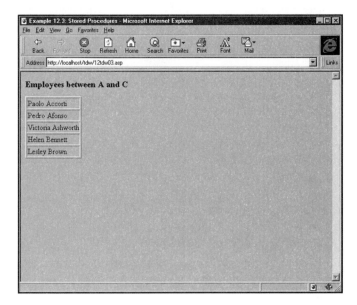

Summary

This chapter has explained the ADO `Command` object in detail and covered the topics of `Parameter`-based queries, precompilation, and executing stored procedures. It has shown you how to use both the `Command` object and its subordinate `Parameters` collection to help save execution time by reusing the same `Command` object and the same query, even when subsequent executions are slightly different.

The `Parameters` collection and its `Parameter` objects are similar to the `Fields` collection and `Field` objects of the `Recordset`. Both collections are responsible for representing a set of modifiable values corresponding to placeholders in a query string. The `Command` object's `Parameters` are primarily used to send values to the database server, but the `Recordset`'s `Fields` are used to examine values sent back.

Q&A

Q Can I use the question mark in a query to replace not just values, but also actual column names?

A No. The question mark replacement operator can be used only to replace values. It's used with precompiled queries or values that aren't easily specified in the query itself. Queries that vary in structure are too difficult to precompile.

Q I have a book on SQL that covers a topic called "Dynamic SQL." In it, they use named variables in queries in situations where you use question marks. Is it possible to use names instead?

A No. The question mark replacement feature is an ODBC standard; ODBC doesn't support other operators or terms.

Q If I'm not going to prepare my `Command`, what advantage do `Parameters` have over simply building up my query from string fragments in VBScript?

A `Parameters` can be used to pass data that's too large or not easily expressed in a query string.

Q Are stored procedures precompiled, too?

A Most likely they are, but that depends on the back-end database server you're accessing.

Q How big can my queries be?

A The maximum size of the query's text depends on the underlying data provider and the back-end database. It can also depend on the programming environment and its ability to manipulate large strings.

12

Q Can I change the name of the `Parameter` objects after I have retrieved them by calling the `Refresh` method?

A No. Once the `Parameter` objects are placed in the `Parameters` collection, their names are read-only. The only way to rename them is to actually remove the `Parameter` objects from the collection, change their names, and append them again.

Quiz

1. Name the property that can be used to precompile a query.

2. List two ways to populate the `Parameters` collection.

3. The `CommandText` property has three well-known states and one ambiguous state. List all four.

4. Name the special character that can be used as a placeholder in a SQL query for a parameter that's supplied later.

5. There are two forms for specifying a stored procedure call in the `CommandText` property: long and short form. Give an example of each for a call to a function named `Spork` that takes two parameters.

6. When specifying stored procedures in short form, what value must the `CommandType` property be set to?

7. When specifying stored procedures in long form, what value must the `CommandType` property be set to?

8. List the first three parameter names of the `Parameters` collection when the `Refresh` method is used to populate it. Assume you have a simple `Parameter`-based query with at least three parameters.

9. State two different ways to assign `Parameters` to the execution of the query, and give examples of each.

10. Name the property used to specify whether a `Parameter` is used for input, output, or both.

Exercises

1. Specify a `Parameter`-based query that uses the Employee table of the Pubs sample database to find an employee, based on ranges for first name, last name, and middle initial.

2. Write a sub-routine that uses a `Command` object to call the `byroyalty` procedure stored in the Pubs sample database. The procedure takes a single-integer `Parameter` name `@percentage` and returns a set of matching records.

12

3. Write a sub-routine that takes a Command object and a few other arguments and uses those arguments as Parameters to a query execution. Choose any table from any datasource you have available.

4. Write a sub-routine that initializes a Command object in preparation for calling the reptq3 stored procedure. The procedure takes two parameters—@lolimit and @hilimit—both of which are currency values. Build your own Parameters collection by using the CreateParameter and Append methods.

5. Write a dynamic Web page that incorporates the sub-routine built in Exercise 4. Build the input form that requests the low and high limits and on submission generates a listing of all matching records.

6. Build a list of situations where repeated execution of Parameter-based queries would make sense. Feel free to use a project you'll be working on or a topic of interest to you.

12

Day 13

Errors and Provider Properties

by Matt Warren

After reading this chapter, you will be able to do the following:

- ☐ Identify where error conditions might happen when processing your dynamic Web page.
- ☐ Use ADO error information to help determine the correct course of action when error conditions do occur.
- ☐ Combine the power of Visual Basic error control with ADO's extended features.
- ☐ Manage error conditions that raise multiple errors.
- ☐ Show how provider properties help you use advanced features otherwise unavailable to your application.
- ☐ Show how provider properties can give you precise control over the interaction between ADO and the underlying data provider.

Errors

Sometimes method calls fail during program execution, and the ActiveX Data Objects are no exception. Many circumstances can cause the ADO component software to abort execution because of inappropriate arguments or failures in required subsystems, such as the operating system or the underlying data provider.

When methods fail, errors are generated and, by default, the program might halt to report the failure. However, unless the error is extremely severe, stopping the program because of an error condition is often considered unacceptable by the users of your application. You have probably been unlucky enough to experience a few software crashes of your own; either the computer freezes up, or the application vanishes and is replaced by a message in a dialog box, telling you something bad just happened.

Fortunately, errors aren't as severe as crashes. Because they don't actually freeze up the application or bring it tumbling down, the program can recover from them. However, if they aren't dealt with immediately after they happen, they often cause the software to abort. Programming environments such as Visual Basic, VBScript, Java, and JavaScript terminate an application when an error or exception occurs, if that error condition isn't handled by the application itself.

An application that terminates because of an error condition is just as suspect as one that crashes because both types of termination can lead to losing data. What if the application aborted in the middle of saving a document? It's better to catch the errors as they happen and work around them. You might even choose to abort the current work and return to the menu or form being accessed just before the process that failed.

Errors in Visual Basic

Visual Basic has a built-in mechanism—the Err object—that can be used to detect errors as they occur. You can access the Err object to discover the error code of the last error generated. The built-in Err object's Number property is the default, so it's automatically accessed when you reference the object.

For example, after a call is made to a sub-routine or method known to be susceptible to errors, you can do a check against either of these terms:

```
<%
y = somefunction( x )
if err <> 0 then
  %>Oops!<%
end if
%>
```

13

If no error occurs, the value of the Err object's intrinsic Number property is zero. Otherwise, it contains the telltale error code.

What you do with the information is up to you. You could generate a message to relay the failure to the user and continue working. You could send the message, and then return the user to a standard input form. You could even take a second try at whatever failed or choose an alternative route through the code.

Of course, you won't even get this far, if you haven't already done something to warn Visual Basic that you want to handle the error condition yourself. If the programming environment has no instructions from you, it automatically aborts the program at the first sign of trouble.

Visual Basic has a built-in phrase that can be used for just this purpose—to let the programming environment know your intentions for handling errors:

```
<% On Error Resume Next %>
```

The On Error command is part of a series of commands available in Visual Basic for controlling the environment's response to error conditions. Visual Basic Script, however, can use only one of them, which is the On Error Resume Next statement. This statement instructs the environment to ignore errors. It quite literally tells Visual Basic to continue executing on the very next instruction even if there's a failure. Instead of aborting its execution, the program continues to run as though no error occurred.

Of course, this puts the onus back on you, the programmer, to handle the error immediately after it happens; otherwise, you could run the risk of the next statement, or one further down the page, failing in a more disastrous way.

This burden of handling the error yourself is exactly why the Err.Number value is at your disposal. In addition to the Number property, the build-in Err object has other properties, such as Description, Source, HelpContext, and HelpFile. Using these properties together, you can not only deduce the error condition, but you can act on it. The other information is available for delivering messages to the end-user or sending data to a log file.

Multiple Errors with ADO

ADO extends this error-reporting ability by magnifying it. Database servers are often very particular beasts. They are capable of raising more than one error condition at a time. A single query can include multiple SQL statements, each of which may fail. Even single SQL statements can generate more information than can be stuffed into the single Err object. In addition to multiple errors, you can often get several warnings accompanying the errors. They can even appear on their own when no error at all has happened.

To make it easier to get to this important repository of information, the ADO Connection object has an additional member called Errors, which is a collection of many Error objects.

Each Error object has its own Number, Description, Source, HelpContext, and HelpFile properties.

Although Recordsets and Commands can take part in generating these types of multiple errors, only the Connection object has a collection of them. The reason for this is simple. Multiple errors occur during the communication to the database server, over the Connection. Only objects linked to an active Connection can possibly generate multiple errors or warnings coming from the back-end.

If you use the Execute method of the Connection object, errors generated by the execution appear in the Errors collection. Likewise, if you use the Open method of the Recordset object, errors generated by the execution appear in the Errors collection of the associated Connection object. Even if you didn't have an associated Connection object before the call to Open, you will have one afterward.

So you can take a look at the errors in the collection by directly referencing the Errors collection from the Connection object:

```
<% Set Errors = cn.Errors %>
```

If you don't have a local variable referencing your Connection object, you can find it indirectly from either the Recordset or the Command object, as shown here:

```
<% Set Errors = rs.ActiveConnection.Errors %>
```

To determine if there are any Error objects in the collection, use the Count property:

```
<%
if myconnection.Errors.Count > 0 then
   '*** do something here ***
end if
%>
```

To determine the numeric codes of the errors that occurred, examine each Error object independently:

```
<%
for i = 0 to cn.Errors.Count - 1
   if cn.Errors(i) = someProviderError then
      '*** handle the specific error ***
   end if
end if
%>
```

Connection Errors

The Errors collection is similar to the Fields and Parameters collection. It holds on to all the Error objects since you last called another ADO method.

Properties of the Errors Collection

Property	Description
Count	The number of Error objects in the collection

NOTE

All properties of the Errors collection and the Error object are read-only.

The Count Property

Contains a Long value

You can use the Count property to determine the current number of Error objects in the Errors collection.

The Errors collection also contains warnings. Sometimes query executions produce warnings from the underlying data provider. Warnings aren't as severe as errors; they don't try to abort the execution of the application. They are, however, useful in the descriptions they provide and can be a way of letting your application users know that the queries might not be executing as efficiently as possible.

TIP

For this reason, it might be best not to use the Count property as a means of determining if errors happened after a call to an ADO object method. Visual Basic and VBScript both have a built-in variable Err that contains the error number of the last issued error. If you can, check this variable for a non-zero value first before examining the Count property of the Errors collection.

13

Methods of the Errors Collection

Method	Description
Clear	Remove all Errors from the collection
Item	Retrieve an individual Error object

The `Clear` Method

```
Errors.Clear
```

You can use the `Clear` method to remove all `Error` objects from the `Errors` collection. Do this before calling a method that may potentially fail to clear out any previous errors or warnings that might be in the collection. After calling the method in question, check the built-in Visual Basic `Err` variable for a value other than zero, or check the `Count` property of the `Errors` collection to see whether any errors or warnings have been added since the call to `Clear`.

The `Item` Method

```
Set error = Errors.Item( index )
```

> `index` The ordinal index of the `Error` object in the `Errors` collection that you want to retrieve

You can use the `Item` method to retrieve an individual `Error` object from the `Errors` collection. This is the default indexing method when using Visual Basic or VBScript. With these languages, you don't need to call the `Item` method directly; instead, simply use the parentheses on the `Errors` collection itself, as shown here:

```
Set error = Errors( index )
```

The `Error` Object

The `Error` object contains all the information about a single error. Only errors raised by the underlying data provider end up as `Error` objects in the `Errors` collection. Other errors are stored in the `Err` object.

Properties of the `Error` Object

The following table lists the properties of the `Error` object:

Property	Description
Description	The description of the error
HelpContext	The context of the error in the help file
HelpFile	The help file associated with the error
NativeError	The error originally generated by the database
Number	The data provider's numeric error code
Source	The software that generated the error
SQLState	The state of the last SQL execution

The `Description` **Property**
Contains a `String` value

You can use the `Description` property to find a character string describing the error in more detail. This information can be useful in determining the true nature of the error, but is more likely used as part of an error log or a message displayed to a sophisticated user who would benefit from knowing more detail about the error condition.

The `HelpContext` **Property**
Contains a `Long` value

You can use the `HelpContext` property to determine the context of the error condition within an appropriate help file. Use this information to identify a topic in the help file that might give the users of your application an understanding of the error condition and ways to avoid it in the future.

If there's no appropriate help information, `HelpContext`'s value is `0`.

The `HelpFile` **Property**
Contains a `String` value

You can use the `HelpFile` property to determine the name of a help file that might have topics related to the error condition. By using it with the `HelpContext` property, you can automatically point your users to information that helps them discover how to correct the current problem or how to avoid similar problems in the future.

If there's no appropriate help information, the value contains an empty string.

The `NativeError` **Property**
Contains a `Long` value

You can use the `NativeError` property to determine a numeric code that explains the error originally generated by the back-end database server. This code may or may not be the same error code reported by the data provider and accessible through the `Number` property.

Use this property if you're familiar with these values and would prefer to base your error-handling code on their more explicit information.

The Number **Property**

Contains a Long value

You can use the Number property to determine the actual error code returned by the ADO method call that failed. This error code is generated by the underlying data provider, so it's not among the error constants covered in this chapter.

The Source **Property**

Contains a String value

You can use the Source property to get a text message describing the application or software object that generated the error. Use this information when building trace logs of activity in the application or to display a message to a sophisticated user who would benefit from knowing the origin of the error condition.

For error messages generated purely in ADO 1.0, the Source strings can be one of the following:

```
ADODB.Command
ADODB.Connection
ADODB.Field
ADODB.Recordset
ADODB.Parameter
ADODB.Property
```

The SQLState **Property**

Contains a String value

You can use the SQLState property to determine the SQL state information at the time of the error. This information is valid only when using an underlying provider that communicates using ODBC, such as the default provider for ADO 1.0—MSDASQL. The SQLState information is a five-character string containing an error code defined by the SQL standard.

Use this property if you're familiar with these values and would prefer to base your error-handling code on their more explicit information.

Taking Advantage of Errors

Errors will arise in your application from time to time whether you like them or not. Using tools such as ADO opens you up to a world of objects and services that aren't always 100 percent reliable. You might not always be successful opening that next Connection object.

The server may be full of requests already, overloading its capacity. The network between your middle-tier Web server and database server could intermittently be overloaded or interrupted because it's an actual piece of wire that can be cut.

The next Command you execute could fail for any number of reasons, but whatever the reason, it's best to make your application or dynamic Web page as foolproof as possible. To do this, turn off Visual Basic's automatic abort feature—if it can be called a feature—and handle the error conditions on your own. You have the Err object in Visual Basic at your disposal that tells you what happened, and there's the ADO Connection object as well. It has an entire collection of Error objects that can be inspected individually; each one provides details for a particular cause of failure.

Known Errors

Table 13.1 is a complete list of the error codes generated by ADO. It's especially important to make use of this list when you're deciding how to respond to an error condition. Some conditions can be expected. You might have alternative code paths that can be executed in case the first attempt fails, but other errors may be considered too severe to handle in such a way.

It's important to note, however, that the codes listed aren't ones found in the Errors collection. Error codes generated by the provider or by the back-end database server aren't known or understood by ADO. Luckily, ADO doesn't disguise this information. Full provider-specific error codes are handed back to your application when an error is generated. The same value appears on the built-in Err object as well as in the collection. The opposite, though, is not true.

The error codes generated by ADO, those shown in Table 13.1, are ones that appear in the Number property of the built-in Err object only. When these error conditions arise, no special provider errors are listed in the Errors collection.

Table 13.1. Values for the Err object's Number property.

Error Constant	Value	Meaning
adErrBoundToCommand	3707	An attempt to change the ActiveConnection property of the Recordset was made, after the Recordset had already been bound to a Command object that had its own, different ActiveConnection.
adErrDataConversion	3421	An system error occurred when ADO was trying to convert data from one type to another.

continues

13

Table 13.1. continued

Error Constant	Value	Meaning
adErrFeatureNotAvailable	3251	The underlying data provider doesn't support a feature that was required to complete the last operation.
adErrIllegalOperation	3219	The last operation was invalid due to the current state of the object.
adErrInTransaction	3246	An error occurred concerning the transaction being attempted or currently in progress.
adErrInvalidArgument	3001	An argument used in the last method call is invalid, given the current state of the object or options in use.
adErrInvalidParamInfo	3708	A Parameter object was specified incorrectly.
adErrItemNotFound	3265	The item requested couldn't be found in the collection.
adErrNoCurrentRecord	3021	The last operation is invalid when the current record position is either BOF or EOF.
adErrObjectClosed	3704	The last operation is invalid when the object is closed.
adErrObjectNotSet	3420	An object required in the last object doesn't exist or isn't set.
adErrObjectOpen	3705	The last operation is invalid when the object is open.
adErrProviderNotFound	3706	The data provider named in the Provider property of the Connection object couldn't be found in the system Registry or located on disk.

Execution

The most common error condition you check for is determining whether your Command executed successfully. The best method is to always check Visual Basic's built-in Err value first; it's the quickest means to find out if something has gone wrong:

```
<%
 Set rs = cn.Execute()
 if Err = 0 then
    '*** proceed with work
  end if
%>
```

If the execution is successful, the value of the Err variable is zero. Otherwise, it contains the explicit error code generated by the method call. You can get more information about the error by continuing to inspect either the built-in Err object or by looking at the Error objects in the Errors collection.

The following code fragment generates an error message for the user by evaluating the Description property of the built-in Err object:

```
<%
  set rs = cn.Execute()
  if Err = 0 then
    '*** proceed with work ***
  else
    %>Error: <%= Err.Description %><%
  else
  end if
%>
```

The next code fragment extends this concept by optionally examining all the values in the Errors collection:

```
<%
  set rs = cn.Execute()
  if Err = 0 then
    '*** proceed with work ***
  else if cn.Errors.Count > 0 then
    for i = 0 to cn.Errors.Count - 1
      if cn.Errors(i) < 0 then
        %>Error: <%= cn.Errors(i).Description %><%
      else
        %>Warning: <%= cn.Errors(i).Description %><%
      end if
    next
  else
    %>Error: <%= Err.Description %><%
  else
  end if
%>
```

Closed Recordsets

13

The second most common error condition you check for is the one you force into existence as a means of testing the resulting Recordset to see whether it's open.

The Recordset returned from the Execute method exists in one of three different states:

- ☐ Open with records
- ☐ Open with no records
- ☐ Closed with no records

The first two conditions happen regularly. If the query is successful, it returns all records matched in the SQL WHERE clause. Sometimes, however, no records match at all, and the Recordset comes back empty. This is perfectly normal, so you don't need to write any special error-handling code for this condition. What you do need to handle, however, is the third condition—a Recordset that's closed.

Some queries never result in data, no matter what. ADO, though, still hands back a Recordset object to the caller, but in this case it's closed. Savvy programmers are aware of the type of queries they make, and which ones in particular are known not to return data. For example, you could use a Command object to execute a query that actually inserts data into a table. This type of query doesn't result in records being sent back to the caller, and so the execution results in a Recordset that's closed.

If you know ahead of time that the Recordset is going to end up closed, you could simply ignore the returned object. If it were that simple, however, you wouldn't need to do any checking for errors.

Imagine, instead, that you're using a Command object to call a procedure stored in the database. You may or may not know what to expect from the procedure. Depending on the parameters supplied, the procedure might generate records to send back or it might not. You may have to be prepared to handle either case.

In a simpler scenario, you might choose to write several generic sub-routines that handle tasks like executing common queries or working with Recordsets passed in. It might be important for you to know whether the Recordset is open, and you might not have total control over how that Recordset came into being. It's better to be certain than sorry.

Unfortunately, the Recordset doesn't have a property named IsOpen. If it did, then going through the checks described here probably wouldn't be necessary. The only way to truly know whether a Recordset is open is to try using it in a way that would be considered invalid if it were actually closed.

For example, trying to access the EOF property is harmless, yet it's considered an invalid operation to perform on a closed Recordset. It generates an error, and if you weren't prepared to handle this minor but distinct condition, your application would halt just the same.

Luckily, you can use this fact to your advantage. Simply access the EOF property and immediately afterward check whether your access generated an error, as shown here:

```
<%
    On Error Resume Next
    Set rs = cn.Execute
    x = rs.EOF
    if Err == adErrObjectClosed then
      %>That object was closed!<%
    else
      '*** do some processing ***
    end if
%>
```

Warnings

Another feature you can take advantage of when using ADO is the ability to retrieve warning information from the Errors collection. Sometimes the data provider returns warnings in addition to errors when things go wrong. Other times, warnings can appear by themselves even when no error has occurred. Only the ADO Errors collection has this information available.

Warnings aren't as severe as errors; they don't cause the execution to abort. The data provider might just be notifying you that a query is executing in a non-optimal fashion, or the state of the database is reaching some sort of limit.

You can find out about warnings by examining the Errors collection when no error has happened. Check the Count property to see whether it's greater than zero. If it is, then the Errors collection is full of warnings. When errors do occur, the collection is cleared and repopulated with the current error information. At other times, when only warnings occur, they're added to the end of the collection and represent a cumulative series of warnings.

NOTE

> You can distinguish the difference between errors and warnings in the Errors collection by checking the sign of the Number property. True errors have negative Number values; warnings have positive ones.

If you decide that it would be useful for your application to keep track of warnings as well as errors, you're going to have to be prepared to clear the Errors collection yourself. If you don't, the warnings will be mixed with the previous error messages and you might mistakenly believe that errors are recurring.

One method to use is clearing the Errors collection after each time you handle a particular error condition. This method keeps the collection empty so that later, when a warning occurs after a call to another ADO method, only the warnings exist in the Errors collection.

Another method is clearing the Errors collection before each call to a method that you expect warnings to be generated from.

You can mix together your error handling and warning checks to give you complete coverage of possible events, as shown here:

```
<%
  On Error Resume Next
  cn.Errors.Clear
  Set rs = cn.Execute( query )
  if Err <> 0 then
    '*** process errors  ***
  elseif cn.Errors.Count > 0 then
    '*** process warnings ***
  end if
%>
```

13

Checking ADO Errors

Listing 13.1 is an example of how you might go about checking for error conditions and handling these abnormalities. It's a dynamic Web page that looks and works much like the examples in Chapter 12, "Commands and Stored Procedures."

First, the user sees a form that asks for two entries: the beginning and end of a range of employee last names. When the information is submitted back to the server, a Parameter-based query is executed based on the entry. The added benefit of this Web page, however, is that when errors happen, instead of the page halting and an error message explaining where in your code the error happened, a message of your choosing is displayed. At the end of the message, the user is offered a button that when clicked restarts the page that generated the fault.

Listing 13.1. Checking errors (13TWD01.ASP).

```
 1: <HTML>
 2: <HEAD>
 3: <TITLE>Example 13.1: Checking Errors</TITLE>
 4: </HEAD>
 5: <BODY>
 6: <% thisPage = "13twd01.asp" %>
 7: <%
 8: '************************************************
 9: '* IsOpen
10: '*
11: Function IsOpen( rs )
12:    On Error Resume Next
13:    bof = rs.BOF
14:    If Err = 0 Then
15:       IsOpen = true
16:    Else
17:       IsOpen = false
18:    End If
19: End Function
20: %>
21: <%
22: '************************************************
23: '* CheckError
24: '*
25: Function CheckError( cn, msg, mode )
26:    If Err <> 0 Then
27:       %>
28:       <H3>
29:       An error has occurred in <%= thisPage %>
30:       while <%= msg %>.
31:       </H3>
32:       <%
33:       '**** display all the errors & warnings ****
```

```
34:     If cn = Nothing Then
35:         %>Error: <%= Err.Description %><%
36:     ElseIf cn.Errors.Count = 0 Then
37:         %>Error: <%= Err.Description %><%
38:     Else
39:         For i = 0 to cn.Errors.Count - 1
40:             If cn.Errors(i) < 0 then
41:                 %>Error: <%= cn.Errors(i).Description %><%
42:             Else
43:                 %>Warning: <%= cn.Errors(i).Description %><%
44:             End If
45:         Next
46:     End If
47:     %>
48:     <FORM METHOD=POST ACTION="<%= thisPage %>">
49:     <INPUT TYPE=SUBMIT VALUE="Continue">
50:     <INPUT TYPE=HIDDEN NAME=mode VALUE="<%= mode %>">
51:     </FORM>
52:     <%
53:     CheckError = True
54:   Else
55:     CheckError = False
56:   End if
57: End Function
58: %>
59: <%
60: '************************************************
61: '* NameRangeForm
62: '*
63: Sub NameRangeForm( action, mode )
64: %>
65: <B>Enter range for matching last names</B>
66: <HR>
67: <FORM METHOD=POST ACTION="<%= action %>">
68: <TABLE BORDER=0>
69: <TR>
70: <TD>From</TD>
71: <TD><INPUT NAME="From"></TD>
72: </TR>
73: <TR>
74: <TD>To</TD>
75: <TD><INPUT NAME="To"></TD>
76: </TR>
77: </TABLE>
78: <HR>
79: <INPUT TYPE=SUBMIT VALUE="Enter">
80: <INPUT TYPE=HIDDEN NAME="mode" VALUE="<%= mode %>">
81: </FORM>
82: <% End Sub %>
83: <%
84: '************************************************
85: '* GenerateTable
86: '*
87: Sub GenerateTable( rs )
```

13

continues

g 13.1. continued

```
88:     '** avoid accidental errors by checking to see
89:     '** if the Recordset is open first
90:     If IsOpen( rs ) Then
91:       %><TABLE BORDER=1><%
92:       ' set up column names
93:       For i = 0 to rs.fields.count - 1
94:         %><TD><B><%= rs(i).Name %></B></TD><%
95:       Next
96:       ' write each row
97:       While Not rs.EOF
98:         %><TR><%
99:         For i = 0 To rs.Fields.Count - 1
100:          v = rs(i)
101:          If isnull(v) Then v = " "
102:          %><TD VALIGN=TOP><%= v %></TD><%
103:        Next
104:        %></TR><%
105:        rs.MoveNext
106:      Wend
107:      %></TABLE><%
108:    End If
109: End Sub
110: %>
111: <%
112: '************************************************
113: '* THE MAIN CODE
114: '*
115: If mode = "" Then
116:   NameRangeForm thisPage, "Names"
117: ElseIf mode = "Names" Then
118:   On Error Resume Next
119:   Set cn = Server.CreateObject("ADODB.Connection")
120:   Set cm = Server.CreateObject("ADODB.Command")
121:   cn.Open "pubs", "sa", ""
122:   If Not CheckError( cn, "connecting to the database", "" ) Then
123:     query = _
124:       "SELECT fname, lname FROM employee" &_
125:       " WHERE lname >= ? AND lname <= ?"
126:     cm.ActiveConnection = cn
127:     cm.CommandText = query
128:     cm.Parameters.Refresh
129:     cm(0) = Request.Form("From")
130:     cm(1) = Request.Form("To")
131:     Set rs = cm.Execute
132:     If Not CheckError( cn, "executing the query", "" ) Then
133:       '** a header
134:       %><B>Employees between [<%
135:       %><%= Request.Form("From") %>] and [<%
136:       %><%= Request.Form("To") %>]</B><HR><%
137:       '** the data
138:       GenerateTable rs
139:     End If
140:   End If
```

```
141: End If
142: %>
143: </BODY>
144: </HTML>
```

The dynamic Web page in Listing 13.1 is primarily composed of a series of sub-routines and functions. Before you delve too deep into them, however, take note of the simple assignment in the first scripting section:

```
<% thisPage = "13tdw01.asp" %>
```

This assignment is used to store the name of this very ASP file into the global variable thisPage. Later, thisPage is used as the ACTION parameter of multiple forms. Using named constants, even ones you invent on your own, always improves the readability of your code. You can even save yourself the work of hunting down all the equivalent references, if and when you decide to change the name of your page.

You should also isolate commonly reused program sequences into their own sub-routines or functions. The previous chapters have made heavy use of both. The second scripting section, at line 7 in Listing 13.1, contains just such a beast, one you should cut-and-paste into your own dynamic pages or code libraries as is.

The IsOpen() function takes a single parameter—a Recordset—and determines whether it's currently open. It does this by making use of the known behavior regarding openness and errors. Properties such as BOF are invalid with the Recordset closed, and so report an error; the BOF property is used to test whether the Recordset is open. If an error is raised, it's ignored by the system because the On Error Resume Next statement is used at the beginning of the function.

> **TIP**
>
> Each sub-routine or function has its own error-controlling state. If you use the On Error Resume Next statement in one sub-routine, you haven't altered how errors are handled in the next one, so you need to repeat it for each sub-routine or function.

13

The second function, CheckError(), has three parameters: a Connection object, a message, and a mode string. The Connection object is used because ADO may report errors and warnings in the Errors collection. The value for the mode string tells the function what you want done next, if an error has truly occurred. The job of CheckError() is to not only determine whether an error was raised from the last method call, but also to generate a detailed message for the user and redirect the application to an appropriate recovery point.

It does this by first checking the built-in `Err` object. If an error has occurred, its `Number` property will be anything but zero. Because the `Number` property is the default item of the built-in `Err` object, you don't need to specify it directly, as shown here:

```
If Err <> 0 Then
```

If an error did happen, a message header is generated. Following the message, the `Connection` object is inspected for extended error information:

```
If cn = Nothing Then
    %>Error: <%= Err.Description %><%
ElseIf cn.Errors.Count = 0 Then
    %>Error: <%= Err.Description %><%
Else
    For i = 0 to cn.Errors.Count - 1
        If cn.Errors(i) < 0 then
            %>Error: <%= cn.Errors(i).Description %><%
        Else
            %>Warning: <%= cn.Errors(i).Description %><%
        End If
    Next
End If
```

You can use the `CheckError()` method even when a `Connection` object isn't available. The first check is to see whether the value `Nothing`, instead of an active connection, was actually passed to the function. In both cases, when there's no `Connection` object, or the `Errors` collection is empty, the `Description` property of the built-in `Err` object is used to generate a message.

> **TIP**
>
> When using Visual Basic, always separate tests for object non-existence from tests against object properties, even when both tests would naturally lead to the same code. Unlike C, C++, or Java, Basic doesn't support short-circuit Boolean evaluation. If you have two expressions combined with an `OR` statement, both will be evaluated, even if the first is good enough to pass the combined test. That means the object property will be accessed even when the object is non-existent, or `Nothing`.

If there are errors and warnings in the `Errors` collection, instead of using the description in the `Err` object, the `CheckError()` function generates separate messages for each item in the collection, distinguishing warnings from errors.

> **NOTE**
>
> If an error has truly occurred, and it was caused by accessing an ADO method or property, the first `Error` object in the ADO `Errors` collection will be equivalent to the built-in `Err` object.

13

The next two sub-routines, NameRangeForm() and GenerateTable(), should be more than familiar to you by now. The NameRangeForm() generates an input form with two input fields: one for beginning of the name range, and the other for the end. The GenerateTable() sub-routine takes a Recordset and generates the appropriate HTML for displaying the data in a table.

It's important to note, however, that the GenerateTable() sub-routine has been enhanced. It now makes use of the IsOpen() function from the top of the file to determine whether the Recordset passed to it is actually open. If it isn't, then no table is generated.

That leaves the only remaining scripting section—The Main Code—that controls the general flow of the page's execution.

When the page is executed for the first time, the NameRangeForm() sub-routine is called to generate the appropriate input form:

```
If mode = "" Then
  NameRangeForm thisPage, "Names"
```

After the Name Range form has been submitted back from the user, the actual processing begins. Before anything else, the On Error Resume Next statement is issued to turn off Visual Basic's automatic abort feature:

```
ElseIf mode = "Names" Then
  On Error Resume Next
```

Immediately following, both a Connection and Command object are created, and the Connection is opened to the Pubs sample database:

```
  Set cn = Server.CreateObject("ADODB.Connection")
  Set cm = Server.CreateObject("ADODB.Command")
  cn.Open "pubs", "sa", ""
```

Because opening a Connection is a method that can fail for many reasons, immediately after the call to the Open method, a check is made for any errors that might have happened:

```
If Not CheckError( cn, "connecting to the database" ) Then
```

If errors did happen, the CheckError() function generates the necessary messages. Only if the CheckError() function reports that no errors occurred at all, does the test succeed and the following code execute:

```
query = _
    "SELECT fname, lname FROM employee" &_
    " WHERE lname >= ? AND lname <= ?"
cm.ActiveConnection = cn
cm.CommandText = query
cm.Parameters.Refresh
cm(0) = Request.Form("From")
cm(1) = Request.Form("To")
```

13

The `Command` object is prepared for execution with the `ActiveConnection` and `CommandText` properties, as well as the two parameters `From` and `To`, filled in. Next, the `Command` is immediately executed, and the `CheckError()` function is used again to determine whether the execution succeeded:

```
Set rs = cm.Execute
If Not CheckError( cn, "executing the query" ) Then
```

Only when there are no errors is the `Recordset` used to generate a table of data. This is done with a call to `GenerateTable()`.

Provider Properties

Each ActiveX Data Object has a set of properties. The `Recordset` object has properties like `EOF` and `BOF` that tell you when the record position has reached either boundary. The `Command` object has properties such as `CommandText`, and the `Connection` object has ones like `ConnectionString`. Each of these properties and the others described in this book so far are all common, ordinary properties that you will make extensive use of when using ADO for data access.

Properties are both bits of information that tell you about the state of an object and a means of changing that state. Often, changes you make to properties control the behavior of methods called in the future. When you assign a value to the `CommandText` property, you're telling the `Command` object which query you want executed the next time you call the `Execute` method or use the `Command` object in a call to the `Recordset`'s `Open` method.

ActiveX Data Objects provide as built-in properties most of the information commonly used to control data access—properties that help you open connections, specify commands, and navigate through records. What they don't give you, however, are built-in properties that control rarely used features or features that aren't common among all data providers. Still, access to these advanced features is available. The goal of ActiveX Data Objects is to make common operations simple and advanced operations possible.

The most complicated, and probably the most misunderstood, feature of ADO is access to provider properties. ADO does give you a means of controlling all the features of a data provider, even ones that are rarely used or are uncommon across all providers. Each ADO object, be it `Recordset`, `Connection`, `Command`, `Field`, or `Parameter`, has a collection called `Properties` attached to it that contains `Property` objects, each one representing a particular provider-specified property.

The first time the `Properties` collection of a particular object is accessed, provider-specific property information is retrieved from the underlying data provider and is used to populate the collection. Each property has a name, value, data type, and attribute.

The complicated part about using provider properties is having to know in advance the name of the property and what it's used for, not to mention whether it's even available from the underlying data provider. Trying to access a property that doesn't exist is treated as an error and halts the execution of your application, unless you have taken measures like the ones covered in the earlier sections of this chapter.

Accessing Provider Properties

Because provider properties are stored in a collection, you can access them the same way you normally access fields from a Recordset and parameters from a Command. You can call the default indexing method of the Properties collection to retrieve any of the properties, as shown here:

```
<% Set prop1 = rs.Properties(0) %>
```

Of course, since not all providers supply properties in exactly the same way, in exactly the same order, being able to guess at a property's ordinal value is going to be tough. It's better to remember the name of the property you want to access and use it instead, as this example does:

```
<% Set prop1 = cn.Properties("Maximum Row Size") %>
```

Just as with the other ADO collections used in Visual Basic, you can skip right past the actual Property object and access the value directly:

```
<% value = cn.Properties("Maximum Row Size") %>
```

This method works because the Value property of the Property object is considered the default method.

Near the end of this chapter, you will find a complete list of property names common to ADO providers built using the OLE DB interface specification. Not all providers supply all the properties in the list, but if they do, they are named as shown and work as described.

The Properties Collection

The term *property* has a twofold meaning in this chapter. It's being used as a general term to describe a built-in member variable of an object, but also to describe a very specific ADO object. A built-in property is an item such as EOF, Count, or CommandText. Each ADO object has a unique and finite set of built-in properties. A Property object is much different. It's an object that reflects a provider-specific state or feature. These properties are normally more advanced than the common data-access properties designed to be built-in features of ADO. They usually allow control over features unique to the underlying data provider.

13

Because ADO doesn't know until runtime which data provider will be used to access data, it can't present these advanced features as built-in properties. Instead, they are gathered into a dynamic collection named Properties. Each ADO object has a Properties collection populated with provider-specific Property objects that are available when you first try to access them or when you explicitly call the Refresh method.

However, the distinction doesn't stop there. The Property objects have their share of properties too. They have built-in properties just as any other object does. The Properties collection even has its own methods because it, too, is an object; all objects have built-in properties and methods.

The following sections list the properties and methods of both the Properties collection and the Property object.

NOTE

> The following descriptions have a phrase on the right-hand side of the page, just after the section title. Each phrase tells you whether the corresponding property is read-write or read-only.

Properties of the Properties Collection

The following table lists the property of the Properties collection:

Property	Description
Count	The total number of properties in the collection

The Count Property

Contains a Long value   Read-Only

You can use the Count property to determine the total number of Property objects in the Properties collection. If the Properties collection isn't already populated with extended properties from the underlying data provider, calling this method causes ADO to request the appropriate properties.

Methods of the Properties Collection

The following table lists the methods of the Properties collection:

13

Method	Description
Item	Used to retrieve an individual property
Refresh	Forces the properties to be read from the provider

The Item Method

```
Set property = Properties.Item( index )
```

    index   A variant containing either the ordinal index of the Property object or its name

You can use the Item method to retrieve an individual Property object from the Properties collection. This is the default indexing method when using Visual Basic or VBScript. With these languages, it isn't necessary to call the Item method directly; instead, simply use the parentheses on the Properties collection itself:

```
Set property = Properties( index )
```

The Refresh Method

```
Properties.Refresh
```

You can use the Refresh method to populate the Properties collection with extended property information from the underlying data provider.

The Property Object

The Property object is used to get, and optionally change, the value of an extended provider-specific property. The standard properties that exist on the ADO objects aren't represented as separate Property objects within the Properties collection.

Properties of the Property Object

The following table lists the properties available directly from the Property object:

Property	Value
Attributes	The Property's behavior
Name	The name of the Property object
Type	The data type of the value
Value	The value of the Property object

13

The Attributes Property

Contains a PropertyAttributesEnum (Long) value   Read-Only

You can use the Attributes property to determine the behavior of the individual Property object. The value of the Attributes property may contain one or more of the following constants:

Attribute Constant	Value	Description
adPropNotSupported	0	The Property is in the list because it's one of the default OLE DB extended properties, but it isn't supported by the actual underlying data provider.
adPropRequired	1	The Property is required by the underlying data provider. The value associated with this property has a distinct effect on the behavior of the ADO object.
adPropOptional	2	The Property isn't required by the underlying data provider, but if set, it has an effect on the behavior of the ADO object.
adPropRead	512	The Property object's Value property can be read from.
adPropWrite	1024	The Property object's Value property can be assigned a value.

TIP   Use the AND operator in Visual Basic to determine which of many attributes are set on any given Property object. The expression (*object*.Properties(0) AND adPropWrite) determines whether the property can be written to.

The Name Property

Contains a String value   Read-Only

You can use the Name property to determine the name of the extended property. Then, use this name as a means to pick out this same Property object from the Properties collection by using the Item() method or the default indexing method, the parentheses operator.

The Type **Property**

Contains a DataTypeEnum (Long) value Read-Only

You can use the Type property to determine the type of data required when setting the Property object's value, or the type to expect when retrieving it. The most important types to distinguish are categories such as integers, floating point, string, date, and binary.

Type Constant	Value	Description
adBigInt	20	8-byte signed integer
adBinary	128	Binary encoded bytes
adBoolean	11	Boolean True or False
adBSTR	8	Unicode character string
adChar	129	ASCII character string
adCurrency	6	Numeric currency
adDate	7	System style date
adDBDate	133	Date encoded as YYYYMMDD
adDBTime	134	Time encoded as HHMMSS
adDBTimeStamp	135	Time stamp
adDecimal	14	Numeric value with fixed precision
adDouble	5	Double-precision floating point
adError	10	System error code
adGUID	72	Globally unique identifier
adIDispatch	9	COM/OLE Automation object
adInteger	3	4-byte signed integer
adIUnknown	13	COM/OLE object
adNumeric	131	Numeric value with fixed precision
adSingle	4	Single-precision floating point
adSmallInt	2	2-byte signed integer
adTinyInt	16	1-byte signed integer
adUnsignedBigInt	21	8-byte unsigned integer
adUnsignedInt	19	4-byte unsigned integer
adUnsignedSmallInt	18	2-byte unsigned integer
adUnsignedTinyInt	17	1-byte unsigned integer
adUserDefined	132	User-defined
adVariant	12	An OLE Automation Variant
adWChar	130	Unicode character string

The `Value` Property

Contains a `Variant` value   Read-Write

You can use the `Value` property to get and set the value of the `Property` object.

In some circumstances, setting the value of a `Property` object is allowed; other times, it isn't. For example, some extended properties can be set on the `Connection` object before it's open. Likewise, some `Recordset` properties can be set before it's open as well. The properties on the `Command` object can always be set; they reflect the properties of a `Recordset` before it's open.

NOTE

> Note, however, that many extended properties are informational only. They can't be assigned new values. Use the `Attributes` property to determine which `Property` objects can be read from or written to.

OLE DB Provider Properties

The following sections list the known set of provider properties used by data providers built for OLE DB 1.0. Providers can, however, have more properties than the ones defined here.

Some properties have tables describing unique values that can be assigned or obtained from the `Property` object. The constant value terms beginning with `DBPROPVAL` might not be available to you as a Visual Basic programmer. These terms are defined in the OLE DB SDK in a header file meant for C/C++. In addition to the named constants, the actual numeric values have been supplied so that you can use them directly or through constants you define in your application.

The actual name of each property precedes the description of its states and behaviors. You need to use these exact quoted strings when retrieving the properties from the `Properties` collection. If you're very familiar with the data provider you're using, and happen to know the exact order that these properties appear in the collection, you can use the ordinal value as an index instead of the string name. However, the order of the properties isn't guaranteed across different providers or even different versions.

Connection Initialization Properties

To have any effect, these properties must be set before the `Connection` object is opened.

The "Connect Timeout" Property

The Connect Timeout property contains a Long value describing the number of seconds to wait for a connection to be established before timing out.

The "Data Source" Property

The Data Source property holds a String containing the name of the datasource to connect to. This is equivalent to the datasource used as the first parameter to the Connection object's Open method, or the DATA SOURCE= property as used in the connection string.

The "Extended Properties" Property

The Extended Properties property holds a String containing a series of property names and values, separated by equals signs (=) and semicolons (;). This information is specified in the exact same form as a connection string. In fact, this same provider property is used by ADO to pass all unrecognized connection string values to the underlying provider. The default provider, MSDASQL, sends these values to ODBC.

The "Locale Identifier" Property

The Locale Identifier property holds a String containing the text version of an LCID— Locale ID—used by the operating system to determine localization behavior.

The "Location" Property

The Location property holds a String containing the server name that the datasource is located on.

The "Mode" Property

The Mode property holds a Long value containing a set of flags that determine the access mode the Connection uses against the datasource. The Mode property may contain zero or more of the following values combined:

Mode Constant	Value	Hex Value
DB_MODE_READ	1	&h1
DB_MODE_WRITE	2	&h2
DB_MODE_READWRITE	3	&h3
DB_MODE_SHARE_DENY_READ	4	&h4
DB_MODE_SHARE_DENY_WRITE	8	&h8
DB_MODE_SHARE_EXCLUSIVE	12	&hC
DB_MODE_SHARE_DENY_NONE	16	&h10

The "Password" Property

The Password property holds a String value containing the password that's used when connecting to the datasource.

The "Persist Security Info" Property

The Persist Security Info property contains a Boolean value that determines whether the data provider is allowed to store sensitive authentication information.

The "Prompt" Property

The Prompt property contains a Long value that determines whether the user will be prompted for initialization information when the Connection is opened. It can be one of the following values:

Prompt Constant	Value
DBPROMPT_PROMPT	1
DBPROMPT_COMPLETE	2
DBPROMPT_COMPLETEREQUIRED	3
DBPROMPT_NOPROMPT	4

The "User ID" Property

The User ID property holds a String value containing the user's account name that's known by the datasource.

The "Window Handle" Property

The Window Handle property holds a Long value containing the window handle (HWND) that's used as the parent window if the user needs to be prompted for initialization information when the Connection object is opened.

Connection Information Properties

Use these connection information properties after a Connection has been established. Most are informational only, so they can't be assigned new values.

The "Active Sessions" Property

The Active Sessions property holds a Long value containing the maximum number of Connection objects that can be opened to the same datasource at any one time.

The "Asynchable Abort" Property

The Asynchable Abort property contains a Boolean value that states whether a transaction can be aborted asynchronously.

The "Asynchable Commit" Property

The Asynchable Commit property contains a Boolean value that states whether a transaction can be committed asynchronously.

The "Pass By Ref Accessors" Property

The Pass By Ref Accessors property contains a Boolean value that states whether OLE DB accessors can be defined to pass data by reference. This only affects how ADO communicates with OLE DB.

The "Catalog Location" Property

The Catalog Location property contains a Long value determining where catalog names appear in relation to table names in fully qualified table names:

Catalog Location Constant	Value
DBPROPVAL_CL_START	1
DBPROPVAL_CL_END	2

The "Catalog Term" Property

The Catalog Term property holds a String value containing the name used by the datasource to describe a catalog.

The "Catalog Usage" Property

The Catalog Usage property contains a Long value describing where catalog names can be used. The property can contain zero or more of the following values added together:

Catalog Usage Constant	Value
DBPROPVAL_CU_DML_STATEMENTS	1
DBPROPVAL_CU_TABLE_DEFINITION	2
DBPROPVAL_CU_INDEX_DEFINITION	4
DBPROPVAL_CU_PRIVILEGE_DEFINITION	8

The "Column Definition" Property

The Column Definition property contains a Long value that describes the terms that can be used when defining columns. The property may contain zero or the following value:

Definition Constant	Value
DBPROPVAL_CD_NOTNULL	1

The "Data Source Name" Property

The Data Source Name property holds a String value containing the name of the datasource that it's connected to.

The "Read-Only Data Source" Property

The Read-Only Data Source property contains a Boolean value determining whether the datasource is read-only.

The "DBMS Name" Property

The DBMS Name property holds a String value containing the name of the database management system that controls the datasource.

The "DBMS Version" Property

The DBMS Version property holds a String value containing the version of the database management system that controls the datasource.

The "Data Source Object Threading Model" Property

The Data Source Object Threading Model property contains a Long value that describes the threading model that's used by the data provider. It can be one of the following values:

Thread Model Constant	Value
DBPROPVAL_RT_FREE	1
DBPROPVAL_RT_APARTMENT	2
DBPROPVAL_RT_SINGLE	4

The "GROUP BY Support" Property

The GROUP BY Support property contains a Long value that describes the support for the GROUP BY clause available from the data provider. It can be zero or more of the following values added together:

Constant	Value
DBPROPVAL_GB_EQUALS_SELECT	1
DBPROPVAL_GB_CONTAINS_SELECT	2
DBPROPVAL_NO_RELATION	4

The "Heterogenous Table Support" Property

The Heterogenous Table Support property contains a Long value that describes the ability of the provider to join tables from different sources in the same query. It may be zero or more of the following values added together:

Constant	Value
DBPROPVAL_HT_DIFFERENT_CATALOGS	1
DBPROPVAL_HT_DIFFERENT_PROVIDERS	2

The "Identifier Case Sensitivity" Property

The Identifier Case Sensitivity property holds a Long value that describes how identifiers are recognized and stored by the data provider. It can be one of the following values:

Constant	Value
DBPROPVAL_IC_UPPER	1
DBPROPVAL_IC_LOWER	2
DBPROPVAL_IC_SENSITIVE	4
DBPROPVAL_IC_MIXED	8

The "Maximum Index Size" Property

The Maximum Index Size property holds a Long value containing the maximum number of bytes that can be used as the key of an index.

The "Maximum Row Size" Property

The Maximum Row Size property holds a Long value containing the maximum number of bytes that can be used for the sum of the length of all columns of an individual record.

13

The "Maximum Row Size Includes BLOB" Property

The Maximum Row Size Includes BLOB property contains a Boolean value that describes whether the maximum row size includes the length of columns designed to hold binary large objects (BLOBs). These are often stored outside the record.

The "Maximum Tables in SELECT" Property

The Maximum Tables in SELECT property contains a Long value that describes the maximum number of tables that can be referenced in a single SQL SELECT statement.

The "Multiple Parameter Sets" Property

The Multiple Parameter Sets property contains a Boolean value that describes whether the data provider permits more than one set of parameters at a time.

The "Multiple Results" Property

The Multiple Results property contains a Boolean value that describes whether the data provider supports returning multiple independent Recordsets from compound queries.

The "Multiple Storage Objects" Property

The Multiple Storage Objects property contains a Boolean value that describes whether the data provider supports having more than one open storage object at a time.

The "Multi-Table Update" Property

The Multi-Table Update property contains a Boolean value that describes whether the data provider can update records that are the result of a multitable query.

The "NULL Collation Order" Property

The NULL Collation Order property contains a Long value that describes where records with NULL value columns are placed in the ordered output. The columns in question must be ones used in the SQL ORDER BY clause. The property can contain one of the following values:

Constant	Value
DBPROPVAL_NC_END	1
DBPROPVAL_NC_HIGH	2
DBPROPVAL_NC_LOW	4
DBPROPVAL_NC_START	8

The "NULL Concatenation Behavior" **Property**

The NULL Concatenation Behavior property contains a Long value that describes what happens when NULL value fields are appended to non-null fields for computed columns or expressions used in queries. It can contain one of the following values:

Constant	Value
DBPROPVAL_CB_NULL	1
DBPROPVAL_CB_NOTNULL	2

The "OLE DB Version" **Property**

The OLE DB Version property holds a String containing the version of the OLE DB provider.

The "OLE Object Support" **Property**

The OLE Object Support property contains a Long value that describes the type of support the data provider has for storing objects in columns. It can be zero or more of the following values added together:

Constant	Value
DBPROPVAL_OO_BLOB	1
DBPROPVAL_STRUCTUREDSTORAGE	2
DBPROPVAL_OO_PERSIST	4

The "ORDER BY Columns in Select List" **Property**

The ORDER BY Columns in Select List property contains a Boolean value that describes whether columns used in the SQL ORDER BY clause must also appear in the select list.

The "Output Parameter Availability" **Property**

The Output Parameter Availability property contains a Long value that describes when output parameters are available after a call to Execute. It can contain zero or more of the following values:

Constant	Value
DBPROPVAL_OA_NOTSUPPORTED	1
DBPROPVAL_OA_ATEXECUTE	2
DBPROPVAL_OA_ATROWRELEASE	4

13

The "Persistent ID Type" Property

The Persistent ID Type property contains a Long value that describes the type of DBIDs used to represent unique tables, indexes, and columns. It can have zero or more of the following values:

Constant	Value
DBPROPVAL_PT_GUID_NAME	1
DBPROPVAL_PT_GUID_PROPID	2
DBPROPVAL_PT_NAME	4
DBPROPVAL_PT_GUID	8

The "Prepare Abort Behavior" Property

The Prepare Abort Behavior property contains a Long value that describes the effect on prepared commands when the current transaction is aborted, whether the command is still prepared or not. The property can be one of the following values:

Constant	Value
DBPROPVAL_CB_DELETE	1
DBPROPVAL_CB_PRESERVE	2

The "Prepare Commit Behavior" Property

The Prepare Commit Behavior property contains a Long value that describes the effect on prepared commands when the current transaction is committed, whether the command is still prepared or not. The property can be one of the following values:

Constant	Value
DBPROPVAL_CB_DELETE	1
DBPROPVAL_CB_PRESERVE	2

The "Procedure Term" Property

The Procedure Term property holds a String value containing the term used by the data provider to describe stored procedures.

The "Provider Name" Property

The Provider Name property holds a String value containing the name of the underlying data provider. For ADO 1.0, it's MSDASQL.DLL.

The "Provider Version" **Property**

The Provider Version property holds a String value containing the version number of the underlying data provider.

The "Quoted Identifier Sensitivity" **Property**

The Quoted Identifier Sensitivity property contains a Long value that describes how the data provider interprets the case sensitivity of quoted identifiers used in query strings. It can be one of the following values:

Constant	Value
DBPROPVAL_IC_UPPER	1
DBPROPVAL_IC_LOWER	2
DBPROPVAL_IC_SENSITIVE	4
DBPROPVAL_IC_MIXED	8

The "Rowset Conversions on Command" **Property**

The Rowset Conversions on Command property contains a Boolean value that describes whether data-type conversion capabilities can be determined in the Command object, before the query is issued and a Recordset is opened.

The "Schema Term" **Property**

The Schema Term property holds a String value containing the term used by the data provider to describe schema names.

The "Schema Usage" **Property**

The Schema Usage property contains a Long value that describes exactly where schema names may be used. It can be zero or more of the following added together:

Constant	Value
DBPROPVAL_SU_DML_STATEMENTS	1
DBPROPVAL_SU_TABLE_DEFINITION	2
DBPROPVAL_SU_INDEX_DEFINITION	4
DBPROPVAL_SU_PRIVILEGE_DEFINITION	8

The "SQL Support" Property

The SQL Support property contains a Long value that describes the level of support of the SQL language. It can contain one item from the first group, zero or more items from the second group, and zero or one item from the last group, all added together:

Constant	Value	Hex Value
Group 1		
DBPROPVAL_SQL_NONE	0	&h0
DBPROPVAL_SQL_ODBC_MINIMUM	1	&h1
DBPROPVAL_SQL_ODBC_CORE	2	&h2
DBPROPVAL_SQL_ODBC_EXTENDED	4	&h4
Group 2		
DBPROPVAL_SQL_ESCAPECLAUSES	256	&h100
DBPROPVAL_SQL_ANSI89_IEF	8	&h8
Group 3		
DBPROPVAL_SQL_ANSI92_ENTRY	16	&h10
DBPROPVAL_SQL_FIPS_TRANSITIONAL	32	&h20
DBPROPVAL_SQL_ANSI92_INTERMEDIATE	64	&h40
DBPROPVAL_SQL_ANSI92_FULL	128	&h80

The "Structured Storage" Property

The Structured Storage property contains a Long value that describes the COM interfaces available on storage objects when retrieved from the database. These interfaces are available to ADO as a means to deliver large-value fields to you through the GetChunk() and AppendChunk() methods. The property can be zero of more of the following values added together:

Constant	Value
DBPROPVAL_SS_ISEQUENTIALSTREAM	1
DBPROPVAL_SS_ISTREAM	2
DBPROPVAL_SS_ISTORAGE	4
DBPROPVAL_SS_ILOCKBYTES	8

The "Subquery Support" Property

The Subquery Support property contains a Long value that describes the clauses in SQL queries that support subqueries. It can be zero or more of the following values:

Constant	Value	Hex Value
DBPROPVAL_SQ_CORRELATEDSUBQUERIES	1	&h1
DBPROPVAL_SQ_COMPARISON	2	&h2
DBPROPVAL_SQ_EXISTS	4	&h4
DBPROPVAL_SQ_IN	8	&h8
DBPROPVAL_SQ_QUANTIFIED	16	&h10

The "Transaction DDL" Property

The Transaction DDL property contains a Long value that describes explicitly which data-definition statements are supported during transactions. It can be one or more of the following values added together:

Constant	Value
DBPROPVAL_TC_NONE	0
DBPROPVAL_TC_DML	1
DBPROPVAL_TC_DDL_COMMIT	2
DBPROPVAL_TC_DDL_IGNORE	4
DBPROPVAL_TC_ALL	8

The "Isolation Levels" Property

The Isolation Levels property contains a Long value that describes the supported transaction isolation levels. It can be zero or more of the following values added together:

Constant	Value	Hex Value
DBPROPVAL_TI_CHAOS	16	&h10
DBPROPVAL_TI_READUNCOMMITTED	256	&h100
DBPROPVAL_TI_BROWSE	256	&h100
DBPROPVAL_TI_CURSORSTABILITY	4096	&h1000
DBPROPVAL_TI_READCOMMITTED	4096	&h1000
DBPROPVAL_TI_REPEATABLEREAD	65536	&h10000
DBPROPVAL_TI_SERIALIZABLE	65536	&h10000
DBPROPVAL_TI_ISOLATED	1048576	&h100000

The "Isolation Retention" Property

The Isolation Retention property contains a Long value that describes the types of retained transactions available from the provider. It can be zero or more of the following values added together. Constants that include a DC in their names refer to actions that may potentially break isolation between transactions; those with a NO refer to actions that always break isolation between transactions. All others refer to actions that *always* preserve isolation between transactions.

Constant	Value	Hex Value
DBPROPVAL_TR_COMMIT_DC	1	&h1
DBPROPVAL_TR_COMMIT	2	&h2
DBPROPVAL_TR_COMMIT_NO	4	&h4
DBPROPVAL_TR_ABORT_DC	8	&h8
DBPROPVAL_TR_ABORT	16	&h10
DBPROPVAL_TR_ABORT_NO	32	&h20
DBPROPVAL_TR_DONTCARE	64	&h40
DBPROPVAL_TR_BOTH	128	&h80
DBPROPVAL_TR_NONE	256	&h100
DBPROPVAL_TR_OPTIMISTIC	512	&h200

The "Table Term" Property

The Table Term property holds a String containing the term used to describe tables.

The "User Name" Property

The User Name property holds a String containing the name of the user, or user ID, used to make the connection to the datasource.

Command and Recordset Properties

The following properties appear on both the Command and Recordset objects. Many of them can be assigned values before the Recordset is opened, but none can be assigned afterward.

Interface Properties

IAccessor
IColumnsInfo
IColumnsRowset
IConnectionPointContainer
IConvertType
IRowset

13

```
IRowsetChange
IRowsetIdentity
IRowsetInfo
IRowsetResynch
IRowsetUpdate
ISupportErrorInfo
```

Each of the previous properties contains a `Boolean` value that determines whether the particular OLE DB interface is available for use by the `Recordset` object.

The `"Preserve on Abort"` Property

The `Preserve on Abort` property contains a `Boolean` value that determines whether the `Recordset` remains open after the governing transaction has been aborted.

The `"Blocking Storage Objects"` Property

The `Blocking Storage Objects` property contains a `Boolean` value that determines whether all other OLE DB methods fail, except for explicit methods that deal with large storage objects when a storage object has been accessed and until it's released. ADO may use storage objects in its implementation of the `GetChunck()` and `AppendChunk()` methods. ADO guards against method calls from failing for you; however, the `GetChunk()` or `AppendChunk()` calling sequence may be reset.

The `"Bookmarkable"` Property

The `Bookmarkable` property contains a `Boolean` value that determines whether the `Recordset` has bookmarks available.

The `"Skip Deleted Bookmarks"` Property

The `Skip Deleted Bookmarks` property contains a `Boolean` value that determines whether the `Recordset` will advance to the next valid record when it's positioned on a bookmark of a deleted record.

The `"Bookmark Type"` Property

The `Bookmark Type` property contains a `Long` value that determines the type of bookmarks supported by the `Recordset`. It can be one of the following values:

Constant	Value
DBPROPVAL_BMK_NUMERIC	1
DBPROPVAL_BMK_KEY	2

The "Fetch Backwards" Property

The Fetch Backwards property contains a Boolean value that determines whether the Recordset has the ability to fetch records in reverse order.

In the ADO Recordset, reading backward is done by setting the CacheSize to a negative number.

The "Hold Rows" Property

The Hold Rows property contains a Boolean value that determines whether the current cache of records can be held while another separate cache is read from the datasource; otherwise, the original cache must be lost. Holding rows is a necessity for the ADO Clone method to work properly.

The "Scroll Backwards" Property

The Scroll Backwards property contains a Boolean value that determines whether the Recordset can be moved to records previously read. This property is necessary for the MovePrevious method to work properly or for the Move method to have a negative offset.

The "Change Inserted Rows" Property

The Change Inserted Rows property contains a Boolean value that determines whether newly inserted rows can be modified.

The "Column Privileges" Property

The Column Privileges property contains a Boolean value that determines whether access privileges are dealt with per column.

The "Command Time Out" Property

The Command Time Out property contains a Long value that determines the maximum number of seconds the execution can take before timing out. A value of zero indicates infinite time.

The "Preserve on Commit" Property

The Preserve on Commit property contains a Boolean value that determines whether the Recordset remains open after the governing transaction has been committed.

13

The "Delay Storage Object Updates" Property

The Delay Storage Object Updates property contains a Boolean value that determines whether storage objects are held until batch-updating Recordsets are explicitly updated by calling UpdateBatch.

The "Immobile Rows" Property

The Immobile Rows property contains a Boolean value that determines whether the order of the records within the Recordset remains fixed, even if records are inserted or updated.

The "Literal Bookmarks" Property

The Literal Bookmarks property contains a Boolean value that determines whether bookmarks can be compared literally against one another.

The "Literal Row Identity" Property

The Literal Row Identity property contains a Boolean value that describes whether unique rows fetched more than once by a single Recordset or multiple clones have literal references to the exact same record.

The "Maximum Open Rows" Property

The Maximum Open Rows property contains a Long value that describes the maximum number of records that can be cached at any one time. A value of zero indicates no limit.

The "Maximum Pending Rows" Property

The Maximum Pending Rows property contains a Long value that describes the maximum number of records that can have pending changes at the same time. A value of zero indicates no limit.

The "Maximum Rows" Property

The Maximum Rows property contains a Long value that describes the maximum number of records that can exist in a Recordset. A value of zero indicates no limit.

The "Others' Inserts Visible" Property

The Others' Inserts Visible property contains a Boolean value the determines whether the Recordset can see inserts made by other Recordsets the next time the cache is re-fetched.

13

The "Others' Changes Visible" Property

The Others' Changes Visible property contains a Boolean value the determines whether the Recordset can see updates or deletions made by other Recordsets the next time the cache is re-fetched.

The "Own Inserts Visible" Property

The Own Inserts Visible property contains a Boolean value that determines whether the Recordset can see its own inserts the next time the cache is re-fetched.

The "Own Changes Visible" Property

The Own Changes Visible property contains a Boolean value that determines whether the Recordset can see its own updates and deletions the next time the cache is re-fetched.

The "Remove Deleted Rows" Property

The Remove Deleted Rows property contains a Boolean value that determines whether deleted records are removed from the cache the next time the cache is re-fetched.

The "Report Multiple Changes" Property

The Report Multiple Changes property contains a Boolean value that describes whether the data provider can determine if multiple rows have been affected by the same update or deletion.

The "Return Pending Inserts" Property

The Return Pending Inserts property contains a Boolean value that describes whether the provider is capable of returning records that are pending insertion when the cache is re-fetched.

The "Row Privileges" Property

The Row Privileges property contains a Boolean value that describes whether access privileges are granted on a per row basis.

The "Row Threading Model" Property

The Row Threading Model property contains a Long value that determines the threading model used by the Recordset when calling into the provider. It can be one of the following values:

13

Constant	Value
DBPROPVAL_RT_FREETHREAD	1
DBPROPVAL_RT_APTMTTHREAD	2
DBPROPVAL_RT_SINGLETHREAD	4

The "Server Cursor" Property

The Server Cursor property contains a Boolean value that determines whether the underlying cursor is restricted to existing only on the server.

The "Strong Row Identity" Property

The Strong Row Identity property contains a Boolean value that determines whether the newly inserted record is guaranteed to be literally the same record in memory when the cache is re-fetched.

The "Updatability" Property

The Updatability property contains a Long value that determines the type of modifications supported by the Recordset. The property can contain zero or more of the following values:

Constant	Value
DBPROPVAL_UP_CHANGE	1
DBPROPVAL_UP_DELETE	2
DBPROPVAL_UP_INSERT	4

Field Properties

The "BASECATALOGNAME" Property

The BASECATALOGNAME property holds a String value containing the name of the catalog this field originates from.

The "BASECOLUMNNAME" Property

The BASECOLUMNNAME property holds a String value containing the name of the column this field originates from.

13

The "BASESCHEMANAME" Property

The BASESCHEMANAME property holds a String value containing the name of the schema this field originates from.

The "BASETABLENAME" Property

The BASETABLENAME property holds a String value containing the name of the table this field originates from.

The "CLSID" Property

The CLSID property holds a String value containing the GUID associated with this field's column.

The "DATETIMEPRECISION" Property

The DATETIMEPRECISION property holds a Long value describing the number of digits in the fractional seconds portion of the field value.

The "DEFAULTVALUE" Property

The DEFAULTVALUE property holds a Variant value containing the field's default value.

The "DOMAINCATALOG" Property

The DOMAINCATALOG property holds a String value containing the catalog name of the domain associated with this field.

The "DOMAINSCHEMA" Property

The DOMAINSCHEMA property holds a String value containing the schema name of the domain associated with this field.

The "DOMAINNAME" Property

The DOMAINNAME property holds a String value containing the name of the domain associated with this field.

The "HASDEFAULT" Property

The HASDEFAULT property holds a Boolean value that determines whether the field has a default value.

The "ISAUTOINCREMENT" Property

The ISAUTOINCREMENT property holds a Boolean value that describes whether the field is based on an auto-incrementing column.

The "ISCASESENSITIVE" Property

The ISCASESENSITIVE property holds a Boolean value that describes whether the field's value must be matched in a case-sensitive fashion.

The "ISSEARCHABLE" Property

The ISSEARCHABLE property holds a Long value that describes how the field can be used as a portion of a query constraint, such as a SQL WHERE clause. It can contain one of the following values:

Constant	Value
DB_UNSEARCHABLE	1
DB_LIKE_ONLY	2
DB_EXCEPT_LIKE	3
DB_SEARCHABLE	4

The "ISUNIQUE" Property

The ISUNIQUE property holds a Boolean value that describes whether the column associated with the field must contain unique values per row.

The "OCTETLENGTH" Property

The OCTETLENGTH property holds a Long value that describes the maximum number of 8-bit bytes that can be used to hold the value of this field.

Taking Advantage of Provider Properties

Provider properties can be used in your application as easily as normal built-in properties can. For the most part, they have the same restrictions. You can assign values to some of them; with others, you can only read the current state. The only real difference is that you have to use the Properties collection to get at them. To do so, you must know, and have available, a string containing the property's name.

The names of provider properties aren't supplied by constants in the ADO code library or in the file ADOVBS.INC. Currently, there are no equivalents to symbols like adOpenKeyset

13

ckOptimistic for provider properties, but that doesn't mean you have to go without.
means you will have to define them yourself.

head of your dynamic Web page, application, or in a separate module if you are using
Visual Basic proper, you can assign the actual property names to variables you will use later,
as shown here:

```
<% adPropMode = "Mode" %>
```

TIP   It's more convenient to write an application using constant terms
instead of embedding strings directly into the code. You're less likely to
have errors due to typing mistakes, especially if you have to use the
same name more than once.

Inside ADO

Provider properties aren't just some extra mechanism built into ADO to reveal provider-
specific capabilities. They are truly integrated into how ADO works. Many of the standard
ADO options and constant values are actually provider properties in disguise. Both ADO
lock types and cursor types are implemented through the internal use of provider properties.

ADO Cursor Types

The following table shows the names of the provider properties that ADO uses when the
particular cursor type constant is used in the Open or Execute methods:

Cursor Type Constant	Provider Properties	Value
adOpenForwardOnly	None	
adOpenKeyset	Other's Changes Visible	True
	Bookmarkable	True
	Scroll Backwards	True
	Hold Rows	True
	IRowsetResynch	True
	Own Inserts Visible	True
	Own Changes Visible	True
	Remove Deleted Rows	True
adOpenDynamic	Other's Changes Visible	True
	Scroll Backwards	True
	Remove Deleted Rows	True

Cursor Type Constant	Provider Properties	Value
adOpenStatic	Own Inserts Visible	True
	Own Changes Visible	True
	Bookmarkable	True
	Scroll Backwards	True
	Hold Rows	True
	IRowsetResynch	True

ADO Lock Types

The following table lists the names of the provider properties that ADO uses when a particular lock type constant is used in Open or Execute methods:

Lock Type Constant	Provider Properties	Value
adLockReadOnly	None	
adLockPessimistic	IRowsetChange	True
	Updatability	7
adLockOptimistic	IRowsetChange	True
	Updatability	7
adLockBatchOptimistic	IRowsetChange	True
	IRowsetUpdate	True
	Updatability	7

Summary

This chapter has covered both the ADO Errors and Properties collections, along with their respective Error and Property objects. It has shown you how to take control of your dynamic Web application when error conditions arise by turning off Visual Basic's automatic abort behavior and handling these conditions yourself. It has also shown you how to retrieve richly detailed error information from the Connection object's Errors collection and how to distinguish errors from warnings.

In addition, this chapter has given you an inside scoop on how ADO interacts with the underlying data provider through assigning provider properties. These properties are available to you through the Properties collection and can be used to override how ADO and the provider work together to deliver data.

Q&A

Q Will the `Errors` collection ever contain error codes generated by failures from other sources?

A No. The `Errors` collection contains just errors and warnings generated by the data provider. Only calls to ADO methods could possibly cause the `Errors` collection to be populated.

Q Will warnings ever occur when there are no errors?

A Yes. Remember, however, the `Errors` collection isn't cleared when a warning occurs on its own; the warning is merely added to the list. The only way to detect that a warning has been issued is to monitor the collection's `Count` property. The easiest way to do this is to clear the collection before making an ADO method call. If the built-in `Err` object has a value of zero, and the `Count` property is greater than zero, then you know there are warnings in the collection.

Q If the listed error codes won't ever appear in the `Errors` collection, where can I find a list of ones that will?

A A complete list of all the possible errors isn't possible. The errors will, however, most likely be either common OLE DB error codes or ODBC ones.

Q If I have two `Recordsets` open and they both use the same `Connection` object, how do I distinguish between errors generated from one to the other?

A There's no direct way to determine the causal relationship, except that because your code is linear, the errors in the collection always represent those generated by the last method call, regardless of which object the call was made on.

One caveat, however, is that if the `Recordsets` are actually executing in parallel (separate simultaneous page hits) and through the built-in `Session` object still share the same `Connection`, the values in the `Errors` collection will seem different. The `Connection` object actually maintains a separate `Errors` collection for each thread of execution. In this specific case, each `Recordset` would have its own list of errors.

Q Why do you have to use the `On Error Resume Next` statement in each sub-routine?

A Each sub-routine represents its own "scope" of error context. You can turn off errors in one sub-routine, as you did with `IsOpen()` in the example, and still leave Visual Basic's normal error abort mechanism for sub-routines such as `NameRangeForm()`.

Q In what common situation would I need to use provider properties?

A No common situation would require the use of provider properties. ADO's standard interface should cover all common access situations. Provider properties

13

should be used to control the behavior of unique database features that aren't covered by the ADO interfaces.

You will find, however, that many of the provider properties listed directly correspond to ADO features. However, ADO doesn't guarantee that these properties are always available.

Quiz

1. Name two different places to find error information when using ADO in Visual Basic Script.

2. In addition to errors, the ADO Errors collection may contain what?

3. Errors generated by the underlying data provider appear in the Errors collection. True or False?

4. Errors generated by ADO itself appear in the Errors collection. True or False?

5. What's the statement you must use to turn off Visual Basic's automatic error abort behavior?

6. How do you distinguish between errors and warnings in the ADO Errors collection?

7. Each time a new warning is generated, the Errors collection is automatically cleared and filled with the new information. True or False?

8. The best way to access provider properties in the Properties collection is by ordinal number or by name?

9. Named constants for each common provider property are declared in the ADOVBS.INC include file. True or False?

10. Some properties in the Properties collection can be used to control database access features not normally available using standard ADO methods and properties. True or False?

Exercises

1. Write your own version of the CheckError() sub-routine that displays your own messages instead of the ones supplied in the Error objects.

2. Take a sample ASP file from an earlier chapter and upgrade it with error checking.

3. Write a dynamic Web page that connects to a database and displays all the current provider properties for the Connection, Command, Recordset, and Field objects.

4. Write an interactive dynamic Web page that extends Exercise 4 by allowing the user to enter the query and connection information.

5. Write a dynamic Web page that re-tries a database query if the first attempt fails.

13

Day 14

Dynamic Web Application: The Meeting Place

by Matt Warren

This entire chapter is devoted to examining a complete dynamic Web application. It's the culmination of this week's study of dynamic Web pages using Microsoft's Active Server Pages and ActiveX Data Objects (ADO).

After reading this chapter, you will be able to do the following:

☐ Identify uses of ADO `Recordset`, `Command`, and `Connection` objects to perform database searches.

☐ List instances of the ADO `Command` object being used to perform `Parameter`-based queries and updates.

☐ Identify uses of ADO-enhanced error detection and VBScript-style error management.

☐ Cite examples of HTML forms being used to not only collect data, but also to provide user-controlled navigation through the application.

☐ Show where HTML tables are being used to format data input and output.

The Meeting Place

The fictional Web site "The Meeting Place" is an example of a medium-scale database application designed to work across the Internet. Its primary goal is to let visitors sign up to reserve conference space in one of many locations.

The application has been broken up into five distinct ASP files, some generating multiple Web pages, depending on the choices made by visitors.

The Main Menu

The first ASP file functions as the main menu and the starting page for people visiting the site. Listing 14.1 shows the HTML and VBScript code that work together to present the menu.

Listing 14.1. The main menu.

```
 1: <HTML>
 2: <% thisPage = "14TWD01.asp" %>
 3: <HEAD>
 4: <TITLE>Example 14.1: Main Menu</TITLE>
 5: </HEAD>

 6: <CENTER>
 7: <H1>The Meeting Place</H1>
 8: <H3>The Premier Conference Room Reservation System</H3>

 9: <% if Session("EventID") > "" then %>
10: <BR>
11: <B>Group  </B><%= Session("GroupName") %>
12:    
13: <B>Event  </B><%= Session("EventName") %>
14: <% end if %>

15: <HR>

16: <TABLE BORDER=0>
```

14

```
17: <TR><TD>
18: <A HREF="14TWD02.asp">Check In</A>
19: </TD></TR>

20: <% if Session("EventID") > "" then %>
21: <TR><TD>
22: <A HREF="14TWD05.asp">Reserve Meeting Space</A>
23: </TD></TR>
24: <TR><TD>
25: <A HREF="14TWD03.asp">View Reservations</A>
26: </TD></TR>
27: <% end if %>

28: </TABLE>

29: <HR>
30: <BR>The Meeting Place is a product of MegaCorp Northwest
31: <BR>1000 Plaza Center
32: <BR>Seattle, WA
33: <BR>
34: <BR>
35: <BR>
36: <BR>For comments regarding this Web site and its content, please contact
37: <BR>
38: <BR><A HREF="mailto:wizard@tmp.com">wizard@tmp.com</A>
39: </CENTER>

40: </HTML>
```

The main menu Web page can take on two different appearances, depending on the information available when the page is generated. The first time a user visits the page, the single item "Check In" is displayed in the center. It's a reference to the second Web page, shown in Listing 14.2. Clicking on this link starts the check-in process, requiring the visitor to designate his or her organization (group) and the account (event).

Figure 14.1 shows the Web page users see the first time they visit the site.

After the visitor has successfully checked in, returning to the first Web page reveals the slightly altered page shown in Figure 14.2.

Checking In

Checking in is by no means a simple process. It might look straightforward to the visitor, but behind the scenes all sorts of intricate database interactions are happening.

The goal of checking in is to give visitors an opportunity to supply both the group and event information for their reservations. Visitors must supply both pieces of information before they can make any room reservations.

14

Figure 14.1.

The main menu of the Meeting Place.

Figure 14.2.

After checking in.

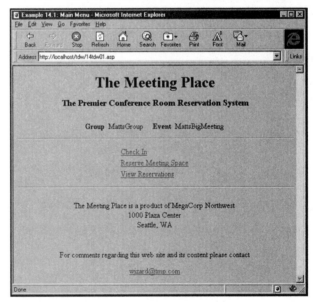

Listing 14.2. The checking-in process.

```
1: <HTML>
2: <% thisPage = "14TWD02.asp" %>
3: <!-- #include file="adovbs.inc" -->
4: <!-- #include file="14TWD04.asp" -->
```

14

```
 5: <%
 6: SUB Header()
 7:     %>
 8:     <HEAD>
 9:     <TITLE>Example 14.2: Check In (Groups & Events)</TITLE>
10:     </HEAD>
11:     <CENTER>
12:     <A HREF="14TWD01.asp">
13:     <H1>The Meeting Place</H1>
14:     </A>
15:     <H3>The Premier Conference Room Reservation System</H3>
16:     <%
17:     if Request.Form("mode") = "" then
18:         Session("GroupID") = ""
19:         Session("GroupName") = ""
20:         Session("EventID") = ""
21:         Session("EventName") = ""
22:     end if
23:     if Session("EventID") > "" then
24:         %>
25:         <BR>
26:         <B>Group  </B><%= Session("GroupName") %>
27:            
28:         <B>Event  </B><%= Session("EventName") %>
29:         <%
30:     end if
31:
32:     %>
33:     <HR>
34:     </CENTER>
35:     <%
36: END SUB

37: SUB ChooseGroupForm( action, mode )
38:     groups = GetItemList( "GroupName", "Groups", "DSN=TMP" )
39:     FormBegin action
40:     %>Select the name of the group or organization that <%
41:     %>you are associated with <%
42:     %>or leave it blank to request a new group name.<%
43:     %><BR><BR><%
44:     %><B>Group  </B><%
45:     FormSelect "GroupName", 40, "", groups
46:     %><BR><BR><%
47:     FormSubmit "Continue", "Continue"
48:     FormEnd mode
49: END SUB

50: SUB CreateGroupForm( action, mode )
51:     FormBegin action
52:     %><H4>Enter Group Information</H4><%
53:     %>
54:     <TABLE BORDER=0>
55:     <TR>
56:     <TD><B>Group Name</B></TD>
57:     <TD><% FormInput "GroupName", 40, "" %></TD>
58:     </TR>
```

14

continues

Listing 14.2. continued

```
59:    <TR><TD> </TD></TR>
60:    <TR><TD><B>Contact Info</B></TD></TR>
61:    <TR><TD><HR></TD><TD><HR></TD></TR>
62:
63:    <TR>
64:    <TD><B>First Name</B></TD>
65:    <TD><% FormInput "FirstName", 20, "" %></TD>
66:    </TR>
67:    <TR>
68:    <TD><B>Last Name</B></TD>
69:    <TD><% FormInput "LastName", 20, "" %></TD>
70:    </TR>
71:    <TR>
72:    <TD><B>Address</B></TD>
73:    <TD><% FormInput "Address1", 40, "" %></TD>
74:    </TR>
75:    <TR>
76:    <TD></TD>
77:    <TD><% FormInput "Address2", 40, "" %></TD>
78:    </TR>
79:    <TR>
80:    <TD><B>City</B></TD>
81:    <TD><% FormInput "City", 20, "" %></TD>
82:    </TR>
83:    <TR>
84:    <TD><B>State</B></TD>
85:    <TD><% FormInput "State", 4, "" %></TD>
86:    </TR>
87:
88:    <TR>
89:    <TD><B>Zip</B></TD>
90:    <TD><% FormInput "Zip", 10, "" %></TD>
91:    </TR>
92:    <TR>
93:    <TD><B>Email</B></TD>
94:    <TD><% FormInput "Email", 40, "" %></TD>
95:    </TR>
96:    </TABLE>
97:    <BR><BR>
98:    <%
99:    FormSubmit "Continue", "Continue"
100:   FormEnd mode
101: END SUB

102: SUB FindGroupID()
103:    ON ERROR RESUME NEXT
104:    IF Session("GroupID") = "" THEN
105:        SET cn = Server.CreateObject("ADODB.Connection")
106:        cn.Open "TMP"
107:        IF CheckError( cn, "" ) THEN EXIT SUB
108:        '** Find the group that was just created
109:        SET rs = cn.Execute( _
```

```
110:                    "SELECT * FROM Groups WHERE GroupName = '" &_
111:                        Request.Form("GroupName") & "'" _
112:                        )
113:            IF CheckError( cn, "" ) THEN EXIT SUB
114:            IF NOT rs.EOF THEN
115:                Session("GroupID") = rs("GroupID")
116:                Session("GroupName") = Request.Form("GroupName")
117:            END IF
118:        END IF
119: END SUB

120: SUB FindEventID()
121:     ON ERROR RESUME NEXT
122:     IF Session("EventID") = "" THEN
123:         SET cn = Server.CreateObject("ADODB.Connection")
124:         cn.Open "TMP"
125:         IF CheckError( cn, "" ) THEN EXIT SUB
126:         '** Find the group that was just created
127:         SET rs = cn.Execute( _
128:             "SELECT * FROM Events WHERE " &_
129:                 "EventName = '" & Request.Form("EventName") &_
130:                 "' AND " &_
131:                 "GroupID = " & CSTR(Session("GroupID")) _
132:                 )
133:         IF CheckError( cn, "" ) THEN EXIT SUB
134:         IF NOT rs.EOF THEN
135:             Session("EventID") = rs("EventID")
136:             Session("EventName") = Request.Form("EventName")
137:         END IF
138:     END IF
139: END SUB

140: SUB CreateNewGroup()
141:     ON ERROR RESUME NEXT
142:     SET cn = Server.CreateObject("ADODB.Connection")
143:     cn.Open "TMP"
144:     IF CheckError( cn, "" ) THEN EXIT SUB
145:     IF Request.Form("FirstName") > "" AND _
146:         Request.Form("LastName") > "" THEN
147:         cn.Execute "INSERT INTO Contacts " &_
148:             "(FirstName, LastName, Address1, Address2, " &_
149:             " City, State, Zip, Email) " &_
150:             "VALUES (" &_
151:             "'" & Request.Form("FirstName") & "', " &_
152:             "'" & Request.Form("LastName") & "', " &_
153:             "'" & Request.Form("Address1") & "', " &_
154:             "'" & Request.Form("Address2") & "', " &_
155:             "'" & Request.Form("City") & "', " &_
156:             "'" & Request.Form("State") & "', " &_
157:             "'" & Request.Form("Zip") & "', " &_
158:             "'" & Request.Form("Email") & "' ) "
159:         IF CheckError( cn, "" ) THEN EXIT SUB
160:         SET rs = cn.Execute( _
161:             "SELECT ContactID FROM Contacts WHERE " &_
162:                 "LastName = '" & Request.Form("LastName") &_
```

continues

14

Listing 14.2. continued

```
163:                      "' AND " &_
164:                      "FirstName = '" & Request.Form("FirstName") &_
165:                      "'" )
166:          IF CheckError( cn, "" ) THEN EXIT SUB
167:             ContactID = rs("ContactID")
168:      ELSE
169:
170:             ContactID = 0
171:      END IF
172:
173:      '** Create New Group record
174:      cn.Execute "INSERT INTO Groups (GroupName, ContactID) VALUES ('" &_
175:          Request.Form("GroupName") & "', " & CSTR(ContactID) & " )"
176:      IF CheckError( cn, "" ) THEN EXIT SUB
177:      '** Find the group that was just created
178:      SET rs = cn.Execute( _
179:          "SELECT * FROM Groups WHERE GroupName = '" &_
180:              Request.Form("GroupName") & "'" )
181:      IF CheckError( cn, "" ) THEN EXIT SUB
182:      Session("GroupID") = rs("GroupID")
183:      Session("GroupName") = Request.Form("GroupName")
184:
185: END SUB

186: SUB ChooseEventForm( action, mode )
187:      ON ERROR RESUME NEXT
188:      SET cn = Server.CreateObject("ADODB.Connection")
189:      cn.Open "TMP"
190:      IF CheckError( cn, "" ) THEN EXIT SUB
191:      SET rs = cn.Execute( _
192:          "SELECT EventName FROM Events WHERE GroupID = " &_
193:              CSTR( Session("GroupID") ) )
194:      IF CheckError( cn, "" ) THEN EXIT SUB
195:      IF NOT rs.EOF THEN
196:          events = rs.GetRows( -1 )
197:      ELSE
198:          events = null
199:      END IF
200:
201:      FormBegin action
202:      %>Select the name of the group or organization that <%
203:      %>you are associated with <%
204:      %>or leave it blank to request a new group name.<%
205:      %><BR><BR><%
206:      %><B>Group  </B><%= Session("GroupName") %><%
207:      %><BR><BR><%
208:
209:      %>Select the name of the event account that <%
210:      %><%= Session("GroupName") %><%
211:      %> will be reserving space for, <%
212:      %> or leave it blank to request a new event account.<%
213:      %><BR><BR><%
214:      %><B>Event  </B><%
215:      FormSelect "EventName", 40, "", events
216:      %><BR><BR><%
```

14

```
217:      FormSubmit "Continue", "Continue"
218:      FormEnd mode
219: END SUB

220: SUB CreateEventForm( action, mode )
221:      FormBegin action
222:      %><H4>Enter Event Information</H4><%
223:      %>
224:      <TABLE BORDER=0>
225:      <TR>
226:      <TD><B>Event Name</B></TD>
227:      <TD><% FormInput "EventName", 40, "" %></TD>
228:      </TR>
229:      <TR><TD> </TD></TR>
230:      <TR><TD><B>Contact Info</B></TD></TR>
231:      <TR><TD><HR></TD><TD><HR></TD></TR>
232:
233:      <TR>
234:      <TD><B>Same as Group Contact</B></TD>
235:      <TD><% FormCheckBox "SameAsGroup", false %></TD>
236:      </TR>
237:
238:      <TR>
239:      <TD><B>First Name</B></TD>
240:      <TD><% FormInput "FirstName", 20, "" %></TD>
241:      </TR>
242:      <TR>
243:      <TD><B>Last Name</B></TD>
244:      <TD><% FormInput "LastName", 20, "" %></TD>
245:      </TR>
246:      <TR>
247:      <TD><B>Address</B></TD>
248:      <TD><% FormInput "Address1", 40, "" %></TD>
249:      </TR>
250:      <TR>
251:      <TD></TD>
252:      <TD><% FormInput "Address2", 40, "" %></TD>
253:      </TR>
254:      <TR>
255:      <TD><B>City</B></TD>
256:      <TD><% FormInput "City", 20, "" %></TD>
257:      </TR>
258:      <TR>
259:      <TD><B>State</B></TD>
260:      <TD><% FormInput "State", 4, "" %></TD>
261:      </TR>
262:
263:      <TR>
264:      <TD><B>Zip</B></TD>
265:      <TD><% FormInput "Zip", 10, "" %></TD>
266:      </TR>
267:      <TR>
268:      <TD><B>Email</B></TD>
269:      <TD><% FormInput "Email", 40, "" %></TD>
270:      </TR>
271:      </TABLE>
```

14

continues

Listing 14.2. continued

```
272:    <BR><BR>
273:    <%
274:    FormSubmit "Continue", "Continue"
275:    FormEnd mode
276: END SUB

277: SUB CreateNewEvent()
278:    ON ERROR RESUME NEXT
279:    SET cn = Server.CreateObject("ADODB.Connection")
280:    cn.Open "TMP"
281:    IF CheckError( cn, "" ) THEN EXIT SUB
282:    IF Request.Form("SameAsGroup") > "" THEN
283:        SET rs = cn.Execute( _
284:            "SELECT ContactID FROM Groups WHERE " &_
285:                "GroupID = " & Session("GroupID") _
286:                )
287:        IF CheckError( cn, "" ) THEN EXIT SUB
288:        IF NOT rs.EOF THEN
289:            ContactID = rs("ContactID")
290:        END IF
291:    ELSEIF Request.Form("FirstName") > "" AND _
292:            Request.Form("LastName") > "" THEN
293:        cn.Execute "INSERT INTO Contacts " &_
294:            "(FirstName, LastName, Address1, Address2, " &_
295:            " City, State, Zip, Email) " &_
296:            "VALUES (" &_
297:            "'" & Request.Form("FirstName") & "', " &_
298:            "'" & Request.Form("LastName") & "', " &_
299:            "'" & Request.Form("Address1") & "', " &_
300:            "'" & Request.Form("Address2") & "', " &_
301:            "'" & Request.Form("City") & "', " &_
302:            "'" & Request.Form("State") & "', " &_
303:            "'" & Request.Form("Zip") & "', " &_
304:            "'" & Request.Form("Email") & "' ) "
305:        IF CheckError( cn, "" ) THEN EXIT SUB
306:        SET rs = cn.Execute( _
307:            "SELECT ContactID FROM Contacts WHERE " &_
308:                "LastName = '" & Request.Form("LastName") &_
309:                "' AND " &_
310:                "FirstName = '" & Request.Form("FirstName") &_
311:                "'" )
312:        IF CheckError( cn, "" ) THEN EXIT SUB
313:        ContactID = rs("ContactID")
314:    ELSE
315:
316:        ContactID = 0
317:    END IF
318:
319:    '** Create New Event record
320:    cn.Execute "INSERT INTO Events " &_
321:        "(EventName, GroupID, ContactID) VALUES ('" &_
322:        Request.Form("EventName") & "', " &_
323:        CSTR(Session("GroupID")) & ", " &_
324:        CSTR(ContactID) & " )"
```

14

```
325:     IF CheckError( cn, "" ) THEN EXIT SUB
326:     '** Find the Event that was just created
327:     SET rs = cn.Execute( _
328:         "SELECT * FROM Events WHERE " &_
329:             "GroupID = " & CSTR(Session("GroupID")) &_
330:             " AND " &_
331:             "EventName = '" & Request.Form("EventName") &_
332:             "'" )
333:     IF CheckError( cn, "" ) THEN EXIT SUB
334:     Session("EventID") = rs("EventID")
335:     Session("EventName") = Request.Form("EventName")
336:
337: END SUB

338: SUB ChooseOperation()
339:     %>
340:     <CENTER>
341:     <TABLE BORDER=0>
342:     <TR><TD>
343:     <A HREF="14TWD02.asp">Check In</A>
344:     </TD></TR>
345:     <TR><TD>
346:     <A HREF="14TWD05.asp">Reserve Meeting Space</A>
347:     </TD></TR>
348:     <TR><TD>
349:     <A HREF="14TWD03.asp">View Reservations</A>
350:     </TD></TR>
351:     </TABLE>
352:     </CENTER>
353:     <%
354: END SUB
355: %>

356: <%
357: mode = Request.Form("mode")
358: if mode = "" then
359:     Header
360:     ChooseGroupForm thisPage, "ChooseGroupForm"
361: elseif mode = "ChooseGroupForm" then
362:     if Request.Form("GroupName") = "" then
363:
364:         Header
365:         CreateGroupForm thisPage, "CreateGroupForm"
366:     else
367:         FindGroupID
368:         if Session("GroupID") > "" then
369:
370:             Header
371:             ChooseEventForm thisPage, "ChooseEventForm"
372:
373:         else
374:
375:             Header
376:             ChooseGroupForm thisPage, "ChooseGroupForm"
377:         end if
378:     end if
```

continues

Listing 14.2. continued

```
379: elseif mode = "CreateGroupForm" then
380:     CreateNewGroup
381:     if Session("GroupID") > "" then
382:
383:         Header
384:         ChooseEventForm thisPage, "ChooseEventForm"
385:     else
386:         Header
387:         ChooseGroupForm thisPage, "ChooseGroupForm"
388:     end if
389: elseif mode = "ChooseEventForm" then
390:     if Request.Form("EventName") = "" then
391:
392:         Header
393:         CreateEventForm thisPage, "CreateEventForm"
394:     else
395:         FindEventID
396:         if Session("EventID") > "" then
397:             Header
398:             ChooseOperation
399:
400:         else
401:
402:             Header
403:             ChooseEventForm thisPage, "ChooseEventForm"
404:         end if
405:     end if
406: elseif mode = "CreateEventForm" then
407:     CreateNewEvent
408:     if Session("EventID") > "" then
409:         Header
410:         ChooseOperation
411:
412:     else
413:
414:         Header
415:         ChooseEventForm thisPage, "ChooseEventForm"
416:     end if
417: end if
418: %>
419: <HR>
420: <CENTER>
421: <BR>For comments regarding this web site and its content please contact
422: <BR>
423: <BR><A HREF="mailto:wizard@tmp.com">wizard@tmp.com</A>
424: </CENTER>
425: </HTML>
```

The first page for checking in is an input form with a single drop-down listbox; it displays the names of all the known groups (organizations) that have used The Meeting Place service before. Instructions advise visitors to keep the selection blank if they want to open an account for a new organization. Figure 14.3 shows the page visitors first see when they start checking in.

Figure 14.3.

Specifying the group.

If you choose to create a new group account by leaving the selection blank and clicking Continue, a separate Web page is generated so visitors can fill in all the pertinent information. (See Figure 14.4.) Visitors must enter both group and contact information.

Figure 14.4.

Adding a new group account.

14

After selecting a group name or entering a new one, you're automatically sent to the next input form. It shows the group name you have decided on and prompts you for an event name. Because a group name corresponds to an organization, such as a company, each group can sponsor many different events, with each one needing conference rooms or meeting space. Figure 14.5 shows the event selection input form.

Figure 14.5.

Specifying the event.

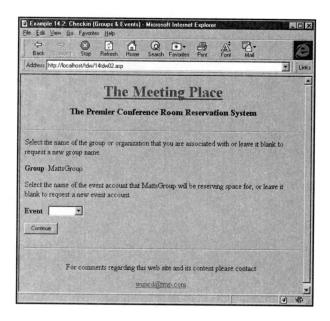

The events listed in the drop-down listbox correspond to the group you have already identified. In the same way you can add a new group name, you can add an event name to the database if it's not in the list. Simply leaving the event selection blank and clicking Continue takes you to the input form for adding new events, shown in Figure 14.6.

Finally, after you've entered information for both the group and the event, the page is regenerated to show a feature menu. If you refer back to Figure 14.2, you can see that the items Reserve Meeting Space and View Reservations have been added.

Viewing Reservations

The View Reservations ASP file generates a report showing all the room reservations made for the current group and event information. It's primarily composed of a sub-routine that uses ADO to query for an explicit range of room reservations and displays them as a generated HTML table.

14

Figure 14.6.

Adding a new event.

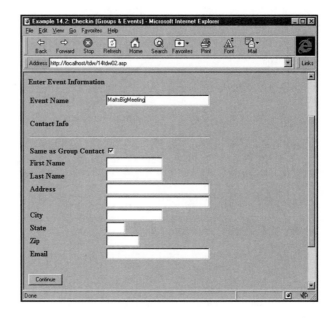

Listing 14.3. Viewing the room reservations.

```
 1: <HTML>
 2: <% thisPage = "14TWD03.asp" %>
 3: <!-- #include file="adovbs.inc" -->
 4: <!-- #include file="14TWD04.asp" -->

 5: <%
 6: SUB Header()
 7:     %>
 8:     <HEAD>
 9:     <TITLE>Example 14.3: Viewing Reservations</TITLE>
10:     </HEAD>
11:     <CENTER>
12:     <A HREF="14TWD01.asp">
13:     <H1>The Meeting Place</H1>
14:     </A>
15:     <H3>The Premier Conference Room Reservation System</H3>
16:     <%
17:     if Session("EventID") > "" then
18:         %>
19:         <BR>
20:         <B>Group  </B><%= Session("GroupName") %>
21:            
22:         <B>Event  </B><%= Session("EventName") %>
23:         <%
24:     end if
25:
```

continues

14

Listing 14.3. continued

```
26:     %>
27:     <HR>
28:     </CENTER>
29:     <%
30: END SUB

31: SUB ListResByDate()
32:     ON ERROR RESUME NEXT
33:     query = _
34:         "SELECT * FROM Reservations, Rooms, Buildings " &_
35:         "WHERE Reservations.BuildingID = Rooms.BuildingID " &_
36:           "AND Reservations.FloorNo = Rooms.FloorNo " &_
37:           "AND Reservations.RoomNo = Rooms.RoomNo " &_
38:           "AND Rooms.BuildingID = Buildings.BuildingID " &_
39:           "AND EventID = " & CStr(Session("EventID")) & " " &_
40:         "ORDER BY StartReserve"
41:
42:     SET cn = Server.CreateObject("ADODB.Connection")
43:     cn.open "TMP"
44:     IF CheckError( cn, "" ) THEN EXIT SUB
45:     SET rs = cn.Execute( query )
46:     IF CheckError( cn, "" ) THEN EXIT SUB
47:     %>
48:     <CENTER>
49:     <TABLE BORDER=1>
50:     <TD>From</TD>
51:     <TD>To</TD>
52:     <TD>Building</TD>
53:     <TD>Room</TD>
54:     <%
55:     WHILE NOT rs.EOF
56:         %>
57:         <TR>
58:         <TD><%= rs("StartReserve") %></TD>
59:         <TD><%= rs("EndReserve") %></TD>
60:         <TD><%= rs("BuildingName") %></TD>
61:         <TD><%= rs("RoomName") & " (" & rs("RoomNo") & ")" %></TD>
62:         </TR>
63:         <%
64:
65:         rs.MoveNext
66:     WEND
67:     %>
68:     </TABLE>
69:     </CENTER>
70:     <%
71: END SUB
72: %>


73: <%
74: if Session("EventID") > "" then
75:     Header
76:     ListResByDate
77: else
```

14

```
78:     %><H4>Event Information Unavailable</H4><%
79: end if
80: %>

81: <HR>
82: <CENTER>
83: <BR>For comments regarding this web site and its content please contact
84: <BR>
85: <BR><A HREF="mailto:wizard@tmp.com">wizard@tmp.com</A>
86: </CENTER>
87: </HTML>
```

Figure 14.7 shows an example of this Web page being used to display room reservations.

Figure 14.7.

Room reservations.

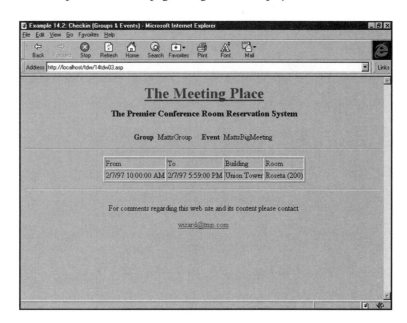

Utilities

The Utilities ASP file, 14TWD04.ASP, isn't actually an ASP file at all; it's used as a file that the server includes in other ASP files. The Utilities file contains helper sub-routines for building input forms and checking for ADO error conditions. The definitions should seem familiar, since they're based on ones used in previous chapters.

14

Listing 14.4. The Utilities file.

```
 1: <%
 2: '*******************************************************
 3: '* ERROR CHECKING

 4: Function IsOpen( rs )
 5:    On Error Resume Next
 6:    bof = rs.BOF
 7:    If Err = 0 Then
 8:       IsOpen = true
 9:    Else
10:       IsOpen = false
11:    End If
12: End Function

13: Function CheckError( cn, mode )
14:    If Err <> 0 Then
15:       %>
16:       <H3>
17:       An error has occurred in <%= thisPage %>.
18:       </H3>
19:       <%
20:       '**** display all the errors & warnings ****
21:       If cn = Nothing Then
22:          %>Error: <%= Err.Description %><%
23:       ElseIf cn.Errors.Count = 0 Then
24:          %>Error: <%= Err.Description %><%
25:       Else
26:          For i = 0 to cn.Errors.Count - 1
27:             If cn.Errors(i) < 0 then
28:                %>Error: <%= cn.Errors(i).Description %><%
29:             Else
30:                %>Warning: <%= cn.Errors(i).Description %><%
31:             End If
32:          Next
33:       End If
34:       %>
35:       <FORM METHOD=POST ACTION="<%= thisPage %>">
36:       <INPUT TYPE=SUBMIT VALUE="Continue">
37:       <INPUT TYPE=HIDDEN NAME=mode VALUE="<%= mode %>">
38:       </FORM>
39:       <%
40:       CheckError = True
41:    Else
42:       CheckError = False
43:    End if
44: End Function

45: '*******************************************************
46: '* FORMS

47: Sub FormBegin( action )
48:    %> <FORM METHOD=POST ACTION=<%= action %>> <%
49: End Sub
```

14

```
50: Sub FormEnd( mode )
51:    %>
52:    <INPUT TYPE=HIDDEN NAME="mode" VALUE="<%=mode%>">
53:    </FORM>
54:    <%
55: End Sub

56: Sub FormInput( name, size, value )
57:    %>
58:    <INPUT TYPE=TEXT SIZE=<%=size%> VALUE="<%=value%>" NAME="<%=name%>" >
59:    <%
60: End Sub

61: Sub FormCheckBox( name, checked )
62:    %>
63:    <INPUT TYPE=CHECKBOX NAME="<%=name%>" >
64:    <%
65: End Sub

66: Sub FormSelect( name, size, value, items )
67:    %>
68:    <SELECT NAME=<%=name%>>
69:    <%
70:    if NOT IsNull(items) then
71:        found = false
72:        for i = 0 to UBound(items,2)
73:          if value = items(0,i) then
74:            Response.Write "<OPTION SELECTED>" + cstr(items(0,i))
75:            found = true
76:          else
77:            Response.Write "<OPTION>" + cstr(items(0,i))
78:          end if
79:        next
80:    end if
81:    if not found then
82:      Response.Write "<OPTION SELECTED>" + cstr(value)
83:    end if
84:    %>
85:    </SELECT>
86:    <%
87: End Sub

88: Sub FormText( name, rows, cols, value )
89:    if isNull(value) then value = ""
90:    %>
91:    <TEXTAREA NAME="<%=name%>" ROWS=<%=rows%> COLS=<%=cols%>
92:    ><%= value %></TEXTAREA>
93:    <%
94: End Sub

95: Sub FormSubmit( name, value )
96:    %>
97:    <INPUT TYPE=SUBMIT NAME=<%=name%> VALUE=<%=value%> >
98:    <%
99: End Sub
```

14

continues

Listing 14.4. continued

```
100: Function GetItemList( fld, table, cn )
101:   set rs = Server.CreateObject("ADODB.Recordset")
102:   rs.Open "select "+fld+" from "+table +" group by "+fld, cn
103:   if IsOpen( rs ) then
104:     GetItemList = rs.GetRows(-1)
105:   end if
106: End Function
107: %>
```

Reserving Space

The last ASP file, 14TWD05.ASP, is the longest and most complex dynamic Web page in this book so far. It has many different types of input forms and information displays that are presented individually. The goal of this Web page is to direct you through selecting several potential room candidates, viewing the times available for each room, and making your final room selection.

Listing 14.5. Reserving a meeting space.

```
 1: <HTML>
 2: <!--#include file="adovbs.inc" -->
 3: <!--#include file="14TWD04.asp" -->
 4: <% thisPage = "14TWD05.asp" %>

 5: <%
 6: SUB Header()
 7:     %>
 8:     <HEAD>
 9:     <TITLE>Example 14.2: Reserving Rooms</TITLE>
10:     </HEAD>
11:     <BODY>
12:     <CENTER>
13:     <A HREF="14TWD01.asp">
14:     <H1>The Meeting Place</H1>
15:     </A>
16:     <H3>The Premier Conference Room Reservation System</H3>
17:     <BR>
18:     <B>Group  </B><%= Session("GroupName") %>
19:        
20:     <B>Event  </B><%= Session("EventName") %>
21:     <HR>
22:     </CENTER>
23:     <%
24: END SUB

25: SUB InitRoomSearchCriteria()
26:     Session("building")      = "all"
```

```
27:     Session("capacity")      = "any"
28:     Session("seated")        = "any"
29:     Session("tables")        = ""
30:     Session("podiums")       = ""
31:     Session("telephones")    = ""
32:     Session("networkports")  = ""
33:     Session("monitors")      = ""
34:     Session("screens")       = ""
35:     Session("vcr")           = ""
36:     Session("sound")         = ""
37:     Session("vidconf")       = ""
38:     Session("avdate")        = Date
39: END SUB

40: SUB SaveRoomSearchCriteria()
41:     Session("building")      = Request.Form("building")
42:     Session("capacity")      = Request.Form("capacity")
43:     Session("seated")        = Request.Form("seated")
44:     Session("tables")        = Request.Form("tables")
45:     Session("podiums")       = Request.Form("podiums")
46:     Session("telephones")    = Request.Form("telephones")
47:     Session("networkports")  = Request.Form("networkports")
48:     Session("monitors")      = Request.Form("monitors")
49:     Session("screens")       = Request.Form("screens")
50:     Session("vcr")           = Request.Form("vcr")
51:     Session("sound")         = Request.Form("sound")
52:     Session("vidconf")       = Request.Form("vidconf")
53: END SUB

54: FUNCTION RoomSearchQueryString()
55:     sqlselect = "SELECT " &_
56:         "BuildingName, " &_
57:         "Buildings.BuildingID, " &_
58:         "FloorNo, " &_
59:         "RoomNo, " &_
60:         "RoomName, " &_
61:         "MaxPersons, " &_
62:         "MaxSeated, " &_
63:         "Chairs, " &_
64:         "Tables, " &_
65:         "Podiums, " &_
66:         "Telephones, " &_
67:         "NetworkPorts, " &_
68:         "VideoMonitors, " &_
69:         "ProjectionScreens, " &_
70:         "VideoPlayback, " &_
71:         "SoundSystem, " &_
72:         "VideoConferencing"
73:     sqlfrom = " FROM Buildings, Rooms"
74:     sqlsort = " ORDER BY BuildingName, RoomNo "
75:     sqlwhere = " WHERE Buildings.BuildingID = Rooms.BuildingID "
76:     if Session("building") <> "all" then
77:         sqlwhere = sqlwhere & " AND BuildingName = '" &_
78:             Session("building") + "'"
79:     end if
80:     if Session("capacity") <> "any" then
```

14

continues

Listing 14.5. continued

```
81:            sqlwhere = sqlwhere & " AND MaxPersons >= " &_
82:                Session("capacity")
83:        end if
84:        if Session("seated") <> "any" then
85:            sqlwhere = sqlwhere & " AND MaxSeated >= " &_
86:                Session("seated")
87:        end if
88:        if Session("tables") <> "" then
89:            sqlwhere = sqlwhere & " AND Tables >= " &_
90:                Session("tables")
91:        end if
92:        if Session("chairs") <> "" then
93:            sqlwhere = sqlwhere & " AND Chairs >= " &_
94:                Session("chairs")
95:        end if
96:        if Session("podiums") <> "" then
97:            sqlwhere = sqlwhere & " AND Podiums >= " &_
98:                Session("podiums")
99:        end if
100:       if Session("telephones") <> "" then
101:           sqlwhere = sqlwhere & " AND Telephones >= " &_
102:               Session("telephones")
103:       end if
104:       if Session("networkports") <> "" then
105:           sqlwhere = sqlwhere & " AND NetworkPorts >= " &_
106:               Session("networkports")
107:       end if
108:       if Session("monitors") <> "" then
109:           sqlwhere = sqlwhere & " AND VideoMonitors >= " &_
110:               Session("monitors")
111:       end if
112:       if Session("screens") <> "" then
113:           sqlwhere = sqlwhere & " AND ProjectionScreens >= " &_
114:               Session("screens")
115:       end if
116:       if Session("vcr") <> "" then
117:           sqlwhere = sqlwhere & " AND VideoPlayback = " &_
118:               cstr( Session("vcr" ) )
119:       end if
120:       if Session("sound") <> "" then
121:           sqlwhere = sqlwhere & " AND SoundSystem = " &_
122:               cstr( Session("sound") )
123:       end if
124:       if Session("vidconf") <> "" then
125:           sqlwhere = sqlwhere & " AND VideoConferencing = " &_
126:               cstr( Session("vidconf") )
127:       end if
128:       RoomSearchQueryString = sqlselect & sqlfrom & sqlwhere & sqlsort
129: END FUNCTION

130: SUB RoomSearchForm( action, mode )
131:     ON ERROR RESUME NEXT
132:     Set cn = Server.CreateObject("ADODB.Connection")
133:     cn.Open "TMP"
```

14

```
134:    IF CheckError( cn, "" ) THEN EXIT SUB
135:    '** Get a list of known buildings...
136:    buildings = GetItemList( "BuildingName", "Buildings", cn )
137:    capacity = GetItemList( "MaxPersons", "Rooms", cn )
138:    seated = GetItemList( "MaxSeated", "Rooms", cn )
139:    FormBegin action
140:    %>
141:    <CENTER>
142:    <TABLE BORDER=0>
143:    <TD>
144:    <TABLE BORDER=0>
145:    <TR>
146:    <TD>Building</TD>
147:    <TD><% FormSelect "building", 60, "all", buildings %></TD>
148:    </TR>
149:    <TR>
150:    <TD>Capacity</TD>
151:    <TD><% FormSelect "capacity", 5, "any", capacity %></TD>
152:    </TR>
153:    <TR>
154:    <TD>Seated Capacity</TD>
155:    <TD><% FormSelect "seated", 5, "any", seated %></TD>
156:    </TR>
157:    <TR>
158:    <TD>Tables</TD>
159:    <TD><% FormInput "Tables", 5, "" %></TD>
160:    </TR>
161:    <TR>
162:    <TD>Podiums</TD>
163:    <TD><% FormInput "Podiums", 5, "" %></TD>
164:    </TR>
165:    <TR>
166:    <TD>Telephones</TD>
167:    <TD><% FormInput "Telephones", 5, "" %></TD>
168:    </TR>
169:    </TABLE>
170:    </TD>
171:    <TD>
172:    <TABLE BORDER=0>
173:    <TR>
174:    <TD>Network Ports</TD>
175:    <TD><% FormInput "NetworkPorts", 5, "" %></TD>
176:    <TR>
177:    <TR>
178:    <TD>Video Monitors</TD>
179:    <TD><% FormInput "Monitors", 5, "" %></TD>
180:    </TR>
181:    <TR>
182:    <TD>Projection Screens</TD>
183:    <TD><% FormInput "Screens", 5, "" %></TD>
184:    </TR>
185:    <TR>
186:    <TD>Video Playback (vcr)</TD>
187:    <TD><% FormCheckBox "Vcr", false %></TD>
188:    </TR>
189:    <TR>
```

continues

14

Listing 14.5. continued

```
190:    <TD>Sound System</TD>
191:    <TD><% FormCheckBox "Sound", false %></TD>
192:    </TR>
193:    <TR>
194:    <TD>Video Conferencing</TD>
195:    <TD><% FormCheckBox "VidConf", false %></TD>
196:    </TR>
197:    </TABLE>
198:    </TD>
199:    </TABLE>
200:    <BR>
201:    <TABLE BORDER=0>
202:    <TD><% FormSubmit "Submit", "Search" %></TD>
203:    </TABLE>
204:    </CENTER>
205:    <%
206:    FormEnd mode
207: END SUB

208: SUB RoomFeatureList()
209:    ON ERROR RESUME NEXT
210:    query = RoomSearchQueryString()
211:    set cn = Server.CreateObject("ADODB.Connection")
212:    cn.Open "TMP"
213:    IF CheckError( cn, "" ) THEN EXIT SUB
214:    set rs = cn.Execute( query )
215:    IF CheckError( cn, "" ) THEN EXIT SUB
216:    %><CENTER><%
217:    %><TABLE BORDER=1><%
218:    %><TD><H4>Building</H4></TD><%
219:    %><TD><H4>Room</H4></TD><%
220:    %><TD><H4>Capacity</H4></TD><%
221:    %><TD><H4>Chairs</H4></TD><%
222:    %><TD><H4>Tables</H4></TD><%
223:    %><TD><H4>Podiums</H4></TD><%
224:    %><TD><H4>Phones</H4></TD><%
225:    %><TD><H4>Ports</H4></TD><%
226:    %><TD><H4>Monitors</H4></TD><%
227:    %><TD><H4>Screens</H4></TD><%
228:    %><TD><H4>VCR</H4></TD><%
229:    %><TD><H4>Sound</H4></TD><%
230:    %><TD><H4>VidConf</H4></TD><%
231:    lastBuilding = ""
232:    WHILE NOT rs.EOF
233:        %><TR><%
234:        if lastBuilding = rs("BuildingName") then
235:            %><TD></TD><%
236:        else
237:            %><TD><%= rs("BuildingName") %></TD><%
238:        end if
239:        %><TD><%= rs("RoomName") & " (" & rs("RoomNo") & ")" %></TD><%
240:        %><TD><%= rs("MaxPersons") & "/" & rs("MaxSeated") %></TD><%
241:        %><TD><%= rs("Chairs") %></TD><%
242:        %><TD><%= rs("Tables") %></TD><%
```

14

```
243:        %><TD><%= rs("Podiums") %></TD><%
244:        %><TD><%= rs("Telephones") %></TD><%
245:        %><TD><%= rs("NetworkPorts") %></TD><%
246:        %><TD><%= rs("VideoMonitors") %></TD><%
247:        %><TD><%= rs("ProjectionScreens") %></TD><%
248:        if rs("VideoPlayback") then
249:            %><TD><FONT COLOR="BLUE">Yes</FONT></TD><%
250:        else
251:            %><TD> </TD><%
252:        end if
253:        if rs("SoundSystem") then
254:            %><TD><FONT COLOR="BLUE">Yes</FONT></TD><%
255:        else
256:            %><TD> </TD><%
257:        end if
258:        if rs("VideoConferencing") then
259:            %><TD><FONT COLOR="BLUE">Yes</FONT></TD><%
260:        else
261:            %><TD> </TD><%
262:        end if
263:        %></TR><%
264:        lastBuilding = rs("BuildingName")
265:        rs.MoveNext
266:    WEND
267:    %></TABLE></CENTER><%
268: END SUB

269: SUB RoomFeatureMenu( action, mode )
270:    %><CENTER><%
271:    FormBegin action
272:
273:    FormSubmit "avsubmit", "Calendar"
274:    FormInput  "avdate", 30, Session("avdate")
275:    FormEnd mode
276:    %></CENTER><%
277: END SUB

278: SUB RoomCalendarMenu( action, mode )
279:    %><CENTER><%
280:    FormBegin action
281:    FormSubmit "avsubmit", "Features"
282:    FormSubmit "avsubmit", "Calendar"
283:    FormInput  "avdate", 30, Session("avdate")
284:    FormSubmit "avsubmit", "Previous"
285:    FormSubmit "avsubmit", "Next"
286:    FormEnd mode
287:    %></CENTER><%
288: END SUB

289: FUNCTION CreateReservationSelectCommand( cn )
290:    SET cm = Server.CreateObject("ADODB.Command")
291:    cm.CommandText = "SELECT * FROM Reservations, Events " &_
292:        "WHERE Events.EventID = Reservations.EventID " &_
293:        " AND BuildingID = ? AND FloorNo = ? AND RoomNo = ? " &_
294:        " AND ( (StartReserve >= ? AND StartReserve <= ?) " &_
295:            " OR (EndReserve >= ? AND EndReserve <= ?) ) "
```

continues

Listing 14.5. continued

```
296:      cm.ActiveConnection = cn
297:      cm.Prepared = true
298:      cm.Parameters.Append cm.CreateParameter( "BuildingID", adInteger )
299:      cm.Parameters.Append cm.CreateParameter( "FloorNo", adInteger )
300:      cm.Parameters.Append cm.CreateParameter( "RoomNo", adInteger )
301:      cm.Parameters.Append cm.CreateParameter( "StartLow", adDBTimestamp )
302:      cm.Parameters.Append cm.CreateParameter( "StartHigh", adDBTimestamp )
303:      cm.Parameters.Append cm.CreateParameter( "EndLow", adDBTimestamp )
304:      cm.Parameters.Append cm.CreateParameter( "EndHigh", adDBTimestamp )
305:      SET CreateReservationSelectCommand = cm
306: END FUNCTION

307: SUB GenerateCalendarHeader( hr1, hr2 )
308:      FOR n = hr1 TO hr2
309:          if n < 10 then
310:              t = "0"+cstr(n)
311:          elseif n < 13 then
312:              t = cstr(n)
313:          elseif n < 22 then
314:              t = "0"+cstr(n-12)
315:          else
316:              t = cstr(n-12)
317:          end if
318:          %><TD><H4><%= t+":00" %></H4></TD><%
319:      NEXT
320: END SUB

321: SUB GenerateCalendarRow( cm, avdate, hr1, hr2, buildingID, floorNo,
➥roomNo )
322:      DIM avhours(24)
323:      ON ERROR RESUME NEXT
324:      dt1 = CDate( avdate + " 12:00 AM" )
325:      dt2 = DateAdd( "h", 24, dt1 )
326:      cm("BuildingID") = buildingID
327:      cm("FloorNo") = floorNo
328:      cm("RoomNo") = roomNo
329:      cm("StartLow") = dt1
330:      cm("StartHigh") = dt2
331:      cm("EndLow") = dt1
332:      cm("EndHigh") = dt2
333:      '*** clear the available hours array ***
334:      FOR hr = 0 TO 23
335:          avhours(hr) = "white"
336:      NEXT
337:      '*** Execute Inner Query to determine availability ***
338:      SET rs = cm.Execute
339:      IF CheckError( cm.ActiveConnection, "" ) THEN EXIT SUB
340:      '*** count each reservation period ***
341:
342:      WHILE NOT rs.EOF
343:          IF rs("EventID") = Session("EventID") THEN
344:              color = "blue"
345:          ELSEIF rs("GroupID") = Session("GroupID") THEN
346:              color = "green"
```

14

```
347:        ELSE
348:            color = "black"
349:        END IF
350:        hrStart = Hour(rs("StartReserve"))
351:        hrEnd = Hour(rs("EndReserve"))
352:        FOR hr = hrStart TO hrEnd
353:            avhours(hr) = color
354:        NEXT
355:        rs.MoveNext
356:    WEND
357:    rs.Close
358:    SET rs = Nothing
359:    '*** generate marker for each hour period ***
360:    FOR hr = hr1 TO hr2
361:        %><TD BGCOLOR="<%= avhours(hr) %>"> </TD><%
362:    NEXT
363: END SUB

364: SUB GenerateLegend()
365:    %>
366:    <TABLE BORDER=0>
367:    <TD BGCOLOR="white">
368:    <FONT COLOR="Black">  Available  </FONT>
369:    </TD>
370:    <TD BGCOLOR="Black">
371:    <FONT COLOR="White">  Reserved  </FONT>
372:    </TD>
373:    <TD BGCOLOR="Green">
374:    <FONT COLOR="White">  Your Group  </FONT>
375:    </TD>
376:    <TD BGCOLOR="Blue">
377:    <FONT COLOR="White">  Your Event  </FONT>
378:    </TD>
379:    </TABLE>
380:    <%
381: END SUB

382: SUB RoomCalendarListForm( action, mode )
383:    ON ERROR RESUME NEXT
384:    query = RoomSearchQueryString()
385:    '** GET LIST OF COMPATIBLE ROOMS
386:    SET cn = Server.CreateObject("ADODB.Connection")
387:    cn.Open "TMP"
388:    IF CheckError( cn, "" ) THEN EXIT SUB
389:    SET rs = cn.Execute( query )
390:    IF CheckError( cn, "" ) THEN EXIT SUB
391:    SET cm = CreateReservationSelectCommand( cn )
392:    '**** START FORM ****
393:    FormBegin action
394:    %><CENTER><%
395:    %><TABLE BORDER=1><%
396:    %><TD><H4>Building</H4></TD><%
397:    %><TD><H4>Room</H4></TD><%
398:    '** generate time-period column headers
399:    GenerateCalendarHeader 7, 22
400:    lastBuilding = ""
```

14

continues

Listing 14.5. continued

```
401:        WHILE NOT rs.EOF
402:            '*** generate row of information
403:            %><TR><%
404:            if lastBuilding = rs("BuildingName") then
405:                %><TD></TD><%
406:            else
407:                %><TD><%= rs("BuildingName") %></TD><%
408:            end if
409:            name = "_" + cstr(rs("BuildingID")) +_
410:                   "_" + cstr(rs("FloorNo")) +_
411:                   "_" + cstr(rs("RoomNo"))
412:            val =  rs("RoomName") & " (" & rs("RoomNo") & ")"
413:            %><TD><% FormSubmit name, val %></TD><%
414:            GenerateCalendarRow cm, Session("avdate"), 7, 22, _
415:                rs("BuildingID"), rs("FloorNo"), rs("RoomNo")
416:            %></TR><%
417:            lastBuilding = rs("BuildingName")
418:            rs.MoveNext
419:        WEND
420:        %></TABLE><%
421:        %><BR><%
422:        GenerateLegend
423:        %></CENTER><%
424:        FormEnd mode
425: END SUB

426: SUB DecodeRoomInRequest()
427:        '** Find The Room encoded in the button name **
428:        FOR EACH name IN Request.Form
429:
430:            IF Left(name,1) = "_" THEN
431:                brk2 = InStr( 2, name, "_" )
432:                brk3 = InStr( brk2 + 1, name, "_" )
433:                Session("BuildingID") = Mid( name, 2, brk2 - 2 )
434:                Session("FloorNo") = Mid( name, brk2 + 1, brk3 - brk2 - 1 )
435:                Session("RoomNo") = Mid( name, brk3 + 1 )
436:
437:            END IF
438:
439:        NEXT
440: END SUB

441: SUB ReserveRoomForm( action, mode )
442:        ON ERROR RESUME NEXT
443:        Dim starttimes(1,16)
444:        Dim endtimes(1, 16)
445:        FOR n = 7 TO 22
446:            if n < 10 then
447:                t = "0"+cstr(n)
448:            elseif n < 13 then
449:                t = cstr(n)
450:            elseif n < 22 then
451:                t = "0"+cstr(n-12)
```

```
452:            else
453:                t = cstr(n-12)
454:            end if
455:            if n < 13 then
456:                starttimes(0,n-7) = t + ":00 AM"
457:                endtimes(0,n-7) = t + ":59 AM"
458:            else
459:                starttimes(0,n-7) = t + ":00 PM"
460:                endtimes(0,n-7) = t + ":59 PM"
461:            end if
462:        NEXT
463:        Set cn = Server.CreateObject("ADODB.Connection")
464:        cn.Open "TMP"
465:        IF CheckError( cn, "" ) THEN EXIT SUB
466:        SET cm = CreateReservationSelectCommand( cn )
467:        '** display the daily calendar for the current room **
468:        %><TABLE BORDER=1><%
469:        GenerateCalendarHeader 7, 22
470:
471:        %><TR><%
472:
473:        GenerateCalendarRow _
474:            cm, _
475:            Session("avdate"), _
476:            7, 22, _
477:            Session("BuildingID"), _
478:            Session("FloorNo"), _
479:            Session("RoomNo")
480:
481:        %></TR><%
482:        %></TABLE><%
483:        %><BR><%
484:        GenerateLegend
485:        %><BR><%
486:        %><B>Make a Reservation</B><%
487:        %><BR><%
488:        FormBegin action
489:        %>
490:        <TABLE BORDER=0>
491:        <TD>Start Time</TD>
492:        <TD><% FormSelect "StartTime", 20, "", starttimes %></TD>
493:        <TD> </TD>
494:        <TD>End Time</TD>
495:        <TD><% FormSelect "EndTime", 20, "", endtimes %></TD>
496:        </TABLE>
497:        <BR>
498:        <%
499:        FormSubmit "Reserve", "Reserve"
500:        FormEnd mode
501: END SUB

502: SUB ReserveRoom()
503:        ON ERROR RESUME NEXT
504:        '** check for conflicting reservations **
505:        Set cn = Server.CreateObject("ADODB.Connection")
506:        cn.Open "TMP"
```

continues

Listing 14.5. continued

```
507:      IF CheckError( cn, "" ) THEN EXIT SUB
508:      SET cm = CreateReservationSelectCommand( cn )
509:      dt1 = CDate( Session("avdate") & " " &_
510:          Request.Form("startTime") )
511:      dt2 = CDate( Session("avdate") & " " &_
512:          Request.Form("endTime") )
513:      cm("BuildingID") = Session("buildingID")
514:      cm("FloorNo") = Session("FloorNo")
515:      cm("RoomNo") = Session("RoomNo")
516:      cm("StartLow") = dt1
517:      cm("StartHigh") = dt2
518:      cm("EndLow") = dt1
519:      cm("EndHigh") = dt2
520:      SET rs = cm.Execute
521:      IF CheckError( cn, "" ) THEN EXIT SUB
522:      '** if the recordset is empty, then no conflict
523:      IF rs.EOF THEN
524:          SET cm = Server.CreateObject("ADODB.Command")
525:          cm.ActiveConnection = cn
526:          cm.CommandText = _
527:              "INSERT INTO Reservations " &_
528:                  "(BuildingID, FloorNo, RoomNo, EventID, " &_
529:                  " StartReserve, EndReserve) " &_
530:                  "VALUES (?, ?, ?, ?, ?, ? )"
531:          cm.Parameters.Append _
532:              cm.CreateParameter( "BuildingID", adInteger )
533:          cm.Parameters.Append _
534:              cm.CreateParameter( "FloorNo", adInteger )
535:          cm.Parameters.Append _
536:              cm.CreateParameter( "RoomNo", adInteger )
537:          cm.Parameters.Append _
538:              cm.CreateParameter( "EventID", adInteger )
539:          cm.Parameters.Append _
540:              cm.CreateParameter( "StartReserve", adDBTimestamp )
541:          cm.Parameters.Append _
542:              cm.CreateParameter( "EndReserve", adDBTimestamp )
543:          cm("BuildingID") = Session("BuildingID")
544:          cm("FloorNo") = Session("FloorNo")
545:          cm("RoomNo") = Session("RoomNo")
546:          cm("EventID") = Session("EventID")
547:          cm("StartReserve") = dt1
548:          cm("EndReserve") = dt2
549:          cm.Execute
550:      ELSE
551:          Session("Error") = "Conflict in reservation times"
552:      END IF
553:
554: END SUB
555: %>

556: <%
557: mode = Request.Form("mode")
558: if mode = "" then
559:
560:      InitRoomSearchCriteria
561:      Header
```

```
562:     RoomSearchForm thisPage, "search"
563: elseif mode = "search" then
564:     SaveRoomSearchCriteria
565:
566:     Header
567:     RoomFeatureMenu thisPage, "menu"
568:     RoomFeatureList
569: elseif mode = "menu" then
570:     if Request.Form("avsubmit") = "Calendar" then
571:         Session("avdate") = Request.Form("avdate")
572:         Header
573:         RoomCalendarMenu thisPage, "menu"
574:         %><BR><%
575:         RoomCalendarListForm thisPage, "pick"
576:     elseif Request.Form("avsubmit") = "Next" then
577:         Session("avdate") = CStr(
             ➥DateAdd( "d", 1, CDate( Session("avdate") ) ) )
578:         Header
579:         RoomCalendarMenu thisPage, "menu"
580:         %><BR><%
581:         RoomCalendarListForm thisPage, "pick"
582:     elseif Request.Form("avsubmit") = "Previous" then
583:         Session("avdate") = CStr(
             ➥DateAdd( "d", -1, CDate( Session("avdate") ) ) )
584:         Header
585:         RoomCalendarMenu thisPage, "menu"
586:         %><BR><%
587:         RoomCalendarListForm thisPage, "pick"
588:     elseif Request.Form("avsubmit") = "Features" then
589:         Header
590:         RoomFeatureMenu thisPage, "menu"
591:         RoomFeatureList
592:     end if
593: elseif mode = "pick" then
594:     DecodeRoomInRequest
595:     Header
596:     ReserveRoomForm thisPage, "reserve"
597: elseif mode = "reserve" then
598:     Session("Error") = ""
599:
600:     ReserveRoom
601:     Header
602:     if Session("Error") > "" then
603:         %><B><%= Session("Error") %></B><%
604:         %><BR><%
605:         ReserveRoomForm thisPage, "reserve"
606:     else
607:         RoomCalendarMenu thisPage, "menu"
608:         %><BR><%
609:         RoomCalendarListForm thisPage, "pick"
610:
611:     end if
612: end if
613: %>
```

14

continues

Listing 14.5. continued

```
614: <HR>
615: <CENTER>
616: <BR>For comments regarding this web site and its content please contact
617: <BR>
618: <BR><A HREF="mailto:wizard@tmp.com">wizard@tmp.com</A>
619: </CENTER>
620: </BODY>
621: </HTML>
```

The first page you see after selecting Reserve Meeting Space on the menu page is an input form for specifying search constraints that should lead you directly to the room or rooms that best fit your needs. You can enter information such as the room's maximum capacity, the number of people who can be comfortably seated, how many video monitors are available, or the number of tables and podiums available. If you leave a field blank or empty, it's considered pertinent to the search. Leaving all the fields blank retrieves *all* the conference rooms.

Figure 14.8 shows the input form for entering search constraints. Clicking the Search button takes you to the next page.

Figure 14.8.

Entering search constraints.

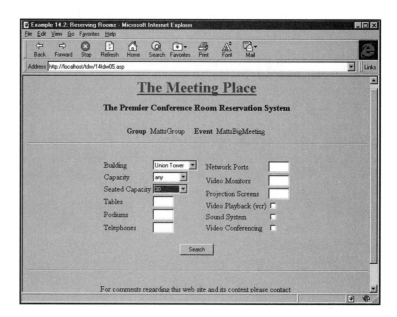

After you have reduced the number of available conference rooms down to a manageable subset, the next dynamically generated Web page is used to confirm your selections. It shows

14

a table of all the conference rooms that match your search criteria and gives you a detailed list of their features and equipment. Figure 14.9 shows the result of selecting the search criteria used in Figure 14.8.

Figure 14.9.

Conference rooms that match the search criteria.

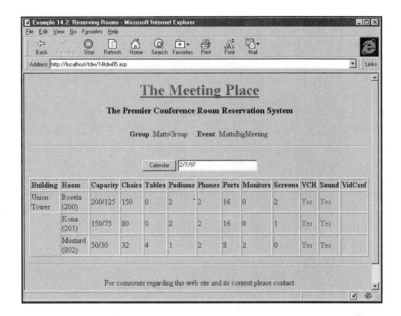

There's nothing you need to enter on this page, no action you need to take. You can stop here, back up to the search page, and specify different criteria if you didn't find the type of room you were looking for. To continue, you need to specify a date in the input field next to the Calendar button. Clicking the Calendar button generates a display of available times for all rooms on the date you entered.

The calendar is actually an HTML table. Each row is a different room, and each column is a particular hour of the day. Figure 14.10 shows the calendar with all the rooms available.

Each cell of the table is encoded by color. A white cell denotes a time period that's not currently reserved, and a black cell marks one that's already taken. Reserved cells can also be encoded with green and blue. Blue denotes a reservation already made by your group for your particular event; green is used for reservations made by your group, but not the event you're currently making reservations for. The encoding is informative enough to let you make a selection, without giving out too much detail about the reservations made by other people.

Figure 14.11 shows the same page with some of the rooms already reserved.

14

Figure 14.10.

The choice of available times is wide-open.

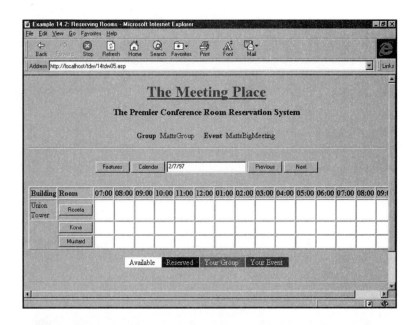

Figure 14.11.

Displaying reserved rooms.

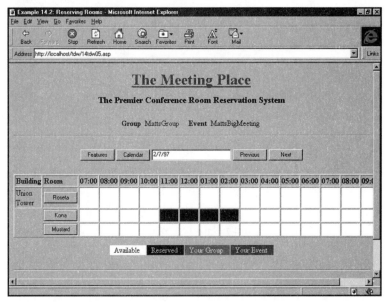

To make a choice, simply click the button displaying the name of the room; the buttons are part of the table itself. This choice takes you to another Web page that displays just the calendar row for the selected room with some input fields for choosing a time period. (See

Figure 14.12.) All you have to do is pick a starting time and an ending time from the drop-down listboxes.

Figure 14.12.

Reserving a time period.

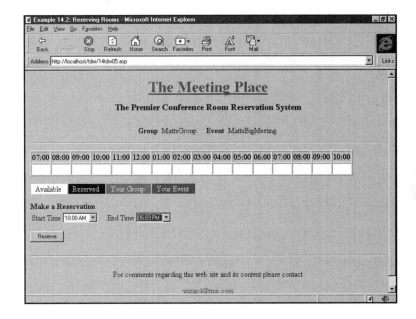

Once you have made your reservation, the dynamic Web page returns you to the previous calendar page that's regenerated to include your new information. From here, you're free to continue making more room reservations for the same event. You can always get back to the application's home page by clicking on the title The Meeting Place.

Summary

This chapter has given you a chance to see a complete dynamic Web site application that uses ADO on the server to manage database interactions and help generate the page contents. You have seen an example of how several dynamic Web pages used together can complete the picture of an entire online application. This chapter has put to use all the objects in the ADO family, using concepts and skills you learned in previous chapters.

Q&A

Q I noticed that you put a bunch of the forms' sub-routines into a separate file and included it in each ASP file. Could you do the same thing with sub-routines that generate a standard page header?

14

A Yes, you certainly could. In fact, if your site has many pages, putting header-generating sub-routines in a single place gives your application a consistent look.

Q In the earlier chapter on Command objects, you told us how parameters should be used instead of concatenating query strings together, yet in your "big" example you do this in many places.

A This is true. Parameter-based queries are useful when you want to reissue the same command many times using the same parameter sets, or when the parameter values are potentially complex and difficult to represent in a simple text string.

With Parameter-based queries, the composition of the query string and the parameters are done by the data provider and can happen on the server itself. However, when no benefit was gained by using Parameter-based queries, a simple concatenation was good enough.

You might also notice that in another part of the example, a Parameter-based query is used because it represents an "abstract" query that can be assigned constraints by using simple text names, without needing to know the query string's syntax or structure.

Q How come you use the %> and <% brackets in the script code instead of using Response.write?

A Personal preference. Somewhere along the way, I decided that using the scripting brackets would remind me that I was actually generating HTML.

Quiz

1. Listing 14.3, "Viewing the room reservations," is used primarily to generate a report. True or False?

2. List the three main application menu items available to a visitor who's "checked in."

3. The process of checking in eventually ends in the visitor specifying two pieces of information. What is that information?

4. Name the sub-routine in Listing 14.5 that uses a prepared Parameter-based command to optimize multiple queries when generating a single Web page.

5. Unlike the examples in earlier chapters, most HTML header information has been isolated into a single sub-routine of what name?

6. Form utilities are included in a separate file. Name the file and the method used to include these utilities in each ASP file.

7. Name at least one sub-routine that uses the FormSelect command to generate a drop-down listbox containing information from a database table.

14

8. Search constraints are remembered by the Web application between successive Web pages by using what Active Server Pages built-in feature?

9. What is the purpose of the Visual Basic statement repeated after each ADO Open or Execute method call?

10. List the name of at least one sub-routine that uses ADO to add new records to a database table.

Exercises

1. Write a new ASP file that manages canceling reservations. Add a new menu item on the application's main menu for this page.

2. Add new code to the View Reservations Web page, file 14TWD03.ASP, that generates several kinds of reports. For example, instead of listing the reservations in chronological order, list them by room.

3. Add a new feature that lets visitors get a report showing all room reservations for a given group, broken down by each event.

4. Add a new menu item and Web page that systematically purges all reservations made for events that have already taken place.

5. Add new ways to display the room reservation calendar that collapse reservation information into groups of time spanning weeks and months.

6. Add a mechanism that requires visitors to enter a password when selecting group and event information.

14

WEEK

2

8

9

10

11

12

13

14

In Review

Chapters 8 though 14 gave you a detailed overview and concrete examples of using Microsoft ActiveX Data Objects with Active Server Pages and Visual Basic Script on the server to build compelling online applications.

Day 8: ActiveX Data Objects (ADO) Overview

In this chapter, you were introduced to the ADO model, learned what these objects are used for, and saw how they can coexist within the Visual Basic Scripting environment available on the server through Active Server Pages and Microsoft Internet Information Server.

The three primary data-access objects—`Connection`, `Command`, and `Recordset`—can be used together or independently to manipulate data on a remote database server. Each object has its area of specialty. The `Connection` object represents a physical link between the Web server and the database server that the other objects use to communicate. The `Command` object can be used to execute `Parameter`-based queries and stored procedures. The `Recordset` is a tool for interacting with the results of a query or for viewing or modifying the data.

Day 9: Dynamic Pages and the ADO Recordset

This chapter delved immediately into creating your first data-centered dynamic Web page. It examined the ADO `Recordset` in detail, along with its `Fields` collection. It showed you how to use the `Recordset` to do the job of all three ActiveX Data Objects: establishing a link, issuing a query, and examining the results. It even gave you your first peek at incorporating these features into your own dynamic Web page. You were shown how to mix Visual Basic and HTML instructions in the same ASP file, how the script code is processed each time the page is accessed, and how data you get through ADO can be used to dynamically generate HTML text.

Day 10: More Dynamic Pages

This chapter continued where Chapter 9 left off. It gave you more concrete examples of using the ADO `Recordset` and also introduced using HTML `<TABLE>` tags for data display, HTML `<FORM>` tags for user input, and server-side scripting embedded in the Active Server Page for data processing. It showed you that a single dynamic Web page can be more than just an HTML-generating template. By using `<FORM>` tags and submitting responses back to the same ASP file, a single page can become an entire application. A user's interactions can drive what happens next, what content is displayed, and what processing gets done.

Day 11: Transactions and the `Connection` Object

This chapter switched gears and brought up the topics of easy execution, shared connections, connection pooling, and transactions. It gave you a detailed breakdown of the `Connection` object and how to fine-tune the communication link between your application and the back-end database server. It showed you how transactions could be used to isolate your database interactions from those occurring from other users or other Web page accesses happening in tandem. Multiple individual SQL statements—inserts, updates, and queries—can be grouped into one seemingly all-or-nothing atomic action. The Connection object can even be used without the Recordset to do any straightforward operation that the database recognizes.

Day 12: Commands and Stored Procedures

Chapter 12 helped you go beyond simple straightforward operations to open up the world of Parameter-based execution: precompiled SQL statements and calling procedures stored in the database itself. You got a complete description of the ADO Command object and its Parameters collection, along with discussion and examples of using each of these features.

Day 13: Errors and Provider Properties

Chapter 13 filled in the holes left by error handling and discrete control of advanced data-access features. The ADO Errors collection offers a way to discover sets of error codes generated by the underlying data provider when commands are executed and data is retrieved. Although the built-in Err object should be used to handle general error conditions for ADO and the rest of your application, the Errors collection is a good place to find more in-depth information about actual conditions and non-threatening warnings. In addition, the Properties collection available on every ActiveX Data Object can be used to discover and set provider-specific properties. Some database providers might have advanced, yet not often used, features. ADO doesn't stand in your way of using them when you need to. The Properties collection can be used to turn these features on.

Day 14: Dynamic Web Application: The Meeting Place

The last chapter of the week combined all the objects and server-based programming techniques into one example: "The Meeting Place," an online conference room reservation system. It used all three primary ADOs along with their respective collections to build a complete multiuser, multipage, multi–ASP-file online application that could be the starting ground for your own work. The sample application uses the ADO Recordset to examine data and generate HTML <TABLE> tags for display; dynamically generated fields and <FORM> tags for user input; and Parameter-based queries to find, insert, and update reservations and share and reuse both Command and Connection objects.

Together, these chapters gave you a firm understanding of how to use ActiveX Data Objects, Active Server Pages, and Visual Basic Script to develop data-aware dynamic Web applications. The data access was done exclusively on the server so that anyone, using any browser, could view and interact with the resulting Web pages. Because of being restricted to the server, high-speed local area networks could be deployed between Web servers and database servers, improving performance and reducing the risk of network failures.

At a Glance

This week is intended to show you how to use the new Microsoft Advanced Data Connector (ADC) framework to construct data-intensive Web applications for use on the Internet or corporate intranets. Several advanced concepts are introduced throughout the week, but as long as you keep ADC's straightforward framework in mind, these concepts will fall easily into place.

The main intention of the ADC development team was to create a simple-to-learn framework for building powerful Web database-centered applications. You will see how easy creating a database application with ActiveX technology can be. Your knowledge of Visual Basic means you're already halfway there to using ADC. This week will guide you to the rest of the information you need to use the power of ADC in your own applications.

The examples developed during this week rely on the ActiveX-framework used by Internet browsers, such as Internet Explorer 3.0 and the upcoming 4.0 edition. As the ActiveX framework is extended, and other browser technologies, such as Netscape Navigator, have plug-ins developed to take full advantage of ADC, you can develop ADC programs that will be used on virtually every hardware and operating system platform. Some advanced tools are introduced during the week, including Microsoft Visual Basic Enterprise Edition 5.0 (VB5) and Microsoft Internet Information Server 3.0 with Active Server Pages (ASP). These tools are introduced gradually and incorporated into hands-on lessons that relate directly to ADC and its multi-tiered model of application development. These tools complement ADC application development, and ADC was designed to work with them.

Where You Are Going

This week takes the skills and knowledge you have accumulated in the previous two weeks—ActiveX Data Objects, Active Server Pages server-side scripting, and so forth—and shows you how to build distributed applications that make the best use of browser, application server, and database components. You will build several applications in the course of the week, from a simple data-publishing application to a partitioned application using business objects and VBScript to manage an online library.

The week starts with an introduction to ADC's architecture and programming model, which will be quite familiar to Visual Basic programmers. From there, you build a small application to learn the main aspects of programming and deploying an ADC application. This hands-on session is followed by a reference guide and programming "cookbook" of ideas for using each of the ADC objects and their services. Once the main architectural and programming issues have been defined, you learn about the Active Server Pages component of Microsoft Internet Information Server 3.0, and see how to use it to build even better and more powerful Web applications with ADC. This topic introduces you to the important application-development concept of *distributed logic partitioning*, the practice of separating presentation logic from business logic and database storage and retrieval, thereby maximizing the reusability of components created for ADC. Next, you see how to develop a large application using Visual Basic business objects, ADC, and ASP pages to put all of this into perspective.

Finally, the week covers issues and considerations raised by distributing your ADC applications, such as digitally signing controls, creating CAB files for your downloadable ADC components, threading models of host client browsers, and manipulating the client-side Registry to mark your custom business objects as `SafeForScripting` and `SafeForInitialization`. This discussion ties up the preceding topics and gives you an opportunity to review the material covered during the week.

How You Get to the Goal

Since this book presents examples using the absolute latest technology from Microsoft, there are a few rough spots. With later releases, there will most likely be much simpler methods for bringing up and accessing the features, but for now, some pretty complex manual configurations are required. In the following few paragraphs, I've tried to make the process as easy as possible, but the steps are very critical. Please follow them closely. Fortunately, these requirements apply to only a couple of chapters.

Setup Instructions for Chapter 16

For the application server, make sure you follow these steps to set it up correctly:

1. Install Internet Information Server (IIS) 3.0 with Active Server Pages (ASP). This installation also includes the ODBC Driver Manager 3.0 and some Microsoft ODBC drivers that include the Access ODBC driver. It also creates an ODBC system DSN called "AdvWorks" that points to an Access database, ADVWORKS.MDB.

2. Create an IIS virtual directory where you'll put the IDC/HTX, HTM, and ASP files. Make sure you grant both Read and Execute rights for the Access privilege. If you need a reminder on how to create virtual directories in IIS, please refer to Chapter 2, "The Client-Server Model," for a review of the steps.

You should be able to run the examples in Listing 16.1 and 16.2 by entering `http://IISServerName/VirtualDirectory/`*`filename.extension`* in the Address text box in Internet Explorer. If you can't run either one of these examples, then consult the ASP online documentation, located under windows\system32\inetsrv\docs\ASPdocs\roadmap.asp after Internet Information Server is installed.

For the rest of the examples throughout the week, you'll need to install Advanced Data Connector (ADC):

NOTE

> OLE DB is the OLE interface that allows applications to access data uniformly; you can download it from this site:
>
> `http://www.microsoft.com/oledb`
>
> Both the OLE DB Software Developer's Kit and Advanced Data Connector can be downloaded from this Web site, too.

1. Install the OLE DB SDK, which installs all the required OLE DB and ADO (ActiveX Data Objects) components for ADC.

2. Install ADC from the oledbsdk\msadc directory and make sure you reboot the system.

3. Verify you have ADO, MSADC, and OLE DB subdirectories under the Program Files\Common Files\System directory. Make sure those subdirectories contain all the files listed as required DLLs in Chapter 16's section "Configuring Your Application and Client Server." If some of the files aren't there, it means the installation failed. You must install either OLE DB SDK or ADC again, depending on which file is missing.

4. Create an IIS virtual directory called "ADCDownload" that points to the MSADC10.CAB file. Make sure you grant both the Read and Execute rights for the access privilege so the client tier can download the necessary files for ADC to run. If this virtual directory is missing and the client machine doesn't have ADC installed, then the client machine can't run the examples; no error message is returned when this happens.

5. Use the SQL script 16TBL.SQL to create tables and insert data into tables in the database server. This script is designed for SQL Server. If you use an Access database as your database server, you'll need to manually modify the script. However, most of the ADC examples used during Week 3 don't run against an Access database, so it's recommended that you use SQL Server as the database server.

   You can run the SQL Script by using ISQL_w. From the Microsoft SQL Server program group, start ISQL_w and connect to SQL Server. Select your database name under the DB listbox and choose File | Open from the menu to bring up the Open File dialog box. In that dialog box, enter the correct path for 16TBL.SQL in the "File name" text box and click the Open button.

   After 16TBL.SQL is open, choose Query | Execute from the menu to run the query.

6. For these examples, the user ID for SQL Server is sa, but there's no password. If your SQL Server has a different user ID and password, you'll have to modify the ODBC connection string throughout the examples. For example, the ODBC connection string will be `DSN=Video;UID=sa;Pwd=demo` instead of `DSN=Video,UID=sa`.

7. In the Control Panel, double-click the ODBC Administration icon to create an ODBC system DSN called "Video." Select the System DSN tab and click the Add button to bring up the ODBC SQL Server Setup dialog box. Enter `Video` in the Data Source Name text box and make sure the Use Trusted Connection checkbox is *unchecked*. You can choose which database you want to use to run this script.

Click the Options button and enter the database name under the Login section. This database is where you store the tables.

8. You can run the example in Listing 16.3 by entering `http://IISServerName/VirtualDirectory/filename.extension` in the Address text box in Internet Explorer. Change the filename to the Web page you're going to run.

Troubleshooting

If no data is returned and no error message is displayed, make sure you have done Step 4 correctly. If you have, go to the Program Files\Common Files\System directory\msadc directory, and re-register the DLLs by issuing `regsvr32 DLLName.DLL`; `DLLName` should be the specific name of the DLL you're re-registering. You should do this from the DOS prompt.

If you get a `Login Failed` error, make sure your SQL Server is running and verify the information you entered in Step 6 again. *This information is critical.*

For both the application server and client machine, follow these steps to set them up correctly:

1. Install Visual Basic Professional Edition or above.

2. If you're running Visual Basic 5.0, the data-aware controls no longer come with the installation. On your VB5 CD-ROM, go to the \tools\controls subdirectory. Follow the instructions described in README.TXT to install the data-aware controls correctly.

3. Make sure the CLASSIDs for the DBGrid, RichText, and 3D Radio controls exist in your Registry:

Control	Filename	CLASSID
DBGrid	TDBGS32.OCX	00028C50-0000-0000-0000-000000000046
RichText	RICHTX32.OCX	3B7C8860-D78F-101B-B9B5-04021C009402
3D Radio	THREED32.OCX	0BA686AA-F7D3-101A-993E-0000C0EF6F5E

4. Click the Start button, choose Run, then enter `RegEdit` to bring up the Registry Editor. Next, search for these controls based on the filename or CLASSID. If the controls aren't correctly registered in your machine, you won't be able to see them displayed in the Web page. To register the controls, use `regsvr32 ControlName.OCX`; fill in the specific control you're registering for `ControlName`.

If the controls are registered but have different CLASSIDs, you'll need to modify the code in the examples to use the CLASSID your controls are registered with.

For the client machine, you need these additional setup steps:

1. Install Internet Explorer 3.01.

2. Make sure the security level is set to Medium or Minimal; otherwise, you won't be able to download the MSADC10.CAB file. To do that, in Internet Explorer, choose View | Security. Select the Security tab, and click the Safety Level button. Select the Medium radio button for the safety level, and click OK after you finish.

After following all these setup instructions, you're ready to run the examples in Chapter 16.

Setup Instructions for Chapter 21

Use the same setup instructions as the ones for Chapter 16, except for some changes to these two steps:

5. Use 21TWDTB.SQL, 21TWDSP.SQL, and 21TWDINS.SQL to create tables, create stored procedures, and insert data into SQL Server. You can run this script in the same database as previously or run it in a different database.

7. Create an ODBC system DSN called "Vlibrary" instead of "Video" and follow the rest of the instructions as described previously. The database for the Vlibrary datasource needs to point to the database you use in Step 5.

Day **15**

The Advanced Data Connector (ADC)

by Alexander Stojanovic

The Advanced Data Connector (ADC) you're studying this week is a new paradigm for developing database applications for the Web and corporate intranets. It's based on the programming model of ActiveX Data Objects (ADO), which you studied last week, and extends this model to include applications that move data between application servers and client browsers.

Unlike previous technologies, which limited this data to non-editable data in the form of HTML tables and other "static" views, ADC allows the data to be cached, edited, and updated from the client. It comes with its own powerful in-memory data cache that allows applications to keep editable data close at hand—on the client. ADC also allows application developers to build distributed applications with server application objects, an advanced feature introduced later in this week. All these ADC features make developing partitioned Web database applications that can communicate with databases and have sophisticated processing and application logic a reality. Even better, since ADC is based on programming models familiar to Visual Basic programmers, learning how to effectively program with ADC is much easier than with rival technologies, such as Cold Fusion and LiveConnect.

You will start by spending some time looking at the origins of ADC and Web data access programming. This is a new class of applications that have started to emerge with the explosion of interest in the World Wide Web as a backbone for application development and data publishing. This background will help you appreciate the advance that ADC represents over traditional Web data-access solutions, based on CGI scripting and static data publishing.

ADC allows developers to put together data-intensive applications for their Internet Explorer browsers, applications that can take existing data-aware ActiveX controls and link them to live data on the client. ADC can automatically manage the connection of data to these ActiveX objects, through a process called *data binding*. Developers can use this feature to quickly and easily connect visual controls and data, making their browser-hosted applications offer richer end-user experiences and more sophisticated editing environments.

With ADC, programmers can also create applications for the Web that rival the classic client-server applications built before the rise of the Web, in terms of visual complexity, processing capability, data access and local storage, and distributed object programming. With all of these features, ADC is an elegant and simple technology to learn how to use. You can master ADC by becoming familiar with a few powerful ADC objects: `AdvancedDataControl`, `AdvancedDataSpace`, `AdvancedDataFactory`, and ADO `Recordset`. After reviewing the background on Web data-access technologies, I'll give you an overview of the ADC architecture and its components, explaining how they fit to make powerful Internet applications. That overview will prepare you for the coming chapters, where you learn how to build increasingly sophisticated applications that can be easily distributed over the Web.

The Origins of the Advanced Data Connector

To understand the role and function of the Advanced Data Connector (ADC), you need to understand the context from which it arose. The context is Web-based interactive programming, with an emphasis on data-intensive application design—applications that process large amounts of data, such as data mining, reporting, OLAP (online analytical processing), complex order processing, and so forth. The current approach to writing these data-intensive applications has some limitations and shortcomings that ADC is engineered to address, within a programming framework that's easy to understand and use. A brief overview of the current server-centered solutions give you a foundation for explaining how ADC changes the

face of Web database programming. The primary approach to Web programming until now has been through using the *Common Gateway Interface*, or *CGI*. The basic idea behind CGI is to define a convention (a *protocol*) for passing data between Web servers and standalone applications; it includes activation, parameter passing, and control flow and is usually written in languages such as Perl, Tcl, C++, or Python.

NOTE

A *protocol* is simply a way to specify how communication takes place between machines. You can think of it as a formal convention for how the machines, modules, or software layers pass information and requests back and forth. The specification includes defining data packet delivery formats, header information, valid parameter types, communication synchronization, conversation verbs, control flow, and activating and deactivating data transfer.

Common protocols include TCP, HTTP, UDP, FTP, and SMTP. HTTP (HyperText Transport Protocol) is the protocol Web programmers and readers of this book are most interested in. A set of protocols that depend on one another are called a *protocol stack*. HTTP-->TCP-->IP is an example of a protocol stack.

Traditional CGI Web Scripting Approaches

User input parameters can be passed to an application by using environment variables or URL strings, and results are passed back to the server for processing and then returned to the client browser that *invoked*, or initiated, the CGI script. The Web server is in charge of analyzing the URL string, and—if a CGI invocation is detected—executing the program and processing its output into HTTP to send to the client application. CGI is a client-server model running on top of HTTP. The diagram in Figure 15.1 illustrates the CGI program control flow.

This diagram shows the three participants in the HTTP transaction: the Web browser, the server, and the CGI application, which is driven by user input. Processing a form, such as logging onto an online banking application, is an example of responding to user input. The code in Listing 15.1 could be used to fetch input, the user name, and a password from the client and trigger an application that validates the name and password.

Figure 15.1.

The CGI program control flow.

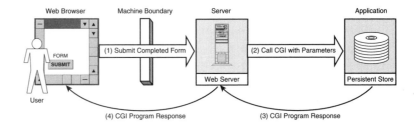

Listing 15.1. Logging on with the online banking application.

```
<HTML><HEAD><TITLE>Online Banking Service</TITLE></HEAD>
<BODY>
<H1>Please enter your name and password.</H1>
<FORM METHOD="GET" ACTION="/cgi-bin/bankservice.pl">
<PRE>
Name:     <INPUT TYPE="TEXT" NAME="name">
Password: <INPUT TYPE="TEXT" NAME="password">
<INPUT TYPE="SUBMIT" name="Submit">  <INPUT TYPE="RESET" name="Reset">
</FORM>
</HTML>
```

The page that's generated would look like the one in Figure 15.2.

Figure 15.2.

The logon screen.

The screen in Figure 15.2 is the one the user would see when he or she downloaded the logon HTML page from the Web server. The user fills in the two input fields with data and, when the request is ready to be submitted, clicks the Submit button in the lower-left corner.

On the client side, the application is triggered by the user clicking the Submit button. The <FORM> tag specifies the HTTP method that's used when the SUBMIT action is triggered. Using the GET method means that the parameters passed to the server and CGI program are encoded

15

in the URL itself. The actual HTTP transaction, the formatted HTTP message sent from the browser to the Web server for this action request, would be as follows:

```
GET HTTP/1.0 /cgi-bin/bankservice.pl?name=AlvinGoldfarb&password=AutomaticPM
```

The URL string encodes all the necessary information needed to process the request from the browser, including the following:

☐ The HTTP method to be used (GET)

☐ The version of HTTP understood by the client browser (1.0)

☐ The directory where the CGI application is located (/cgi-bin)

☐ The name of the application (bankservice.pl)

☐ The input parameters to the application (name and password)

The question mark indicates the start of the input parameters list, and the apostrophes separate the parameters. The Web server would analyze this URL string and invoke the CGI application (BANKSERVICE.PL), passing along the two parameters.

Once the BANKSERVICE.PL program has finished processing the HTTP transaction, it returns its output parameters in two parts: a full or partial HTTP header that describes the format of the data being returned (for example, HTML, ASCII text, GIF, JPEG), and the body of the response. The header is separated from the body by a blank line. Assuming that the logon failed because of an incorrect password being submitted, the output of BANKSERVICE.PL might look like this:

```
Content-type: text/html

<HTML><HEAD><TITLE>Logon Failure</TITLE></HEAD>
<BODY>
<H1>Sorry Alvin, your logon failed due to an invalid password.</H1>
</BODY>
</HTML>
```

The BANKSERVICE.PL application generates a dynamic Web page, inserting the user's name, and then adds a standard response banner informing the user that the logon request has failed. This is a simple use of CGI, but one that exhibits its most important features. This CGI approach has some limitations, the most serious of which is the static nature of the data returned. In this case, it's a simple HTML page with one element, a header with the error message. The majority of data-access solutions currently available suffer from this limitation: that the data returned is static and not very useful for client-side programming. Although CGI allows for interactive Web programs, the interactivity is seriously constrained by the response's format, which is typically static HTML and HTML forms. Microsoft has developed technologies such as IIS 3.0 and ADC to supply this missing dimension—interactivity—to Web application developers.

CGI applications can be used to process the results of HTML form input, generate dynamic Web pages, act as gateways to Internet facilities—such as e-mail, file transfer, and search services—and retrieve data from corporate databases. CGI defines the way the Web server and external program communicate, and the Web server is left to translate the results of the CGI program into a format—HTTP—compatible with the Web client. The CGI framework can be extended by using *server-side includes* (*SSIs*), directives placed within HTML to execute other programs or output data. The use of SSI depends, too, on the Web server used because not all Web servers support SSIs; Microsoft Internet Information Server 3.0, however, does.

How ADC Differs from Traditional CGI Programming

Advanced Data Connector (ADC) is a technology designed to expressly address the limitation of returning static data. ADC allows server applications to return "live" data, not just static HTML pages with tables and non-interactive data. Like CGI, ADC is based on HTTP as the application-level protocol for communication between browser applications and servers, but ADC takes HTTP and builds a truly interactive programming model on top of it. ADC does this, while allowing the programmer to interact with the results returned by HTTP servers, in the well-known Visual Basic client-server paradigm—complete with datasource controls and standard data-aware controls, such as the DBGrid and DBList ActiveX controls. Visual Basic programmers can leverage their knowledge to get involved in Web application programming without having to learn completely new programming languages and protocols.

Advanced Data Connector, like its predecessor CGI, is a technology designed to provide distributed application processing. Unlike CGI, however, ADC leverages the model of Visual Basic to offer a framework that supports several unique and powerful features:

- ☐ Drop-in support for data-aware ActiveX controls to view dynamic, updatable data in Web applications
- ☐ Efficient caching of results on server and client, through a compact and powerful in-memory database called the Virtual Table Manager (VTM)
- ☐ Plug-and-Play database connectivity over HTTP to ODBC and OLE DB datasources
- ☐ Visual Basic–style data-binding application construction, with easy porting of existing Visual Basic applications onto the Web
- ☐ Remote OLE Automation object method calls over HTTP and DCOM, allowing custom-built business objects in Visual Basic to be invoked and used in distributed applications

The following section introduces the components of the ADC framework, which work together to offer fast data access, navigation, updating, and marshaling.

NOTE

> *Marshaling* is the process of moving data from one address space or process into another. When you marshal data to an HTTP server from a browser, you're sending the data from the browser's process space into another's—the server's—by using HTTP.
>
> The logon application example illustrates this concept: The name and password parameters are marshaled through the HTTP message to the HTTP server. The term *marshaling* comes from remote procedure call (RPC) programming, in which input parameters to remote functions are copied from the program's address space into another machine's or process's address space. Marshaling does, however, cause a performance penalty on data access, so try to avoid it when possible. Writing distributed applications with ADC requires marshaling, but ADC avoids marshaling data unnecessarily. A synonym for marshaling is *remoting*.

What Is Advanced Data Connector?

The Microsoft Advanced Data Connector (ADC) delivers a new Web data-access technology that allows developers to create data-centered applications within ActiveX-enabled browsers, such as Microsoft Internet Explorer. ADC erects a framework that permits seamless interaction with databases on corporate intranets and over the Internet. Along with these advances, ADC's design offers a programming model that's easy to use and familiar to millions of Visual Basic developers. ADC offers the advantages of client-side caching of data results, update capability on cached data, and data-aware ActiveX control integration.

ADC's Approach to Web Database Programming

ADC goes beyond the current generation of Web data-access tools by allowing clients to update the data they see. End-users aren't restricted to staring at a static HTML results table. With ADC, end-users can alter, add, and delete data they have queried and retrieved. All changes are buffered locally and can be submitted to the server for inspection, processing, and, if appropriate, storage in the database. The benefits of traditional client-server technology have been migrated to the Web, and the read-only, static client is a thing of the past. Being able to use a local data cache means the end-user can navigate through large datasets without costly server round-trips.

Using drop-in ActiveX data controls, such as grids, lists, and combo boxes, programmers can create sophisticated user interfaces that allow end-users to view and change data with a minimum of programming. By taking advantage of many available Visual Basic data-aware controls, ADC delivers a more compelling interaction model for the Web and makes the job of putting the application together easier.

Partitioning Application Logic

Microsoft's ADC gives you the ability to invoke remote objects over HTTP, allowing you to develop Web applications that effectively partition application logic between Visual Basic Scripting Edition code on the client and server objects. OLE Automation objects written in Visual Basic can make services available to client-side applications, yet protect the client's logic and data from being distributed. Developers are no longer restricted to choosing among "thin" or "fat" clients and servers; they can make an informed choice and partition their data and logic accordingly.

The Microsoft Advanced Data Connector is the new face for distributed data access through the Web. By supplying data manipulation over retrieved data, efficient client-side caching, and integration with data-aware ActiveX controls within an elegant and powerful programming model, ADC makes data-centered Web application development a reality for Visual Basic developers. The speed and efficiency offered by ADC technologies, such as the Virtual Table Manager, make this framework an attractive one for applications that need navigation of large result sets, fast updating, and coherent caching with distributed transaction support.

ADC Framework Components

The ADC framework consists of several integrated components that work together to deliver live data, updatability, caching, and server object-invocation services. As a VBScript and Visual Basic programmer, you will seldom need to understand the intricacies of the Virtual Table Manager, for example, but understanding the underlying architecture will help you decide how to place your application logic on the client, application server, and database. Each of the components are described in the following sections.

The first feature you should notice is the availability of live data on the client. The browser has access to a dynamic, in-memory cache, where relational and object data can be stored, retrieved, and modified. Updates can, at the programmer's discretion, be transmitted to the application server, where the changes can be immediately stored in the database or processed further by server business objects.

15

These application objects are typically used to encapsulate business logic. By *business logic*, I mean the specific rules that a business, such as a bank, has for processing and dealing with data. It typically consists of rules coded into the application logic of the Server object's methods. A banking application, for example, might have a Loan object with a method called ProcessLoanApplication. This method would contain the rules for determining whether a prospective customer qualifies for the loan program offered by the bank. A bank probably wouldn't want to have its rules and practices available in the form of VBScript code on HTML pages. To keep the rules confidential, the banking application would create one or more of these business objects on the server, where they could process data but not be downloaded for examination and "hacking" on the client.

ADC can operate without a connection being held open on the server, yet still retain the transactional state of cached objects and data. This context can be used on the application server later to reconnect objects to their datasources and commit changes made in distributed and local transactions.

While on the client, data is stored in the *in-memory cache*, called the *Virtual Table Manager* (VTM). This cache supports the notion of transactional isolation (explained in the following section, "Understanding Transactions"). Programming the VTM is done implicitly by using ADO Recordset objects. Visual Basic/VBScript programmers never have to program the VTM directly; instead, they can rely on the ADO programming model, which was covered in Week 2, "Server-Side Rowsets with ActiveX Data Objects." This feature makes using the VTM easier for HTML/VBScript developers. The VTM is discussed in more detail in Chapter 20, "Business Objects and ADO."

NOTE   Sharing transactional workspaces isn't available in the current version of the Advanced Data Connector. It will be available with version 2.0. For now, every Recordset gets its own transactional workspace.

The diagram in Figure 15.3 shows ADC's main components interacting to process an application request, much as the components interacted in the CGI-based program flow in Figure 15.1. Notice that, with ADC, server objects—each with its own life span, transactional scope, and unique identity—are used to process requests from the client browser. ADC facilitates the easy introduction of object-oriented programming for the Web by extending the Visual Basic object model with the concept of *proxies* for distributed objects. A *proxy* is a stand-in for a remote object within a local address space.

Figure 15.3.
The ADC program flow.

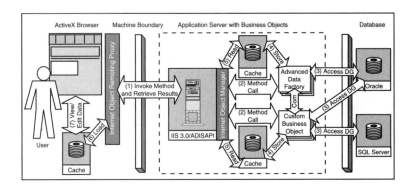

NOTE

A *proxy* takes the place of a server object, intercepting calls to the object and handling the marshaling of input and output parameters over HTTP or DCOM, the two transport protocols supported by ADC. From the perspective of the client-side programmer, the proxy *is* the Server object, which simplifies using distributed objects in a Web application.

The *Internet Object Remoting Proxy* (*IORP*) is the generic HTTP proxy used by ADC. For DCOM proxies, ADC uses the registered proxies in the local system registry to create object instances and marshal data. Visual Basic programmers don't have to know a thing about how the proxy mechanism works; they simply program with the instantiated proxies (created by the AdvancedDataSpace object's CreateObject() method).

Components that are usually associated with the client—that is, the browser—side of the framework enable local caching of data and invoking remote object methods on server application objects. The VTM supplies the underlying mechanism by which all the results retrieved in the course of a Web application's program flow can be stored in transaction workspaces on the client and used by several visual controls.

Understanding Transactions

A *transaction* is a logical unit of work; it can be started, aborted, or committed. Once a transaction is started, all subsequent work up to the first abort or commit is considered to be occurring *within* the transaction. A transaction encompasses critical business processing events and actions and can be thought of as the carrier of business logic, as opposed to

15

programming logic. A transaction has four properties that make it very useful—indeed, necessary—for doing any sort of distributed application design:

☐ **Atomicity:** A transaction, although it may encompass many data transformations and processes, always either completely works or completely fails. If a transaction fails, then all changes done within it are rolled back to their *pre-transaction state*, and the system is left as though the transaction had never occurred.

☐ **Consistency:** A transaction never leaves the database, the stored data of the system, in an inconsistent state. If a change is made to the system, it's one that can be undone if the transaction fails at some later point.

☐ **Isolation:** A transaction works as though it were in complete isolation from all other transactions in a system. Although several transactions can use a piece of data, or change the state of a system, they do so without knowing what transformations were made to that system by other transactions.

☐ **Durability:** A transaction's changes, once committed, persist beyond any system failures. Once a transaction's changes are committed, any subsequent failures of the system won't undo the committed transaction's changes to existing data structures.

Collectively, these properties are known by the acronym *ACID* properties of transactions. The ACID properties allow an application to guarantee that the data it uses in the course of its control flow is consistent with the database and, should any problems arise, that the database is left in a consistent state. This consistency is imperative in systems such as financial management software, where lack of transaction consistency can lead to serious problems. For example, if debits are made from one account but the credits to the other account fail and are never recorded, then the money has been subtracted from the account but ends up "lost" electronically. Imagine that this is your 401K investment being rolled over from one plan to another, and you begin to see the value of a data cache that understands and operates with the idea of a transactional workspace.

 NOTE

A *transactional workspace* is an abstraction of the Isolation property described for transactions' ACID properties. A workspace should be thought of as a boundary in which objects exist. All objects within this boundary can potentially see changes made to other objects that they might be affected by. Take, for example, an ActiveX control that displays the subtotal for an invoice. The total is based on the aggregate total of objects edited in another ActiveX control—a visual grid where users enter product identifiers, descriptions, and totals. As the user enters new item rows, the Subtotal control—a basic text field—would be refreshed with the new running total.

> This refreshing happens because the subtotal field and the order-entry grid are in the same transactional workspace and can "see" changes made to one another. The mechanism through which this happens in ADC is the VTM, which sends change notifications to objects in the same workspace—that is, feeding off the same ADO `Recordset`. In this way, should the transaction be aborted, all the ActiveX controls displaying the `Recordset`'s edited data would be reset to the `Recordset`'s state before the transaction began. This illustrates the Atomicity property of transactions—either all the changes performed within the scope of the transaction are made durable (saved to a permanent storage system) or they are all undone.

A related concept, called *isolation level*, describes how much visibility ongoing changes to data objects in a distinct transaction have. Visibility ranges from having no access to these uncommitted changes, called READ COMMITTED isolation, to having full view of the changes. The "right" isolation for an application depends mostly on the business logic. Application developers must remember that uncommitted changes they see (that is, changes that haven't been made durable) can be aborted and discarded.

ADC Component Descriptions

The following components are considered client components in the ADC framework:

- ☐ Virtual Table Manager (VTM)
- ☐ Internet Object Remoting Proxy (IORP)
- ☐ `AdvancedDataControl` (ADC)
- ☐ `AdvancedDataSpace` (ADS)
- ☐ `AdvancedDataFactory` (ADF)
- ☐ ADOR `Recordset`

These components are considered server components in the ADC framework:

- ☐ Advanced Data Connector Internet Server Extension (ADISAPI)
- ☐ Internet Object Manager (IOM)
- ☐ `AdvancedDataFactory` (ADF)
- ☐ ADOR `Recordset`
- ☐ ActiveX Data Objects (ADO) Library (`Connection`, `Command`, and `Recordset`)
- ☐ Advanced Data Tablegram (ADTG)

The descriptions of these components are given in the following sections. For more detailed descriptions, refer to Chapter 17, "The AdvancedDataControl and the ADO Recordset." Several of ADC's components could be considered both server *and* client (those that are have been indicated in the following sections), meaning they can be created and used in browser application code, using VBScript or JavaScript, or on application servers with the Internet Object Manager.

Virtual Table Manager

The Virtual Table Manager (VTM), which can appear on the server or client, is an in-memory relational data cache that makes OLE DB interfaces available for data access and manipulation. It supports marshaling its contents through IMarshal and IPersistStream interfaces among multiple server tiers and provides client-side cursor models over its cache elements.

NOTE

> A *cursor* is a view of the data inside the VTM, including a notion of looking at a specific position or row called *currency*. Data-aware ActiveX controls use these cursors to access data in the VTM and to keep their displays synchronized with the current position of the VTM's Recordset data. VTM's cursors are said to be *disconnected*, meaning that cursor and data storage keep all the Recordset's data on the client. This is a requirement for Internet scenarios, when the server can't be expected to maintain portions of a Recordset, which might be thousands of rows, while also servicing thousands of ADC requests from clients. Having disconnected cursors reduces the load on the server and also allows much faster data access at the client, because all the data is cached on the client in the VTM's "workspaces," which might contain one or more Recordsets of data.

The VTM maintains relational data, client updates, and record status information. Visual Basic programmers can use ADO objects, primarily Recordsets, to access, update, and store data in the VTM.

Internet Object Remoting Proxy

The Internet Object Remoting Proxy (IORP) is a client-side remoting component used to marshal data into and out of the ADC VTM and to the Server objects. The IORP provides the HTTP proxy for business objects that can be accessed through HTTP, rather than DCOM. The Internet Object Remoting Proxy is a non-visual object; it's created whenever the `AdvancedDataSpace`'s `CreateObject()` method is used to create an HTTP proxy. Here's the VBScript code to create the IORP:

```
SUB GetRecordsetTest
    Dim myProxy
    Dim myRecordet
    Set myProxy = myADS.CreateObject("MYPROGID", "http://Server")
    Set myRecordset = myProxy.GetServerRecordsets(25)
END SUB
```

This code creates an instance of an object proxy, called `myProxy`, which can then be used to invoke methods on the remote object—in this case, to return `Recordsets` from the `Server` object. The IORP is the client-side piece of ADC's HTTP object-remoting infrastructure. The server-side piece is the Internet Object Manager, which is a logical part of the ADISAPI dynamic link library registered with IIS 3.0. The IORP handles the marshaling of object requests, input parameters, and the unmarshaling of return parameters, including populating the VTM cache with the results.

The `AdvancedDataControl` Object

The `AdvancedDataControl` object is a datasource control compatible with Internet Explorer 3.0 and a data-binding manager for Internet Explorer–based applications. It allows for Visual Basic–style data-access programming in VBScript/HTML Web pages. `AdvancedDataControl` is a non-visual, drop-in control that's embedded on Web pages with an `<OBJECT>` tag to enable database access and update support to Web applications using the ADC framework. Here's an example of its initialization:

```
<OBJECT CLASSID="clsid:9381D8F2-0288-11d0-9501-00AA00B911A5"
    ID="ADCControl1"
    WIDTH=1 HEIGHT=1>
    <PARAM NAME="BINDINGS" VALUE="Grid1;">
    <PARAM NAME="SQL" VALUE="select * from customers">
    <PARAM NAME="SERVER" VALUE="http://webserver">
    <PARAM NAME="CONNECT" VALUE="DSN=TESTCON1;uid=test1;pwd=test1;">
</OBJECT>
```

The four main properties made available by the `AdvancedDataControl` object are `Bindings`, `SQL`, `Connect`, and `Server`. These four properties supply the underpinning for ADC's programming model. By setting them, the VBScript programmer gets simple, effective data access, without resorting to object proxies, writing custom objects, and worrying about `AdvancedDataSpace` "workspaces." The data retrieved through this simple model is stored in the VTM and can be updated later through ActiveX data-aware controls, such as those specified in the `Bindings` property. These updates can then be pushed back to the server, where they can be permanently stored in the database.

15

The AdvancedDataSpace Object

The AdvancedDataSpace (ADS) object is a non-visual, drop-in object constructor for creating in-process OLE Automation objects, HTTP proxies, and DCOM marshaling proxies. It manages the transactional workspace used to establish communication to remote OLE Automation servers over HTTP. Its role as a transaction space coordinator for application developers permits partitioning Recordsets and data cache states. Each object proxy created by a specific ADS is considered to be within that ADS's transactional workspace. The following example creates two AdvancedDataSpace objects, an AdvancedDataControl object, and a few HTTP proxies:

```
<!-- These are embedded on the HTML Page -->

<OBJECT CLASSID="clsid:99586d40-db60-11cf-9d87-00aa00b91181"
    ID=ADS1>
</OBJECT>

<OBJECT CLASSID="clsid:99586d40-db60-11cf-9d87-00aa00b91181"
    ID=ADS2>
</OBJECT>

<OBJECT CLASSID="clsid:9381D8F2-0288-11d0-9501-00AA00B911A5"
    ID=ADC1>
    <PARAM NAME="BINDINGS" VALUE="Grid;">
    <PARAM NAME="SQL" VALUE="Select Company_name, Order_id from Orders">
    <PARAM NAME="CONNECT" VALUE="DSN=TESTDSN1;UID=test1;PWD=test1;">
    <PARAM NAME="SERVER" VALUE="http://webserver1">
    <PARAM NAME="DATASPACE" VALUE="ADS1">
</OBJECT>

<!-- Later, these objects are programmatically created with VBScript code -->
SUB TestWorkspaceIsolation
    Dim myProxy1
    Dim myProxy2
    Set myProxy1 = ADS1.CreateObject("MYPROGID", "http://webserver1")
    Set myProxy2 = ADS2.CreateObject("MYNEWPROGID", "http://webserver1")
END SUB
```

The first object proxy, myProxy1, and the AdvancedDataControl object, ADC1, both share the same transactional workspace within the VTM because they're associated with the same AdvancedDataSpace object. Any query results stored and updated through the Recordset associated with ADC1 can be seen immediately by the owner of myProxy1, if the proxy has an open Recordset that shares some columns with the Recordset of ADC1.

NOTE

As I mentioned earlier, sharing transactional workspaces isn't available in the current version of the Advanced Data Connector. It will be available with version 2.0. For now, every Recordset gets its own transactional workspace.

The `AdvancedDataFactory` Object

The `AdvancedDataFactory` (ADF) object, which can appear on the server or client, is a SQL query and update control used with `AdvancedDataControl` objects to retrieve and post data to back-end datasources that support ODBC. `AdvancedDataFactory` functions as a utility object and template to develop business objects compatible with the ADC framework for distributed application development. It's marked as a `SafeForScripting` object, so it can be used on both client machines and application servers.

Several of the methods made available by the `AdvancedDataControl` object are wrappers for underlying ADF methods. When programmers set the four properties on the `AdvancedDataControl` object to get easy data access, they're indirectly using the ADF object to perform the querying and update operations.

The following code shows how an ADF method is invoked directly rather than indirectly through the `AdvancedDataControl` object. An ADF HTTP proxy is created within an event handler, and the `Query()` method is invoked, causing the actual `Server` object (ADF) to process the query and return a `Recordset` containing the query's. This `Recordset` is marshaled back to the client browser by the Internet Object Manager, and the ADOR `Recordset` return value is assigned to a local variable called `myResultSet`. The VBScript code makes use of a server variable called `SERVER_NAME`, indicating that it's part of an ASP file and that the target HTML specifying the actual IIS server name will be dynamically determined—that is, *late bound*—when the page is downloaded to the browser.

```
SUB LoadPage
Dim myQueryEngine
Dim myResultSet
Set myQueryEngine = ADS1.CreateObject("AdvancedDataFactory",
➡"http://<%=Request.ServerVariables("SERVER_NAME")%>")
Set myResultSet = myQueryEngine.Query("DSN=DEMO1;UID=test1;PWD=test1;",
➡"select customerid, customername from customerprofile for browse")
END SUB
```

ADISAPI (Advanced Data Internet Server API) and Internet Object Manager

The ADISAPI is an Internet Information Server (IIS) 3.0 ISAPI extension library that offers data analyzing, OLE Automation control, `Recordset` marshaling, and Advanced Data TableGram packaging, streaming, and unpackaging. The ADISAPI component takes HTTP posts with multipart MIME for parameters and converts them into a sequence of standard COM interface calls. The return value and error code is marshaled back to the client through multipart MIME.

15

This extension library performs the work needed to create object instances, invoke their services through OLE Automation interfaces, and process the return parameters for transport back to the calling client through the *tabular data-streaming protocol*. This format, called ADTG, is defined for sending tabular data, such as rows from a SQL database query result, over HTTP. The format is very efficient and used by ADC components to move the tabular data across the HTTP. The IORP object makes it possible to marshal OLE-DB Rowsets from one machine to another over HTTP.

The Internet Object Manager (IOM) component is responsible for invoking objects and methods and managing the life cycle of objects. With ADC 1.5, custom business objects written by programmers in Visual Basic can be stored on the server between method calls, allowing complex transactional states to be cached on both the client and server sides of the HTTP stream. The IOM is also responsible for performing security look-ups on requested objects to verify that they are SafeForScripting and SafeForInitialization objects.

The ADOR Recordset

ADC supports disconnected Recordset marshaling as parameters over HTTP and DCOM protocols, based on the ADOR Recordset (which can appear on the server or client) implementation supplied by the ActiveX Data Objects (ADO) team. These Recordset objects can be reconnected to datasources on the application server (middle-tier), allowing convenient distributed data processing for Internet scenarios. In Chapter 17, these objects are described in detail, especially the different marshaling options available to the VBScript programmer—such as marshaling only changed data back to the application server, instead of the entire result set. This option makes data transport more efficient and speeds up application processing. Imagine querying for 100,000 rows, updating only one or two of them, and then having to marshal all the rows, both changed and unchanged, back to the application server over a slow, 28.8 modem. ADC's ADOR Recordsets default to marshaling only the changed rows of a Recordset back to the client.

ActiveX Data Objects (ADO)

The primary programming model for ADC is ActiveX Data Objects, which has been covered extensively in Week 2. ADC custom business objects and server scripts use ADO objects (which can appear on the server or client) extensively for all data access and programming. ADC fully supports ADO Connection, Command, and Recordset objects, including all methods and properties. ADO Recordset objects can't be marshaled; that is, they can't be moved from one address space to another, especially over HTTP.

ADC remedies this problem through a simple property setting. The Visual Basic object builder just needs to set the CursorLocation property on an ADODB Recordset to get a Recordset object that can be marshaled. This Recordset can then be moved to the client, where VBScript programming can further manipulate it, and the results can be displayed through ActiveX data-aware controls. The following code is a short example of a custom business object method that returns an ADODB Recordset that can be marshaled to the client:

```
Public Function ListPublications() As Variant
    Dim myRecordset As New ADODB.Recordset
    Dim mySql As String

    mySql = "Select publisher_name, author, title from publishers, titles"

    myRecordset.CursorLocation = adUseClientBatch
myRecordset.Open mySql, "DSN=TESTDSN1;UID=test1;PWD=test1;",
➥adUnspecified, adLockBatchOptimistic, adCmdUnspecified

    Set ListPublications = myRecordset
End Function
```

This Recordset is packaged and streamed to the client application by the Internet Object Manager and ADISAPI. On the client side, the Internet Object Remoting Proxy unpacks the Recordset, creates the VTM, loads the Recordset into a transactional workspace, and then returns control to the calling program. The client-side script can then access the Recordset and its data, and bind the Recordset to AdvancedDataControl objects, or use it in subsequent calls to other remote object methods.

Advanced Data TableGram (ADTG) Streaming Protocol

ADTG is a compact, wire-efficient application protocol for streaming tabular and object status data across application protocols, such as HTTP. The protocol defines a *tablegram*, a self-describing data BLOB that supports transport of any type of data. The ADTG is one of two methods used to populate the VTM; the other is using OLE DB interfaces made available by the cache component.

VBScript programmers almost never need to examine the ADTG streams. The ADTG streams carry all the relational and object states of application server objects to the browser-client. The ADTG tablegram is also used in synchronizing and reconciling disconnected VTM caches after updates are performed against database servers for data cached locally. These status tablegrams carry update result status information, error information, new values and time stamps, and other information necessary for maintaining a coherent cache after an update operation is performed on a persistent data store. ADTG is the glue that keeps disconnected VTMs and application instances that are running on different machines or different processes synchronized and coherent in a distributed transaction framework.

15

15

The ADC components are explained in more detail, by examining each object and its methods and properties, in Chapter 17. For now, you have enough information to discuss the ADC programming model and dive into a short programming exercise. You will build a small contact database for use within Internet Explorer so you can learn how to program data access and update with the AdvancedDataControl object by itself. More advanced concepts, such as custom business objects, Active Server Page scripting, and transactions, are introduced in Chapter 17.

The ADC Programming Model

This section briefly introduces the simple ADC programming model. ADC actually offers two distinct models, depending on the requirements of the VBScript programmer and the need for custom object processing. This section covers just the simple model; the advanced model is explained in Chapter 16, "Using the AdvancedDataControl Object." I already mentioned the simple model when describing the ADC client-side components; it consists of just the following elements:

☐ An AdvancedDataControl object with the following properties set: Bindings, SQL, Connect, and Server. Setting these properties through the <OBJECT> tag PARAM syntax, or setting them by writing code in the OnLoad event, is enough to perform simple data access, marshal the data to the client-side VTM cache, and populate the data-aware controls that have been designated in the Bindings property.

☐ One or more ActiveX data-aware controls associated with the AdvancedDataControl object. These controls can be complex data-aware controls, such as the Sheridan SSDBGrid, or simple controls, such as the built-in Internet Explorer 3.0 text fields. An arbitrarily large set of controls can be managed by a single AdvancedDataControl, and multiple AdvancedDataControls can be embedded on a page, each with a different Recordset and query.

☐ One or more event handlers for invoking SubmitChanges() and CancelUpdates() events. This element is required only if the programmer wants to let the user interact with the data displayed. You can create a simple event handler, such as SUB Update_OnClick, which internally calls ADC.SubmitChanges(). This is a wrapper around the ADC method calls, which internally delegate all update processing on the AdvancedDataFactory proxy.

NOTE

A *wrapper* is a method or object that conceals some internal functioning, delegation, or logic. In this case, the ADC hides the existence of the ADF. The ADC's methods internally invoke the ADF, a detail that a

> new programmer might not really need to know about. This limits the
> number of objects that the client programmer has to keep track of and
> use in simple applications. It's a "convenience function"— something
> to make the programmer's job easier.

This simple model intentionally omits most of the mechanics of client-side caching, use of
Internet Object Remoting Proxies, and programming control of the Recordset object, which
contains the state of the data access query. It's an ideal model for simple data publishing and
can be used to construct fairly sophisticated Web database applications. Until an application
needs to implement application server objects, this model is adequate for building pages with
dynamic data access, updates, and high-performance data navigation.

I haven't yet discussed most of the details on configuring system datasource names (DSNs),
ODBC drivers to target datasources, and the configuration of IIS 3.0 for use with ADC.
These topics form the first part of Chapter 16. Like VBScript programming for ADC on the
client, the configuration of the server components is a straightforward task.

Summary

You have covered a good deal of material in this introductory section. Starting with CGI
programming for the Web, you have learned about the Microsoft Advanced Data Connector,
a component technology designed to address some limitations of CGI programming and to
create a framework for developing high-performance Web database applications within
ActiveX browsers. The main components of the ADC framework—AdvancedDataControl,
AdvancedDataFactory, AdvancedDataSpace, and ADO Recordsets—create an elegant and
powerful programming model for developing data-intensive applications. ADC also offers
update support and data remoting, which frees the application developer to concentrate on
implementing application logic, rather than coding server scripts to perform database
updating.

You have also learned about the importance of the VTM and its role as an in-memory
database for storing relational and object data. All this information might sound a bit
overwhelming, but ADC's core ideas represent an immense simplification of the database
programming chores typically required when writing Web applications. Visual Basic
programmers are given the opportunity to re-use their knowledge of ActiveX controls, which
can be embedded and used in ADC Web applications just as they can in Visual Basic
standalone development. The AdvancedDataControl object is actually a Web-enhanced
version of the datasource control familiar to Visual Basic programmers. Anyone familiar with
the RDO control can instantly recognize the usefulness and purpose of the

15

AdvancedDataControl. In the next chapter, you put this knowledge to use. For now, review the ADC component descriptions, try the quiz questions and exercises, and then take a well-earned rest.

Q&A

Q **What is the purpose of the `AdvancedDataFactory`? What other ADC object makes heavy use of its methods?**

A The purpose of the ADF is to provide simple data querying and updating capabilities against any ADC-compatible datasources. The `AdvancedDataControl` makes heavy use of the ADF; it re-introduces the query and update methods of the ADF to create a simpler programming model.

Q **What is a transaction workspace? How are these workspaces created and defined?**

A A transaction workspace is a partitioning mechanism in the Virtual Table Manager. It allows data from different transactions to reside within the same cache without causing the transactions' ACID properties to be jeopardized. The workspaces are defined by the `AdvancedDataSpace` (ADS) objects embedded on the downloaded HTML page or Active Server Page.

Objects associated with the same ADS—that is, that have been created with the `CreateObject()` method of the same ADS—will have all their result sets' (`Recordsets`) share state. This means that these `Recordsets` might instantly see changes made to other "associated" `Recordsets`. The default behavior for `AdvancedDataControl` objects, if the `ActiveDataSpace` property isn't set to a specific value, is to create a new ADS, thereby creating a new transaction workspace in the VTM. So, by default, all query results have their own workspace and don't have the same share state as other query results.

Q **What are the advantages of using ADC over other Web database access technologies?**

A ADC was designed with a few priorities in mind: making dynamic, live data available to ActiveX browser developers, offering a high-performance, easy-to-learn programming model to Visual Basic developers, and providing an extensible application model that supports cache coherency and custom server object development. ADC runs on top of OLE DB and ODBC, meaning it's accessible by the largest possible number of compatible databases. By starting with a well-known Visual Basic programming model and datasource controls, and extending the concept to Web browsers, ADC allows programmers to actually use what they have previously learned directly and effectively.

Quiz

1. What's an ADOR `Recordset`? Why is it useful in developing Web applications? Where are they stored on the client side? What other programming object is it directly related to?

2. What are the four core properties of the `AdvancedDataControl`? What are they used for? Describe each of them.

3. What is the primary programming model for ADC on the server? What are the components of that model? (Hint: You have been studying it for over a week now.)

4. What's the role of the Internet Object Remoting Proxy? What is the server-side component that complements it? What protocols does the IORP support? Can you think of some protocols it should support but currently doesn't?

5. What do the following terms mean?

    transaction
    marshaling
    proxy
    protocol

6. Name at least two protocols mentioned in this chapter. (These terms are used continuously throughout Week 3, so knowing what they mean is vital!)

7. What are the client-side components of ADC? What are the server-side components?

8. What is the purpose of Advanced Data TableGrams? Why are they necessary in the ADC framework? Give at least one example of how a tablegram is used.

9. What two browser scripting languages is ADC compatible with?

10. What is the VTM? What role does it play in making data navigation more efficient? What are the workspaces it supports? Why would these be important to programmers?

11. What ADC component can be used in VBScript code to create HTTP and DCOM proxies through programming? Why would someone use a proxy instead of the object itself on the Web page? Discuss Web security issues, such as `SafeForScripting`. Does this have something to do with using proxies? What would be the danger in creating a non-`SafeForScripting` object on the client machine? Can you think of some scenarios where creating arbitrary objects on the client could lead to disastrous results?

Exercise

Try to load and run the sample application that you will be developing tomorrow from the Samples folder. Load the VBScript code and look it over, seeing whether you can identify the AdvancedDataControl object and determine the values of the Bindings, SQL, Connect, and Server properties. Look over the event handlers, and note the AdvancedDataControl methods being invoked.

Day 16

Using the AdvancedDataControl Object

by Joyce Chia-Hsun Chen

Yesterday, you learned about the concept of Advanced Data Connector—how it's different from traditional CGI programming and its approach to Web database programming. You also saw the roles of the server and client components in the Advanced Data Connector framework. By now, you should have an overall understanding of what you can do with Advanced Data Connector and have a basic grasp of Advanced Data Connector components, such as `AdvancedDataControl`, `AdvancedDataSpace`, and `AdvancedDataFactory`.

One of the drawbacks of traditional Web database programming is that the returned result set is static; there's no way to directly manipulate the data at runtime. This drawback restricts the Web database application's ability to interact with the data. Advanced Data Connector has addressed this problem by providing an important feature: the ability to manipulate live data. *Live data* exists in an active cache on the client machine, rather than being just a static local copy on the Web page. With the data stored in an active cache, you can manipulate it to get true interactive Web database programming. This is how Advanced Data Connector can help you develop data-intensive interactive Web database programming.

Advanced Data Connector stores live data by using the Virtual Table Manager, which was briefly discussed in Chapter 15, "The Advanced Data Connector (ADC)." Today, however, you'll go into more depth on exactly how the Virtual Table Manager handles live data in the client machine and learn how to use AdvancedDataControl objects in a Web page to manipulate live data and bind it to data-aware Visual Basic controls. The properties and methods of AdvancedDataControl objects are also discussed in depth throughout today's lesson. After today, you will be able to program AdvancedDataControl objects in your Web page and bind the live data to Visual Basic data-bound controls. Specifically, after reading this chapter, you will be able to do the following:

- ☐ Explain how you can manipulate live data with Advanced Data Connector
- ☐ List the components of the client tier of the Advanced Data Connector architecture
- ☐ List the methods and properties of the AdvancedDataControl object
- ☐ Use AdvancedDataControl objects in a Web page
- ☐ Bind live data to input fields
- ☐ Bind live data to data-aware VB4 or VB5 controls

NOTE

> To run the examples in this chapter, please make sure you refer to the setup instructions included in "Week 3 at a Glance."

Manipulating Data on the Client Tier

Advanced Data Connector's availability of live data makes it distinct from other technologies. Advanced Data Connector differs from IDC/HTX (Internet Database Connector and HTML extension files) and ActiveX Data Objects (ADO) in its ability to return live data instead of HTML pages with static tables containing non-interactive data. With AdvancedDataControl, you can also bind the live data with Visual Basic data-aware controls, which gives you more flexibility for manipulating the data at runtime.

16

Using IDC/HTX for Web Pages

Microsoft Internet Information Server 1.0 introduced the idea of IDC and HTX. IDC allows you to specify a query, an ODBC datasource, and a template file so that you can submit the query result into the HTML template on a Web page. The IDC file has information about the datasource name, user ID, password, SQL statement, and template HTX filename. The query is sent to the ODBC datasource specified under the `Datasource` keyword in the IDC file when the Web page is loaded or refreshed. The returned data from the query is static in the client machine and on the Web page, so you can't interact with it onscreen. Listing 16.1 is an example of how you could use IDC and HTX files to retrieve data from a table and place it into the HTML template on a Web page.

Listing 16.1. The IDC file (16TWD01.IDC).

```
Datasource: AdvWorks
Username: idcsmpl1
Template: 16exc01.htx
SQLStatement: SELECT ContactFirstName, ContactLastName from Customers
```

In this example, you use the Microsoft Access database file ADVWORKS.MDB that ships with Internet Information Server 3.0 with Active Server Pages. First, create a system datasource named AdvWorks. You want to retrieve data to fill the ContactFirstName and ContactLastName columns from the Customers table. In the IDC file, specify the ODBC datasource name `AdvWorks` for the `Datasource` parameter and the user ID `sa` for the `Username` parameter. No password is required for sa, so you can omit the `password` parameter. For the `SQLStatement` parameter, use `SELECT ContactFirstName, ContactLastName from Customers`. Once you get the returned result set, an HTX template is populated with the data and displayed in a Web page. The HTX template is specified under the `Template` parameter; in this example, it's called 16TWD01.HTX. Listing 16.2 shows the content of the file.

Listing 16.2. The HTX template file (16TWD01.HTX).

```
1: <HTML>
2: <HEAD>
3: <TITLE>Teach Yourself Active Web Databases with VB in 21 Days</TITLE>
4: </HEAD>
5: <BODY BGCOLOR="ffffff" TEXT="000000" LINK="000080" LANGUAGE="VBS">
6: <CENTER>
7: <H1><font size=4>
➥Teach Yourself Active Web Databases with VB in 21 Days</H1></font>
8: <H2><font size=3>Using IDC/HTX to retrieve data</H2></font>
9: <BR>
10: <HR size=4 width=80%>
```

continues

Listing 16.2. continued

```
11: <BR><BR>
12: <TABLE align=center COLSPAN=8 CELLPADDING=5 BORDER=0 WIDTH=200>
13: <!-- BEGIN column header row -->
14: <TR>
15: <TD  VALIGN=TOP BGCOLOR="#800000">
16: <FONT STYLE="ARIAL NARROW" COLOR="#ffffff" SIZE=1>First Name</FONT>
17: </TD>
18: <TD ALIGN=CENTER BGCOLOR="#800000">
19: <FONT STYLE="ARIAL NARROW" COLOR="#ffffff" SIZE=1>Last Name</FONT>
20: </TD></TR>
21: <%begindetail%>
22: <TR>
23: <TD BGcolor ="f7efde" align=center>
24: <font style ="arial narrow" size=1>
25: <%ContactFirstName%></TD><TD BGcolor ="f7efde" align=center>
26: <font style ="arial narrow" size=1>
27: <%ContactLastName%></TD></TR>
28: <%enddetail%>
29: </font></align></center></FONT></TABLE>
30: </BODY>
31: </HTML>
```

The most important thing in this HTX file is indicating where you want your returned results displayed. To specify where you're going to display the returned data of the ContactFirstName and ContactLastName columns in the HTX template, you need to use the <%*column name*%> format. In this example, <%ContactFirstName%> and <%ContactLastName%> in the HTX template show where the data should be displayed. Use <%begindetail%> and <%enddetail%> to mark the section where the returned result is inserted. Verify the following steps before running the IDC/HTX example:

1. Install Microsoft Internet Information Server 1.0 or higher. For downloading information, please see Appendix A, "Where to Find Everything."

2. Put the IDC and HTX files in the same virtual directory and grant both Read and Execute for the access privileges. For a review on how to set up IIS and virtual directories in IIS, please refer to Chapter 2, "The Client-Server Model."

3. From Internet Explorer, enter http://IISServerName/VirtualDirectory/ 16twd01.idc in the Address text box and click the Refresh button or press Enter. For downloading information on Internet Explorer, please see Appendix A.

From the screen shown in Figure 16.1, you can see that all the data from the ContactFirstName and ContactLastName columns has been selected from the Customer table and the returned result set has been listed in a table structure. Note that this data is a static part of the HTML page, so you can't interact with it at runtime.

Figure 16.1.

The result of using IDC/HTX to retrieve data.

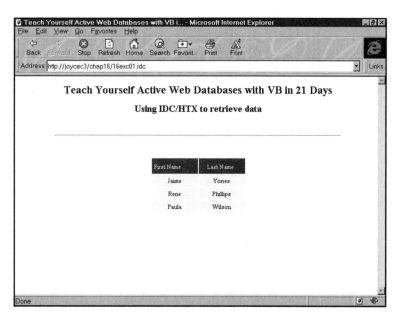

Using ASP/ADO for Web Pages

Now take a look at ActiveX Data Objects (ADO). Microsoft Internet Information Server 3.0 with Active Server Pages (ASP) allows you to build HTML Web pages with VBScript. You can use ADO in VBScript to query the ODBC datasource and populate the HTML page with the result set. ASP combined with ADO in a Web page allows you to retrieve data in a more complex manner, but you can retrieve data *only* at the time the Web page is loaded or refreshed. Once the data is fetched and stored in your Web browser, it's no longer live data; it exists in your Web page as static, non-interactive data. For instance, you can't dynamically scroll the data or perform any insert/update/delete operations on it.

Listing 16.3 shows how to use ADO to retrieve data and display the results on a Web page. Note that the extension for ASP files is .ASP.

Listing 16.3. Using ADO to retrieve and display data (16TWD02.ASP).

```
1: <%@ LANGUAGE = VBScript %>
2: <HTML>
3: <TITLE>Teach Yourself Active Web Databases with VB in 21 Days</TITLE>
4: </HEAD>
5: <BODY BGCOLOR="ffffff" TEXT="000000" LINK="000080" LANGUAGE="VBS">
6: <CENTER>
7: <H1><font size=4>
➥Teach Yourself Active Web Databases with VB in 21 Days</H1></font>
```

continues

Listing 16.3. continued

```
 8: <H2><font size=3>Using ASP/ADO to retrieve data</H2></font>
 9: <BR>
10: <HR size=4 width=80%>
11: <%set myConnection = server.CreateObject("ADODB.Connection")
12: myConnection.Open "AdvWorks"
13: SQLQuery = "select ContactFirstName,ContactLastName from customers"
14: set RSCustomerList =  myConnection.Execute(SQLQuery)%>
15: <br><br>
16: <center>
17: <TABLE align=center COLSPAN=8 CELLPADDING=5 BORDER=0 WIDTH=200>
18: <!-- BEGIN column header row -->
19: <TR>
20: <TD   VALIGN=TOP BGCOLOR="#800000">
21: <FONT STYLE="ARIAL NARROW" COLOR="#ffffff" SIZE=1>First Name</FONT>
22: </TD>
23: <TD ALIGN=CENTER BGCOLOR="#800000">
24: <FONT STYLE="ARIAL NARROW" COLOR="#ffffff" SIZE=1>Last Name</FONT>
25: </TD></TR>
26: <!-- Get Data -->
27: <% do while not RScustomerList.EOF %>
28: <TR>
29: <TD BGcolor ="f7efde" align=center>
30: <font style ="arial narrow" size=1>
31: <%=RScustomerList("contactfirstname")%>
32: </font></td>
33: <TD BGcolor ="f7efde" align=center>
34: <font style ="arial narrow" size=1>
35: <%=RScustomerList("contactlastname") %>
36: </font></td>
37: <% RScustomerList.MoveNext%>
38: <%loop %>
39: <!-- Next Row -->
40: </align></center></TD></TR></FONT></TABLE>
41: </BODY>
42: </HTML>
```

With ASP, you can use the VB language in a Web page. Notice that in the IDC/HTX method, there's no way you can process the data one record at a time. With ASP, however, you can process the data in more sophisticated ways. In the preceding example, <%@LANGUAGE =VBScript%> indicates that VBScript is used in this code. For any VB language you use in the file, <% specifies the beginning of the VBScript and %> marks where it ends. The CreateObject() method creates an ADO object, and then you connect to the ODBC datasource by using the Open() method.

The SQL statement is specified by the SQLQuery property of the ADO object; the ODBC datasource and SQL statement are the same as those used in the IDC example. You execute the SQL statement by using the Execute method of the ADO object. RSCustomer points to the returned result set. Finally, you can process the records one at a time by looping through the result set and populating the Web page's table structure with data until there's no more data. In this example's VBScript, notice that the data is submitted all at once; you don't have the option of performing scrolled retrieval. ADO gives you more options for handling data than the IDC/HTX method does, but you still can't update or scroll the data onscreen.

Review the following steps before running the ASP file:

1. Install Microsoft Internet Information Server 3.0 or higher with Active Server Pages.
2. Put the ASP file in a virtual directory and grant both Read and Execute for the Access privileges.
3. From Internet Explorer, enter `http://IISServerName/VirtualDirectory/16twd02.asp` in the Address text box and click the Refresh button or press Enter.

As you can see in Figure 16.2, the returned result set is exactly the same as in the IDC example, but you need only one ASP file to do what IDC/HTX does.

Figure 16.2.

The result of using ADO to retrieve data.

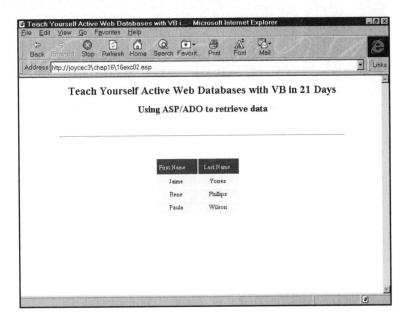

Using the AdvancedDataControl Object in Web Pages

Now that you've seen how IDC/HTX and ASP/ADO work, it's time to see how the Advanced Data Connector architecture makes data-centered interactive Web programming possible. With Advanced Data Connector architecture, the results stay active in a cache in the Virtual Table Manager (VTM), which allows you to manipulate the data. You can scroll

data and do inserts, updates, and deletions, and you can dynamically scroll the
page, treating the data there as a Recordset. Listing 16.4 gives you an example
of the Advanced Data Connector's components: the AdvancedDataControl

Listing 16.4. Using the AdvancedDataControl object to retrieve data.

```
1: <HTML>
2: <TITLE>Teach Yourself Active Web Databases with VB in 21 Days</TITLE>
3: </HEAD>
4: <BODY LANGUAGE="VBS" onload ="Init" >
5: <CENTER>
6: <H1><font size=3>
➥Teach Yourself Active Web Databases with VB in 21 Days</H1></font>
7: <P><font size=2>Using AdvancedDataControl Object to retrieve data</p></font>
8: <HR size=4 width=80%>
9: <OBJECT ID="Grid1" WIDTH=400 HEIGHT=150
10:      CLASSID="CLSID:00028C00-0000-0000-0000-000000000046">
11: </OBJECT><BR>
12: <BR>
13: <table>
14:      <tr><td>ADC Server:<td><INPUT NAME=Server SIZE=70>
15:      <tr><td>Connection:<td><INPUT NAME=Connect SIZE=70>
16:      <tr><td>Query:<td><INPUT NAME=SQL SIZE=70>
17: </table>
18: <BR>
19: <INPUT TYPE=BUTTON NAME="First" VALUE="&First" onClick="MoveFirst">
20: <INPUT TYPE=BUTTON NAME="Next" VALUE="&Next" onClick="MoveNext">
21: <INPUT TYPE=BUTTON NAME="Prev" VALUE="&Prev" onClick="MovePrev">
22: <INPUT TYPE=BUTTON NAME="Last" VALUE="&Last" onClick="MoveLast">
23: <INPUT TYPE=BUTTON NAME="Run" VALUE="&Execute Query!" onClick="Requery">
24: </CENTER>
25: <OBJECT CLASSID="clsid:9381D8F2-0288-11d0-9501-00AA00B911A5"
26:      ID=ADC HEIGHT=10 WIDTH = 10
27:      CODEBASE="http://<%=Request.ServerVariables("Server_Name")%>
➥/ADCDownload/msadc10.cab">
28:      <PARAM NAME="BINDINGS" VALUE="Grid1">
29: </OBJECT>
30: <SCRIPT LANGUAGE= "VBS">
31: SUB MoveFirst
32:      ADC.MoveFirst
33: END SUB
34: SUB MoveNext
35:      ADC.MoveNext
36: END SUB
37: SUB MovePrev
38:      ADC.MovePrevious
39: END SUB
40: SUB MoveLast
41:      ADC.MoveLast
42: END SUB
43: SUB Requery
44:      ADC.Server = Server.Value
```

16

```
45:        ADC.Connect = Connect.Value
46:        ADC.SQL = SQL.Value
47:        ADC.Refresh
48: END SUB
49: SUB Init
50:        Server.Value = "http://<%=Request.ServerVariables("Server_name")%>"
51:        Connect.Value = "DSN=AdvWorks"
52:        SQL.Value = "SELECT ContactFirstName, ContactLastName FROM Customers"
53: END SUB
54: </SCRIPT>
55: </BODY>
56: </HTML>
```

Figure 16.3 illustrates the Web page before you run the SQL statement.

Figure 16.3.

Using the Advanced-
DataControl *object*
to retrieve data.

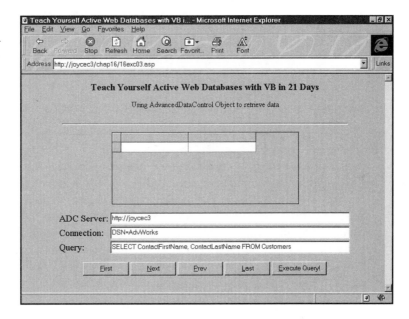

To run this example, you'll need to follow the setup instructions described in the section "Configuring Your Application and Client Server." You'll explore this program in greater detail later on, but right now, just concentrate on the returned result set. Follow these steps to see how AdvancedDataControl works in this Web page:

1. Enter the ODBC datasource (DSN=AdvWorks, in this example) in the Connection: field.

2. In the ADC Server: field, enter the HTTP server's URL.

3. Enter the SQL statement in the Query: field.

4. Click the Execute Query! button to execute the SQL statement.

Figure 16.4 shows what the Web page looks like after the SQL statement has been executed.

Figure 16.4.

The result of clicking the Execute Query! button.

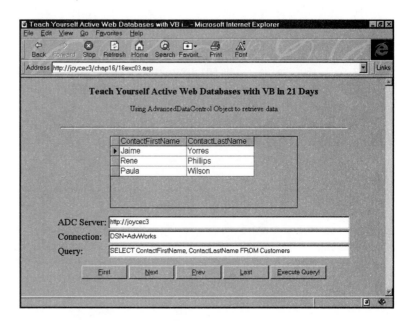

Notice that the data fills the grid control onscreen. You can move backward and forward through he records, and the text in the grid control scrolls accordingly. The data has become "active," so you can dynamically scroll it in the Web page by clicking the First, Next, Prev, and Last buttons. You don't have to load or refresh the Web page to manipulate the data. This feature is what data-centered interactive Web programming means. You can also modify this sample by changing the query to another SQL statement, such as `Select ContactFirstName, ContactLastName, BillingAddress from customers`. You can also change the connection string to any ODBC datasources that have already been set up in the Microsoft Internet Information Server (IIS).

As you can see in Figure 16.5, I changed the connection string to `DSN=video;UID=sa` and the query to `SELECT * from Video_Detail`. You can see the result displayed dynamically in the grid control, which isn't tied to a specific query. The information on how to set up the video ODBC datasource and Video_Detail table are described in the section "Configuring Your Application and Client Server." You can use any of the ODBC system DSNs in your machine to perform other queries.

16

Figure 16.5.

Changing the connection string and query.

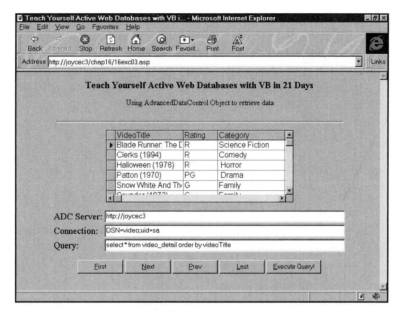

Advanced Data Connector's Three-Tier Architecture

The preceding example demonstrates true data-centered interactive Web programming. How does Advanced Data Connector do this? By using its three-tier architecture to manipulate live data.

NOTE

A *tier* represents a separate process space or machine boundary. A traditional client-server application is two-tiered. The database application resides on the client machine (the client tier) and the database server contains the database. For example, you can have an ODBC application running on your local machine while an Oracle or SQL Server database resides on a different server machine. The ODBC application, in this case, is in the client tier and the machine running Oracle or SQL Server is the application server tier. The ODBC application holds all the business and programming logic, but the database server contains only data.

In Advanced Data Connector's three-tier architecture, the *client tier* is the Web database application, the *middle tier* is the application server (for example, Internet Information Server), and the location of the database server is the third tier. The location of the database server is specified in the ODBC datasource on the application server, which is responsible for processing the request from the client tier and accessing the data in the database server. When the client tier requests data from the application server, the application server processes the request and retrieves the data from the database server. The application server then packages the data and sends it over to the Web browser (in the client tier).

The client tier stores the data in a cache that's managed by one of the Advanced Data Connector's client framework components, the Virtual Table Manager (VTM). The *Virtual Table Manager* is a dynamic, in-memory cache that stores the relational and object data. The data stays in the Virtual Table Manager until it's discarded or refreshed in the client tier. With live data stored in the Virtual Table Manager, Advanced Data Connector allows you to bind the data to Visual Basic ActiveX controls, scroll through the data, and perform insert/update/delete operations at runtime on the data stored in the VTM. If you change the data and want to apply those changes to the database server, the VTM submits only the changed data to the application server. The application server can then apply the changed data to the database server. With this capability, Advanced Data Connector really helps you build data-intense interactive Web database programs.

NOTE
In a small office or intranet setup, Advanced Data Connector may operate in a two-tier fashion, with the database server residing on the same machine as Internet Information Server. However, this configuration is still generally treated as three-tiered because the application and database server aren't the same process.

Middle-Tier (Application Server) Architecture

The application server uses an ODBC datasource to connect to the database server, but the client tier doesn't maintain any connection with the database server. The application server interacts with the database server, packages the data, and sends the data back to the client tier. The client tier component unpacks the data and stores it in a cache so that the client database Web application can manipulate the data. The application server framework includes the following components: Advanced Data Connector Internet Server Extension (ADISAPI), Internet Object Manager (Business Object), and the `AdvancedDataFactory` (ADF) and ADO `Recordset`.

16

The ADISAPI component is an Internet Information Server 3.0 ISAPI extension library. It's responsible for marshaling OLE DB rowsets from the application server to the client tier and also across the machine boundary. ADISAPI also converts the requests sent from the client tier into a sequence of standard OLE COM interface calls and creates an instance of the business objects.

The idea of using business objects is to separate the data storage and business logic from the application logic. With the business logic and access to the database server contained in the business objects, you can protect your business rules and data from being distributed. Business objects can be just like any generic ActiveX controls created with Visual Basic or Visual C++.

AdvancedDataFactory, which is the default business object if no custom business object is specified, implements methods that provide read/write access to the database server specified in the ODBC datasource. It doesn't contain any business rules—it simply supplies read/write access to the data.

The ADO Recordset serves as a wrapper for the OLE DB rowset; business objects use it to retrieve the OLE DB rowset information.

This section has given you a brief introduction to the middle-tier components. Chapter 19, "Client-Server Business Objects," explores the architecture of the middle tier and the relationship of its components in greater detail.

Advanced Data Connector's Client-Tier Architecture

The client-tier framework includes the following components: Virtual Table Manager (VTM), Internet Object Remoting Proxy (Business Object Proxy), AdvancedDataControl (ADC), AdvancedDataSpace (ADS), and ADOR Recordset (ADOR). The Virtual Table Manager, an in-memory relational data cache, maintains relational data, client updates, and record status information in the OLE DB rowset format. Programming with the VTM is done by using the ADOR Recordset, so you never have to program with the VTM directly.

Today's lesson concentrates on the client tier and shows you how to use Advanced Data Connector for live data in the client tier. The diagram in Figure 16.6 illustrates the client tier of the Advanced Data Connector architecture and how each component interacts with the others.

When the data is requested from a Web page, AdvancedDataControl objects check with the Virtual Table Manager to see whether the data exists in the VTM's temporary table. If it does, the Virtual Table Manager sends the data in an OLE DB rowset format to the AdvancedDataControl object.

Figure 16.6.

The client tier of the Advanced Data Connector architecture.

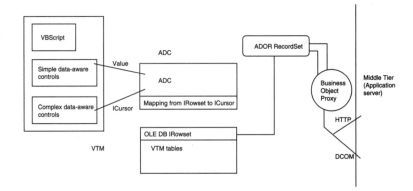

NOTE

A *rowset* is the central concept of OLE DB. Rowsets allow the OLE DB providers to display data in a tabular form. You can interact with the rowsets through the OLE DB interface. Think of rowsets as rows and columns holding the data supplied by OLE DB providers.

If the requested data is bound to a simple data-bound control or simple data-aware control, it's assigned to the controls' Values property. However, if the requested data is bound to a complex data-aware control, AdvancedDataControl must convert that data from the OLE DB rowset format to the ICursor format used in complex data-aware controls. After the data is retrieved into the Virtual Table Manager by calling the Refresh method, you can interact with the data by using the MoveFirst(), MoveNext(), MovePrevious(), and MoveLast() methods of the AdvancedDataControl object.

If the requested data isn't in the Virtual Table Manager's temporary table, a business object proxy is created implicitly by the AdvancedDataSpace object, if the CreateObject() method of the AdvancedDataSpace object isn't used. The purpose of the *business object proxy* is to access the business object in the application server across the process and machine boundary and also communicate with the ADISAPI. It's responsible for marshaling and unpacking the information about the business object. The business object proxy module communicates with the ADISAPI module, which is placed in the application server through HTTP.

The invoked methods, properties, and parameter values of the business object are packed into MIME format and marshaled to the ADISAPI module in the application server. The result of whether the specified methods, properties, and parameter values are correct is packed into the same MIME format and marshaled from the ADISAPI module in the application server back to the business object proxy in the client tier. The business object proxy unpacks the MIME packaging information into return values and output parameters for the method call.

The data retrieved through the business object in the application server is initially in OLE DB rowset format. It's packed into an Advanced Data TableGram Streaming Protocol (ADTG) stream and sent over to the client tier. ADTG is a compact, wire-efficient application for streaming tabular and object-state data across applications such as HTTP. ADTG defines a concept for a *tablegram*, a self-describing data blob that supports transporting any type of data.

The business object proxy in the client tier receives this ADTG stream data from the middle tier. Because the data is in the ADTG stream, the business object proxy invokes the ADOR `Recordset` to unpack that data into OLE DB rowsets and store it in the Virtual Table Manager's temporary table. Once the data is in the Virtual Table Manager's temporary storage, it's passed back to the `AdvancedDataControl`, which handles the OLE DB rowset and ICursor mapping described earlier.

The Virtual Table Manager temporarily stores the data in a table structure. The data is normalized so that updates, inserts, and deletions are more efficient and integrated. On top of the temporary table structure is the OLE DB IRowset layer. The ADOR `Recordset` and `AdvancedDataControl` are used to interact with the OLE DB IRowset layer. As I mentioned earlier, programming with the Virtual Table Manager is done implicitly through the ADOR `Recordset`. The ADOR `Recordset` wraps on top of the OLE DB rowset and is responsible for unpacking the data from the ADTG stream into the OLE DB rowset format. The ADOR `Recordset` is also responsible for converting the OLE DB rowset's information into an ADTG stream so that it can be marshaled across the process/machine boundary into the middle tier. The ADOR `Recordset` is covered more extensively over the next few days of lessons.

Now that you understand how the data is marshaled back from the application server to the client tier and how the data is stored in the Virtual Table Manager, you might be wondering whether the database connection still exists between the application server and the database server, since the data is stored in the client tier. Well, with data stored in the Virtual Table Manager, Advanced Data Connector can still operate while disconnected. An active connection between the application server and database server isn't necessary. Even without a connection being held open on the server, the Advanced Data Connector can still keep the transactional state of the cached object and data stored in the Virtual Table Manager. This information can be used on the application server later to reconnect objects to their datasources and commit changes for distributed and local transactions.

NOTE

Microsoft Internet Information Server (IIS) 3.0 and Active Server Pages (ASP) take advantage of one of the new features introduced in ODBC 3.0—*connection pooling*. With connection pooling, you can reuse the

active connection from a pool. When you disconnect your ODBC
connection, the ODBC Driver Manager can store the connection in
the pool instead of fully disconnecting.

By now, you should understand the client-tier architecture and how the Virtual Table
Manager stores data so that Advanced Data Connector can interact with the live data. The
AdvancedDataControl objects serve as binding managers to handle the data mapping between
ICursor and OLE DB rowsets. With this client-tier concept in mind, you're now ready to
use an AdvancedDataControl object in a Web page after learning about its properties and
methods in the following sections. Before continuing, however, you need to go through the
Advanced Data Connector setup to get your machine ready.

Configuring Your Application and Client Server

There are some software requirements for running Advanced Data Connector on both your
client and server machine. You also need to set up an ODBC system datasource for your
application server to connect to a database server or local database. Your database server can
be SQL Server or Access database. You also need to consider some security factors. The details
for configuring your application server and client machine are described in the following
sections.

Software Requirements for the Application Server

You need the following software components to run Advanced Data Connector:

- ☐ NT 4.0 Server with Service Pack 2
- ☐ Internet Information Server 3.0 with Active Server Pages
- ☐ Any Level 2–compliant ODBC drivers and database (for example, Access database
  and SQL Server 6.5 with Service Pack 2)
- ☐ Internet Explorer 3.01
- ☐ OLE DB SDK (OLE DB SDK installs ADO and also supplies the
  MSADC10.EXE ADC installation program in the MSADC subdirectory)
- ☐ Visual Basic Professional Edition or above (you'll need the data-aware controls that
  come with VB)

Check Appendix A for downloading information on any of these components.

16

Installation for the Application Server

Run MSADC10.EXE to install Advanced Data Connector components to your application server machine. The installation creates a subdirectory called "MSADC" under the \%SystemRoot%\Program Files\Common Files\System directory. The installation will fail if you don't have NT 4.0 Server with Service Pack 2 and Internet Information Server 3.0 with Active Server Pages. One of the Advanced Data Connector components installed on the server machine is MSADC10.CAB. This file is specified in a Web page, using the CODEBASE parameter to take advantage of HTML's automatic downloading capability. Specifying the CODEBASE parameter and the MSADC10.CAB file enables downloading and installing Advanced Data Connector components on the client machine. For more information on downloading and CAB files, please refer to Chapter 6, "Using an ActiveX Control." Besides MSADC10.CAB, there are some DLLs you need to know about, listed in Table 16.1.

Table 16.1. DLLs required for Advanced Data Connector.

Filename	Version	Timestamps
MSADCC10.DLL	1.00.1211.0	12/11/96
MSADCB10.DLL	1.00.1211.0	12/11/96
MSADCO10.DLL	1.00.1211.0	12/11/96
MSADCF10.DLL	1.00.1211.0	12/11/96
MSADCS10.DLL	1.00.1211.0	12/11/96

Advanced Data Connector relies on ADO and OLE DB to work correctly. Tables 16.2 and 16.3 list the ADO and OLE DB DLLs required for Advanced Data Connector.

Table 16.2. Required ADO DLLs.

Filename	Version	Timestamps
MSADER10.DLL	1.00.994	11/25/96
MSADO10.DLL	1.00.994	11/25/96
MSADOR10.DLL	1.00.995	12/6/96

Table 16.3. Required OLE DB DLLs.

Filename	Version	Timestamps
MSADC.DLL	01.10.2326	11/26/96
MSDAENUM.DLL	01.10.2326	11/26/96

continues

Table 16.3. continued

Filename	Version	Timestamps
MSDAER.DLL	01.10.2326	11/26/96
MSDASQL.DLL	01.10.2326	11/26/96
MSDASQLR.DLL	01.10.2326	11/26/96
MSDATL.DLL	01.10.2326	11/26/96
MSDATT.DLL	01.10.2326	11/26/96

Setting Up an ODBC System Datasource

Microsoft Internet Information Server uses the NT service World Wide Publishing Service to access the ODBC datasource, so you need to set up an ODBC system datasource by following these steps:

1. In the Control Panel, click on the ODBC Data Source Administrator icon.
2. Select the System DSN tab.
3. Click the Add button.
4. Enter your server or database name, depending on what kind of ODBC drivers you're using. If you are using SQL Server, make sure the Use Trusted Connection checkbox is unchecked.
5. Click the Options button if you're using SQL Server. Enter the database name under the Login section. This database is where you store the tables.
6. After you're done, click OK.

This information will be used in the `Connect` property of an `AdvancedDataControl` object.

Enabling Connection Pooling

With connection pooling, you can reuse the existing connection; this feature enhances performance by saving connection time. The default for connection pooling is `Off`, but you can enable it by using the Registry Editor:

1. Click the Start button, and then choose Run.
2. Enter `RegEdit` and click OK.
3. Open the following folders in the Registry Editor's left-hand window:

   `HKEY_LOCAL_MACHINE\System\CurrentControlSet\Services\W3SVC\ASP\Parameters`

4. One of the value names in the right-hand window is `StartConnectionPooling`. If you don't see that name, choose Edit | New | DWORD Value from the menu to

create an entry in the right-hand window. Enter `StartConnectionPooling` on the highlighted value name or right-click on the newly created value and select Rename to modify the value name. Double-click on that value name.

5. In the Edit DWORD Value dialog box that opens, change the value of the Value Data field to 1 to enable connection pooling.

6. After modifying the entry, bring up your Internet Server Manager from the Microsoft Internet Server program group. Select WWW service and choose Properties | Stop Service from the menu to stop the service. After the WWW service is stopped, choose Properties | Start Service from the menu to restart it. The connection pooling setting doesn't take effect until the WWW service is restarted.

Now your server is all set, so take a look at what you need to do for the client machine.

Software Requirements for the Client Tier

You need the following software components on your client machine to run Advanced Data Connector:

☐ NT 4.0 Server, NT 4.0 Workstation, or Win95
☐ Internet Explorer 3.01

NOTE

> The client tier doesn't necessarily need data-aware controls on its machine if the application server has used the `CODEBASE` download feature for the controls in its Web page. In this week's examples, you don't specify any `CODEBASE` downloading information for data-aware controls, so the client tier needs Visual Basic Professional Edition or higher for the data-aware controls.

Security Considerations on the Client Tier

By default, security in Internet Explorer is set at high. High security prevents files from loading. For Advanced Data Connector, Internet Explorer's security level needs to be set at medium so that the required files, such as MSADC10.CAB, can be downloaded to the client machine. To change the security level in Internet Explorer, follow these steps:

1. In Internet Explorer, choose View | Security.
2. Select the Security tab, and click the Safety Level button.
3. Select the Medium radio button for the safety level.
4. Click OK after you finish.

Now your machine is ready for Advanced Data Connector programming. Before you start working with AdvancedDataControl objects, however, you need to set up an ODBC system datasource for all the following examples.

Assume you have a virtual video rental store that people can browse, and you want to set up a Web page so these people can reserve videos. Table 16.4 shows the structure of the first table. The SQL script needed to create this table and insert records is available is on the book's CD-ROM. The filename is 16TBL.SQL.

NOTE   You can choose which database you want to use to create these tables. Depending on which database you use, enter the database name in the ODBC Data Source Setup dialog box.

Table 16.4. The structure of the Video_Detail table.

Column Name	Length	Constraints
VideoTitle	char(50)	Not null, unique
Rating	char(10)	Not null
Category	char(20)	Not null
ReleaseDate	datetime	Not null
Description	text	Allow null
ReservedID	int	Default -1
DueDate	datetime	Allow null
ReservedFlag	int	Default 0

This Video_Detail table stores information on the videos. You can assume that the video's title is unique, so the unique index key for the Video_Detail table is VideoTitle. There is only one copy available of each video, so only one customer can reserve it at a time. By default, the ReservedID is -1, meaning no one has reserved the video yet. If the video is reserved, the customer information is stored in the ReservedID column to reflect who reserved the video. The Rating column stores the video's rating, such as PG-13. The Category column is used to describe the type of video, such as Comedy. The Description column stores a brief description of the video, and the ReleaseDate column specifies when the video is available in the store. The ReservedFlag column stores information about whether the video has been reserved. The default for this column is 0, meaning the video hasn't been reserved yet.

16

The ReservedID and ReservedFlag columns are used for similar purposes, but the ReservedID is hidden behind the scene, so the customer can't change the data stored in it. Once a customer has reserved a video, the ReservedFlag becomes 1, and then you insert the customer ID information into the ReservedID column. The ReservedFlag column is created so you can bind this column with a data-aware control.

For the following examples to work, you need to create an ODBC system datasource called "Video," and the database server for the datasource must be SQL Server. With Advanced Data Connector 1.0, you can update only data that's in SQL Server. You can still use the Access database for any of the examples that don't require updating, but for those examples that do, you must have an ODBC SQL Server datasource.

You also need to set up an Internet Information Server virtual directory called ADCDownload that contains the MSADC10.CAB file. Whenever the Web page is accessed, the MSADC10.CAB file installs the required ADC files to the client machine.

The User ID for the database server is sa, and there's no password. If your database server has a different user ID and password, you'll need to modify the ODBC connect string, as described in the section "The `Connect` Property."

The `AdvancedDataControl` Object

`AdvancedDataControl` objects give you binding and mapping capabilities. With an `AdvancedDataControl` object, you can bind returned result sets to data-aware controls on a Web page, depending on the binding information specified in the `Bindings` property. You can bind more than one data-aware control to a returned result set; however, an `AdvancedDataControl` object can have only one `Recordset` associated with it.

When you use `AdvancedDataControl` objects, the default business object is used to access the data in the application server without having to explicitly specify the business object. The default business object is `AdvancedDataFactory`, which is covered in more depth in Chapter 19. You can use `AdvancedDataControl` to retrieve data explicitly by using `AdvancedDataSpace` and `AdvancedDataFactory`, but you also need to specify its CLASSID in the `Object` parameter in the Web page. The CLASSID for the `AdvancedDataControl` object is `9381D8F2-0288-11d0-9501-00AA00B911A5`. So to use an `AdvancedDataControl` object in your Web page, make sure you include the following code:

```
<OBJECT CLASSID="clsid:9381D8F2-0288-11d0-9501-00AA00B911A5"
➥ID=ADC1 HEIGHT=1 WIDTH = 1
➥CODEBASE="http://<%=Request.ServerVariables("IIS")%>
➥/ADCDownload/msadc10.cab">
➥</OBJECT>
```

NOTE The CLASSID, a unique, 128-bit number, of an OLE object identifies it to the system. The CLASSID needs to be registered in the local computer's system registry so other users can use the OLE object.

The AdvancedDataControl object is invisible, so you can specify 1 for both the height and width; the ID of this AdvancedDataControl object is set as ADC1. Later in the scripting section, you use ADC1 to identify this AdvancedDataControl object. Next, you use the CODEBASE keyword to take advantage of HTML's automatic downloading capability. By specifying MSADC10.CAB in the CODEBASE parameter, you allow the AdvancedDataControl components to be downloaded and installed on the client machine when the Web page is loaded.

In the CODEBASE parameter, use one of the Active Server Pages objects to specify the location of the MSADC10.CAB file in the application server. With Internet Information Server 3.0 and Active Server Pages, you can dynamically retrieve the host name of the application server you sent the HTTP request to. You can use the Request object with its ServerVariables to retrieve the server name. The ServerVariables collection supplies information about the environment variables. Using the ServerVariables collection, you don't have to hard-code the server name. The file extension needs to be .ASP instead of .HTM to use Active Server Pages.

With this basic structure, how do you specify where the application server is, and how do you issue a SQL statement to a database server? The answer lies in the AdvancedDataControl object's properties.

AdvancedDataControl **Properties**

There are five properties available in an AdvancedDataControl object: Server, Connect, SQL, Bindings, and Recordset. The following sections describe each of the properties in detail. All the properties are optional except the Bindings property when you're using AdvancedDataFactory.

The Server **Property**

Use the Server property to specify the application server by supplying a URL. You also use this property to create an instance of the business object and define the ODBC datasource. You can specify the server name at design time, which is shown in Listing 16.5, or change it at runtime by using the Refresh method.

Listing 16.5. Specifying the server name at design time.

```
 1: <HTML>
 2: <HEAD>
 3: <TITLE>Teach Yourself Active Web Databases with VB in 21 Days</TITLE>
 4: </HEAD>
 5: <BODY>
 6: <OBJECT CLASSID="clsid:9381D8F2-0288-11d0-9501-00AA00B911A5"
 7: ID=ADC1 HEIGHT=1 WIDTH = 1
➥CODEBASE="http://<%=Request.ServerVariables("Server_name")%>
➥/ADCDownload/msadc10.cab">
 8: <PARAM NAME="Server"
➥VALUE="http://<%=Request.ServerVariables("Server_name")%>">
 9: </OBJECT>
10: </BODY>
11: </HTML>
```

Listing 16.5 uses the Parameter method to specify the Server property of the AdvancedDataControl object. The property name is supplied after the PARAM NAME= keyword. As you can see in Listing 16.6, you can change the Server property at runtime by using the AdvancedDataControl.property = value syntax.

Listing 16.6. Specifying the Server property at runtime.

```
 1: <HTML>
 2: <HEAD>
 3: <TITLE>Teach Yourself Active Web Databases with VB in 21 Days</TITLE>
 4: </HEAD>
 5: <BODY LANGUAGE="VBS" onload ="Init" >
 6: <OBJECT CLASSID="clsid:9381D8F2-0288-11d0-9501-00AA00B911A5"
 7: ID=ADC1 HEIGHT=1 WIDTH = 1
➥CODEBASE="http://<%=Request.ServerVariables("Server_name")%>
➥/ADCDownload/msadc10.cab">
 8: </OBJECT>
 9: <SCRIPT LANGUAGE= "VBS">
10: SUB Init
11: ADC1.Server = "http://IISServerName"
12: End Sub
13: </SCRIPT>
14: </BODY>
15: </HTML>
```

Keep in mind that you can always use the ServerVariable to dynamically retrieve the server name, so you don't have to hard-code the server name. In Listing 16.6, the Body language is Visual Basic, and the onLoad parameter is Init(). This value for the onLoad parameter means that when this Web page is loaded, the Init sub-routine is invoked. If no initial sub-routine is specified, the Window_OnLoad sub-routine is used.

16

Later, you place the Init sub-routine in the <SCRIPT> section and choose to set AdvancedDataControl's Server property at runtime to http://IISServerName. Please note that if you're using ServerVariable to dynamically get the server name, the file extension must be .ASP to enable Active Server Pages.

You're finished setting up the application server, but how about the ODBC datasource defined in the application server? Take a look at the Connect property described in the following section.

The Connect Property

The Connect property is where you enter the ODBC connection string. Before you can do this, however, you need to make sure that the ODBC datasource is in the application server and that it's a system datasource. Also, the user ID and password must be valid to connect to the database server. You can specify the Connect property by using the PARAM method or assign its value at runtime, as shown in Listing 16.7.

Listing 16.7. Assigning the Connect property at runtime.

```
 1: <HTML>
 2: <HEAD>
 3: <TITLE>Teach Yourself Active Web Databases with VB in 21 Days</TITLE>
 4: </HEAD>
 5: <BODY LANGUAGE="VBS" onload ="Init" >
 6: <OBJECT CLASSID="clsid:9381D8F2-0288-11d0-9501-00AA00B911A5"
 7: ID=ADC1 HEIGHT=1 WIDTH = 1
➥CODEBASE="http://<%=Request.ServerVariables("Server_name")%>
➥/ADCDownload/msadc10.cab">
 8: </OBJECT>
 9: <SCRIPT LANGUAGE= "VBS">
10: SUB Init
11: ADC1.Server = "http://<%=Request.ServerVariables("Server_name")%>"
12: ADC1.Connect = "DSN=Video;UID=sa"
13: End Sub
14: </SCRIPT>
15: </BODY>
16: </HTML>
```

In Listing 16.7, the ODBC system datasource name is Video and the user ID is =sa. There's no password in this example, but if you need to assign one for your datasource, use PWD=. With the Server and Connect properties finished, you need only the SQL statement, which is assigned in the SQL property.

The SQL Property

The SQL property indicates the SQL statement you want to use on the ODBC datasource. You can change this property at runtime, too.

You can use normal SQL statement syntax. If you want to update the data, add for browse to the end of the SQL statement. The for browse operation works only with a SQL Server datasource for the 1.0 release. The for browse statement adds information to the requested columns to make sure the update is correctly matched to the original data in the ODBC datasource. Listing 16.8 is an example of how to define the SQL property.

Listing 16.8. Defining the SQL property at runtime.

```
 1: <HTML>
 2: <HEAD>
 3: <TITLE>Teach Yourself Active Web Databases with VB in 21 Days</TITLE>
 4: </HEAD>
 5: <BODY LANGUAGE="VBS" onload ="Init" >
 6: <OBJECT CLASSID="clsid:9381D8F2-0288-11d0-9501-00AA00B911A5"
 7: ID=ADC1 HEIGHT=1 WIDTH = 1
➥CODEBASE="http://<%=Request.ServerVariables("Server_name")%>
➥/ADCDownload/msadc10.cab">
 8: </OBJECT>
 9: <SCRIPT LANGUAGE= "VBS">
10: SUB Init
11: ADC1.Server = "http://<%=Request.ServerVariables("Server_name")%>"
12: ADC1.Connect = "DSN=Video;UID=sa"
13: ADC1.SQL =" Select * from Video_detail"
14: End Sub
15: </SCRIPT>
16: </BODY>
17: </HTML>
```

In Listing 16. 8, Select * from Video_Detail is the SQL statement issued against the Video ODBC datasource defined in the application server. The returned result set of the SQL statement is stored in the VTM so that you can manipulate the data in the client tier. So far, you have defined the values of the properties because the user doesn't need to know the Server, Connect, and SQL properties in the video example. However, what if you want to allow more flexibility by defining the properties on the Web page? To allow users to enter their own Server, Connect, and SQL properties, create three input text boxes in the Web page, as shown in Listing 16.9.

16

Listing 16.9. Adding the input text boxes.

```
 1: <HTML>
 2: <TITLE>Teach Yourself Active Web Databases with VB in 21 Days</TITLE>
 3: </HEAD>
 4: <BODY LANGUAGE="VBS" onload ="Init" >
 5: <CENTER>
 6: <H1><font size=4>
�íTeach Yourself Active Web Databases with VB in 21 Days</H1></font>
 7: <IMG SRC="video.gif" ALT="Virtual Video Store">
 8: <H2><font size=3>Using Server, Connect, and SQL properties</H2></font>
 9: <HR size=4 width=80%>
10: <BR>
11: <table>
12:      <tr><td>ADC Server:<td><INPUT NAME=Server SIZE=70>
13:      <tr><td>Connection:<td><INPUT NAME=Connect SIZE=70>
14:      <tr><td>Query:<td><INPUT NAME=SQL SIZE=70>
15: </table>
16: </CENTER>
17: <OBJECT CLASSID="clsid:9381D8F2-0288-11d0-9501-00AA00B911A5"
18:      ID=ADC1 HEIGHT=10 WIDTH = 10
➍CODEBASE="HTTP://<%=Request.ServerVariables("Server_name")%>
19: /ADCDownload/msadc10.cab">
20: </OBJECT>
21: <SCRIPT LANGUAGE= "VBS">
22: Sub Init
23: Server.Value = "http://<%=Request.ServerVariables("Server_name")%>"
24: Connect.Value = "DSN=Video;UID=sa"
25: SQL.Value ="select VideoTitle,Rating,Category, ReleaseDate,
➍ReservedFlag, Description from video_Detail order by VideoTitle"
26:      ADC1.Connect = Connect.Value
27:      ADC1.SQL = SQL.Value
28:      ADC1.Server = Server.Value
29: End Sub
30: </SCRIPT>
31: </BODY>
32: </HTML>
```

Listing 16.9 creates the ADC Server, Connection, and Query input text boxes for the user to define the Server, Connect, and SQL properties, respectively. In this example, you supply your own initial values for the input text boxes; the results are shown in Figure 16.7.

As you can see in Figure 16.7, the values of the Connection and Query input boxes have been initialized with this statement:

```
"DSN=Video;UID=sa",
➍"select VideoTitle,Rating,Category, ReleaseDate, ReservedFlag,
➍Description from video_Detail order by VideoTitle"
```

The application server name has been dynamically assigned. However, in your video example, you won't allow users to define the Server, Connect and SQL properties because you're going to hide them. For your own practice, though, you can still set up those input text boxes in your Web page to see the results.

Figure 16.7.

Allowing user-defined values for the Server, Connect, *and* SQL *properties.*

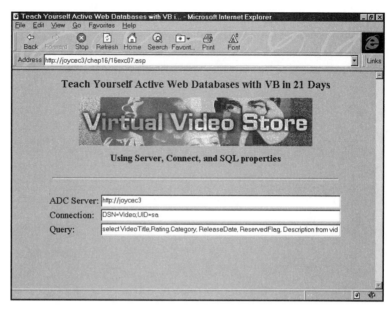

So far, you have defined the URL of the application server, the ODBC datasource, and the SQL statement you want to use, and you know that the returned result set is stored in the VTM on the client tier. But how are you going to show the results in your Web page? Remember, I mentioned that the `AdvancedDataControl` object handles binding data to a data-aware control; this function is specified in the `Bindings` property.

The `Bindings` **Property**

The `Bindings` property binds the returned result set with the data-aware controls. You can bind more than one control to a `Recordset`. Unlike the previous three properties, the `Bindings` property can't be changed at runtime; it must be defined at design time.

Visual Basic has three types of data-bound controls: simple controls, simple data-aware controls, and complex data-aware controls. `AdvancedDataControl` objects treat simple controls and simple data-aware controls in the same manner—they simply set and retrieve the value of the controls without doing any mapping. SimpleEdit, MaskedEdit, RichText, 3D Panel, 3D Check Box, and 3D Radio are all simple data-aware controls.

NOTE

You must be using at least the Professional Edition of Visual Basic to get the data-aware controls. Visual Basic Standard Edition doesn't have them.

For complex data-aware controls, `AdvancedDataControl` objects map the data from OLE DB rowset to ICursor, which is used in controls that handle scrolling. DBCombo and DBGrid are both complex data-aware controls.

Now that you understand the difference between simple data-aware controls and complex data-aware controls, take a look at some examples. In Listing 16.10, you bind the returned result set of the VideoTitle column to a RichText simple data-aware control.

Listing 16.10. Binding to a RichText control.

```
1: <OBJECT CLASSID="CLSID:3B7C8860-D78F-101B-B9B5-04021C009402"
2: ID=Text1 height=30 width=100>
3: </OBJECT>
4: <BR>
5: <OBJECT CLASSID="clsid:9381D8F2-0288-11d0-9501-00AA00B911A5"
6:      ID=ADC1 HEIGHT=10 WIDTH = 10
7:      CODEBASE="HTTP://<%=Request.ServerVariables("Server_name")%>
➥/ADCDownload/msadc10.cab">
8:         <PARAM NAME="BindingS" VALUE="Text1.Text=VideoTitle">
9: </OBJECT>
```

The CLASSID for the RichText control is 3B7C8860-D78F-101B-B9B5-04021C009402, and its size is defined in Width and Height parameters: 30 for the height and 100 for the width. The name of the control, Text1, is specified in the ID parameter. Later on, you use the name of the control to specify the binding. In the Bindings property of the AdvancedDataControl object, you assign the returned result from the VideoTitle column, one of the columns defined in the SQL property, to the RichText data-aware control named Text1. Because RichText is a simple data-aware control, you need to assign the data to its Text property.

Now take a look at how to bind the entire return result set to a DBGrid complex data-aware control, as shown in Listing 16.11.

Listing 16.11. Binding the result set to a DBGrid control.

```
1: <OBJECT CLASSID="CLSID: 00028C50-0000-0000-0000-000000000046"
2: ID=Grid1 height=100 width=200>
3: </OBJECT>
4: <BR>
5: <OBJECT CLASSID="clsid:9381D8F2-0288-11d0-9501-00AA00B911A5"
6:      ID=ADC1 HEIGHT=10 WIDTH = 10
7:      CODEBASE="HTTP://<%=Request.ServerVariables("Server_name")%>
➥/ADCDownload/msadc10.cab">
8:         <PARAM NAME="BindingS" VALUE="Grid1">
9: </OBJECT>
```

16

The CLASSID for the DBGrid control is 00028C50-0000-0000-0000-000000000046. Its height is 100, its width is 300, and its name is Grid1. The DBGrid control is a complex data-aware control, so you don't need to specify which column fills the control; *all* the columns defined in the SQL property are bound to the DBGrid control.

You aren't limited to defining only one data-aware control in the AdvancedDataControl's Bindings property. You can define more than one, as shown in Listing 16.12.

Listing 16.12. Binding a Recordset to several controls.

```
 1: <OBJECT CLASSID="CLSID:3B7C8860-D78F-101B-B9B5-04021C009402"
 2: ID=Text1 height=30 width=100>
 3: </OBJECT>
 4: <BR>
 5: <OBJECT CLASSID="CLSID: 00028C50-0000-0000-0000-000000000046"
 6: ID=Grid1 height=100 width=200>
 7: </OBJECT>
 8: <BR>
 9: <OBJECT CLASSID="clsid:9381D8F2-0288-11d0-9501-00AA00B911A5"
10:     ID=ADC1 HEIGHT=10 WIDTH = 10
11:     CODEBASE="HTTP:// <%=Request.ServerVariables("Server_name")%>
➥/ADCDownload/msadc10.cab">
12:     <PARAM NAME="BindingS" VALUE="Text1.Text=VideoTitle;Grid1">
13: </OBJECT>
```

You can bind one returned result set to more than one control by using a delimiter to separate the controls. In Listing 16.12, you bind the data to the grid control and the data for the VideoTitle column to the RichText control.

Now that you know how to bind data to data-aware controls, you might be wondering what kind of controls are available in Visual Basic 4.0. Table 16.5 lists the most commonly used controls in Visual Basic 4.0.

Table 16.5. List of available Visual Basic 4.0 controls.

Control	Filename	CLASSID
DBGrid	TDBGS32.OCX	00028C50-0000-0000-0000-000000000046
DBListBox	DBList32.OCX	02A69B00-081B-101B-8933-08002B2F4F5A
DBComboBox	DBList32.OCX	FAEEE760-117E-101B-8933-08002B2F4F5A
RichText	RichTx32.OCX	3B7C8860-D78F-101B-B9B5-04021C009402
MhImage	MHIMAG32.OCX	D93D83B0-9426-11CE-BDAB-00AA00575482
SSDBCombo	SSDATB32.OCX	BC496AE5-9B4E-11CE-A6D5-0000C0BE9395
SSDBGrid	SSDATB32.OCX	BC496AE0-9B4E-11CE-A6D5-0000C0BE9395
3D Radio	THREED32.OCX	0BA686AA-F7D3-101A-993E-0000C0EF6F5E

Now try using some of these data-aware controls in your video store example, as shown in Listing 16.13.

Listing 16.13. Binding data-aware controls.

```
1: <HTML>
2: <TITLE>Teach Yourself Active Web Databases with VB in 21 Days</TITLE>
3: </HEAD>
4: <BODY LANGUAGE="VBS" onload ="Init">
5: <CENTER>
6: <H1><font size=4>
➥Teach Yourself Active Web Databases with VB in 21 Days</H1></font>
7: <IMG SRC="video.gif" ALT="Virtual Video Store">
8: <H2><font size=4>Bind data to a DBGrid control</H2></font>
9: <HR size=4 width=80%>
10: <OBJECT ID="Grid1" WIDTH=600 HEIGHT=150
11:     CLASSID="CLSID:00028C00-0000-0000-0000-000000000046">
12: </OBJECT>
13: <BR>
14: </CENTER>
15: <OBJECT CLASSID="clsid:9381D8F2-0288-11d0-9501-00AA00B911A5"
16:     ID=ADC1 HEIGHT=10 WIDTH = 10 CODEBASE-"HTTP://
➥<%=Request.ServerVariables("Server_name")%>/ADCDownload/msadc10.cab">
17:         <PARAM NAME="Server" VALUE="HTTP://<%=Request.ServerVariables
➥("Server_name")%>"> <PARAM NAME="Connect" VALUE="DSN=Video;UID=sa">
18:         <PARAM NAME="SQL" VALUE="select VideoTitle,Rating,Category,
➥ReleaseDate,ReservedFlag, Description from video_Detail order by
➥VideoTitle">
19:         <PARAM NAME="BINDINGS" VALUE="Grid1">
20: </OBJECT>
21: <SCRIPT LANGUAGE= "VBS">
22: SUB Init
23: END SUB
24: </SCRIPT>
25: </BODY>
26: </HTML>
```

The code in Listing 16.13 binds the returned result set of the SQL statement Select * from Video_Detail to a DBGrid data-aware control. The ID for the DBGrid control is Grid1, and its binding is specified in the Bindings property. For the DBGrid control, you don't need to define the column name; the whole returned result set is automatically bound to the Grid1 DBGrid control. So far, you haven't used any of the AdvancedDataControl methods, you will be defining the Server, Connect, and SQL properties at design time so that the data can be fetched into the data-aware DBGrid control.

The data, displayed on the Web page, can be scrolled with the DBGrid control. (See Figure 16.8.) The data is no longer static; rather, it's dynamic, so it responds to scrolling even though there's no database connection being maintained. The interactive data is on the client tier because it's stored in the VTM.

Now that you have successfully bound returned result sets to a grid control, try working on some more examples.

Figure 16.8.

Using the Server, Connect, SQL, *and* Bindings *properties.*

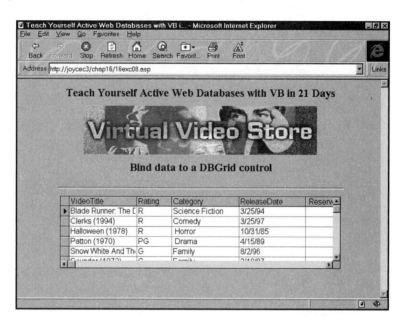

For the next example in Listing 16.14, you're going to bind the returned result set to a 3D Radio, a RichText, and a DBGrid control. You want to control which column you display on the grid control and use the 3D Radio and RichText control to display the rest of the columns.

Listing 16.14. Binding a result set to more controls.

```
 1: <TITLE>Teach Yourself Active Web Databases with VB in 21 Days</TITLE>
 2: </HEAD>
 3: <BODY LANGUAGE="VBS" onload ="Init">
 4: <CENTER>
 5: <H1><font size=4>
➥Teach Yourself Active Web Databases with VB in 21 Days</H1></font>
 6: <IMG SRC="video.gif" ALT="Virtual Video Store">
 7: <H2><font size=3>Bind data to DBGrid, RichText and Radio controls</H2>
➥</font>
 8: <HR size=4 width=80%>
 9: <BR>
10: <OBJECT ID="Grid1" WIDTH=500 HEIGHT=100
11:     CLASSID="CLSID:00028C00-0000-0000-0000-000000000046">
12: </OBJECT>
13: <BR>
```

continues

Listing 16.14. continued

```
14: <OBJECT CLASSID="CLSID:3B7C8860-D78F-101B-B9B5-04021C009402"
15:      ID=Text1 height=40 width=400>
16: </OBJECT>
17: <OBJECT ID="Radio1" WIDTH=100 HEIGHT=50
18:      CLASSID="CLSID:0BA686AA-F7D3-101A-993E-0000C0EF6F5E">
19:      <PARAM NAME="Caption" VALUE="Reserved">
20: </OBJECT>
21: </CENTER>
22: <OBJECT CLASSID="clsid:9381D8F2-0288-11d0-9501-00AA00B911A5"
23:      ID=ADC1 HEIGHT=1 WIDTH = 1
24:      CODEBASE="HTTP://<%=Request.ServerVariables("Server_name")%>
➥/ADCDownload/msadc10.cab">
25:      <PARAM NAME="Server" VALUE="HTTP://
➥<%=Request.ServerVariables("Server_name")%>">
26:      <PARAM NAME="Connect" VALUE="DSN=Video;UID=sa">
27:      <PARAM NAME="SQL" VALUE="Select VideoTitle,Rating,Category,
➥ReleaseDate,ReservedFlag, Description from Video_detail">
28:      <PARAM NAME="BINDINGS" VALUE="Grid1;Text1.Text=description;
➥Radio1.Value=ReservedFlag"></OBJECT>
29: <SCRIPT LANGUAGE= "VBS">
30: Sub Init
31:      Grid1.Columns(4).Visible = FALSE
32:      Grid1.Columns(5).Visible = FALSE
33: End Sub
34: </SCRIPT>
35: </BODY>
36: </HTML>
```

In Listing 16.14, you use three data-aware controls for binding: DBGrid, RichText, and 3D Radio. Their IDs are Grid1, Text1, and Radio1. The SQL statement used this time just retrieves data from the VideoTitle, Rating, Category, ReleaseDate, ReservedFlag, and Description columns of the Video_Detail table.

The data in the Description column could be fairly large, so you want to display this column in a RichText control. Also, you need to use a 3D Radio control to indicate whether the video has been reserved.

In the Bindings property, you specify that the data from the Description column is bound to Text1, and the data for the ReservedFlag column is bound to Radio1. For Grid1, you don't have to specify the column name because all the columns are automatically bound to complex data-aware controls.

Because you're already displaying the Description and ReservedFlag columns in the RichText and Radio controls already, you want to hide those two columns in Grid1. You do this by assigning a value of FALSE to the column's Visible property. In the preceding example, the Description column is in column 4 of the grid and ReservedFlag is in column 5, so set the Visible property of the Grid1.Column(4) Grid1.Column(5) to FALSE.

16

As you can see in Figure 16.9, you can scroll through the DBGrid control. The content of the RichText control reflects the data from the Description column of the current record, and the 3D Radio control indicates whether the video has been reserved. With `Server`, `Connect`, `SQL`, and `Bindings` properties set, you can now retrieve data and scroll through it dynamically.

Figure 16.9.

Binding data to DBGrid, RichText, and 3D Radio controls.

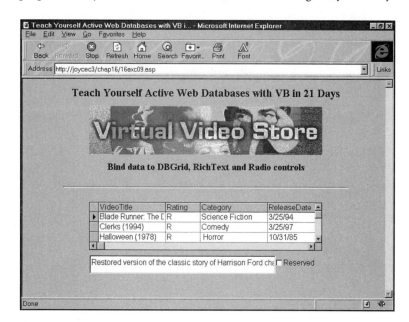

The `Recordset` **Property**

The `AdvancedDataControl` object has one more property: the `Recordset` property, which specifies the `Recordset` name. This property is normally used when you use `AdvancedDataSpace` to create a custom business object and you want to associate the ADO `Recordset` of the business object to your `AdvancedDataControl` object. If `AdvancedDataSpace` is being used, then `AdvancedDataControl` links with the business object's `Recordset` by assigning the ADO `Recordset`'s value of a business object to `AdvancedDataControl`'s `Recordset` property. The data in the ADO `Recordset` of this business object is bound to the data-aware control specified in the `Bindings` property of the `AdvancedDataControl` object. That property is covered in more detail during the next few days of lessons.

The following code shows that a method of a custom business object has been invoked to return an ADOR `Recordset`:

```
Dim myBusObj
Dim myBusObjRS
set myBusObj = ads.CreateObject("project.myBus,
➥"http:// <%=Request.ServerVariables("Server_name")%>")
```

```
SUB LOAD
set myBusObjRS = myBusObj.myRecordSet()
adc.RecordSet = myBusObjRS
END SUB
```

At this point, you already know how to use the AdvancedDataControl object's properties to retrieve data and use the DBGrid control to scroll the data, so the following sections introduce you to the AdvancedDataControl object's methods.

AdvancedDataControl **Methods**

There are six methods available for the AdvancedDataControl object: MoveNext(), MoveFirst(), MovePrev(), MoveLast(), Refresh(), and SubmitChanges(). These methods allow you to scroll through the Recordset, requery the data, and submit the changed data. None of these methods require input parameters.

The MoveNext() **Method**

The MoveNext() method moves the current row to the next row of the returned result set. With this method, you can add a button to the previous example and invoke the MoveNext() method whenever the Next button is clicked, as shown in Listing 16.15. Adding this method will let the customer scroll the entire returned result set.

Listing 16.15. Using the MoveNext() **method.**

```
 1: <TITLE>Teach Yourself Active Web Databases with VB in 21 Days</TITLE>
 2: </HEAD>
 3: <BODY LANGUAGE="VBS" onload ="Init">
 4: <CENTER>
 5: <H1><font size=4>
➡Teach Yourself Active Web Databases with VB in 21 Days</H1></font>
 6: <IMG SRC="video.gif" WIDTH=400 HEIGHT=100 ALT="Virtual Video Store">
 7: <HR size=2 width=80%>
 8: <H2><font size=3>Using MoveFirst methods.</H2></font>
 9: <BR>
10: <OBJECT ID="Grid1" WIDTH=500 HEIGHT=100
11:     CLASSID="CLSID:00028C00-0000-0000-0000-000000000046">
12: </OBJECT>
13: <BR>
14: <OBJECT CLASSID="CLSID:3B7C8860-D78F-101B-B9B5-04021C009402"
15:     ID=Text1 height=40 width=400>
16: </OBJECT>
```

16

```
17: <OBJECT ID="Radio1" WIDTH=100 HEIGHT=50
18:     CLASSID="CLSID:0BA686AA-F7D3-101A-993E-0000C0EF6F5E">
19:       <PARAM NAME="Caption" VALUE="Reserved">
20: </OBJECT>
21: <BR><BR>
22: <INPUT TYPE=BUTTON NAME="Next" VALUE="&Next" onClick="MoveNext">
23: </CENTER>
24: <OBJECT CLASSID="clsid:9381D8F2-0288-11d0-9501-00AA00B911A5"
25:     ID=ADC1 HEIGHT=1 WIDTH = 1
26:     CODEBASE="HTTP://<%=Request.ServerVariables("Server_name")%>
➥/ADCDownload/msadc10.cab">
27:       <PARAM NAME="Server" VALUE="HTTP://
➥<%=Request.ServerVariables("Server_name")%>">
28:       <PARAM NAME="Connect" VALUE="DSN=Video;UID=sa">
29:       <PARAM NAME="SQL" VALUE="Select VideoTitle,Rating,Category,
➥ReleaseDate, ReservedFlag, Description from Video_detail
➥order by VideoTitle">
30:       <PARAM NAME="BINDINGS" VALUE="Grid1;Text1.Text=description;
➥Radio1.Value=ReservedFlag">
31: </OBJECT>
32: <SCRIPT LANGUAGE= "VBS">
33: Sub MoveNext
34:       ADC1.MoveNext
35: End Sub
36: Sub Init
37:       Grid1.Columns(4).Visible = FALSE
38:       Grid1.Columns(5).Visible = FALSE
39: End Sub
40: </SCRIPT>
41: </BODY>
42: </HTML>
```

In Listing 16.15, you create a button on the Web page by using the <INPUT> tag, which defines an element such as a button, radio button, checkbox, or text box. The TYPE parameter defines the type of element; in this example, the type of element is a button. The NAME parameter is the application's internal name for the button, and the VALUE parameter defines the labels associated with the button—in this example, it's Next. The OnClick parameter assigns the sub-routine invoked when you click the button; for this example, assign the Refresh sub-routine to the OnClick parameter.

Notice that you can click the Next button to scroll to the next row of the released videos. (See Figure 16.10.) You can move the record to the next available video title in the store. So how about moving the record to the previous one, the first one in the Recordset, and the last one in the Recordset? The methods to do all that are explained in the following sections.

Figure 16.10.

Using the
`MoveNext()` *method.*

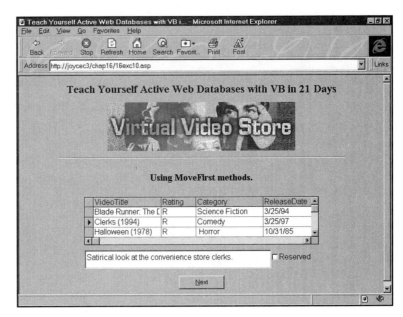

The `MoveFirst()` Method

The `MoveFirst()` method moves the current row to the next row of the `Recordset`. The following example shows how you invoke the `MoveFirst()` method by clicking the First button on the Web page:

```
<INPUT TYPE=BUTTON NAME="First" VALUE="&First" onClick="MoveFirst">
SUB MoveFirst
ADC1.MoveFirst
END SUB
```

The `MovePrevious()` Method

The `MovePrevious()` method moves the current row to the next row of the `Recordset`. You can invoke the `MovePrevious()` method by clicking the Prev button on the Web page, as shown in this example:

```
<INPUT TYPE=BUTTON NAME="Prev" VALUE="&Prev" onClick="MovePrev">
SUB MovePrev
ADC1.MovePrevious
END SUB
```

16

The `MoveLast()` Method

The `MoveLast()` method moves the current row to the last row of the `Recordset`. The following example shows how you can invoke the `MoveLast()` method by clicking the Last button on the Web page:

```
<INPUT TYPE=BUTTON NAME="Last" VALUE="&Last" onClick="MoveLast">
SUB MoveLast
ADC1.MoveLast
END SUB
```

In Listing 16.16, you're going to combine the `MoveFirst()`, `MovePrevious()`, `MoveNext()`, and `MoveLast()` methods to give the `AdvancedDataControl` object the ability to scroll data.

Use the `<INPUT>` tag to define four buttons: First, Next, Prev, and Last. Next, associate the `MoveFirst()` sub-routine with the First button through the `OnClick` parameter, the `MoveNext()` sub-routine with the Next button, the `MovePrev()` sub-routine with the Prev button, and the `MoveLast()` sub-routine with the Last button. Now you can click the buttons and scroll through the entire video list, both forward and backward.

Listing 16.16. Adding scrolling ability to the `AdvancedDataControl` object.

```
 1: <TITLE>Teach Yourself Active Web Databases with VB in 21 Days</TITLE>
 2: </HEAD>
 3: <BODY LANGUAGE="VBS" onload ="Init">
 4: <CENTER>
 5: <H1><font size=5>
➥Teach Yourself Active Web Databases with VB in 21 Days</H1></font>
 6: <IMG SRC="video.gif" WIDTH=400 HEIGHT=100 ALT="Virtual Video Store">
 7: <HR size=2 width=80%>
 8: <H2><font size=3>Using the
➥MoveFirst, MovePrevious, MoveNext(), and MoveLast Methods</H2></font>
 9: <BR>
10: <OBJECT ID="Grid1" WIDTH=500 HEIGHT=100
11:     CLASSID="CLSID:00028C00-0000-0000-0000-000000000046">
12: </OBJECT>
13: <OBJECT CLASSID="CLSID:3B7C8860-D78F-101B-B9B5-04021C009402"
14:     ID=Text1 height=40 width=400>
15: </OBJECT>
16: <OBJECT ID="Radio1" WIDTH=100 HEIGHT=50
17:     CLASSID="CLSID:0BA686AA-F7D3-101A-993E-0000C0EF6F5E">
18:     <PARAM NAME="Caption" VALUE="Reserved">
19: </OBJECT>
20: <BR><BR>
21: <INPUT TYPE=BUTTON NAME="First" VALUE="&First" onClick="MoveFirst">
22: <INPUT TYPE=BUTTON NAME="Next" VALUE="&Next" onClick="MoveNext">
23: <INPUT TYPE=BUTTON NAME="Prev" VALUE="&Prev" onClick="MovePrev">
24: <INPUT TYPE=BUTTON NAME="Last" VALUE="&Last" onClick="MoveLast">
```

continues

16

Listing 16.16. continued

```
25:  </CENTER>
26:  <OBJECT CLASSID="clsid:9381D8F2-0288-11d0-9501-00AA00B911A5"
27:       ID=ADC1 HEIGHT=1 WIDTH = 1       CODEBASE="HTTP://
➡<%=Request.ServerVariables
➡("Server_name")%>/ADCDownload/msadc10.cab">
28:       <PARAM NAME="Server" VALUE="HTTP:
➡//<%=Request.ServerVariables("Server_name")%>">
29:       <PARAM NAME="Connect" VALUE="DSN=Video;UID=sa">
30:       <PARAM NAME="SQL" VALUE="Select VideoTitle,Rating,Category,
➡ReleaseDate, ReservedFlag, Description from Video_detail
➡order by VideoTitle">
31:       <PARAM NAME="BINDINGS" VALUE="Grid1;Text1.Text=description;
➡Radio1.Value=ReservedFlag">
32:  </OBJECT>
33:  <SCRIPT LANGUAGE= "VBS">
34:  SUB MoveFirst
35:       ADC1.MoveFirst
36:  END SUB
37:  SUB MoveNext
38:       ADC1.MoveNext
39:  END SUB
40:  SUB MovePrev
41:       ADC1.MovePrevious
42:  END SUB
43:  SUB MoveLast
44:       ADC1.MoveLast
45:  END SUB
46:  Sub Init
47:       Grid1.Columns(4).Visible = FALSE
48:       Grid1.Columns(5).Visible = FALSE
49:  End Sub
50:  </SCRIPT>
51:  </BODY>
52:  </HTML>
```

Figure 16.11 shows the result of clicking the MoveLast button. With AdvancedDataControl, you can see how easy it is to scroll the data dynamically with the data-aware controls. Notice that when you're scrolling the data, you don't have to connect to the ODBC datasource to retrieve the data. All the data manipulations are done through the data in the Virtual Table Manager. If you want to do the same thing in ASP/ADO, you must open a connection with the ODBC datasource each time you want to scroll the data. You have to internally keep track of which record is current and carefully compare the record to display the correct row that users are scrolling. With AdvancedDataControl, these tasks are taken care of by the Virtual Table Manager; all you need to do is invoke the MoveNext(), MovePrevious(), MoveFirst(), and MoveLast() methods.

16

Figure 16.11.

Using the
`MoveFirst()`,
`MovePrevious()`,
`MoveNext()`, *and*
`MoveLast()`
methods.

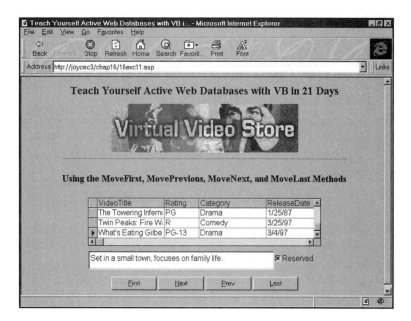

Now you can scroll through the whole list of released videos, but what if you want to see only the released videos that haven't been checked out yet?

The `Refresh` Method

The `Refresh` method requeries the ODBC datasource specified in the `Connect` property and refreshes the `Recordset`. This method requires `Connect`, `Server`, and `SQL` properties to connect to the application server and ODBC datasource.

Listing 16.17 shows how to invoke the `Refresh` method by clicking the Refresh button on the video store Web page. If there's a pre-existing `Recordset`, then it's released and any unsaved changes are discarded. In this example, the `Refresh` method is used to query the ODBC datasource with the SQL statement specified in the `SQL` property.

Listing 16.17. Refreshing the `Recordset`.

```
1: <TITLE>Teach Yourself Active Web Databases with VB in 21 Days</TITLE>
2: </HEAD>
3: <BODY LANGUAGE="VBS" onload ="Init">
4: <CENTER>
5: <H1><font size=4>
➥Teach Yourself Active Web Databases with VB in 21 Days</H1></font>
```

continues

Listing 16.17. continued

```
 6: <IMG SRC="video.gif" WIDTH=400 HEIGHT=100 ALT="Virtual Video Store">
 7: <HR size=1 width=80%>
 8: <H2><font size=3>Using the Refresh Method</H2></font>
 9: <BR>
10: <OBJECT ID="Grid1" WIDTH=500 HEIGHT=100
11:     CLASSID="CLSID:00028C00-0000-0000-0000-000000000046">
12: </OBJECT>
13: <OBJECT CLASSID="CLSID:3B7C8860-D78F-101B-B9B5-04021C009402"
14:     ID=Text1 height=40 width=400>
15: </OBJECT>
16: <OBJECT ID="Radio1" WIDTH=100 HEIGHT=50
17:     CLASSID="CLSID:0BA686AA-F7D3-101A-993E-0000C0EF6F5E">
18:     <PARAM NAME="Caption" VALUE="Reserved">
19: </OBJECT>
20: <BR><BR>
21: <INPUT TYPE=BUTTON NAME="First" VALUE="&First" onClick="MoveFirst">
22: <INPUT TYPE=BUTTON NAME="Next" VALUE="&Next" onClick="MoveNext">
23: <INPUT TYPE=BUTTON NAME="Prev" VALUE="&Prev" onClick="MovePrev">
24: <INPUT TYPE=BUTTON NAME="Last" VALUE="&Last" onClick="MoveLast">
25: <INPUT TYPE=BUTTON NAME="Refresh" VALUE="&Refresh">
26: </CENTER>
27: <OBJECT CLASSID="clsid:9381D8F2-0288-11d0-9501-00AA00B911A5"
28:     ID=ADC1 HEIGHT=1 WIDTH = 1
29:     CODEBASE="HTTP://<%=Request.ServerVariables("Server_name")%>
➥/ADCDownload/msadc10.cab">
30:     <PARAM NAME="BINDINGS"
➥VALUE="Grid1;Text1.Text=description;Radio1.Value=ReservedFlag">
31:     </OBJECT>
32: <SCRIPT LANGUAGE= "VBS">
33: SUB MoveFirst
34:     ADC1.MoveFirst
35: END SUB
36: SUB MoveNext
37:     ADC1.MoveNext
38: END SUB
39: SUB MovePrev
40:     ADC1.MovePrevious
41: END SUB
42: SUB MoveLast
43:     ADC1.MoveLast
44: END SUB
45: SUB Refresh_OnClick
46:     ADC1.Refresh
47: END SUB
48: Sub Init
49:     ADC1.Server ="http://<%=Request.ServerVariables("Server_name")%>"
50:     ADC1.Connect ="DSN=Video;UID=sa"
51:     ADC1.SQL ="Select VideoTitle,Rating,Category, ReleaseDate,
➥ReservedFlag, Description from Video_detail order by VideoTitle"
```

16

```
52:        ADC1.Refresh
53:        Grid1.Columns(4).Visible = FALSE
54:        Grid1.Columns(5).Visible = FALSE
55: End Sub
56: </SCRIPT>
57: </BODY>
58: </HTML>
```

When this Web page is loaded, the Init sub-routine is invoked. Within that sub-routine, you assign the Connect, Server, and SQL properties at runtime because you can use the Refresh method to query the data. Init then invokes the Refresh method to use the SQL statement specified in the SQL property.

Since this is the first time the SQL statement is used, there's no existing returned result set in the Virtual Table Manager, so a business object proxy is created. Once the data is retrieved in the application server, it's packed and sent over to the client tier. The data then appears on the data-aware controls you define in the Bindings property.

In the preceding example, you also create a Refresh button to invoke the Refresh method. However, this time there's no sub-routine specified to associate with the OnClick action. By default, when the button is clicked, it calls the button_OnClick sub-routine; in this case, it invokes the Refresh_OnClick sub-routine. Figure 16.12 is the result displayed on the Web page. Clicking the Refresh button invokes the Refresh method and refreshes the list of videos.

Figure 16.12.

Using the Refresh *method.*

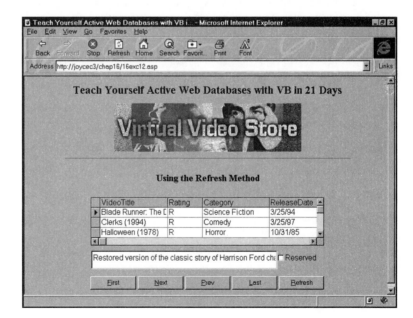

In Listing 16.18, you're going to give the customer a choice of seeing only the available videos or only the reserved videos in the virtual video store.

Listing 16.18. Showing available or reserved videos.

```
 1: <TITLE>Teach Yourself Active Web Databases with VB in 21 Days</TITLE>
 2: </HEAD>
 3: <BODY LANGUAGE="VBS" onload ="Init">
 4: <CENTER>
 5: <H1><font size=4>
➥Teach Yourself Active Web Databases with VB in 21 Days</H1></font>
 6: <IMG SRC="video.gif" WIDTH=400 HEIGHT=100 ALT="Virtual Video Store">
 7: <HR size=1 width=80%>
 8: <H2><font size=3>Show Videos</H2></font>
 9: <BR>
10: <OBJECT ID="Grid1" WIDTH=500 HEIGHT=100
11:     CLASSID="CLSID:00028C00-0000-0000-0000-000000000046">
12: </OBJECT>
13: <OBJECT CLASSID="CLSID:3B7C8860-D78F-101B-B9B5-04021C009402"
14:     ID=Text1 height=40 width=400>
15: </OBJECT>
16: <OBJECT ID="Radio1" WIDTH=100 HEIGHT=50
17:     CLASSID="CLSID:0BA686AA-F7D3-101A-993E-0000C0EF6F5E">
18:     <PARAM NAME="Caption" VALUE="Reserved">
19: </OBJECT>
20: <BR><BR>
21: <INPUT TYPE=BUTTON NAME="First" VALUE="&First" onClick="MoveFirst">
22: <INPUT TYPE=BUTTON NAME="Next" VALUE="&Next" onClick="MoveNext">
23: <INPUT TYPE=BUTTON NAME="Prev" VALUE="&Prev" onClick="MovePrev">
24: <INPUT TYPE=BUTTON NAME="Last" VALUE="&Last" onClick="MoveLast">
25: <INPUT TYPE=BUTTON NAME="ShowRev" VALUE="Show &Reserved Video">
26: <INPUT TYPE=BUTTON NAME="ShowAvail" VALUE="Show &Available Video">
27: </CENTER>
28: <OBJECT CLASSID="clsid:9381D8F2-0288-11d0-9501-00AA00B911A5"
29:     ID=ADC1 HEIGHT=1 WIDTH = 1
30:     CODEBASE="HTTP://<%=Request.ServerVariables("Server_name")%>
➥/ADCDownload/msadc10.cab">
31:     <PARAM NAME="BINDINGS"
➥VALUE="Grid1;Text1.Text=description;Radio1.Value=ReservedFlag">
32: </OBJECT>
33: <SCRIPT LANGUAGE= "VBS">
34: SUB MoveFirst
35:     ADC1.MoveFirst
36: END SUB
37: SUB MoveNext
38:     ADC1.MoveNext
39: END SUB
```

```
40: SUB MovePrev
41:      ADC1.MovePrevious
42: END SUB
43: SUB MoveLast
44:      ADC1.MoveLast
45: END SUB
46: SUB ShowRev_OnClick
47:      ADC1.SQL ="Select VideoTitle,Rating,Category, ReleaseDate,
➡ReservedFlag, Description from Video_detail where
➡ReservedFlag != 0 order by VideoTitle"
48:      ADC1.Refresh
49:      Grid1.Columns(4).Visible = FALSE
50:      Grid1.Columns(5).Visible = FALSE
51: END SUB
52: SUB ShowAvail_OnClick
53:      ADC1.SQL ="Select VideoTitle,Rating,Category, ReleaseDate,
➡ReservedFlag, Description from Video_detail where
➡ReservedFlag =0  order by VideoTitle"
54:      ADC1.Refresh
55:      Grid1.Columns(4).Visible = FALSE
56:      Grid1.Columns(5).Visible = FALSE
57: END SUB
58: Sub Init
59:      ADC1.Server ="http://<%=Request.ServerVariables("Server_name")%>"
60:      ADC1.Connect ="DSN=Video;UID=sa"
61: End Sub
62: </SCRIPT>
63: </BODY>
64: </HTML>
```

In this example, you remove the Refresh button and add two new buttons: Show Reserved Videos and Show Available Videos. When the customer clicks the Show Reserved Videos button, all the videos that have already been reserved are displayed. Clicking the Show Available Videos button displays only the videos that haven't been reserved yet.

Remember that the Refresh method requires SQL, Connect, and Server properties. The Connect and Server properties remain the same as before. For the SQL property, modify the SQL statement used when the customer clicks the Show Reserved Videos button, as shown here:

```
Select VideoTitle, Rating, Category, ReleaseDate,
➡ ReservedFlag, Description from Video_detail where ReservedFlag !=0
```

When the Show Available button is clicked, this is the SQL statement used:

```
Select VideoTitle, Rating, Category, ReleaseDate,
➡ ReservedFlag, Description from Video_detail where ReservedFlag =0
```

This SQL statement is used to select the videos that have a `ReservedFlag` equal to `0`. The SQL statement uses for the Show Reserved Videos sub-routine contains one extra column: `DueDate`. This column is displayed so that the customer knows when the video might be available again.

In Figure 16.13, the DBGrid control displays all the reserved videos after the Show Reserved button is clicked. As you scroll down, notice that the Reserved checkbox is marked for all the videos. In the Video_Detail table, you had already defined "Snow White and The Seven Dwarves" and "What's Eating Gilbert Grape? (1993)" as reserved. After you click the Show Reserved Video button, you can see that both videos are displayed.

Figure 16.13.

Showing the reserved videos.

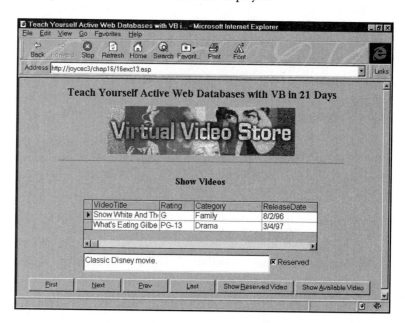

In Figure 16.14, the DBGrid control displays all the available videos when the Show Available Video button is clicked. As you can see, neither "Snow White And The Seven Dwarves" or "What's Eating Gilbert Grape? (1993)" are displayed.

Once customers can see which video is reserved or available, the next thing they might want to do is reserve a video to rent. The method to do that is covered in the next section.

Figure 16.14.

Showing all the available videos.

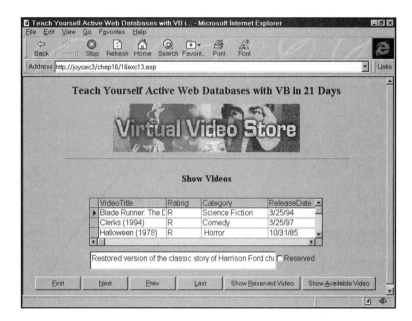

The SubmitChanges Method

The SubmitChanges method submits the changed data to the application server. Once this method is invoked, the Virtual Table Manager collects all the data that has been changed, packages the changed data, and sends it to the application server. The changed data works in a batch mode: Either it all succeeds or it all fails. You need to call the Refresh method immediately after the SubmitChanges method to keep the time stamp of the changed data in the Virtual Table Manager in sync. You can use the SubmitChanges method only with the default business object (meaning AdvancedDataFactory), not with a custom business object.

Remember, if you want to be able to update the data, you can add for browse to the end of the SQL statement. The for browse operation works only with a SQL Server datasource for the 1.0 release; it adds information to the requested columns to make sure the update is correctly matched to the original data in the ODBC datasource.

Listing 16.19 modifies the video example you have been working on to allow the user to reserve the video.

Listing 16.19. Reserving a video.

```
 1: <TITLE>Teach Yourself Active Web Databases with VB in 21 Days</TITLE>
 2: </HEAD>
 3: <BODY LANGUAGE="VBS" onload ="Init">
 4: <CENTER>
 5: <H1><font size=4>
➥Teach Yourself Active Web Databases with VB in 21 Days</H1></font>
 6: <IMG SRC="video.gif" WIDTH=400 HEIGHT=100 ALT="Virtual Video Store">
 7: <HR size=2 width=80%>
 8: <H2><font size=3>Using SubmitChanges Method</H2></font>
 9: <BR>
10: <OBJECT ID="Grid1" WIDTH=500 HEIGHT=100
11:     CLASSID="CLSID:00028C00-0000-0000-0000-000000000046">
12:     </OBJECT>
13: <BR>
14: <OBJECT CLASSID="CLSID:3B7C8860-D78F-101B-B9B5-04021C009402"
15:     ID=Text1 height=40 width=400>
16:     <PARAM NAME="ALLOWUPDATE" VALUE="TRUE;">
17: </OBJECT>
18: <OBJECT ID="Radio1" WIDTH=100 HEIGHT=50
19:     CLASSID="CLSID:0BA686AA-F7D3-101A-993E-0000C0EF6F5E">
20:     <PARAM NAME="ALLOWUPDATE" VALUE="TRUE;">
21:     <PARAM NAME="Caption" VALUE="Reserved">
22: </OBJECT>
23: <BR><BR>
24: <INPUT TYPE=BUTTON NAME="First" VALUE="&First" onClick="MoveFirst">
25: <INPUT TYPE=BUTTON NAME="Next" VALUE="&Next" onClick="MoveNext">
26: <INPUT TYPE=BUTTON NAME="Prev" VALUE="&Prev" onClick="MovePrev">
27: <INPUT TYPE=BUTTON NAME="Last" VALUE="&Last" onClick="MoveLast">
28: <BR>
29: <INPUT TYPE=BUTTON NAME="ShowRev" VALUE="Show &Reserved Video">
30: <INPUT TYPE=BUTTON NAME="ShowAvail" VALUE="Show A&vailable Video">
31: <INPUT TYPE=BUTTON NAME="SubmitChanges" VALUE="&SubmitChanges">
32: </CENTER>
33: <OBJECT CLASSID="clsid:9381D8F2-0288-11d0-9501-00AA00B911A5"
34:     ID=ADC1 HEIGHT=1 WIDTH = 1
35:     CODEBASE="HTTP://<%=Request.ServerVariables("Server_name")%>
➥/ADCDownload/msadc10.cab">
36:     <PARAM NAME="BINDINGS"
➥VALUE="Grid1;Text1.Text=description;Radio1.Value=ReservedFlag">
37: </OBJECT>
38: <SCRIPT LANGUAGE= "VBS">
39: SUB MoveFirst
40:     ADC1.MoveFirst
41: END SUB
42: SUB MoveNext
43:     ADC1.MoveNext
44: END SUB
45: SUB MovePrev
46:     ADC1.MovePrevious
47: END SUB
```

16

```
48: SUB MoveLast
49:      ADC1.MoveLast
50: END SUB
51: SUB ShowRev_OnClick
52:      ADC1.SQL ="Select VideoTitle,Rating,Category, ReleaseDate,
➥ReservedFlag, Description from Video_detail where
➥ReservedFlag !=0 order by VideoTitle"
53:      ADC1.Refresh
54:      Grid1.Columns(4).Visible = FALSE
55:      Grid1.Columns(5).Visible = FALSE
56: END SUB
57: SUB ShowAvail_OnClick
58:      ADC1.SQL ="Select VideoTitle,Rating,Category, ReleaseDate,
➥ReservedFlag, Description from Video_detail where
➥ReservedFlag =0 order by VideoTitle for browse"
59:      ADC1.Refresh
60:      Grid1.Columns(4).Visible = TRUE
61:      Grid1.Columns(5).Visible = FALSE
62: END SUB
63: SUB SubmitChanges_onClick
64:      ADC1.SubmitChanges
65:      ADC1.Refresh
66:      Grid1.Columns(4).Visible = FALSE
67:      Grid1.Columns(5).Visible = FALSE
68: END SUB
69: Sub Init
70:      ADC1.Server ="http://<%=Request.ServerVariables("Server_name")%>"
71:      ADC1.Connect ="DSN=Video;UID=sa"
72: End Sub
73: </SCRIPT>
74: </BODY>
75: </HTML>
```

To update the data in the 3D Radio, RichText, or Grid controls, you need to set the AllowUpdate property to TRUE and include the for browse keyword. The customer can reserve a video by checking the Reserved checkbox, and, because the data is directly bound to the Grid control, the customers can move to the video they want and click the SubmitChanges button to submit their requests. They can also uncheck videos they have reserved to take them off the reserved list.

After you submit the changes, the videos you have requested are no longer available in the Grid control because the Refresh method is invoked after you submit the changes. The change has been committed to the database and reflected right away.

This example demonstrates how simple and easy it is to manipulate data through the AdvancedDataControl object. Click the Show Available Video button and check the Reserved checkbox to reserve "Blade Runner: The Director's Cut (1982)." (See Figure 16.15.)

Figure 16.15.

Using the Submit-Changes *method.*

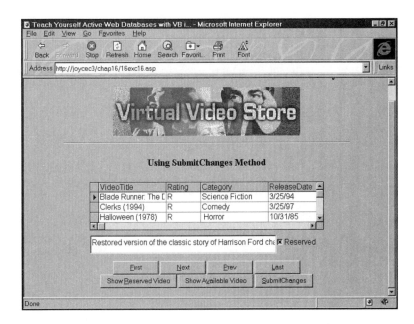

Next, click the SubmitChanges button and notice the change in Figure 16.16. "Blade Runner: The Director's Cut (1982)" no longer shows up in the Grid control.

Figure 16.16.

The result of clicking the SubmitChanges button.

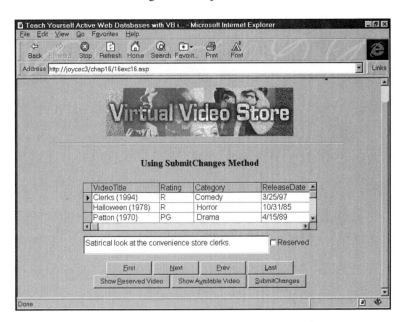

Figure 16.17 shows you the result after clicking the Show Reserved Video button. "Blade Runner: The Director's Cut (1982)" once again shows up in the Grid control.

Figure 16.17.

The result of clicking the Show Reserved Video button.

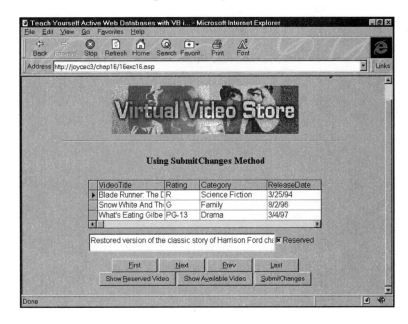

You can make several video requests and send them all at once. `AdvancedDataControl` marks all the changes in the Virtual Table Manager. Once a `SubmitChanges` method is invoked, all the changed data is packaged and sent over to the application server, which lets the client tier work while disconnected and then reconnect when the changed data is submitted. Details on how the reconnect works are covered in Chapter 20, "Business Objects and ADO."

After you mark the videos the customers want to check out, you might change your mind before they submit the request. You might want to cancel all the requests. The next method gives you the ability to cancel the pending changes.

The `CancelUpdate` Method

The `CancelUpdate` method cancels all the pending changes. The following example shows how to invoke the `CancelUpdate` method by clicking the CancelUpdate button on a Web page:

```
<INPUT TYPE=BUTTON NAME="CancelUpdate" VALUE="&CancelUpdate!"
onClick="CancelUpate">
SUB CancelUpdate
ADC1.CancelChange
END SUB
```

The Virtual Table Manager internally keeps both a copy of the original values and the changes. The `CancelUpdate` method empties the changes and the bound data-aware control is refreshed.

Virtual Video Store Example

In the last example for this chapter, you're going to modify the virtual video store so that customers can enter their customer IDs and see what videos they have reserved or reserve more videos. To do this, you need to modify the `SubmitChanges_OnClick` sub-routine. When the customer clicks the Submit Changes button after marking the reserved videos, you need to scan through the `Recordset` and update the `ReservedID` column to reflect the customer ID. The modified `SubmitChanges_OnClick` sub-routine looks like this:

```
SUB SubmitChanges_onClick
    IF CustomerID.Value="" Then
        MsgBox "Please enter customer ID before reserving the video"
    ELSE
        ADC1.MoveFirst
        ADC1.Recordset.MoveFirst
        while not ADC1.Recordset.EOF
            if ADC1.Recordset("reservedFlag").Value <> 0 then
                Text2.Text=CustomerID.Value
            end if
            ADC1.MoveNext
            ADC1.Recordset.MoveNext
        wend
        ADC1.SubmitChanges
        ADC1.Refresh
    END IF
END SUB
```

First, this sub-routine checks whether the customer ID is empty. If it is, a message box is displayed informing the customer that he or she must enter a customer ID to reserve videos. If there is a customer ID, then you scroll through the `AdvancedDataControl` `Recordset` and set the ReservedID equal to the Customer ID when the ReservedFlag has been checked. You set the ReservedID through a hidden RichText control, `Text2`, which is bound to the ReservedID column of the Video_Detail table. If you modify the `Text2` data, you're actually making changes to the `Recordset`. Notice that you're scrolling the Grid control along with the `Recordset` (using `ADC.MoveNext`) so that the `Text2` control reflects the current row of the `Recordset`. After you make changes to the `Text2` RichText control, you submit them by using the `SubmitChanges` method. Take a look at the complete example in Listing 16.20.

16

Listing 16.20. Modifying the SubmitChanges_OnClick sub-routine.

```
 1: <TITLE>Teach Yourself Active Web Databases with VB in 21 Days</TITLE>
 2: </HEAD>
 3: <BODY LANGUAGE="VBS" onload ="Init">
 4: <CENTER>
 5: <H1><font size=4>
➥Teach Yourself Active Web Databases with VB in 21 Days</H1></font>
 6: <IMG SRC="video.gif" WIDTH=400 HEIGHT=100 ALT="Virtual Video Store">
 7: <HR size=2 width=80%>
 8: <H2><font size=3>Reserve Videos Based on Customer ID</H2></font>
 9: <table><font size=1>
10:        <tr><td>Customer ID:<td><INPUT NAME=CustomerID SIZE=6>
11: </table></font>
12: <OBJECT ID="Grid1" WIDTH=500 HEIGHT=100
13:        CLASSID="CLSID:00028C00-0000-0000-0000-000000000046">
14: </OBJECT>
15: <BR>
16: <OBJECT CLASSID="CLSID:3B7C8860-D78F-101B-B9B5-04021C009402"
17:        ID=Text1 height=40 width=400>
18:        <PARAM NAME="ALLOWUPDATE" VALUE="TRUE;">
19: </OBJECT>
20: <OBJECT ID="Radio1" WIDTH=100 HEIGHT=50
21:        CLASSID="CLSID:0BA686AA-F7D3-101A-993E-0000C0EF6F5E">
22:        <PARAM NAME="Caption" VALUE="Reserved">
23:        <PARAM NAME="ALLOWUPDATE" VALUE="TRUE;">
24: </OBJECT>
25: <BR>
26: <OBJECT CLASSID="CLSID:3B7C8860-D78F-101B-B9B5-04021C009402"
27:        ID=Text2 height=1 width=1>
28:        <PARAM NAME="ALLOWUPDATE" VALUE="TRUE;">
29:        <PARAM NAME="Visible" VALUE="FALSE;">
30:        </OBJECT>
31: <BR><BR>
32: <CENTER>
33: <INPUT TYPE=BUTTON NAME="First" VALUE="&First" onClick="MoveFirst">
34: <INPUT TYPE=BUTTON NAME="Next" VALUE="&Next" onClick="MoveNext">
35: <INPUT TYPE=BUTTON NAME="Prev" VALUE="&Prev" onClick="MovePrev">
36: <INPUT TYPE=BUTTON NAME="Last" VALUE="&Last" onClick="MoveLast">
37: <BR>
38: <INPUT TYPE=BUTTON NAME="ShowAVail" VALUE="Show &Available">
39: <INPUT TYPE=BUTTON NAME="ShowReserved" VALUE="&Show Reserved"
➥onClick="ShowR">
40: <INPUT TYPE=BUTTON NAME="Reserve" VALUE="&Reserve" onClick="Con">
41: </CENTER>
42: <OBJECT CLASSID="clsid:9381D8F2-0288-11d0-9501-00AA00B911A5"
43:        ID=ADC1 HEIGHT=10 WIDTH = 10
➥CODEBASE="http://<%=Request.ServerVariables("Server_name")%>
➥/ADCDownload/msadc10.cab">
44:        <PARAM NAME="BINDINGS"
➥VALUE="Grid1;TEXT1.Text=Description;Radio1.Value=ReservedFlag;
➥Text2.Text=ReservedId">
```

continues

Listing 16.20. continued

```
45:        </OBJECT>
46: <BR><BR>
47: <SCRIPT LANGUAGE= "VBS">
48: SUB MoveFirst
49:        ADC1.MoveFirst
50: END SUB
51: SUB MoveNext
52:        ADC1.MoveNext
53: END SUB
54: SUB MovePrev
55:        ADC1.MovePrevious
56: END SUB
57: SUB MoveLast
58:        ADC1.MoveLast
59: END SUB
60: SUB Con
61:        IF CustomerID.Value="" Then
62:            MsgBox "Please enter customer ID before reserving the video"
63:        ELSE
64:            ADC1.MoveFirst
65:            ADC1.Recordset.MoveFirst
66:            while not ADC1.Recordset.EOF
67:                if ADC1.Recordset("reservedFlag").Value <> 0 then
68:                    Set Text2.Text=CustomerID.Value
69:                end if
70:                    ADC1.MoveNext
71:                    ADC1.Recordset.MoveNext
72:            wend
73:            ADC1.SubmitChanges
74:            ADC1.Refresh
75:            Grid1.Columns(4).Visible = FALSE
76:            Grid1.Columns(5).Visible = FALSE
77:            Grid1.Columns(6).Visible = FALSE
78:        END IF
79: END SUB
80: SUB ShowAvail_OnClick
81:        ADC1.SQL ="select VideoTitle,Rating,Category,ReleaseDate,
➥ ReservedID,Description,Reservedflag
➥ from Video_detail where Reservedflag = 0
➥ order by VideoTitle FOR BROWSE"
82:        ADC1.Refresh
83:        Grid1.Columns(4).Visible = FALSE
84:        Grid1.Columns(5).Visible = FALSE
85:        Grid1.Columns(6).Visible = FALSE
86: END SUB
87: SUB ShowR
88:        if CustomerID.Value =  "" THEN
89:        ELSE
90:            ADC1.SQL = "select VideoTitle,Rating,Category, ReleaseDate,
➥ ReservedID,Description,ReservedFlag from Video_detail
➥ where ReservedID = " & CustomerID.Value & " for browse"
```

16

```
91:          ADC1.Refresh
92:          Grid1.Columns(4).Visible = TRUE
93:          Grid1.Columns(5).Visible = FALSE
94:          Grid1.Columns(6).Visible = FALSE
95:      END IF
96: END SUB
97: SUB Init
98:      ADC1.Server = "http://<%=Request.ServerVariables("Server_name")%>"
99:      ADC1.Connect = "DSN=Video;UID=sa"
100:      CustomerID.Value=""
101: END SUB
102: </SCRIPT>
103: </BODY>
104: </HTML>
```

In this example, you add another RichText control, Text2, and set the Visible property of Text1 to FALSE because you don't want the customer to see this control. You also change the ShowR() sub-routine so that it retrieves only the videos that have been reserved by the specified customer. The SQL statement is dynamically constructed to specify Customer ID information in the ReservedID column of the WHERE condition for the search criteria.

Figure 16.18 shows you the screen after you click the Show Available Video button.

Figure 16.18.

Clicking the Show Available Video button.

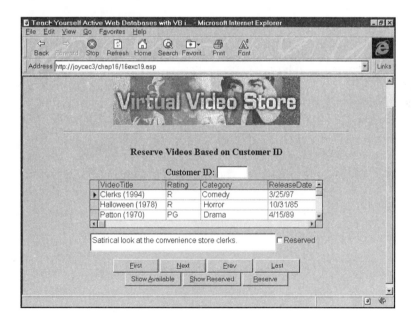

Figure 16.19 shows you the result after you enter 3 as the customer ID, select the "Clerks (1994)" video, and click the Reserve button to reserve that video.

Figure 16.19.

Entering the customer ID and clicking the Reserve button.

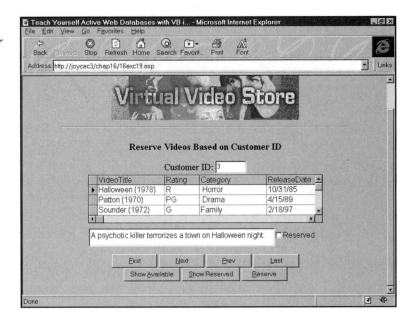

Figure 16.20 shows you the result after you enter 3 for the customer ID and click the Show Reserved Video button. The "Clerks (1994)" video shows up in the Grid control.

Figure 16.20.

Reserving the video and clicking the Show Reserved Video button.

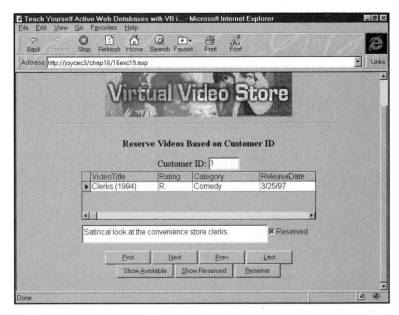

So far, all these examples require application logic to process the information—for example, queries that differ from `select all the videos in the store` to `select all the available videos in the store`. No business rules have been defined to more carefully control the client application. In Chapter 19, you will learn how to define a business object so that all the business rules can be hidden on the application server tier, and the client application can retrieve the data just by invoking the business objects and their methods.

Summary

Today, you have learned the client-tier architecture of Advanced Data Connector and seen how each of the client framework components interact with each other. You have also explored the properties and methods of the `AdvancedDataControl` object in depth and worked through many examples using `AdvancedDataControl` objects and the default business object to manipulate data. By now, you should be comfortable programming the `AdvancedDataControl` by using the default business object, and you should have an understanding of how the `AdvancedDataControl` can be useful for data-centered interactive Web programming.

One of the client-tier components is the ADOR `Recordset`, which is discussed in more detail in Chapter 19. Also, the `AdvancedDataSpace` object is covered in Chapters 19 and 20 when business objects are introduced.

Q&A

Q Where can I find downloading information for all the technology mentioned in this chapter?

A You'll find the information in Appendix A.

Q Why can't I get any of the ADC examples to work, but there's no error message?

A First, you want to use the example in Listing 16.4 to make sure your ADC environment is set up correctly. If the Listing 16.4 example doesn't work, please check Appendix A on how to set up your environment correctly to run the examples in this chapter.

Q How does Advanced Data Connector differ from IDC/HTX and ASP with ADO?

A Advanced Data Connector allows you to interact with active data at runtime, but IDC/HTX and ASP with ADO handle only static data.

Q When I invoke the SubmitChanges method, is all the data submitted or only the changed data?

A Only the changed data is submitted.

Q **When I use the SubmitChanges method to update data, I get a Rowset not updatable error.**

A You probably didn't create a unique index key for your table. The SubmitChanges method relies on the unique index key to act properly.

Q **For some reason, I just can't update data!**

A You need to check the following things: Set the AllowUpdate property of the controls to TRUE, and use the for browse keyword for the SQL statement. The database server must be SQL Server 6.5 with Service Pack 2. Finally, make sure the table you're updating has a unique index key.

Quiz

1. What are the methods and properties of an AdvancedDataControl object?

2. Can you bind more than one control to an AdvancedDataControl object?

3. Can you have more than one returned result set for a AdvancedDataControl object?

4. What kind of properties are required when you invoke the Requery method of an AdvancedDataControl object?

5. What's the different between simple data-aware controls and complex data-aware controls?

Exercise

Create an online ticket reservation system for a virtual theater.

16

Day 17

The AdvancedDataControl and the ADO Recordset

by Matt Warren

Interactive Web pages aren't tied to the automatic data binding the Advanced Data Connector (ADC) supplies. They can offer a richer user experience by combining automatic binding with non–data-bound controls and data-aware scripts. To do this, the Web page developer can take advantage of ADC and ADO (ActiveX Data Objects) at the same time. Both Microsoft products are designed to work together to achieve more than either one could alone.

After reading this chapter, you will be able to do the following:

- [ ] Describe what a client-side Recordset is.
- [ ] Show how the ADO Recordset performs data access tasks that the Advanced Data Connector can't.
- [ ] Use the ADO Recordset to modify the AdvancedDataControl's current position.
- [ ] Use the ADO Recordset to access records outside the AdvancedDataControl's monitoring.
- [ ] Use the ADO Recordset to read fields that aren't bound to Edit controls.
- [ ] Show how to use the ADO Recordset and the ADC AdvancedDataControl together to perform updates through programming.

 NOTE

> To run the examples in this chapter, please make sure you refer to the setup instructions included in "Week 3 at a Glance."

A Recordset **for the Client**

The Advanced Data Connector extends database access across the Internet. It sends query results anywhere, allowing interactive manipulation of the individual records on the client machine. This feature means that ActiveX controls and even ordinary HMTL input fields can be used to display, edit, and update database records.

Web pages can be designed to incorporate the Advanced Data Connector as a downloadable object, specifying its construction and connections to other page components by using standard HTML instructions. The ADC takes the place of the datasource controls familiar to Microsoft Visual Basic and Microsoft Visual C++ programmers.

What the ADC doesn't do on its own, however, is provide a general programming interface for data access. There's no way to get at the actual data fields from within scripting code. Certainly, the ADC's AdvancedDataControl has its own properties and methods for connecting to the middle-tier server, and even some for synchronizing the current record position with all the bound controls, but there's no equivalent to the ADO Recordset's Fields collection. In other words, you can't actually pull data out of the AdvancedDataControl and place it in a program variable.

Fortunately, there's already an object that gives you direct field access; it is, of course, the ADO Recordset. The Advanced Data Connector comes complete with its own Recordset object. The ADC coordinates data between Edit controls, and the Recordset interacts with scripting code. The two complement each other functionally. In fact, the ADC is built on the same technology as the Recordset. The two are merely different interfaces on top of the same data store. Changes made to fields through the interactive use of Edit controls are reflected immediately in the data visible to the Recordset.

The ADC's Recordset, however, is slightly different from the Recordset described in Chapter 9, "Dynamic Changes and the ADO Recordset." It's a specialized Recordset meant to transfer quickly and easily from a Web server to a client browser. To do this and keep transmission time to a minimum, the Recordset object was redesigned to include only a subset of the methods and properties available to its big brother. Some of its functions were sacrificed in a quest to make the object as small as possible, while still allowing ease of use for common data-access situations.

The ADC's Recordset is referred to as the *ADOR Recordset*, as opposed to the ADODB Recordset used extensively in Chapters 9 through 14. *ADOR* stands for *ActiveX Data Objects Recordset-Only.*

Getting at the Recordset

Before you can use the ADOR Recordset within client-side scripting code, you have to get hold of one. You don't need to use the CreateObject() method or even HTML <OBJECT> tags to create your own because the ADC already has one it's quite willing to share. In fact, it has a property called Recordset that's meant for that purpose. The function you use looks like this:

```
<script language="vbs">

Function GetRecordset( connector )
  Set GetRecordset = connector.recordset
End Function

</script>
```

You probably won't even need to write a function like GetRecordset(), but it demonstrates how easily you can get the Recordset object.

Getting at the Data

Just as with the full ADO Recordset, the smaller sibling has a Fields collection, with each Field object corresponding to a database column. You can still use Visual Basic's shorthand notation for accessing individual columns:

```
<Script language="vbs">

  Set rs = GetRecordset( c )
  field1 = rs(0)
```

```
    field2 = rs(1)
    field3 = rs(2)

</Script>
```

Naturally, the same still goes for accessing fields by name, as shown here:

```
<Script language="vbs">

  Set rs = GetRecordset( c )
  firstname = rs("FirstName")
  lastname  = rs("LastName")
  phone     = rs("PhoneNumber")

</Script>
```

If you've decided to access each and every field, one by one, a FOR...NEXT loop is still the preferred choice, and the Fields collection still guides you to the last element, as shown here:

```
<Script language="vbs">

  Set rs = GetRecordset( c )

  for n = 0 to rs.fields.count - 1
    value = rs.fields(n)
  next

</Script>
```

Navigating the Recordset

For the most part, accessing data with the newer, leaner Recordset is exactly the same. For that matter, so is navigation. To move between records, you use the same commands that take the same parameters. The ADOR Recordset has both the MoveNext() and MovePrevious() methods, as well as MoveFirst() and MoveLast(). It even has the seldom-used Move() method that takes both a bookmark and an offset count as parameters.

Taking a bookmark as a parameter would, of course, lead you to believe that the ADOR Recordset still supports bookmarks, which is true. The Bookmark property can be used to both get and set the current bookmark value. However, just as with the full ADODB Recordset, bookmarks are supported only when the underlying data provider supports them. Fortunately, the ADC's underlying Internet-friendly data provider does support bookmarks, so it's safe to assume they're available when you're accessing data over the Internet.

The last two members of the navigation team are, as you've probably guessed, the EOF and BOF properties. They, too, are part of the ADOR Recordset. Without them, you wouldn't know when you reached the beginning or end of the data. Here's how they're used in scripting code:

```
<script language="vbs">

sub WalkForward( rs )
```

```
    rs.MoveFirst
    while not rs.EOF
      for n = 0 to rs.fields.count - 1
        value = rs( n )
      next n
      rs.MoveNext
    wend
end sub

sub WalkBackward( rs )
  rs.MoveLast
  while not rs.BOF
    for n = 0 to rs.fields.count - 1
      value = rs( n )
    next n
    rs.MovePrevious
  wend
end sub

</script>
```

What's Missing?

This is the million-dollar question: What features don't you get when you choose to use the ADOR Recordset instead of the ADODB Recordset? The answer is: quite a few.

First of all, there are no Connection or Command objects. Even if you somehow managed to bring them down to the client from the ADODB library on the server and had authorization to do so, they aren't designed to work with the ADOR Recordset. So forget any notions of shared Connections or prepared and Parameter-based commands. However, all hope is not lost. Later on, in Chapters 19, "Client-Server Business Objects," and 20, "Business Objects and ADO," you find out how to use both the ADODB objects on the server with the ADOR Recordset on the client to get the best of both worlds. For the sake of argument, though, pretend that isn't possible for now.

Second, you can get data only by using either the ADC itself or the Recordset's Open() method to establish a link, query the database, and populate the Recordset. Worse than that, there are no options. You can't choose between forward-only and keyset cursors, and you have no control over the locking mode or whether you're even allowed to update data at all. You take what you get. The underlying data provider has full control; it decides what you can and cannot do.

Again, this limitation isn't necessarily entirely bad. The underlying data provider used by the ADC offers a bidirectional cursor, with bookmarks and updates that use the batch-optimistic mode.

Still, these limitations are only the start. The Field objects have been stripped bare. Yes, you can still get the value of the corresponding field for the current record position by using the

Value property, but that's about all. The only other property on the Field object is the Name property. There are no Attributes, OriginalValue, or UnderlyingValue, and no methods like GetChunk() or AppendChunk().

The ADOR Recordset

The ADOR Recordset is a different code library from that of ADODB. It's packaged with the ADC client-side downloadable CAB file and can be automatically transferred to a user's workstation via a reference in a Web page.

It is important to understand the differences between the two objects. Although they're both called Recordset, many of the features have been removed from the ADOR version to reduce the amount of bits that need to be transferred over the network. It's technically possible to write client-side applications with the ADODB object family, but that topic is beyond the scope of this book.

The properties and methods available to the ADOR Recordset are described in the following sections.

Properties of the ADOR Recordset

Property	Description
BOF	Beginning of the file
Bookmark	Bookmark of the current record position
EOF	End of the file
MarshalOptions	Determines which records to transmit

NOTE

> The following descriptions have a phrase on the right-hand side of the page, just after the section title. The words to the left of the separating slash (/) pertain to the Recordset before it's been opened, and those to the right apply while it's open.

The BOF Property

Contains a Boolean value   NA / Read-Only

The BOF property, which can have the value of TRUE or FALSE, can be used to determine whether the current record position is actually before the first record of the set. This can happen when you're trying to move the position backward by using MovePrevious() or when you're specifying a negative offset to the Move() method.

The Bookmark **Property**

Contains a Variant value   NA / Read-Write

The Bookmark property can be used to get a reference marker to the current record position and to move the current record position to the referenced row. Assigning the Bookmark property is equivalent to calling the Move() method, with a valid bookmark and a count (of how many records to move to beyond the bookmark) of zero.

The EOF **Property**

Contains a Boolean value   NA / Read-Only

The EOF property, which can have a value of TRUE or FALSE, is used to determine whether the current record position is actually after the last record of the set. This can happen when you're trying to move the position forward by using MoveNext() or when you're specifying a positive offset to the Move() method.

The MarshalOptions **Property**

Contains one of the following values: NA / Read-Only

Marshal Constant	Value	Description
adMarshalAll	0	Marshal all records
adMarshalModifiedOnly	1	Marshal only modified records

The MarshalOptions property can be used to limit the type of records transmitted between the client and the server. A business object that wants to send a Recordset back to the client typically uses adMarshalAll, but a piece of scripting code on the client that wants to send only the changes back to the server needs to use adMarshalModifiedOnly.

The Advanced Data Connector uses this property internally when requesting data from the ADC middle-tier server and submitting changes back. If you're using method calls on the ADC object to send and receive data, you don't need to modify this property.

Methods of the ADOR Recordset

The methods of the ADOR Recordset correspond to similar methods found in the ADODB Recordset. The following table lists only those methods that are part of the ADOR Recordset.

Method	Description
Close	Close the Recordset
Move	Move to the specified position

continues

Method	Description
MoveFirst	Move to the first position
MoveLast	Move to the last position
MoveNext	Move to the next position
MovePrevious	Move to the previous position
Open	Open the Recordset

The Close() Method

Recordset.Close

You can use the Close() method to indicate that you're done using the Recordset to access records from the query. Any resources used by the Recordset are then released.

Closing the Recordset happens by default as soon as no references to the Recordset remain. This lack of references might happen because the variables used as references to the Recordset were limited to the scope of a function or script that's no longer being executed or because you have reassigned that variable to a new value or object. If you don't explicitly close the Recordset object, it's automatically closed for you.

The Move() Method

Recordset.Move count, start

count   The number of records to move in relation to the start position. A value of 1 means "move to one record after the start position," and a value of -1 means "move to one record before the start position."

start   A bookmark declaring the start position of the Move() method. This parameter is optional. If it isn't specified, the move is made in relation to the current record position.

You can use the Move() method—by far the most powerful of all the move methods—to change the current record position. A single statement can move many records forward or backward at the same time.

Not all Recordsets can move the current position backward, however. Recordsets opened with adOpenForwardOnly for the CursorType can move forward only, so records can't be returned to.

 NOTE

> A move that would cause the position to be placed anywhere after the end of the set instead places the current position in a special location that is considered to be immediately after the last record. For example,

imagine two separate calls to `Move()`: one requesting a move to the last record plus one, and another requesting a move to the last record plus ten. After either call, the current record position is placed after the end of the records. In both cases, the final position is exactly the same. The edges of the `Recordset` act like barriers. There's only one imaginary spot beyond each edge.

WARNING

A move made in relation to the current position (when the current position is either after the end of the set or before the beginning of the set) that would cause the position to be moved even further beyond the edge is considered an error.

The `MoveFirst` Method

Recordset.MoveFirst

You can use the `MoveFirst` method to move the current record position to the first record in the set so that the `Recordset` is automatically positioned on the first record when it's opened.

`Recordsets` opened with `adOpenForwardOnly` for the `CursorType` or those without bookmark support may not move back to the first record once the current position has moved beyond it.

The `MoveLast` Method

Recordset.MoveLast

You can use the `MoveLast` method to move the current record position to the last record in the set. However, `Recordsets` opened without bookmark support may not allow you to move directly to the last record. Instead, you'll have to use `MoveNext`.

The `MoveNext` Method

Recordset.MoveNext

You can use the `MoveNext` method to move the current record position to the very next record in the set. If the current position is the last record in the set, the `EOF` property is assigned the value `TRUE` after the call to `MoveNext`.

If `MoveNext` is repeatedly called while the current position is after the end of the `Recordset`, an error is generated.

The MovePrevious **Method**

Recordset.MovePrevious

You can use the MovePrevious method to move the current record position to the previous record in the set. If the current position is the first record in the set, the BOF property is assigned the value TRUE after the call to MovePrevious.

If MovePrevious is repeatedly called while the current position is after the end of the Recordset, an error is generated.

Not all Recordsets can move the current position backward. Recordsets opened with adOpenForwardOnly for the CursorType can move forward only. Because of this, records can't be returned to.

The Open() **Method**

Recordset.Open *source, connection*

source	A string containing a query acceptable to the database server
connection	A string containing connection information descriptive enough to establish a connection to a database server

You can use the Open() method to both establish a connection to a database server and execute a query. The Recordset that's opened is the default type supported by the provider. The general ADO provider MSDASQL defaults to a forward-only, read-only cursor. If the Recordset comes from the Advanced Data Connector instead of being opened with the Open method, the Recordset is bidirectional and capable of supporting bookmarks.

The connection string can have the special argument sequence *Provider=<name>*; that's used to change the data provider.

Properties of the ADOR Fields **Collection**

Like the ADODB Recordset's Fields collection, there's only one property.

Property	*Description*
Count	The number of fields in the collection

The Count **Property**

Contains an Integer value   NA / Read-Only

You can use the Count property to determine the total number of fields in the Fields collection.

Methods of the ADOR `Fields` Collection

In addition to having only one property, the ADOR `Recordset`'s `Fields` collection has only a single method.

Method	Description
Item	The default method that retrieves field objects

The `Item` Method

```
Set field = Fields.Item( index )
```

index   The name or ordinal position of the requested `Field` object

The `Item` method is the default method called when you use the parentheses as indexing operators on the `Recordset` or the `Fields` collection. This method is normally hidden from view inside program editors that understand the type-library format of OLE Automation objects.

Properties of the ADOR `Field` Object

The ADOR `Field` object has only two properties and no methods. The `Field` object has been trimmed down to only the most essential properties used for accessing `Recordset` data values.

Property	Description
Name	The name of the field
Value	The value based on the current position

The `Name` Property

Contains a `String` value   NA / Read-Only

You can use the `Name` property to determine the name of the field as specified in the query. This same name can be used as a key when you're retrieving the `Field` object from the `Fields` collection.

The `Value` Property

Contains a `Variant` value   NA / Read-Write

You can use the `Value` property to get the data value for the corresponding field of the current record. The ADOR `Recordset` object doesn't support updating in its initial release. However, changes can still be made to the data by using data-bound controls and the Advanced Data Connector.

Using Recordsets in Client Scripts

There are many reasons, and just as many ways, to use a Recordset object in client-side scripting code. Automatic data binding, made possible by the Advanced Data Connector's AdvancedDataControl, is only the first step into bringing interactive data access to the client. Many applications need to go beyond the canned interactions that data-bound controls are limited to. In the same way that scripting enhances static HTML pages by allowing the page designer to do more than what's described by HTML, data access done through programming lets applications go beyond the limited scope of prepackaged controls. One of those prepackaged controls is the ADC AdvancedDataControl itself.

Roll-Your-Own Data Binding

You may find the ADC's automatic binding capabilities too limited. The ADC is good at supplying data for simple HTML input fields, like text boxes and buttons, and other complex data-bound controls, like the Grid control that comes with ADC and the data-bound Grid control packaged with Visual Basic Enterprise Edition. It's not very good, however, at feeding data into other, often more useful, ActiveX controls.

For example, you could have a perfectly good Graph control that draws histograms, bar charts, or even fancy scientific impedance charts, but because the Graph control accepts data only in the form of arrays or files, you can't use the ADC.

You might find it quite normal to write the following Visual Basic code to initialize this hypothetical Graph control:

```
Dim x(3)
Dim y(3)
x(0) = "94"
y(0) = 2500
x(1) = "95"
y(1) = 2790
x(2) = "96"
y(2) = 4310
x(3) = "97"
y(4) = 8192
graph.barplot x, y
```

With a Recordset available, you could easily supply data from a remote database, over the Internet, to that control. In the following example, the variable sales is an instance of an

17

AdvancedDataControl connected to the Sales database. This example uses the entire Recordset to fill a pair of arrays:

```
Sub BarChartButton_OnClick()

  Set rs = Sales.Recordset
  Dim x(rs.RecordCount)
  Dim y(rs.RecordCount)

  rs.MoveFirst
  For item = 0 to rs.RecordCount - 1
    x(item) = rs("Year")
    y(item) = rs("Sales")
    rs.MoveNext
  Next

  graph.BarPlot x, y

End Sub
```

In one control, such as a Grid, you could display the entire data set, and in the other, a Graph control, you could give a visual overview of the same information. Without combining the ADC and the Recordset to bring the information to the client, the only other method of generating the graphic would be doing it on the server, which isn't interactive and takes up too much time on the server.

You have several choices, however, for making this Graph control example interactive. The information coming from the ADC isn't static. You can re-specify the query, collect new data, and regenerate the Graph at any time, perhaps in response to the user clicking a button or some other sort of interaction.

The type of interaction that the ADC is good at is synchronization. When you tell the ADC to advance to the next record by calling MoveNext(), all the bound fields follow suit, each displaying the appropriate information from the same record. The Grid control can even scroll its window to keep the highlight bar in step with the advancing records. What you might want to do is somehow keep a non–data-bound control, like the Graph, in sync with the rest of controls.

You could re-query by using a second ADC AdvancedDataControl each time the current position is changed. Based on information in the current record, you could query for more detailed data from another table. This second AdvancedDataControl and its Recordset object could be used to generate a graph. What's harder to understand, however, is how to use the current position, which all the data-bound controls magically seem to know about, within the scripting code.

Keeping in Step

Although the Recordset that's available from the Advanced Data Connector doesn't use the automatic data binding that keeps the other controls linked, you can still synchronize the Recordset with the AdvancedDataControl. In normal ADO terms, the Recordset you get from the AdvancedDataControl is actually a "clone" of the true Recordset being used to synchronize the data-bound controls. What this means is that you can go about using the Recordset, navigating back and forth, without disturbing the information being displayed onscreen. If you reset your Recordset to the first record in the set, the onscreen controls don't change to reflect this new state. The screen is *not* updated when you call MoveNext() on the Recordset.

However, this might be exactly what you want. Each record might be designed to contain information that would be interesting to display by graph. Instead of displaying sales over time, your graph could display information from different columns of the same table. In this case, you would certainly want the graph to match the record being displayed by the other controls. However, because the Recordset you have available is disconnected from the rest of the controls, it doesn't have a current position that matches.

The question is, how do you determine which record in the set is the current one being displayed, and how can you navigate your own Recordset to point to the same one? There *is* a way—called *manual synchronization*—and it's simple to use, but somehow it got missed when the documentation for the Advanced Data Connector was being prepared.

TIP

> The Advanced Data Connector's AdvancedDataControl has its own Bookmark property that matches the Recordset's Bookmark property. You can use the value you get from one to assign to the other. Assigning the first bookmark to the other causes them to become synchronized.

If you need to use manual synchronization, you can do it just before you need to access the data. In the following code fragment, the Graph control is drawn by using information from the current record position:

```
Sub DrawGraph()
  Dim x(3)
  Dim y(3)

  x(0) = "Sales Q1"
  x(1) = "Sales Q2"
  x(2) = "Sales Q3"
  x(3) = "Sales Q4"

  Set rs = sales.Recordset
  rs.bookmark = sales.bookmark
```

```
y(0) = rs("SalesQ1")
y(1) = rs("SalesQ2")
y(2) = rs("SalesQ3")
y(3) = rs("SalesQ4")

graph.BarPlot x, y

End Sub
```

You still need to add one more step to make the whole process happen automatically. Unlike the other data-bound controls, your Graph control isn't told when the current record position changes.

You can, however, tell your Graph control directly, if you're using your own HTML buttons as a navigation interface, as shown here:

```
Sub ButtonNext_OnClick()
  sales.MoveNext
  DrawGraph
End Sub
```

In this code fragment, each time the ButtonNext button is clicked, the Data control `Sales` is told to advance the current position. After it has been moved, a call to the `DrawGraph()` sub-routine defined earlier draws the graph corresponding to the new record position.

Accessing Unbound Fields

Of course, you might find reasons to use the `Recordset` that aren't so grandiose, such as simply accessing a field that's not currently displayed onscreen by a control.

Another simple reason for using the `Recordset` could be to verify that the values in a couple of input fields match a constraint secretly held by the program but not known by the users, as shown in this example:

```
Sub ComputeBonus()

  Set rs = sales.Recordset
  rs.Bookmark = sales.Bookmark

  if document.salesform.q1 > rs("minsales") then
    document.salesform.bonus = 1000
  else
    document.salesform.bonus = 0
  end if

End Sub
```

In this code, the `bonus` input field is auto-initialized when the sales for quarter one (q1) are above a minimum sales value per record. A sub-routine like this might be useful for enhancing a sales-entry form.

You might also want to collapse an entire dataset down into a set of totals on demand, without requiring a secondary query to the remote data server; the code to do that looks like this:

```
Sub ComputeTotals()

   '** initialize counters
   q1 = 0
   q2 = 0
   q3 = 0
   q4 = 0

   '** compute totals
   Set rs = sales.Recordset
   rs.MoveFirst
   While not rs.EOF
     q1 = q1 + rs("SalesQ1")
     q2 = q2 + rs("SalesQ2")
     q3 = q3 + rs("SalesQ3")
     q4 = q4 + rs("SalesQ4")
     rs.MoveNext
   Wend

   '** assign totals to form fields for display
   document.form1.q1 = q1
   document.form1.q2 = q2
   document.form1.q3 = q3
   document.form1.q4 = q4

End Sub
```

Updating Records

Of all the tasks that the ADOR Recordset can and can't perform, it seems rather arbitrary for it not to support updating fields. After all, the ADC supports updating. If a user changes the value of a bound field, that value is changed in the Recordset; when the SubmitChanges() method is called on the ADC's Data control, all the changed records are sent back to the server to update the original database.

It's exactly because the AdvancedDataControl supports updating, however, that the Recordset can't. The ADODB Recordset object has very complex semantics when it comes to the ability to update, insert, and delete records. The communication between cloned Recordsets becomes rather tricky and is directly tied into the ability of the Recordset to send out notifications of changes, in much the same way that bound controls communicate with one another. But the ADC doesn't operate in the same way. The code to support it would have weighed the library down so much that it wouldn't seem feasible to transmit across the Internet.

The AdvancedDataControl and the Recordset are clones of one another; changes to one affect the other directly. Because the ADOR Recordset was reduced to such a small subset of the

ADODB `Recordset`, no mechanism was left to interpret or react to changes made by another source. Therefore, the `AdvancedDataControl` is free to change the field values without dealing with the complexities of notifying the `Recordset` clone. It has to deal only with notifications to bound controls. The `Recordset` must discover these changes later, on its own, when scripting code is used to access values.

Updating Through Scripting Code

Inevitably, Web page designers are going to find reasons for updating field values automatically, such as writing scripting code that calculates changes to fields and updates them directly into the `Recordset`. Since the `Recordset` can't be used to update data, you can't assign the field values directly, so your only recourse is to use an old HTML trick.

Many Web page designers' favorite trick is to use hidden input fields to hold values that never get seen by the person viewing the page because they aren't displayed. You have already been using this trick. Chapters 10 through 14 used it every time an HTML input form was displayed—the mode field was typed as hidden, as you can see here:

```
<INPUT TYPE=HIDDEN NAME="Mode">
```

You can use the same trick to help you make updates to field values in scripting code. The only difference is that you're going to be using a data-bound ActiveX control instead of a standard HTML input field. On your Web page, define a hidden ActiveX control for all fields needing to be calculated but not already being displayed. Tie them into the `AdvancedDataControl` by specifying them in the `BINDINGS` parameter used in the `AdvancedDataControl`'s `<OBJECT>` specification.

The following segment of a dynamic Web page processes each record in the query, updating the bonus field:

```
<!-- declare 'sales' data control -->
<OBJECT CLASSID="clsid:9381D8F2-0288-11d0-9501-00AA00B911A5"
  ID="sales"
  CODEBASE="HTTP://myserver/MSADC/msadc10.cab"
  WIDTH=1 HEIGHT=1>
  <PARAM NAME="BINDINGS" VALUE="fldBonus.Text=Bonus" >
  <PARAM NAME="Connect" VALUE="DSN=MyDB;UID=MyID;PWD=MyPWD;">
  <PARAM NAME="Server" VALUE="http://myserver ">
  <PARAM NAME="SQL" VALUE="Select * from Sales">
</OBJECT>

<!-- declare hidden field -->
<OBJECT ID="fldBonus"
  WIDTH=0 HEIGHT=0
  CODEBASE="HTTP://myserver/MSADC/Samples/Sheridan.cab"
  CLASSID="3BB7C8860-D78F-101B-B9B5-04021C009402"
  >
```

17

```
</OBJECT>

<!-- process update -->

<SCRIPT LANGUAGE="VBS">

  Set rs = sales.rs

  rs.MoveFirst
  while not rs.EOF
    sales.Bookmark = rs.Bookmark

    if rs("salesQ1") > rs("minSales") then
       document.fldBonus = 1000
    end if

    rs.MoveNext
  wend

  sales.SubmitChanges

</SCRIPT>
```

This example isn't truly interactive and could probably have been done just as well with a SQL UPDATE command, but it does illustrate the use of hidden fields as a way to allow updates through scripting code.

Note how the Bookmark property is being used to synchronize the AdvancedDataControl and the Recordset. A few pages back, you were shown how the AdvancedDataControl was used to synchronize the Recordset. This time it's going in reverse because the Recordset is the one that's smarter about navigation—it has the EOF property that tells the code when to stop looping. In this example, the bookmark is used to synchronize the AdvancedDataControl to guarantee that bound fields always correspond to the data in the current record.

Client HTML Generation

Back in Chapter 8, "ActiveX Data Objects (ADO) Overview," I mentioned that it might be useful to actually generate HTML during client scripting in addition to the normal server-side generation done by Active Server Pages. A dynamic Web page can be created in either place. There are many reasons not to generate HTML during client scripting; for instance, the extra scripting code would require a longer transmission time. Most Web designers don't want to inflict that penalty on their users.

Of course, there's the other side of the coin. Web sites and servers with huge volumes of hits often want to keep the processing on the server to a minimum. For many, server-side processing can be too expensive because it takes up too much time and ties the processor to doing other tasks instead of responding to Web page requests. Besides faster response time, one of the primary reasons for adding built-in interaction on the client is to reduce the number of round trips and the workload on the server.

It might actually take less information to transmit the code that generates the page instead of the entire, pre-generated page, as shown in this example:

```
<HTML>
<HEAD>
<TITLE>HTML Generation</TITLE>
</HEAD>

<BODY>

<OBJECT CLASSID="clsid:9381D8F2-0288-11d0-9501-00AA00B911A5"
  ID="adc"
  CODEBASE="HTTP://myserver/MSADC/msadc10.cab"
    WIDTH=1 HEIGHT=1>
  <PARAM NAME="Connect" VALUE="DSN=MyDB;UID=MyID;PWD=MyPWD;">
  <PARAM NAME="Server" VALUE="http://myserver ">
  <PARAM NAME="SQL" VALUE="SELECT * FROM FLAVORS">
</OBJECT>

<script language="vbs">

  '** generate flavor picker **

  document.write("<SELECT NAME=s1>")

  Set rs = adc.Recordset
  rs.MoveFirst
  While not rs.EOF

    document.write( "<OPTION>" )
    document.write( rs("flavor") )

    rs.MoveNext
  Wend

  document.write("</SELECT>")

</script>

</BODY>

</HTML>
```

Using the browser's built-in method Document.Write(), you can add HTML tags to the document while it's being processed. Everything in the document is parsed and processed in order from top to bottom. In the preceding example, the AdvancedDataControl is created first, and then the scripting code within the script block is parsed and executed. All this happens before the page is displayed to the viewer.

The Document.Write() method works just like the Response.Write() method available on the server. The Document.Write() method inserts HTML where the method is called, just as Response.Write() does on the server. The example actually builds a <SELECT> input field, containing all the flavors from the Flavor table. Although this table could be quite large, the scripting code sent to the client is much smaller. The data still has to be transmitted either way, but the data transmission takes less time through the AdvancedDataControl than it would take for the server to generate the equivalent list and send the full HTML sequence to the client browser.

Custom Searching Example

The ASP file in Listing 17.1 shows how you can use the ADOR Client Recordset with the ADC's automatic data binding to offer more than just the physical display of data fields. You can actually extend both the Recordset's and the Data control's features.

Listing 17.1 is an example of what you might do in your own Web page. It adds the ability to search for records in a Recordset that match particular criteria. ADODB has a feature to filter the Recordset, but even if you had the full ADODB Recordset on the client, those filters don't work on all fields at once.

The Web page produced from Listing 17.1 lists all the fields of a database table onscreen by using data-bound ActiveX controls. The ADC is used to bring the results of a query across the Internet and into those same controls. Below the fields are a series of VCR-style buttons that move the currently displayed record to the first or last record in the set or to the next or previous record from the current position.

In addition to the VCR-style buttons, there's an extra input field for specifying a matching string. Once a value is entered into this field, the screen displays only records that have the exact sequence somewhere in one of the fields.

Listing 17.1. Custom searching (17TWD01.ASP).

```
 1: <HTML>
 2: <HEAD>
 3: <TITLE>Example 17.1: Custom Searching</TITLE>
 4:
 5: <H1>Custom Searching</H1>
 6: </HEAD>
 7:
 8:
 9: <BODY LANGUAGE="VBS" onLoad="btnFirst_OnClick">
10:
11: <!-- #include file="17twd02.inc" -->
12:
```

```
13:
14: <!-- ******** THE DISPLAY ******** -->
15:
16: <CENTER>
17:
18: <TABLE>
19:
20: <TR>
21: <TD>First Name</TD>
22: <TD><% DataField "first", 100 %></TD>
23: </TR>
24:
25: <TR>
26: <TD>Last Name</TD>
27: <TD><% DataField "last", 100 %></TD>
28: </TR>
29:
30: <TR>
31: <TD>
32:
33: </TABLE>
34:
35: <BR>
36:
37: <INPUT TYPE=BUTTON NAME=btnFirst VALUE="<<">
38: <INPUT TYPE=BUTTON NAME=btnPrev VALUE="<">
39: <INPUT TYPE=BUTTON NAME=btnNext VALUE=">">
40: <INPUT TYPE=BUTTON NAME=bntLast VALUE=">>">
41:
42: <BR>
43: <BR>
44: <B>Find Matching Names</B>
45: <INPUT NAME=fldFind VALUE="" WIDTH=100>
46:
47: </CENTER>
48:
49:
50:
51:
52: <!-- **** VB SCRIPT THAT RUNS ON THE SERVER **** -->
53:
54: <%
55: '**** GENERATE A DATA CONTROL *****
56:
57: DataControl "adc", _
58:     "first.Text=fname;last.Text=lname;foo.Text=lname", _
59:     "SELECT * FROM Employee FOR BROWSE", _
60:     "DSN=pubs;UID=sa;PWD=;"
61: %>
62:
63:
64: <!-- **** VB SCRIPT THAT RUNS ON THE CLIENT **** -->
65:
66: <SCRIPT LANGUAGE="VBS">
67:
68: SUB btnFirst_OnClick()
```

continues

Listing 17.1. continued

```
69:
70:    IF fldFind.value > "" THEN
71:      FindNext adc
72:    ELSE
73:      adc.MoveFirst
74:    END IF
75:
76: END SUB
77:
78: SUB btnLast_OnClick()
79:    IF fldFind.value > "" THEN
80:      FindLast adc
81:    ELSE
82:      adc.MoveLast
83:    END IF
84: END SUB
85:
86: SUB btnNext_OnClick()
87:    IF fldFind.value > "" THEN
88:      FindNext adc
89:    ELSE
90:      adc.MoveNext
91:    END IF
92: END SUB
93:
94: SUB btnPrev_OnClick()
95:    IF fldFind.value > "" THEN
96:      FindPrevious adc
97:    ELSE
98:      adc.MovePrevious
99:    END IF
100: END SUB
101:
102: SUB fldFind_OnChange()
103:
104:    IF fldFind.value > "" THEN
105:      FindAny adc
106:    END IF
107:
108: END SUB
109:
110:
111:
112: '** FIND **********************************
113:
114:
115: '** DOES THE CURRENT RECORD CONTAIN THE VALUE IN ANY FIELD?
116:
117: FUNCTION RecordContainsFind( rs, v )
118:
119:    FOR f = 0 TO rs.fields.count - 1
120:
121:      IF InStr( CStr(rs(f).value), v ) > 0 THEN
```

```
122:         RecordContainsFind = true
123:       END IF
124:
125:    NEXT
126:
127:    RecordContainsFind = false
128:
129: END FUNCTION
130:
131:
132:
133: '** FIND THE NEXT MATCH
134:
135: SUB FindNext( dc )
136:
137:    SET rs = dc.Recordset
138:    rs.Bookmark = dc.Bookmark
139:
140:    rs.MoveNext
141:
142:    WHILE NOT rs.EOF
143:
144:       IF RecordContainsFind( rs, fldFind.value ) THEN
145:
146:          adc.Bookmark = rs.Bookmark
147:
148:          EXIT SUB
149:
150:       END IF
151:
152:       rs.MoveNext
153:    WEND
154:
155: END SUB
156:
157:
158: '** FIND THE PREVIOUS MATCH
159:
160: SUB FindPrevious( dc )
161:
162:    SET rs = dc.Recordset
163:    rs.Bookmark = dc.Bookmark
164:
165:    rs.MovePrevious
166:
167:    WHILE NOT rs.BOF
168:
169:       IF RecordContainsFind( rs, fldFind.value ) THEN
170:
171:          adc.Bookmark = rs.Bookmark
172:
173:          EXIT SUB
174:
175:       END IF
176:
177:       rs.MovePrevious
```

17

continues

Listing 17.1. continued

```
178:    WEND
179:
180: END SUB
181:
182:
183: '** FIND THE FIRST MATCH
184:
185: SUB FindFirst( dc )
186:
187:    SET rs = dc.Recordset
188:
189:    rs.MoveFirst
190:
191:    WHILE NOT rs.EOF
192:
193:       IF RecordContainsFind( rs, fldFind.value ) THEN
194:
195:          adc.Bookmark = rs.Bookmark
196:
197:          EXIT SUB
198:
199:       END IF
200:
201:       rs.MoveNext
202:    WEND
203:
204: END SUB
205:
206:
207: '** FIND THE LAST MATCH
208:
209: SUB FindLast( dc )
210:
211:    SET rs = dc.Recordset
212:
213:    rs.MoveLast
214:
215:    WHILE NOT rs.BOF
216:
217:       IF RecordContainsFind( rs, fldFind.value ) THEN
218:
219:          adc.Bookmark = rs.Bookmark
220:
221:          EXIT SUB
222:
223:       END IF
224:
225:       rs.MovePrevious
226:    WEND
227:
228: END SUB
229:
230:
231: SUB FindAny( dc )
```

17

```
232:
233:    SET rs = dc.Recordset
234:
235:    '** try forward
236:
237:    rs.Bookmark = dc.Bookmark
238:
239:    WHILE NOT rs.EOF
240:
241:      IF RecordContainsFind( rs, fldFind.value ) THEN
242:
243:        adc.Bookmark = rs.Bookmark
244:
245:        EXIT SUB
246:
247:      END IF
248:
249:      rs.MoveNext
250:    WEND
251:
252:
253:    '** try reverse
254:
255:    rs.Bookmark = dc.Bookmark
256:
257:    WHILE NOT rs.BOF
258:
259:      IF RecordContainsFind( rs, fldFind.value ) THEN
260:
261:        adc.Bookmark = rs.Bookmark
262:
263:        EXIT SUB
264:
265:      END IF
266:
267:      rs.MovePrevious
268:    WEND
269:
270:    Alert "Cannot find any matches"
271:
272: END SUB
273:
274: </SCRIPT>
275:
276:
277: </BODY>
278: </HTML>
```

A separate file is created to act as a library and hold sub-routines that automatically generate the appropriate HTML sequences to add data controls to your Web page. The controls used in Listing 17.2 are supplied by the Advanced Data Connector distribution. By using subroutines, you can remove the clutter of complex object declarations and the need to remember the rather terse globally unique identifiers known as CLASSIDs.

Listing 17.2. ADC-distributed controls (17TWD02.INC)

```
 1: <% host = Request.ServerVariables("SERVER_NAME") %>
 2:
 3:
 4: <% SUB DataControl( name, bind, sql, connect ) %>
 5:
 6: <OBJECT
 7:    ID=<%= name %>
 8:    CLASSID="clsid:9381D8F2-0288-11d0-9501-00aa00b911a5"
 9:    CODEBASE="http://<%= host %>/MSADC/msadc10.cab"
10:    WIDTH=1 HEIGHT=1
11:    >
12: <PARAM NAME="Server" VALUE="http://<%= host %>" >
13:
14: <% if bind <> "" then %>
15:    <PARAM NAME="Bindings" VALUE="<%= bind %>">
16: <% end if %>
17:
18: <% if connect <> "" then %>
19:    <PARAM NAME="Connect" VALUE="<%= connect %>">
20: <% end if %>
21:
22: <% if sql <> "" then %>
23:    <PARAM NAME="SQL" VALUE="<%= sql %>">
24: <% end if %>
25:
26: </OBJECT>
27:
28: <% END SUB %>
29:
30:
31: <% SUB DataGrid( name, width, height ) %>
32:
33: <OBJECT
34:    ID="<%= name %>"
35:    WIDTH=<%= width %>
36:    HEIGHT=<%= height %>
37:    CLASSID="CLSID:BC496AE0-9B4E-11CE-A6D5-0000C0BE9395"
38:    CODEBASE="HTTP://<%= host %>/MSADC/Samples/Sheridan.cab">
39: </OBJECT>
40:
41: <% END SUB %>
42:
43:
44: <% SUB DataField( name, width ) %>
45:
46: <OBJECT
47:    ID=<%= name %>
48:    WIDTH=<%= width %>
49:    HEIGHT=27
50:    CODEBASE="HTTP://<%= host %>/MSADC/Samples/Sheridan.cab"
51:    CLASSID="CLSID:3B7C8860-D78F-101B-B9B5-04021C009402">
52:    >
```

17

```
53:  </OBJECT>
54:
55:  <% END SUB %>
56:
57:
58:  <% SUB HiddenField( name ) %>
59:
60:  <OBJECT
61:      ID=<%= name %>
62:      WIDTH=0
63:      HEIGHT=0
64:      CODEBASE="HTTP://<%= host %>/MSADC/Samples/Sheridan.cab"
65:      CLASSID="CLSID:3B7C8860-D78F-101B-B9B5-04021C009402">
66:      >
67:  </OBJECT>
68:
69:  <% END SUB %>
```

17

ANALYSIS   It's best to get an understanding of the include file first. It contains a handful of sub-routines that can be used to generate the <OBJECT> tag sequence that adds the ActiveX controls to your Web page. These sub-routines are actually executed on the server as part of Active Server Pages in Internet Information Server. The sub-routines are DataControl(), DataGrid(), DataField(), and HiddenField().

Only the sub-routines DataControl() and DataField() are used in this example. The others are supplied for your convenience if you choose to take this include file and add it to your own project.

The DataControl() sub-routine builds the appropriate <OBJECT> tag to generate the Advanced Data Connector's AdvancedDataControl object. The sub-routine generates the <PARAM> tags only for the parameters that are fully specified. If you pass blank strings for any number of the sub-routine's actual parameters, they aren't converted into HTML <PARAM> tags.

If you don't assign the Connect parameter or the SQL parameter, the AdvancedDataControl doesn't automatically try to query for data when the page loads. This can be useful when you don't yet know what query or database you intend to access. All the object's <PARAM> tags can also be assigned through Visual Basic Script. The AdvancedDataControl has properties matching the <PARAM> names used by the <OBJECT> declaration syntax.

The other sub-routines generate data-bound controls. DataGrid() generates an entire scrollable display grid that shows all the fields and all the rows in the query. DataField() generates a data-bound edit field that shows only one field for one record at a time. HiddenField() works just like DataField(), except that it doesn't appear onscreen and the user can't access it. It stays hidden by setting the WIDTH and HEIGHT parameters to 0. Hidden fields are generally useful when you're performing automatically generated updates.

Listing 17.1 shows the actual code for this example. It primarily contains a section of field declarations for the data-bound record display, followed by a series of buttons used as VCR controls. After that comes the declaration of an ADC AdvancedDataControl and a bunch of scripting code that defines sub-routines to handle button clicks and navigation through the data.

The first four sub-routines are all explicit handlers for OnClick events, executed when the user clicks the corresponding button. The next sub-routine is a handler for an OnChange event that occurs when the user changes the value in the Find field. The OnClick event handlers are all set up to first check whether the user has specified a value in the fldFind input field. If there is a value, a special Find method is called to handle the special case. Otherwise, the normal ADC AdvancedDataControl method is called to move the current position.

The Find versions of the navigation methods—First, Last, Next, and Previous—all rely on a function called RecordContainsFind() that determines whether the current record in the Recordset parameter rs contains the value v in any of its fields. If it does, the function returns TRUE; if not, the function returns FALSE.

The Find navigation sub-routines use the RecordContainsFind() inside WHILE...WEND loops, as they search in their own manner for a matching record. When a match is found, the AdvancedDataControl is synchronized to the matching record by assigning the Recordset's Bookmark property to the AdvancedDataControl. When this happens, the onscreen data-bound controls automatically adjust to display the new record.

The only really peculiar sub-routine is FindAny(). Its job is to find a match no matter where one exists, but instead of simply starting with the first record list as FindFirst() does, it starts at the current position, heading down the list if it can't find a match. If all else fails, it starts over at the AdvancedDataControl's current position and continues its search, heading back toward the top. If no record can be found at all, it displays an Alert message warning the user that the displayed record doesn't actually match the criteria.

Taking a Look at the Web Page in Action

Figure 17.1 shows the Web page as it first appears when loaded. The first record in the query is shown in the data-bound Edit control.

Clicking the next-record button, denoted as > on the VCR-style button pad, moves the shared current record position to the next record in the set. Figure 17.2 shows the next record.

Clicking the last-record button, denoted as >> on the screen, moves the shared current record position to the last record in the set. Figure 17.3 shows the last record.

Filling in the Find value in the input field causes the Web application to filter out the records that don't have the Find value. Figure 17.4 shows a Find value being specified.

Figure 17.1.

Start your engines.

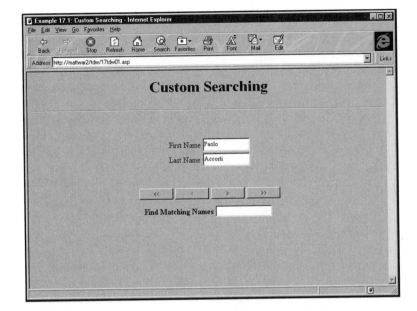

Figure 17.2.

The next record.

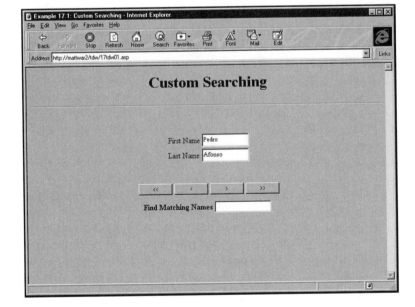

Figure 17.3.

The last record.

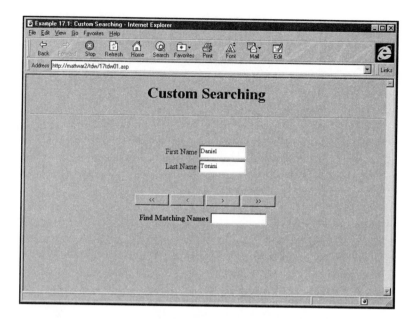

Figure 17.4.

Filtering the data.

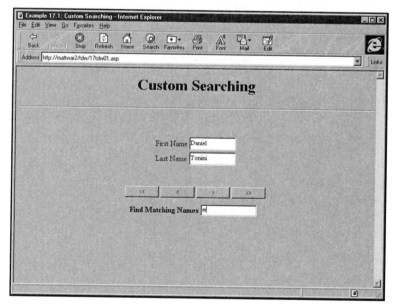

Pressing Tab or clicking outside the Find input field causes the Web application to automatically search for a nearby match. Figure 17.5 shows the page after it has found the first one.

Figure 17.5.

The first match.

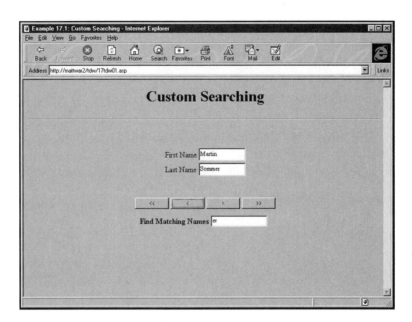

To prove that the records are truly being filtered, click the << button to move to the first record in the set. Notice that the record found isn't the first record that appeared when the page was loaded. Figure 17.6 shows the first record in the filtered data.

Figure 17.6.

The first in the filter.

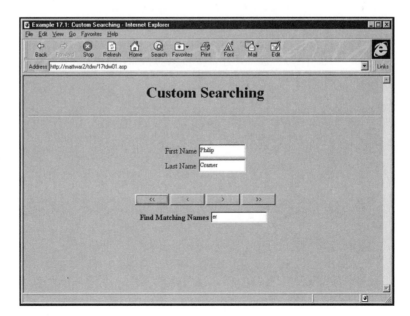

Summary

This chapter has shown you how to take advantage of the ADOR client-side Recordset object that comes with the Advanced Data Connector. The ADOR Recordset has functions and features that are a subset of the ADODB Recordset's, but it brings to the Advanced Data Connector the ability to access data through programming in client-side scripting code.

This chapter has also shown you how to use the ADOR Recordset with the ADC AdvancedDataControl and its other data-bound controls to go beyond simple automatic data binding. Working with the whole family of objects helps you create data-aware Web pages that are interactive and offer a richer user experience.

Q&A

Q Can I have more than one AdvancedDataControl on my Web page?

A Yes. You can have as many as you need to build the Web page you want.

Q Can I have an AdvancedDataControl that isn't bound to any fields but can still be used through the ADOR Recordset?

A Yes. You may find many compelling reasons to perform data access that doesn't involve direct user participation.

Q Can I load data into an AdvancedDataControl/Recordset after the page has been loaded and the user has clicked a button or two?

A Yes, just don't specify the <PARAM> tags within the AdvancedDataControl's <OBJECT> tag. You can later assign these values in scripting code. The ADC AdvancedDataControl uses all the familiar <PARAM> arguments and properties on the AdvancedDataControl itself.

Q Can I use bookmarks from one ADOR Recordset with a Recordset associated with a different AdvancedDataControl?

A No. You can share bookmarks only with objects that are technically "clones" of one another. The ADOR Recordset and its associated AdvancedDataControl are actually clones of each other. They share the same set of records but provide separate current record positions.

Q If I know that my client computers already have access to ADODB, can I use it instead of ADOR?

A Yes and no. The ADC AdvancedDataControl creates ADOR Recordsets when you instruct it to query for data from the ADC middle-tier data server.

    However, if you have an ADODB Recordset that's already opened, you can assign it to the Recordset property of an AdvancedDataControl, and the AdvancedDataControl will use it.

Unfortunately, in ADODB 1.0, you can't use the `Open()` method and query for data from the ADC middle-tier server.

Q **If I change a value using a data-bound control, and then immediately try to access the data with the ADOR `Recordset`, will I get the changed value back?**

A Yes, as long as you manually synchronize the bookmark of the ADOR `Recordset` to match the bookmark of the `AdvancedDataControl`.

Q **The ADOR `Recordset`'s `Field` object has no `Type` property. How can I determine the data type it's going to pass back through the `Value` property?**

A You can't. Visual Basic Script has no strong typing, so except for convenience, this property wasn't necessary. Limiting the interface to the bare minimum reduced the object's size considerably. In fact, the ADOR `Recordset` compresses to less than 15K and can be transferred from the server to the client about as quickly as any small Web-page graphic.

Quiz

1. From which property of the ADC `AdvancedDataControl` do you get the ADOR `Recordset`?

2. The ADOR `Recordset`, once you get it from the ADC `AdvancedDataControl`, is automatically synchronized with the current record position shared by the data-bound controls. True or False?

3. List the properties available on the ADOR `Recordset`'s `Field` object.

4. The ADOR `Recordset` has an `Open()` method that you might not ever need to use. What two arguments does it share with its bigger sibling, the ADODB `Recordset`?

5. When generated by the ADC `AdvancedDataControl`, what cursor type and lock type is the ADOR `Recordset` using?

6. List the five navigation methods that can be used to change the current record position controlled by the ADOR `Recordset`.

7. In addition to the five navigation methods, name one property that can be used to change the current record position.

8. Name the two properties that the ADOR `Recordset` shares with the ADODB `Recordset` in determining the boundaries of the data.

9. What property on the ADOR `Recordset` and the ADC `AdvancedDataControl` can be used to manually synchronize the two objects?

10. The ADOR `Recordset` can be used to both read and write field values shared with the ADC `AdvancedDataControl`. True or False?

17

Exercises

1. Write a sub-routine that uses the ADOR `Recordset` object to calculate the totals of all the order-detail prices in a query from the AdvWorks datasource.

2. Write a sub-routine that uses the ADOR `Recordset` to search for the next record with the same value in one of the columns of the current record.

3. Write a sub-routine that uses the ADOR `Recordset` to count the number of records.

4. Build a Web page that uses automatic data-binding through the ADC `AdvancedDataControl` and a set of VCR-style navigation buttons.

5. Expand Exercise 4 to include an auto-computed field that doesn't exist in the query. Use the ADOR `Recordset` and manual synchronization to auto-compute this field.

6. Find an ActiveX control that's not already data-bound that you would like to use in your own Web page. Use the ADOR `Recordset` to feed it information from the current record.

7. Build your own Web page that uses the trick of hidden data-bound fields to allow you to automatically generate updates to that field without the user intervening.

Day 18

Data Validation

by Matt Warren

This chapter is less about ADO and ADC than it is about using client scripting. The goal of any database-centered application, whether it exists over the Web or as a standalone product, is to maintain reliable information. Without data integrity, the results garnered from any study of the collected information will be faulty, rife with errors.

The best method for getting rid of errors in your data is to prevent them from entering the database in the first place. Your back-end database probably has mechanisms for specifying integrity rules and even for performing custom validation by routing requests through stored procedures. These are both good methods, so you should use them often. However, the first line of defense is always the best.

Catching the errors before they're sent to the database will minimize the work the server must do and reduce the frustration caused by slow-responding error messages.

After reading this chapter, you will be able to do the following:

- ☐ Explain why data validation is valuable.
- ☐ Explain why data validation on the client is even more valuable.
- ☐ State the differences between the three major types of data validation that can occur on the client.
- ☐ Show how auto-correction, auto-completion, and auto-anticipation can be advantageous for the user of your Web page.
- ☐ Show how to use the Advanced Data Connector interactively to help limit user input to only valid data.
- ☐ Define in simple terms the meaning of *domain* and *range* in a data-validation context.

Keeping Tabs on the Data

The interactive nature of client-side scripting gives you a way to automatically detect when the user is making a mistake. Each time an onscreen field value is changed, the focus is moved between controls, or the user takes an explicit action, you have an opportunity to look over the information and make certain it meets your standards.

Keeping tabs on the data in this manner is possible because of the event model built right into the browser. *Events* are messages sent from one place to another to indicate that something important has happened. They are triggers that automatically invoke a response from the scripting code. You can use events to bring your own custom responses to life. By attaching your own sub-routines to events, you can guarantee that your code takes action whenever the user moves the mouse, clicks a button, or types in a field.

You have already been using events, even though you might not know it. In the previous chapter and elsewhere in the book, sample code has used peculiarly named sub-routines to respond to button clicks, such as this one:

```
<INPUT TYPE=BUTTON NAME=MyButton>

<SCRIPT LANGUAGE="VBS">

SUB MyButton_OnClick()

    ' do something interesting here

END SUB

</SCRIPT>
```

The input field is named MyButton, and the corresponding sub-routine is named MyButton_OnClick. An *association* is made between an event and a button by combining the names of each into the name of your sub-routine. Because of this association, when the user clicks the button, the sub-routine is executed.

You can use this knowledge to your advantage. For example, the button might actually be the Submit button used in last week's reading, or a close facsimile. Through scripting code, you can control exactly what happens before a form is submitted; you can even keep it from being submitted at all.

With the Advanced Data Connector, you probably aren't writing a dynamic Web page that submits data back to the server using standard HTML form features. However, you might still want to send a batch of record changes back. You can do this by using the SubmitChanges() method of the ADC AdvancedDataControl. You can call this method directly inside the sub-routine that has the matching OnClick name.

To make this sub-routine work, define a button that's not actually a true HTML Submit button, but one that only appears to be, as shown here:

```
<INPUT TYPE=BUTTON NAME=Submit VALUE="SUBMIT">
```

Next, add a sub-routine that hooks into the OnClick() event method by using the name of the button control:

```
<SCRIPT LANGUAGE="VBS">

SUB Submit_OnClick()
  ' do something interesting here
  datactl.SubmitChanges
END SUB

</SCRIPT>
```

Inside the sub-routine, do any work that needs to be done before the data is submitted to the server, and then call the SubmitChanges() method on the AdvancedDataControl. When the button is clicked, your code is executed and the changes are submitted.

Of course, what you choose to do before you call the SubmitChanges() method is important. This is one of the places in the code where you should judge whether the data is safe to send back to the server. If it isn't, then perhaps SubmitChanges() shouldn't be called at all. Take a look at Listing 18.1 to see an example of making judgments about the safety of data.

Listing 18.1. Validating the total.

```
1: <SCRIPT LANGUAGE="VBS">
2:
3: SUB Submit_OnClick()
4:   SET rs = datactl.Recordset
```

continues

Listing 18.1. continued

```
 5:    totalCost = 0
 6:
 7:    '*** tally the total cost ****
 8:    rs.MoveFirst
 9:    WHILE not rs.EOF
10:      totalCost = totalCost + rs("item_cost")
11:      rs.MoveNext
12:    WEND
13:
14:    IF totalCost > 100 THEN
15:      MessageBox "Total Cost exceeds $100.00", "Cannot Submit"
16:    ELSE
17:      DataCtl.SubmitChanges
18:    END IF
19:
20: END SUB
21:
22:
23: </SCRIPT>
```

This short example shows how you can use the OnClick() event notification to validate that the total cost of all items being sent back to the server doesn't exceed 100 dollars. The total is calculated by using the ADOR Recordset you get from the ADC AdvancedDataControl with the standard WHILE...WEND looping syntax. Once you know the total, you can decide whether to send the changes.

User-Interface Events

Many types of validations can be performed on your data, and there are many places such checks can be made. Any time a user changes the value of a field, some fixed relationship between data fields could be disturbed. It's best to pick the appropriate event and quickly validate the change.

You can use the following list of browser events as a reference for data validation. Any of these events can be associated with your own VBScript code, which can have the built-in smarts to cross the *T*s and dot the *I*'s of every field in your Recordset.

Event Name	Description
OnLoad	Sent just after the Web page is loaded
OnUnload	Sent just before the Web page is unloaded
OnSubmit	Sent when the user presses a Submit button
OnClick	Sent when the user clicks a button
OnFocus	Sent when a control gets focus

Event Name	Description
OnBlur	Sent when a control loses focus
OnChange	Sent when the value of a control changes
OnSelect	Sent when an item is chosen from a list

The OnLoad Event

Use the OnLoad event to do any processing before the user has a chance to interact with the Web page. To specify which sub-routine is executed for this event, assign the value to the OnLoad property in the <BODY> tag of the HTML, as shown here:

```
<BODY LANGUAGE="VBS" OnLoad="OnLoad">

<!--- Some HTML stuff in here

<SCRIPT LANGUAGE="VBS">

SUB OnLoad()
  '*** Process something here
END SUB

</SCRIPT>

</BODY>
```

Actions

- ☐ Assign a SQL statement and force an AdvancedDataControl to issue a query against an ADC data server.

- ☐ Get an ADOR Recordset and do a first pass/check over the result of an ADC AdvancedDataControl query.

- ☐ Set up initial values in onscreen Edit controls that might not already be bound to a data control.

The OnUnload Event

Use the OnUnload event to do any processing just before the Web page is about to be switched for another. To specify which sub-routine is executed for this event, assign the value to the OnUnload property in the <BODY> tag of the HTML, as shown here:

```
<BODY LANGUAGE="VBS" OnUnload="OnUnload">

<!--- Some HTML stuff in here

<SCRIPT LANGUAGE="VBS">

SUB OnUnload()
  '*** Process something here
```

18

```
END SUB

</SCRIPT>

</BODY>
```

Actions

- ☐ Perform final validations.
- ☐ Submit final changes to the data server using `SubmitChanges()`.
- ☐ Start a new communication with the data server to log the length of time the user visited your Web page.

The `OnSubmit` Event

Use the `OnSubmit` event to do any processing just before an HTML form is gathered into an HTTP message to be sent back to the Web server. To specify which sub-routine is executed for this event, assign the value of the `OnSubmit` property in the `<FORM>` tag of an HTML input form, as follows:

```
<FORM LANGUAGE="VBS" OnSubmit="OnSubmit">

<!--- Some HTML input fields go here

</FORM>

<SCRIPT LANGUAGE="VBS">

SUB OnSubmit()
  '*** Process something here
END SUB

</SCRIPT>
```

Actions

- ☐ Calculate the values of "hidden" form fields.
- ☐ Validate forms' edit fields.
- ☐ Validate all records in an ADC `AdvancedDataControl`'s `Recordset`.

Data validation is not just for Web pages with fully interactive data access; it can be used quite competently with ordinary server-generated dynamic Web pages. However, the client browser must be capable of executing the type of scripting language you choose to program with.

18

The `OnClick` **Event**

Use the `OnClick` event to do any processing just after the user clicks on the associated button control. This event is probably one of the most useful events for data validation. Quite often, button controls are used to define new-page–specific events. For example, the previous chapter used button controls to generate Next and Previous messages that moved the current record position held by the ADC `AdvancedDataControl`. These button controls caused the displayed record to change to the next or previous record. Adding data validation to these events dramatically improves your chances of catching errors.

To specify which sub-routine is executed when the user clicks on a button control, either declare the sub-routine directly in the <INPUT> tag of the button declaration, or simply declare a sub-routine joining the names of the button and the event.

Here's the code you should declare in the <INPUT> tag:

```
<INPUT NAME=MyButton LANGUAGE="VBS" OnClick="SomebodyClickedMe">

<SCRIPT LANGUAGE="VBS">

SUB SomebodyClickedNe()
  '*** respond to click here
END SUB

</SCRIPT>
Associated by subroutine name:
<INPUT NAME=MyButton>

<SCRIPT LANGUAGE="VBS">

SUB MyButton_OnClick()
  '*** respond to click here
END SUB

</SCRIPT>
```

Actions

- ☐ Repopulate an ADC `AdvancedDataControl` with results from a new query.
- ☐ Move the current record position shared by all the data-bound Edit controls.
- ☐ Validate the state of the current record.
- ☐ Cache the "current" values of the current record so you can later implement an Undo feature.
- ☐ Check the integrity of the values in the current record, comparing the field values against known acceptable values.
- ☐ Submit all user changes to the database server.

The OnFocus Event

Use the OnFocus event to do any processing when the user's input cursor is first moved into the Edit control, but before the user has had a chance to modify the control's value.

To specify which sub-routine is executed when the focus is changed between Edit controls, declare the sub-routine directly in the <INPUT> tag of the control declaration, or simply declare a sub-routine joining the names of the control and the event.

This is the code declared in the <INPUT> tag:

```
<INPUT NAME=Field1 LANGUAGE="VBS" OnFocus="IHaveFocus">

<SCRIPT LANGUAGE="VBS">

SUB IHaveFocus()
   '*** do something here
END SUB

</SCRIPT>
Associated by subroutine name:
<INPUT NAME=Field1>

<SCRIPT LANGUAGE="VBS">

SUB Field1_OnFocus()
  '*** respond to focus change here
END SUB

</SCRIPT>
```

Actions

- ☐ Save the value of the Edit control so you can restore it if the user enters a wrong value.
- ☐ Auto-calculate the field value based on other known fields.
- ☐ Validate the field value before the user starts editing.

The OnBlur Event

Use the OnBlur event to do any processing of the field just after the user has expressed the intent to move the edit focus to another field, but before the move has actually taken place.

To specify which sub-routine is executed when the focus is lost on a particular Edit control, declare the sub-routine directly in the <INPUT> tag of the control declaration, or simply declare a sub-routine joining the names of the control and the event.

Here's the code you declare in the <INPUT> tag:

```
<INPUT NAME=Field1 LANGUAGE="VBS" OnBlur ="ILostFocus">

<SCRIPT LANGUAGE="VBS">
```

```
SUB ILostFocus()
  '*** do something here
END SUB

</SCRIPT>
Associated by subroutine name:
<INPUT NAME=Field1>

<SCRIPT LANGUAGE="VBS">

SUB Field1_OnBlur()
  '*** respond to focus change here
END SUB

</SCRIPT>
```

Actions

☐ Validate the field's value. If it matches an appropriate entry, force the focus to stay on this field by calling the Focus() method on the Edit control.

☐ Auto-calculate other fields based on the new value of this field.

The OnChange Event

Use the OnChange event to do any validation checks each time individual changes are made to the edit field's value. This event is sent when the focus is leaving the field, but only if the field value has been changed since the field got focus.

To specify which sub-routine is executed when the value is changed on a particular Edit control, declare the sub-routine directly in the <INPUT> tag of the control declaration, or simply declare a sub-routine joining the names of the control and the event.

This is the code you declare in the <INPUT> tag:

```
<INPUT NAME=Field1 LANGUAGE="VBS" OnChange ="IWasChanged">

<SCRIPT LANGUAGE="VBS">

SUB IWasChanged()
  '*** do something here
END SUB

</SCRIPT>
Associated by subroutine name:
<INPUT NAME=Field1>

<SCRIPT LANGUAGE="VBS">

SUB Field1_OnChange()
  '*** respond to value change here
END SUB

</SCRIPT>
```

Actions

☐ Validate the field's value.

☐ Auto-calculate other fields based on the new value of this field.

☐ Keep a series of data-bound controls in sync with the current value of the input field by using the `Recordset` object to search for matches, and synchronize the ADC `AdvancedDataControl` by using the `Bookmark` property.

The `OnSelect` Event

Use the `OnSelect` event to do any validation checks each time individual selections are made to an HTML `<SELECT>` field. To specify which sub-routine is executed when the selection is changed on a particular listbox control, declare the sub-routine directly in the `<SELECT>` tag of the control declaration, or simply declare a sub-routine joining the names of the control and the event.

Here's the code you declare in the `<SELECT>` tag:

```
<SELECT NAME=Field1 LANGUAGE="VBS" OnSelect="IWasSelected">
<OPTION>Apple
<OPTION>Banana
<OPTION>Cherry
<OPTION>Lemon-Lime
<OPTION>Orange
<OPTION>Watermelon
</SELECT>

<SCRIPT LANGUAGE="VBS">

SUB IWasSelected()
   '*** do something here
END SUB

</SCRIPT>
Associated by subroutine name:
<SELECT NAME=Field1>
<OPTION>Apple
<OPTION>Banana
<OPTION>Cherry
<OPTION>Lemon-Lime
<OPTION>Orange
<OPTION>Watermelon
</SELECT>
<INPUT NAME=Field1>

<SCRIPT LANGUAGE="VBS">

SUB Field1_OnSelect()
   '*** respond to selection change here
END SUB

</SCRIPT>
```

18

Actions

- ☐ Validate the field's value.
- ☐ Auto-calculate other fields based on the new value of this field.
- ☐ Keep a series of data-bound controls in sync with the current value of the selection field by using the Recordset object to search for matches, and synchronize the ADC AdvancedDataControl by using the Bookmark property.
- ☐ Use an AdvancedDataControl to query the database and generate more information based on the selection. Pipe this information into other data-bound controls.

Validating Fields

Before you get too deep into contemplating all the possible ways you could use user-interface events to hook in your own data validation code, you need some background knowledge of the types of validation that are possible. Not all data validations are alike.

Validating fields is entirely different from validating entire records or even an entire Recordset. Field values aren't as crucial to the database's integrity as relationships between values in records or across tables are. Still, you want a chance to verify that the value a user enters fits into a known constraint of your application's data model.

Simple Checks

Phone number fields should include an area code, prefix, and number in a recognizable, consistent format. Consistency might be especially important to another application running on the server that runs reports against the database and needs phone numbers to always look the same.

E-mail addresses are the same. They might be vital pieces of information you're trying to capture from the visitors to your site, so you want to make sure that what they enter at least looks like a valid e-mail address. It should have an e-mail account name followed by an @ symbol, followed by the network address of the e-mail computer. Here's a sample validation routine for e-mail addresses:

```
<SCRIPT LANGUAGE="VBS">

SUB Email_OnBlur()

  pos = InStr( 1, email.value, "@" )

  IF pos = 0 OR pos < 2 OR pos = Len( email.value ) THEN

    Alert "You must enter a valid email address"

    Email.Focus
```

```
END IF

END SUB

</SCRIPT>
```

It's easy to see in this small code fragment that the work it takes to actually make a field validation is rather nominal. When the user tries to "leave" an input field, the `OnBlur()` method is fired by the browser, causing the Visual Basic sub-routine `Email_OnBlur()` to execute. This sub-routine simply checks the current value of the field to see if it looks somewhat like an e-mail address. If it doesn't, it alerts the user to the mistake and refocuses the input caret back onto the same edit field.

Auto-Correction

However, that's not the only measure you can take. Sometimes it's easier to simply fix the entry yourself than to make the user go back and retype it. Many common typos can be anticipated, or items that aren't even typos but merely have many common forms of expression can be caught and automatically corrected.

Mistakes often occur in abbreviations for mailing addresses. Sometimes people use full words; other times they use abbreviations. Also, not all abbreviations are the same. When a large corporation has legions of data-entry operators all trained to do data input in exactly the same way, many of these problems are nonexistent. However, when data input is delegated to individual users, all sorts of non-uniform entries can happen.

The following code fragment catches and fixes common typos:

```
<SCRIPT LANGAUGE="VBS">

SUB Address_OnChange()

  x = instr( 1, LCase(Address.value), "street" )
  if x > 0 then
    Address.value = left( Address.value, x - 1 ) &_
      "St" & mid( Address.value, x + 6, 100 )
  end if

  x = instr( 1, LCase(Address.value), "avenue" )
  if x > 0 then
    Address.value = left( Address.value, x - 1 ) &_
      "Ave" & mid( Address.value, x + 6, 100 )
  end if

  x = instr( 1, LCase(Address.value), "boulevard" )
  if x > 0 then
    Address.value = left( Address.value, x - 1 ) &_
      "Blvd" & mid( Address.value, x + 9, 100 )
  end if

END SUB
</SCRIPT>
```

18

This code actually checks the current value of the input field, looking for words known to appear often in addresses. When they do occur, the code automatically re-edits the input field, changing the discovered words into their more database-friendly forms.

The words and their "friendly" forms have been chosen merely to point out an example of what could be done, not to insist that address fields be populated with abbreviations instead of full words.

Auto-Anticipation

The flip-side to auto-correction is auto-anticipation. Sometimes, given a previous user entry, you might be able to guess the values of one or more fields the user has yet to interact with. This could save the user time by not having to enter what's already obvious.

There are at least two types of interesting anticipation scenarios: One is anticipating another field in a single record; the second is anticipating a field or fields in a new record. For example, the user might have already entered many records in which several of the fields from the same column contain the same values. After the user enters data for the same column in a new record, you can check the current entry against previous ones and make a guess at the whole value. Word processors refer to this feature as *auto-completion*, and an example of it is given in Listing 18.2.

Listing 18.2. Auto-completion.

```
 1: <SCRIPT LANGUAGE="VBS">
 2:
 3: SUB Fld1_OnChange()
 4:
 5:    SET rs = DataCtl.Recordset
 6:    bmk = DataCtl.bookmark
 7:
 8:    WHILE NOT rs.EOF
 9:
10:      rsValue = rs(0)
11:
12:      '*** don't compare against yourself ****
13:      IF bmk <> rs.Bookmark THEN
14:
15:        '** if this matches then ask if we can change it
16:        IF Left( rsValue, Len(Fld1.value) ) = Fld1.value THEN
17:
18:          IF confirm("Did you mean to enter [" + rsValue + "]? ") THEN
19:            Fld1.Value = rsValue
20:            EXIT SUB
21:          END IF
22:
23:        END IF
24:
```

continues

Listing 18.2. continued

```
25:    END IF
26:
27:        rs.MoveNext
28:    WEND
29:
30: END SUB
31:
32: </SCRIPT>
```

This script fragment responds to a field change and automatically checks whether the value entered is an abbreviated form of another value in the same column of the same table. It uses the ADOR Recordset supplied by the AdvancedDataControl to loop through all the previous records, taking special care not to accidentally compare the field value with the equivalent field in the current record.

After determining which, if any, previous values partially match the entered value, the code brings up a confirmation dialog box, asking the user if the value was meant to be one of the previous values. You could always just automatically swap the values without prompting the user for permission, but that might cause valid entries to be disallowed instead of changing them to a previous value that just happens to contain more text.

The auto-anticipation example in Listing 18.3 is similar in that it either searches known values for previous edits or makes use of special cases hard-coded into the script.

Listing 18.3. Fixed auto-anticipation.

```
 1: <SCRIPT LANGUAGE="VBS">
 2:
 3: SUB FldProduct_OnSelect()
 4:
 5:    IF FldProduct.value = "Eggs" THEN
 6:      FldQty = 12
 7:    ELSEIF FldProduct.value = "Soda" THEN
 8:      FldQty = 6
 9:    END
10:
11: END SUB
12:
13: </SCRIPT>
```

In this grocery store example, a select field is used to pick a product name. Some of the products come in known quantities; eggs, for example, often come by the dozen, and most cans of soda are sold in six-packs. For those particular cases, the script has been augmented to auto-initialize the fldQty quantity field when either of those choices are made. The customer might want 24 eggs, not 12, or one can of soda instead of six, but those are the exceptions, not the rule. Most of the time people buy predictable quantities. Another auto-anticipation procedure is shown in Listing 18.4.

Listing 18.4. Historic auto-anticipation.

```
 1: <SCRIPT LANGAUGE="VBS">
 2:
 3: SUB FldPayee_OnChange()
 4:
 5:    SET rs = RecurringPaymentsCtl.Recordset
 6:    SET payee = rs("payee")
 7:
 8:    WHILE NOT rs.EOF
 9:
10:      IF LCase(payee) = LCase(FldPayee.value) THEN
11:
12:         FldCashType.value = rs("cashtype")
13:         FldCashAmount.value = rs("cashamt")
14:         FldComments.value = rs("comments")
15:
16:         EXIT SUB
17:
18:      END IF
19:
20:      rs.MoveNext
21:    WEND
22:
23: END SUB
24:
25: </SCRIPT>
```

This "historic" example models a data anticipation-validation that might occur in an online-checkbook application. The sub-routine assumes you have a Data control that has already been queried to contain a list of unique recurring payments. Whenever the payee for the new record matches a previously known payee, the rest of the input fields are auto-initialized with the same values that were entered before.

Validating Records

Beyond field validation lies the entirely separate world of record validation, which is much more complex. In fact, record validation includes most, if not all, of field validation's tasks. Many field validations can be held off until the record is considered "complete." This is often known when the user decides to take some explicit action, such as moving on to the next record or clicking a button that implies an operation over the entire record.

18

Record Validations

Record validations are often used to perform one or more of the following tasks:

- ☐ Guarantee that individual fields are validated.
- ☐ Guarantee that field values are consistent with each other, that subtotals add up to totals, and so forth.
- ☐ Guarantee the uniqueness of records, making sure the user doesn't accidentally enter the same information twice.

Field-Wise Validation

Field validity is most commonly checked at record-validation time. Many applications prefer not to interfere with the user until a form's entry is complete. When the user signals that the form is finished and he or she wants it submitted, then each field is checked, one by one, for validity.

This is exactly the kind of validation that occurs when processing responses from dynamic Web pages that have submitted forms back to the server. Your Web application has the chance to validate the fields before they're actually used to modify the database. You have no choice—the only opportunity you have to validate the fields are one record at a time or one form submission at a time. For example, look at Listing 18.5.

Listing 18.5. Restaurant employee.

```
 1: <SCRIPT LANGUAGE="VBS">
 2:
 3: FUNCTION ValidateName( f )
 4:
 5:    IF f.value > "" AND Instr(1,f.value," ") = 0 THEN
 6:        ValidateName = true
 7:    ELSE
 8:        Alert f.name + " must have a value"
 9:        f.focus
10:        ValidateName = false
11:    END IF
12:
13: END FUNCTION
14:
15: FUNCTION ValidatePosition( f )
16:
17:    IF f.value = "Cook" OR _
18:        f.value = "Waiter" OR _
19:        f.value = "Host" OR _
20:        f.value = "Busboy" OR _THEN
21:        ValidatePosition = true
22:    ELSE
```

18

```
23:       Alert f.value & " is not a valid position"
24:       f.focus
25:       ValidatePosition = false
26:     END IF
27:
28: END FUNCTION
29:
30: FUNCTION ValidateSalary( f )
31:
32:     IF f.value < 15000 OR f.value > 28000 THEN
33:        Alert "The salary in not within the valid range"
34:        f.focus
35:        ValidateSalary = true
36:     ELSE
37:        ValidateSalary = true
38:     END IF
39:
40: END FUNCTION
41:
42:
43: SUB AddButton_OnClick()
44:
45:     IF NOT ValidateName(fldFName) THEN EXIT SUB
46:     IF NOT ValidateName(fldLName) THEN EXIT SUB
47:     IF NOT ValidatePosition( fldPosition ) THEN EXIT SUB
48:     IF NOT ValidateSalary( fldSalary ) THEN EXIT SUB
49:
50:     AddNewEmployee
51:
52: END SUB
53:
54: </SCRIPT>
```

This code has four separate routines: three validation functions and one button-click sub-routine. The three validation functions take a field Edit control as an input parameter. Instead of writing special event-handling code for each input field, the rules have been generalized so they can apply to multiple fields.

The final sub-routine at line 43, however, is fixed to the Add button. When the Add button is clicked, all the edit fields are validated before the AddNewEmployee() sub-routine is called. If one of the validate functions returns a Boolean type FALSE, the sub-routine is aborted. It's assumed that the functions themselves take care of warning the user, which is exactly what happens in each of the validation functions. If the specific validation fails, an alert message is displayed to the user, and the focus is reset to the field in question.

Record Consistency

Consistency checking means making sure the individual fields of a record agree with each other, not just with some special formatting rules. Usually, you have some self-understood relationship between the columns of your database tables. For example, an individual record can contain a set of weighted columns, each containing a percentage, with the total number always adding up to 100 percent.

Another example, shown in Listing 18.6, is a record that represents a line item of an order form. The quantity, the unit cost, and the discount must all combine to come up with the entered total item cost.

Listing 18.6. Tea totalling.

```
 1: <SCRIPT LANGAUGE="VBS">
 2:
 3: SUB UpdateTeaOrderBtn_OnClick()
 4:
 5:    SET rs = orderCtl.Recordset
 6:    rs.bookmark = orderctl.bookmark
 7:
 8:    IF rs("discount") > rs("qty") * rs("cost") THEN
 9:       Alert("Discount cannot be greater than cost")
10:       fldDiscount.focus
11:       EXIT SUB
12:    END IF
13:
14:    IF rs("discount") > rs("qty") * rs("price") * 0.20 THEN
15:       Alert("Discount cannot be greater than 20% of price")
16:       fldDiscount.focus
17:       EXIT SUB
18:    END IF
19:
20:    IF rs("qty") * rs("price") - rs("discount") <> rs("total") THEN
21:      IF Confirm("Total does not match.  Auto-calculate?") THEN
22:        rs("total") = rs("qty") * rs("price") - rs("discount")
23:      ELSE
24:         fldTotal.focus
25:         EXIT SUB
26:      END IF
27:    END IF
28:
29:    DoActualOrderUpdate
30:
31: END SUB
32:
33: </SCRIPT>
```

The Tea Totalling example demonstrates how you can validate the relationships between record fields when the record is expected to be in a consistent state. In this example, that validation time is when the user has asked that the edit be added back to the database.

If you're the using the Advanced Data Connector to interact with data, you would probably implement the DoActualOrderUpdate() sub-routine to do nothing, except clear the fields and call the AddNew() method of the AdvancedDataControl in preparation for yet another record.

18

That's because the ADC is actually isolated from the database and can accept multiple record changes in a batch operation, submitting them all at once. This batch submission saves you processing time when the changes must be transmitted across the Internet.

If you are using standard HTML forms, you would probably implement DoActualOrderUpdate() to actually call the Submit() method of the input form. This choice forces the browser to perform the equivalent operation that would normally have happened if the user clicked on a true HTML Submit button, as shown here:

```
<SCRIPT LANGUAGE="VBS">

SUB DoActualOrderUpdate()
  document.orderForm.submit
END SUB

</SCRIPT>
```

Record Uniqueness

Checking record uniqueness is a method of guaranteeing that the user hasn't accidentally entered the same information twice. This mistake is normally caught by the database when the actual records are submitted back to the server, but it's better to catch it before you have wasted the time of transmitting the data. The user would rather know right away than wait until the server processes the submission and generates the response page. Take a look at the example in Listing 18.7.

18

Listing 18.7. Tweedle Dee.

```
 1: <SCRIPT LANGUAGE="VBS">
 2:
 3: SUB UpdateRecordBtn_OnClick()
 4:
 5:    SET rs = datactl.Recordset
 6:    bmk = datactl.Bookmark
 7:
 8:    rs.Bookmark = bmk
 9:    f0 = rs(0)
10:    f1 = rs(1)
11:    f2 = rs(2)
12:
13:    rs.MoveFirst
14:    WHILE NOT rs.EOF
15:
16:      IF bmk <> rs.Bookmark THEN
17:
18:        IF r0 = rs(0) AND  _
19:            f1 = rs(1) AND _
20:            f2 = rs(2) THEN
21:
```

continues

Listing 18.7. continued

```
22:            IF NOT Confirm( _
23:                "This record matches a previous record." &_
24:                " Do you wish to update it anyway?" ) THEN
25:                EXIT SUB
26:            END IF

27:        END IF
28:
29:        rs.MoveNext
30:    WEND
31:
32:    DoActualUpdate
33:
34: END SUB
35:
36: </SCRIPT>
```

This example is quite straightforward. A Recordset is requested from an active AdvancedDataControl, and the current record position is remembered by getting a bookmark to it. The important key-field values are stored in variables, and then the entire Recordset is looped over, checking the key fields against the stored "current" values.

If another record with matching key fields is discovered, the user is prompted with a message to confirm the update. If the update isn't confirmed, the button's OnClick() method is aborted, and the user is back to editing the same record.

Validating the Submission

In most data-access scenarios, validating the entire record is equivalent to validating the submission, but this isn't true in the case of the Advanced Data Connector. Since the ADC batches multiple updates, at submission time many records can be pending transfer back to the database server.

This is a complication, but it's also an opportunity. Simple HTML entry forms enhanced with client-side scripting don't have the capability to validate multiple records at once, unless somehow the form is large enough to encompass a fixed number of records. Normally, an input form equates to a single record.

Some applications might be able to make use of this opportunity. You could validate that totals and subtotals across multiple records actually add up to what you expect. For an example, look at Listing 18.8.

Listing 18.8. Reimbursements.

```
 1: <SCRIPT LANGUAGE="VBS">
 2:
 3: SUB SubmitAllBtn_OnClick()
 4:
 5:    SET rs = datactl.Recordset
 6:
 7:    totalCost = 0
 8:
 9:    rs.MoveFirst
10:    WHILE NOT rs.EOF
11:
12:       totalCost = totalCost + rs("cost")
13:
14:       rs.MoveNext
15:    WEND
16:
17:    IF totalCost > 1000 THEN
18:       Alert "You cannot submit more than $1000.00 worth of " &_
19:             "reimbursements using this form."
20:       EXIT SUB
21:    END IF
22:
23:    datactl.SubmitChanges
24:
25: END SUB
26:
27: </SCRIPT>
```

The reimbursement example tallies the Cost field of the Recordset and then eventually checks it against the maximum allowable reimbursement from petty cash. If the submission actually contains records with total costs higher than the known maximum, a message is displayed alerting the user to the error, and the operation is aborted. The user is left to decide whether to alter the records in the submission and try again or to find another way to get reimbursed.

Domains and Ranges

If you have a lot of experience building database applications, you have probably already heard the terms *domain* and *range* used in the context of data storage. If you're an authority on advanced data-modeling techniques or you're just responsible for what some companies might call their "data dictionary," you probably know more about these terms than this book could even attempt to describe.

Fortunately, it's not important that you have a thorough understanding—a basic one is enough. *Domains* are like data types, though often more explicit than storage types used by the database server. *Ranges* are unique sets of values within a domain that a table's column is limited to. A column's domain might be the domain of "all colors," and the range could be specifically red, blue, or green. The domain might be the domain of phone numbers, with the range being a particular list.

You have probably noticed the parallel between a domain and a column and a range and table. These parallels aren't always accurate, but they're close enough for what you need to understand for this book. For example, you might have a table with multiple color columns: shirt color, pants color, sock color, and shoe color. They are all columns having the domain "color," but there are different columns that most likely have uniquely different ranges of possible values.

Advanced database servers have ways to constrain column values to fit within domains and to limit ranges within domains. The server can be set up so that constrained columns are limited to values only within their dictated ranges. However, as the argument went earlier in this chapter, it's better for the user's sake to validate the fields before the records are transmitted to the server. It saves time and aggravation.

One way to validate the fields beforehand is to require the user to pick from a selection list—probably the best way to constrain input using standard user-interface features. You can build selection lists on the server by using Active Server Pages. However, if multiple input fields require the same large selection list, the generated page can get huge very fast. It would be better to reuse the Advanced Data Connector technology to pull down the list just one time and reuse it for multiple selection lists.

Fortunately, this is exactly what you can do using the ADC and a data-bound Selection control. Listing 18.9 shows an example of using data-bound Selection controls along with a pair of `AdvancedDataControls` to restrict user entry to only valid ranges.

Listing 18.9. Constraining user entries to valid ranges.

```
 1:
 2: <HTML>
 3:
 4: <HEAD>
 5: <TITLE> Example 18.1: Constrained Input </TITLE>
 6: <CENTER>
 7: <H1>Constrained Input</H1>
 8: </CENTER>
 9: <HR>
10: </HEAD>
11:
12:
13: <BODY LANGUAGE="VBS" OnLoad="OnLoad">
14:
15: <% host = Request.ServerVariables("SERVER_NAME") %>
16:
17:
18: <CENTER>
19: <TABLE BORDER=0>
20:
```

```
21: <!-- Product Type Selection -->
22:
23: <TR>
24: <TD><B>Choose Product Type </B></TD>
25:
26: <TD>
27: <OBJECT
28:     ID=prodtypelist
29:     WIDTH=200
30:     HEIGHT=30
31:     CLASSID="CLSID:BC496AE5-9B4E-11CE-A6D5-0000C0BE9395"
32:     CODEBASE="HTTP://<%= host %>/MSADC/Samples/Sheridan.cab">
33: <PARAM NAME="DataFieldList" VALUE="ProductType">
34: </OBJECT>
35: </TD>
36: </TR>
37:
38: <TR>
39: <TD><B>Choose Product Name </B></TD>
40:
41: <TD>
42: <OBJECT
43:     ID=prodnamelist
44:     WIDTH=200
45:     HEIGHT=30
46:     CLASSID="CLSID:BC496AE5-9B4E-11CE-A6D5-0000C0BE9395"
47:     CODEBASE="HTTP://<%= host %>/MSADC/Samples/Sheridan.cab">
48: <PARAM NAME="DataFieldList" VALUE="ProductName">
49: </OBJECT>
50: </TD>
51: </TR>
52:
53: </TABLE>
54: </CENTER>
55:
56: <!-- ProductType Data Control -->
57: <OBJECT
58:     ID=prodtype
59:     WIDTH=1 HEIGHT=1
60:     CLASSID="clsid:9381D8F2-0288-11d0-9501-00aa00b911a5"
61:     CODEBASE="http://<%= host %>/MSADC/msadc10.cab" >
62:     <PARAM
63:       NAME="Server"
64:       VALUE="http://<%= host %>" >
65:     <PARAM
66:       NAME="Bindings"
67:       VALUE="prodtypelist;">
68:     <PARAM
69:       NAME="Connect"
70:       VALUE="DSN=AdvWorks;">
71:     <PARAM
72:       NAME="SQL"
73:       VALUE="Select ProductType From Products GROUP BY ProductType">
74: </OBJECT>
75:
76: <!-- Product Data Control -->
77: <OBJECT
```

18

continues

Listing 18.9. continued

```
78:     ID=product
79:     WIDTH=1 HEIGHT=1
80:     CLASSID="clsid:9381D8F2-0288-11d0-9501-00aa00b911a5"
81:     CODEBASE="http://<%= host %>/MSADC/msadc10.cab" >
82:     <PARAM
83:       NAME="Server"
84:       VALUE="http://<%= host %>" >
85:     <PARAM
86:       NAME="Bindings"
87:       VALUE="prodnamelist;">
88:     <PARAM
89:       NAME="Connect"
90:       VALUE="DSN=AdvWorks;">
91: </OBJECT>
92:
93:
94:
95: <SCRIPT LANGUAGE="VBS">
96:
97:
98: '** CloseUp is an event sent by the drop-down table
99: SUB ProdTypeList_CloseUp()
100:
101:   IF prodtypelist.text > "" THEN
102:
103:     '*** re-query for product names of the appropriate type
104:
105:     query = "SELECT ProductName FROM Products "
106:     query = query & "WHERE ProductType = '" & prodtypelist.text & "'"
107:
108:     product.SQL = query
109:     product.Refresh
110:   END IF
111:
112: END SUB
113:
114:
115: SUB OnLoad()
116:     '** force first list into existence
117:     ProdTypeList.MoveFirst
118:     ProdTypeList_CloseUp
119: END SUB
120:
121: </SCRIPT>
122:
123:
124: </BODY>
125: </HTML>
```

18

The example consists primarily of four ActiveX controls and two event-based VBScript sub-routines. Two of the controls are data-bound selection lists, and the other two are their respective AdvancedDataControls feeding them the actual data.

One sub-routine responds to the selection made in the first selection list; the other sub-routine is an OnLoad event bootstrapping mechanism. Whenever a new value is chosen in the first selection list, the event sub-routine is executed. What it actually does is form a new query for the second selection list's AdvancedDataControl. The new query is based on the selected value in the first control.

Using VBScript as a little scripting glue between the two controls, they are now both kept in sync with one another. The first control contains the product type, and each type is limited to several specific products in the database's Products table. Using these two controls together, you can systematically narrow your choice down to an actual product name without having to wade through the set of all possible products.

The second sub-routine is executed automatically when the page is loaded because a reference to OnLoad in the <BODY> tag instructs the OnLoad event to execute the VBScript sub-routine of the same name.

Full Data-Validation Example

Listing 18.10 is an example of a Web page using data validation. It's a more elaborate form of the auto-correction example from earlier in the chapter combined with field-wise record validation.

Listing 18.10. Data validation (18TWD10.ASP).

```
 1: <HTML>
 2:
 3: <HEAD>
 4: <TITLE> Example 18.10: Data Validation </TITLE>
 5: <CENTER>
 6: <H1>Data Validation</H1>
 7: </CENTER>
 8: <HR>
 9: </HEAD>
10:
11:
12: <BODY>
13: <BR>
14: <BR>
15: <BR>
16:
17:
18: <CENTER>
19: <TABLE BORDER=0>
20:
```

continues

Listing 18.10. continued

```
21: <TR>
22: <TD><B>Name</B></TD>
23: <TD><INPUT NAME=fldName WIDTH=80></TD>
24: </TR>
25:
26: <TR>
27: <TD><B>Address</B></TD>
28: <TD><INPUT NAME=fldAddr1 WIDTH=80></TD>
29: </TR>
30:
31: <TR>
32: <TD></TD>
33: <TD><INPUT NAME=fldAddr2 WIDTH=80></TD>
34: </TR>
35:
36: <TR>
37: <TD><B>City</B></TD>
38: <TD><INPUT NAME=fldCity WIDTH=20></TD>
39: </TR>
40:
41: <TR>
42: <TD><B>State</B></TD>
43: <TD><INPUT NAME=fldState WIDTH=4></TD>
44: </TR>
45:
46: <TR>
47: <TD><B>Zip Code</B></TD>
48: <TD><INPUT NAME=fldZip WIDTH=20></TD>
49: </TR>
50:
51: </TABLE>
52:
53: <BR>
54: <BR>
55: <BR>
56:
57: <INPUT TYPE=BUTTON NAME=Submit VALUE="SUBMIT">
58:
59: </CENTER>
60:
61:
62:
63: <SCRIPT LANGUAGE="VBS">
64:
65: SUB FldName_OnBlur()
66:
67:    FixName fldName
68:
69: END SUB
70:
71:
72: SUB FldAddr1_OnBlur()
73:
74:    FixAddress fldAddr1
75:
```

```
 76: END SUB
 77:
 78:
 79: SUB FldAddr2_OnBlur()
 80:
 81:    FixAddress fldAddr2
 82:
 83: END SUB
 84:
 85:
 86:
 87: SUB Submit_OnClick()
 88:
 89:    IF NOT Validate( fldName ) THEN EXIT SUB
 90:
 91:    IF NOT Validate( fldAddr1 ) THEN EXIT SUB
 92:
 93:    IF NOT Validate( fldCity ) THEN EXIT SUB
 94:
 95:    IF NOT Validate( fldState ) THEN EXIT SUB
 96:
 97:    IF NOT Validate( fldZip ) THEN EXIT SUB
 98:
 99:    Alert "The data has been submitted"
100:
101: END SUB
102:
103:
104:
105: SUB FixAddress( fld )
106:
107:    Replace fld, "Avenue", "Ave"
108:    Replace fld, "Boulevard", "Blvd"
109:    Replace fld, "Street", "St"
110:    Replace fld, "Court", "Ct"
111:    Replace fld, "Lane", "Ln"
112:    Replace fld, "Route", "Rt"
113:
114:    Replace fld, "North", "N"
115:    Replace fld, "South", "S"
116:    Replace fld, "East", "E"
117:    Replace fld, "West", "W"
118:    Replace fld, "NorthWest", "N W"
119:    Replace fld, "NorthEast", "N E"
120:    Replace fld, "SouthWest", "S W"
121:    Replace fld, "SouthEast", "S E"
122:
123:    Replace fld, "First", "1st"
124:    Replace fld, "Second", "2nd"
125:    Replace fld, "Third", "3rd"
126:    Replace fld, "Fifth", "5th"
127:    Replace fld, "Sixth", "6th"
128:    Replace fld, "Seventh", "7th"
129:    Replace fld, "Eighth", "8th"
130:    Replace fld, "Ninth", "9th"
131:
```

18

continues

Listing 18.10. continued

```
132: END SUB
133:
134: SUB FixName( fld )
135:
136:    Replace fld, "Doctor", "Dr."
137:
138: END SUB
139:
140:
141:
142: SUB Replace( fld, oldVal, newVal )
143:
144:    fldVal = fld.value
145:
146:    lcFld = LCase(fldVal)
147:    lcValue = LCase( oldVal )
148:
149:    cVal = Len(lcValue)
150:
151:    x = InStr( 1, lcFld, lcValue )
152:
153:    WHILE x > 0
154:
155:      before = mid( lcFld, x - 1, 1 )
156:      after = mid( lcFld, x + cVal, 1 )
157:
158:      IF (before = "" OR Before = " " ) AND (after = "" OR after = " " ) THEN
159:
160:        fldVal = left( fldVal, x - 1 ) & newVal & mid( fldVal, x + cVal,
  ➥ Len(fldVal))
161:
162:        lcFld = LCase(fldVal)
163:
164:      END IF
165:
166:      x = InStr( x + 1, lcFld, lcValue )
167:
168:    WEND
169:
170:
171:    IF fldVal <> fld.value THEN
172:
173:      fld.value = fldVal
174:
175:    END IF
176:
177: END SUB
178:
179:
180: FUNCTION Validate( fld )
181:
182:    Validate = true
```

```
183:
184:    IF Fld.value = "" THEN
185:
186:      Alert "A Required field is empty."
187:
188:      fld.focus
189:
190:      Validate = false
191:
192:    END IF
193:
194: END FUNCTION
195:
196:
197: </SCRIPT>
198:
199:
200:
201: </BODY>
202:
203: </HTML>
```

ANALYSIS This example focuses entirely on the data-validation aspect of a Web page. The code to actually submit records to a database server has been left out to simplify the context.

The example is primarily a series of input fields, organized into a nice display with the help of an HTML table, and a bunch of client-side scripting code.

Both the name field and the two address fields are subject to validation when you're finished editing the field. This is done by trapping the OnBlur event that's sent whenever the corresponding edit field loses focus, caused by tabbing out of the field or clicking onto someplace else. Each time this happens, the matching OnBlur() sub-routine takes over.

The name field's OnBlur() sub-routine calls the FixName() sub-routine, and the other two field's OnBlur() sub-routines call the FixAddress() sub-routine. Both FixName() and FixAddress() use the Replace() sub-routine, which in turn does a search-and-replace operation on the passed-in field's value. The FixAddress() sub-routine requests that all the familiar long-form names be exchanged for their more condensed forms. The FixName() sub-routine does the same, except its list is limited to transforming the word *doctor* into the abbreviation *Dr.*.

The other half of the validation occurs when the user clicks the Submit button. This is a cue to the Web page to validate the record before it's actually submitted. In this case, all the required fields are checked by calling the plain-vanilla Validate() sub-routine.

18

Summary

This chapter has given you the means to perform data validation interactively on the client by using Visual Basic Script. You have learned the difference between normal field-level validations and record-level validations and seen how to attach your own sub-routines to user-interface events. It has also offered an in-depth discussion on many facets of each type of validation, including a special submission-level validation that's possible when using the Advanced Data Connector.

Q&A

Q What happens if I don't validate the data on the client?

A One of two things. Either the database server automatically validates records when it receives them, or they just do not get validated.

In the former case, only script database constraints can be automatically validated by the server. If the validations fail, then the data submission fails. The only result is that you have to force the user to re-enter the data anyway, and the time-lag could be frustrating.

In the latter case, the database simply fills up with improper data.

Q How can I guarantee that all clients can execute my client script?

A You can't. This section of the book assumes that you have made a decision to accept potential incompatibility with the full range of possible browsers to gain more advanced capabilities. Instead of taking a least-common-denominator approach, you have chosen to confine your application distribution to a well-understood market.

Q Can I auto-correct users' input as they type in data, not waiting for them to hit Enter or Tab?

A Not using standard HTML input fields or standard browser notifications. The Win32 platform has a much richer event model, but it's not evident when using the browser as a platform.

It could, however, easily be done given ActiveX Edit controls that use a richer event model.

Q Is it possible to make the input fields allow only formatted input, like specifying the data format mm/dd/yyyy where the cursor is allowed to move only over the m, d, and y?

A Again, not using the standard HTML input fields. A richer set of ActiveX controls would be the obvious solution. The best you can get with plain input fields is to validate the text after it's been entered.

18

Q You have code that auto-anticipates other fields based on ones you just entered. Would it be possible to auto-anticipate fields or entire records that are in another table?

A Certainly. The auto-anticipate method is not bound to any particular technology. You can do whatever you think necessary as long as it can be done in the scripting language you're using.

Q Can you give me an example of what you might do in the OnFocus event? I can see how using the OnBlur and the OnChange events is interesting because they happen just after the field value is changed, but OnFocus doesn't seem useful.

A The OnFocus event can be just as useful as the other two. The examples in the chapter are biased toward using OnChange and OnBlur, but that doesn't need to be the case.

Q I want to write a validation routine that uses the same Recordset based on the same data, but in two different ways at the same time. ADODB had a clone method that would build a separate Recordset that could be at a different position, but it was really using the same data. Can I do the same thing with ADC? It doesn't seem possible.

A Yes, in fact you can. You need to create a second ADOR Recordset object separately by using the <OBJECT> syntax. Then, in scripting code, use the Open() method, passing in the original ADOR Recordset as the source parameter. This does the same thing as the ADODB Recordset's clone method. In fact, you can actually do this with the ADODB Recordset as well, as shown here:

```
<SCRIPT LANGUAGE="VBS">
   adorRS2.Open adorRS1
</SCRIPT>
```

Quiz

1. Describe the difference between auto-completion and auto-anticipation.
2. Record validation is a superset of field validation. True or False?
3. Field validations may occur each time a field value is changed. True or False?
4. Record validations may occur each time the cursor is moved between fields. True or False?
5. List at least two different types of record validation that can't be considered outgrowths of field validation.
6. What two events are sent each time the focus is changed between edit fields? In what order are they sent?
7. List at least one event that's sent only if the data value is changed in an edit field.

8. Show two different ways to bind your own script code to a field and a user-interface event.

9. Name at least one type of data validation scenario where it would be useful to calculate totals.

10. Describe at least one type of action you might take when attaching script code to the OnSubmit event.

Exercises

1. Write a validation sub-routine that capitalizes all names in a name field.

2. Write a validation sub-routine that makes certain a name field has at least a first and last name.

3. Write a validation sub-routine that forces names fields to appear in the order "last name, first name, middle initial."

4. Write a validation sub-routine that combines Exercises 1 and 3.

5. Take any full example from Chapters 10 to 13 and add validation support.

6. On paper, take a data model from a small project you're working on or have worked on and list the column domain and value ranges you can recall.

7. Write a dynamic Web page that uses both client- and server-side validation support within VBScript.

Day **19**

Client-Server Business Objects

by Joyce Chia-Hsun Chen

In the last few days, you have learned about the Advanced Data Connector components in the client tier. You have learned about the `AdvancedDataControl` object, the client-tier architecture, and the ADOR `Recordset` and how to program them in a client-tier Web page. So far, the lessons have concentrated on client-tier programming and its components. Using the `AdvancedDataControl` object and ADOR `Recordset` in the client tier, you have put most of the programming and business logic in the client tier, with the application server reading and writing data to the database server. With most programming logic in the client tier, the `AdvancedDataControl` framework uses a default business object in the application server to perform reads and writes to the database server. The result is that you rely heavily on the client tier to process the data properly and to contain all the programming and business logic.

The overview of the Advanced Data Connector in Chapter 15, "The Advanced Data Connector (ADC)," mentions that one of the ADC's approaches to Web programming is to partition the business logic between the client tier and application server. With Advanced Data Connector, you can invoke remote business objects over HTTP so you can develop a Web application that effectively partitions application logic between the VBScript on the client tier and the application Server object. The application Server object contains all the business logic and data manipulation and protects it from unwanted distribution. In general, you call the application Server objects *business objects* because you want them to have business rules to follow. Today, you're going to focus on business objects; you'll see how to create them in both Visual Basic 4.0 and 5.0. After reading this chapter, you will be able to do the following:

- Describe the middle-tier (application server) architecture
- Describe business objects
- Describe the AdvancedDataSpace and AdvancedDataFactory objects
- Use Visual Basic 4.0 to create business objects
- Use Visual Basic 5.0 to create business objects
- Construct Web pages to access custom business objects

You have learned that Advanced Data Connector normally works in a logical three-tier fashion. The client tier uses the client-side cache to allow AdvancedDataControl to interact with live data, and the application server handles communication with the database server and creates instances of business objects. You also find the Virtual Table Manager and ADO Recordset in the application server to handle the OLE DB rowset.

To use a business object in the application server, a *business object proxy* is needed in the client tier for marshaling and unpacking the invoked methods, properties, and parameter values of the business object in the application server. But what is a business object exactly, and why use one?

NOTE
To run the examples in this chapter, please make sure you refer to the setup instructions included in "Week 3 at a Glance."

Why Use Business Objects?

The idea of business objects is based on partitioning application and business logic. *Business logic* means business rules that are defined for a certain need; for example, a business rule can be "if the video is released within the week, the rental price is $3.99; otherwise, it's $2.99." Normally, you want to hide the business rule from the client tier and be able to change it frequently to suit your needs. Ideally, you would like to put the business rule in the application server so that the client tier doesn't know the business rules. This placement of business rules is precisely one of the ADC's goals. The Advanced Data Connector architecture allows you to separate the application and business rules and data between the client tier and the application server. The business rules and data stay in the application server, and the client tier contains only the necessary application logic.

With business rules, and data access to the database server in the business objects, you can effectively protect your business rules and data from redistribution. Business objects need to exist only on the application server, so the client tier doesn't know the business logic within the business objects. You can customize your own business objects, easily changing them to adjust to your needs, because the business object exists only in the application server.

What Are Business Objects?

Business objects can be any OLE Automation objects created by Visual Basic, Visual C++, C++, or Java. The name *business object* was chosen because the goal is to separate the business rules and put them into objects. Business objects can be as simple as objects used just to handle data reads and writes or they could contain much more complex business rules. For example, Advanced Data Connector supplies a default business object called `AdvancedDataFactory` that simply does data reads and writes. This default business object is invoked implicitly if no business object is specified. Business objects can be invoked as in-process servers or called through HTTP or DCOM/RPC (Distributed Common Object Model/Remote Procedure Call).

The actual communication with business objects in the Advanced Data Connector architecture is done through business object proxies and ADISAPI. The ADISAPI component is an Internet Information Server 3.0 ISAPI extension library. Business object proxies in the client tier are in charge of marshaling the invoking method, parameter, and data to the ADISAPI in the application server. Business objects are instantiated by ADISAPI for each method call and destroyed after the method call is finished. This communication module in the Advanced Data Connector architecture allows the client tier to access remote business objects on the application server. Because you're allowing the client tier to access remote objects, you need to mark any custom business object as safe for scripting to ensure a safe Internet environment; you'll learn how to do that later in the section "Business Objects." First, take a look at the example in Listing 19.1 of a business object created in Visual Basic.

19

Listing 19.1. Creating a business object in Visual Basic.

```
1: Public Function GetAllVideos()
2: Dim myADF As Object
3: Dim rs As ADOR.Recordset
4: Dim SQLString
5:     Set myADF = CreateObject("AdvancedDataFactory")
6:     SQLString = "select VideoTitle,Rating,Category, ReleaseDate,
➥ReservedFlag, Description from video_Detail order by VideoTitle"
```

continues

Listing 19.1. continued

```
7:      Set rs = myADF.Query("dsn=video;uid=sa", SQLString)
8:      Set GetAllVideos = rs
9: End Function
```

The business object in Listing 19.1 has one function, `GetAllVideos()`. This function returns the ADOR `Recordset`, generated by the `Select * from video_Detail` SQL statement, to the calling function. Later in this chapter, you will use this example again to see how to create it in both Visual Basic 4.0 and 5.0 and how to access business objects from a Web page.

Middle-Tier (Application Server) Architecture

Now that you understand what business objects are and why you should use them, you can see how business objects fit into the application server and the Advanced Data Connector architecture. You're also ready to learn how the client tier invokes remote business objects through HTTP and how the data gets marshaled back and forth.

The client tier chooses whether to invoke a custom business object. If no custom business object is specified, the default business object, `AdvancedDataFactory`, is used. The way to invoke the business object in the client tier is through the `AdvancedDataSpace` object, which is responsible for creating a business object proxy. Once a business object proxy is created, the client tier can invoke the business object's method. The business object proxy marshals the invoked methods, properties, and parameter values of the business object in MIME format to the ADISAPI module in the application server by using HTTP. (See Figure 19.1.)

Figure 19.1.

The ADC's middle-tier (application server) architecture.

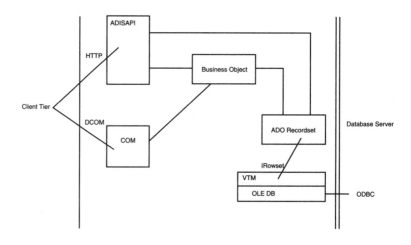

After receiving the MIME format information from the client tier, the ADISAPI module unpacks the information into methods, properties, and parameters of the business object, and then creates an instance of the business object in the application server. If an ADTG data stream is being passed along with the MIME information, ADO Recordsets are invoked to unpack the ADTG stream data.

After the business object is instantiated by ADISAPI, ADISAPI makes the method call on the business object, depending on the content of the MIME information. ADISAPI is responsible for marshaling the OLE DB rowset from the application server to the client tier and also across the machine boundary. ADISAPI also converts the request sent from the client tier into a sequence of standard OLE COM interface calls and then instantiates the business object.

The business object is responsible for making a connection with the ODBC datasource through the ADO Recordset and OLE DB ODBC provider. The data returned from the ODBC datasource is stored in the Virtual Table Manager (VTM) in OLE DB rowset format. ADO Recordsets act as a wrapper on top of the OLE DB interface and are in charge of getting the data from the OLE DB rowset to the ADOR Recordset so that it can be packaged into ADTG to send over to the client tier. If AdvancedDataControl's SubmitChanges method is used, the Virtual Table Manager creates a table based on the changed data, and the OLE DB ODBC provider makes the change to that ODBC datasource according to the content of the table in the VTM.

After the data is retrieved or updated in the application server, the retrieved data is packaged into ADTG and the result of whether the specified methods, properties, and parameter values are correct is packed into the same MIME format and sent over to the client tier. All this information is marshaled from the ADISAPI module in the application server back to the business object proxy in the client tier.

Now that you understand how the application server works, take a look at the default business object and AdvancedDataSpace before you delve into the custom business object.

The AdvancedDataSpace Object

AdvancedDataSpace is one of the client-tier framework components. It creates business object proxies in the client tier for the business objects on the application server. The *business object proxy* is responsible for the communication between the client tier and the application server. With business object proxies, you can invoke the methods of the business object in the application server to do data manipulation.

You can use one AdvancedDataSpace object to create more than one business proxy. Each returned ADOR Recordset from the invoking business object method can be associated with an `AdvancedDataControl` object. The end result is that you can have more than one `AdvancedDataControl` object associated with the same `AdvancedDataSpace`. To use `AdvancedDataSpace` in your Web page, you need to include the `<OBJECT>` section in your code. The CLASSID for `AdvancedDataSpace` is `99586D40-DB60-11CF-9D87-00AA00B91181`; because `AdvancedDataSpace` is invisible on the Web page, you can set both its width and height to 1. Here's an example of what you need to include in your Web page:

```
<OBJECT ID="AdvancedDataSpace1" WIDTH=1 HEIGHT=1
    CLASSID="CLSID:99586D40-DB60-11CF-9D87-00AA00B91181">
</OBJECT>
```

`AdvancedDataSpace` doesn't have any properties, but it does have one method, `CreateObject()`, associated with it. This method is described in more detail in the following section.

The `CreateObject` Method

The `CreateObject()` method allows you to create a business object proxy, which is responsible for packing the requested methods, properties, and parameter values into MIME format and marshaling the data to the ADISAPI in the application server. When ADISAPI gets that information from the business object proxy, it instantiates the business object. `AdvancedDataSpace` can invoke business objects through an in-process server, HTTP, or DCOM, and the `CreateObject()` method allows you to specify which method you want to use to invoke the business object on the application server.

The `CreateObject()` method accepts two parameters. First, specify the PROGID for the business object you want to use in the first parameter. For the second parameter, if you're accessing the business object through HTTP, specify the URL of the application server; if you're accessing through DCOM, specify the computer name; and if you're accessing the business object as an in-process server, you don't have to supply anything in the second parameter. After this method is invoked, a business object proxy is created so that you can invoke methods and parameters of the business object on the application server.

NOTE

PROGID is used to identify an OLE object in Visual Basic instead of the raw CLASSID because Visual Basic can't read the C/C++ header to pull out the CLASSID information. PROGID serves as an alternative language-independent symbolic name.

The information on how a CLASSID is associated with the PROGID is stored under HKEY_CLASSES_ROOT\CLSID in the Registry. You can also find the CLASSID for your OLE object there and a PROGID key that specifies the PROGID for the OLE object. For example, the CLASSID for `AdvancedDataSpace` is `99586D40-DB60-11CF-9D87-00AA00B91181`, and the PROGID is `AdvancedDataSpace`.

Here are some examples of how to use the CreateObject() method. First, to create a business object through an in-process server, you could use this statement:

```
Set myProxy = AdvancedDataSpace1.CreateObject("myProxy", "")
```

Second, you can create a business object through HTTP, as shown here:

```
Set myProxy = AdvancedDataSpace1.CreateObject("myProxy", "http://IISServerName")
```

Finally, you can also create a business object through DCOM, as shown in this example:

```
Set myProxy = AdvancedDataSpace1.CreateObject("myProxy", "IISServerName")
```

Using what you have learned so far, you should be able to construct a Web page that uses AdvancedDataSpace to invoke a business object. Before you get into the details on how to create a business object, you're going to try creating a business object proxy for the default business object, AdvancedDataFactory, as shown in Listing 19.2.

Listing 19.2. Creating a business object proxy.

```
 1: <HTML>
 2: <HEAD>
 3: <TITLE>
➥Teach Yourself Active Web Databases with VB in 21 Days</TITLE>
 4: </HEAD>
 5: <BODY BGCOLOR="ffffff" TEXT="000000" LINK="000080"
➥LANGUAGE="VBS" onload = "Init">
 6: <CENTER>
 7: <BR>
 8: <IMG SRC="video.gif" ALT="Virtual Video Store">
 9: <BR>
10: <H3>Teach Yourself Active Web Databases with VB in 21 Days</H3>
11: <BR>
12: <HR size=4 width="80%">
13: <!-- AdvancedDataSpace -->
14:     <OBJECT ID="AdvancedDataSpace1" WIDTH=1 HEIGHT=1
15:      CLASSID="CLSID:99586D40-DB60-11CF-9D87-00AA00B91181">
16:     </OBJECT>
17: <BR>
18: <SCRIPT LANGUAGE="VBScript">
19: Option Explicit
20: Dim myAdvancedDataFactory
21: Sub Init
22:     Set myAdvancedDataFactory =AdvancedDataSpace1.CreateObject
➥("AdvancedDataFactory", "http://IISServerName")
23: End Sub
24: </SCRIPT>
25: </BODY>
26: </HTML>
```

At the beginning of the code, you include the AdvancedDataSpace object; because it's invisible, you assign 1 for both the width and height. Under the VBScript section, you create a business object proxy for the default business object, `AdvancedDataFactory`. The first parameter of the `CreateObject()` method is `AdvancedDataFactory`, indicating that you're creating a business object proxy for `AdvancedDataFactory`, and the second parameter is the application server name `http://IISServerName`, which means that the `AdvancedDataFactory` is on the Microsoft Internet Information server.

In this example, you aren't invoking any `AdvancedDataFactory` methods yet. In the next section, you'll add more code to invoke the methods of business objects and go into more depth about exactly what `AdvancedDataFactory` does and what methods are available.

With the `CreateObject()` method, you can create business object proxies for any custom business objects you want to use. In this chapter, you're going to create business object proxies only through HTTP. In the next chapter, you will see how to set up your machine and create business objects through DCOM.

The `AdvancedDataFactory` Object

`AdvancedDataFactory` reads and writes data to the database server; it resides on the application server in a DLL format and is the default business object used to get data access to the database server in the Advanced Data Connector architecture. It returns the result set to the client tier and applies the updated data received from the client tier to the database server. The result sets that are being marshaled back and forth are in ADOR `Recordset` format.

For any kind of business object, you need to mark it as safe for scripting to ensure a safe Internet environment. You also need to register the PROGID for the business object under the ADCLaunch key in the Registry. `AdvancedDataFactory` is automatically marked as safe for scripting and is registered under the ADCLaunch key during the Advanced Data Connector's installation.

You can invoke the `AdvancedDataFactory` object through the `CreateObject()` method of the `AdvancedDataSpace` object. If you don't create a business object proxy in the Advanced Data Connector architecture, by default, `AdvancedDataFactory` is the business object that's implicitly invoked to give `AdvancedDataControl` data access to the database server.

`AdvancedDataFactory` is provided by the Advanced Data Connector architecture so that you can use `AdvancedDataControl` objects without using a custom business object. `AdvancedDataFactory`, as the default business object, simply does data reads and writes; it doesn't contain any business logic. You can replace `AdvancedDataFactory` with any custom business objects to apply your own business rules. You can also build a custom business object on top of the `AdvancedDataFactory` to take advantage of its data access capability and build your own business rules.

By default, when `AdvancedDataFactory` is used implicitly, `AdvancedDataControl`'s `SQL` and `Connect` properties are passed to `AdvancedDataFactory` so that it can have the necessary

19

information to access data in the database server. After the result set is generated, it's placed in an ADOR Recordset so it can be marshaled back to the client tier. Once the client tier receives the ADOR Recordset, it's automatically assigned to the Recordset property of the AdvancedDataControl object so that the returned result set can be placed in data-aware controls.

The example you saw earlier in the AdvancedDataSpace section demonstrates how to invoke the AdvancedDataFactory explicitly. There's no result set returned yet because you haven't used any AdvancedDataFactory methods to return the data, but as you learn about these methods, you will see how to send back an ADOR Recordset to the client tier.

Like AdvancedDataSpace, AdvancedDataFactory doesn't have any properties, but it does have three methods associated with it: Query, Submitchanges, and CreateRecord.

The Query Method

The Query method accepts two input parameters: The first one defines the ODBC connection string, and the second one specifies the SQL statement. The Query method issues the SQL statement in the second parameter to the ODBC datasource specified in the first parameter. The returned output parameter for this method is a Recordset that's the result set of the SQL statement. This returned result set is in ADOR Recordset format so it can be marshaled back to the client tier.

In the next example in Listing 19.3, you're going to invoke the Query method and assign the returned result set to an AdvancedDataControl object so that the data-aware controls can be populated with data. Before you start the next example, however, take another look at the virtual video store example used in Chapter 16, "Using the AdvancedDataControl Object." To refresh your memory, assume you're running a virtual video store that allows customers to reserve videos over the Web. Basically, they can view a list of videos and reserve them. The table structure is shown in Table 19.1.

19

Table 19.1. The Video_Detail table.

Column Name	Length	Constraints
VideoTitle	char(50)	Not null, unique
Rating	char(10)	Not null
Category	char(20)	Not null
ReleaseDate	datetime	Not null
Description	text	Allow null
ReservedID	int	Allow null
DueDate	datetime	Allow null
ReservedFlag	int	Allow null

> **NOTE**
>
> For more information on the description of this table and how to create it, please refer to Chapter 16, "Using the AdvancedDataControl Object," in the section "Configuring your Application and Client Server."

Listing 19.3. Using the Query method to retrieve data.

```
 1: <TITLE>Teach Yourself Active Web Databases with VB in 21 Days</TITLE>
 2: </HEAD>
 3: <BODY LANGUAGE="VBS">
 4: <CENTER>
 5: <H1><font size=5>
➥Teach Yourself Active Web Databases with VB in 21 Days
➥</H1></font>
 6: <IMG SRC="video.gif" WIDTH=400 HEIGHT=100 ALT="Virtual Video Store">
 7: <HR size=2 width=80%>
 8: <H2><font size=3>Using AdvancedDataFactory's Query Method</H2></font>
 9: <BR>
10: <OBJECT ID="Grid1" WIDTH=500 HEIGHT=100
11:       CLASSID="CLSID:00028C00-0000-0000-0000-000000000046">
12: </OBJECT>
13: <OBJECT CLASSID="CLSID:3B7C8860-D78F-101B-B9B5-04021C009402"
14:       ID=Text1 height=40 width=400>
15: </OBJECT>
16: <OBJECT ID="Radio1" WIDTH=100 HEIGHT=50
17:         CLASSID="CLSID:0BA686AA-F7D3-101A-993E-0000C0EF6F5E">
18:         <PARAM NAME="Caption" VALUE="Reserved">
19: </OBJECT>
20: <BR>
21: <!-- AdvancedDataSpace -->
22:     <OBJECT ID="ADS1" WIDTH=1 HEIGHT=1
23:       CLASSID="CLSID:99586D40-DB60-11CF-9D87-00AA00B91181">
24: </OBJECT>
25: <BR>
26: <INPUT TYPE=BUTTON NAME="First" VALUE="&First" onClick="MoveFirst">
27: <INPUT TYPE=BUTTON NAME="Next" VALUE="&Next" onClick="MoveNext">
28: <INPUT TYPE=BUTTON NAME="Prev" VALUE="&Prev" onClick="MovePrev">
29: <INPUT TYPE=BUTTON NAME="Last" VALUE="&Last" onClick="MoveLast">
30: <INPUT TYPE=BUTTON NAME="Refresh" VALUE="&Refresh" onClick="Refresh">
31: </CENTER>
32: <OBJECT CLASSID="clsid:9381D8F2-0288-11d0-9501-00AA00B911A5"
33:     ID=ADC1 HEIGHT=10 WIDTH = 10
34: CODEBASE="http://<%=Request.ServerVariables("Server_name")%>
➥/ADCDownload/msadc10.cab">
35:     <PARAM NAME="BINDINGS" VALUE=
➥"Grid1;Text1.Text=description;Radio1.Value=ReservedFlag">
36: </OBJECT>
37: <BR><BR>
38: <SCRIPT LANGUAGE= "VBS">
39: Dim myADF
40: SUB MoveFirst
41:     ADC1.MoveFirst
42: END SUB
```

```
43: SUB MoveNext
44:      ADC1.MoveNext
45: END SUB
46: SUB MovePrev
47:      ADC1.MovePrevious
48: END SUB
49: SUB MoveLast
50:      ADC1.MoveLast
51: END SUB
52: SUB Refresh
53:      Set rs  = myADF.Query("dsn=video;uid=sa","Select VideoTitle,Rating,
➥Category, ReleaseDate, ReservedFlag, Description
➥from Video_detail order by VideoTitle")
54:      ADC1.Recordset = rs
55:      Grid1.Columns(4).Visible = FALSE
56:      Grid1.Columns(5).Visible = FALSE
57: END SUB
58: Sub Window_OnLoad()
59: Dim rs
60:      Set myADF = ADS1.CreateObject("AdvancedDataFactory", _
61:                      "http://<%=Request.ServerVariables("Server_name")%>")
62:      Set rs  = myADF.Query("dsn=video;uid=sa","Select VideoTitle,Rating,
➥Category, ReleaseDate, ReservedFlag, Description
➥from Video_detail order by VideoTitle")
63:      ADC1.Recordset = rs
64:      Grid1.Columns(4).Visible = FALSE
65:      Grid1.Columns(5).Visible = FALSE
66: End Sub
67: </SCRIPT>
68: </BODY>
69: </HTML>
```

In this example, you use AdvancedDataSpace's CreateObject() method to create a business object proxy for AdvancedDataFactory. The first parameter of AdvancedDataSpace's CreateObject() is AdvancedDataFactory, and the second parameter is the location of the application server:

```
http://<%=Request.ServerVariables("Server_name")%>
```

You store the business object proxy reference in a global variable called myADF; it's declared right after <<SCRIPT LANGUAGE= "VBS">, rather than inside a subroutine, so that you can use this variable later in the Refresh method. After you get the business object proxy for AdvancedDataFactory, you invoke the Query method of the AdvancedDataFactory business object.

For the first parameter of the Query method, specify the ODBC connection string as dsn=video;uid=sa. Because there's no password for the user ID in the database server, omit the password. If a password is needed, use dsn=video;uid=sa;pwd=password instead. For the second parameter, use this SQL statement to retrieve data from the application server:

```
Select VideoTitle, Rating, Category, ReleaseDate, ReservedFlag,
➥Description from Video_detail order by VideoTitle
```

19

The parameters for the Query method and the Query method itself are packed in MIME format and sent over to ADISAPI in the application server. ADISAPI instantiates AdvancedDataFactory and converts the MIME format data into the actual Query method, which executes the following SQL statement to retrieve data from the database server specified in the second parameter:

```
Select VideoTitle, Rating, Category, ReleaseDate, ReservedFlag,
➡Description from Video_detail order by VideoTitle
```

The returned result set is marshaled back in ADOR Recordset format. You then get this ADOR Recordset and bind the returned result set to the DBGrid (Grid1), RichText (Text1), and Radio (Radio1) data-aware controls. One of AdvancedDataControl's properties, Recordset, is used to associate the returned ADO Recordset from the business object to an ADC1 object. With this in mind, you assign the returned Recordset from AdvancedDataFactory to the Recordset property of the AdvancedDataControl object (ADC1), which now has the returned result set, and the data is bound to Grid1, Text1, and Radio1 controls. The data is displayed in these data-aware controls; you can scroll the records by clicking the MoveFirst, MoveNext, MovePrev, and MoveLast buttons to invoke the AdvancedDataControl object's methods. From the Refresh button, you have invoked the Query method again to retrieve the data. Because you use myADF to store the reference to the business object proxy, you don't have to use CreateObject() to create a business object proxy again.

In Chapter 16, I mentioned that all the AdvancedDataControl properties are optional except the Bindings property. The example in Listing 19.3 has clearly demonstrated that. You used the default business object explicitly to retrieve the data and get the same functions as you do when using AdvancedDataControl objects alone. In Listing 19.4, however, you don't use AdvancedDataFactory explicitly, but you get the same effect by using just the AdvancedDataControl object.

Listing 19.4. Using the default business object.

```
 1: <HTML>
 2: <HEAD>
 3: <TITLE>Teach Yourself Active Web Databases with VB in 21 Days</TITLE>
 4: </HEAD>
 5: <BODY BGCOLOR="ffffff" TEXT="000000" LINK="000080"
➡LANGUAGE="VBS" onload = "Init">
 6: <CENTER>
 7: <BR>
 8: <IMG SRC="video.gif" ALT="Virtual Video Store">
 9: <BR>
10: <H3>Teach Yourself Active Web Databases with VB in 21 Days</H3>
11: <BR><BR><BR>
12: <OBJECT ID="Grid1" WIDTH=550 HEIGHT=200
13:       CLASSID="CLSID:00028C00-0000-0000-0000-000000000046">
14: </OBJECT>
15: <OBJECT ID="Radio1" WIDTH=100 HEIGHT=50
16:       CLASSID="CLSID:0BA686AA-F7D3-101A-993E-0000C0EF6F5E">
```

```
17:         <PARAM NAME="Caption" VALUE="Reserved">
18:         <PARAM NAME="ALLOWUPDATE" VALUE="TRUE;">
19: </OBJECT>
20: <BR><BR><BR>
21: <OBJECT CLASSID="CLSID:3B7C8860-D78F-101B-B9B5-04021C009402"
22:      ID=Text1 height=100 width=300>
23:         <PARAM NAME="ALLOWUPDATE" VALUE="TRUE;">
24: </OBJECT>
25: <BR>
26: <!-- AdvancedDataSpace -->
27:         <OBJECT ID="AdvancedDataSpace1" WIDTH=1 HEIGHT=1
28:         CLASSID="CLSID:99586D40-DB60-11CF-9D87-00AA00B91181">
29:         </OBJECT>
30: <BR><BR><BR>
31: <INPUT TYPE=BUTTON NAME="First" VALUE="&First" onClick="MoveFirst">
32: <INPUT TYPE=BUTTON NAME="Next" VALUE="&Next" onClick="MoveNext">
33: <INPUT TYPE=BUTTON NAME="Prev" VALUE="&Prev" onClick="MovePrev">
34: <INPUT TYPE=BUTTON NAME="Last" VALUE="&Last" onClick="MoveLast">
35: <INPUT TYPE=BUTTON NAME="Refresh" VALUE="&Refresh" onClick="Refresh">
36: </CENTER>
37: <OBJECT CLASSID="clsid:9381D8F2-0288-11d0-9501-00AA00B911A5"
38:      ID=ADC1 HEIGHT=10 WIDTH = 10
➥CODEBASE="http://<%=Request.ServerVariables("Server_name")%>
➥/ADCDownload/msadc10.cab">
39:         <PARAM NAME="BINDINGS"
➥VALUE="Grid1;Text1.Text=description;Radio1.Value=Reserved">
40:         </OBJECT>
41: <BR><BR>
42: <SCRIPT LANGUAGE= "VBS">
43: SUB MoveFirst
44:      ADC1.MoveFirst
45: END SUB
46: SUB MoveNext
47:      ADC1.MoveNext
48: END SUB
49: SUB MovePrev
50:      ADC1.MovePrevious
51: END SUB
52: SUB MoveLast
53:      ADC1.MoveLast
54: END SUB
55: SUB Refresh
56:      ADC1.Refresh
57: END SUB
58: Sub Init
59:      ADC1.Server = "http://<%=Request.ServerVariables("Server_name")%>"
60:      ADC1.Connect = "DSN=Video;UID=sa"
61:      ADC1.SQL =" VideoTitle,Rating,Category, ReleaseDate, ReservedFlag,
➥ Description from Video_detail order by VideoTitle "
62:      ADC1.Refresh
63:      Grid1.Columns(4).Visible = FALSE
64:      Grid1.Columns(5).Visible = FALSE
65: End Sub
66: </SCRIPT>
67: </BODY>
68: </HTML>
```

19

In this example, you don't use `AdvancedDataFactory`; you use the `AdvancedDataControl` object and assign the necessary properties to get the returned result set. You don't have to assign the returned result set to `AdvancedDataControl`'s `Recordset` property because all this is handled implicitly by the `AdvancedDataControl` object. Both of these examples provide the same functions, but one uses `AdvancedDataFactory` explicitly and the other uses it implicitly. Figure 19.2 shows the results onscreen.

Figure 19.2.

The result of using AdvancedDataFactory's Query *method.*

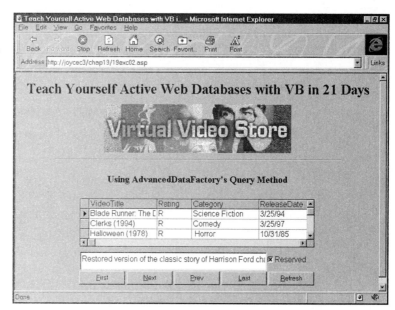

You can use the First, Prev, Next, and Last buttons to scroll the records. As usual, you have intentionally hidden some of the columns of the `DBGrid` control because you want to use other data-aware controls to display the data. So far, you can scroll the data, but how about submitting the changed data? When you use `AdvancedDataFactory` implicitly, you usually invoke `AdvancedDataControl`'s `SubmitChanges` method. Now that you have used `AdvancedDataFactory` explicitly, how are you going to submit the changed data to the application server and database server? One of the `AdvancedDataFactory` methods, `SubmitChanges`, handles it.

The `SubmitChanges` Method

The `SubmitChanges` method submits changes in a `Recordset` to the database server. It accepts two input parameters: The first one defines the ODBC connection string, and the second one specifies the ADOR `Recordset`. The ADOR `Recordset` specified in the second parameter contains only the changed record, not the whole `Recordset`.

The SubmitChanges method can be used only with the AdvancedDataFactory object; other business objects can't use this method. In ADC 1.0, the changes either all succeed or all fail. When you use AdvancedDataFactory implicitly, you use AdvancedDataControl's SubmitChanges method to submit the changed data. In the example in Listing 19.5, you see how to use the SubmitChanges method of AdvancedDataFactory explicitly.

Listing 19.5. Using AdvancedDataFactory's SubmitChanges method.

```
 1: <TITLE>Teach Yourself Active Web Databases with VB in 21 Days</TITLE>
 2: </HEAD>
 3: <BODY LANGUAGE="VBS">
 4: <CENTER>
 5: <H1><font size=5>
➥Teach Yourself Active Web Databases with VB in 21 Days</H1></font>
 6: <IMG SRC="video.gif" WIDTH=400 HEIGHT=100 ALT="Virtual Video Store">
 7: <HR size=2 width=80%>
 8: <H2><font size=3>Using AdvancedDataFactory's SubmitChangesmethod</H2></font>
 9: <BR>
10: <OBJECT ID="Grid1" WIDTH=500 HEIGHT=100
11:       CLASSID="CLSID:00028C00-0000-0000-0000-000000000046">
12: </OBJECT>
13: <OBJECT CLASSID="CLSID:3B7C8860-D78F-101B-B9B5-04021C009402"
14:      ID=Text1 height=40 width=400>
15: </OBJECT>
16: <OBJECT ID="Radio1" WIDTH=100 HEIGHT=50
17:       CLASSID="CLSID:0BA686AA-F7D3-101A-993E-0000C0EF6F5E">
18:       <PARAM NAME="Caption" VALUE="Reserved">
19: </OBJECT>
20: <BR>
21: <INPUT TYPE=BUTTON NAME="First" VALUE="&First" onClick="MoveFirst">
22: <INPUT TYPE=BUTTON NAME="Next" VALUE="&Next" onClick="MoveNext">
23: <INPUT TYPE=BUTTON NAME="Prev" VALUE="&Prev" onClick="MovePrev">
24: <INPUT TYPE=BUTTON NAME="Last" VALUE="&Last" onClick="MoveLast">
25: <INPUT TYPE=BUTTON NAME="Refresh" VALUE="&Refresh" >
26: <INPUT TYPE=BUTTON NAME="Confirm" VALUE="&Confirm" >
27: <BR>
28: <!-- AdvancedDataSpace -->
29:       <OBJECT ID="ADS1" WIDTH=1 HEIGHT=1
30:       CLASSID="CLSID:99586D40-DB60-11CF-9D87-00AA00B91181">
31: </OBJECT>
32: <BR>
33: <OBJECT CLASSID="clsid:9381D8F2-0288-11d0-9501-00AA00B911A5"
34:      ID=ADC1 HEIGHT=10 WIDTH = 10
35: CODEBASE="http://<%=Request.ServerVariables("Server_name")%>
➥/ADCDownload/msadc10.cab">
36:       <PARAM NAME="BINDINGS"
➥VALUE="Grid1;Text1.Text=description;Radio1.Value=ReservedFlag">
37: </OBJECT>
38: <BR><BR>
39: <SCRIPT LANGUAGE= "VBS">
40: Dim myADF
41: SUB MoveFirst
```

19

continues

Listing 19.5. continued

```
42:      ADC1.MoveFirst
43: END SUB
44: SUB MoveNext
45:      ADC1.MoveNext
46: END SUB
47: SUB MovePrev
48:      ADC1.MovePrevious
49: END SUB
50: SUB MoveLast
51:      ADC1.MoveLast
52: END SUB
53: SUB Refresh_OnClick
54:      ADC1.recordset  = ADF.Query("dsn=video;uid=sa","Select
➧VideoTitle,Rating,Category, ReleaseDate, ReservedFlag, Description
➧from Video_detail order by VideoTitle FOR BROWSE")
55:      ADC1.Refresh
56:      Grid1.Columns(3).Visible = FALSE
57:      Grid1.Columns(4).Visible = FALSE
58: END SUB
59: SUBConfirm_OnClick
60: ADC1.Server = "http://<%=Request.ServerVariables("Server_name")%>"
61:      ADC1.Connect="dsn=video;uid=sa"
62:      ADC1.MoveLast
63:      ADC1.MoveFirst
64:      ADF.SubmitChanges "dsn=video;uid=sa", ADC1.recordset
65:      ADC1.recordset  = ADF.Query("dsn=video;uid=sa","Select VideoTitle,
➧Rating,Category, ReleaseDate, ReservedFlag, Description
➧from Video_detail order by VideoTitle FOR BROWSE")
66:      ADC1.Refresh
67:      Grid1.Columns(4).Visible = FALSE
68:      Grid1.Columns(5).Visible = FALSE
69: END SUB
70: Sub Window_OnLoad()
71:      Set ADF = ADS1.CreateObject("AdvancedDataFactory",
➧ "http://<%=Request.ServerVariables("Server_name")%>")
72:    ADC1.recordset  = ADF.Query("dsn=video;uid=sa","Select VideoTitle,
➧Rating,Category, ReleaseDate, ReservedFlag, Description
➧from Video_detail order by VideoTitle FOR BROWSE")
73:      Grid1.ALLOWUPDATE=TRUE
74:      Grid1.Columns(4).Visible = FALSE
75:      Grid1.Columns(5).Visible = FALSE
76: End Sub
77: </SCRIPT>
78: </BODY>
79: </HTML>
```

In Listing 19.5, you add one more button to handle the SubmitChanges method. Remember, before you can change any data in a data-aware control, you need to set the controls to allow updates. If you click the Confirm button, the AdvancedDataFactory's SubmitChanges method is invoked. You specify the ODBC connection string dsn=video;uid=sa for the first parameter, and the Recordset ADC1.Recordset for the second parameter. After the changes are submitted, you refresh the AdvancedDataControl object's Recordset.

Uncheck the video "Blade Runner: The Director's Cut (1982)" to indicate that you don't want to reserve the video anymore, and submit the changes. (See Figure 19.3.)

Figure 19.3.

The result of using AdvancedDataFactory's SubmitChanges *method.*

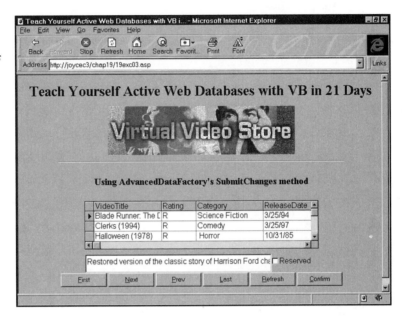

The CreateRecord **Method**

The CreateRecord method accepts one input parameter and returns one output parameter. It creates a specific type of Recordset based on the input column's information. The returned Recordset works in a disconnected fashion. This method is particularly useful if you're dealing with data of a non-SQL type. The following example shows how you can create an empty Recordset:

```
Dim ColInfo(2), c0(3)
Dim x
'the name of the column
c0(0) = "Videotitle"
'the type of the column. 129 is adChar and -1 is adInteger
c0(1) = CInt(129)
'the size of the column
c0(2) = CInt(40)
'whether the data is nullable or not
c0(3) = False
ColInfo(0) = c0
AdvancedDataControl.Recordset = AdvancedDataFactory.CreateRecordSet(ColInfo)
```

This example creates a `Recordset` with a column named VideoTitle. The data type is char with a size equal to 40 characters; this column doesn't allow null values.

So far, you're dealing only with data from an ODBC datasource. The `CreateRecord` method gives you the advantage of creating a `Recordset` from a non-SQL source. Take a look at the following example:

```
Sub GetVideoTemplate() As Variant
Dim tempSet As New ASODB.Recordset
Dim tempEngine as Object
Dim ColInfo(2), c0(3)
Dim x
'the name of the column
c0(0) = "VideoTitle"
'the type of the column. 129 is adChar and -1 is adInteger
c0(1) = CInt(129)
'the size of the column
c0(2) = CInt(40)
'whether the data is nullable or not
c0(3) = False
ColInfo(0) = c0
Set tempEngine = CreateObject("AdvancedDataFactory")
Set tempSet  = AdvancedDataFactory.CreateRecordSet(ColInfo)
Dim fields(0)
field(0) = c0(0)
Dim Data(0)
Data(0) = 'Forrest Gump'
tempSet.AddNew fields, Data
tempSet.MoveFirst
Set GetVideoTemplate = tempSet
Exit function
Error:
GetVideoTemplate = ERROR
Exit Funciton
```

This example creates a `Recordset` that has one column. As in the previous example, the column name is VideoTitle, the size is 40, and null values aren't allowed. You then insert one record—in this case, Forrest Gump—into this `Recordset` by using the `AddNew` method. After the new record is inserted, the `Recordset` is returned.

You've covered the methods of `AdvancedDataSpace` and `AdvancedDataFactory`; you know that if you use the `AdvancedDataControl` object and specify the `Server`, `Connect`, and `SQL` properties, you're implicitly using `AdvancedDataSpace` and `AdvancedDataFactory`. If there are no business rules involved, you can simply use `AdvancedDataFactory` implicitly, without concerning yourself about `AdvancedDataFactory`. `AdvancedDataSpace` and `AdvancedDataFactory` come into play when you start developing your own business objects. You need `AdvancedDataSpace` to create business object proxies, and `AdvancedDataFactory` as a base for your custom business object.

As stated before, `AdvancedDataFactory` doesn't contain any business rules; it simply does data reads and writes to the database server. If you want to protect the data or maintain some kind of business rules for the application and servers, you must create your own custom business object. In the next section, you're going to see how to create a custom business object in Visual Basic 4.0 and 5.0. It's also important to know how to mark business objects as safe for scripting to ensure a secure Internet environment because the client tier needs to invoke a remote object in the application server.

Business Objects

Earlier in this chapter, I mentioned that the idea behind business objects is to protect the data and business rules from being redistributed. Business objects can be any OLE objects created by Visual Basic, Visual C++, C++, or Java, and they can be written as DLLs or EXEs. If the business object is written as a DLL, it's accessed through HTTP or DCOM. When you access the business object through HTTP, you need to register it on the application server so that it can be instantiated in the application server. If the business object is written as an EXE, it can be accessed through DCOM. In this chapter, you're going to concentrate only on business objects written as DLLs and accessed through HTTP. The default business object that you have been using so far AdvancedDataFactory, is written as a DLL.

To ensure a safe Internet environment, business objects need to be marked as safe for scripting. The application server also has control over whether the business object can be launched by using the Registry database. All these security measures are taken because any client tier can try to invoke the business object, and it's impossible to validate the user based on the user ID since all the users are logged in as "anonymous." To solve this problem, use the Registry database to control whether you want anyone to launch the business object. If the PROGID of the business object doesn't show up under the ADCLaunch key in the Registry database, no one can invoke the object. Throughout this section, you're going to see how to create business objects in Visual Basic 4.0 and 5.0, how to mark your business object as safe for scripting, and how to allow users to launch business objects.

Before you delve into how to create a business object in Visual Basic 4.0 or 5.0, first look at the business object you're going to create. In the virtual video store example, say you're going to let the customer enter a five-digit number. If the number matches up with a random lucky number, the customer gets a free video rental. You will have only one business rule that validates the number the customer entered against the lucky number generated by a randomizing function. The business rule is called Draw, and the business object is named VideoVB4 or VideoVB5u, depending on which version of Visual Basic you use to create the object. To generate a lucky number, use one of the Visual Basic functions—Rnd—to generate a random number, as shown here:

```
Public Function Draw(myNumber As Long) As Variant
    Randomize
    LuckyNumber = Int((100000 * Rnd) + 1)
    If myNumber = LuckyNumber Then
```

19

```
        Draw = 0
    Else
        Draw = LuckyNumber
    End If
End Function
```

If the number entered matches the computer-generated random number, you return 1 to indicate that those two numbers match and the customer can get a free video rental. If the numbers don't match, you return the lucky number to the client tier.

Creating Business Objects in Visual Basic 4.0

Business objects are like OLE objects that can be created in Visual Basic. To create OLE objects from Visual Basic 4.0 and 5.0, you define a class, then define, within that class, methods and business rules that can be invoked. Follow these steps to create business objects in Visual Basic 4.0:

1. Create a normal Visual Basic project by choosing File | New Project from the menu.

2. You need to name the project; this name is the first part of the object name you refer to when using the CreateObject() method or Dim statement. To name the project, choose Tools | Options from the menu.

3. Select the Project tab and enter VideoVB4 in the Project Name text box.

4. Because business objects don't need a form, you must remove the default form. Choose View | Project from the menu to bring up the Project Window.

5. Next, select Form1 with Projects1 from the Project window, and then choose File | Remove File from the menu.

6. Now that the default form is removed, you need to tell the program where the entry point will be—that is, which function will be invoked first. In Visual Basic, the Sub Main procedure is normally where the first entry point is, and you can supply this sub-routine by inserting a new module. To do that, choose Insert | Module from Module1 Window from the menu. Next, enter Sub Main in the Module window and press Enter; the code is automatically entered.

7. Now you're ready to create the business object. First, you need to define a class by using the class module. Choose Insert | Class Module from the menu to bring up the Class window.

8. Next, choose View | Properties to open the Properties window. Select "2 - Creatable Multiuse" for the Instancing properties. This choice means you can create this object both inside and outside the project by using either the CreateObject() method or Dim statement.

19

9. Set the `Public` property to `TRUE` to indicate that this class is visible both inside and outside the project and application. Enter `VideoVB4Cls` as the class name (it will be the second part of your business object's name).

10. Next, choose View | Code to open the Class window, and enter the function you want to implement, as follows:

```
Public Function Draw(myNumber As Long) As Variant
    Randomize
    LuckyNumber = Int((100000 * Rnd) + 1)
    If myNumber = LuckyNumber Then
        Draw = 0
    Else
        Draw = LuckyNumber
    End If
End Function
```

11. After you enter the function, choose File | Save Project to save the project and modules as `VideoVB4.vbp` and `VideoVB4.cls`.

12. The project is ready for you to compile. Business objects can be in-process servers or standalone files; in this example, your business object is going to be an OLE DLL file. To do this, choose File | Make OLE DLL File from the menu.

13. Next, click the Option button, select the Auto-Increment checkbox, and click OK. Make sure the file has no compile errors.

14. Before you can use this business object, however, you need to register it in the Registry by using REGSVR32.EXE. To do this, click the Start button on the desktop, choose Run, and enter `regsvr32 VideoVB4.dll`.

TIP Before exiting Visual Basic, it's always a good idea to test the business object in the Visual Basic environment before you try to use it in a Web page. To do this, follow the steps in the next section.

19

Testing the Business Object in Visual Basic 4.0

To test your new business object in the Visual Basic environment, follow these steps:

1. Create a Visual Basic project by choosing File | New Project from the menu.

2. To tell your project to refer to the `VideoVB4` object, choose Tools | References from the menu to bring up the Reference window.

3. Under Available References options, select the VideoVB4 object. If the `VideoVB4` object doesn't show up there, you need to use REGSVR32 to register the object.

4. Create a TextBox control and a CommandButton control on the default form. You don't have to change their names; by default, the TextBox ID is Text1 and the CommandButton ID is Command1. Double-click on the CommandButton control, and the sub-routine corresponding to the Click event of the CommandButton is displayed.

5. Enter the following code within the body of the function:

```
Private Sub Command1_Click()
Dim myObj As New VideoVB4.VideoVB4Cls
Dim ret As Long
ret = myObj.Draw(Text1.Text)
If (ret = 1) Then
    MsgBox "Congratulations! You have won a free video rental"
Else
    MsgBox "Sorry! The lottery number is: " & ret
End If
End Sub
```

VideoVB4.VideoVB4Cls is the PROGID for the business object you created in Visual Basic 4.0. The Dim myObj As New VideoVB4.VideoVB4Cls statement allows you to create a reference to the VideoVB4 object and assign it to myObj variable. This myObj variable acts like a business object proxy. You can then call any of the methods of the VideoVB4.VideoVB4Cls business object. The Draw method requires one input parameter and one output parameter. You pass whatever the customer enters in the text box for the input parameter and use the ret variable to get the result. If the ret variable is equal to 1, it means that the numbers matched, and the customer can get a free video rental. Otherwise, you use a message box to display the lottery number.

6. Run the Visual Basic application. Next, enter a number and click the command button (the default name is Command1; in this example, it's Draw) to see whether the number matches the lucky number. If the entered number matches the lucky number, it displays a message box to congratulate you; otherwise, it displays the lucky number.

You can see how easy it is to create a business object and use it in Visual Basic 4.0. Now, with a custom business rule at hand, you want to know how to access it from the Web page. Before you do that, though, you need to prepare your business object for the environment and make sure it's safe for scripting.

Marking the Business Object as Safe for Scripting

Before using a business object, you need to mark it as safe for scripting to ensure a secure Internet environment. To invoke a custom business object through the Advanced Data Connector, its CLASSID needs to be entered into the Registry as safe for scripting. The default business object, `AdvancedDataFactory`, is already registered as safe for scripting. Follow these steps to mark your business object as safe for scripting:

1. To manually mark your business object as safe for scripting, you must create a file with a .REG extension. The file needs to contain the following information:

```
REGEDIT4
[HKEY_CLASSES_ROOT\CLSID\<MyBusinessObjectGUID>\Implemented Categories
➥{7DD95801-9882-11CF-9FA9-00AA006C42C4}]
[HKEY_CLASSES_ROOT\CLSID\<MyBusinessObjectGUID>\Implemented Categories
➥{7DD95802-9882-11CF-9FA9-00AA006C42C4}]
```

In this code, `<MyBusinessObjectGUID>` is the GUID number of your business object. The CLASSID for the `VideoVB4` object is `C788D8AD-86B5-11D0-A88D-00A0C911B4F2`, so your VIDEOVB4SAFE.REG file will look like this:

```
[HKEY_CLASSES_ROOT\CLSID\{C788D8AD-86B5-11D0-A88D-00A0C911B4F2} \Imple-
mented
➥Categories{7DD95801-9882-11CF-9FA9-00AA006C42C4}]
[HKEY_CLASSES_ROOT\CLSID\{C788D8AD-86B5-11D0-A88D-00A0C911B4F2} \Imple-
mented
➥Categories{7DD95802-9882-11CF-9FA9-00AA006C42C4}]
```

There's no easy way to find out the CLASSID of a object except by going to the Registry database. The CLASSID information is stored under \HKEY_CLASSES_ROOT\CLSID.

2. Save your VIDEOVB4SAFE.REG file, and merge it into the Registry database. To do this, click the Start button, choose Run, and enter `RegEdit` to bring up the Registry Editor. Choose Registry | Import Registry File from its menu. You can also double-click on your file in Windows Explorer.

The business object created in Visual Basic 5.0 can be automatically marked as safe for scripting; I will explain how to do this after the section on creating the business object in Visual Basic 5.0.

Checking the Business Object's Required Registry Entry

To launch the business object through `AdvancedDataControl`, you need to enter the business object's PROGID into the Registry under the ADCLaunch key, as shown in these steps:

1. Create a file with the .REG extension that has the following information:

```
REGEDIT4
[HKEY_LOCAL_MACHINE\SYSTEM\CurrentControlSet\Services\W3SVC\Parameters\
➥ADCLaunch\VideoVB4.VideoVB4Cls]
```

2. Save this file and merge it into the Registry. To do this, click the Start button, choose Run, and enter `REGEDIT` to bring up the Registry Editor. From its menu, choose Registry | Import Registry File.

19

Testing Your VB4 Business Object in a Web Page

Now try using this business object in your Web page. The code to do this is given in Listing 19.6.

Listing 19.6. Creating a business object in Visual Basic 4.0.

```
 1: <TITLE>Teach Yourself Active Web Databases with VB in 21 Days</TITLE>
 2: </HEAD>
 3: <BODY LANGUAGE="VBS">
 4: <CENTER>
 5: <H1><font size=5>
➥Teach Yourself Active Web Databases with VB in 21 Days</H1></font>
 6: <IMG SRC="video.gif" WIDTH=400 HEIGHT=100 ALT="Virtual Video Store">
 7: <HR size=2 width=80%>
 8: <H2><font size=3>Using VB4 business objects</H2></font><table>
 9:      <tr><td>Please enter your lottery Number:<td><INPUT NAME=LotteryNumber
➥ SIZE=10>
10:      </table>
11: <INPUT TYPE=BUTTON VALUE="Draw" NAME="Draw">
12: <!-- AdvancedDataSpace -->
13:      <OBJECT ID="ADS1" WIDTH=1 HEIGHT=1
14:      CLASSID="CLSID:99586D40-DB60-11CF-9D87-00AA00B91181">
15:      </OBJECT>
16: <BR>
17: <SCRIPT LANGUAGE="VBScript">
18: Option Explicit
19: Dim myObj
20: Dim ret
21: Sub Window_OnLoad()
22: End Sub
23: Sub Draw_OnClick()
24: Set myObj = ADS1.CreateObject("VideoVB4.VideoVB4Cls",
➥ "http://<%=Request.ServerVariables("Server_name")%>")
25: ret = myObj.Draw(LotteryNumber.Value)
26: If (ret = 1) Then
27:      MsgBox "Congratulations! You have won a free video rental"
28: Else
29:      MsgBox "Sorry! The lottery number is: " & ret
30:   End If
31: End Sub
32: </SCRIPT>
33: </BODY>
34: </HTML>
```

First, you include the AdvancedDataSpace object in the Web page and use its CreateObject() method to create a business object proxy for the VideoVB4.VideoVB4Cls object. The first parameter of the CreateObject() method is the business object's PROGID; the second parameter is the application server name. After you create the business object, invoke the Draw method of the business object to see whether the number entered in LotteryNumber text box matches the lottery number. A message box displays the result.

Figure 19.4 shows you the screen before you enter a number.

Figure 19.4.

Using a VB4 business object in a Web page.

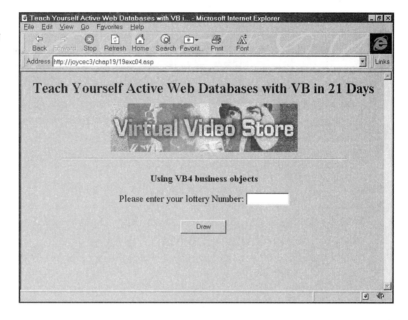

Figure 19.5 shows you the screen after you enter a number. If the entered number doesn't match, a message box is displayed with the correct number.

Figure 19.5.

The Web page after you enter a number.

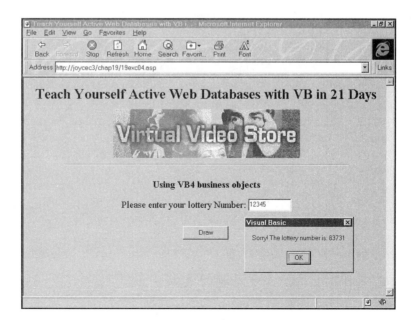

Now that you understand how to create a business object in Visual Basic 4.0 and how to access it from both Visual Basic 4.0 and a Web page, try creating the same business object in Visual Basic 5.0.

Creating Business Objects in Visual Basic 5.0

Visual Basic 5.0 makes it easier to create a business object than Visual Basic 4.0 does. In Visual Basic 4.0, the business objects are called OLE Automation objects. In Visual Basic 5.0, you call them ActiveX objects. The steps to create a business object in Visual Basic 5.0 are as follows:

NOTE

> As part of Internet fever, OLE objects have been renamed ActiveX objects. The name *ActiveX objects* has a broader meaning because you can not only access these objects through Visual Basic, C, and C++, but also through Microsoft Internet Explorer.

1. In Visual Basic 5.0, choose File | New to bring up the New Project window. In the New tab, select ActiveX DLL and click OK to close the window.

    This is the first difference you will notice between Visual Basic 5.0 and 4.0. Depending on the type of project you want to create, Visual Basic 5.0 constructs the necessary forms or class modules for you.

2. To name your project, choose Projects | Project1 Properties to bring up the Projects Properties window. Enter VideoVB5 for the project name, and then click OK to close the window.

3. In the Class Module window on the right-hand side of the screen, enter in VideoObjVB5 for the class name (the second part of the object name). Make sure you have "5 - MultiUse" selected for the Instancing properties.

4. Choose View | Code to bring up the Class window. In the main window, enter the code for the Draw function:

```
Public Function Draw(myNumber As Long) As Variant
    Randomize
    LuckyNumber = Int((100000 * Rnd) + 1)
    If myNumber = LuckyNumber Then
        Draw = 0
    Else
        Draw = LuckyNumber
    End If
End Function
```

5. Choose File | Save Project to save the project and class module.

6. Now you compile this project and make a business object. Choose File | Make VideoObjVB5.DLL from the menu.

After `VideoObjVB5.DLL` is successfully compiled, follow the steps mentioned earlier to make sure the business object's PROGID appears in the ADCLaunch key and the business object is marked as safe for scripting. One new feature in Visual Basic 5.0 is that you don't have to manually mark the business object as safe for scripting; learn more about this new feature in the following section. For how to create the business object's PROGID under the ADCLaunch key, please refer to the previous section, "Creating Business Objects in Visual Basic 4.0."

Marking Business Objects as Safe for Scripting in Visual Basic 5.0

If you create a business object in Visual Basic 5.0, you can use one of its tools to mark it as safe for scripting; follow these steps:

1. Start the Visual Basic Application Setup Wizard from your Visual Basic 5.0 program group, and click the Next button in the introduction window.

2. Enter <path>\ `VideoVb5.vbp` for the project name text box. Next, select the Create Internet Download Setup radio button for the Option group box. Click Next to move to the next window.

3. Pick a destination for your business object's CAB file in the Internet Distribution Location window. Click Next to go to the next window.

4. Click the Safety button in the Internet Package window. In the Safety dialog box, check the "Safe for scripting" option, and then click OK. Click Next to move to the next window.

5. Click Next again in the ActiveX Components window. The next window, File Summary, shows you what files are needed for shipping. Click Next to advance to the next window, and finally, click Next in the Finish! window.

Now your business object is marked as safe for scripting. An HTM Web page and a CAB file are generated in the destination directory to allow downloading. The content of the HTM file is as follows:

```
<HTML>
<OBJECT
    classid="clsid:D6C106CC-82DA-11D0-AEE6-444553540000"
    id=test
    codebase="VideoVB5.CAB#version=1,0,0,0">
</OBJECT>
</HTML>
```

This HTM file is automatically generated by the Visual Basic Application Setup Wizard. You can put this information in your Web page to take advantage of the automatic-downloading feature. When the Web page is loaded, the CAB file is downloaded and installed as a business object on the client machine. For the business objects you're using in this chapter, you don't need to use the automatic-downloading feature because the business objects need to exist only in the application server, since you're accessing them through HTTP.

19

Keep in mind, this process just marks your Visual Basic 5.0 business objects as safe for scripting; it doesn't add their PROGIDs under the ADCLaunch key in the Registry. The REG file you create to register the ADCLaunch key for this object is as follows:

```
REGEDIT4
[HKEY_LOCAL_MACHINE\SYSTEM\CurrentControlSet\Services\W3SVC\Parameters\
➡ADCLaunch\VideoVB5.VideoVB5Cls]
```

Testing the Business Object in Visual Basic 5.0 and a Web Page

To test your business object in the Visual Basic 5.0 environment, follow these steps:

1. Create a Visual Basic project by choosing File | New Project from the menu and selecting Standard EXE.

2. Create a TextBox control and a CommandButton control on the default form. You don't have to change their names; by default, the TextBox's ID is Text1. Double-click on the CommandButton control, and the sub-routine corresponding to the Click event of the CommandButton is displayed. Enter the following code within the body of the function:

   ```
   Private Sub Command1_Click()
   Dim ret As Integer
   ret = Draw(26540)
   If (ret = 1) Then
       MsgBox "Congratulations! You have won a free video rental"
   Else
       MsgBox "Sorry! The lottery number is: " & ret
   End If
   End Sub
   ```

3. To tell your project to reference the VideoVB5 object, choose Project | Reference from the menu to bring up the Reference window. Scroll down the Available References Options list and select the Video1 object you would like to reference. Compile the program.

Run the Visual Basic application. You can enter a number and click the Draw button to see whether the number entered matches the lucky number. If the entered number matches the lucky number, it displays a message box to congratulate you; otherwise, it displays the lucky number.

You reference a Visual Basic 5.0 business object from a Web page the same way you do for Visual Basic 4.0 business objects. You can use the same Web page you used in Listing 19.6 and modify the business object's PROGID to VideoVB5.VideoVB5Cls:

```
Sub Draw_OnClick()
Set myObj = ADS1.CreateObject("VideoVB5.VideoVB5Cls ",
➡ "http://<%=Request.ServerVariables("Server_name")%>")
ret = myObj.Draw(LotteryNumber.Value)
If (ret = 1) Then
    MsgBox "Congratulations! You have won a free video rental"
Else
```

```
      MsgBox "Sorry! The lottery number is: " & ret
   End If
End Sub
```

You have changed the first parameter of the `CreateObject()` method to reflect the new PROGID: `VideoVB5.VideoVB5Cls`. The rest of the code is the same as what was given in Listing 19.6. The result of using `VideoVB5.VideoVB5Cls` in the Web page is the same as what's shown in Figures 19.4 and 19.5.

Using `AdvancedDataControl` Objects to Access Custom Business Objects

So far, you have created a simple business object that compares a user-entered number with a computer-generated random number and returns the result to the client Web page for display, but doesn't interact with the database server. Can you use this business object to interact with the database server? Before I show you an example, review the Advanced Data Connector architecture briefly, because what you learned earlier will come into play as you're developing business objects.

In Chapter 16, you learned that the data getting marshaled back and forth needs to be an ADOR `Recordset` so that it can be packed as an ADTG data stream. This requirement is very important when you develop business objects because if the business object needs to return a `Recordset` to the client side, it must be returned as an ADOR `Recordset` for marshaling to work correctly. Also, keep in mind that you use an ADOR `Recordset` in the application server to interact with the database server.

Earlier, you learned that the default business object, `AdvancedDataFactory`, does data reads and writes only while accessing the database server. You're going to work on a business object, using the virtual video rental store example from Chapter 16, that will simply return a `Recordset` to the client tier by using `AdvancedDataFactory`.

For this example, the business object you create will have a method that returns all the videos to the client Web page. You can use either Visual Basic 4.0 or 5.0 to create this new business object, and you're still going to keep the `Draw` method for this business object. The business object is named `VVstoreObj.VVstoreObjCls`. Here's the code for the new method, called `GetAllVideos`:

```
Public Function GetAllVideos()
Dim myADF As Object
Dim rs As ADOR.Recordset
Dim SQLString
    Set myADF = CreateObject("AdvancedDataFactory")
SQLString = "select VideoTitle,Rating,Category, ReleaseDate,
➥ReservedFlag, Description from video_Detail Order by VideoTitle"
    Set rs = myADF.Query("dsn=video;uid=sa", SQLString)
    Set GetAllVideos = rs
End Function
```

19

To use the ADOR Recordset in your Visual Basic project, you need to reference it first. Choose Project | Reference from the menu to bring up the Reference window. Scroll down the Available References Options list and select the "Microsoft Active Data Objects/ Recordset 1.0" item.

You have declared three variables in this function: myADF is of the type Object; the second one, rs, is an ADOR Recordset; and the third one is SQLString. myADF serves as a reference to the AdvancedDataFactory object, and rs is the ADOR Recordset you're going to send back to the client tier. SQLString stores the SQL statement you're going to issue against the database server in case you select all the videos in the store.

After you declare all the variables, use Visual Basic's CreateObject() method to create an AdvancedDataFactory object and assign the reference of AdvancedDataFactory back to the myADF variable. The CreateObject() method creates and returns an ActiveX object. After you get a reference of AdvancedDataFactory, use AdvancedDataFactory's Query method to generate a returned result set based on the ODBC database and the Select VideoTitle,Rating,Category, ReleaseDate, ReservedFlag, Description from video_Detail Order by VideoTitle SQL statement.

The returned result set is assigned back to an ADOR Recordset, which is returned to the calling function. Now take a look at how you received this ADOR Recordset on the client tier in Listing 19.7.

> **NOTE**
>
> Remember to mark VVstoreObj.VVstoreObjCls as safe for scripting, and make sure the PROGID appears under the ADCLaunch key in the Registry.

Listing 19.7. Using VVStoreObj to get all the videos.

```
 1: <TITLE>Teach Yourself Active Web Databases with VB in 21 Days</TITLE>
 2: </HEAD>
 3: <BODY LANGUAGE="VBS">
 4: <CENTER>
 5: <H1><font size=5>
➡Teach Yourself Active Web Databases with VB in 21 Days</H1></font>
 6: <IMG SRC="video.gif" WIDTH=400 HEIGHT=100 ALT="Virtual Video Store">
 7: <HR size=2 width=80%>
 8: <H2><font size=3>Using VVStoreObj to Get All the Videos</H2></font>
 9: <!-- AdvancedDataSpace -->
10:     <OBJECT ID="ADS1" WIDTH=1 HEIGHT=1
```

19

```
11:        CLASSID="CLSID:99586D40-DB60-11CF-9D87-00AA00B91181">
12: </OBJECT>
13: <OBJECT CLASSID="clsid:9381D8F2-0288-11d0-9501-00AA00B911A5"
14:        ID=ADC1 HEIGHT=1 WIDTH = 1        CODEBASE="HTTP://
➥<%=Request.ServerVariables("Server_name")%>/ADCDownload/msadc10.cab">
15:        <PARAM NAME="BINDINGS"
➥VALUE="Grid1;Text1.Text=description;Radio1.Value=ReservedFlag">
16: </OBJECT>
17: <BR>
18: <OBJECT ID="Grid1" WIDTH=500 HEIGHT=100
19:        CLASSID="CLSID:00028C00-0000-0000-0000-000000000046">
20: </OBJECT>
21: <BR>
22: <OBJECT CLASSID="CLSID:3B7C8860-D78F-101B-B9B5-04021C009402"
23:        ID=Text1 height=40 width=400>
24: </OBJECT>
25: <OBJECT ID="Radio1" WIDTH=100 HEIGHT=50
26:        CLASSID="CLSID:0BA686AA-F7D3-101A-993E-0000C0EF6F5E">
27:        <PARAM NAME="Caption" VALUE="Reserved">
28: </OBJECT>
29: <BR><BR>
30: <INPUT TYPE=BUTTON NAME="First" VALUE="&First" onClick="MoveFirst">
31: <INPUT TYPE=BUTTON NAME="Next" VALUE="&Next" onClick="MoveNext">
32: <INPUT TYPE=BUTTON NAME="Prev" VALUE="&Prev" onClick="MovePrev">
33: <INPUT TYPE=BUTTON NAME="Last" VALUE="&Last" onClick="MoveLast">
34: <INPUT TYPE=BUTTON NAME="GetAllVideo" VALUE="&Get All Videos"
➥onClick="GetAll">
35: <SCRIPT LANGUAGE="VBScript">
36: Option Explicit
37: Dim myObj
38: Dim ret
39: Dim rs
40: SUB MoveFirst
41:        ADC1.MoveFirst
42: END SUB
43: SUB MoveNext
44:        ADC1.MoveNext
45: END SUB
46: SUB MovePrev
47:        ADC1.MovePrevious
48: END SUB
49: SUB MoveLast
50:        ADC1.MoveLast
51: END SUB
52: Sub GetAll()
53:        Set rs = myObj.GetAllVideos()
54:        ADC1.Recordset = rs
55: End SUB
56: Sub Window_OnLoad()
57:        Set myObj = ADS1.CreateObject("VVStoreObj.VVStoreObjCls",
➥  "HTTP://<%=Request.ServerVariables("Server_name")%>")
58: End Sub
59: </SCRIPT>
60: </BODY>
61: </HTML>
```

19

continues

You created five buttons in this example: First, Next, Prev, Last, and Get All Videos. The new button, Get All Videos, invokes the GetAllVideos() method on the custom business object. Two variables, Mystore and rs, are used to store the information on the business object proxy and ADOR Recordset returned from the GetAllVideos() method.

In the Window_OnLoad sub-routine, use AdvancedDataSpace's CreateObject() method to create a business object proxy for the VVStoreObj.VVStoreObjCls business object. Window_OnLoad is used by default if you don't specify any default function. After you create the myStore business object proxy, invoke the GetAllVideos() method in the GetAll sub-routine to get an ADOR Recordset for all the videos in the store. With an ADOR Recordset at hand, you can then assign the ADOR Recordset to the AdvancedDataControl object, ADC1, so that the data is bound to the data-aware controls.

Figure 19.6 shows you the screen after you click the Get All Videos button; the data is displayed in the data-aware bound controls.

Figure 19.6.

The result of using VVStore's GetAllVideos() method.

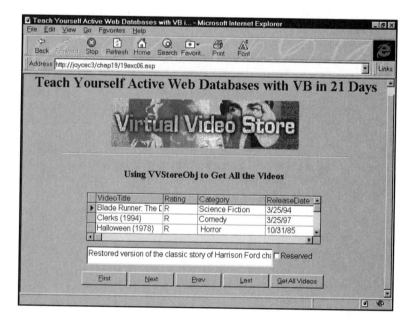

Now try creating two more methods for your business object before you finish this chapter. Besides being able to return all the videos, you should be able to retrieve only the videos that haven't been checked out yet. To do this, you call the function, GetAllAvailableVideos():

```
Public Function GetAllAvailableVideos() As Variant
Dim myADF As Object
Dim rs, SQLString
        Set myADF = CreateObject("AdvancedDataFactory")
```

```
SQLString = "select VideoTitle,Rating,Category, ReleaseDate,
➥ReservedFlag, Description from video_Detail where ReservedFlag = 0
➥order by VideoTitle"
        Set rs = myADF.Query("dsn=video;uid=sa", SQLString)
        Set GetAllAvailableVideos = rs
End Function
```

This function is basically the same as `GetAllVideos()` except you use a different query—selecting all the videos with the `ReservedFlag` equal to `0`. You also need a function that returns the videos reserved by a specific customer ID. To do this, you can call the function `GetReservedVideos()`:

```
Public Function GetReservedVideos(ByVal CustomerID As Integer) As Variant
Dim myADF As Object
Dim rs, SQLString
        Set myADF = CreateObject("AdvancedDataFactory")
SQLString = "select VideoTitle,Rating,Category,
➥ReleaseDate, ReservedFlag, Description from Video_detail
➥where ReservedID = " & CustomerID & " order by VideoTitle"
        Set rs = myADF.Query("dsn=video;uid=sa", SQLString)
        Set GetReservedVideos = rs
End Function
```

This function uses a SQL statement that selects all the videos reserved by a specific customer ID. With these two new functions, you're going to add two more buttons in the Web page to handle the `GetAllAvailableVideos()` and `GetReservedVideos()` methods, as shown in Listing 19.8. The input parameter of the `GetReservedVideos()` method is based on the customer ID the user enters.

Listing 19.8. Adding the `GetAllAvailableVideos()` and `GetReservedVideos()` methods.

```
 1: <TITLE>Teach Yourself Active Web Databases with VB in 21 Days</TITLE>
 2: </HEAD>
 3: <BODY LANGUAGE="VBS">
 4: <CENTER>
 5: <H1><font size=5>
➥Teach Yourself Active Web Databases with VB in 21 Days</H1></font>
 6: <IMG SRC="video.gif" WIDTH=400 HEIGHT=100 ALT="Virtual Video Store">
 7: <HR size=2 width=80%>
 8: <H2><font size=3>Using VVStoreObj to Get Videos</H2></font>
 9: <!-- AdvancedDataSpace -->
10:     <OBJECT ID="ADS1" WIDTH=1 HEIGHT=1
11:     CLASSID="CLSID:99586D40-DB60-11CF-9D87-00AA00B91181">
12: </OBJECT>
13: <OBJECT CLASSID="clsid:9381D8F2-0288-11d0-9501-00AA00B911A5"
14:     ID=ADC1 HEIGHT=1 WIDTH = 1
15:     CODEBASE="HTTP://<%=Request.ServerVariables("Server_name")%>
➥/ADCDownload/msadc10.cab">
16:     <PARAM NAME="BINDINGS" VALUE=
➥"Grid1;Text1.Text=description;Radio1.Value=ReservedFlag">
```

continues

Listing 19.8. continued

```
17: </OBJECT>
18: <BR>
19: <table><font size=3>
20:     <tr><td>Customer ID:<td><INPUT NAME=CustomerID SIZE=10>
21:     </table></font>
22: <BR>
23: <OBJECT ID="Grid1" WIDTH=500 HEIGHT=100
24:     CLASSID="CLSID:00028C00-0000-0000-0000-000000000046">
25: </OBJECT>
26: <BR>
27: <OBJECT CLASSID="CLSID:3B7C8860-D78F-101B-B9B5-04021C009402"
28:     ID=Text1 height=40 width=400>
29: </OBJECT>
30: <OBJECT ID="Radio1" WIDTH=100 HEIGHT=50
31:     CLASSID="CLSID:0BA686AA-F7D3-101A-993E-0000C0EF6F5E">
32:     <PARAM NAME="Caption" VALUE="Reserved">
33: </OBJECT>
34: <BR><BR>
35: <INPUT TYPE=BUTTON NAME="First" VALUE="&First" onClick="MoveFirst">
36: <INPUT TYPE=BUTTON NAME="Next" VALUE="&Next" onClick="MoveNext">
37: <INPUT TYPE=BUTTON NAME="Prev" VALUE="&Prev" onClick="MovePrev">
38: <INPUT TYPE=BUTTON NAME="Last" VALUE="&Last" onClick="MoveLast">
39: <BR>
40: <INPUT TYPE=BUTTON NAME=
➥"GetAllVideo" VALUE="&Get All Videos" onClick="GetAll">
41: <INPUT TYPE=BUTTON NAME="GetReserv" VALUE="Get &Reserved" >
42: <INPUT TYPE=BUTTON NAME="GetAvail" VALUE="&Get &Available">
43: <SCRIPT LANGUAGE="VBScript">
44: Option Explicit
45: Dim myObj
46: Dim ret
47: Dim rs
48: SUB MoveFirst
49:     ADC1.MoveFirst
50: END SUB
51: SUB MoveNext
52:     ADC1.MoveNext
53: END SUB
54: SUB MovePrev
55:     ADC1.MovePrevious
56: END SUB
57: SUB MoveLast
58:     ADC1.MoveLast
59: END SUB
60: Sub GetAll()
61:     Set rs = myObj.GetAllVideos()
62:     ADC1.Recordset = rs
63: End SUB
64: Sub GetReserv_OnClick()
```

```
65:      Dim myDefaultID
66:      myDefaultID =-2
67:      IF CustomerID.Value <> "" Then
68:         myDefaultID = CustomerID.Value
69:      END IF
70:      ADC1.Recordset = myObj.GetReservedVideos(myDefaultID)
71: End SUB
72: Sub GetAvail_OnClick()
73:      Set rs = myObj.GetAllAvailableVideos()
74:      ADC1.Recordset = rs
75: End SUB
76: Sub Window_OnLoad()
77:      Set myObj = ADS1.CreateObject("VVStoreObj.VVStoreObjCls",
➥ "HTTP://<%=Request.ServerVariables("Server_name")%>")
78: End Sub
79: </SCRIPT>
80: </BODY>
81: </HTML>
```

In this example, AdvancedDataSpace's CreateObject() method creates a business proxy for the business object. Next, two new buttons for the GetAllAvailableVideos() and GetReservedVideos() methods are created. When the Get Available button is clicked, the GetAvail_OnClick sub-routine is invoked, which in turn calls the GetAllAvailableVideos() method to retrieve the videos that aren't reserved yet. The returned Recordset is assigned to the ADC1 Recordset.

When the Get Reserved button is clicked, the GetReserv_OnClick sub-routine is invoked. First, it checks whether the customer ID is empty. If it is, you pass -2 to the GetReservedVideos() function to indicate that there's no valid ID entered. If the customer ID isn't empty, pass the entered customer ID to the GetAllAvailableVideos() function. Figure 19.7 shows the page as it's first seen.

As you can see in Figure 19.7, all the videos are displayed, including the "Snow White And The Seven Dwarves (1937)" video, which is, by default, reserved by customer 2.

After you click the Get Available button, however, the "Snow White And The Seven Dwarves (1937)" video is no longer displayed in the Grid control; only the available videos are displayed. (See Figure 19.8.)

As you can see in Figure 19.9, only the videos reserved by a specific customer are displayed after you click the Get Reserved button. The "Snow White And The Seven Dwarves (1937)" video is displayed in the Grid control for customer 2.

19

Figure 19.7.

The result of invoking the GetAllVideos() *method.*

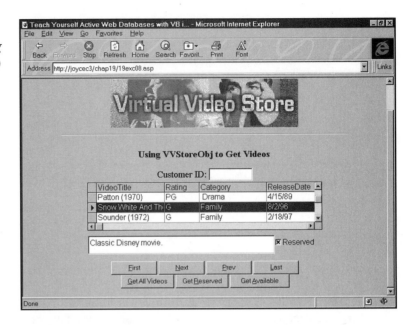

Figure 19.8.

The result of invoking the GetAllAvailable-Videos() *method.*

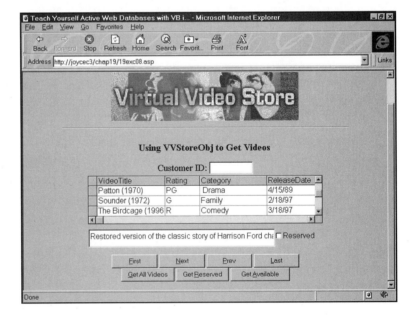

19

Figure 19.9.

The result of invoking the GetReserved-Videos() *method.*

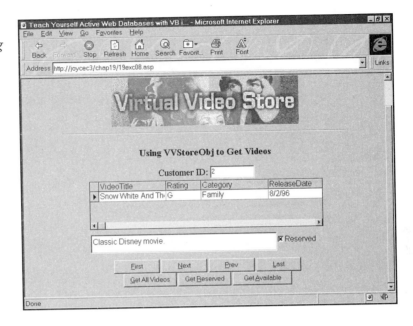

Summary

Today, you have taken a close look at the AdvancedDataControl application server architecture. You know how to use AdvancedDataSpace and AdvancedDataFactory to interact with business objects and how to create business objects in both Visual Basic 4.0 and 5.0. During the last few days, you have learned enough concepts about the Advanced Data Connector for you to have a clear picture of how to use these objects to construct interactive Web pages. You have seen examples of how to use AdvancedDataControl, AdvancedDataSpace, AdvancedDataFactory, and custom business objects. So far, you have used AdvancedDataFactory as a base to create your custom business objects, and the custom business objects you created today don't include any data validation. In the next chapter, you're going to learn how to use ADO for custom business objects.

Q&A

Q **What kind of advantage will I get if I use more than one AdvancedDataControl object in one AdvacedDataSpace?**

A The original idea of allowing more than one AdvancedDataControl object in an AdvancedDataSpace is that you can associate the Recordsets of different

AdvancedDataControl objects together. The data changes in one Recordset are reflected in the other as long as they're created by the same AdvancedDataSpace. However, this concept hasn't been implemented yet in version 1.0 of the ADC.

Q Why do I get a `cannot create object` error?

A It's possible you forgot to mark your business object as safe for scripting, or you forgot to register it under the ADCLaunch key.

Quiz

1. What are the methods of AdvancedDataSpace?

2. What are the methods of AdvancedDataFactory?

3. What is the default business object?

4. How do you mark a business object as safe for scripting?

Exercise

Create a business object that handles an online ticket reservation system for a virtual theater. This exercise is similar to the exercise in Chapter 16, except you will be using a business object.

Day 20

Business Objects and ADO

by Joyce Chia-Hsun Chen

In yesterday's lesson, you learned the purpose of business objects—to help you protect your business logic and data from distribution. Business objects aren't limited to any particular language; you can use C++ or Visual Basic, among others. You have learned how to use Visual Basic 4.0 and 5.0 to build business objects, how to mark the business object as safe for scripting, and how to put the PROGID under the ADCLaunch key to ensure a safe Internet environment and launch the business object. You have also seen how to create a business object proxy in the client tier by using AdvancedDataSpace and how to invoke the business object's methods.

By now, you have covered almost everything about the Advanced Data Connector components: `AdvancedDataControl` objects, ADOR `Recordsets`, `AdvancedDataSpace`, `AdvancedDataFactory`, and, most important, business objects. What else is missing from this picture?

You know how to create a business object using `AdvancedDataFactory` and how to create a `Recordset` and submit its changes with `AdvancedDataFactory`'s `Query` and `SubmitChanges` methods. However, using `AdvancedDataFactory` limits your ability to do more data validation and manipulation because it provides just data reading and writing—nothing else. So you'd like to build a more powerful business object, but how do you go about that?

In Week 2, you learned about ADO (ActiveX Data Objects), which is based on OLE DB and provides a uniform interface to data. Because it's language-neutral, you can use it in C/C++, Java, Visual Basic, or VBScript. ADO offers a feature for creating a disconnected `Recordset` and later reconnecting to the `Recordset` to apply changes. This feature is particularly useful for intranet/Internet environments because the `Recordsets` need to be disconnected in the client tier.

For those reasons, ADO is the best technology to use for building your more powerful business object. Today, you'll see how to use ADO to perform more data manipulation in business objects. You're going to build business objects using ADO and learn how you can apply changed records to the database server through ADO.

After this chapter, you will know how to do the following:

- Use ADO to create a business object.
- Pass a disconnected `Recordset` from application server to the client tier.
- Pass a modified `Recordset` from the client to the application server.
- Reconnect to an active `Connection`.

NOTE

> To run the examples in this chapter, please make sure you refer to the setup instructions included in "Week 3 at a Glance."

Using `AdvancedDataFactory` in a Business Object

In the previous chapter, you learned how to use `AdvancedDataFactory` to create a business object and how to use its `Query` method, which does all the data retrieval and packaging, to get a `Recordset` and marshal this `Recordset` back to the client tier. You simply supply the SQL statement and ODBC connection string information and invoke the Query method to get a Recordset that can be marshaled to the client tier. AdvancedDataFactory hides the Recordset creation and retrieving it for marshaling. Although you won't be using AdvancedDataFactory in today's lesson, you *will* be duplicating its work to create your new business object.

AdvancedDataFactory's Query method uses ADODB to generate a Recordset that's converted to an ADOR Recordset (which, as you might recall, is the "lightweight" version of the ADODB Recordset) that contains the base table metadata. The *base table metadata* contains information necessary for reconstructing the table structure and the data for the Recordset. This metadata is marshaled with the ADOR Recordset to the client tier, which uses the table metadata information to generate the table structure in the Virtual Table Manager so that the Recordset can stay disconnected.

The business objects you created in Chapter 19, "Client-Server Business Objects," take advantage of this convenient ADOR Recordset. You use the Query method to get a Recordset that's already converted into an ADOR Recordset, and then simply marshal this Recordset back to the client tier, without worrying about the conversion between an ADODB Recordset and an ADOR Recordset.

Using AdvancedDataFactory for your business objects saves you some programming work, but there's not much you can do about the Recordset in the business object. If you want to scan through the record and make adjustments, you can't do that with AdvancedDataFactory objects. Also, you can't validate any of the record's data in the Recordset, and you can submit only what the client tier has changed to the database server.

With these limitations in mind, you can see the need for using ADO to get more functions and features. The trade-off is that you must convert the ADODB and ADOR Recordsets yourself and set some options to reconnect to the Recordset later. As you work through the examples in this chapters, the rewards for using ADO in your business object will become clearer—and so will the pitfalls you need to watch out for.

Using ADO to Create a Business Object

20

Generating an ADODB Recordset in the business object is the same as creating a normal ADODB Recordset in a VB application. However, you do need to be careful about how you format the Recordset you want to marshal back and how to prepare the Recordset properly so you can get it back after the client tier makes changes, and then apply the changes to the database server.

There are two types of Recordsets: ADODB and ADOR. ADOR Recordsets are the "lightweight" version of ADODB Recordsets; they contain the base table metadata used to regenerate the table. In an intranet/Internet situation, it's importantly to have a Recordset containing all the information about the data and table structure so it doesn't have to rely on a continuously active connection with the database server. The ADOR Recordset can stay disconnected from the database server, so if you use ADODB to create a Recordset, you should convert it into an ADOR Recordset before you marshal it to the client tier.

After the Recordset is marshaled to the client tier, the client tier might make some changes to the Recordset. This changed Recordset can then be marshaled back to the business objects. Business objects need to be "smart" enough to understand the changes and somehow apply just those changes to the database server.

If the original Recordset has ten records and only one record has been modified in the client tier, how does the client tier decide whether to marshal the whole Recordset or only the changed record to the business object? How is the business object going to apply the changed record to the database server? Does the business object need to scan through the whole Recordset and compare each record to see whether the data has been changed? Furthermore, how does the business object know what kind of SQL statement is used for generating the Recordset?

The perfect solution is to allow the business object to reconnect to the Recordset. By *reconnecting*, I mean treat the Recordset as though you had made the modification inside the same function, and the Recordset had never been marshaled anywhere. After you reconnect to the Recordset, you can use a normal method to apply the changes to the database server. To allow reconnection later on, you need to set some options for the Recordset before you marshal it to the client tier.

Now, take a look at a business object that's using an ADODB Recordset:

```
Public Function GetAllVideos() As Object
    Dim rs As ADODB.Recordset
    Set rs = CreateObject("ADODB.Recordset")
rs.Open "select VideoTitle, Rating, Category, ReleaseDate, ReservedFlag,
➥ Description from Video_detail order by videoTitle for browse", _
"dsn=video;uid=sa;pwd=;", adOpenUnspecified,
➥ adLockUnspecified, adCmdUnspecified
    Set GetAllVideos = rs
End Function
```

rs is the reference to the ADODB Recordset, and the Open method creates a Recordset. You return this Recordset from the GetAllVideos function. For the SQL statement, continue to use the Virtual Video Rental example. You want to create a Recordset based on the VideoTitle, Rating, Category, ReleaseDate, ReservedFlag, and Description columns in the Video_Detail table.

To use the ADODB Recordset in your Visual Basic business object, you need to check the reference for the ADODB object so that it's available to your business object. To do that, choose Project | Reference from the menu to bring up the Reference window. Scroll down the

20

Available References Option list and select Microsoft Active Data Object / Recordset 1.0 and Microsoft OLE DB ActiveX Data Objects 1.0 Library. The Microsoft Active Data Object / Recordset 1.0 is for using ADOR Recordsets, and the filename is MSADOR10.DLL. The Microsoft OLE DB ActiveX Data Objects 1.0 Library is for using ADODB, and the filename is MSADO10.DLL.

NOTE

> The ADODB methods aren't explained in detail because ADODB was covered thoroughly in Week 2. However, I'll explain all the properties that are important to the Advanced Data Connector. If you have any questions about the methods, please refer to the lessons in Week 2.

The preceding code gives you a basic structure for creating a GetAllVideos function for the business object. But what about converting the ADODB Recordset to an ADOR Recordset and getting the Recordset ready so you can reconnect later?

The answer to both those questions lies in one of ADODB's properties: CursorLocation. The CursorLocation property, which allows you to mark an ADODB Recordset as ready for marshaling, has three options: adUseClient, adUseServer, and adUseClientBatch. With the adUseClientBatch option set, the ADODB Recordset is converted into an ADOR Recordset that can function in a disconnected fashion and later be reconnected to apply changes.

Once you set the adUseClientBatch option for a Recordset's CursorLocation property, this ADOR Recordset is ready to be marshaled to the client tier. It contains the base table metadata used to regenerate the table in the Virtual Table Manager so that it can operate in a disconnected fashion. With this option available, you can now add adUseClientBatch to the GetAllVideos function and finish the business object:

```
Public Function GetAllVideos() As Object
    Dim rs As ADODB.Recordset
    Set rs = CreateObject("ADODB.Recordset")

SQLString = "select VideoTitle,Rating,Category, ReleaseDate,
➥ ReservedFlag, Description from Video_detail
order by VideoTitle for browse"

    rs.CursorLocation = adUseClientBatch
rs.Open SQLString, "dsn=video;uid=sa;pwd=;", adOpenUnspecified,
➥ adLockUnspecified, adCmdUnspecified

    Set GetAllVideos = rs
End Function
```

20

NOTE

> By default, ADODB uses the ODBC OLE DB provider, which operates internally only with the adUseServer and adUseClientBatch options. In general, OLE DB doesn't have a standard property that ADODB can use to instruct the provider how to function. The CursorLocation property is rigged through the "back door" into the ODBC OLE DB provider.

You need to set adUseClientBatch for the CursorLocation property before creating a Recordset. First, use the Open method to create a Recordset. Note that you didn't specify any settings for CursorType, LockType, and Options; you just used default settings.

NOTE

> In the ADC 1.0 documentation, it mentions that you need to specify adLockBatchOptimistic for the LockType property so that the Recordset can use the key and time stamp fields for updating. However, this information is incorrect because the underlying OLE DB doesn't "like" the adLockBatchOptimistic option combined with ADC. If you set up adLockBatchOptimistic for the LockType property, you will get an unexpected error.

Now you can make a business object out of this function, and the client tier can use this function to get a Recordset. One thing worth mentioning repeatedly is that if you want the client tier to be able to update the Recordset, you need to use the for browse keyword in your SQL statement, as shown here:

```
select VideoTitle, Rating, Category, ReleaseDate,
➡ ReservedFlag, Description from Video_detail
➡ order by videoTitle for browse
```

With Advanced Data Connector 1.0, you can do updates only on data in SQL Server.

NOTE

> Remember to mark the business object as safe for scripting and register it under the ADCLaunch key; these procedures were explained in Chapter 19.

With this business object handy, you can create a Web page to invoke the GetAllVideos method and bind the returned result to the data-aware controls. Listing 20.1 shows the Web page.

Listing 20.1. A Web page invoking the `GetAllVideos` method.

```
 1: <TITLE>Teach Yourself Active Web Databases with VB in 21 Days</TITLE>
 2: </HEAD>
 3: <BODY LANGUAGE="VBS">
 4: <CENTER>
 5: <H1><font size=5>
➡ Teach Yourself Active Web Databases with VB in 21 Days</H1></font>
 6: <IMG SRC="video.gif" WIDTH=400 HEIGHT=100 ALT="Virtual Video Store">
 7: <HR size=2 width=80%>
 8: <H2><font size=3>Using VVStoreADOObj to Get All the Videos</H2></font>
 9: <!-- AdvancedDataSpace -->
10:     <OBJECT ID="ADS1" WIDTH=1 HEIGHT=1
11:     CLASSID="CLSID:99586D40-DB60-11CF-9D87-00AA00B91181">
12: </OBJECT>
13: <OBJECT CLASSID="clsid:9381D8F2-0288-11d0-9501-00AA00B911A5"
14:     ID=ADC1 HEIGHT=1 WIDTH = 1
15:     CODEBASE="HTTP://<%=Request.ServerVariables("Server_name")%>
➡ /ADCDownload/msadc10.cab">
16:     <PARAM NAME="BINDINGS"
➡ VALUE="Grid1;Text1.Text=description;Radio1.Value=ReservedFlag">
17: </OBJECT>
18: <BR>
19: <OBJECT ID="Grid1" WIDTH=500 HEIGHT=100
20:     CLASSID="CLSID:00028C00-0000-0000-0000-000000000046">
21: </OBJECT>
22: <BR>
23: <OBJECT CLASSID="CLSID:3B7C8860-D78F-101B-B9B5-04021C009402"
24:     ID=Text1 height=40 width=400>
25: </OBJECT>
26: <OBJECT ID="Radio1" WIDTH=100 HEIGHT=50
27:     CLASSID="CLSID:0BA686AA-F7D3-101A-993E-0000C0EF6F5E">
28:     <PARAM NAME="Caption" VALUE="Reserved">
29: </OBJECT>
30: <BR><BR>
31: <INPUT TYPE=BUTTON NAME="First" VALUE="&First" onClick="MoveFirst">
32: <INPUT TYPE=BUTTON NAME="Next" VALUE="&Next" onClick="MoveNext">
33: <INPUT TYPE=BUTTON NAME="Prev" VALUE="&Prev" onClick="MovePrev">
34: <INPUT TYPE=BUTTON NAME="Last" VALUE="&Last" onClick="MoveLast">
35: <INPUT TYPE=BUTTON NAME="GetAll" VALUE="&Get All Videos">
36: <SCRIPT LANGUAGE="VBScript">
37: Option Explicit
38: Dim myObj
39: Dim ret
40: Dim rs
41: SUB MoveFirst
42:     ADC1.MoveFirst
43: END SUB
44: SUB MoveNext
45:     ADC1.MoveNext
46: END SUB
47: SUB MovePrev
48:     ADC1.MovePrevious
49: END SUB
50: SUB MoveLast
```

continues

20

Listing 20.1. continued

```
51:        ADC1.MoveLast
52: END SUB
53: Sub GetAll_OnClick()
54:        Set rs = myObj.GetAllVideos()
55:        ADC1.Recordset = rs
56:        Grid1.Columns(4).Visible = FALSE
57:        Grid1.Columns(5).Visible = FALSE
58: End SUB
59:
60: Sub Window_OnLoad()
61:        Set myObj = ADS1.CreateObject("VVStoreADOObj.VVStoreADOObjCls",
➥ "HTTP://<%=Request.ServerVariables("Server_name")%>")
62: End Sub
63: </SCRIPT>
64: </BODY>
65: </HTML>
```

The PROGID for the business object is VVStoreADOObj.VVStoreADOObjCls. First, you create the business object proxy myObj for this business object, and then invoke the GetAllVideos method when the user clicks the Get All Videos button. The returned ADOR Recordset is bound into the Grid1, Text1, and Radio1 data-aware controls. This Web page is similar to the one in Chapter 19, but the underlying business object logic has been changed from using AdvancedDataFactory to ADODB. The client tier simply changes the reference from one business object to another one.

This example again demonstrates how the business logic is hidden from the client tier and how you can change the business object logic easily without the client tier being aware of the change. Figure 20.1 shows the result when the Get All Videos button is clicked.

Now try modifying the business object and adding the functions you learned in Chapter 19. First, add the GetAllAvailableVideos function:

```
Public Function GetAllAvailableVideos() As Object
    Dim rs As ADODB.Recordset
    Dim SQLString

    SQLString = "select VideoTitle,Rating,Category, ReleaseDate,
➥ ReservedFlag, Description from video_Detail
➥ where ReservedFlag =0 order by VideoTitle"

    Set rs = CreateObject("ADODB.Recordset")
    rs.CursorLocation = adUseClientBatch
    rs.Open SQLString, "dsn=video;uid=sa;pwd=;",
➥ adOpenUnspecified, adLockUnspecified, adCmdUnspecified

    Set GetAllAvailableVideos = rs
End Function
```

20

Figure 20.1.

Invoking the
`GetAllVideos`
method of the
`VVStoreADOObj`
business object.

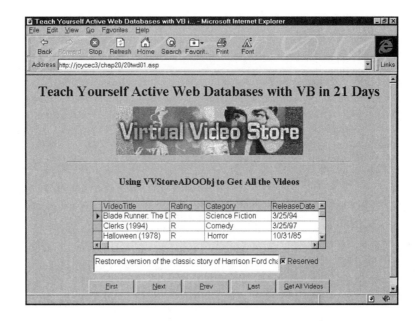

Again, instead of using `AdvancedDataFactory`, you use ADODB. You want to return the videos that haven't been reserved yet to the client tier. First, use the following SQL statement to create the `Recordset`:

```
select VideoTitle,Rating,Category, ReleaseDate, ReservedFlag,
➡ Description from video_Detail where ReservedFlag = 0
➡ order by VideoTitle
```

The rest of the code is the same as what's in the `GetAllVideos` function. Specify `adUseClientBatch` for the `CursorLocation` property and use the default values for the `CursorType` and `LockType` properties. Now take a look at the `GetReservedVideos` function:

```
Public Function GetReservedVideos(ByVal CustomerID As Integer) As Object
    Dim rs As ADODB.Recordset
    Dim SQLString

    SQLString = "select VideoTitle,Rating,Category, ReleaseDate,
➡ ReservedFlag, Description from Video_detail where ReservedID = " _
➡     & CustomerID & " order by VideoTitle"

    Set rs = CreateObject("ADODB.Recordset")
    rs.CursorLocation = adUseClientBatch
    rs.Open SQLString, "dsn=video;uid=sa;pwd=;",
➡ adOpenUnspecified, adLockUnspecified, adCmdUnspecified

    Set GetReservedVideos = rs
End Function
```

20

The `GetReservedVideos` function takes one input parameter that specifies the customer ID; the SQL statement is constructed based on this customer ID. This function returns all the videos reserved by the specified customer ID.

After adding all these new functions, you can compile the business object. Next, you're going to modify the Web page to retrieve the available and reserved videos, but this time you allow customers to pick which type of videos they want to see. Instead of using three buttons to differentiate the video type, you're going to use radio buttons so the customer can choose the video type. Take a look at the following HTML code:

```
<P>Video Type: <INPUT NAME="VideoType" TYPE=RADIO VALUE="All"
➡ onclick ="VideoTypeClick(1)">All
<INPUT NAME="VideoType" TYPE=RADIO VALUE="Available"
➡ onclick ="VideoTypeClick(2)">Available
<INPUT NAME="VideoType" TYPE=RADIO VALUE="Reserved"
➡ onclick ="VideoTypeClick(3)">Reserved
```

Three radio buttons offer choices for video types. However, because VBScript does not support radio button control arrays, you specify a sub-routine for each radio button's `OnClick` event to pass in a different value. If the customer clicks All for the video type, the value is set to 1. Later, you can use this value to indicate the method you need to invoke. The `VideoTypeClick` sub-routine looks like this:

```
Dim VType
VType=0
SUB VideoTypeClick(curvalue)
VType = curValue
END SUB
```

A global variable, `VType`, is declared to store the video type information; its value is 0. This global variable is used to provide information about the video type for other sub-routines. After the customer selects the video type and clicks the Get Videos button, a method corresponding to the type of video—All, Available, or Reserved—is invoked. Here is the sub-routine:

```
SUB GetVideos_OnClick()
    IF VType = 0 THEN
        MsgBox "Please select a video type"
        exit sub
    END IF
    IF VType = 1 THEN
        Set rs = myObj.GetAllVideos()
    ELSEIF VType = 2 THEN
        Set rs = myObj.GetAllAvailableVideos()
    ELSEIF VType = 3 AND ISEMPTY(Customer_id.value) THEN
        MsgBox
➡ "Please enter the customer ID before viewing the reserved videos"
    ELSEIF VType = 3 THEN
        Set rs = myObj.GetReservedVideos(Customer_id.value)
    END IF

    ADC1.Recordset = rs
```

```
      ADC1.Refresh
      Grid1.Columns(4).Visible = FALSE
      Grid1.Columns(5).Visible = FALSE
End SUB
```

If the VType is 0, that means the customer hasn't chosen any video type, so you inform the customer of that with a message box that says Please select a video type. When the VType variable is 1, you invoke the GetAllVideos method; when it's 2, you invoke the GetAllAvailableVideos. Since the GetReservedVideos method expects one input parameter, you need to make sure that the Customer_id input field isn't empty. If the Customer_id field isn't empty, you invoke the GetReservedVideos method and pass the value of the Customer_id field to it. Your new modified Web page is ready; the complete code for it is in Listing 20.2.

Listing 20.2. A Web page that includes radio buttons for choosing the type of video.

```
 1: <TITLE>Teach Yourself Active Web Databases with VB in 21 Days</TITLE>
 2: </HEAD>
 3: <BODY LANGUAGE="VBS">
 4: <CENTER>
 5: <H1><font size=5>
➡ Teach Yourself Active Web Databases with VB in 21 Days</H1></font>
 6: <IMG SRC="video.gif" WIDTH=400 HEIGHT=100 ALT="Virtual Video Store">
 7: <HR size=2 width=80%>
 8: <P><font size=3>Using VVStoreADOObj to Get Videos by Type</P></font>
 9: <font size=2>Customer ID: <INPUT NAME="customer_id" SIZE="20">
10:
11: <P>Video Type: <INPUT NAME="VideoType" TYPE=RADIO VALUE="All" onclick
➡ ="VideoTypeClick(1)">All
12: <INPUT NAME="VideoType" TYPE=RADIO VALUE="Available" onclick
➡ ="VideoTypeClick(2)">Available
13: <INPUT NAME="VideoType" TYPE=RADIO VALUE="Reserved"
➡ onclick ="VideoTypeClick(3)">Reserved
14: <P></font>
15:
16: <!-- AdvancedDataSpace -->
17:     <OBJECT ID="ADS1" WIDTH=1 HEIGHT=1
18:     CLASSID="CLSID:99586D40-DB60-11CF-9D87-00AA00B91181">
19: </OBJECT>
20: <OBJECT CLASSID="clsid:9381D8F2-0288-11d0-9501-00AA00B911A5"
21:     ID=ADC1 HEIGHT=1 WIDTH = 1
22:     CODEBASE="HTTP://<%=Request.ServerVariables("Server_name")%>
➡ /ADCDownload/msadc10.cab">
23:     <PARAM NAME="BINDINGS"
➡ VALUE="Grid1;Text1.Text=description;Radio1.Value=ReservedFlag">
24: </OBJECT>
25: <BR>
26: <OBJECT ID="Grid1" WIDTH=500 HEIGHT=100
27:     CLASSID="CLSID:00028C00-0000-0000-0000-000000000046">
28: </OBJECT>
29: <BR>
```

20

continues

Listing 20.2. continued

```
30: <OBJECT CLASSID="CLSID:3B7C8860-D78F-101B-B9B5-04021C009402"
31:     ID=Text1 height=40 width=400>
32: </OBJECT>
33: <OBJECT ID="Radio1" WIDTH=100 HEIGHT=50
34:     CLASSID="CLSID:0BA686AA-F7D3-101A-993E-0000C0EF6F5E">
35:     <PARAM NAME="Caption" VALUE="Reserved">
36: </OBJECT>
37: <BR><BR>
38: <INPUT TYPE=BUTTON NAME="First" VALUE="&First" onClick="MoveFirst">
39: <INPUT TYPE=BUTTON NAME="Next" VALUE="&Next" onClick="MoveNext">
40: <INPUT TYPE=BUTTON NAME="Prev" VALUE="&Prev" onClick="MovePrev">
41: <INPUT TYPE=BUTTON NAME="Last" VALUE="&Last" onClick="MoveLast">
42: <INPUT TYPE=BUTTON NAME="GetVideos" VALUE="&Get Videos">
43: <SCRIPT LANGUAGE="VBScript">
44: Option Explicit
45: Dim myObj
46: Dim ret
47: Dim rs
48: Dim VType
49: VType=0
50: SUB VideoTypeClick(curvalue)
51: VType = curValue
52: END SUB
53: SUB MoveFirst
54:     ADC1.MoveFirst
55: END SUB
56: SUB MoveNext
57:     ADC1.MoveNext
58: END SUB
59: SUB MovePrev
60:     ADC1.MovePrevious
61: END SUB
62: SUB MoveLast
63:     ADC1.MoveLast
64: END SUB
65: SUB GetVideos_OnClick()
66:     IF VType = 0 THEN
67:         MsgBox "Please select a video type"
68:         exit sub
69:     END IF
70:     IF VType = 1 THEN
71:         Set rs = myObj.GetAllVideos()
72:     ELSEIF VType = 2 THEN
73:         Set rs = myObj.GetAllAvailableVideos()
74:     ELSEIF VType = 3 AND (customer_id.value="") THEN
75:         MsgBox
➡ "Please enter the customer ID before viewing the reserved videos"
76:     ELSEIF VType = 3 THEN
77:         Set rs = myObj.GetReservedVideos(Customer_id.value)
78:     END IF
79:
80:     IF NOT ISEMPTY(rs) THEN
81:         ADC1.Recordset = rs
82:         ADC1.Refresh
```

20

```
83:         Grid1.Columns(4).Visible = FALSE
84:         Grid1.Columns(5).Visible = FALSE
85:      END IF
86: End SUB
87:
88: Sub Window_OnLoad()
89:      Set myObj = ADS1.CreateObject("VVStoreADOObj.VVStoreADOObjCls",
➥ "HTTP://<%=Request.ServerVariables("Server_name")%>")
90: End Sub
91: </SCRIPT>
92: </BODY>
93: </HTML>
```

In this code, an input field is added to accept the customer ID entered by the customer, and both the VideoTypeClick and GetVideosOnClick sub-routines were added. Figure 20.2 shows the message box displayed if the customer doesn't choose a video type.

Figure 20.2.

The message box displayed if the video type isn't selected.

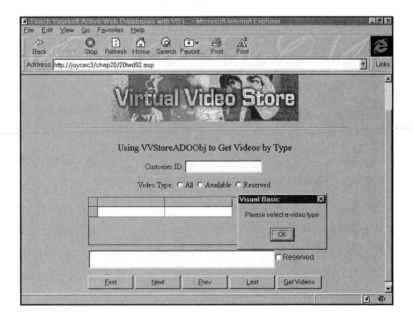

Figure 20.3 shows the result of choosing All as the video type and clicking the Get Videos button. As you can see, both the reserved and available videos are showing up in the grid control.

In Figure 20.4, the customer chose Available as the video type before clicking the Get Videos button. As you can see, only the available videos are showing up in the grid control.

Figure 20.3.

Choosing to get all the videos.

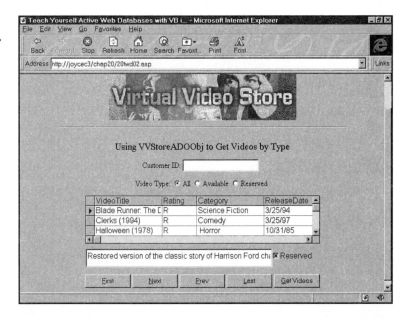

Figure 20.4.

Choosing to get just the available videos.

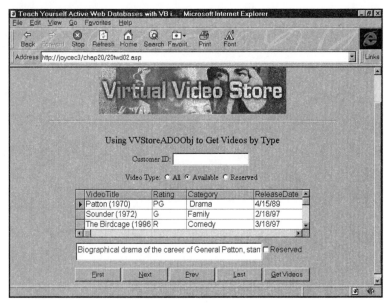

Figure 20.5 shows the result of choosing Reserved as the video type and clicking the Get Videos button without entering the customer ID. A message box informs the customer that a customer ID is required.

Figure 20.5.

The message box displayed when a customer ID isn't entered.

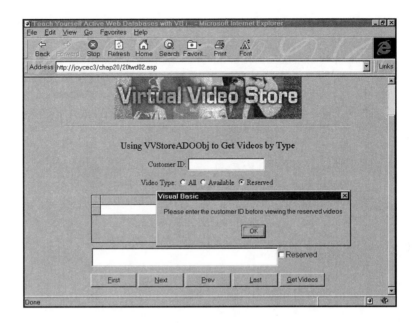

In Figure 20.6, the customer has entered the customer ID, chosen Reserved as the video type, and clicked the Get Videos button. As you can see, only the videos that have been reserved by the specified customer are showing up in the grid control.

Figure 20.6.

Choosing to get the reserved videos.

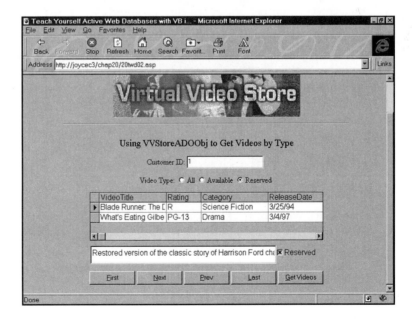

20

So far, you have successfully used ADODB to implement a business object and passed the ADOR Recordset to the client tier. As you might have noticed, none of the SQL statements you have used have the for browse keyword, which means you're not allowing any updates in the DBGrid control. With all the knowledge you have gained, you're probably anxious to allow the client tier to modify the data in the DBGrid control, as you learned to do Chapter 18, "Data Validation." Without update capability, these business objects are just retrieving data from the database server, which makes them a little boring.

Passing the ADOR Recordset from the Client to the Application Server

For the client tier to modify the data, you need to add the for browse keyword to the SQL statement in the business object. The GetAllVideos function you have been using so far can be modified as follows:

```
Public Function GetAllVideos() As Object
    Dim rs As ADODB.Recordset
    Set rs = CreateObject("ADODB.Recordset")

    SQLString = "select VideoTitle,Rating,Category, ReleaseDate,
➥ ReservedFlag, Description from Video_detail
➥ order by VideoTitle for browse"

    rs.CursorLocation = adUseClientBatch
    rs.Open SQLString, "dsn=video;uid=sa;pwd=;", adOpenUnspecified,
➥ adLockUnspecified, adCmdUnspecified

    Set GetAllVideos = rs
End Function
```

Simple enough—but what about the HTML code in the client tier? The preceding modified code just means you can now change data in the DBGrid and Radio Button data-aware controls. How are you going to marshal the ADOR Recordset back to the business object? And what kind of record are you going to marshal back to the application server?

Creating a Function to Marshal the Recordset to the Business Object

First, you need to create a function in your business object to accept the Recordset from the client tier. This function is named SetData, and its code is as follows:

```
Public Function SetData(rso As Object)
'function that get the recordset from the client tier
' and apply the changed data to the application server
End Function
```

This function accepts one input parameter that's a Recordset marshaled from the client tier. Now you can invoke this function in the client tier. But are you marshaling the whole Recordset from the client tier to the business object or just the changed record?

Marshaling the Changed Recordset to the Business Object

Ideally, you want to marshal only the changed record to the business object. When you marshal the Recordset from the business object to the client tier, there's no doubt you need to marshal the complete Recordset based on the SQL statement. However, when you marshal the Recordset from the client tier to the business object, normally, you don't really care about the unchanged records.

The purpose of marshaling data back to the business object is so that you can apply the changed data to the database server and maybe do some data validation in the business object before applying the data to the database server. You have many reasons to do something with the changed data, but in general, the unchanged data isn't important. So, to enhance the performance, marshal only the changed records to the business object to reduce the traffic and speed up the process.

 NOTE Whether you want to marshal the whole Recordset or only the changed record really depends on your business logic. The trade-off is that the speed of marshaling a smaller set of records is obviously faster than marshaling a larger set.

How do you tell the Recordset you're going to marshal only the changed data? With the MarshalOptions property, one of the properties of the ADOR Recordset. There are two options for this property: adMarshalModifiedOnly and adMarshalAll. The adMarshalModifiedOnly option tells the Recordset to marshal only the changed records, and the adMarshalAll option allows you to marshal the complete Recordset.

The HTML code doesn't understand adMarshalModifiedOnly and adMarshalAll options, so you need to specify their actual values; the value for adMarshalModifiedOnly is 1, and it's 0 for the adMarshalAll option. Here's how you specify MarshalOptions in the client tier:

```
set rso = Adc1.Recordset
rso.MarshalOptions=1
myObj.SetData rso
```

20

Reconnecting in the Business Object

The client tier marshals the changed records to the business object, and it's up to the business object to apply the changes to the database server. Your business object has the Recordset with the changed records, how are you going to apply the changed Recordset to the database server? Perhaps you're going to have to compare the record against the database server and apply the change yourself? If you do, how are you going to know what kind of SQL statement was used for this Recordset? It will be a huge headache if you need to keep track of all this information.

The answer to all these questions is proof that Advanced Data Connector is slick technology. The Advanced Data Connector architecture allows you to reconnect to the marshaled ADODB Recordset and apply all the changed records to the database server. Remember you set the adUseClientBatch option for the CursorLocation. One of the reasons for doing this is to allow the Recordset to function in a disconnected fashion, and then later be reconnected. Reconnecting means you can preserve all the Recordset's time stamp information and use it to apply the update. Here's how to reconnect to the marshaled Recordset:

```
Public Function SetData(rso As Object)
Dim rs As New ADODB.Recordset

rs.Open rso, "dsn=Video;uid=sa;pwd=;"
rs.UpdateBatch

End Function
```

First, you create a reference to the ADODB Recordset, as usual. The tricky part is that when you use the Open method, you want to use the marshaled Recordset as the first parameter instead of using a SQL statement; this allows reconnection to the Recordset. After you reconnect to the Recordset, you can call one of the ADODB methods, UpdateBatch, to apply all the changes to the database server. The reconnect capability and the UpdateBatch method take care of all the headaches for you. You don't have to worry about comparing the changed record to the original record and carefully applying only the changed columns or rows. All this is taken care of behind the scenes.

In the next example, you're going to let the customer reserve a video and use the SetData function to apply the reservation to the database server.

The Complete Example

You need to add one more sub-routine to the business object: SetData(). You also need to change the SQL statement for the GetAllAvailableVideos function to allow the user to reserve the videos. The GetAllVideos function is still just for browsing, not updating. Here's the SetData function:

```
Public Function SetData(rso As Object)
Dim rs As New ADODB.Recordset

rs.Open rso, "dsn=video;uid=sa;pwd=;"
rs.UpdateBatch

End Function
```

This is the GetAllAvailableVideos function:

```
Public Function GetAllAvailableVideos() As Object
    Dim rs As ADODB.Recordset
    Dim SQLString

    SQLString = "select VideoTitle,Rating,Category, ReleaseDate,
➥ ReservedFlag, Description from video_Detail where ReservedFlag =0
➥ order by VideoTitle  for browse"

    Set rs = CreateObject("ADODB.Recordset")
    rs.CursorLocation = adUseClientBatch
    rs.Open SQLString, "dsn=video;uid=sa;pwd=;", adOpenUnspecified,
➥ adLockUnspecified, adCmdUnspecified

    Set GetAllAvailableVideos = rs
End Function
```

For the client tier Web page, you're going to add a button to invoke the SetData function. Listing 20.3 gives you the complete HTML code.

Listing 20.3. A Web page with the SetData and GetAllAvailableVideos functions.

```
 1: <TITLE>Teach Yourself Active Web Databases with VB in 21 Days</TITLE>
 2: </HEAD>
 3: <BODY LANGUAGE="VBS">
 4: <CENTER>
 5: <H1><font size=5>
➥ Teach Yourself Active Web Databases with VB in 21 Days</H1></font>
 6: <IMG SRC="video.gif" WIDTH=400 HEIGHT=100 ALT="Virtual Video Store">
 7: <HR size=2 width=80%>
 8: <P><font size=3>Using VVStoreADOObj to Reserve Videos</P></font>
 9: <font size =2>Customer ID: <INPUT NAME="customer_id" SIZE="20">
10:
11: <P>Video Type: <INPUT NAME="VideoType" TYPE=RADIO VALUE="All"
➥ onclick ="VideoTypeClick(1)">All
12: <INPUT NAME="VideoType" TYPE=RADIO VALUE="Available"
➥ onclick ="VideoTypeClick(2)">Available
13: <INPUT NAME="VideoType" TYPE=RADIO VALUE="Reserved"
➥ onclick ="VideoTypeClick(3)">Reserved
14: <P></font>
15:
16: <!-- AdvancedDataSpace -->
17:     <OBJECT ID="ADS1" WIDTH=1 HEIGHT=1
18:     CLASSID="CLSID:99586D40-DB60-11CF-9D87-00AA00B91181">
```

20

continues

Listing 20.3. continued

```
19: </OBJECT>
20: <OBJECT CLASSID="clsid:9381D8F2-0288-11d0-9501-00AA00B911A5"
21:        ID=ADC1 HEIGHT=1 WIDTH = 1
22:        CODEBASE="HTTP://<%=Request.ServerVariables("Server_name")%>
➥ /ADCDownload/msadc10.cab">
23:        <PARAM NAME="BINDINGS"
➥ VALUE="Grid1;Text1.Text=description;Radio1.Value=ReservedFlag">
24: </OBJECT>
25: <BR>
26: <OBJECT ID="Grid1" WIDTH=500 HEIGHT=100
27:        CLASSID="CLSID:00028C00-0000-0000-0000-000000000046">
28: </OBJECT>
29: <BR>
30: <OBJECT CLASSID="CLSID:3B7C8860-D78F-101B-B9B5-04021C009402"
31:        ID=Text1 height=40 width=400>
32: </OBJECT>
33: <OBJECT ID="Radio1" WIDTH=100 HEIGHT=50
34:        CLASSID="CLSID:0BA686AA-F7D3-101A-993E-0000C0EF6F5E">
35:        <PARAM NAME="Caption" VALUE="Reserved">
36: </OBJECT>
37: <BR><BR>
38: <INPUT TYPE=BUTTON NAME="First" VALUE="&First" onClick="MoveFirst">
39: <INPUT TYPE=BUTTON NAME="Next" VALUE="&Next" onClick="MoveNext">
40: <INPUT TYPE=BUTTON NAME="Prev" VALUE="&Prev" onClick="MovePrev">
41: <INPUT TYPE=BUTTON NAME="Last" VALUE="&Last" onClick="MoveLast">
42: <INPUT TYPE=BUTTON NAME="GetVideos" VALUE="&Get Videos">
43: <INPUT TYPE=BUTTON NAME="Update" VALUE="&Update" >
44: <SCRIPT LANGUAGE="VBScript">
45: Option Explicit
46: Dim myObj
47: Dim ret
48: Dim rs
49: Dim VType
50: VType=0
51: Dim rso
52:
53: SUB VideoTypeClick(curvalue)
54: VType = curValue
55: END SUB
56: SUB MoveFirst
57:        ADC1.MoveFirst
58: END SUB
59: SUB MoveNext
60:        ADC1.MoveNext
61: END SUB
62: SUB MovePrev
63:        ADC1.MovePrevious
64: END SUB
65: SUB MoveLast
66:        ADC1.MoveLast
67: END SUB
68: SUB GetVideos_OnClick()
69:        IF VType = 0 THEN
70:            MsgBox "Please select a video type"
```

```
71:         exit sub
72:     END IF
73:     IF VType = 1 THEN
74:         Set rs = myObj.GetAllVideos()
75:     ELSEIF VType = 2 THEN
76:         Set rs = myObj.GetAllAvailableVideos()
77:         ELSEIF VType = 3 AND (ISEMPTY(Customer_id.value)
➡ OR Customer_id.value ="") THEN
78: MsgBox "Please enter the customer ID before viewing the reserved videos"
79:     ELSEIF VType = 3 THEN
80:         Set rs = myObj.GetReservedVideos(Customer_id.value)
81:     END IF
82:
83:     ADC1.Recordset = rs
84:     ADC1.Refresh
85:     Grid1.Columns(4).Visible = FALSE
86:     Grid1.Columns(5).Visible = FALSE
87: End SUB
88:
89: SUB Update_OnClick()
90:     set rso = ADC1.Recordset
91:     IF (VType =2 or VType=3) AND NOT ISEMPTY(rso) THEN
92:         ADC1.MoveFirst
93:         ADC1.MoveLast
94:         rso.MarshalOptions=1
95:         myObj.SetData rso
96:         GetVideos_OnClick
97:     END IF
98: End SUB
99:
100: Sub Window_OnLoad()
101:     Set myObj = ADS1.CreateObject("VVStoreADOObj.VVStoreADOObjCls",
➡ "HTTP://<%=Request.ServerVariables("Server_name")%>")
102: End Sub
103: </SCRIPT>
104: </BODY>
105: </HTML>
```

A sub-routine is added to invoke the SetData function once the user checks the Reserved checkbox and clicks the Update button. Check to see whether the video type is Available or Reserved and whether the Recordset is empty before you invoke the SetData function. You call AdvancedDataControl's MoveFirst and MoveNext methods to make sure the change in the radio button applies to the Recordset. Next, you set 1 for the MarshalOption property to indicate you want to marshal only the changed records. You then invoke the SetData method and pass the changed Recordset as the input parameter for the method. After the changed Recordset is applied to the database server, you need to refresh the Recordset of the AdvancedDataControl object, so call the GetVideos_OnClick sub-routine to get the videos for the selected video type.

Figure 20.7 shows you the available videos. The Reserved 3D radio button is checked for the first video in the DBGrid control.

20

Figure 20.7.

Reserving videos.

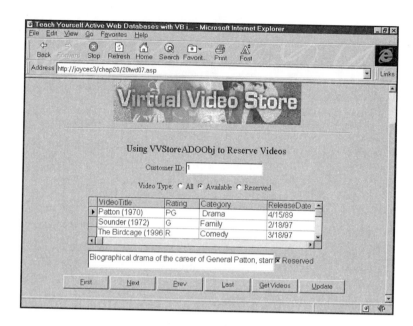

Figure 20.8 shows you the result after you click the Update button to reserve the first video. The videos you saw earlier no longer appear in the DBGrid control.

Figure 20.8.

After clicking the Update button.

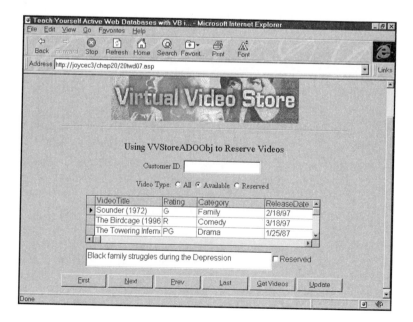

20

Notice how easy it is for you to change the data in the client tier and use the UpdateBatch method in the business object to apply the changes. Here's a review of the steps you went through to do that:

1. Set the adUseClientBatch option for the CursorLocation property before you marshal the Recordset to the client tier.

2. Set MarshalOptions to indicate whether you're marshaling a complete or modified Recordset before marshaling it to the business object.

3. Reconnect to the Recordset and use the UpdateBatch method to apply the changes to the database server.

Wow—all you need are three simple steps, and no more headaches over making a disconnected Recordset work, taking care of reconnecting an active connection, and making sure the data is accurately applied to the database server.

The next task is doing more data manipulation in the business object. For example, when customers reserve videos, you want to associate the video with the customer ID so that customers can view their reserved videos. Why not simply modify the information in the client tier? Well, your overall goal is to separate the business logic from the client tier. You want to protect the data and business rules and not let the client tier know about the business logic. Furthermore, in the Advanced Data Connector, you can't modify the Recordset except in the data-aware bound controls.

In the SetData function, you're reconnecting to the Recordset by using the ADODB Recordset, and you're using UpdateBatch to apply the changed records. Before you issue the UpdateBatch method, you can use the ADODB Recordset method to scan through the record and change the data any way you want to. Here's the SetData function that puts the customer ID information in the changed records:

```
Public Function SetData(rso As Object, ByVal CID As Integer)
Dim rs As New ADODB.Recordset

rs.Open rso, "dsn=video;uid=sa;pwd=;"
rs.MoveFirst
While Not rs.EOF
If rs("ReservedFlag") <> 0 Then
    rs("ReservedID") = Str(CID)
Else
    rs("ReservedID") = Str(-1)
End If
rs.MoveNext
Wend

rs.UpdateBatch

End Function
```

20

The SetData function accepts two input parameters: the changed Recordset, and the customer ID you apply to the changed records. Once you reconnect to the changed Recordset, scan through it. If the ReservedFlag is not equal to 0, which means the customer has reserved the video, modify the ReservedID column and change it to the specified customer ID. If the ReservedFlag *is* equal to 0, which means the customer has "unreserved" the video, modify the ReservedID column and change it to -1, meaning this video is now available.

Modifying the data in the business object also ensures the data's security. Even if some hackers change the data you want to protect, you can always validate it and make the proper changes.

NOTE

> You can't modify any of the index key columns. The UpdateBatch method relies on the index key columns to actually apply the changes. You will get an unexpected error if you try to modify the Recordset's index key columns.

Before you move on to the Web page, you need to make some changes to the GetAllAvailableVideos and GetReservedVideos functions. First, include the ReservedID column in the SQL statement for both functions. Second, add the for browse keyword to the GetReservedVideos function so the customer can unreserve a video. Here are the modified versions of the GetAllAvailableVideos and GetReservedVideos functions:

```
Public Function GetAllAvailableVideos() As Object
    Dim rs As ADODB.Recordset
    Dim SQLString

    SQLString = "select VideoTitle,Rating,Category, ReleaseDate,
➡ ReservedFlag, Description,ReservedID from video_Detail
➡ where ReservedFlag =0 order by VideoTitle  for browse"

    Set rs = CreateObject("ADODB.Recordset")
    rs.CursorLocation = adUseClientBatch
    rs.Open SQLString, "dsn=video;uid=sa;pwd=;", adOpenUnspecified,
➡ adLockUnspecified, adCmdUnspecified

    Set GetAllAvailableVideos = rs
End Function

Public Function GetReservedVideos(ByVal CustomerID As Integer) As Object
    Dim rs As ADODB.Recordset
    Dim SQLString

    SQLString = "select VideoTitle,Rating,Category, ReleaseDate, ReservedFlag,
➡ Description,ReservedID from Video_detail where ReservedID = " _
    & CustomerID & " order by VideoTitle  for browse"

    Set rs = CreateObject("ADODB.Recordset")
```

20

```
        rs.CursorLocation = adUseClientBatch
        rs.Open SQLString, "dsn=video;uid=sa;pwd=;", adOpenUnspecified,
➡ adLockUnspecified, adCmdUnspecified

        Set GetReservedVideos = rs
End Function
```

In the Web page, you need to pass in one more parameter for the SetData method and make sure the customer ID is entered before invoking the SetData function. Here's the modified Update_OnClick sub-routine:

```
SUB Update_OnClick()
        set rso = ADC1.Recordset
        IF ISEMPTY(Customer_id.value) THEN
            MsgBox "Please enter the customer ID before reserving videos"
            EXIT SUB
        END IF
        IF (VType =2 or VType=3) AND NOT ISEMPTY(rso) THEN
            ADC1.MoveFirst
            ADC1.MoveLast
            rso.MarshalOptions=1
            myObj.SetData rso, Customer_id.value
            GetVideos_OnClick
        END IF
End SUB
```

If the customer ID is empty, a message box asks the customer to enter an ID and exit the sub-routine. If the customer ID is entered, you use the same basic steps as in the last example, except you pass the customer ID as the second parameter for the SetData method. Since the SQL statements in the business object have one more column now, you also need to hide the column in the grid control for the ReservedID. Listing 20.4 gives you the complete HTML code.

Listing 20.4. A Web page with a request for the customer ID.

```
 1: <TITLE>Teach Yourself Active Web Databases with VB in 21 Days</TITLE>
 2: </HEAD>
 3: <BODY LANGUAGE="VBS">
 4: <CENTER>
 5: <H1><font size=5>
➡ Teach Yourself Active Web Databases with VB in 21 Days</H1></font>
 6: <IMG SRC="video.gif" WIDTH=400 HEIGHT=100 ALT="Virtual Video Store">
 7: <HR size=2 width=80%>
 8: <P><font size=3>Using VVStoreADOObj to Reserve Videos</P></font>
 9: <font size =2>Customer ID: <INPUT NAME="customer_id" SIZE="20">
10:
11: <P>Video Type: <INPUT NAME="VideoType" TYPE=RADIO VALUE="All" onclick
➡ ="VideoTypeClick(1)">All
12: <INPUT NAME="VideoType" TYPE=RADIO VALUE="Available" onclick
➡ ="VideoTypeClick(2)">Available
13: <INPUT NAME="VideoType" TYPE=RADIO VALUE="Reserved"
➡ onclick ="VideoTypeClick(3)">Reserved
```

20

continues

Listing 20.4. continued

```
14: <P></font>
15:
16: <!-- AdvancedDataSpace -->
17:       <OBJECT ID="ADS1" WIDTH=1 HEIGHT=1
18:       CLASSID="CLSID:99586D40-DB60-11CF-9D87-00AA00B91181">
19: </OBJECT>
20: <OBJECT CLASSID="clsid:9381D8F2-0288-11d0-9501-00AA00B911A5"
21:       ID=ADC1 HEIGHT=1 WIDTH = 1
22:       CODEBASE="HTTP://<%=Request.ServerVariables("Server_name")%>
➥ /ADCDownload/msadc10.cab">
23:       <PARAM NAME="BINDINGS"
➥ VALUE="Grid1;Text1.Text=description;Radio1.Value=ReservedFlag">
24: </OBJECT>
25: <BR>
26: <OBJECT ID="Grid1" WIDTH=500 HEIGHT=100
27:       CLASSID="CLSID:00028C00-0000-0000-0000-000000000046">
28: </OBJECT>
29: <BR>
30: <OBJECT CLASSID="CLSID:3B7C8860-D78F-101B-B9B5-04021C009402"
31:       ID=Text1 height=40 width=400>
32: </OBJECT>
33: <OBJECT ID="Radio1" WIDTH=100 HEIGHT=50
34:       CLASSID="CLSID:0BA686AA-F7D3-101A-993E-0000C0EF6F5E">
35:       <PARAM NAME="Caption" VALUE="Reserved">
36: </OBJECT>
37: <BR><BR>
38: <INPUT TYPE=BUTTON NAME="First" VALUE="&First" onClick="MoveFirst">
39: <INPUT TYPE=BUTTON NAME="Next" VALUE="&Next" onClick="MoveNext">
40: <INPUT TYPE=BUTTON NAME="Prev" VALUE="&Prev" onClick="MovePrev">
41: <INPUT TYPE=BUTTON NAME="Last" VALUE="&Last" onClick="MoveLast">
42: <INPUT TYPE=BUTTON NAME="GetVideos" VALUE="&Get Videos">
43: <INPUT TYPE=BUTTON NAME="Update" VALUE="&Update" >
44: <SCRIPT LANGUAGE="VBScript">
45: Option Explicit
46: Dim myObj
47: Dim ret
48: Dim rs
49: Dim VType
50: VType=0
51: Dim rso
52:
53: SUB VideoTypeClick(curvalue)
54: VType = curValue
55: END SUB
56: SUB MoveFirst
57:       ADC1.MoveFirst
58: END SUB
59: SUB MoveNext
60:       ADC1.MoveNext
61: END SUB
62: SUB MovePrev
63:       ADC1.MovePrevious
64: END SUB
65: SUB MoveLast
66:       ADC1.MoveLast
```

```
67: END SUB
68: SUB GetVideos_OnClick()
69:     IF VType = 0 THEN
70:         MsgBox "Please select a video type"
71:         exit sub
72:     END IF
73:     IF VType = 1 THEN
74:         Set rs = myObj.GetAllVideos()
75:     ELSEIF VType = 2 THEN
76:         Set rs = myObj.GetAllAvailableVideos()
77:      ELSEIF VType = 3 AND (ISEMPTY(Customer_id.value)
➥ OR Customer_id.value ="") THEN
78:         MsgBox
➥ "Please enter the customer ID before viewing the reserved videos"
79:     ELSEIF VType = 3 THEN
80:         Set rs = myObj.GetReservedVideos(Customer_id.value)
81:     END IF
82:
83:     ADC1.Recordset = rs
84:     ADC1.Refresh
85:     Grid1.Columns(4).Visible = FALSE
86:     Grid1.Columns(5).Visible = FALSE
87: End SUB
88:
89: SUB Update_OnClick()
90:     set rso = ADC1.Recordset
91:     IF (VType =2 or VType=3) AND NOT ISEMPTY(rso) THEN
92:         ADC1.MoveFirst
93:         ADC1.MoveLast
94:         rso.MarshalOptions=1
95:         myObj.SetData rso
96:         GetVideos_OnClick
97:     END IF
98: End SUB
99:
100: Sub Window_OnLoad()
101:     Set myObj = ADS1.CreateObject("VVStoreADOObj.VVStoreADOObjCls",
➥ "HTTP://<%=Request.ServerVariables("Server_name")%>")
102: End Sub
103: </SCRIPT>
104: </BODY>
105: </HTML>
```

20

Besides the changes to the Update_OnClick sub-routine, you have also modified the GetVideos_OnClick sub-routine to hide the ReservedID column. You hide the sixth column of the resulting Recordset if the video type is Available or Reserved because you're adding only the ReservedID column to the GetAllAvailableVideo and GetReservedVideos methods.

You might be wondering whether users can trick the system by changing the ReservedID, but this is taken care of in the SetData function. No matter what kind of information is entered in the ReservedID column, you can override it in the SetData function, so the ReservedID data is protected. Once again, data validation is one of the reasons you want to use business objects.

Figure 20.9 shows you the available videos. The Reserved 3D radio button is checked for the first video in the DBGrid control.

In Figure 20.10, the customer has clicked the Update button to reserve the first video. The videos you saw in Figure 20.9 no longer appear in the DBGrid control.

Figure 20.9.

Reserving videos by customer ID.

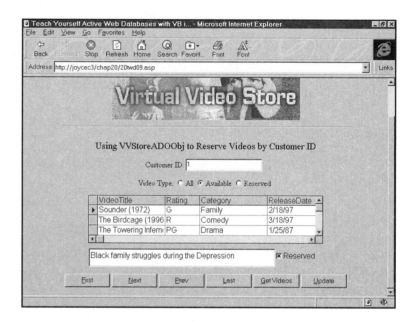

Figure 20.10.

After clicking the Update button, the available videos are displayed for that customer ID.

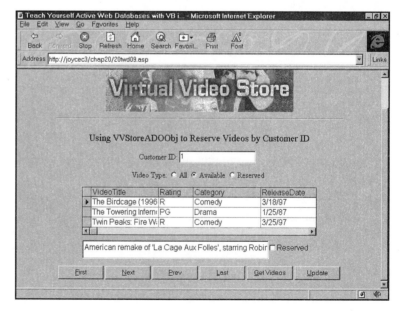

In Figure 20.11, the customer has changed the video type to Reserved and clicked the Get Videos button. For the video just reserved, the specified customer ID has shown up in the DBGrid control.

Figure 20.11.

Viewing the reserved videos.

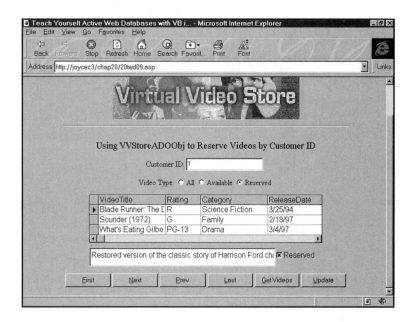

You have successfully changed the record in the business object without too much programming involved. The Advanced Data Connector architecture has made your Web database programming much easier and far more powerful.

Using ADC in Visual Basic

So far this week, you have been using Advanced Data Connector components in the Web page. You might be wondering whether you can use the Advanced Data Connector components within Visual Basic? The answer is yes.

You can use an `AdvancedDataSpace` object to create a client-tier business object proxy that references a business object in the application server through HTTP. The following code demonstrates how to do that:

```
Dim rs As Object
    Dim adf As Object
    Dim ads As Object

    Set ads = CreateObject("AdvancedDataSpace")
    Set adf = ads.CreateObject("AdvancedDataFactory", "http://IISServerName")
```

```
Set rs = adf.query("DSN=pubs;UID=sa;PWD=", "select au_lname from authors")
While Not rs.EOF
    Print rs!au_lname
    rs.MoveNext
Wend
```

The variable ads is used to reference the AdvancedDataSpace object, and the CreateObject method creates a business proxy. The location of the business object is in the application server http://IISServerName. After you create the business object proxy, then you can use AdvancedDataFactory's Query method to return a Recordset. This method certainly opens up a new way for Visual Basic applications to reference a remote business object through HTTP. For all the business objects you have created earlier, you can use this same method to access them through Visual Basic. HTTP access is no longer limited to HTML code.

NOTE

Remember to check the reference for the Advanced Data Connector object library in your Visual Basic project so that the ADC components are available to your project. To do this, choose Project | Reference to bring up the Reference window. Scroll down the list and select AdvancedDataSource Type Library and AdvancedDataSource Type Library. These two libraries have the same name, but different file-names: One is MSADCC10.DLL and the other is MSADCB10.DLL.

Note that with Advanced Data Connector 1.0, you can't use the AdvancedDataControl object to bind the Recordset to the Visual Basic data-aware controls. You will get a method not supported error.

Distributed Component Object Model (DCOM)

In an intranet situation, you can access business objects without using HTTP. Your business objects might be in a remote NT server, so you can use DCOM to access them without going through HTTP. Basically, you can use DCOM to marshal the methods and parameters across the network.

When DCOM is used instead of COM, proxies and stubs replace HTTP, the business object proxy, and ADISAPI components. The MIME format, discussed in Chapter 16, "Using the AdvancedDataControl Object," no longer applies to DCOM. Its marshaling code has been implemented in such a way that the methods and parameters are transported in the native DCE/NDR (Distributed Computing Environment/Network Data Representation) format.

The way to use DCOM is by specifying the `ServerName` instead of `http://servername/` in the `CreateObject` method. `ServerName` uses `CoCreateInstanceEx` to create a DCOM proxy for the specified object on the server.

NOTE
You can access business objects in DLL format through DCOM. First, you need to set up the Microsoft Transaction Server. When it's processing objects, it maintains the business object's state across multiple client calls. In this situation, the `AdvancedDataSpace` in the client tier is replaced by the Microsoft Transaction Server's `Transaction Context` object.

Summary

Today you have learned about one of Advanced Data Connector's most important features: disconnected `Recordsets`. They allow the client tier to modify the `Recordset` and marshal the changed records back to the application server. The application server can then reconnect to the `Recordset` and apply changes to the database server. You have seen examples of how to validate changed data in the business object and apply the changes to the database server, and you have learned how to use Advanced Data Connector components in Visual Basic. Tomorrow, you're going to use what you have learned this week to create a complete example.

Q&A

Q Why do I get a `login failed` error?

A You probably didn't use a system ODBC DSN or check the Trusted Connection option in your ODBC DSN, or perhaps the user ID or password you used isn't valid.

Q Every time I recompile my business object and try to make the DLL, it gives me a `permission denied` error. Why?

A What you're encountering is a caching feature of IIS. IIS loads DLLs (such as your custom business object) and holds onto them long after you have navigated to another page. There's no way to flush this DLL cache. Even though your business object instance is released after the method returns, the DLL for the object is still loaded in memory, which makes it impossible to overwrite/recompile.

So before you recompile the business object, you need to stop the IIS service to release the business object and restart it again.

20

Quiz

1. What do you need to do to marshal an ADODB `Recordset` from the application server to the client tier?

2. How do you marshal the complete `Recordset`?

3. What do you need to do to marshal just the modified records?

4. Can you modify the ADOR `Recordset` in the client tier without using data-bound VB controls?

5. Can you use the `for browse` keyword with an Access database?

6. Do you need to specify `adLockBatchOptimistic` for the lock type?

Exercise

Create a Web page that allows customers to register their personal information and get customer IDs. Tie this Web page to the example you used in this chapter so that the customer ID doesn't have to be to predefined.

Day **21**

Interactive Web Application: The Virtual Library

by Joyce Chia-Hsun Chen

Today, you're going to use what you've learned this week to build an online virtual library that lets a Web user register and become a member of the virtual library. You will also build a search engine for the library's books. After a member locates a book, he or she can reserve the book and check it out later.

After this chapter, you will know how to do the following:

- ☐ How to use Advanced Data Connector components to create a search engine.
- ☐ How to validate data in the business object.
- ☐ How to apply changes.

Before you start the example, here is the required software for building the example:

Microsoft Windows NT Server 4.0 with Service Pack 2

Microsoft SQL Server 6.5 with Service Pack 2

Microsoft Internet Information Server 3.0 with Active Server Pages

Microsoft Advanced Data Connector 1.0

Microsoft OLE DB SDK 1.1

Microsoft ActiveX Data Objects 1.0

Visual Basic 4.0 or 5.0

NOTE   To run the examples in this chapter, please make sure you refer to the setup instructions included in "Week 3 at a Glance."

What Does the Virtual Library Do?

The goal of this chapter is to create an online virtual library that has four components you will build: the member login/registration procedure, a search engine for specific books, the reservation list, and the component for checking out and extending time for books.

The member login and registration component lets a user log into the main library system. If users aren't members of the library yet, they can register to become members. Once they become members, they can enter the library and reserve or check out books based on their member IDs. Figure 21.1 shows you the complete member-registration page.

Once members enter the library, they can use the search engine to search for books based on book title, author, keyword, ISBN, or library. The author, keyword, and library information is retrieved from the database server and displayed in DBCombo controls so that members can simply select the information they want to search for. If the search is based on book title or ISBN, members need to enter the book title or ISBN information. The results of the search are displayed in a DBGrid control. Figure 21.2 shows you the search engine page.

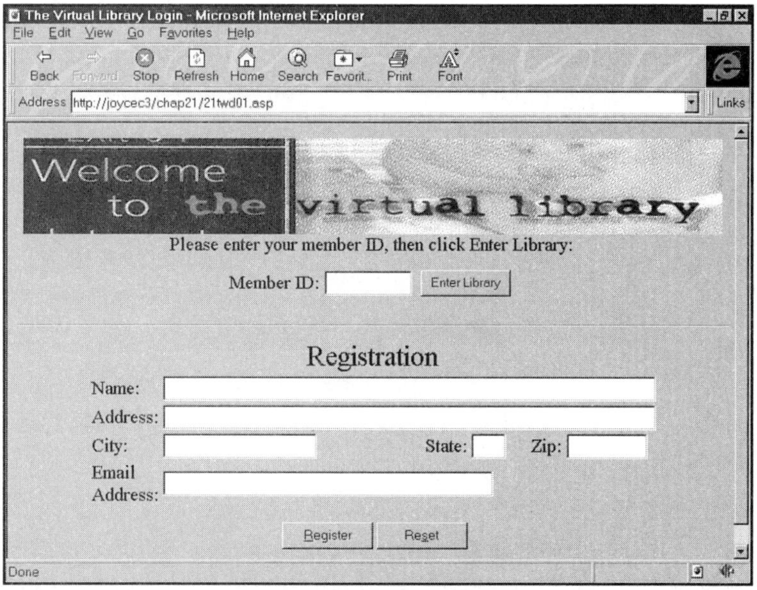

Figure 21.1.

The Virtual Library member login and registration page.

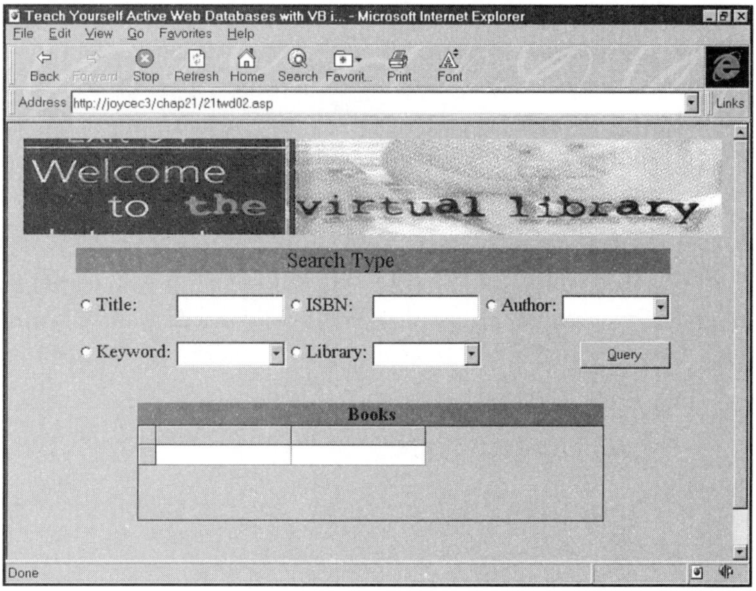

Figure 21.2.

The Virtual Library's search engine.

Members can use the reserving books component to reserve books before checking them out. They can enter books they want to check out in a DBGrid control for the temporary reserve list; they can also remove books from this list in the DBGrid control. In Figure 21.3, the reservation list has been added to the page.

Figure 21.3.

The Virtual Library's reservation list.

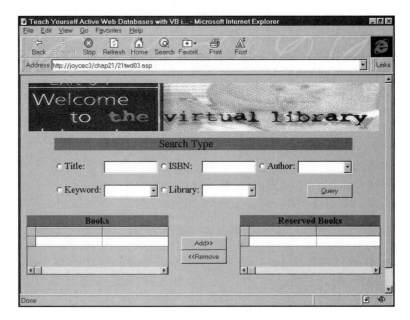

The component for checking out and extending time for books allows members to check out all the books in the temporary reserve list. Once books are checked out, members can't "uncheck" them. This component also allows a member to extend a book's loan period, if necessary. You can enforce an "extend book" business rule that says a book can be checked out for only a month. Members can't extend that checkout period beyond a month. In Figure 21.4, the checkout/extend component has been added to the page.

Now that you know what these four components do in the Virtual Library, you can move on to create tables, stored procedures, business objects and methods, and HTML code to build your own online library.

21

Figure 21.4.

The Virtual Library's checkout/extend component.

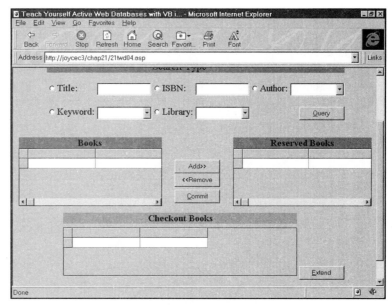

The Member Login/Registration Component

First, you need to create an ODBC system DSN called "Vlibrary" to refer to the database server. You can use the script file 21TWDTB.SQL from this book's CD-ROM to create all the tables described in the following sections. Use 21TWDSP.SQL to create stored procedures and 21TWDINS.SQL to insert data into tables. Tables and stored procedures are created in the database server, business objects need to be created in the application server, and last, but not least, the HTML code is created in the client tier. All the tables have the "VLib" prefix and all the stored procedures have the VLib_sp_ prefix.

The reason you use stored procedures is so the data's controls can reside in the database server. If for some reason a table structure is changed, you can easily change the stored procedure for the business object.

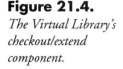

Tables for the Member Login/Registration Component

Your first table is used to hold the member information. Users enter their names, addresses, and e-mail information to register.

The VLib_Member Table

The member ID is automatically generated, and the e-mail address must be unique.

Table 21.1. The VLib_Member table.

Column Name	Data Type	Constraints
ID	`int`	Identity(1,1), not null
Name	`char(100)`	Not null
Address	`text`	Not null
City	`char(50)`	Not null
State	`char(2)`	Not null
Zip	`char(9)`	Not null
EmailAddress	`char(100)`	Not null, unique

Stored Procedures for the Member Login/ Registration Component

You need three stored procedures: checking to see whether a user is already a member, registering a user, and, finally, retrieving the member ID for an e-mail address.

The `VLib_sp_GetMember_ID` Stored Procedure

The `VLib_sp_GetMember_ID` retrieves the member ID based on the e-mail address:

```
create proc VLib_sp_GetMemberID
@cemailaddress   char(100)
as
select ID from  VLib_member
where emailaddress= @cemailaddress
```

The `VLib_sp_InsertMember` Stored Procedure

The `VLib_sp_InsertMember` stored procedure inserts a record in the VLib_Member table based on the name, address, city, state, zip, and e-mail address that the member enters. Notice that you're not inserting data for the ID column because the SQL server automatically generates this information. Here's the code for the stored procedure:

```
create proc VLib_sp_InsertMember
@cname char(100),
@caddress char(200),
@ccity char(100),
@cstate char(2),
@czip char(9),
@cemailaddress  char(100)
as
insert into VLib_member(name, address, city, state, zip, emailaddress)
values(@cname, @caddress, @ccity, @cstate, @czip, @cemailaddress)
```

The `VLib_sp_IsMemberExist` Stored Procedure

The `VLib_sp_IsMemberExist` procedure checks to see whether the specified e-mail address is already associated with a member ID:

```
create proc VLib_sp_IsMemberExist
@cemailaddress  char(100)
as
select count(*) from  VLib_member
where emailaddress= @cemailaddress
```

Business Objects and Methods for the Member Login/Registration Component

You're going to create a business object called `VLibMemberObj.VLibMemberObjCls`. Only one method is needed in this business object:

```
Public Function InsertMember(CName As String, CAddress As String, _
CCity As String, CState As String, CZip As String, CMail As String) As Integer
Dim conn As New ADODB.Connection
conn.Open "dsn=VLibrary;uid=sa;pwd"

Dim rsInsert As New ADODB.Recordset
Dim rsIsMemberExist As New ADODB.Recordset
Dim rsGetMemberID As New ADODB.Recordset
Dim SQLString As String

SQLString = "exec VLib_sp_IsMemberExist '" & CMail & "'"
Set rsIsMemberExist = conn.Execute(SQLString)
rsIsMemberExist.MoveFirst
If rsIsMemberExist(0) = 0 Then
    SQLString = "exec VLib_sp_insertMember '" & CName & "','" & CAddress & "','"
➥ _
    CCity & "','" & CState & "','" & CZip & "','" & CMail & "'"
    Set rsInsert = conn.Execute(SQLString)
    SQLString = "exec VLib_sp_GetMemberID '" & CMail & "'"
    Set rsGetMemberID = conn.Execute(SQLString)
    rsGetMemberID.MoveFirst
```

21

```
        InsertMember = rsGetMemberID(0)
Else
        InsertMember = -1
End If

End Function
```

The `InsertMember` method first calls `VLib_sp_IsMemberExist` to see whether the specified e-mail address already exists in the VLib_Member table. If it does, the function returns -1 to inform the user that he or she is already a member. If not, it calls the `VLib_sp_InsertMember` stored procedure to insert the user and calls the `VLib_sp_GetMemberID` stored procedure to return the member ID.

HTML Code for the Member Login/Registration Component

To enter the library, users enter their member IDs and click the Enter Library button. If users aren't members, but would like to join the Virtual Library, they can enter some information and click the Register button to register. The HTML code you need is shown in Listing 21.1.

Listing 21.1. The member login/registration component.

```
 1: <HTML>
 2: <HEAD><TITLE>The Virtual Library Login</TITLE></HEAD>
 3: <BODY>
 4: <center>
 5: <IMG SRC="vlibrary.gif" ALT="Virtual Library">
 6: <br><br><br><br>
 7: Please enter your member ID, then click Enter Library:
 8:
 9: <FORM name="form1" METHOD="POST" ACTION="search.asp">
10: <P>
11: Member ID: <INPUT NAME="MemberID" SIZE="10">
➥<INPUT TYPE=Submit Value="Enter Library">
12: </FORM>
13: <HR><br><br><br><br>
14: <font size=5> Registration</font><br><br><br>
15: <table width=300 border=0>
16: <b><font size =2>
17: <tr>
18: <td colspan=1>Name:</td>
19: <td colspan=4><INPUT NAME="CName" SIZE="72"></td>
20: </tr>
21:
22: <tr><td colspan=1>Address:</td>
23: <td colspan=4><INPUT NAME="CAddress" SIZE="72"></td>
24: </tr>
25:
26: <tr><td colspan=1>City:</td>
```

21

```
27: <td colspan=1><INPUT NAME="CCity" SIZE="20"></td>
28: <td colspan=1 align="RIGHT">State:</td>
29: <td><INPUT NAME="CState" SIZE="2" maxlength=2>
30: </td>
31: <td colspan=1 align="RIGHT">Zip:
32: <INPUT NAME="CZip" SIZE="9" maxlength=9>
33: </td></tr>
34:
35: <tr><td colspan=1>Email Address: </td>
36: <td colspan=3><INPUT NAME="CEmail" SIZE="47">
37: </td></tr>
38:
39: </table><p>
40: <INPUT TYPE=BUTTON NAME="Register" VALUE="&Register">
41: <INPUT TYPE=BUTTON NAME="Reset" VALUE="&Reset"></p>
42: </center>
43: <!-- AdvancedDataSpace -->
44:     <OBJECT ID="ADS1" WIDTH=1 HEIGHT=1
45:     CLASSID="CLSID:99586D40-DB60-11CF-9D87-00AA00B91181">
46: </OBJECT>
47:
48: <SCRIPT LANGUAGE="VBScript">
49: Sub Reset_OnClick
50: CAddress.Value =""
51: CName.Value =""
52: CCity.Value =""
53: CZip.Value =""
54: CState.Value =""
55: CEMail.Value =""
56: End Sub
57: Sub Register_OnClick
58: Dim myObj
59: Dim myID
60: myID=-2
61:
62: Set myObj = ADS1.CreateObject("VLibMemberObj.VLibMemberObjCls",
 ➥ "HTTP://<%=Request.ServerVariables("Server_name")%>")
63: IF CAddress.Value ="" or CName.Value ="" or CCity.Value =""
 ➥or CZip.Value ="" or CState.Value ="" or CEMail.Value ="" THEN
64:    MsgBox "You need to enter all the data in order to register"
65: ELSE
66:    myID = myObj.InsertMember(CName.Value,
 ➥CAddress.Value,CCity.Value,CState.Value,CZip.Value,CEMail.Value)
67: END IF
68: IF myID = -1 THEN
69:    MsgBox "You have already registered"
70: ELSE
71:    MsgBox "You member ID is :" &myID &
 ➥". You can click Enter Library to enter the virtual library."
72:    Document.form1.MemberID.Value=myID
73: END IF
74: End Sub
75: </script>
76: </BODY>
77: </HTML>
```

21

ANALYSIS In this code, you use a Form object to navigate. Once users enter their member ID and click the Enter Library button, they can jump to the main library Web page, which is named in the ACTION parameter. In this code, you use SEARCH.ASP as the main library Web page. If your main library Web page's filename is different, you need to change this parameter.

If users want to register, they must enter the requested information and click the Register button. The register_OnClick sub-routine checks to see whether all the information is entered. If not, it displays a message box asking the user to enter the information. Otherwise, it invokes the InsertMember method of the VLibMemberObj.VLibmemberObjCls object. If the method returns -1, that means the user is already registered; otherwise, it returns the member ID.

With the member login/registration component completed, Figure 21.5 shows you a user entering all the information and clicking the Register button to register. However, you can't click the Enter Library button because you haven't built the search engine yet.

Figure 21.5

The member login/registration component.

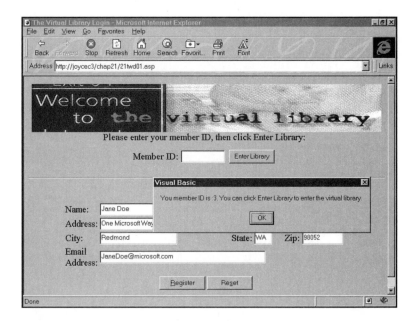

The Search Engine Component

Members can use the search engine to search for books based on title, author, keyword, library, or ISBN information. The member can choose the search type and then enter the search criteria or pick one from the list. If no information is entered or selected, the search is conducted as a wildcard search to get all the books.

Tables for the Search Engine Component

You need to create five tables to hold the book information: VLib_Keyword, VLib_Author, VLibrary, VLib_Book, and VLib_BookLocation.

The VLib_Keyword Table

The VLib_Keyword table stores all the keyword information that's available for books. The data in this table is displayed in a DBCombo control when members use the search engine. Members can choose the keyword—the subject matter or topic, for example—they want the search based on.

Table 21.2. The VLib_Keyword table.

Column Name	Data Type	Constraints
ID	int	Primary key
Name	char(100)	Not null

The VLib_Author Table

The VLib_Author table stores all the available author information for the Virtual Library's books. Members can choose an author name as the search criteria. The author information is displayed in a DBCombo control when members use the search engine.

Table 21.3. The VLib_Author table.

Column Name	Data Type	Constraints
ID	int	Primary key
Name	char(100)	Not null

The VLibrary Table

The VLibrary table stores information about library branches; members can select a specific branch library name to have the books from that branch listed. This table's data is displayed in a DBCombo control, too.

Table 21.4. The VLibrary table.

Column Name	Data Type	Constraints
ID	int	Primary key
Name	char(100)	Not null

21

The VLib_Book Table

The VLib_Book table—the core of the Virtual Library system—stores all the book information. It refers to VLib_Author for the author ID and VLib_Keyword for the keyword ID. Each book can have three keywords. The search engine uses the search criteria to conduct the search on the VLib_Book table. The matching records are displayed in a DBGrid control.

Table 21.5. The VLib_Book table.

Column Name	Data Type	Constraints
ID	integer	Primary key
Title	char(100)	Not null
AuthorID	int	Reference to VLib_Author.ID
Keyword1	int	Reference to VLib_Keyword.ID
Keyword2	int	Reference to VLib_Keyword.ID
Keyword3	int	Reference to VLib_Keyword.ID
ISBN	char(100)	Allow null
Description	text	Allow null

The VLib_BookLocation Table

The VLib_BookLocation table stores information about which library books are located in; it links the book and library information.

Table 21.6. The VLib_BookLocation table.

Column Name	Data Type	Constraints
BookID	integer	Reference to Vlib_book.ID
LibraryID	integer	Reference to Vlibrary.ID
Copies	integer	Not null

Stored Procedures for the Search Engine Component

You need to create stored procedures that retrieve books based on the author, title, keyword, and library information. In case no search type is selected, you also need to create a stored procedure to retrieve a list of all the books.

The `VLib_sp_GetBookbyAuthor` **Stored Procedure**

The `VLib_sp_GetBookbyAuthor` stored procedure retrieves all books with the author name matching the specified author name:

```
create proc VLib_sp_GetBookbyAuthor
@authorName varchar(100)
as
select a.title, b.name, a.isbn, c.name keyword1, d.name keyword2,
➥e.name  keyword3, a.description,a.id ID
➥from vlib_book a, vlib_author b, vlib_keyword c,
➥vlib_keyword d,  vlib_keyword e
Where a.authorid = b.id
and b.name like @AuthorName
and a.keyword1 *= c.id
and a.keyword2 *= d.id
and a.keyword3 *= e.id
order by a.title
```

Note that the SQL statement also needs to retrieve the author name and keyword name, instead of just using authorID and keywordID from the table.

The `VLib_sp_GetBookbyKeyword` **Stored Procedure**

The `VLib_sp_GetBookbyKeyword` stored procedure retrieves all books with a keyword matching the specified keyword:

```
create proc VLib_sp_GetBookbyKeyword
@KeywordName varchar(100)
as
select a.title, f.name , a.isbn, c.name keyword1,
➥d.name keyword2, e.name  keyword3, a.description,a.id  ID
➥from vlib_book a, vlib_keyword b
➥, vlib_keyword c, vlib_keyword d, vlib_keyword e,vlib_author f
Where b.name like @KeywordName
and f.id = a.authorid
and ( a.keyword1 = b.id or
 a.keyword2 = b.id or
a.keyword3 = b.id )
and a.keyword1 *= c.id
and a.keyword2 *= d.id
and a.keyword3 *= e.id
order by a.title
```

The `VLib_sp_GetBookbyLibrary` **Stored Procedure**

The `VLib_sp_GetBookbyLibrary` stored procedure retrieves all the books that belong to the library branch indicated in the search criteria:

```
create proc VLib_sp_GetBookbyLibrary
@LibraryName varchar(100)
as
select a.title, a.isbn, d.name keyword1,
```

21

```
➥e.name keyword2, f.name  keyword3, a.description,a.id  ID
from vlib_book a, vLibrary b
,vLib_Booklocation c
, vlib_keyword d, vlib_keyword e, vlib_keyword f,vlib_author g
Where b.name like @LibraryName
and g.id = a.authorid
and a.id=c.bookid
and c.libraryid = b.id
and ( a.keyword1 = b.id or
 a.keyword2 = b.id or
a.keyword3 = b.id )
and a.keyword1 *= d.id
and a.keyword2 *= e.id
and a.keyword3 *= f.id
order by a.title
```

The `VLib_sp_GetBookbyTitle` Stored Procedure

The `VLib_sp_GetBookbyTitle` stored procedure retrieves all the books with a title matching the specified title:

```
create proc VLib_sp_GetBookbyTitle
@TitleName varchar(100)
as
select a.title, a.isbn, d.name keyword1,
➥e.name keyword2, f.name  keyword3, a.description,a.id ID
from vlib_book a,
vlib_keyword d, vlib_keyword e, vlib_keyword f,vlib_author g
Where a.title like @TitleName
and g.id = a.authorid
and a.keyword1 *= d.id
and a.keyword2 *= e.id
and a.keyword3 *= f.id
order by a.title
```

The `VLib_sp_GetBookbyISBN` Stored Procedure

The `VLib_sp_GetBookbyISBN` stored procedure retrieves all the books with an ISBN matching the specified ISBN:

```
create proc VLib_sp_GetBookbyISBN
@ISBN varchar(100)
as
select a.title, a.isbn, d.name keyword1,
➥e.name keyword2, f.name  keyword3, a.description ,a.id ID
from vlib_book a, vlib_keyword d, vlib_keyword e, vlib_keyword f
Where a.isbn like @ISBN
and a.keyword1 *= d.id
and a.keyword2 *= e.id
and a.keyword3 *= f.id
order by a.title
```

21

The `VLib_sp_GetAllBooks` Stored Procedure

The `VLib_sp_GetAllBooks` procedure retrieves all the books:

```
create proc VLib_sp_GetAllBooks
as
select a.title, b.name, a.isbn, d.name keyword1,
➥e.name keyword2, f.name  keyword3, a.description,a.id  ID
from vlib_book a,vlib_author b,
vlib_keyword d, vlib_keyword e, vlib_keyword f
Where b.id = a.authorid
and a.keyword1 *= d.id
and a.keyword2 *= e.id
and a.keyword3 *= f.id
order by a.title
```

Business Objects and Methods for the Search Engine Component

You're going to create the business object `VLibObj.VLibObjCls` for the search engine component. This same business object will be used for the reserve and checkout/extend book components.

You need to create methods for each search type and one more method for searching all the books, if no search type is specified. You also want to create a general method, `ProcessQuery`, that's used internally by other methods in the business object.

The `ProcessQuery` Method

The `ProcessQuery` method issues the SQL statement used for a search type to the database server and returns the `Recordset`:

```
Public Function ProcessQuery(ByVal strSQL As String)
    Dim rs As ADODB.Recordset
    Set rs = CreateObject("ADODB.Recordset")

    rs.CursorLocation = adUseClientBatch
    rs.Open strSQL, "dsn=VLibrary;uid=sa;pwd=;",
➥adOpenUnspecified, adLockUnspecified, adCmdUnspecified
Set ProcessQuery = rs
End Function
```

The `GetBooksBasedOnAuthor` Method

The method `GetBooksBasedOnAuthor` calls the `VLib_sp_GetBookbyAuthor` stored procedure and returns the `Recordset` to the client tier:

```
Public Function GetBooksBasedOnAuthor(ByVal AuthorName As String) As Object
    Dim rs As New ADODB.Recordset
    Dim SQLString As String
```

21

```
    SQLString = "exec Vlib_sp_GetBookbyAuthor '" & AuthorName & "'"
    Set rs = ProcessQuery(SQLString)
    Set GetBooksBasedOnAuthor = rs
End Function
```

The `GetBooksBasedOnKeyword` Method

The `GetBooksBasedOnKeyword` method calls the `VLib_sp_GetBookByKeyword` stored procedure and returns the `Recordset` to the client tier:

```
Public Function GetBooksBasedOnKeyword(ByVal KeywordName As String) As Object
    Dim rs As New ADODB.Recordset
    Dim SQLString As String

    SQLString = "exec Vlib_sp_GetBookbyKeyword '" & KeywordName & "'"
    Set rs = ProcessQuery(SQLString)
    Set GetBooksBasedOnKeyword = rs
End Function
```

The `GetBooksBasedOnLibrary` Method

The `GetBooksBasedOnLibrary` method calls the `VLib_sp_GetBookByLibrary` stored procedure and returns the `Recordset` to the client tier:

```
Public Function GetBooksBasedOnLibrary(ByVal LibraryName As String) As Object
    Dim rs As New ADODB.Recordset
    Dim SQLString As String

    SQLString = "exec Vlib_sp_GetBookbyLibrary '" & LibraryName & "'"
    Set rs = ProcessQuery(SQLString)
    Set GetBooksBasedOnLibrary = rs
End Function
```

The `GetBooksBasedOnTitle` Method

The `GetBooksBasedOnTitle` method calls the `VLib_sp_GetBookByTitle` stored procedure and returns the `Recordset` to the client tier:

```
Public Function GetBooksBasedOnTitle(ByVal TitleName As String) As Object
    Dim rs As New ADODB.Recordset
    Dim SQLString As String

    SQLString = "exec Vlib_sp_GetBookbyTitle '" & TitleName & "'"
    Set rs = ProcessQuery(SQLString)
    Set GetBooksBasedOnTitle = rs
End Function
```

The `GetBooksBasedOnISBN` Method

The `GetBooksBasedOnISBN` method calls the `VLib_sp_GetBookByISBN` stored procedure and returns the `Recordset` to the client tier:

```
Public Function GetBooksBasedOnISBN(ByVal ISBNName As String) As Object
    Dim rs As New ADODB.Recordset
    Dim SQLString As String

    SQLString = "exec Vlib_sp_GetBookbyISBN '" & ISBNName & "'"
    Set rs = ProcessQuery(SQLString)
    Set GetBooksBasedOnISBN = rs
End Function
```

The `GetAllBooks` Method

The `GetAllBooks` method calls the `VLib_sp_GetAllBooks` stored procedure and returns the `Recordset` to the client tier:

```
Public Function GetAllBooks() As Object
    Dim rs As New ADODB.Recordset
    Dim SQLString As String

    SQLString = "exec Vlib_sp_GetAllBooks "
    Set rs = ProcessQuery(SQLString)
    Set GetAllBooks = rs
End Function
```

HTML Code for the Search Engine Component

You're going to create five radio buttons that members can use to choose the search type. You use two text boxes, for the title and ISBN criteria, and three DBCombo controls, which are bound with three `AdvancedDataControl` objects for retrieving the author, keyword, and library information. These DBCombo controls provide listboxes so members can simply pick one of the search criteria.

Once a search type and criterion is defined, members click the Query button to display the book data in a DBGrid control. The complete HTML code for the search engine is shown in Listing 21.2. You need to use the Web page from the section "The Member Login/ Registration Component" to jump to the following Web page. Next, modify the `ACTION` parameter in the member login/registration component's Web page to reflect the filename of the search engine's Web page.

Listing 21.2. The search engine component.

```
1: <HTML>
2: <HEAD>
3: <TITLE>Teach Yourself Active Web Databases with VB in 21 Days</TITLE>
4: </HEAD>
5: <center>
6: <IMG SRC="vlibrary.gif" ALT="Virtual Library">
7: <br><br><br><br>
8: <table border="0" cellpadding="0" cellspacing="0" width="70%"
```

21

continues

Listing 21.2. continued

```
 9: bordercolor="#008080">
10:     <tr>
11:         <td colspan="2" width="30%" bgcolor="#008080"> </td>
12:         <td colspan="2" bgcolor="#008080"><font size="4">Search
13: Type</font></td>
14:         <td colspan="2" bgcolor="#008080"> </td>
15:     </tr>
16:     <tr>
17:         <td> </td>
18:         <td> </td>
19:     </tr>
20:     <tr>
21:         <td valign="top" width="5%" nowrap>
22:             <input type="radio"name="SearchType" value="Title"
23:             onclick="SearchTypeClick(3)">Title:
24:         </td>
25:         <td valign="top" width="25">
26:             <input type="text" size="13" name="TitleParameter">
27:         </td>
28:         <td valign="top" width="4%" nowrap>
29:             <input type="radio"name="SearchType" value="ISBN"
30:             onclick="SearchTypeClick(5)">ISBN:
31:         </td>
32:         <td valign="top" width="25%" nowrap>
33:             <input type="text"size="13" name="ISBNParameter">
34:         </td>
35:         <td valign="top" width="5%" nowrap>
36:             <input type="radio"name="SearchType" value="Author"
37:             onclick="SearchTypeClick(1)">Author:
38:         </td>
39:         <td align="right" valign="top" width="25%" nowrap>
40:             <object id="VBComboAuthor"
➥classid="clsid:FAEEE760-117E-101B-8933-08002B2F4F5A"
41:             align="baseline" border="0" width="117" height="28">
42:             <param name="ListField" value="AuthorName">
43:             </object>
44:         </td>
45:     </tr>
46:     <tr>
47:         <td> </td>
48:         <td> </td>
49:         <td> </td>
50:         <td> </td>
51:         <td> </td>
52:         <td> </td>
53:     </tr>
54:     <tr>
55:         <td valign="top" width="5%" nowrap>
56:             <input type="radio"name="SearchType" value="Keyword"
57:             onclick="SearchTypeClick(3)">Keyword:
58:         </td>
59:         <td valign="top" width="25%">
60:             <object id="VBComboKeyword"
➥classid="clsid:FAEEE760-117E-101B-8933-08002B2F4F5A"
61:             align="texttop" border="0" width="117" height="28">
```

```
62:                    <param name="ListField" value="KeywordName">
63:                </object>
64:            </td>
65:            <td valign="top" width="4%" nowrap>
66:                <input type="radio"name="SearchType" value="Library"
67:                onclick="SearchTypeClick(4)">Library:
68:            </td>
69:            <td valign="top" width="25%" nowrap>
70:                <object id="VBComboLibrary"
➥classid:"clsid:FAEEE760-117E-101B-8933-08002B2F4F5A"
71:                align="baseline" border="0" width="117" height="28">
72:                <param name="ListField"value="LibraryName">
73:                </object>
74:            </td>
75:            <td align="right" valign="bottom" colspan="2" width="30%">
76:                <p align="right">
77:                <input type="button" name="Query"value="&Query"></p>
78:                <p align="right"> </p>
79:            </td>
80:        </tr>
81: </table>
82: </center></div><div align="center"><center>
83: <table border="0" cellpadding="0" cellspacing="0" width="50%">
84:        <tr>
85:            <th colspan="1" width="50%" bgcolor="#008080">Books</th>
86:            <th align="left"> </th>
87:        </tr>
88:        <tr>
89:            <td rowspan="5" colspan="1" width="50%" nowrap>
90:                <object id="GridBook"
➥classid:"clsid:00028C00-0000-0000-0000-000000000046"
91:                    align="center" border="0" hspace="0" width="500"
92:                    height="200">
93:                </object>
94:            </td>
95:        </tr>
96: </table>
97: </center></div><div align="center"><center>
98: <br><br>
99: </center></div>
100: <p> </p>
101: <!-- AdvancedDataSpace -->
102:        <OBJECT ID="ADS1" WIDTH=1 HEIGHT=1
103:        CLASSID="CLSID:99586D40-DB60-11CF-9D87-00AA00B91181">
104: </OBJECT>
105: <OBJECT CLASSID="clsid:9381D8F2-0288-11d0-9501-00AA00B911A5"
106:        ID=ADCAuthor HEIGHT=1 WIDTH = 1
107:        CODEBASE="HTTP://<%=Request.ServerVariables("Server_name")%>
➥/ADCDownload/msadc10.cab">
108:        <PARAM NAME="BINDINGS" VALUE="VBComboAuthor">
109:        <PARAM NAME="server" VALUE="http://
➥<%=Request.ServerVariables("Server_name")%>">
110:        <PARAM NAME="Connect" VALUE="DSN=VLibrary;uid=sa">
111:        <PARAM NAME="SQL" VALUE="SELECT rtrim(name) AuthorName
➥FROM vlib_author  order by name">
```

continues

21

Listing 21.2. continued

```
112: </OBJECT>
113: <OBJECT CLASSID="clsid:9381D8F2-0288-11d0-9501-00AA00B911A5"
114:     ID=ADCKeyword HEIGHT=1 WIDTH = 1
115:     CODEBASE="HTTP://<%=Request.ServerVariables("Server_name")%>
➥/ADCDownload/msadc10.cab">
116:     <PARAM NAME="BINDINGS" VALUE="VBComboKeyword">
117:     <PARAM NAME="server" VALUE="http://
➥<%=Request.ServerVariables("Server_name")%>">
118:     <PARAM NAME="Connect" VALUE="DSN=VLibrary;uid=sa">
119:     <PARAM NAME="SQL" VALUE="SELECT rtrim(name) KeywordName
➥FROM vlib_keyword  order by name">
120: </OBJECT>
121: <OBJECT CLASSID="clsid:9381D8F2-0288-11d0-9501-00AA00B911A5"
122:     ID=ADCLibrary HEIGHT=1 WIDTH = 1
123:     CODEBASE="HTTP://<%=Request.ServerVariables("Server_name")%>
➥/ADCDownload/msadc10.cab">
124:     <PARAM NAME="BINDINGS" VALUE="VBComboLibrary">
125:     <PARAM NAME="server" VALUE="http://
➥<%=Request.ServerVariables("Server_name")%>">
126:     <PARAM NAME="Connect" VALUE="DSN=VLibrary;uid=sa">
127:     <PARAM NAME="SQL" VALUE="SELECT RTRIM(name) LibraryName
➥FROM vlibrary order by name">
128: </OBJECT>
129: <OBJECT CLASSID="clsid:9381D8F2-0288-11d0-9501-00AA00B911A5"
130:     ID=ADCBook HEIGHT=1 WIDTH = 1
131:     CODEBASE="HTTP://<%=Request.ServerVariables("Server_name")%>
➥/ADCDownload/msadc10.cab">
132:     <PARAM NAME="BINDINGS" VALUE="GridBook;Description.text=description">
133: </OBJECT>
134: <SCRIPT LANGUAGE="VBScript">
135: Option Explicit
136: Dim myObj
137: Dim ret
138: Dim rs
139: Dim SType
140: Dim MemberID
141: SType=0
142: Dim rso
143: SUB SearchTypeClick(curvalue)
144: SType = curValue
145: END SUB
146:
147: SUB Query_OnClick()
148:     Dim mytest
149:     IF SType = 0 THEN
150:       set rs = myObj.GetAllBooks
151:     ELSEIF SType = 1 THEN
152:       myTest = RTrim(VBComboAuthor.Text)
153:       IF myTest ="" THEN
154:         myTest ="%"
155:       END IF
156:       set rs = myObj.GetBooksBasedOnAuthor(myTest)
```

```
157:      ELSEIF SType = 2 THEN
158:       myTest = RTrim(TitleParameter.value)
159:       IF myTest ="" THEN
160:           myTest ="%"
161:       END IF
162:       set rs = myObj.GetBooksBasedOnTitle(myTest)
163:      ELSEIF SType = 3 THEN
164:       myTest = RTrim(VBComboKeyword.Text)
165:       IF myTest ="" THEN
166:           myTest ="%"
167:       END IF
168:       set rs = myObj.GetBooksBasedOnKeyword(myTest)
169:      ELSEIF SType = 4 THEN
170:       myTest = RTrim(VBComboLibrary.Text)
171:       IF myTest ="" THEN
172:           myTest ="%"
173:       END IF
174:       set rs = myObj.GetBooksBasedOnLibrary(myTest)
175:      ELSEIF SType = 5 THEN
176:       myTest = RTrim(ISBNParameter.Value)
177:       IF myTest ="" THEN
178:           myTest ="%"
179:       END IF
180:       set rs = myObj.GetBooksBasedOnISBN(myTest)
181:      END IF
182:
183:      IF NOT ISEmpty(rs) THEN
184:          AdcBook.Recordset = rs
185:      END IF
186: End SUB
187:
188:
189: Sub Window_OnLoad()
190:      Set myObj = ADS1.CreateObject("VlibObj.VLibObjCls",
➥ "HTTP://<%=Request.ServerVariables("Server_name")%>")
191:      MemberID = <%=request.form("MemberID")%>
192:
193: End Sub
194: </SCRIPT>
195: </BODY>
196: </HTML>
```

ANALYSIS   The ADCAuthor control retrieves data from the VLib_Author table and binds the data into the GridAuthor control. The ADCKeyword control retrieves data from the VLib_Keyword table and binds the data into the GridKeyword control, and the ADCLibrary control retrieves data from the VLib_Library table and binds the data into the GridLibrary control. ADCGrid binds data into the GridBook control, which displays the search results.

When a member selects any one of the radio buttons, the SearchTypeClick sub-routine is called to pass a value according to the search type. This value is stored in a global variable so that later on you can invoke different methods of the VLibObj business object based on the search type.

21

The search type defaults to 0, which invokes the `GetAllBooks` method. Here's what the other values result in:

Value	Method Invoked
1	GetBooksBasedOnAuthor
2	GetBooksBasedOnTitle
3	GetBooksBasedOnKeyword
4	GetBooksBasedOnLibrary
5	GetBooksBasedOnISBN

If no search criterion is entered for the search type, a wildcard search is conducted.

At this point, the search engine for the Virtual Library is complete. Members can search for books based on author, keyword, title, ISBN, or library branch. The author, keyword, and library branch information is retrieved and displayed in listboxes so that members can simply select search information from the list. Figure 21.6 shows you the Web page before any search begins.

Figure 21.6.

The search engine component for the Virtual Library.

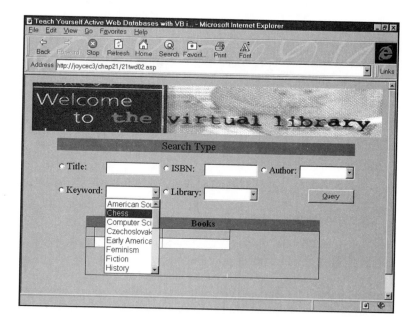

Figure 21.7 shows you the results of a member selecting a keyword for the search criteria.

21

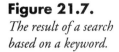

Figure 21.7.
The result of a search based on a keyword.

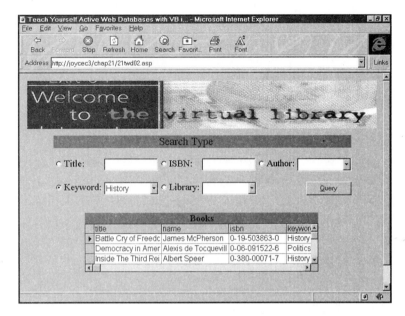

Try testing the search engine by selecting different search types and search criteria.

The Reserve Book Component

Now you need to set up a component so members can temporarily reserve books. If they change their minds about books they've reserved, those books can be removed from the temporary reserved list.

After members finish reserving books, they can then check out all the reserved books. When the books are checked out, all the books reserved for those particular members are deleted.

Also, you want to enforce a rule: Once a book is already reserved or checked out by a member, the member can't reserve it again. Only one copy of the book can be reserved or checked out for a member.

Tables for the Reserve Book Component

You need to create two tables for the reserve book component: VLib_TmpReserved and VLib_CheckOut.

The VLib_TmpReserved Table

The VLib_TmpReserved table stores information about books that have been temporarily reserved.

Table 21.7. The VLib_TmpReserved table.

Column Name	Data Type	Constraints
MemberID	integer	Not null
BookID	integer	Not null
BookTitle	char(100)	Not null
LibraryID	integer	Not null

The VLib_Checkout Table

The VLib_Checkout table stores information on books that have been checked out.

Table 21.7. The VLib_Checkout table.

Column Name	Data Type	Constraints
MemberID	integer	Not null
LibraryID	integer	Not null
CheckoutDate	smalldatetime	Not null
DueDate	smalldatetime	Not null

Stored Procedures for the Reserve Book Component

You need to create three stored procedures for the reserve book component that handle inserting, deleting, and retrieving records in the VLib_TmpReserved table.

One more stored procedure needs to be added to enforce the rule mentioned earlier, so before you allow a record to be added to the VLib_TmpReserved table, you must make sure it isn't already in the VLib_TmpReserved or VLib_Checkout tables.

The VLib_sp_GetTmpReserved Stored Procedure

The VLib_sp_GetTmpReserved stored procedure retrieves all the books reserved under a specific member ID from the VLib_TmpReserved table:

```
create proc VLib_sp_GetTmpReserved
@memberID integer
as
select b.title title, c.name libraryname, a.bookid bookid, a.libraryid libraryid
from Vlib_TmpReserved a, vlib_book b, vlibrary c
where a.memberid=@memberid
and a.bookid=b.id
and a.libraryid=c.id
```

The `VLib_sp_InsertTmpReserved` Stored Procedure

The `VLib_sp_InsertTmpReserved` stored procedure inserts a record into the VLib_TmpReserved table based on the member ID and book ID:

```
create proc VLib_sp_InsertTmpReserved
@memberID integer,
@BookID integer
as
declare @libraryID integer
declare @BookTitle char(100)
select @LibraryID=libraryid from vlib_BookLocation where BookID = @BookID
select @BookTitle=title from vlib_Book where ID = @BookID
insert into Vlib_TmpReserved(Memberid, BookID, LibraryID, booktitle)
➥values(@MemberID, @BookID, @LibraryID, @booktitle)
```

The first library branch that has the book is used for the LibraryID column of the inserted record.

The `VLib_sp_RemoveTmpReserved` Stored Procedure

The `VLib_sp_RemoveTmpReserved` stored procedure removes the book from the VLib_TmpReserved table for the specified member ID and book ID:

```
create proc VLib_sp_RemoveTmpReserved
@memberID integer,
@BookID integer
as
delete from Vlib_TmpReserved where Memberid = @Memberid and BookID = @BookID
```

The `VLib_sp_RemoveAllTmpReserved` Stored Procedure

The `VLib_sp_RemoveAllTmpReserved` stored procedure removes all the books from the VLib_TmpReserved table for the specified member ID:

```
create proc VLib_sp_RemoveAllTmpReserved
@memberID integer
as
delete from Vlib_tmpReserved
where memberid=@memberid
```

21

The `VLib_sp_IsBookIDExist` Stored Procedure

The `VLib_sp_IsBookIDExist` stored procedure checks whether a book has already been reserved or checked out by a particular member:

```
create proc VLib_sp_IsBookIDExist
@MemberID integer,
@BookID integer
as
declare @count1 integer
declare @count2 integer
select @count1=count(*) from Vlib_Checkout
where BookID =@BookID and MemberID =@MemberID
select @count2=count(*) from Vlib_TmpReserved
where BookID =@BookID and MemberID =@MemberID
if (@count1 <>0 ) or (@count2 <>0)
    select 1
else
    select 0
```

Business Objects and Methods for the Reserve Book Component

You are going to add methods for the reserve book component to the `VLibObj.VLibObjCls` business object. These methods are `GetTmpReserved`, `InsertTmpReserved`, and `RemoveTmpReserved`.

The `GetTmpReserved` Method

The `GetTmpReserved` method calls the `VLib_sp_GetTmpReserved` stored procedure to retrieve the reserved books from the VLib_TmpReserved table for the specified customer ID:

```
Function GetTmpReserved(ByVal MemberID As Integer) As Object
Dim rs As New ADODB.Recordset
Dim SQLString As String

SQLString = "exec Vlib_sp_GetTmpReserved " & MemberID
Set rs = ProcessQuery(SQLString)
Set GetTmpReserved = rs

End Function
```

The `InsertTmpReserved` Method

The `InsertTmpReserved` method calls the `VLib_sp_IsBookIDExist` stored procedure to see whether the specified book ID is already reserved or checked out:

```
Function InsertTmpReserved(ByVal MemberID As Integer, ByVal BookID As Integer)
➥As Integer
Dim rs, rs1 As New ADODB.Recordset
Dim SQLString As String
```

21

```
SQLString = "exec Vlib_sp_IsBookIDExist " & MemberID & "," & BookID
Set rs = ProcessQuery(SQLString)
rs.MoveFirst
If rs(0) = 0 Then
   SQLString = "exec Vlib_sp_InsertTmpReserved " & MemberID & "," & BookID
   Set rs1 = ProcessQuery(SQLString)
   InsertTmpReserved = 1
Else
   InsertTmpReserved = 0
End If
End Function
```

If the book has already been reserved or checked out, the method returns 0. Otherwise, the method calls the VLib_sp_InsertTmpReserved stored procedure to insert a record into the VLib_TmpReserved table based on the specified customer ID and book ID and returns 1.

The RemoveTmpReserved Method

The RemoveTmpReserved method calls the VLib_sp_RemoveTmpReserved stored procedure to remove a record from the VLib_TmpReserved table for the specified customer ID and book ID:

```
Function RemoveTmpReserved(ByVal MemberID As Integer, ByVal BookID As Integer)
➥As Integer
Dim SQLString As String
Dim rs As New ADODB.Recordset

SQLString = "exec Vlib_sp_RemoveTmpReserved " & MemberID & "," & BookID
Set rs = ProcessQuery(SQLString)
RemoveTmpReserved = 1
End Function
```

The RemoveAllTmpReserved Method

The RemoveAllTmpReserved method calls the VLib_sp_RemoveAllTmpReserved stored procedure to remove all the records from the VLib_TmpReserved table for the specified customer ID:

```
Function RemoveAllTmpReserved(ByVal MemberID As Integer)
Dim SQLString As String
Dim rs As New ADODB.Recordset

SQLString = "exec Vlib_sp_RemoveAllTmpReserved " & MemberID
Set rs = ProcessQuery(SQLString)
End Function
```

HTML Code for the Reserve Book Component

You need a DBGrid control to hold the reserved book list and two more buttons for adding and removing reserved books. The complete HTML code is shown in Listing 21.3. Like the

Web page in the search engine component, you need to use the Web page from the section "The Member Login/Registration Component" to jump to the following Web page. Also, you must modify the ACTION parameter in the member login/registration component's Web page to reflect the filename of the reserve book component's Web page.

Listing 21.3. The reserve book component.

```
 1: <HTML>
 2: <HEAD>
 3: <TITLE>Teach Yourself Active Web Databases with VB in 21 Days</TITLE>
 4: </HEAD>
 5: <center>
 6: <IMG SRC="vlibrary.gif" ALT="Virtual Library">
 7: <br><br><br><br>
 8: <BODY LANGUAGE="VBS">
 9: <table border="0" cellpadding="0" cellspacing="0" width="70%"
10: bordercolor="#008080">
11:     <tr>
12:         <td colspan="2" width="30%" bgcolor="#008080"> </td>
13:         <td colspan="2" bgcolor="#008080"><font size="4">Search
14:         Type</font></td>
15:         <td colspan="2" bgcolor="#008080"> </td>
16:     </tr>
17:     <tr>
18:         <td> </td>
19:         <td> </td>
20:     </tr>
21:     <tr>
22:         <td valign="top" width="5%" nowrap>
23:             <input type="radio"name="SearchType" value="Title"
24:             onclick="SearchTypeClick(3)">Title:
25:         </td>
26:         <td valign="top" width="25">
27:             <input type="text" size="13" name="TitleParameter">
28:         </td>
29:         <td valign="top" width="4%" nowrap>
30:             <input type="radio"name="SearchType" value="ISBN"
31:             onclick="SearchTypeClick(5)">ISBN:
32:         </td>
33:         <td valign="top" width="25%" nowrap>
34:             <input type="text"size="13" name="ISBNParameter">
35:         </td>
36:         <td valign="top" width="5%" nowrap>
37:             <input type="radio"name="SearchType" value="Author"
38:             onclick="SearchTypeClick(1)">Author:
39:         </td>
40:         <td align="right" valign="top" width="25%" nowrap>
41:             <object id="VBComboAuthor"classid="
➡clsid:FAEEE760-117E-101B-8933-08002B2F4F5A"
42:                         align="baseline" border="0" width="117" height="28">
43:                         <param name="ListField" value="AuthorName">
44:             </object>
45:         </td>
46:     </tr>
47:     <tr>
```

21

```
48:          <td> </td>
49:          <td> </td>
50:          <td> </td>
51:          <td> </td>
52:          <td> </td>
53:          <td> </td>
54:      </tr>
55:      <tr>
56:          <td valign="top" width="5%" nowrap>
57:              <input type="radio"name="SearchType" value="Keyword"
58:               onclick="SearchTypeClick(3)">Keyword:
59:          </td>
60:          <td valign="top" width="25%">
61:              <object id="VBComboKeyword"
➡classid="clsid:FAEEE760-117E-101B-8933-08002B2F4F5A"
62:                      align="texttop" border="0" width="117" height="28">
63:                      <param name="ListField" value="KeywordName">
64:              </object>
65:          </td>
66:          <td valign="top" width="4%" nowrap>
67:              <input type="radio"name="SearchType" value="Library"
68:               onclick="SearchTypeClick(4)">Library:
69:          </td>
70:          <td valign="top" width="25%" nowrap>
71:              <object id="VBComboLibrary"
➡classid="clsid:FAEEE760-117E-101B-8933-08002B2F4F5A"
72:                      align="baseline" border="0" width="117" height="28">
73:                      <param name="ListField"value="LibraryName">
74:              </object>
75:          </td>
76:          <td align="right" valign="bottom" colspan="2" width="30%">
77:              <p align="right">
78:              <input type="button" name="Query"value="&Query"></p>
79:              <p align="right"> </p>
80:          </td>
81:      </tr>
82: </table>
83: </center></div><div align="center"><center>
84: <table border="0" cellpadding="0" cellspacing="0" width="76%">
85:      <tr>
86:          <th colspan="3" width="40%" bgcolor="#008080">Books</th>
87:          <th align="left"> </th>
88:          <th colspan="3" bgcolor="#008080">Reserved Books</th>
89:      </tr>
90:      <tr>
91:          <td rowspan="5" colspan="3" width="40%" nowrap>
92:              <object id="GridBook"
➡classid="clsid:00028C00-0000-0000-0000-000000000046"
93:                      align="left" border="0" hspace="0" width="305"
94:                      height="200">
95:              </object>
96:          </td>
97:          <td width="20%"> </td>
98:          <td rowspan="5" colspan="3" width="40%" nowrap>
99:              <object id="GridTmpReserved"
➡classid="clsid:00028C00-0000-0000-0000-000000000046"
```

continues

Listing 21.3. continued

```
100:                          align="baseline" border="0" width="300" height="200">
101:                </object>
102:             </td>
103:          </tr>
104:          <tr>
105:             <td align="center" width="20%" nowrap><input
106:             type="button" name="AddBook" value="Add&gt;&gt;" </td></td>
107:          </tr>
108:          <tr>
109:             <th width="20%"><input type="button" name="RemoveBook"
110:             value="&lt;&lt;Remove" </td></th>
111:          </tr>
112:          <tr>
113:             <td align="center" width="20%" nowrap></td>
114:          </tr>
115: </table>
116: </center></div><div align="center"><center>
117: <br><br>
118: </center></div>
119: <p> </p>
120: <!-- AdvancedDataSpace -->
121:     <OBJECT ID="ADS1" WIDTH=1 HEIGHT=1
122:     CLASSID="CLSID:99586D40-DB60-11CF-9D87-00AA00B91181">
123: </OBJECT>
124: <OBJECT CLASSID="clsid:9381D8F2-0288-11d0-9501-00AA00B911A5"
125:     ID=ADCAuthor HEIGHT=1 WIDTH = 1
126:     CODEBASE="HTTP://<%=Request.ServerVariables("Server_name")%>
➥/ADCDownload/msadc10.cab">
127:     <PARAM NAME="BINDINGS" VALUE="VBComboAuthor">
128:     <PARAM NAME="server" VALUE="http://
➥<%=Request.ServerVariables("Server_name")%>">
129:     <PARAM NAME="Connect" VALUE="DSN=VLibrary;uid=sa">
130:     <PARAM NAME="SQL" VALUE="SELECT rtrim(name) AuthorName
➥FROM vlib_author  order by name">
131: </OBJECT>
132: <OBJECT CLASSID="clsid:9381D8F2-0288-11d0-9501-00AA00B911A5"
133:     ID=ADCKeyword HEIGHT=1 WIDTH = 1
134:     CODEBASE="HTTP://<%=Request.ServerVariables("Server_name")%>
➥/ADCDownload/msadc10.cab">
135:     <PARAM NAME="BINDINGS" VALUE="VBComboKeyword">
136:     <PARAM NAME="server" VALUE="http://
➥<%=Request.ServerVariables("Server_name")%>">
137:     <PARAM NAME="Connect" VALUE="DSN=VLibrary;uid=sa">
138:     <PARAM NAME="SQL" VALUE="SELECT rtrim(name) KeywordName
➥FROM vlib_keyword  order by name">
139: </OBJECT>
140: <OBJECT CLASSID="clsid:9381D8F2-0288-11d0-9501-00AA00B911A5"
141:     ID=ADCLibrary HEIGHT=1 WIDTH = 1
142:     CODEBASE="HTTP://<%=Request.ServerVariables("Server_name")%>
➥/ADCDownload/msadc10.cab">
143:     <PARAM NAME="BINDINGS" VALUE="VBComboLibrary">
144:     <PARAM NAME="server" VALUE="http://
➥<%=Request.ServerVariables("Server_name")%>">
145:     <PARAM NAME="Connect" VALUE="DSN=VLibrary;uid=sa">
146:     <PARAM NAME="SQL" VALUE="SELECT RTRIM(name) LibraryName
➥FROM vlibrary order by name">
```

```
147: </OBJECT>
148: <OBJECT CLASSID="clsid:9381D8F2-0288-11d0-9501-00AA00B911A5"
149:     ID=ADCBook HEIGHT=1 WIDTH = 1
150:     CODEBASE="HTTP://<%=Request.ServerVariables("Server_name")%>
➥/ADCDownload/msadc10.cab">
151:     <PARAM NAME="BINDINGS" VALUE="GridBook; ">
152: </OBJECT>
153: <OBJECT CLASSID="clsid:9381D8F2-0288-11d0-9501-00AA00B911A5"
154:     ID=ADCTmpReserved HEIGHT=1 WIDTH = 1
155:     CODEBASE="HTTP://<%=Request.ServerVariables("Server_name")%>
➥/ADCDownload/msadc10.cab">
156:     <PARAM NAME="BINDINGS" VALUE="GridtmpReserved">
157: </OBJECT>
158: <SCRIPT LANGUAGE="VBScript">
159: Option Explicit
160: Dim myObj
161: Dim ret
162: Dim rs
163: Dim SType
164: Dim MemberID
165: SType=0
166: Dim rso
167: SUB SearchTypeClick(curvalue)
168: SType = curValue
169: END SUB
170:
171: SUB Query_OnClick()
172:     Dim mytest
173:     IF SType = 0 THEN
174:         set rs = myObj.GetAllBooks
175:     ELSEIF SType = 1 THEN
176:         myTest = RTrim(VBComboAuthor.Text)
177:         IF myTest ="" THEN
178:             myTest ="%"
179:         END IF
180:         set rs = myObj.GetBooksBasedOnAuthor(myTest)
181:     ELSEIF SType = 2 THEN
182:         myTest = RTrim(TitleParameter.value)
183:         IF myTest ="" THEN
184:             myTest ="%"
185:         END IF
186:         set rs = myObj.GetBooksBasedOnTitle(myTest)
187:     ELSEIF SType = 3 THEN
188:         myTest = RTrim(VBComboKeyword.Text)
189:         IF myTest ="" THEN
190:             myTest ="%"
191:         END IF
192:         set rs = myObj.GetBooksBasedOnKeyword(myTest)
193:     ELSEIF SType = 4 THEN
194:         myTest = RTrim(VBComboLibrary.Text)
195:         IF myTest ="" THEN
196:             myTest ="%"
197:         END IF
198:         set rs = myObj.GetBooksBasedOnLibrary(myTest)
199:     ELSEIF SType = 5 THEN
200:         myTest = RTrim(ISBNParameter.Value)
```

21

continues

Listing 21.3. continued

```
201:        IF myTest ="" THEN
202:            myTest ="%"
203:        END IF
204:        set rs = myObj.GetBooksBasedOnISBN(myTest)
205:     END IF
206:
207:     IF NOT ISEmpty(rs) THEN
208:         AdcBook.Recordset = rs
209:     END IF
210: End SUB
211:
212: SUB AddBook_OnClick()
213:     dim myBookID
214:     dim myRet
215:
216:     myBookID = GridBook.Columns("ID").Text
217:     myRet = myObj.InsertTmpReserved(MemberID, myBookID)
218:     IF myRet = 0 THEN
219:         MsgBox "This book has already been reserved or checkout by you"
220:     ELSE
221:         set rs = myObj.GetTmpReserved(MemberID)
222:         AdcTmpReserved.recordset = rs
223:     END IF
224: END SUB
225:
226: SUB RemoveBook_OnClick()
227:     dim myBookID
228:     dim myret
229:
230:     myBookID = GridTmpReserved.Columns("BookID").Text
231:     myret = myObj.RemoveTmpReserved(MemberID, myBookID)
232:     set rs = myObj.GetTmpReserved(MemberID)
233:     AdcTmpReserved.recordset = rs
234: END SUB
235:
236:
237: Sub Window_OnLoad()
238:     Set myObj = ADS1.CreateObject("VlibObj.VLibObjCls",
  ➥ "HTTP://<%=Request.ServerVariables("Server_name")%>")
239:     GridTmpReserved.AllowAddNew = True
240:     MemberID = <%=request.form("MemberID")%>
241:     set rs = myObj.GetTmpReserved(MemberID)
242:     AdcTmpReserved.recordset = rs
243:
244: End Sub
245: </SCRIPT>
246: </BODY>
247: </HTML>
```

21

A new ADC control and DBGrid are added to hold the reserved books: `ADCTmpReserved` and `GridTmpReserved`. When the Add button is clicked, the `AddBook_OnClick` sub-routine is called.

The `AddBook_OnClick` sub-routine retrieves the book ID of the current record into the GridBook control and invokes the `InsertTmpReserved` method. If the `InsertTmpReserved` method returns `0`, it displays a message box informing the member that he or she has already reserved or checked out that book. If the `InsertTmpReserved` method returns `1`, it refreshes the DBTmpReserved control by invoking the `GetTmpReserved` method.

When the Remove button is clicked, the `RemoveBook_OnClick` sub-routine is called; it invokes the `RemoveTmpReserved` method to remove a book from the VLib_TmpReserved table. After the record is removed, it refreshes the DBTmpReserved control by invoking the `GetTmpReserved` method.

The reserve book component is now complete, and you can try testing how it works. Figure 21.8 shows you the reserve book component after a member searches for books based on the specified author.

Figure 21.8.

The reserve book component.

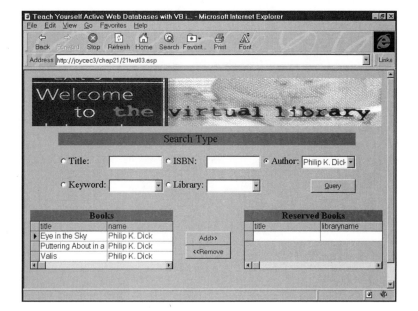

In Figure 21.9, the member has clicked the Add button to reserve two books.

Figure 21.9.

Reserving two books.

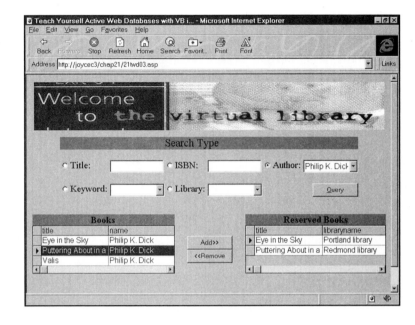

In Figure 21.10, the member has clicked the Remove button to remove one of the books from the reserved list.

Figure 21.10.

Removing a book from the reserved list.

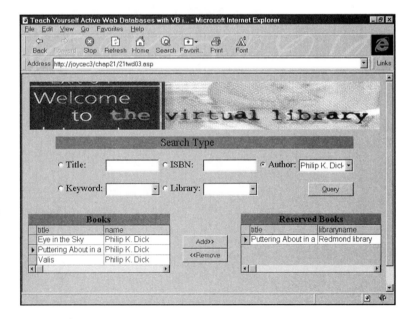

The Checkout/Extend Books Component

The checkout/extend books component allows you to check out all the books in the reserved list and extend a book's due date.

Once the reserved books are checked out, the books on that member's reserved list need to be removed. For extending a book's due date, you want to enforce the rule that the maximum loan period for a book is 30 days. If the member tries to extend the book's due date past 30 days, the extension is refused.

Tables for the Checkout/Extend Books Component

The tables used in this component are VLib_TmpReserved and VLib_Checkout. These two tables were described in the section on the reserve books component.

Stored Procedures for the Checkout/Extend Books Component

You need to create stored procedures to get a list of books that have been checked out and insert them into the VLib_Checkout table. You also need a stored procedure to check whether a book's due date can be extended. If it can, you need a stored procedure to update the due date.

The `VLib_sp_GetCheckout` Stored Procedure

The `VLib_sp_GetCheckout` stored procedure retrieves all the books checked out by the specified member ID from the VLib_Checkout table:

```
create proc VLib_sp_GetCheckout
@memberID integer
as
select a.title, f.duedate, b.name,a.isbn,c.name keyword1,
➥d.name keyword2, e.name  keyword3,  a.description ,a.id BookID
from vlib_book a, vlib_author b, vlib_keyword c,
vlib_keyword d,  vlib_keyword e, VLib_CheckOut f
Where a.authorid = b.id
and a.id = f.Bookid
and f.MemberId = @memberID
and a.keyword1 *= c.id
and a.keyword2 *= d.id
and a.keyword3 *= e.id
order by a.title
```

21

The `VLib_InsertCheckout` **Stored Procedure**

The `VLib_InsertCheckout` stored procedure inserts a record into the VLib_Checkout table based on the member ID, book ID, and library ID:

```
create proc VLib_sp_InsertCheckout
@memberID integer,
@BookID integer,
@LibraryID integer
as
insert into Vlib_Checkout(Memberid, BookID, LibraryID,
➥checkoutdate, duedate, extend)
values(@MemberID, @BookID, @LibraryID, getdate(),
➥DATEADD(day, 7, getdate()), 1)
```

The data for the CheckoutDate column of the inserted record is the current system date, and the data for the DueDate column is seven days plus the current system date, which means the member can borrow the book for seven days.

The `VLib_CheckExtend` **Stored Procedure**

The `VLib_CheckExtend` stored procedure, as shown here, performs two checks:

```
create proc VLib_sp_CheckExtend
@memberID integer,
@BookID integer
as
declare @CheckOutPeriod integer
select @CheckOutPeriod =datediff(day,getdate(), checkoutdate)
from vlib_checkout
where bookid=@bookid
and memberid=@memberid
if @CheckOutPeriod > 23
select 0
else
select 1
```

First, it checks whether the book is already overdue. If it is, the member can't extend it. Second, it checks the book's check-out date. If the current system date is more than 23 days past the date indicated in the CheckoutDate column, the member can't extend the book's due date because a book can't be loaned out for more than 30 days. The stored procedure returns 0 if the extension is denied and returns 1 if it's OK to extend the due date.

The `VLib_UpdateDueDate` **Stored Procedure**

The `VLib_UpdateDueDate` stored procedure updates the book's due date, indicated in the DueDate column of the VLib_Checkout table:

```
create proc Vlib_sp_UpdateDueDate
@memberID integer,
@BookID integer
as
update vlib_Checkout
```

```
set duedate = dateadd(day,7,duedate)
where bookid=@bookid
and memberid=@memberid
go
```

The new due date is the old due date plus seven days.

Business Objects for the Checkout/Extend Books Component

You need to add methods for inserting and retrieving checked-out books. You also need to add a method to extend a book's due date.

The GetCheckout Method

The GetCheckout method calls the VLib_sp_GetCheckout stored procedure to retrieve the checked-out books from the VLib_Checkout table for the specified member ID:

```
Function GetCheckout(ByVal MemberID As Integer) As Object
Dim rs As New ADODB.Recordset
Dim SQLString As String

    SQLString = "exec VLib_sp_GetCheckout " & MemberID

    Set rs = ProcessQuery(SQLString)
    Set GetCheckOut = rs

End Function
```

The InsertCheckout Method

The InsertCheckout method reconnects to the reserved book Recordset, then scans through all the records and calls the VLib_sp_InsertCheckout stored procedure to insert a record in the VLib_Checkout table based on the customer ID and book ID of the record in the reserved book Recordset:

```
Public Function InsertCheckout(rso As Object, ByVal MemberID As Integer)
Dim conn As New ADODB.Connection
Dim rsInsert As New ADODB.Recordset
Dim rs As New ADODB.Recordset
Dim SQLString As String

conn.Open "dsn=VLibrary;uid=sa;pwd"
rs.Open rso, "dsn=VLibrary;uid=sa;pwd=;"

rs.MoveFirst
While Not rs.EOF

SQLString = "exec VLib_sp_InsertCheckout " & MemberID & "," _
& rs("BookID") & "," & rs("LibraryID")
```

21

```
Set rsInsert = conn.Execute(SQLString)
rs.MoveNext
Wend
End Function
```

The ExtendBook **Method**

The ExtendBook method first calls the CanExtend stored procedure to see whether a book's due date can be extended:

```
Function ExtendBook(ByVal MemberID As Integer, ByVal BookID As Integer) As
Integer
    Dim myRet As Integer

    myRet = CanExtend(MemberID, BookID)
    If myRet = 1 Then
        myRet = UpdateDueDate(MemberID, BookID)
        ExtendBook = 1
    Else
        ExtendBook = 0
    End If
End Function
```

If the due date can be extended, the method calls the VLib_UpdateDueDate stored procedure to extend the book's due date and returns 1 to indicate that it's done so successfully. Otherwise, the method returns 0 to indicate that the extension has failed.

HTML Code for the Checkout/Extend Books Component

You need an ADC and a DBGrid control to hold the checked-out book list, a button for checking out the reserved book, and a button to extend the selected book's due date. The complete HTML code is shown in Listing 21.4.

Listing 21.4. The checkout/extend books component.

```
 1: <HTML>
 2: <HEAD>
 3: <TITLE>Teach Yourself Active Web Databases with VB in 21 Days</TITLE>
 4: </HEAD>
 5: <BODY LANGUAGE="VBS">
 6: <center>
 7: <IMG SRC="vlibrary.gif" ALT="Virtual Library">
 8: <br><br><br><br>
 9: <table border="0" cellpadding="0" cellspacing="0" width="70%"
10: bordercolor="#008080">
11:     <tr>
12:         <td colspan="2" width="30%" bgcolor="#008080"> </td>
13:         <td colspan="2" bgcolor="#008080"><font size="4">Search
```

```
14:          Type</font></td>
15:          <td colspan="2" bgcolor="#008080"> </td>
16:      </tr>
17:      <tr>
18:          <td> </td>
19:          <td> </td>
20:      </tr>
21:      <tr>
22:          <td valign="top" width="5%" nowrap>
23:              <input type="radio"name="SearchType" value="Title"
24:              onclick="SearchTypeClick(3)">Title:
25:          </td>
26:          <td valign="top" width="25">
27:              <input type="text" size="13" name="TitleParameter">
28:          </td>
29:          <td valign="top" width="4%" nowrap>
30:              <input type="radio"name="SearchType" value="ISBN"
31:              onclick="SearchTypeClick(5)">ISBN:
32:          </td>
33:          <td valign="top" width="25%" nowrap>
34:              <input type="text"size="13" name="ISBNParameter">
35:          </td>
36:          <td valign="top" width="5%" nowrap>
37:              <input type="radio"name="SearchType" value="Author"
38:              onclick="SearchTypeClick(1)">Author:
39:          </td>
40:          <td align="right" valign="top" width="25%" nowrap>
41:              <object id="VBComboAuthor"
➥classid="clsid:FAEEE760-117E-101B-8933-08002B2F4F5A"
42:                      align="baseline" border="0" width="117" height="28">
43:                  <param name="ListField" value="AuthorName">
44:              </object>
45:          </td>
46:      </tr>
47:      <tr>
48:          <td> </td>
49:          <td> </td>
50:          <td> </td>
51:          <td> </td>
52:          <td> </td>
53:          <td> </td>
54:      </tr>
55:      <tr>
56:          <td valign="top" width="5%" nowrap>
57:              <input type="radio"name="SearchType" value="Keyword"
58:               onclick="SearchTypeClick(3)">Keyword:
59:          </td>
60:          <td valign="top" width="25%">
61:              <object id="VBComboKeyword" classid="
➥clsid:FAEEE760-117E-101B-8933-08002B2F4F5A"
62:                      align="texttop" border="0" width="117" height="28">
63:                  <param name="ListField" value="KeywordName">
64:              </object>
65:          </td>
66:          <td valign="top" width="4%" nowrap>
67:              <input type="radio"name="SearchType" value="Library"
```

21

continues

Listing 21.4. continued

```
68:                    onclick="SearchTypeClick(4)">Library:
69:           </td>
70:           <td valign="top" width="25%" nowrap>
71:               <object id="VBComboLibrary"classid="
➥clsid:FAEEE760-117E-101B-8933-08002B2F4F5A"
72:                    align="baseline" border="0" width="117" height="28">
73:                    <param name="ListField"value="LibraryName">
74:               </object>
75:           </td>
76:           <td align="right" valign="bottom" colspan="2" width="30%">
77:               <p align="right">
78:               <input type="button" name="Query"value="&Query"></p>
79:               <p align="right"> </p>
80:           </td>
81:      </tr>
82: </table>
83: </center></div><div align="center"><center>
84: <table border="0" cellpadding="0" cellspacing="0" width="76%">
85:      <tr>
86:           <th colspan="3" width="40%" bgcolor="#008080">Books</th>
87:           <th align="left"> </th>
88:           <th colspan="3" bgcolor="#008080">Reserved Books</th>
89:      </tr>
90:      <tr>
91:           <td rowspan="5" colspan="3" width="40%" nowrap>
92:               <object id="GridBook"
➥classid="clsid:00028C00-0000-0000-0000-000000000046"
93:                    align="left" border="0" hspace="0" width="305"
94:                    height="200">
95:               </object>
96:           </td>
97:           <td width="20%"> </td>
98:           <td rowspan="5" colspan="3" width="40%" nowrap>
99:               <object id="GridTmpReserved"
➥classid="clsid:00028C00-0000-0000-0000-000000000046"
100:                   align="baseline" border="0" width="300" height="200">
101:              </object>
102:          </td>
103:      </tr>
104:      <tr>
105:           <td align="center" width="20%" nowrap><input
106:           type="button" name="AddBook" value="Add&gt;&gt;" </td></td>
107:      </tr>
108:      <tr>
109:           <th width="20%"><input type="button" name="RemoveBook"
110:           value="&lt;&lt;Remove" </td></th>
111:      </tr>
112:      <tr>
113:           <td align="center" width="20%" nowrap><input
114:           type="button" name="Commit" value="&amp;Commit"></td>
115:      </tr>
116: </table>
117: </center></div><div align="center"><center>
118: <br><br>
119: <table border="0" cellpadding="0" cellspacing="0" width="60%">
120:      <tr>
```

```
121:        <td> </td>
122:        <td> </td>
123:        <td> </td>
124:        <td> </td>
125:        <td> </td>
126:        <td> </td>
127:        <td> </td>
128:        <th width="50%" bgcolor="#FF00FF">Checkout Books</th>
129:        <td> </td>
130:        <th width="50%"> </th>
131:    </tr>
132:    <tr>
133:        <td rowspan="5" width="10%"> </td>
134:        <td rowspan="5"> </td>
135:        <td rowspan="5"> </td>
136:        <td rowspan="5"> </td>
137:        <td rowspan="5"> </td>
138:        <td rowspan="5"> </td>
139:        <td rowspan="5"> </td>
140:        <td align="right" rowspan="5" width="90%">
141:            <object id="GridCheckout"
➥classid="CLSID:00028C00-0000-0000-0000-000000000046"
142:                    align="baseline" border="0" width="500" height="259">
143:            </object>
144:        </td>
145:        <td> </td>
146:        <td width="10%"> </td>
147:    </tr>
148:    <tr>
149:        <td> </td>
150:        <td width="10%"> </td>
151:    </tr>
152:    <tr>
153:        <td> </td>
154:        <td width="10%"> </td>
155:    </tr>
156:    <tr>
157:        <td> </td>
158:        <td width="10%"> </td>
159:    </tr>
160:    <tr>
161:        <td> </td>
162:        <td align="right" valign="bottom" width="10%"><input
163:        type="button" name="Extend" value="&amp;Extend"></td>
164:    </tr>
165: </table>
166: </center></div>
167: <p> </p>
168: <!-- AdvancedDataSpace -->
169:     <OBJECT ID="ADS1" WIDTH=1 HEIGHT=1
170:     CLASSID="CLSID:99586D40-DB60-11CF-9D87-00AA00B91181">
171: </OBJECT>
172: <OBJECT CLASSID="clsid:9381D8F2-0288-11d0-9501-00AA00B911A5"
173:     ID=ADCAuthor HEIGHT=1 WIDTH = 1
174:     CODEBASE="HTTP://<%=Request.ServerVariables("Server_name")%>
➥/ADCDownload/msadc10.cab">
```

continues

Listing 21.4. continued

```
175:        <PARAM NAME="BINDINGS" VALUE="VBComboAuthor">
176:        <PARAM NAME="server" VALUE="http://
➥<%=Request.ServerVariables("Server_name")%>">
177:        <PARAM NAME="Connect" VALUE="DSN=VLibrary;uid=sa">
178:        <PARAM NAME="SQL" VALUE="SELECT rtrim(name) AuthorName
➥FROM vlib_author  order by name">
179: </OBJECT>
180: <OBJECT CLASSID="clsid:9381D8F2-0288-11d0-9501-00AA00B911A5"
181:        ID=ADCKeyword HEIGHT=1 WIDTH = 1
182:        CODEBASE="HTTP://<%=Request.ServerVariables("Server_name")%>
➥/ADCDownload/msadc10.cab">
183:        <PARAM NAME="BINDINGS" VALUE="VBComboKeyword">
184:        <PARAM NAME="server" VALUE="http://
➥<%=Request.ServerVariables("Server_name")%>">
185:        <PARAM NAME="Connect" VALUE="DSN=VLibrary;uid=sa">
186:        <PARAM NAME="SQL" VALUE="SELECT rtrim(name) KeywordName
➥FROM vlib_keyword  order by name">
187: </OBJECT>
188: <OBJECT CLASSID="clsid:9381D8F2-0288-11d0-9501-00AA00B911A5"
189:        ID=ADCLibrary HEIGHT=1 WIDTH = 1
190:        CODEBASE="HTTP://<%=Request.ServerVariables("Server_name")%>
➥/ADCDownload/msadc10.cab">
191:        <PARAM NAME="BINDINGS" VALUE="VBComboLibrary">
192:        <PARAM NAME="server" VALUE="http://
➥<%=Request.ServerVariables("Server_name")%>">
193:        <PARAM NAME="Connect" VALUE="DSN=VLibrary;uid=sa">
194:        <PARAM NAME="SQL" VALUE="SELECT RTRIM(name) LibraryName
➥FROM vlibrary order by name">
195: </OBJECT>
196: <OBJECT CLASSID="clsid:9381D8F2-0288-11d0-9501-00AA00B911A5"
197:        ID=ADCBook HEIGHT=1 WIDTH = 1
198:        CODEBASE="HTTP://<%=Request.ServerVariables("Server_name")%>
➥/ADCDownload/msadc10.cab">
199:        <PARAM NAME="BINDINGS" VALUE="GridBook;Description.text=description">
200: </OBJECT>
201: <OBJECT CLASSID="clsid:9381D8F2-0288-11d0-9501-00AA00B911A5"
202:        ID=ADCTmpReserved HEIGHT=1 WIDTH = 1
203:        CODEBASE="HTTP://<%=Request.ServerVariables("Server_name")%>
➥/ADCDownload/msadc10.cab">
204:        <PARAM NAME="BINDINGS" VALUE="GridtmpReserved">
205: </OBJECT>
206: <OBJECT CLASSID="clsid:9381D8F2-0288-11d0-9501-00AA00B911A5"
207:        ID=ADCGetCheckout HEIGHT=1 WIDTH = 1
208:        CODEBASE="HTTP://<%=Request.ServerVariables("Server_name")%>
➥/ADCDownload/msadc10.cab">
209:        <PARAM NAME="BINDINGS" VALUE="GridCheckout">
210: </OBJECT>
211: <SCRIPT LANGUAGE="VBScript">
212: Option Explicit
213: Dim myObj
214: Dim ret
215: Dim rs
216: Dim SType
217: Dim MemberID
218: SType=0
```

```
219: Dim rso
220: SUB SearchTypeClick(curvalue)
221: SType = curValue
222: END SUB
223:
224: SUB Query_OnClick()
225:     Dim mytest
226:     IF SType = 0 THEN
227:        set rs = myObj.GetAllBooks
228:     ELSEIF SType = 1 THEN
229:        myTest = RTrim(VBComboAuthor.Text)
230:        IF myTest ="" THEN
231:           myTest ="%"
232:        END IF
233:        set rs = myObj.GetBooksBasedOnAuthor(myTest)
234:     ELSEIF SType = 2 THEN
235:        myTest = RTrim(TitleParameter.value)
236:        IF myTest ="" THEN
237:           myTest ="%"
238:        END IF
239:        set rs = myObj.GetBooksBasedOnTitle(myTest)
240:     ELSEIF SType = 3 THEN
241:        myTest = RTrim(VBComboKeyword.Text)
242:        IF myTest ="" THEN
243:           myTest ="%"
244:        END IF
245:        set rs = myObj.GetBooksBasedOnKeyword(myTest)
246:     ELSEIF SType = 4 THEN
247:        myTest = RTrim(VBComboLibrary.Text)
248:        IF myTest ="" THEN
249:           myTest ="%"
250:        END IF
251:        set rs = myObj.GetBooksBasedOnLibrary(myTest)
252:     ELSEIF SType = 5 THEN
253:        myTest = RTrim(ISBNParameter.Value)
254:        IF myTest ="" THEN
255:           myTest ="%"
256:        END IF
257:        set rs = myObj.GetBooksBasedOnISBN(myTest)
258:     END IF
259:
260:     IF NOT ISEmpty(rs) THEN
261:        AdcBook.Recordset = rs
262:     END IF
263: End SUB
264:
265: SUB AddBook_OnClick()
266:     dim myBookID
267:     dim myRet
268:
269:     myBookID = GridBook.Columns("ID").Text
270:     myRet = myObj.InsertTmpReserved(MemberID, myBookID)
271:     IF myRet = 0 THEN
272:        MsgBox "This book has already been reserved or checked out by you"
273:     ELSE
274:        set rs = myObj.GetTmpReserved(MemberID)
```

continues

21

Listing 21.4. continued

```
275:        AdcTmpReserved.recordset = rs
276:     END IF
277: END SUB
278:
279: SUB RemoveBook_OnClick()
280:     dim myBookID
281:     dim myret
282:
283:     myBookID = GridTmpReserved.Columns("BookID").Text
284:     myret = myObj.RemoveTmpReserved(MemberID, myBookID)
285:     set rs = myObj.GetTmpReserved(MemberID)
286:     AdcTmpReserved.recordset = rs
287: END SUB
288:
289:
290: SUB Commit_OnClick()
291:     set rso = AdcTmpReserved.Recordset
292:     rso.MarshalOptions=0
293:     myObj.InsertCheckout rso, MemberID
294:     set rs = myObj.GetCheckout(MemberID)
295:     ADCGetCheckout.recordset = rs
296:     myObj.RemoveAllTmpReserved(MemberID)
297:     set rs = myObj.GetTmpReserved(MemberID)
298:     AdcTmpReserved.recordset = rs
299: End SUB
300:
301: SUB Extend_OnClick()
302:     dim myRet
303:     myRet=myObj.ExtendBook(MemberID, GridCheckout.Columns("BookID").Text)
304: IF myRet = 1 THEN
305:     set rs = myObj.GetCheckout(MemberID)
306:     ADCGetCheckout.recordset = rs
307: ELSE
308:    MsgBox "You can not extend this book"
309: END IF
310: End SUB
311:
312: Sub Window_OnLoad()
313:     Set myObj = ADS1.CreateObject("VlibObj.VLibObjCls",
➥ "HTTP://<%=Request.ServerVariables("Server_name")%>")
314:     GridTmpReserved.AllowAddNew = True
315:     MemberID = <%=request.form("MemberID")%>
316:     set rs = myObj.GetCheckout(MemberID)
317:     ADCGetCheckout.recordset = rs
318:     set rs = myObj.GetTmpReserved(MemberID)
319:     AdcTmpReserved.recordset = rs
320:
321: End Sub
322: </SCRIPT>
323: </BODY>
324: </HTML>
```

21

ANALYSIS ADCGetCheckout binds the checked-out Recordset with the GridCheckout control. When a member clicks the Commit button, the Commit_OnClick sub-routine is called to invoke the InsertCheckout method and pass all records in the ADCTmpReserved Recordset as the first input parameter of the method. All the records in ADCTmpReserved are committed to the VLib_Checkout table; after the commit is done, it invokes the RemoveAllTmpReserved method to remove all the reserved books from the VLib_TmpReserved table.

When a member clicks the Extend button, the Extend_OnClick sub-routine is called to invoke the UpdateDueDate method, which extends the current record in the GridReserved control. If the return code of UpdateDueDate is 0, it means the member can't extend the book's due date; otherwise, the book's due date is successfully extended, and the GetReserved method is invoked again to refresh the ADCGetCheckout Recordset.

The checkout/extend component is done, so your Virtual Library is finished. Now you need to combine the member login/registration, search engine, reserve book, and check out/extend components.

Combining All the Components

After combining the member login/registration, search engine, reserve book, and checkout/extend book components into the main library Web page, the Virtual Library's functions are complete. In the main library Web page, members can search for books based on search criteria, reserve books, check out books, and even extend books' due dates.

The security of the main library Web page is controlled by the member login/registration Web page. Only members can enter the main library Web page. They must enter a valid member ID in the member login/registration Web page to enter the main library Web page. Non-members must register before they can enter the main library Web page.

With all these components combined, you have a powerful online library system. From this example, you learn how to build an online system step by step and one component at a time, and then make them work together.

Figure 21.11 shows you the result after extending the due date of one of the checked-out books.

21

Figure 21.11.

Extending one book's due date.

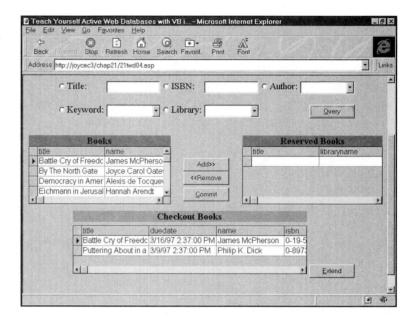

Summary

This chapter has incorporated everything you've learned this week and applied that knowledge to construct the Virtual Library. This example has demonstrated how the Advanced Data Connector makes dynamic Web programming easier and allows you to interact with live data in the client tier. While building this example, you have also seen how valuable business objects are and how to use them to protect your data and business rules.

Q&A

Q **Why do I have to use stored procedures to retrieve or update data?**

A Using stored procedures prevents you from changing the business object every time you need to modify SQL statements. If you need to make changes to a particular SQL statement, you need to modify only one stored procedure instead of re-compiling the whole business object.

Q **Can I use Oracle databases with ADC?**

A For retrieving data only, yes. Keep in mind that updates work only with SQL Server when you're using ADC 1.0. You need to make sure the SQL*Net version is 2.3.2.1.4, and that you have Oracle 7.1 Client and Oracle 7.3 Workgroup for Windows installed.

Quiz

1. How do you get data from the previous Web page? For example, how do you get the member ID from the member login/registration component's Web page into the search engine's Web page?
2. Can you update data through ADC with an Oracle database?
3. What keyword do you have to use in your SQL statement to update records?

Exercise

Add a business rule to the Virtual Library to calculate a member's balance. For example, if books are overdue, the member must pay certain amount of money as an overdue fine.

21

In Review

Chapters 15 through 21 gave you a detailed overview and examples using Microsoft Advanced Data Connector components, along with the ActiveX Data Objects, Active Server Pages, Visual Basic Script, and Visual Basic, to build powerful database-intensive Web applications.

In Chapter 15, "The Advanced Data Connector (ADC)" you learned about the architecture and programming model of Advanced Data Connector. Traditional CGI Web programming was introduced, followed by the ADC architecture. The differences between CGI and ADC were explored in depth, and several CGI programming limitations that have been addressed in ADC were discussed. The chapter explained the purpose of the ADC and its approach to Web database programming. All the ADC framework components and a quick overview of the component descriptions were introduced.

Chapter 16, "Using the AdvancedDataControl Object," took a closer look at the client-tier architecture of the Advanced Data Connector. The ADC client-tier components and their relationships were discussed in detail. The chapter showed you the steps to get your machine ready for being the ADC application server and client tier, and then took you through the properties and methods of the AdvancedDataControl object. Visual Basic data-aware controls were introduced to work with the Bindings property of the AdvancedDataControl object, and many small examples showed you how to use the individual properties and methods of the AdvancedDataControl object. Finally, the chapter combined the properties and methods of AdvancedDataControl objects into a virtual Video Store example to show you how ADC achieves interactive Web programming.

Chapter 17, "The AdvancedDataControl and the ADO Recordset," showed you how to get at data directly in your own client-side scripting code. Instead of restricting interactive data access to prepackaged Edit controls, you can manipulate the individual field values by using your own programming instructions. A subset of the ActiveX Data Objects, the ADOR Recordset is available through a property of the AdvancedDataControl. Although its features are limited compared to the full ADODB Recordset found on the server, the access to data it provides through programming is fundamental for developing highly interactive Web pages.

Chapter 18, "Data Validation," introduced you to data validation and showed you how to take advantage of data access through the ADOR Recordset by putting it to use validating the consistency and correctness of the data entered on the client machine. You saw many different ways to validate data: validations per field, per record, and across the entire Recordset. You can make these validations happen any time the user performs specific interactions, such as pressing buttons or entering or exiting individual edit fields. You also learned how to attach your own programming instructions to these events that could perform any type of validation task.

The middle tier (application server) of the ADC architecture was introduced in Chapter 19, "Client-Server Business Objects." The application server components and their relationships were discussed in detail. You learned what business objects are and what their purpose is. The properties of the AdvancedDataSpace object were introduced and followed by examples of how to use them. You then learned about the default business object and the AdvancedDataFactory object and its properties. You saw how to create a custom business object in both Visual Basic 4.0 and 5.0, learned the importance of marking business objects as safe for scripting, and saw how to allow the business object to be launched in the ADC environment. The chapter then concluded with a discussion on how to use the AdvancedDataSpace object to interact with custom business objects.

Chapter 20, "Business Objects and ADO," continued where Chapter 19 left off. It showed you how to use ADO to create custom business objects and introduced one of ADC's important features: disconnected Recordsets. You learned how to prepare your Recordset in the application server so it can be marshaled to the client tier and work in a disconnected fashion. You also saw how you can marshal the complete Recordset, or only the changed records, from the client tier to the application server. The chapter also discussed how to validate changed data in the custom business object, apply the changes to the database server, and how to use Advanced Data Connector components in Visual Basic.

The last chapter of the week, 21, "Interactive Web Application: The Virtual Library," combined what you have learned throughout the week in one complete example: "The Virtual Library," an online virtual library system. It showed you how to use AdvancedDataControl objects and data-aware Visual Basic controls to retrieve data, how to build custom business objects to enforce business rules with ADODB, and how to validate data in the business object. This virtual library example showed you how to build a search engine using AdvancedDataControl objects and how to hide the business logic and protected data from the client tier in the custom business object.

Together, these chapters gave you a firm understanding of how to use business objects and Advanced Data Connector's components and how to use Visual Basic to develop interactive Web database applications.

APPENDIX A

Where to Find Everything

This appendix is meant to be a guide to finding just about anything related to this book's subject matter. Most of the products mentioned in this book are produced by Microsoft and can be found at the Microsoft site (www.microsoft.com). Some of the products are free, but you might have to pay for some.

You need three kinds of products: first, a full-blown application or operating system; second, an upgrade (referred to as a *Service Pack*); and third, a component that can be part of an application but isn't the entire application.

Software Requirements for Chapter Examples

Microsoft Windows NT Server 4.0 with Service Pack 2. The service pack is a requirement of Microsoft Internet Information Server 3.0 and is automatically installed as part of the IIS 3.0 installation.

Microsoft SQL Server 6.5 with Service Pack 2.

Microsoft Internet Information Server 3.0 with Active Server Pages. The only download file you really *need* is ASP.EXE.

Microsoft Advanced Data Connector 1.0.

Microsoft OLE DB SDK 1.1. You can download this product from the same page as the Advanced Data Connector page.

Microsoft ActiveX Data Objects 1.0. If you installed the ASP.EXE mentioned previously, then you have this component installed.

Visual Basic 4.0 or 5.0.

Microsoft Web Technologies and Products

Microsoft has provided most of the technologies used in this book. The following sections list where you can find the product pages.

Microsoft Internet Information Server (IIS) with Active Server Pages (ASP)

IIS is Microsoft's professional Web server. It supports HTTP, FTP, and Gopher, as well as Secure Sockets Layer (SSL). It must run on an NT Server or NT Workstation machine. At the time of this printing, IIS 3.0 is the most current version; it includes the Active Server Pages as well as the ActiveX Data Objects server technology. The languages currently supported are English, French, Spanish, and German, but more languages are planned.

The following list includes Web sites for products, documentation, and developer information:

☐ **http://www.microsoft.com/iis**

This is the Microsoft Internet Information Server product. You can download the 3.0 product from this site, but your machine must already have the 1.0 product installed. IIS 1.0 is part of the Windows NT 4.0 Server and Workstation installations.

☐ **http://kencox.corinet.com/kencscripts/index.asp**

This site contains demos of cool Active Server Pages.

☐ **http://www.genusa.com/asp/**

This site contains complete developer information on ASP and ISAPI. It also has a list of server-side objects for sale.

☐ **http://www.signmeup.com/faq/**

This site has a growing list of Frequently Asked Questions on many Internet server topics, including ASP, ADO, and IIS. If you have a question you want answered, you can e-mail it to webmaster@signmeup.com.

☐ **http://www.halcyon.com/qvr/asp.htm**

This site is a general Internet server site and offers great links to other sites about Internet servers.

Microsoft ActiveX Data Objects (ADO) 1.0

ADO is the technology used to connect server-side script pages (ASP) to datasources. It's installed as part of the IIS 3.0 installation, but you can find information about it at these sites:

☐ **http://www.microsoft.com/ado**

This is the offical site for ActiveX Data Objects.

☐ **http://www.aqiml.net/udaynet/**

This site is dedicated to ADC only, but has a good range of material.

☐ **http://www.genusa.com/asp/**

This site gives you complete developer information on ADO and also lists server-side objects for sale.

☐ **http://www.signmeup.com/faq/**

This site has a growing list of Frequently Asked Questions on many Internet server topics, including ASP, ADO, and IIS. If you have a question you want answered, you can e-mail it to webmaster@signmeup.com.

Microsoft Advanced Data Connector (ADC) 1.0

ADC is the technology that makes both client and server technologies faster and more efficient. Visit this site for more information and downloading on ADC and its components:

☐ **http://www.microsoft.com/adc**

This is the offical Advanced Data Connector site. It contains explanations, documentation, downloads, and examples.

Microsoft Visual Basic Script (VBScript)

VBScript is a subset of Visual Basic that can be executed on the client's machine (through the Internet Explorer 3.0 browser). VBScript can also be executed on the server within Active Server Pages scripting. You can get more information on VBScript and download it by visiting this site:

☐ **http://www.microsoft.com/vbscript**

This is the official VBScript site. It contains downloads and documentation and has links to related products.

Microsoft Windows NT Server 4.0

NT Server 4.0 is the operating system that IIS 3.0 runs on. It's a multitasking, multithreaded, secure operating system. Find out more about NT Server 4.0 at this site:

☐ **http://www.microsoft.com/ntserver**

This is the official Windows NT Server site. It contains information on planning and deployment, support, and training, as well as where to buy the product. It doesn't offer a free download of the released product.

Microsoft SQL Server 6.5

SQL Server 6.5 is a relational database that includes ODBC drivers, so it can be used with ADO/ADC technologies. Visit this site for more information on SQL Server:

☐ **http://www.microsoft.com/sql**

This site is the official SQL Server site, containing documents and downloads. You can download an evaluation copy of MS SQL Server from this site. Check out the free utility tools.

Microsoft Access

Microsoft Access is a relational database. It, too, has ODBC drivers so it can be used with ADO/ADC technologies. It's generally used for small-business or non-transactioned information. You can find more information on Access by visiting this site:

☐ `http://www.microsoft.com/msaccess`

This is the offical Access site. However, Access can't be downloaded at this site; it's part of the MS Office suite of products and can be purchased at most office and computer stores. This site does have cool Access add-ins, as well as links to the rest of the MS Office products.

Microsoft ActiveX

Microsoft's ActiveX Web gallery has many third-party ActiveX controls that can be used when you're doing data access. Most of these third-party controls can be downloaded from this site for a trial-period. For more information, check out these sites:

☐ `http://www.microsoft.com/gallery`

This is the official ActiveX gallery from Microsoft. It contains everything you need to get going with ActiveX, as well as some ActiveX third-party controls you can try.

☐ `http://www.activexserver.com/BBS1/login.asp`

This is a Web-based bulletin board system for ActiveX.

Microsoft Open Database Connectivity (ODBC)

ODBC is the interface that lets applications access SQL databases by using the SQL language. You can find out more about ODBC by visiting this site:

☐ `http://www.microsoft.com/odbc`

This is the official ODBC site. It may contain a free download of the product (a limited-time offer that may expire by the time the book is published). If you have installed IIS 3.0 or SQL Server 6.5, then you should already have a copy of ODBC on your machine. A quick way to check is to open the Control Panel. If you have an icon for ODBC, then the software is already installed. Make sure the version is 3.0 because earlier versions don't work with ASP, ADP, and ADC.

Microsoft OLE DB

OLE DB is the new database-connectivity software from Microsoft. It integrates ODBC with OLE and is a necessary component of both ADO and ADC. You can find out more about OLE DB by visiting this site:

☐ `http://www.microsoft.com/oledb`

This is the official OLE DB site. It contains product information, the API specification, downloads, and other links to help you get started on programming OLE DB.

Other Web Sites of Interest

The Web technologies mentioned in the preceding sections are those developed by Microsoft. The following sections list other organizations with a strong interest in the Web.

World Wide Web Consortium (www3)

The World Wide Web consortium controls and guides Web technology protocols, including HTML. Check out this site for the latest information on Web developments and protocol standards:

☐ `http://www.w3.org`

Netscape

Netscape is the leader in browser market share and is making extensions to the HTML programming language. You can download the product with a credit-card charge. Check out this site for more information on Netscape:

☐ `http://www.netscape.com`

Netscape Navigator (the Web browser) doesn't support the technologies covered in this book.

Oracle

Oracle is one of leading database providers for middle-tier UNIX systems. Microsoft is trying to make sure their middleware is compatible with Oracle technology. Check out this site to keep abreast of Oracle developments:

☐ `http://www.oracle.com`

Appendix B

Answers to Quiz Questions

Chapter 1 Answers

1. What's the difference between HTML and Active Server Pages?

    HTML is executed only on the client, and Active Server Pages are executed only on the Web server. VBScript can be executed in either place, depending on the syntax.

2. What's the difference between ADO and ADC?

    ADO is part of the Active Server Page technology and is executed on the server. ADC is a technology that has part of its components on the client and part on the server.

3. What HTML component can load different Web pages into the same browser space?

    Frames

4. Where can the rules for HTML be found?

    `http://www.w3.org`

5. Where can ADO be found?

    `http://www.microsoft.com/iis`

6. Where can ADC be found?

    `http://www.microsoft.com/adc`

Chapter 2 Answers

1. What are some of the protocols on the Web?

    TCP/IP and HTML

2. What's the difference between HTTP and TCP/IP?

    HTTP makes a type of request of the Web server, and TCP/IP breaks the request and transports it across the network.

3. How does the response/request model follow the client-server model?

    The response/request model is similar to the client-server model in that one machine is asking for work to be done, and the other machine is doing the work.

4. What does HTTP's PUT command do? Why is it typically not used?

    HTTP's PUT command places a file on the Web server. Few Web administrators allow such open access to a critical application.

5. What does HTTP's DELETE command do? Why is it generally not implemented?

HTTP's DELETE command deletes a file on a Web server. The Web is meant to be a resource for everyone, so there's usually a system for propagating Web pages to the server. The DELETE command would interfere with that methodology.

6. What is the difference between the functions of TCP and IP?

TCP breaks the request up into packets, and IP transports the packets.

7. What is a virtual root?

A virtual root is a mapping from a physical location to a Web location.

8. What does the execute permission do on a virtual root?

The execute permission is critical for allowing execution of a file, such as a CGI script, ISAPI, or ASP file.

9. How do you add default pages beyond DEFAULT.HTM?

This list is comma-delimited, so add a comma and the next default page, such as DEFAULT.ASP.

Chapter 3 Answers

1. What is data normalization used for?

Data normalization keeps the related data in a single table so that updates are hitting just necessary rows, instead of many duplicate rows.

2. What are indexes, unique identifiers, and primary keys used for?

They are methods of speeding up a search.

3. What is ODBC?

ODBC is a connection tool that sits between a programming language and a database.

4. What keyword is used to narrow a search criteria based on a column value?

WHERE

5. What keyword is used to eliminate duplicate values from a search?

DISTINCT

6. What is the difference between dropping a table and deleting a row?

Deleting a row doesn't get rid of all the other rows or the table, but dropping the table does.

Chapter 4 Answers

1. What is an HTML tag used for?

   To indicate to the browser that the text should be interpreted as HTML.

2. What does the `<A>` tag stand for, and what types are there?

   It stands for *anchor*. You can have an internal anchor, referencing another part of the same page, or an external anchor, referencing a different page.

3. What's the difference between the ordered list and the unordered list?

   The ordered list can be numbered and start at a certain number. The unordered list is usually a bulleted list.

4. What tag is used to pass information from the browser to the Web server? What object tag must be inside the `<FORM></FORM>` tags?

   The `FORM` tag. The Submit button must be included.

5. How do you embed one table into another?

   Have the outer table's cell contain the `<TABLE></TABLE>` tags.

6. What is used to send mail as part of the Web page?

   `<A HREF="email:webmaster@acme.com">Webmaster</A>`

7. If you, as the Web administrator, wanted to retrieve information from the user, what would you use?

   A form

8. If you wanted to add a line between one paragraph and the next, what would you use?

   The horizontal rule tag `<HR>`

Chapter 5 Answers

1. What's the syntax for passing parameters to a subprocedure?

   `method="function_Name param_1"`

2. What `Link` property gives you the name of the frame a page was opened into?

   `Target`

3. Why do some of the objects contain arrays?

   Because a Web page can have more than one of these objects, such as a `Link` or `Anchor`.

4. What is VBScript?

   The scripting language supported by Microsoft Internet Explorer.

5. What is the tag that enables scripting, and how can you make sure any non–script-supporting browser can still read your page?

```
<SCRIPT Language="VBScript">
<!--
-->
</SCRIPT>.
```

6. What is the topmost object of the object model?

   The `Window` object is the topmost object. Any object can be accessed through this object.

Chapter 6 Answers

1. What's the file extension for an ActiveX control?

   .OCX

2. Where can you set the properties of a control?

   You can set properties in the `DATA` attribute of the `<OBJECT>` tag, in the `<PARAM>` tag, or within VBScript.

3. What's the difference between a method and an event?

   A method is a procedure of the control that you can call at any time. An event is triggered only by certain occurrences, such as a mouse click.

4. What's the syntax for passing parameters to a method?

   `Control.Method (param1,param2)`

5. Where are ActiveX controls listed?

   They're listed in the operating system's Registry.

6. What does the `CODEBASE` attribute of the `<OBJECT>` tag allow you to do?

   Download the control and register it on the client machine.

Chapter 7 Answers

1. What's the file extension for an Active Server Page?

   .ASP or .INC

2. What permissions do you have to set on a virtual root to have the Active Server Page process correctly?

   Read and Execute privileges

3. If you have a single file of global functions that all Active Server pages may need to get to, how can you access that file?

   `<!--#INCLUDE FILE="menu.inc"-->`

4. How do you create a virtual root?

   From Internet Service Manager's application for MS Internet Information Server

5. What is considered an *application* in Active Server Page terminology?

   A virtual root and all its subdirectories; an application-level variable can be set or accessed from any file in this virtual root or subdirectories.

6. What is the syntax for passing parameters to a method?

   `Control.Method (param1,param2)`

7. What is buffering?

   Buffering is a mechanism to make the Active Server Page process all the script on a page before returning that page to the client's browser.

8. What does `Response.Write` do?

   Posts information to the returned Web page.

Chapter 8 Answers

1. List all three main ADO objects.

   `Connection`, `Command`, and `Recordset`

2. What does the acronym ADO stand for?

   ActiveX Data Objects

3. What's the name of Visual Basic Script's built-in function that's used to create individual ADO objects?

   `CreateObject()`

4. To do its work, the ADO `Recordset` depends on what two other objects?

   `Connection` and `Command`

5. Although the ADO `Recordset` object depends on other objects to do its work, the programmer doesn't need to manipulate them directly. True or False?

   True

6. The prefix ADODB, used when creating ADO objects, refers to what?

   ActiveX Data Objects for OLE DB data providers

7. ADO can be used in which programming languages or environments?

   Visual Basic, C/C++, Java, Office Application macros, Visual Basic Script,

Microsoft's JScript, or any programming environment supporting OLE Automation

8. ADO objects are, in fact, ActiveX objects. True or False?

True

Chapter 9 Answers

1. The Open method can be used to perform two distinct operations. What are they?

   Establishing a connection to the database, and issuing a query

2. Name two properties of the Recordset object you can use to determine whether the query just issued resulted in any records.

   RecordCount and EOF

3. List all methods of the Recordset that can be used to explicitly change the current record position.

   MoveFirst, MoveLast, MoveNext, MovePrevious, and Move (AbsolutePosition and Bookmark can change the current record position, but they are properties, not methods).

4. Name two states that the current record position can be in other than pointing at a valid record.

   Before the start of the records (BOF), and after the end of the records (EOF)

5. Show at least two different ways to reference the data value held in the first field of the Recordset.

   There are four possibilities:

   X = rs(0)

   X = rs(0).value

   X = rs.fields(0)

   X = rs.fields(0).value

6. List the methods that can be used to change the current record position of a default style Recordset.

   MoveNext() and possibly MoveLast()

7. It isn't necessary to call the Close method before the end of the scripting code in an HTML document. True or False?

   True

8. You can access the fields of the Recordset object before the Recordset is opened. True or False?

   False

9. List the standard parts of the WHILE loop used to step forward through each record of the Recordset.

☐ The check for boundary expression: WHILE NOT rs.EOF or WHILE NOT rs.BOF

☐ The body of the loop

☐ The statement that changes position: rs.MoveNext or rs.MovePrevious

☐ The end of the loop: WEND

10. Name a property that can be used to determine the total number of fields in each record of the Recordset.

Count, as in rs.fields.count

Chapter 10 Answers

1. List the HTML tags used for generating tables and explain the role played by each.

<TABLE> declares the start of a table
</TABLE> declares the end of a table
<TR> declares the start of a row
</TR> declares the end of a row
<TD> declares the start of a data item
</TD> declares the end of a data item

2. Given a Recordset named rs, write the HTML instructions that generate a text input field for the field named "title." This input field has a display size of 40 characters and defaults to the current value of the Recordset.

<INPUT NAME="title" WIDTH=40 VALUE="<%= rs("title") %>">

3. A Session object can be used to keep information across multiple page accesses. True or False?

True

4. A single Session object is shared by all users accessing the same Web page. True or False?

False

5. List all types of input fields that can be used with input forms.

Text, Hidden, Button, Checkbox, Password, Radio, Submit, Reset, TextArea, and Select

6. List all types of input fields that can be defined by using the <INPUT> tag.

Text, Hidden, Button, Checkbox, Password, Radio, Submit, and Reset

7. List three primary ways to turn static HTML Web pages into dynamic Web pages.

In general, you have three options: data display (tables), user input (forms), and processing submissions (`Request.Form`).

8. Describe two different ways you can use the `Recordset` object to update a record.

☐ Assign each field independently and call the `Update()` method.

☐ Call `Update()` with an array of field values and an array of field names/indexes.

9. Describe two different ways you can use the `Recordset` object to add a new record.

☐ Call the `AddNew()` method, independently assign each field a new value, and then call the `Update()` method.

☐ Call the `AddNew()` method with an array of field values and an array of field names/indexes.

10. List the four types of locking that can be performed with a `Recordset`.

`adLockReadOnly, adLockPessimistic, adLockOptimistic,` and `adLockBatchOptimistic`

Chapter 11 Answers

1. List the three kinds of information needed to open a connection.

Datasource, user ID, and password

2. A `Connection` object establishes a link to a single datasource. True or False?

True

3. A `Connection` object can be used by only one `Recordset` at a time. True or False?

False

4. What is a connection string?

A string containing information that the underlying data provider uses to determine how a connection is established. It's a series of argument names and values, separated by equals signs and semicolons. Some of the `Connection` properties and `Open()` parameters can also be specified in the command string.

5. Transactions make a series of database interactions look like a single one. True or False?

True

6. What is the method you can call to stop a transaction and undo all previous changes?

`RollbackTrans()`

7. After a transaction is committed, all associated `Recordsets` are immediately closed. True or False?

   False

8. Retained transactions automatically restart after they have been committed. True or False?

   True

9. What property can be used to control the "retained" behavior of a transaction?

   `Attributes`

10. Connection pooling allows `Connections` with three or more `Recordsets` to travel along the "fast lane" of communication bandwidths, bypassing most network bandwidths. True or False?

    False. Connection pooling is a feature provided by the ODBC Driver Manager that keeps connections "secretly" alive after you have closed them. The next time you request a connection to the same database server, a link might already be established.

Chapter 12 Answers

1. Name the property that can be used to precompile the query.

   `Prepared`

2. List two ways to populate the `Parameters` collection.

   ☐ Use the `Refresh()` method to have the `Command` object request the parameters from the database server.

   ☐ Create them yourself by using the `CreateParameter()` and `Append()` methods.

3. The `CommandText` property has three well-known states and one ambiguous state. List all four.

   `adCmdText, adCmdTable, adCmdStoredProc`, and `adCmdUnknown`

4. Name the special character that can be used as a placeholder in a SQL query for a parameter that's supplied later.

   The question mark

5. There are two forms for specifying a stored procedure call in the `CommandText` property: long and short form. Give an example of each for a call to a function named `Spork` that takes two parameters.

   ☐ `"Spork"` when the `CommandType` property is set to `adCmdStoredProc`

   ☐ `"{ call Spork( ?, ? ) }"`

6. When specifying stored procedures in short form, what value must the `CommandType` property be set to?

`adCmdStoredProc`

7. When specifying stored procedures in long form, what value must the `CommandType` property be set to?

`adCmdText`

8. List the first three parameter names of the `Parameters` collection when the `Refresh` method is used to populate it. Assume you have a simple `Parameter`-based query with at least three parameters.

`Param1`, `Param2`, and `Param3`

9. State two different ways to assign `Parameters` to the execution of the query, and give examples of each.

   ☐ Assign each parameter individually:
   ```
   cm(0) = "A"
   cm(1) = "B"
   set rs = cm.Execute
   ```

   ☐ Pass an array of parameter values to the `Execute` command:
   ```
   Dim P(1)
    P(0) = "A"
   P(1) = "B"
   Set rs = cm.Execute( , P )
   ```

10. Name the property used to specify whether a `Parameter` is used for input, output, or both.

`Direction`

Chapter 13 Answers

1. Name two different places to find error information when using ADO in Visual Basic Script.

   The built-in `Err` object and the ADO `Errors` collection found on the `Connection` object

2. In addition to errors, the ADO `Errors` collection may contain what?

   Warnings

3. Errors generated by the underlying data provider appear in the `Errors` collection. True or False?

   True

4. Errors generated by ADO itself appear in the `Errors` collection. True or False?

   False

5. What's the statement you must use to turn off Visual Basic's automatic error abort behavior?

   `On Error Resume Next`

6. How do you distinguish between errors and warnings in the ADO `Errors` collection?

   True errors have an error code less than zero, but warnings always have a positive value.

7. Each time a new warning is generated, the `Errors` collection is automatically cleared and filled with the new information. True or False?

   False. Warnings accumulate in the collection, but the occurrence of an error clears the collection of previous information.

8. The best way to access provider properties in the `Properties` collection is by ordinal number or by name?

   By name; the ordinal number is not guaranteed.

9. Named constants for each common provider property are declared in the ADOVBS.INC include file. True or False?

   False. Only constants for standard ADO properties and parameters are supplied in the ADOVBS.INC file.

10. Some properties in the `Properties` collection can be used to control database access feature not normally available using standard ADO methods and properties. True or False?

    True

Chapter 14 Answers

1. Listing 14.3, file 14TWD03.ASP, is used primarily to generate a report. True or False?

   True

2. List the three main application menu items available to a visitor who's "checked in."

   Check In (to check in again as a new group or event), Reserve Meeting Space, and View Reservations

3. The process of checking in eventually ends in the visitor specifying two pieces of information. What is that information?

   The group and the event

4. Name the sub-routine in Listing 14.5 that uses a prepared `Parameter`-based command to optimize multiple queries when generating a single Web page.

Either `RoomCalendarListForm()` or `GenerateCalendarRow()` is correct.

5. Unlike the examples in earlier chapters, most HTML header information has been isolated into a single sub-routine of what name?

`Header()`

6. Form utilities are included in a separate file. Name the file and the method used to include these utilities in each ASP file.

The file is named 14TWD04.ASP and the server-side include method is used to include the utilities in each ASP file.

7. Name at least one sub-routine that uses the `FormSelect` command to generate a drop-down listbox containing information from a database table.

`ChooseGroupForm()` or `ChooseEventForm()`

8. Search constraints are remembered by the Web application between successive Web pages by using what Active Server Pages built-in feature?

The `Session` object

9. What is the purpose of the Visual Basic statement repeated after each ADO `Open` or `Execute` method call?

The `CheckError()` function determines whether the preceding ADO method resulted in any errors. If it did, warnings are generated in the resulting HTML page, and the current sub-routine is aborted.

10. List the name of at least one sub-routine that uses ADO to add new records to a database table.

`CreateNewGroup()`, `CreateNewEvent()`, or `ReserveRoom()`

Chapter 15 Answers

1. What's an ADOR `Recordset`? Why is it useful in developing Web applications? Where are they stored on the client side? What other programming object is it directly related to?

An ADOR `Recordset` is a `Recordset` that can be marshaled; it's designed to be lightweight and easy to transport across HTTP.

ADOR `Recordsets` are directly consumed by `AdvancedDataControl` objects—either explicitly, by a programmer setting the `Recordset` property of the `AdvancedData-Control`, or implicitly, when the four core properties are set. In the latter case, a query is generated, processed on the server, and the resulting ADOR marshaled back to the client where it's automatically associated with the `AdvancedDataControl`.

The ADOR has the advantage of being very small and easy to download over slower links, and it provides a subset of the full ADODB Recordset functionality. The ADOR is directly related to the full ADO Recordset object and is required by AdvancedDataControl objects.

2. What are the four core properties of the AdvancedDataControl? What are they used for? Describe each of them.

The AdvancedDataControl's four core properties are Connect, Server, SQL, and Bindings:

☐ Connect specifies a connection string used by the AdvancedDataFactory server object to connect to a data provider on the middle tier. A connection string includes a system DSN, an optional user name, and an optional password.

☐ Server designates the Web server where the AdvancedDataControl should establish a connection and execute its SQL query.

☐ SQL is used to define the database statement that should be executed when the AdvancedDataControl is loaded. The statement can be a simple Select * from tabname1... query or any well-formed SQL-92 string, including invoking stored procedures or DDL operations, such as Create Table.

☐ Bindings indicates the set of data-aware ActiveX controls that the AdvancedDataControl is providing data binding services for. The ActiveX controls are specified in a semicolon-delimited string that states the names of the bound controls and the properties that data should be bound to. Simple controls, such as text fields, usually have their Text properties set. For complex data-aware controls, such as the Sheridan SSDBGrid and DBList ActiveX controls, only the name of the control needs to be provided; the ADC runtime system automatically binds data to the right property.

3. What is the primary programming model for ADC on the server? What are the components of that model? (Hint: You have been studying it for over a week now.)

The primary programming model for ADC on the server consists of server *business objects* that encapsulate business logic processing and data access. The server-side model includes the ADISAPI extension library; the Internet Object Manager, which handles creating business objects and invoking methods of those objects; and the ActiveX Data Objects (ADO) library. Business objects, written in Visual Basic, Visual C++, or Visual J++, implement methods that internally use the ADO library or AdvancedDataFactory helper object to query the back-end datastore and return ADOR Recordsets to the client. The Internet Object Manager (IOM) handles marshaling ADOR Recordsets to the client from the server, where the Recordset is reconstructed and available for access through scripting code or direct association with an AdvancedDataControl.

4. What's the role of the Internet Object Remoting Proxy? What is the server-side component that complements it? What protocols does the IORP support? Can you think of some protocols it should support but currently doesn't?

The role of the Internet Object Remoting Proxy (IORP) is to provide a gateway over HTTP for clients to invoke server business objects. The IORP acts as a proxy on the client for remote server objects. The VBScript programmer can write scripts that treat the IORP like local "objects," invoking methods on the proxy. These method calls are intercepted and translated into a format suitable for transport to Web server components of the ADC architecture.

The IORP handles translating client-side requests into multi-part MIME packets that can be efficiently transported to the Web server and turned into a sequence of server-side calls. The complementary component on the Web server is the Internet Object Manager—the object that handles actually creating business objects, passing arguments to object methods, and passing return values to the client IORP.

5. What do the following terms mean?

Transaction
Marshaling
Proxy
Protocol

A *transaction* is a logical unit of work, defined by the ACID properties (atomicity, consistency, isolation, and durability). These properties ensure that the transaction, which can consist of many separate data transformations and operations, is treated as a "logical" unit—either completely succeeding or failing. Transactions are absolutely fundamental for building scalable, distributed applications.

Marshaling means transferring data from one address space to another, which could be from one process to another on the same machine or from one machine to another over the Internet. ADOR Recordsets are primary examples of "marshaling" vehicles in the ADC architecture. They can marshal across the network, providing the results of a database query to a client machine.

A *proxy* is an object that acts as a surrogate for another. In ADC programming, the AdvancedDataFactory can create proxy objects for server business objects through its CreateObject() method.

A *protocol* is a formally defined way for two components to communicate with one another and pass information between themselves. It includes communication format specification, ordering of arguments, connection and disconnection procedures, and a host of other rules to make sure there's no ambiguity in the communication exchanges and that data is neither lost nor misinterpreted.

6. Name at least two protocols mentioned in this chapter. (These terms are used continuously throughout Week 3, so knowing what they mean is vital!)

   A primary protocol used by ADC is HTTP, the HyperText Transfer Protocol. Others are the File Transfer Protocol (FTP) and Distributed COM (DCOM).

7. What are the client-side components of ADC? What are the server-side components?

   Client-side components of ADC include `AdvancedDataSpace`, `AdvancedDataControl`, ADOR `Recordset`, and any proxy objects created by the `AdvancedDataSpace` object, such as the IORP component. The server-side components include the ADISAPI extension library, Internet Object Manager (IOM), `AdvancedDataFactory`, ADOR `Recordset`, ActiveX Data Objects library, and any custom-built business objects.

8. What is the purpose of Advanced Data TableGrams? Why are they necessary in the ADC framework? Give at least one example of how a tablegram is used.

   The purpose of ADTG tablegrams is to provide wire representations of tabular data, such as ADOR `Recordset`s, including information on changed fields, new rows, deleted rows, and (in the future) reconciliation information. The ADTG format is very efficient for streaming large amounts of tabular data across application protocols, such as HTTP and DCOM. It provides a uniform, self-describing layout for the tabular data and separates the metadata information from the actual "rows" of data that constitute the `Recordset`.

   The tablegram format was designed to be compact and efficient, especially for slower connections, such as 28.8 baud dial-up lines. An example of an ADTG tablegram is an "update tablegram," sent from the client to the server. The tablegram would contain, by default, only the changed rows of the original tabular dataset transmitted from the server. This tablegram would be received by the `AdvancedDataFactory` server object, which then uses the tablegram to perform an actual update operation against the target datastore.

9. What two browser scripting languages is ADC compatible with?

   ADC is compatible with Microsoft VBScript and Netscape's JavaScript. VBScript is the preferred scripting language for client-side ADC application design, since it's also used in Active Server Pages (ASP) programming.

10. What is the VTM? What role does it play in making data navigation more efficient? What are the workspaces it supports? Why would these be important to programmers?

    The Virtual Table Manager (VTM) is the in-memory cache for live, disconnected data on the client. It makes efficient navigation possible by being local and in-memory; moving through a large `Recordset` is very quick compared to fetching data from, say, a server-side cursor or reading it from a physical storage device or system file.

VTM workspaces are constructs for allowing transactional isolation on the client. Each workspace is the equivalent of a logical unit of work, or transaction. Each workspace stores one `Recordset` and makes sure the `Recordset` isn't overwritten by changes elsewhere in the VTM. Workspaces are important to programmers because they ensure that changes made to one `Recordset` in the VTM's cache don't contaminate the data of another, unrelated `Recordset`. This ability makes the VTM a useful data store for multiple results, allowing for more sophisticated partitioning of applications and easier client-side programming.

11. What ADC component can be used in VBScript code to create HTTP and DCOM proxies through programming? Why would someone use a proxy instead of the object itself on the Web page? Discuss Web security issues, such as `SafeForScripting`. Does this have something to do with using proxies? What would be the danger is creating a non-`SafeForScripting` object on the client machine? Can you think of some scenarios where creating arbitrary objects on the client could lead to disastrous results?

The `AdvancedDataFactory` object is used to create proxies for HTTP and DCOM protocols. The advantages of using a proxy are numerous: a smaller footprint on the client, control over distribution of business rules (which are implemented through business objects), and flexible partitioning. Distributed-application designers have the choice of how to partition their application with ADC technology. They may opt for "thin" or "fat" clients or a balanced partitioning designed to maximize the application's scalability in OLTP contexts.

The proxy also makes sure that damage to the local machine is impossible or very difficult. With HTTP proxies, the actual "code" of the business object is executing on the application server, where the object is a known quantity and the server has presumably been configured to run the business object. Designers might create business objects, such as those used primarily for validation of forms and user input, that can be downloaded to the client machine and instantiated locally.

You could argue that having the validation "logic" close to the user interface makes sense, and proxies shouldn't be used. The delay and resources consumed on the application server associated with the business objects processing might be deemed inefficient compared with simply shipping the object to the client. To do this, however, designers must "mark" their objects to make sure they're recognized as real business objects, not malicious computer viruses. Therefore, they mark them as SafeForScripting and SafeForInitialization, which is a conscious decision to allow the business object to be created on the client. It's not a side-effect of using the `ADS.CreateObject()` method, but a design decision made with a full knowledge of the possibility that client-instantiated business objects could access the client's file system, Registry, and so forth.

B

ADC blocks VBScript script writers and client developers from inadvertently doing this by blocking the `AdvancedDataSpace` object from creating true business objects (either in-process or standalone EXEs). The situation simply can't happen. Proxies add a layer of security for the client machine; the business object's code doesn't affect the client machine.

A typical "disaster scenario" might be a Word macro virus disguised as a benign business object that's downloaded to the client and executed. The macro invokes Word 97 and executes a hard disk reformat. Before anyone knows what's going on, the virus could destroy the file directory table for the disk partition and wipe out important data. ADC protects the novice programmer from such a situation by blocking the local instantiation of business objects, unless they have been declared SafeForScripting and SafeForInitialization, and the business object's PROGID is added as a value of the ADCLaunch key in the local machine's Registry. This triple-redundancy system makes ADC a safe system for distributed application development. By always using proxy objects, the application developer and VBScript writer has an even more robust system of safeguarding client machines from mischief.

Chapter 16 Answers

1. What are the methods and properties of an `AdvancedDataControl` object?

   The properties are `Bindings`, `Connect`, `Recordset`, `Server`, and `SQL`. The methods are `CancelUpdate`, `MoveFirst`, `MovePrevious`, `MoveNext`, `MoveLast`, `Refresh`, and `SubmitChanges`.

2. Can you bind more than one control to an `AdvancedDataControl` object?

   Yes

3. Can you have more than one returned result set for an `AdvancedDataControl` object?

   No

4. What kind of properties are required when you invoke the `Refresh` method of an `AdvancedDataControl` object?

   The `Refresh` method requires `Connect`, `Server`, and `SQL` properties to connect to the application server and the ODBC datasource.

5. What's the different between simple data-aware controls and complex data-aware controls?

   For simple data-aware controls, `AdvancedDataControl` objects don't do any mapping; they just set and retrieve the value of the controls. For complex data-aware controls, `AdvancedDataControl` objects map the data from the OLE DB rowset to ICursor, which is used in complex data controls that handle scrolling.

Chapter 17 Answers

1. From which property of the ADC `AdvancedDataControl` do you get the ADOR `Recordset`?

   The `Recordset` property

2. The ADOR `Recordset`, once you get it from the ADC `AdvancedDataControl`, is automatically synchronized with the current record position shared by the data-bound controls. True or False?

   False

3. List the properties available on the ADOR `Recordset`'s `Field` object.

   `Name` and `Value`

4. The ADOR `Recordset` has an `Open()` method that you might not ever need to use. What two arguments does it share with its bigger sibling, the ADODB `Recordset`?

   `Source` and `ActiveConnection`

5. When generated by the ADC `AdvancedDataControl`, what cursor type and lock type is the ADOR `Recordset` using?

   The cursor type is equivalent to `adOpenStatic`, and the lock type is `adLockBatchOptimistic`.

6. List the five navigation methods that can be used to change the current record position controlled by the ADOR `Recordset`.

   `MoveFirst()`, `MoveLast()`, `MoveNext()`, `MovePrevious()`, and `Move()`

7. In addition to the five navigation methods, name one property that can be used to change the current record position.

   The `Bookmark` property

8. Name the two properties that the ADOR `Recordset` shares with the ADODB `Recordset` in determining the boundaries of the data.

   `EOF` and `BOF`

9. What property on the ADOR `Recordset` and the ADC `AdvancedDataControl` can be used to manually synchronize the two objects?

   The `Bookmark` property

10. The ADOR `Recordset` can be used to both read and write field values shared with the ADC `AdvancedDataControl`. True or False?

    False. The ADOR v1.0 `Recordset` can be used only to read field values.

Chapter 18 Answers

1. Describe the difference between auto-completion and auto-anticipation.

   Auto-completion affects the field you just changed, but auto-anticipation affects fields you haven't edited yet.

2. Record validation is a superset of field validation. True or False?

   True. Most of what occurs during field validation could be done at record validation time, too.

3. Field validations may occur each time a field value is changed. True or False?

   True

4. Record validations may occur each time the cursor is moved between fields. True or False?

   False. Record validation should occur each time users perform an explicit action that requires the record to be in a consistent state. This could be when they're using the AdvancedDataControl or Recordset to change the current record position, but not when they're tabbing between individual fields.

5. List at least two different types of record validation that can't be considered outgrowths of field validation.

   Record consistency and record uniqueness

6. What two events are sent each time the focus is changed between edit fields? In what order are they sent?

   OnChange and OnBlur, in that order

7. List at least one event that's sent only if the data value is changed in an edit field.

   OnChange

8. Show two different ways to bind your own script code to a field and a user-interface event.

   ☐ Name the explicit sub-routine when you declare the field:

   ```
   <INPUT NAME="Foo" LANGUAGE="VBS" OnChange="DoChangeThang">
   ```

   ☐ Write a VBScript sub-routine with a name formed from the input field's name and the name of the event:

   ```
   SUB Foo_OnChange()
   ```

9. Name at least one type of data-validation scenario where it would be useful to calculate totals.

   Record validation or submission validation

10. Describe at least one type of action you might take when attaching script code to the `OnSubmit` event.

    These are all submission validations, which could include a set of record validations.

Chapter 19 Answers

1. What are the methods of `AdvancedDataSpace`?

   There is only one method: `CreateObject`.

2. What are the methods of `AdvancedDataFactory`?

   They are `CreateRecordset`, `Query`, and `SubmitChanges`.

3. What is the default business object?

   `AdvancedDataFactory`

4. How do you mark a business object as safe for scripting?

   You can use one of the Visual Basic 5.0 tools—the Basic Application Setup Wizard—to automate the process or create the following REG file and merge it into the Registry manually:

   ```
   REGEDIT4

   [HKEY_CLASSES_ROOT\CLSID\<MyBusinessObjectGUID>\Implemented
   ➥Categories{7DD95801-9882-11CF-9FA9-00AA006C42C4}]

   [HKEY_CLASSES_ROOT\CLSID\<MyBusinessObjectGUID>\Implemented
   ➥Categories{7DD95802-9882-11CF-9FA9-00AA006C42C4}]
   ```

   In this code, `<MyBusinessObjectGUID>` is the GUID of your business object.

Chapter 20 Answers

1. What do you need to do to marshal an ADODB `Recordset` from the application server to the client tier?

   Use the `adUseClientBatch` option for the `CursorLocation`.

2. How do you marshal the complete `Recordset`?

   Set `MarshalOptions` equal to 0.

3. What do you need to do to marshal just the modified records?

   Set `MarshalOptions` equal to 1.

4. Can you modify the ADOR Recordset in the client tier without using data-bound VB controls?

No

5. Can you use the for browse keyword with an Access database?

No

6. Do you need to specify adLockBatchOptimistic for the lock type?

No

Chapter 21 Answers

1. How do you get data from the previous Web page? For example, how to you get the member ID from the member login/registration component's Web page into the search engine's Web page

In today's example, you use the Request collection to retrieve data from a Form object.

2. Can you update data through ADC with an Oracle database?

No, you can just retrieve data.

3. What keyword do you have to use in your SQL statement to update records?

The for browse keyword

Index

Teach Yourself Microsoft Visual InterDev in 21 Days

Michael Van Hoozer

Using the day-by-day format of the best-selling *Teach Yourself* series, this easy-to-follow tutorial gives you a solid understanding of Visual InterDev, Microsoft's new Web application–development environment. In no time, you learn how to perform front-end scripting, database and query design, content creation, server-side scripting, and more.

☐ Shows how Active Desktop features, such as HTML, Java, JScript, VBScript, and ActiveX, help developers build Web applications on intranets and the Internet

The CD-ROM contains Internet Explorer 3.0, Microsoft ActiveX and HTML development tools, plus ready-to-use templates, graphics, scripts, Java applets, and ActiveX controls.

$39.99 USA; $56.95 CDN;   1-57521-093-2;   800 pp.   New—Casual—Accomplished

Visual J++ Unleashed

Bryan Morgan, et al.

Java is the hottest programming language being learned today. Microsoft's Windows version of Java, code-named Visual J++, might prove to be even hotter because Microsoft has added several new development features, such as graphic designing, to the Java language. *Visual J++ Unleashed* shows you how to make use of the Java development potential of Visual J++.

☐ Shows how to add interactivity and Java applets to Web pages

☐ Explains how the Windows enhancements to the Java environment can be used for "quick and easy" programming

The CD-ROM includes powerful utilities and source code from the book.

$49.99 USA; $70.95 CDN;   1-57521-161-0;   1,000 pp.   Accomplished—Expert

Web Programming with Visual J++

Mike Cohn, Jay Rutten, and James Jory

Readers get up to speed quickly with this comprehensive new reference on Microsoft's licensed Windows version of Java: Visual J++. This book shows you how to develop feature-rich Visual J++ applications in the Windows environment.

☐ Explores the advanced features of Visual J++

The CD-ROM includes third-party tools, utilities, and demonstrations.

$39.99 USA; $56.95 CDN;   1-57521-174-2;   600 pp.   Accomplished—Expert

Visual Basic for Applications Unleashed

Paul McFedries

Combining both power and ease of use, Visual Basic for Applications (VBA) is the common language for developing macros and applications across all Microsoft Office components. Using the format of the best-selling *Unleashed* series, you can master the intricacies of this popular language and use the full power of VBA.

☐ Covers user-interface design, database programming, networking programming, Internet programming, and standalone application creation

The CD-ROM is packed with sample code, sample spreadsheets, databases, projects, templates, utilities, and evaluation copies of third-party tools and applications.

$49.99 USA; $70.95 CDN;   0-672-31046-5;   800 pp.   Accomplished—Expert

Teach Yourself Visual Basic 5 in 21 Days, Fourth Edition

Nathan Gurewich and Ori Gurewich

Using a logical, easy-to-follow approach, this international bestseller teaches readers the fundamentals of developing Visual Basic 5 programs. It starts with the basics of writing a program and then moves on to adding voice, music, sound, and graphics.

☐ Uses shaded syntax boxes, techniques, and Q&A, Do/Don't, and Workshop sections to highlight key points and reinforce learning

$29.99 USA; $42.95 CDN;   0-672-30978-5;   1,000 pp.   New—Casual

Teach Yourself Database Programming with Visual Basic 5 in 21 Days, Second Edition

Michael Amundsen and Curtis Smith

Visual Basic 5, the 32-bit programming language from Microsoft, is used by programmers to create Windows, Windows 95, and Web applications. This book shows you how to design, develop, and deploy Visual Basic applications for the World Wide Web.

☐ Presented in a daily format, with each week focusing on a different area of database development

☐ Written by a Microsoft Certified Visual Basic Professional

The CD-ROM includes sample code and third-party utilities.

$45.00 USA; $63.95 CDN;   0-672-31018-X;   1,000 pp   New—Casual—Accomplished

Teach Yourself Database Programming with JDBC in 21 Days

Ashton Hobbs

Linking both corporate and home databases to the Web is critical for a Web site to be successful, and Sun's Java API enables you to do just that! Following a step-by-step approach, you learn how to develop Java database components to create complete database applications for Web connection.

☐ Explores database basics, JDBC interfaces, database connectivity and transactions, and more

The CD-ROM is packed with all the source code from the book, two complete, real-world database examples, and a Web page linking to several useful Java resources.

$39.99 USA; $56.95 CDN;   1-57521-123-8;   600 pp.   New—Casual—Accomplished

Teach Yourself Database Programming with Visual J++ in 21 Days

John Fronckowiak and Gordon McMillan

Using a step-by-step, easy-to-follow format, this complete resource takes you beyond the basic product information and guides you through database integration and interface development.

☐ Highlights new technologies, including JavaBeans, JDBC, DAO Library, RDO Library, ActiveX, and COM

The CD-ROM is loaded with scripting and author source code.

$39.99 USA; $56.95 CDN;   1-57521-262-5;   750 pp.   Casual—Accomplished

Add to Your Sams.net Library Today
with the Best Books for Internet Technologies

ISBN	Quantity	Description of Item	Unit Cost	Total Cost
0-672-30978-5		Teach Yourself Visual Basic 5 in 21 Days, Fourth Edition	$29.99	
0-672-31018-X		Teach Yourself Database Programming with Visual Basic 5 in 21 Days, Second Edition (Book/CD-ROM)	$45.00	
1-57521-174-2		Web Programming with Visual J++ (Book/CD-ROM)	$39.99	
1-57521-123-8		Teach Yourself Database Programming with JDBC in 21 Days (Book/CD-ROM)	$39.99	
1-57521-262-5		Teach Yourself Database Programming with Visual J++ in 14 Days (Book/CD-ROM)	$39.99	
1-57521-093-2		Teach Yourself Microsoft Visual InterDev in 21 Days (Book/CD-ROM)	$39.99	
1-57521-161-0		Visual J++ Unleashed (Book/CD-ROM)	$49.99	
0-672-31046-5		Visual Basic for Applications Unleashed (Book/CD-ROM)	$49.99	
		Shipping and Handling: See information below.		
		TOTAL		

Shipping and Handling: $4.00 for the first book, and $1.75 for each additional book. If you need to have it NOW, we can ship product to you in 24 hours for an additional charge of approximately $18.00, and you will receive your item overnight or in two days. Overseas shipping and handling adds $2.00. Prices subject to change. Call between 9:00 a.m. and 5:00 p.m. EST for availability and pricing information on latest editions.

201 W. 103rd Street, Indianapolis, Indiana 46290

1-800-428-5331 — Orders   1-800-835-3202 — FAX   1-800-858-7674 — Customer Service

Book ISBN 1-57521-139-4

MACMILLAN COMPUTER PUBLISHING USA

A VIACOM COMPANY

Technical ---- Support:

If you need assistance with the information in this book or with a CD/Disk accompanying the book, please access the Knowledge Base on our Web site at **http://www.superlibrary.com/general/support**. Our most Frequently Asked Questions are answered there. If you do not find the answer to your questions on our Web site, you may contact Macmillan Technical Support **(317) 581-3833** or e-mail us at **support@mcp.com**.

Installing the CD-ROM

The companion CD-ROM contains all the source code and project files developed by the authors, plus an assortment of evaluation versions of third-party products. To install it, please follow the steps in the following sections.

Windows 95/NT 4 Installation Instructions

1. Insert the CD-ROM into your CD-ROM drive.
2. From the Windows 95 or NT 4 desktop, double-click on the My Computer icon.
3. Double-click on the icon representing your CD-ROM drive.
4. Double-click on the icon called SETUP.EXE to run the CD-ROM installation program.

This program creates a program group with the icons to run the programs on the CD-ROM. No files are copied to your hard drive during this installation.

NOTE   If you have Windows 95 and the Autoplay feature is enabled, the SETUP.EXE program is executed automatically once the CD-ROM is inserted into the drive.

Windows NT 3.51 Installation Instructions

1. Insert the CD-ROM into your CD-ROM drive.
2. From the File Manager or Program Manager, choose File | Run from the menu.
3. Type `<drive>\setup.exe` and press Enter; `<drive>` corresponds to the drive letter of your CD-ROM drive. For example, if your CD-ROM drive is D:, type `D:\SETUP.EXE` and press Enter.
4. The installation creates a program group containing the icons to browse the CD-ROM and install third-party utilities.